The End of Empire and the Making of Malaya

Modern Malaya was born in a period of war, insurrection and monumental social upheaval. This study is the first of its kind, and it examines the achievement of independence in 1957, not primarily through the struggle between Imperial Britain and nationalist elites, but through the internal struggles that late colonial rule fostered at all levels of Malayan society. In this unique study, Dr Harper argues that the late colonial state was a pivotal force in Malaya after the Second World War, particularly in British attempts to mould Malaya's plural society into a viable nation-state. Through new research on the Malayan Emergency, social policy and rural development, and urbanisation and popular culture, this study charts the responses of Malaya's communities to more intrusive forms of government and to rapid social change. Dr Harper emphasises the conflicting visions of independence which emerged in this period, and suggests that although the experiments of late colonialism were frustrated, they left an enduring legacy for the politics of independent Malaya. Thus this book sheds new light on the dynamics of nationalism, ethnicity and state-building in modern Southeast Asia.

T. N. HARPER is a Fellow of Magdalene College, Cambridge and is a University Lecturer in History. He has written for many publications including *Modern Asian Studies*, *Southeast Asian Affairs* and the *Journal of Southeast Asian Studies*.

The End of Empire and the Making of Malaya

T. N. HARPER

CAMBRIDGE
UNIVERSITY PRESS

PUBLISHED BY THE PRESS SYNDICATE OF THE UNIVERSITY OF CAMBRIDGE
The Pitt Building, Trumpington Street, Cambridge CB2 1RP, United Kingdom

CAMBRIDGE UNIVERSITY PRESS
The Edinburgh Building, Cambridge, CB2 2RU, United Kingdom
40 West 20th Street, New York, NY 10011–3211, USA
10 Stamford Road, Oakleigh, Melbourne 3166, Australia

First published 1999

Printed in the United Kingdom at the University Press, Cambridge

Typeset in Erhardt 9.5/12 pt   [CE]

A catalogue record for this book is available from the British Library

Library of Congress Cataloguing in Publication data
Harper, T. N. (Timothy Norman), 1965–
The end of empire and the making of Malaya / T. N. Harper.
p.   cm.
Includes bibliographical references.
ISBN 0 521 59040 X (hardbound)
1. Malaya – History.   I. Title.
DS596.6.H32   1999
959.5′105   dc21   97–28961   CIP

ISBN 0 521 59040 X hardback

For Norman and Collette

'And he felt, through the brandy, that this was perhaps the only country in the world for any man who cared about history.'

Anthony Burgess, *Beds in the East*.

Contents

Tables

Preface

————•————

Modern Malaya was born in a time of war and revolution. This book is an account of the ways in which its people sought to create a nation from a plural society caught in the flux of crisis and social change. A central purpose of the doctoral thesis in which this book had its genesis was to analyse the extent to which the late colonial state shaped the political landscape of independent Malaya. This early emphasis has been retained. The anatomy of late colonialism that follows is a contribution to the comparative history of western expansion and retreat. But as I spent more time in Malaysia the book became an exercise in Southeast Asian social history. The achievement of independence is examined, not primarily through the metropolitan mind of colonialism, but through the struggle within Malayan society for its soul. Many of the ideas and forces this brought to prominence still dominated political life during the late 1980s and 1990s – a period of great change in Malaysia – and my comprehension of them has been coloured by what Malaysians had to say about them at the time. The first lesson of my own historical schooling was that every history is foremost a history of its own making. Other authors have begun to rewrite Malaysian history in new directions, and I hope I have done credit to the richness of their work. New work on late colonialism supports many of the themes I dwell upon here: studies of counter-insurgency have been displaced by a new understanding of the experience of terror; the ideological and institutional impact of colonial rule is being traced in more subtle ways. This book is an attempt to understand the making of modern Malaysian society, but I hope it addresses comparative questions about the nature of the social and ideological forces that create a nation; the role of the state; the development of civil society and the nature of freedom. I hope it speaks to the human concerns of how dilemmas of social change have been faced with dignity and resource. If this book often highlights the conflicts nation-building has created, it is informed by a real sense of Malaysia's achievements, of its possibilities, and a historical understanding of its disappointments.

I received nothing but help and kindness during my extended periods of research in Malaysia and Singapore. The bulk of the fieldwork was conducted from January

1989 to September 1990. It was made possible through the co-operation and assistance of the Socio-Economic Research Unit of the Prime Minister's Department. An invaluable base and hospitality were provided at the Institute of Advanced Studies, Universiti Malaya, for which I thank the Dean and staff, and by Asmara Bestari, Universiti Malaya, for which I thank the then master, Dr Hj. Firdaus Hj. Abdullah. The Institute of Southeast Asian Studies was host to me in Singapore for three months in 1990 and again in 1995 and 1996. I made preliminary visits to the region in 1987 and 1988 and nine further extended visits between 1991 and 1995. Throughout this period I have been particularly grateful to the staff of the Arkib Negara Malaysia, Kuala Lumpur, but also the Perpustakaan Universiti Malaya, Kuala Lumpur; Perpustakaan Universiti Sains Malaysia, Pulau Pinang; Perpustakaan Negara Malaysia, Kuala Lumpur; the library of the Co-operative College of Malaysia and of Seminari Teologi Malaysia. In Singapore: the National Archives, Singapore; the library of the Institute of Southeast Asian Studies; the library of the National University of Singapore; and especially the Southeast Asia collection of the National Library of Singapore. In the United Kingdom: Dr Lionel Carter and the library of the Centre of South Asian Studies, Cambridge; Cambridge University Library, and the library of the Royal Commonwealth Society deposited there; Rhodes House Library, Oxford; the library of the London School of Oriental and African Studies; the Public Record Office, London. Research between 1987 and 1994 was funded by the Economic and Social Research Council; the Governing Body of Peterhouse, Cambridge, the Smuts, Bartle Frere, Mary Euphrasia Moseley and University Travel Funds of Cambridge University. I am especially grateful to the Managers of the Smuts Memorial Fund for electing me to the Hinduja Smuts Fellowship in Commonwealth Studies at the Centre of South Asian Studies, Cambridge and to the Master and Fellows of Magdalene who provide conditions under which work can be done.

Friends in Kuala Lumpur taught me more about Malaysia than any archive or library: I mention especially Oommen George, S. Kannapper, Sheryll Stothard, Kathy Roland, Adeline Tan, Geetha Kumaran, Vinayagaraj Rajaratnam and Fiona Pereira, who also helped in the archives and whose family provided kind hospitality. Portions of drafts were read and improved by Ronald Hyam, Chandran Jeshuran, Jomo K.S., Lee Kam Hing, Tan Liok Ee, Tony Stockwell and Diana Wong. None of them, of course, is responsible for what follows. For advice and assistance I am grateful to Peter Carey, Jeya Kathirithamby-Wells, Paul Kratoska, Loh Wei Leng, Khoo Kay Kim and the Southeast Asian Research Network on Indigenous Minorities and Regional Development. Tony Williams-Hunt and Colin Nicholas were my guides to the Orang Asli. John Roxborough and Robert Hunt made available material on the churches. Samantha Tsao and Laura Stevenson provided the index. In England, Stuart Martin and Sandeep Kapur contributed nothing to the early completion of this work but were helpful in other ways. I was particularly fortunate to benefit from the guidance of Lim Teck Ghee who supervised this work in Kuala Lumpur. In Cambridge, Raj Chandavarkar, Ronald Hyam, John Iliffe, Gordon Johnson, Joanna

Lewis and Anthony Low have been generous with advice and encouragement. John Lonsdale's writing and teaching provoked many ideas that appear here. I owe a special debt to Chris Bayly who supervised the original thesis: no one could ask for more, or expect as much, from a teacher. Phyllis and Yeow Hai have shown me countless kindnesses over the years. Without Carolyn none of this would have happened. My greatest debt is acknowledged in the dedication. What follows is as much their work as it is mine.

Abbreviations

ACCC   Associated Chinese Chambers of Commerce
ACL   Assistant Commissioner for Labour
ADO   Assistant District Officer
AJU   Anti-Japanese Union
Alfsea   Allied Land Forces South East Asia
AMCJA   All-Malaya Council of Joint Action
API   Angkatan Pemuda Insaf
ASAS 50   Angkatan Sasterawan [19]50
ASEAN   Association of Southeast Asian Nations
AWAS   Angkatan Wanita Sedar
BA   British Adviser
BMA   British Military Administration
CCP   Chinese Communist Party
CDL   China Democratic League
CIAM   Central Indian Association of Malaya
CID   Criminal Intelligence Department
CIM   China Inland Mission
CLC   Communities' Liaison Committee
CLR   Controller of Land Revenue
CSSH   *Comparative Studies in Society and History*
DCCAO   Deputy Chief Civil Affairs Officer, BMA
DCL   Deputy Commissioner for Labour
DO   District Officer
EPF   Employees' Provident Fund
GLU   General Labour Union
IMP   Independence of Malaya Party
INA   Indian National Army
JAS   *Journal of Asian History*

JMBRAS	*Journal of the Malay[si]an Branch of the Royal Asiatic Society*
JSEAH	*Journal of Southeast Asian History*
JSEAS	*Journal of Southeast Asian Studies*
[M]JTG	*[Malayan] Journal of Tropical Geography*
KMM	Kesatuan Melayu Muda
KMT	Kuomintang
KRIS	Kesatuan Rakyat Istimewa
LDMR	Labour Department Monthly Report
MARA	Majlis Amanah Rakyat
MAS	*Modern Asian Studies*
MATA	Majlis Agama Tertinggi
MCA	Malayan Chinese Association
MCP	Malayan Communist Party
MDU	Malayan Democratic Union
MIC	Malayan Indian Congress
MMEA	Malayan Mining Employers' Association
MNLA	Malayan National Liberation Army
MNP	Malay Nationalist Party
MPAJA	Malayan People's Anti-Japanese Army
MPIEA	Malayan Planting Industry Employers' Association
MRSA	Monthly Report on Subversive Activities
MTUC	Malayan Trade Union Council
NAP	National Association of Perak
NDYL	New Democratic Youth League
NEP	New Economic Policy
OAG	Officer Administering Government
OCAJA	Overseas Chinese Anti-Japanese Army
PAP	People's Action Party
PAS	Parti Islam SeMalaysia
PETA	Ikatan Pemuda Tanah Ayer
PETA	Pembela Tanah Ayer
PMFTU	Pan-Malayan Federation of Trade Unions
PMGLU	Pan-Malayan General Labour Union
PMIP	Pan-Malayan Islamic Party
PMU	Peninsular Malay Union
PUTERA	Pusat Tenaga Rakyat
RC	Resident Commissioner
RIDA	Rural and Industrial Development Authority
RIMA	*Review of Indonesian and Malayan Affairs*
SAO	State Agricultural Officer
SCAO	Senior Civil Affairs Officer, BMA

List of abbreviations

SEAC	South East Asia Command
SFO	State Forest Officer
SMCY	San Min Chu Yi
TOL	Temporary Occupation Licence
UMNO	United Malays National Organisation
UPAM	United Planting Association of Malaya
ZOPFAN	Zone of Peace, Freedom and Neutrality

Glossary of non-English terms

adat	customary law
bagi dua	sharecropping
baju	clothing
belukar	secondary jungle growth
bendang	wet rice field
bidan	midwife
bomoh	Malay spiritual healer
bumiputera	lit. 'son of the soil'
dulang	plate for washing tin
fitrah	tithe at end of fasting month
gantang	a gallon measure of rice
haj, haji	pilgrimage, pilgrim to Mekka
jampai	the incantations of the bomoh
joget moden	popular dance, usually with professional cabaret dancers
kampong	village
kangani	South Indian labour foreman
kati, katty	one and a third pounds in weight
kaum ibu	women's union
kelong	off-shore fishing platform
kepala	head, usually of labour
kerajaan	government, lit. 'that which pertains to the raja'
ketua kampong	village headman
ladang	forest clearing
lalang	long grass
madrasah	religious school
Mentri Besar	chief minister of a Malay State
merdeka	independence, freedom

min yuen	civil branch of MNLA
mukim	administrative division below a district
Nanyang	South Seas [Chinese]
Orang Asli	lit. 'original people', aborigine
padi kuncha, padi ratus	forms of agricultural credit, see Chapter 6
pemuda	youth
penghulu	headman, administrative head of a *mukim*
perjuangan	struggle
persatuan	association
pondok	village Quran school
rakyat	people, masses
riba	interest forbidden under Islamic law
ronggeng	popular music form
saka	hereditary area of Temiar community
sakai	derogatory term for Orang Asli
sarekat, syarikat	partnership in business
sawah	wet rice fields
sekolah rakyat	people's school
shari'a	Islamic law
tengku	prince or other high royalty
towkay	Chinese trader, usually middleman
tuan besar	lit. 'great lord', used of Europeans
ummah	community of Muslims
zakat	tithe payable after fasting month

Introduction

To write the history of a nation's march to independence is to scrutinise some of its most contested foundation myths. The rise of the nation-state lies at the heart of the modern Southeast Asian experience. Yet it provokes fundamental questions about the distinctiveness of the region and the autonomy of its history: the degree to which the nation is the product of movements deep within Southeast Asian civilisation or the legacy of colonial rule; the extent to which Southeast Asia's encounter with Europe shaped its internal dynamics and values. European rule, and the manner in which colonial authority charted out its dominion, has been seen by historians as pivotal to the emergence of the modern nation-state.[1] Historians have described how, through the prism of the colonial state, nationalists envisaged the unity of their homeland. They have shown how the rulers of post-colonial nations have employed the power of the state to bind the unity of the nation. This writing has sought to examine the dynamics for national integration, and the capacity of politicians to imagine new nations into being. Yet colonial modernity and anti-colonial nationalism have been closely intertwined. Their histories stand in an uneasy relationship to each other, and the lineage between them is neither as simple nor as direct as is often argued. Historians are now uncoupling the concepts and questioning western constructions of the nation-state in Southeast Asia. Many historians emphasise long continuities and draw useful myths from Southeast Asia's past. They seek to show how the sovereignty of the nation-state is derived from pre-colonial traditions. Colonial rule is thus merely an interruption to a longer continuum of state-formation. Other writers emphasise the difficulties of creating a modern nation-state in a region whose pluralism mocks the nation-state's claims to cultural and linguistic exclusiveness. Here, history gives voice to the dissonances within the region's imagined communities.

   Such debates are, of course, common to all post-colonial situations. Similar questions are being asked of Africa and of South Asia. Scholars have begun to

---

[1] For example, of course, Benedict Anderson, *Imagined communities: reflections on the origins and spread of nationalism* (2nd revised edition, London, 1991), especially pp. 163–85.

1

demand new histories for the state, more critical analyses of the construction of national and ethnic identities, and a richer understanding of the making of indigenous civil societies.[2] In analysing their emergence historians of empire have begun to look more closely at the pivotal configuration of the late colonial state.[3] In this, the history of Malaya has much to offer for comparative insight. Modern Malaya has often been perceived as a monument to colonial administrative and political arrangements. By the British it is seen as a model of successful decolonisation. Its institutions, economic structure and ethnic mosaic all have recognisable origins in the colonial period. The country's politics are still dominated by alliances born under British rule. Nationalist leaders have repeatedly turned their rhetoric against the institutional and ideological burdens of the past as they rail against obstacles to their attempts to transform Malaya's politics and society. When their attempts are frustrated, failure is laid at the feet of colonial rule. Yet, the highest expression of the colonial inheritance – the modern state – is also the main instrument of change that the successor regime has at its disposal as it seeks to affirm its post-colonial identity through monumental projects of social engineering. What follows is a historical examination of these frustrations.

This book addresses questions that have dominated the country's historiography since Malaya first became a geographical expression. To what extent did colonial rule make Malaya? How then could it be shaped into a viable nation-state? In Malaya, where Malay, Chinese and Indian populations have created the classic plural society, historians have sought to explain how politicians and governments have attempted to create community, new cultures of belonging. The standard political accounts of decolonisation emphasised how ethnic parties forged a nationalist Alliance, dominated by Malay nationalism, to which the British could devolve power, and how it used this power to promote a common Malayan, later Malaysian, identity. However, the integrationalist assumptions of this kind of nation-building have now been questioned. Pluralism did not give way to assimilation, nor ethnic politics to multi-racialism. Historians now look to explain why this has been so, and now see the nation as more contested than they have done in the past, not only between the constituent ethnic communities, but also within the majority Malay nationalism itself. However, historians differ profoundly on whether primordial political loyalties or more recent processes of social and economic change dictate the politics of community. As they address these questions, J. S. Furnivall's Hobbesian vision of colonial Southeast Asia continues to cast a shadow over the writing of its history. Writing from his experience of the inter-war years, Furnivall described the disruptive impact of the colonial rule:

---

[2] Two exemplary texts are Jean-François Bayart, *The state in Africa: the politics of the belly* (London, 1993); Gyan Pandey, *The construction of communalism in colonial North India* (Delhi, 1993).

[3] For example, see the work of John Lonsdale on Kenya in Lonsdale and B. Berman, *Unhappy valley: conflict in Kenya and Africa* (London, 1992); for the Dutch case see Robert Cribb (ed.), *The late colonial state in Indonesia: political and economic foundations of the Netherlands Indies, 1880–1942* (Leiden, 1994).

Everywhere a native social order, with the plural features characteristic of a society based on personal relations, has been converted into a definitively plural society, with three or more component sections, living side by side but separately, and with no common social life. The plural society has a distinctive plural economy, and a characteristic political constitution.[4]

This book describes how this loose agrarian pluralism was transformed into a corporatist and communal Malaysian polity where, in the words of the present Prime Minister, 'those who say "forget race" are either naive or knaves': the transition from Furnivall to Mahathir.[5] It looks for the roots of this transition in the climacteric years before independence and, by tracing the response of Malayan society to the late colonial state, aims to shed new light on its inner dynamics.

At issue is the capacity of the state to configure social and economic relations. Historians of Malaya have understood the state in a variety of different ways. The first is as an agent of modernity. This perspective emerged out of the work of a long line of colonial scholar-administrators who combined the development of modern administration with pioneering enquiries into the character of indigenous arrangements. History was a necessary adjunct of the practical business of government. This kind of writing has been able to incorporate a significant range of social and economic analyses within its rubric, and many of its assumptions have been transposed into the post-colonial era. Its values are those of secular modernity. It is a Whig interpretation of Malayan history, that emphasises the evolution of its institutions from the feudal dark ages to the creation of a democratic nation–state. It has emphasised the development of the state, and its increasing autonomy as a continuity of institutional, coercive and bureaucratic practices. The end of empire is portrayed as a gradual substitution of one set of personnel for another; anti-colonialism as a struggle for political control of the state. With the advent of mass politics, the state becomes a bargaining ground for the allocation of resources. In the nation-building idiom, what is under examination is the state's relative success as an agent and example of modernisation. A dominant image of the state is that of a more-or-less autonomous set of institutions holding the ring either in the face of political power struggles or of imminent communal disaster. This view was inherited by those who directed the post-colonial state. As one senior Malaysian official remarked at a briefing in 1981, 'our first interest is the salvation and solidarity of the polity'.[6] This theme recurs because of its relevance to a system of political engagement in contemporary Malaysia which emphasises the ability of the state to restructure the economy along ethnic lines, and to determine the relative access of ethnic communities and their leadership to economic and political opportunities. By the 1980s the primacy of the state as an object of study was still very much in vogue. The state's dominance over society was highlighted at the expense of the

[4] J. S. Furnivall, *Progress and welfare in Southeast Asia: a comparison of colonial policy and practice* (New York, 1941), p. 61.
[5] Mahathir bin Mohamad, *The Malay dilemma* (Singapore, 1970), p. 175.
[6] Reported in A. F. Robertson, *The people and the state: an anthropology of planned development* (Cambridge, 1984), p. 288.

nationalisms and social movements which excited earlier generations of scholars. American historical sociology had brought 'the state back in' to analyses of political systems. This found a sympathetic audience among historians of Southeast Asia: military rule and authoritarianism in the region created a pressing concern for scholars to account for the nature of the beast.[7] However, the course of events worked to undermine this perspective. Popular challenges to military government, even unsuccessful ones; attempts at democratisation, even the most fragile, led the ascendency of state power in Southeast Asia to be questioned.

A second body of thought has dismissed these classic accounts of the state in Malaya as static and socially conservative, the work of historians who value order above change. As a counterpoint to this, critics have placed the penetration of external economic forces as a central dynamic of Malayan history, through which the state is conceived 'as an outcome and as a determinate of on-going class contention', the origins of which can be traced to the pre-colonial period.[8] Whilst this perspective highlights the conflicts and antagonisms generated by economic change, its understanding of the European impact is rather one-dimensional: colonial power is seen to rest on its engagement with and shaping of the economic environment, and the colonial state and its agencies, and big business, are still attributed with a power and a degree of co-ordination they rarely, if ever, possessed. However, the very limitations of this perspective, fortified by a general scepticism towards explanations of change in Southeast Asia that minimise the role of indigenous agency led other historians to re-examine colonial rule from below. A much richer understanding of the colonial state, of its social policy, land law, immigration regulations and municipal controls emerged that emphasised the space that subjects of colonial rule carved out for themselves beneath these overarching structures of power. A swelling body of historical writing celebrated a subaltern vision of the underside of Southeast Asian history through the 'collective biography' of the labouring poor.[9] The ideologies of these groups were viewed through the reconstruction of popular *mentalités*, and by examination of counter-hegemonic responses to the impositions of the state and its agents.[10] This trend was mirrored in contem-

---

[7] For example, R. H. Taylor, *The state in Burma* (London, 1987). J. A. C. Mackie, 'Analysing Southeast Asian political systems: changing circumstances and changing approaches', ASAA Conference, Singapore, 1–3 February 1989.

[8] Patrick Sullivan, 'A critical appraisal of historians of Malaya: the theory of society implicit in their work', in Richard Higgott and Richard Robison (eds.), *Southeast Asia: essays in the political economy of structural change* (London, 1985), pp. 65–92; Jomo K. S., *A question of class: capital, the state, and uneven development in Malaya* (Singapore, 1986), pp. 283–4.

[9] James F. Warren, *Rickshaw Coolie: a people's history of Singapore (1880–1940)* (Singapore, 1986); P. J. Rimmer and L. Allen (eds.), *The underside of Malaysian history: pullers, prostitutes and plantation workers* (Singapore, 1990).

[10] Cheah Boon Kheng, 'The erosion of ideological hegemony and royal power and the rise of post-war Malay nationalism', *JSEAS*, 19, 1 (1988), 1–26; his *The peasant robbers of Kedah 1900–1929: historical and folk perceptions* (Singapore, 1988); James C. Scott, *Weapons of the weak: everyday forms of peasant resistance* (New Haven, 1985).

porary perspectives. Civil society began to re-assert itself. The role of non-government organisations – consumers' associations, environmental protection agencies, movements of religious renewal, campaigns for human rights and other pressure groups – as vehicles of this change drew scholarly attention.[11] The recent history of political and social change disclosed more complex patterns in the relationship of state and society in modern Southeast Asia.

In parallel to this, there is a further tradition of history-writing in Malaya, a tradition that eschews secular modernity. It has its beginnings in a tradition of courtly writings in the Malay States from Melaka onwards. This perspective celebrated the continuing evolution of the Malay social and political systems and their ideological world. It found resonance within international scholarship. The tools of cultural anthropology were brought to bear on the notional and psychological world of indigenous kingship. The old historiography was denounced as 'colonial records history', trapped in a bureaucratic discourse based upon the preoccupations of colonial administrators, in which Malay society and indigenous power structures were only considered in so far as they impinged on these institutional concerns.[12] Although its cultural sensitivity and distance from Eurocentrism was not in question, this work drew fire from the 'unrepentant functionalists' for its somewhat static and idealised vision of the Malay political and moral order and for neglecting the discontinuities in its history, for failing to incorporate a sense of social change over time and locality.[13] However, the content of these imaginative histories remains very much the stuff of contemporary politics. Chronicles have been re-examined as part of debates over the position of the *raja* within Malay society, as a source of indigenous notions of accountability. They have been trawled by historians of early modern Southeast Asia, examining the statecraft of the Malay world, looking for the antecedents for the managing of pluralism within an Islamic context; seeking templates for the capacity of the state to foster Malay entrepreneurialism and economic growth. Post-colonial historical writing, appropriated to the needs of nation-building, has sought to explore Malay religion and culture in the colonial period. A growing body of research utilised vernacular sources to explore ways in which subjects related to these political structures. By this token, behind the edifice of colonial rule, the people of Malaya found a surprising degree of social space through which they could mount their own critique on colonial rule and their own societies. A variety of strategies were articulated and a range of outcomes were possible. The early historians of nationalism, it is maintained, minimised dissonance and conflict in their study of

[11] Lim Teck Ghee, 'Non-government organisations and human development: the ASEAN experience', in Lim Teck Ghee (ed.), *Reflections on development in Southeast Asia* (Singapore, 1988), pp. 160–91.

[12] A. C. Milner, *Kerajaan: Malay political culture on the eve of colonial rule* (Tucson, 1982); 'Colonial records history: British Malaya', *MAS*, 21, 4 (1987), 773–92.

[13] J. M. Gullick, 'The condition of having a Raja: a review of *Kerajaan*, by A. C. Milner', *RIMA*, 21, 2 (1982), 109–29.

anti-colonial movements.[14] Post-modernist thought has recently resurrected these older narratives and questioned the assumption that the narrative structures of the professional history of the west should necessarily take precedence over the older tradition.[15] Indeed, it has been argued that internal perceptions of a society, what a society itself perceives to be of importance must dictate the agenda of the historian; history celebrates the particular rather than seeks within a society for the universal.[16] The assertion of indigenous narrative of Malaya's past reflects a more general intellectual mood, from which Malaysian politicians have argued for the authenticity of their institutional experience, and challenged the legitimacy of exogenous critiques that attempt to hold them to account.

The writing of history reflects wider dilemmas within Malaysian political thought. They were sharply drawn in the late colonial period. The need to reconcile an understanding of the nation that was founded upon the historical and cultural experience of the Malays to an ideological and legal framework of nation-building and citizenship that derived from a European tradition was a profound challenge for Malay nationalism. The template for the nation that was being offered by the British had been created by colonial rule. The British too were torn between their obligations as the protecting power of the Malay States and the requirements of governing a multi-racial society. Moreover, non-Malays were unsure as to their place within either vision of nationhood, and felt that their contribution to the history and culture of Malaya had not received its just recognition. The approach of independence intensified these predicaments, and independence left them unresolved. Present-day leaders continue to address them as they strive to create distinctly Malaysian institutions and an authentically Malaysian national identity. Yet, whilst they resist the insensitivity of western thought to Malaysian realities and predicaments, they must also work within institutions which are still largely derived from the colonial tradition. This is a dilemma to which historians might usefully speak. If historians of colonial rule have been blind to the nuances of Malaysian social life that underpinned it, bearers of the indigenous narrative have been slow to examine the ways in which it was permeated by new ideas and shaped by processes of change in the period of British rule. A central premise of this book is that a clearer perception of the state in its colonial form is needed, not least to fortify our understanding of the social forces and nationalisms which challenged it, and the kinds of state-building which supplanted it.

This book examines the divergent responses of colonial government and the communities of Malaya as to a series of social and political crises that demanded the establishment of new forms of community. In particular it examines the social policy and practice of the late colonial state, the spontaneous emergence of movements of

[14] See, for example, Shaharil Talib's introduction to the second edition of W. R. Roff, *The origins of Malay nationalism* (Kuala Lumpur, 1994).

[15] A. C. Milner, 'Post-modern perspectives on Malay biography', *Kajian Malaysia*, 9, 2 (1991), 24–38.

[16] Khoo Kay Kim, 'Malaysian historiography: a further look', *Kajian Malaysia*, 10, 1 (1992), 37–62.

communal self-help and the tensions that erupted between them. A distinguished line of writers have attempted to draw conclusions about state-formation, or nation-building in an earlier parlance, from the experience of revolt and counter-insurgency in British Malaya. Yet for various reasons – lack of sources, the continued sensitivity of the issues at stake, the concentration of scholarship on the Malayan Union period and the Emergency to the near exclusion of everything else – the 1940s and 1950s remain one of the least understood periods of modern Malaysian history. Exemplary research by Malaysian historians has now begun to ask new questions about the period.[17] However, the period is still dominated by the late imperial rubric of counter-insurgency and nation-building. In the most recent work on the Emergency a central theme has been the growth of the state: the growth of apparatus for internal pacification, the widening of its revenue base, and the enlargement of its administrative capacity and reach. This analysis has been broadened by the consideration of ways in which social and political development initiatives were exploited to win the 'allegiance' of the subject populations and to structure the post-colonial order.[18] However, there is a need to disentangle the period from the nationalist and post-colonial mythologies which have grown up around it, and to locate the colonial inheritance more precisely in the social history of modern Malaysia. The argument here departs significantly from existing perspectives: it opens up new areas of argument and reassesses old ones. Late colonialism is anatomised here primarily through its engagement with social and economic change. Its impact is measured in areas beyond the counter-insurgency: in patterns of labour; in agrarian change; in urbanisation and civic sociability; in the transformation of popular culture; in debates on the nature of political freedom. The colonial inheritance will not merely be traced in the structure of Malayan politics, but in the manner in which they were conducted. As ambitious as the colonial state's response to crisis and change was, the autonomy and authority of the state were repeatedly compromised by its participation in these social processes, and its ability to control or direct change undermined by the vitality of indigenous responses to them. These too were deeply divided in their intent. They were also inconclusive. However, their history is fundamental to any understanding of modern Malaysia, and out of the myriad confrontations that arose in these years an independent polity emerged.

Three themes will dominate the chapters that follow. The first is social crisis. An unfolding pattern of migration on the forest frontier has shaped the Malay peninsula throughout its incorporation in the wider world. Practices of cultivation and labour were constantly adapting to the changing social ecology of the internal frontier and

---

[17] In particular the work of Leong Yee Fong on labour; Francis Loh on Kinta society; Tan Liok Ee on Chinese education and politics; Ramlah Adam on the biography of Malay nationalism.

[18] Richard Stubbs, *Hearts and minds in guerrilla warfare: the Malayan Emergency, 1948–1960* (Singapore, 1989), pp. 260–4; and Zakaria Haji Ahmad and Kernial Singh Sandhu, 'The Malayan Emergency: event writ large', in Kernial Singh Sandhu and Paul Wheatley (eds.), *Melaka: the transformation of a Malay capital, c.1400–1980*, 2 vols. (Kuala Lumpur, 1983), I, pp. 388–420.

the advance of the colonial economy. The Pacific war was a watershed in this process. A period of violence and vendetta displaced the townsmen and the industrial labourers of the lowlands into the interior. It broke the existing bonds of patronage and labour discipline, and allowed new forms of leadership to emerge. This crisis underlaid the origins of the Malayan Emergency. The suppression of the revolt did not, in the short term, bring stability to the peninsula. The resettlement of the Malayan Chinese, the greatest developmental project undertaken by any colonial government, tied the agriculturalists back down to the roads and waterways. However, serious new agrarian problems emerged as the cultivators sought to secure and stabilise subsistence in the face of great disruption. Problems of tenancy and poverty were also more intensely felt within rural Malay society. Urbanisation created new social and economic communities, but also created many casualties in the process. These movements of population, as much as the policies of the colonial state, transformed the geography and politics of the peninsula.

A second recurring motif is colonialism as a social force. Whilst at one level, the developing colonial discourse about the nature of Malay society and the character of Malaya's pluralism represented the racial stereotyping inherent within colonial paternalism, in a more sophisticated form it became increasingly prescriptive of action by the colonial state to redress the delicate social balance. Cautious interventions began during the slump. The aftermath of war made larger-scale initiatives unavoidable. War was midwife to a new colonial orthodoxy: a hybrid between the older tradition of Malayan scholar-administrators and social welfare ideologies. It was a register of late imperial ideological confidence that not only was a social reconstruction of Malaya attempted, but also a transformation of its culture. The advance of the new imperialism was greatly accelerated by the Malayan Emergency. Fought to preserve Malaya from the consequences of post-war social crisis, the Emergency was the making of modern Malaya. The state became a presence in the lives of many Asians for the first time. The militarisation of society it necessitated created closer structures of authority. Violence, although in the short term it disintegrated existing loyalties, forced the pace of the creation of new ones. It condemned Malaya to communalism, sometimes literally by the physical separation of populations through resettlement and regroupment. Yet the main motif of colonial government was a sustained attempt to dissolve these old attachments and to re-create community through loyalty and a sense of obligation to the colonial state, articulating a multi-racial Malayan identity. The success of this experiment was contingent on locating indigenous leadership which would nurture it through the transfer of power. Diverse strategies – social welfare, community development, cultural patronage – and the technological revolution that accompanied state expansion, especially the creation of a vast propaganda machine – were employed to this end. However, in many ways technology – in the shape of enhanced road communications, printing, even cinema – empowered Asians. Everywhere, the new enthusiasms these colonial initiatives were intended to arouse, began to advance identities of a different kind.

The third theme is the emergence of a new form of society. Modern Malaya is not the legacy of a primordial past. A concomitant of social crisis was the transformation of amorphous local leaderships into an integrated urban leadership. Violence destroyed old communities, they were to be forged again by the building of new forms of clientage and these new solidarities were articulated in communal terms. However, these divers constituencies were deeply divided, more so than was apparent in the euphoria of independence, as to what the identity, and indeed the end, of the nation ought to be. Cultural agendas were advanced in harness to responses to the material fall-out of social crisis. For the Chinese these centred on land rights, and an openness to new leadership which could guarantee a minimum of interference in their economic and cultural affairs. For the Indians on the estates, it meant unionism and movements of social reform. For the Malays, it meant grappling with the root cause of Malay poverty, through self-help and political mobilisation. In all of these areas of change, a foothold in the interventionist state system became a crucial determinant of communal achievement. Urban leadership began increasingly to mobilise their clients to this end. The colonial leadership, although it disapproved of this basis for mass politics, could not prevent it. Behind the elites stood alternative religious and secular leadership, which – whether through new forms of political mobilisation, education or even popular culture and literature – sought to challenge the assumptions on which the compromises between communal leaderships had been reached.

The following chapter introduces these themes and suggests ways in which they marked the development of state and society before and during the Pacific war. It examines the new state-building policies pursued by the Japanese military against the background of heightened ethnic antagonisms, displacement of population, food shortage, malnutrition and a resurgence of endemic and epidemic disease. Japanese rule, although it did not create anti-colonial nationalism, challenged the established leadership of the community notables through which the British had dealt previously. Tensions came to the fore in the interregnum following the Japanese surrender. This is a primary theme of Chapter 2: an attempt at the close of Pacific war to rebuild the British presence in Malaya from a defeat that was unprecedented in British imperial history. This not only entailed political and administrative rehabilitation, but a reworking of the colonial state's relationship with Malaya's society: an attempt to draw a mushrooming growth of social movements into a new pattern of partnership. The tensions within this experiment, its abandonment, and the reconstruction of colonial authority cast a long shadow over Malayan politics. However, a new language of mass participation and political accountability had been introduced into Malayan politics which underlaid the emergence of new radical forces.

Chapter 3 locates the origins of the Malayan Emergency within the post-war crisis. It was the culmination of a longer process of migration and settlement on the periphery, rather than merely a chain of urban-led subversion, revolt and counter-insurgency. Care is taken to avoid considering the Emergency as primarily a Chinese problem and to see it in relation to economic change and patterns of social organisation, violence and anxiety in the countryside as a whole. The Malay peasant community was torn between Communist, Islamic and millenarian leaders who struggled to fill a vacuum of local leadership and was confronted with fears of economic marginalisation and communal violence. The chapter will examine efforts by the colonial state to reassert its authority in the countryside. Policy towards land, rice cultivation and crop preferences is understood against a menacing environmental crisis precipitated by a new wave of agricultural pioneering on the forest frontier. This provoked the colonial government into a campaign to reassert its presence in these peripheral areas in order to conserve rainforest, prevent soil erosion and assist the recovery and modernisation of the plantation economy. The endemic instability in the rural areas is subjected to new scrutiny and related directly to the reimposition of controls on forest reserves and the occupation of land, and to the labour unrest in the towns. This provoked a pattern of evasion and often violent resistance to authority which forced the pace of the confrontation between the Malayan Communist Party and the British government.

A central assumption of British policy was that the cycle of terror could only be met by the forging of political obedience and loyalty to the colonial state. In Chapter 4 we examine the experience of violence during the Emergency: how it was perceived by those responsible for its suppression; by the rural communities who were subject to it; and how it was validated and constrained. In the eyes of the colonial government, terror criminalised the Chinese population. In political terms, its pacification entailed the guaranteeing of Chinese citizenship rights and accommodation with Malay nationalism. However, the domestication of the Malayan Chinese was also prescriptive of a wider enterprise to secure the allegiance of the Chinese to the colonial state. Counter-terror entailed an attempt to remake both the social and economic as well as the ethnic geography of the peninsula through the resettlement and regroupment of the rural population into protected settlements, and the provision of land for the rural Chinese. The moral reconstruction of Chinese society was pursued through welfare and missionary work and the implanting of civic virtue. Attempts by the Chinese leaders of the towns to re-establish links of patronage with the rural hinterland and to get a purchase on the natural constituency of the Communists in the New Villages – through Chinese education and various experiments in local democracy – were a precursor of large communal mobilisations during the transfer of power and beyond. The Emergency had repercussions beyond the rural fringe, which are examined in Chapter 5. It witnessed the birth of the modern Malayan state and rapid economic change. Labour conditions are examined through employers' attempts to re-establish work discipline, but also through the ways in which south Indian labourers lent support to movements of moral and religious reform and a reconstructed trade unionism, which was to become a vehicle of communal identity. The Emergency years also were a time of rapid urbanisation and of its attendant social evils. In the larger towns a small but politically significant Asian middle class sprung up, which was to be at the forefront of British attempts to promote non-communist, non-communal 'Malayan' politics.

Counter-insurgency also encouraged an attempt to recast the economic structure of the peninsula through reform of the Malay rural economy. This was a period when changing patterns of economy and society provoked the Malays into their own series of undertakings to advance the position of their community, and into an examination of the root causes of Malay poverty. In Chapter 6 the condition of the Malay economy is examined against the cultivator and fisherman's relationship to commercialised agriculture and wage labour. Although the plural characteristics of the rural economy were being modified by growing economic differentiation within the Malay community as a whole, agrarian inequalities continued to be perceived in ethnic terms. Development initiatives, in which senior Malay administrators were at the forefront, focused on restoring economic and social initiative to Malay kampongs, through principles of self-help and the co-operative movement. Again, they were a means of recasting local communities and tutoring local leadership. The failure of these schemes had a profound impact on nationalist thought regarding the position of the Malaya *bumiputera* – son of the soil – and the term reflected a new emphasis on the Malay's entitlement to special rights and privileges in economic life. Attempts were made to create a Malay stake in commerce and industry, both by the state, and by a range of social and political organisations. Although Malay writers interpreted poverty and its alleviation in very different ways, it was increasingly to the authority of the state, as a corporate trust of the Malays, that a generation of Malay politicians looked to redeem the position of the rural Malays, and a new pattern of custody and intercession emerged. The cumulative effects of the settlement of the forest frontier and the ethnic mobilisation of the economy are measured by the experience of the indigenous minorities – the Orang Asli – of the peninsula.

The new arrangements of rural life did not conform to the ideals of community which British rule saw as its duty to implant. As Chapter 7 will show, the 1950s were a period of moral crisis and cultural uncertainty, which witnessed a process of colonial state-building that sought to rationalise old loyalties and construct new ones. A 'Malayan' nationalism and national culture were promoted through new techniques of collaboration. This stood at the apex of the colonial mission. Nowhere was political contest more evident than in the propaganda and sponsorship of cultural renewal. Much of the fabric of Malayan social life stood removed from the cultural experiments of late colonialism. Powerful cultural and political alternatives emerged from outside the colonial paradigm, and sought to effect their own reconstructions of national identity through art, performance, language and literature. Chapter 8 shows how social policy, community development and experiments in local democracy were exploited to entrench a distinction between legitimate and illegitimate forms of popular participation in the political process. However, sponsorship of political activities consonant with the colonial experiments broke down. With the approach of independence, the cultural particularism of the New Villages, the complex reorientations of Malay elites at a local level, and politically resurgent Islam revealed that the social and economic dislocation of the preceding years had subverted the colonial politics of collaboration and its timetables for political advancement.

In initiating policies to counter the consolidation of communal identity by advancing a Malayan sensibility, the colonial government was participating in a process of social change, accelerating new mobilisations, and inadvertently assisted the consolidation of communal identity. By becoming a part of these social processes it succeeded to a point in preserving a measure of social control. Its partial successes had a profound impact on the character of the independent polity, as people looked more and more to the state to accomplish their political and social ambitions. Ultimately this condemned Malaya to communalism. Yet the Malaya that emerged from the end of empire would not stand still. The processes of social and ideological change which had been unleashed at its birth could not be controlled. As the structures of government became more complex and made greater demands on the population, the greater were the opportunities for them to be challenged, or evaded by autonomous action on the part of those subject to them. This was a central paradox of colonial rule. This paradox remained at the heart of the complex relationship between an inherited colonial state system, its corporatist ethos, and the dynamic cohabitation of self-divided communal associations, Malay political primacy and Islamic resurgence in independent Malaysia.

CHAPTER ONE
'On the ruins of Melaka fort'

In Malacca, beside a large reconstruction of the palace of its kings, housed in the old British Club where Somerset Maugham set his short story 'Footprints in the jungle', is an exhibition of over 500 years of Malaysian history. It portrays old Melaka as the centre of a great maritime Malay Islamic civilisation, and charts the town's place in the unfolding story of a nation. In the years before independence, colonial Malacca had declined into something of a backwater. Yet it was still of immense symbolic significance for Malayan nationalists. It was at a Malay Nationalist Party conference in Malacca in the heady year 1945 that the radical, Dr Burhanuddin Al-Helmy, one of Malay nationalism's most important ideologues, declaimed the famous *pantun*:

> *Di atas robohan Melaka*
> *Kita dirikan jiwa merdeka*
> *Bersatu padulah segenap baka*
> *Membela hak keadilan pusaka*
>
> On the ruins of Melaka fort
> We build the soul of independence
> Be united every race
> Defend the right of justice inherited.[1]

It was here in early 1956 that Tunku Abdul Rahman announced the date for the transfer of power: 31 August 1957. His partner in independence, the leader of the Malayan Chinese Tan Cheng Lock, was the quintessential man of Malacca. The town today has been designated a *bandaraya bersejarah*, a living museum: its architecture, its tableaux, the tombs of its heroes have become symbolic of many of the foundation myths of modern Malaysia. The 'soul of independence' has been envisaged in many different ways. The various histories of Melaka offer an insight into the differing genealogies that have been constructed for Malaysia. Some scholars have celebrated

---

[1] There are several variants of this *pantun*. I have taken the version, and slightly modified the translation, in Ahmad Kamal Abdullah et al. (eds.), *History of modern Malay literature* (Kuala Lumpur, 1992), II, p. 22.

the town as a symbol of the historical pluralism of the region, of cultural hybridity as its natural condition.[2] Yet to many Malay scholars, Melaka is a focal point in a continuum of Malay history. Melaka's past is a bridge into the present from which the sovereignty of the nation-state is derived. European rule merely arrested a deeper process of state-formation.[3] In the years before independence, many Malay nationalist politicians read history in the same way. Yet the historical environment of the Malay world changed dramatically in the colonial period. The 'original sovereignty' of the Malays proved hard to reconcile to the new historical reality of the peninsula's plural society. This is a central dilemma of Malay nationalism. Its inability to come to terms with Malaya's colonial history, critics argue, has been an impediment to its attempts to fashion a common purpose with other communities.[4] A central theme of the making of the independent nation-state was the attempts by Malaya's statesmen to reconcile the claims of its competing lineages.

Any exegesis of the colonial inheritance must be attentive to the more protracted shifts in Malaya's history. This chapter identifies the processes of change that created the communities of the peninsula and examines the ways in which the British sought to channel and control them. It isolates three crucial facets of the European impact: the creation of the colonial state, the birth of a new plural society and the fostering of internal movements of social and political reconstruction. Although colonial rule contributed much to the emergence of the plural society, it was not the sole agent in its consolidation. The British rarely possessed the capacity to intervene decisively in social and economic life. This weakness was underscored by indigenous economic initiatives, the self-awareness of new communities and new patterns of thought and leadership. These countervailing forces gathered momentum after the turn of the century. The peninsular Malays explored the anxieties generated by the condition of Islam under European rule and by secular modernity. They began to define their community and imagine their homeland as a whole. Chinese and Indian politics began to reconcile the claims of the motherland to their local predicament. As they did so, innovative political doctrines were introduced into Malaya. These had already made an imprint by the time of the First World War. The inter-war slump saw the passing of the era of high imperialism, the collapse of its assumptions of unbroken prosperity and the erosion of European racial supremacy. Challenges to the colonial order arose, spearheaded by native elites nurtured by European rule. They were deepened by the

---

[2] Kernial Singh Sandhu and Paul Wheatley (eds.), *Melaka: the transformation of a Malay capital* (Kuala Lumpur, 1983); Louis Filipe Thomaz, 'The Malay Sultanate of Melaka', in Anthony Reid (ed.), *Southeast Asia in the early modern era: trade, power and belief* (Ithaca, 1993), pp. 69–90.

[3] Muhammad Yusoff Hashim, *The Malay Sultanate of Malacca: a study of various aspects of Malacca in the fifteenth and sixteenth centuries in Malaysian history* (Kuala Lumpur, 1992), pp. xxii, 281–3.

[4] Muhammad Ikmal Said, 'Ethnic perspectives on the left in Malaysia', in Joel Kahn and Francis Loh Kok Wah (eds.), *Fragmented vision: culture and politics in contemporary Malaysia* (Sydney, 1992), pp. 254–81.

vibrant popular cultures of the towns and by the pockets of Malayan society that had stood beyond the pale of colonial power. The British reacted with resolute and uncompromising assertions of their imperial authority when, in 1939, they found themselves in the throes of a new world crisis. Yet Britain, by herself, was no longer strong enough to fulfil her obligations as the protecting power in the Malay States. The illusion of colonial omnipotence evaporated in late 1941, when the imperial Japanese army conquered Malaya. The gyre of social change was unfettered during the war years: it was a time of disequilibrium that would, over time, create a new society.

The momentum of the Malay world

'The Malay world,' Professor Wolters tells us, 'had a momentum of its own.'[5] And this world remained in motion throughout the colonial period. Many of the dynamics of change attributed to the expansion of Europe were already found within. The indigenous history of the state was unbroken by colonial rule. The early modern state reached its apogee in Melaka: a state based on trade, whose hegemony reached over much of the western archipelago; a richly cosmopolitan world, and the centre of the *darul Islam* in the east. After the Portuguese conquest of Melaka in 1511 the Malay world lost its centre of unity, yet Melaka remained an institutional prototype: a paradigm of statecraft and a point of cultural reference for successor states such as Johor-Riau, Perak and Pahang. They looked to Melaka for legitimacy and competed to inherit its mantle. There were important divergences in experience: other Malay states – Kedah and Trengganu, for example – claimed different lineages. But through courtly chronicles composed after its fall – the *Sejarah Melayu*, or Malay Annals, and the stories of its hero Hang Tuah, *Hikayat Hang Tuah* – the Melaka tradition was transmitted onwards and fostered a vigorous ethos of Malay, *Melayu*, identity. These chronicles were a source of instruction for Melaka's successor regimes; they enshrined the sanctity and authority, the *daulat*, of the Ruler, his role in maintaining the cohesion of the realm, and legitimated the increasingly absolutist visage these states adopted in the competitive environment created by the European traders.[6] In years to come, Melaka's remembrance would lie at the forefront of Malay nationalist thought. Successive colonial regimes also self-consciously sought to build upon it.

Migration is a second dynamic of the early modern world that was transmitted into the modern. The civilisations of the Malay world are founded on movements of people rather than settled accumulations of population. Although the coming of European rule was associated with large influxes of population, migration was deeply rooted in the culture of the region as a resource from pre-colonial times in state-

---

[5] O.W. Wolters, *The fall of Srivijaya in Malay history* (London, 1970), p. 176.
[6] Virginia Matheson, 'Concepts of Malay ethos in indigenous Malay writings', *JSEAS*, 10, 2 (1979), 351–71; J. Kathirithamby-Wells, 'The Johor-Malay world, 1511–1784: changes in political ideology', *Sejarah*, 1 (1988), 35–62.

building and economic development, and as a vital stimulus to the emergence of court cultures and indigenous entrepreneurship. A long history of external migrations introduced Indian learning and Islam; the great tradition of internal migration carried the new cultures throughout the region. By the eighteenth century, migrations within Southeast Asia were undergoing a slow sea-change, moving more from east to west and from south to north. In this period, the Malay peninsula was a fractured and fluid political world. It was a constellation of riverine kingdoms that derived their power from control of the river systems that snaked into the interior. It was a frontier economy where control of trade in forest resources and the opening of land was a major prerogative of political power, and the manpower to exploit this the measure of its effectiveness. Wealth was measured in men. Migration could help build states, but it could also lead to political instability and fragmentation. The history of the peninsula in the eighteenth and nineteenth centuries is a story of interloping kings and communal colonisations of land by migrants from other parts of the archipelago.[7] The characteristic relations between the coast and the hinterland, upriver and downriver, *hulu* and *hilir*, were fraught with tensions. Migrations exacerbated them. The rolling landscape of the west coast behind Melaka attracted from the fourteenth century onwards large numbers of Minangkabau settlers. This migration gained momentum in the seventeenth century as the settlers carved out the nine chiefdoms of Negri Sembilan. Bugis migrants, driven westwards from Sulawesi, usurped control of existing states such as Johor, and played a crucial role in the foundation of new ones, such as Selangor. Immigrant Malay trading classes and agriculturists opened up large areas of new land, especially in Perak. Shared poverty bound them together and led them to forge new relationships with Malay chiefs. These migrant populations showed a great sensitivity to new market linkages and forged wide credit relationships with the trading communities of the European settlements.[8] On the eve of colonial rule, a rich cultural and linguistic patchwork of Malay settlement emerged: for example, pockets of Kerinchi, Mandaling, Acehnese, Banjarese settlement in Selangor and Perak. Populations moved downwards from Patani and Kelantan. These large influxes of population from within the Malay world increased dramatically in the colonial period. The regional identities they created had a profound impact on Malayan politics.[9]

The advent of colonial rule also coincided with, and stimulated, a resumption of migrations from outside the region which would become a predominant theme of Malayan history in the first half of the twentieth century. Resident communities of Chinese, Arab and South Indian Muslims had already emerged with distinctive

---

[7] Wang Gungwu, 'Migration patterns in history: Malaysia and the region', *JMBRAS*, 58 (1985), 43–57.

[8] J. M. Gullick, 'The entrepreneur in late nineteenth century Malay peasant society', *JMBRAS*, 58, (1985), 59–70.

[9] Tunku Shamsul Bahrin, 'The Indonesian immigrants and the Malays of West Malaysia: a study in assimilation and integration', *Geographica*, 6 (1970), 1–12.

Straits, or *Peranakan,* identities. However, economic expansion drew in new flows of people. Commercialised agriculture on a large scale was pioneered by Chinese gambier and tapioca cultivation, which by the nineteenth century may have involved at least half a million acres. Chinese tin mines in Perak and Selangor directly imported labour, but increasingly men came on their own account, leaguing together to work medium-sized holdings through a tribute system.[10] New work on the history of Chinese labour in Malaya has highlighted the importance of the primary unit of economic and social authority, the *kongsi,* which combined traditions of brotherhood with economic partnership, to constitute a system of 'little republics' where central political authority was weak. The British recognised their leaders as *kapitan China* and revenue farmers to capitalise on their economic success, and to relieve themselves of governing the turbulent frontier. However, in the nineteenth century the rivalries between the *kongsi* exploiters of the hinterlands with the older established Straits Chinese mercantile interests of the colonial towns rose in intensity. As the Chinese merchants, or *towkay,* adapted to European business practices and began to work within colonial institutions the British came to perceive the fraternities as criminal rather than economic, and by the 1870s and 1880s, the era of *laissez-faire* had come to an end. Conflicts within Chinese society provided the immediate *casus belli* for colonial intervention in the western Malay States.[11]

By the early nineteenth century these local dynamics collided with changing patterns of international trade. The European stake in Southeast Asia grew after the lifting of restrictions on the China trade in 1729. Local states acquired a pivotal role in the exchange of Indian opium and cottons in the western archipelago for tin, spices and exotica for the Chinese market under the nose of Dutch monopoly. This trade disrupted power relationships in the Malay peninsula. States struggled to keep a grip on trade and rebuff potential challengers by fortifying royal authority. Some rulers made alliance with the Europeans; others took more direct control of their territory. Local chiefs challenged rulers by sea raiding and piracy. Minority traders caught in the middle of these conflicts began to court the support of the Europeans, who complained loudly that they were hostage to the whims of oriental despots. The strategic importance of Southeast Asia grew during the European war between Britain and the Dutch in 1780–4. A 1784 Treaty permitted English navigation in Dutch seas and encouraged local princes to apply to the East India Company for protection. In 1786 the island of Penang was ceded to the English Company by the Ruler of Kedah. During the Napoleonic wars internal conflicts and Malay privateering intensified and confirmed British perceptions of political decay in the Malay world. The Dutch

---

[10] J. C. Jackson, *Planters and speculators: Chinese and European agricultural enterprise in Malaya, 1786–1921* (Kuala Lumpur, 1968), p. 6; R. N. Jackson, *Immigrant labour and the development of Malaya* (Kuala Lumpur, 1960), pp. 79–90.

[11] Wang Tai Peng, *The origins of Chinese kongsi* (Petaling Jaya, 1994); Carl A. Trocki, *Opium and empire: Chinese society in colonial Singapore, 1800–1910* (Ithaca, 1990); Khoo Kay Kim, *The Western Malay States, 1850–73* (Kuala Lumpur, 1972).

monopoly was seen as its root cause, and European war gave Britain the opportunity to seize Dutch possessions and extend her power in the archipelago. In 1819, one of the chief architects of this advance, Stamford Raffles, founded a new trading settlement at Singapore. The Anglo–Dutch Treaty of 1824 established rival spheres of influence, leaving the British dominant on the peninsula, and the Dutch paramount in the islands, whilst permitting the British to trade freely there. It marked the beginning of the era of formal colonial conquest. In 1826, Penang, Singapore and Malacca combined to form the Straits Settlements. They became enclaves for foreign traders, and as their economies expanded, so too did British involvement in the Malay States. A campaign against piracy in the western islands altered patterns of trade; it saw the final decline of local sea-power and an assertion of Company authority over the hinterland, which was becoming increasingly troubled as local elites and Chinese miners squabbled to control resources. In 1873 a contender for power in Perak, Raja Abdullah, requested that the British send a Resident in return for his recognition as Sultan. In early 1874 the Pangkor Engagement formalised this arrangement, which was extended to Selangor and parts of Negri Sembilan in the same year. The murder of the British Resident of Perak in 1875 provoked a consolidation of colonial authority. Treaties of protection were extended to Selangor, Perak, Negri Sembilan and Pahang, and the four states became the Federated Malay States in 1895. Between 1909 and 1914 the remaining peninsular states – Kedah, Perlis, Kelantan, Trengganu and Johore – came under British control as Unfederated Malay States.[12] In the rationalising mind of the Victorian, although not yet in the minds of its people, 'Malaya' had become something more than a geographical expression.

'A moral-forcing system'

Any study of the colonial state in British Malaya is complicated by the fact that, strictly speaking, the British presence was not a state at all, or rather it worked on the pretence that it was not a state. Theoretically it was not sovereign. British authority rested on treaty relationships with the Malay Rulers, and was exercised through the Malay State administrations. The Straits Settlements were exceptions to this and were the wellsprings of colonial modernity in Malaya. Whatever the realities of British power, the architects of indirect rule insisted on this fiction. The Pangkor Engagement of 1874 stipulated that a Resident's advice 'must be acted upon on all questions other than those touching Malay religion and customs'. The areas to which 'custom' extended were left largely undefined. Wide variations of administrative practice emerged. On the one hand, Britain was the custodian of Malay government, and custody enjoined the development of the Malay States from independent decadence to prosperity and good government. On the other hand, the colonial government was an external agent of modernisation, the vehicle of highly commercialised and labour-

---

[12] B.W. and L.Y. Andaya, *A History of Malaysia* (London, 1982), chs. 3–4.

intensive forms of production. It sought to resolve this dilemma of trusteeship by forcing the pace of progress along a historical evolutionary scale borrowed from Whig constitutionalist thought: the Malay States had been found in a state of feudal disintegration and they were to be coaxed through the stages of development of English history and so to be spared its turbulence and the darker side of industrialism. The Pangkor Agreement was seen as Malaya's Magna Carta, an accommodation between the king and the barons. Thereafter the Malay States were to be led down a slow path of tranquil political evolution as the British 'set about the task of moulding their history'. Protection was a 'moral-forcing system'.[13]

A hallmark of colonial rule was the reinvention of traditional forms. Malay monarchy was made more comprehensible to Englishmen; its Durbars were elaborate pantomimes that symbolised the colonial reordering of the realm. For the Maharajah of Johore and the Bendahara of Pahang, a powerful incentive to sign treaties with Britain in 1885 and 1887 was the acquisition of the title 'Sultan' as a gift of sovereignty from Queen Victoria.[14] Local administration was under the supervision of British District Officers, although it was reliant on the co-operation of Malay officials. The system was perfected by Sir Hugh Low, Resident in Perak from 1878 until 1889, who learnt from service with Rajah James Brooke in Borneo how to govern a large country cheaply with a handful of Europeans. The bottom layer of rural administration was rationalised by giving the *penghulu*, or village headmen, a more active role in government, although this varied greatly from state to state.[15] Existing Malay elites were gradually incorporated within a larger bureaucratic structure. A vivid image of this new alliance is an episode at Kuala Kangsar in 1894, where the District Magistrate played chess with the Tengku Temenggong with Malays as chessmen.[16] The Anglo-Malay combine was strengthened in 1905, when a new school for Malays was opened, the Malay College of Kuala Kangsar: to Malays it was the 'Bab-ud-Darajat', the gateway to high position. The Malay Administrative Service, a second-division civil service built up from educated Malays, was launched in 1910. It was low paid and only twenty-seven Malays were promoted into the elite Malayan Civil Service (MCS) by the time of the Second World War. Yet it was an early assertion of the principle that the Malays, being 'sons of the soil', should receive preferential government employment.[17] As the non-Malay population grew, British officials –

---

[13] Paul H. Kratoska, *The Chettiar and the Yeoman: British cultural categories and rural indebtedness in Malaya* (ISEAS, Occasional paper No. 32, Singapore, 1975), pp. 2–8; Hugh Clifford, 'Life in the Malay peninsula: as it was and is', in Paul H. Kratoska (ed.), *Honourable intentions: talks on the British Empire in Southeast Asia delivered at the Royal Colonial Institute, 1874–1928* (Singapore, 1983), pp. 224–48.

[14] Aruna Gopinath, *Pahang, 1880–1933: a political history* (Kuala Lumpur, 1991), p. 86.

[15] J. M. Gullick, *Malay society in the late nineteenth century: the beginnings of change* (Singapore, 1987), pp. 75–88.

[16] W. R. Roff, 'Colonial pursuits', *Journal of the Historical Society, University of Malaya*, 6 (1967/68), 52.

[17] Yeo Kim Wah, 'The grooming of an elite: Malay administrators in the Federated Malay States, 1903–1941', *JSEAS*, 11, 2 (1980), 287–319.

especially those who had carved out their own careers within the system of protection – stressed the 'Malayness' of the Malay States and the political legitimacy they drew from traditional power.

The durability of the Malay States was not solely the consequence of indirect rule. European accounts of Malay government drew poetic contrasts between the ceremonials of courts and the substance of British power. However, although frequently traumatised by change, the ideological world of the Malay polity, the *kerajaan*, remained intact. The internal unrest and resistance associated with colonial conquest indicated important internal shifts in power in which the traditional ruling class generally lost more power than the Ruler. The British boosted the Ruler's prestige by treating him as an absolute monarch whose powers had been usurped by unruly subjects. Succession disputes no longer interfered with the peace of the realm, although, as in the case of Selangor in 1936, on occasion they came close to doing so. The Rulers displayed great aptitude for the statecraft of indirect rule.[18] The general trend lay towards the rationalisation and bureaucratisation of Malay government. But this was not exclusively the work of European mandarins. The Sultans of Johore created an energetic modernising monarchy with administrative departments in the British tradition, which, despite Johore being on the doorstep of Singapore, saved it from early British intervention. Moreover, Malay aristocracies were not as indolent as the British suggested. They used their advantageous position to apply for agricultural and mining concessions on favourable terms and then passed them on to Chinese capitalists. They provided new services and reworked older ones – the hiring of elephants for transportation, the using of traditional rights to labour for irrigation and public works – and although they did not constitute an entrepreneurial class as such, they exploited economic change through trade and bureaucracy and slowly carved out a system of 'achieved status by role', which preserved old forms of inequalities into a new age.[19] The self-strengthening of Malay governments schooled new leadership in religious academies and bureaucracies which were in many ways outside the inner orbit of colonial power. In Kelantan, where 'he who controlled the *imam* commanded the State', Islamic administration became a counterweight to colonial government. It was also given a more regularised institutional position in the western Malay States, and Rulers exploited this to respond to Islamic modernism in the Middle East. Moreover, in the early nineteenth century the writ of central religious authority did not run far: village disputes were settled at the local level where charismatic figures could mobilise the people around Islam.[20] Rebellions, such as the Pahang war of

---

[18] A. C. Milner, *Kerajaan: Malay political culture on the eve of colonial rule* (Tucson, 1982); for the politics of indirect rule, J. M. Gullick, *Rulers and Residents: influence and power in the Malay States, 1870–1920* (Singapore, 1992).

[19] Heather Sutherland, 'The taming of the Trengganu elite', in Ruth T. McVey (ed.), *Southeast Asian transitions: approaches through social history* (New Haven, 1978), pp. 50–2; Shaharil Talib, *After its own image: the Trengganu experience, 1881–1941* (Singapore, 1984), pp. 69–104; Gullick, *Malay society*, esp. pp. 79–80, 258.

[20] William R. Roff, 'The origin and early years of the *Majlis Ugama*', in Roff (ed.), *Kelantan:*

1891–5, were caused in some sense by the internal pressures of self-strengthening, but as they gathered momentum they could take on more anti-colonial and millenarian features. Later mobilisations occurred around old sites of resistance, often hidden from the view of the conquerors: *perang sabil*, holy war, was a living tradition.[21]

The most powerful challenge to British colonial rule, however, came from within the colonial system itself, from those educated by it and exposed to its governing assumptions. The moral charge of protection was to regenerate Malay society, promote change without upheaval, impart industry and time discipline. Malay education was promoted amongst the Malay elite at the expense of English language education. In 1906, education reforms went further in introducing Malays to modernity, by widening the Malay world-view through language and literature, and, in a momentous experiment in cultural engineering, began the romanisation of Malay script. They were a product of a conservative imagination. Colonial schools reproduced Malay tradition as a mirror to the technological supremacy of the west and as a rationale for British intervention. Yet through their accent on individual reading and self-improvement they supplied a very different ethos of education from that of the Quranic system. They provided an audience for modernity, a tool of communal self-analysis, through which Malays began to develop their own conceptions of being modern. There was nothing radically new about modernity, and more than one route to it. For centuries new ideas and attitudes had been disseminated through the region's tradition of inter-migration. In the nineteenth century, Singapore became a central locus for this. For Malays, it contained relicts of the Johor-Riau courtly culture. It was the centre of communications of the eastern Islamic world, a starting point for the *haj* and a refuge from the Dutch authorities. It was home to the mission presses and more importantly, in terms of what was read, to a network of Muslim publishers. Singapore's Javanese, Arab and Indian Muslim minorities took the lead in creating a vibrant print culture. After 1840, 85 per cent of books in Malay came from Singapore: books of instruction – *kitabs*, chronicles – *hikayat*, and a verse form – *syair*; luxury products, distributed by catalogues, mail order, networks of local agents, through vernacular school inspectors, mosques and *madrasahs*, or by itinerant seafarers and traders. Malay publications also came from Bombay, Cairo and Mecca. A new idea of literature was facilitated by the new technology: one that was contemporary, authored by named individuals, that was read as an internal mental process, rather than uttered as a social transaction. In 1890 the registered fortnightly output of the Singapore Muslim presses alone eclipsed the entire production in literary manuscripts to that date of several centuries. Yet it must be stressed that the advent of print did not bring a dramatic disjuncture in world-view. The 'traditional'

---

religion, society and politics in a Malay State (Kuala Lumpur, 1974), pp. 101–52; 'The institutionalization of Islam in the Malay peninsula: some problems for the historian', in Sartomo Kartodirdjo (ed.), *Profiles of Malay culture: historiography, religion and politics* (Jakarta, 1976), pp. 66–72.

[21] Gopinath, *Pahang*, pp. 133–59; Abdul Rahman Haji Abdullah, *Gerakan anti penjajahan di Malaysia, 1511–1950: pengaruh agama dan tarikat* (Kuala Lumpur, 1994).

and the 'modern' developed side-by-side within the new technology.[22] The biography of the Malay educator Haji Abdul Majid bin Zainuddin shows the key intermediary role some Malays played between the intellectual culture of the Malay world and the colonial sphere: it celebrates a literati of great vitality, many of them men employed by the colonial regime, who 'appear now to me', Abdul Majid reminisced, 'as the last links to the old civilisation that is at last being replaced by a new one!'[23] The turn of the century saw an explosion in periodical publications which, although they varied in temper, began to share a new style and method of public utterance. A landmark was *Al-Imam* (1906–10) established by the religious reformer Sayyid Shaykh Al-Hadi. Through its columns and that of a successor, *Neracha* (1911–15), Islamic reform and Middle Eastern issues were debated with a new immediacy in Malaya. *Utusan Melayu* (1907–21), edited by the son of Minangkabau merchant, Mohd. Eunos Abdullah, began to speak to a nation, a *bangsa*, to explain to its audience the new languages of politics and government that had been brought by the Europeans and to fashion its own.[24]

By the century's turning the impact of colonial modernity was registered in the deeper presence of the state. Social and economic change demanded the creation of new structures of authority. Revenues rose dramatically: from $8,434,083 in 1896 to $25,246,863 in 1909. So too did population levels. The first Protected Malay States census in 1891 gave a population of 232,172 'Malaysians', 163,821 Chinese and 20,177 Indians; in 1921 the population had risen to 511,000 'Malaysians', 495,000 Chinese and 305,000 Indians. However, the British protectorates were no longer solely 'Malay' states: in 1901 in Perak the numbers of Chinese exceeded those of Malays by 18,348; in Selangor by 74,771.[25] The mechanisms of indirect rule which had largely absorbed Europeans in Asian polities were changing: Asians were now to be encapsulated in European systems. The colonial state embraced areas of government untouched by the Malay *ancien régime*, services supernumerary to protection. It was a new kind of state entirely. Its power was not negotiable. Its law reflected a new concept of the person that challenged old notions of status and community. It possessed new systems of administrative accounting in the field of revenue, and laid a host of new charges upon the people. It was torn between authoritarian responses to the Asian situation

---

[22] Rex Stevenson, *Cultivators and administrators: British educational policy towards the Malays, 1875–1906* (Kuala Lumpur, 1975); Ian Proudfoot, *Early Malay printed books: a provisional account of materials published in the Singapore-Malaysia area up to 1920, noting holdings in major public collections* (Kuala Lumpur, 1993), Introduction; Hadijah bte Rahmat, 'The printing press and the changing concepts of literature, authorship and notions of self in Malay literature', *JMBRAS*, 69, 1 (1996), 64–84.

[23] William R. Roff (ed.), *The wandering thoughts of a dying man: the life and times of Haji Abdul Majid bin Zainuddin* (Kuala Lumpur, 1978), p. 60.

[24] A. C. Milner, *Invention of politics in colonial Malaya: contesting nationalism and the expansion of the bourgeois public sphere* (Cambridge, 1995), pp. 114–36, 249–51.

[25] Jagjit Singh Sidhu, *Administration in the Federated Malay States, 1896–1920* (Kuala Lumpur, 1981), pp. 67, 80; Emily Sadka, *The Protected Malay States, 1874–95* (Kuala Lumpur, 1968), p. 188.

and its belief in the supremacy of the rule of its law. Migration, the withdrawal of oneself and one's movable wealth, was a traditional way in which Southeast Asians had met the demands of the old regimes. The new Leviathans were very different: 'compared to the kingdoms they replaced they left few places to hide'.[26]

The colonial state was constructed on four pillars: the first was a reformed administration. The racial and bureaucratic ethos of the late Victorian empire discouraged intimacy with Asians. The frontier receded. Administration became professionalised with a more uniform set of values; recruited not from local adventurers, but by examination of cadets for the MCS in London.[27] In 1896, the Protected Malay States were brought together as the Federated Malay States. Although this in no sense created a central government, the accretion of power to new federal bodies continued in the first decade of the twentieth century and was compounded by the First World War. A second pillar was the introduction of a new rule of property for Malaya. After 1891 a systematic land tenure was introduced that acknowledged customary title with leases in perpetuity, and sought to create a rooted landed yeoman peasantry in a manner that disregarded much of the ways in which Malays had viewed the land.[28] The creation of new centres of power was a third pillar of state. Colonial law was administered from new towns such as Kuala Lumpur, Ipoh, Taiping, Telok Anson and Kuantan, which rapidly eclipsed the traditional court centres. Sanitary boards were established in the 1890s which became important conduits for local opinion and, for many Asians, their first direct exposure to western institutional practice.[29] A fourth pillar of state was the enhanced technological competence of government. By the early twentieth century the colonial state embraced a spectrum of new functions: education, social reform, censi, vast works of irrigation, transportation, sanitary engineering, town planning and agricultural research. Malaya became a centre of research in tropical medicine as it became host to vast battalions of indentured labour whose experience was largely one of disease and premature death.[30] Imperial technocracy was not motivated by humanitarianism and progress alone, it generated its own momentum. 'Every Resident,' commented an official in 1915, 'is a Socialist in his own state'.[31] A pool of expertise was developed that laid the foundations for the spectacular projects of post-war colonial rule.

A central objective of state-building in Malaya was the imposition of more effective

---

[26] James C. Scott, *The moral economy of the peasant: rebellion and subsistence in Southeast Asia* (New Haven, 1976), p. 94.

[27] James de Vere Allen, 'The Malayan civil service, 1874–1941: colonial bureaucracy/Malay elite', *CSSH*, 12, 2 (1970), 158–9.

[28] Paul H. Kratoska, 'The peripatetic peasant and land tenure in British Malaya', *JSEAS*, 16, 1 (1985), 16–45.

[29] Khoo Kay Kim, 'Malaysian historiography: a further look', *Kajian Malaysia*, 10, 1 (1992), 56–8.

[30] Lenore H. Manderson, *Sickness and the state: health and illness in colonial Malaya, 1870–1940* (Cambridge, 1996).

[31] Goh Ban Lee, *Urban planning in Malaysia: history, assumptions and issues* (Petaling Jaya, 1991), p. 36.

controls over the labour of its people. In their hunger for labour, and their readiness to import it from overseas, Europeans were following an entrenched local practice. Yet labour was not easy to secure, particularly that of the Chinese who preferred to work for themselves. In the 1870s and 1880s 'militant *laissez-faire*' held sway. British officials were conscious of the abuses of the 'truck' system by which most of the Chinese were employed, yet humanitarian concern did not lead to intervention. It was depressed conditions in Chinese tin mines that led the British to assist key *kapitans* such as Yap Ah Loy of Selangor to manage Chinese labour through coolie-entrepreneurs. The rationale was control, especially through closing the option of Chinese labour to desert to better employers – a traditional form of protest. By 1895 the regulations on the conditions of Chinese workers were written into a Labour Code. To offset the rising numbers of Chinese in the Malay States, and to aid the establishment of the European plantation industry, British administrators turned after 1883 to what were seen as the poverty-stricken, docile peasantry of South India. Indenture was 'a new system of slavery'. During the rubber boom of 1899, 5,249 indentured migrants came to Malaya from Madras; 9,174 in 1900. However, after this date, Indians came increasingly on their own, recruited by labour agents: 15,176 in 1899 and 30,752 in 1900. After 1908 this new flow was regulated by government and industry through a Tamil Immigration Fund; after 1909 all Indians travelled freely, although indenture contracts ran on until 1913.[32] The increase in the Chinese population was unabated: between 1911 and 1921 it was 258,000; between 1921 and 1931, 534,615.[33] Another counterweight to this was settlement from the Dutch East Indies. The 'Malaysian' population rose between the 1891 and 1921 censi from 232,172 to 511,000. However, as we shall see, British attempts to shepherd these massive flows of people were not uniformly successful.

The British dilemma lay in imposing order on native disorder, without extinguishing the native enterprise that had made British Malaya a working proposition in the first place. European business was slow to avail itself of economic opportunities. Sir Frank Swettenham famously observed that 'the prosperity of the Malay States was due to the enterprise and labour of the Chinese . . . The progress made in development was due to local effort and Asiatic capital.' There was no net inflow of capital or imports to the Malay States, at least until the First World War.[34] In 1906 only 10–15 per cent of tin production was in western hands. It was only after this period that more capital-intensive, technologically advanced production gave European business the edge over the more labour-intensive forms of Chinese enterprise. Expansion was financed largely through the reinvested profits of local businesses, the capital and the expertise of Asian compradores, through the expansion of the old

---

[32] Philp Loh, *The Malay States, 1877–95* (Singapore, 1969); Hugh Tinker, *A new system of slavery: the export of Indian labour overseas, 1830–1920* (London, 1974), pp. 57, 315.

[33] Victor Purcell, *The Chinese in Malaya* (Kuala Lumpur, 1967), p. 206.

[34] Frank Swettenham, *British Malaya* (London, 1948), p. 351; J. H. Drabble, 'Some thoughts on the economic development of Malaya under British administration', *JSEAS*, 5, 2 (1974), 203.

Agency House and Straits Trading Companies. Guthrie and Company bought Chinese-mined tin; Boustead and Company expanded into plantations through the marketing of smallholders' produce from the eastern States. Europeans invested through Chettiars, or the larger Chinese concerns, who were better able to assess the credit-worthiness of local borrowers and willing to bear their losses.[35] Although British commercial enterprises were favoured at the expense of local producers, a fixed identity of interest between planters and civil servants of British Malaya did not exist in the face of the subtle hierarchies of the European community.[36] More than this, the vitality of indigenous economy limited the incisiveness of the colonial state as a naked instrument of foreign economic dominance.

Impressive as the aggregate indices of growth were, they only reflect penetration of a relatively small part of the country. Even by 1921 men had settled only 2.5 per cent of the territory of Pahang.[37] Much of the peninsula was a forest frontier, along which the commercial economy impacted in varying degrees. In the pre-colonial era, although wet padi, *sawah*, was introduced from Siam, dry padi cultivation was more important and was practised through shifting, or *ladang*, cultivation. This persisted over much of the peninsula in the colonial era, and it was this kind of land that attracted plantation interests. At the turn of the century only Kedah, Kelantan and Perlis, where the majority of the population was involved in padi production, exported surplus rice. Slowly, a new spatial pattern of production began to emerge, most markedly on the western side of the central range. There were the core areas of colonial enterprise – Perak, Selangor and parts of Negri Sembilan and Johore – where modern mining and plantation industry was concentrated. Adjacent to this were what we might term semi-core areas of food cultivation. It was here that the British directed the main thrust of their agricultural policy to bolster commercial food production for consumption in the towns, mines and estates. These areas – Krian and Sungei Manik in Perak and, by the 1930s, Tanjong Karang in Selangor – were the focus of migrations from within Malaya and from the Dutch East Indies. It was here too that forms of rural indebtedness were becoming more pronounced within Malay rural society. Beyond these areas lay the periphery, the *hulu*, which occupied a marginal place in the colonial economy and where padi was grown solely for consumption. Here the indigenous minorities of the peninsula, the Orang Asli, were crucial intermediaries in the economy of the forest and its fringes.[38] These geographical contrasts must not be interpreted too rigidly, but they would become increasingly significant as the reach of the commercial economy lengthened.

Historians have highlighted ways in which the colonial state created an 'ethnic

---

[35] Rajeswary Ampalavarnar Brown, *Capital and entrepreneurship in Southeast Asia* (London, 1994), pp. 77–122, 142–72.

[36] John Butcher, *The British in Malaya, 1880–1941* (Kuala Lumpur, 1983), pp. 156, 128–9.

[37] R. G. Cant, *An historical geography of Pahang* (Kuala Lumpur, 1972), pp. 100, 29.

[38] Cheng Siok Hwa, 'The rice industry of Malaya: a historical survey', *JMBRAS*, 42, 2 (1969), 130–44; Donald M. Nonini, *British colonial rule and the resistance of the Malay peasantry, 1900–1957* (New Haven, 1992), pp. 80–5.

division of labour' in Malaya: discrete ethnic entities in counterpoise with each other, each with their own economic specialisation: Malays in the padi fields; Chinese in the mines and shops; Indians on the plantations. It is argued that this was a consistent and intentional consequence of colonial policy. The central thrust of post-colonial state-building has been directed at reversing this process.[39] Certainly colonial policy towards the local economy was informed by a series of racial assumptions. Perceptions of the Chinese as the most turbulent and individualistic of races had a direct influence on the indirect manner in which they were governed. The planters' vision of Tamils – 'abject, cowardly and generally lacking in vitality' – entrenched a paternalistic approach to labour management.[40] Notions of the deterioration of the Malay character were developed by a long line of scholar-administrators, in which its chief trait was identified, in Swettenham's phrase, as 'a disinclination to work', or, put another way, resistance to wage labour. For the British, this was the mainspring of Malay economic backwardness and vulnerability, and it led them to see their duty in establishing and safeguarding a settled Malay yeoman-peasantry.[41] Yet the colonial state did not possess the capacity to enforce a rigid 'ethnic division of labour', economic choice also played a part in shaping the rural economy, and British perceptions of a community's economic role were not unchallenged.[42] Malay peasants were very mobile and continued to seek a more flexible access to land than the contractually-based secure tenure offered by the colonial government. Speculators in land emerged, which horrified officials who perceived it to be central to Malay life. Yet padi had always been supported by other activities. The difficulties facing its cultivation under the new economic dispensation heightened the importance of these alternatives for the Malays. The advent of land transportation, the opportunities for casual labour, the provision of supplies to estates, all dictated new opportunities for rural Malays within a wide radius. In Negri Sembilan, for example, networks of rural markets, *pekan*, assisted the expansion of the money economy, and were centres for the circulation of people, commodities and ideas. In such areas Malays were quick to avail themselves of the opportunities presented by the expansion of rubber cultivation. By 1921, 37 per cent of rubber was produced by smallholdings and Malay smallholders accounted for 12–15 per cent of the total world consumption of rubber. Rubber pressurised forest ecology, yet brought new settlement patterns; a revolution in material culture; greater investment in religious life, in pilgrimage and mosque construction.[43] In a similar

[39] Maurice Freedman, 'The growth of a plural society in Malaya', *Pacific Affairs*, 33, 2 (1960), 158–68; Lim Teck Ghee, 'British colonial administration and the "ethnic division of labour" in Malaya', *Kajian Malaysia*, 1, 2 (1984), 28–66.

[40] Leopold Ainsworth, *The confessions of a planter in Malaya: a chronicle of life and adventures in the jungle* (London, 1933), p. 65.

[41] Lim Teck Ghee, *Origins of a colonial economy: land and agriculture in Perak, 1874–1897* (Penang, 1976), pp. 1–41.

[42] Paul H. Kratoska, 'Rice cultivation and the ethnic division of labour in British Malaya', *CSSH*, 24, 2 (1982), 280–314.

[43] Tsuyoshi Kato, 'When rubber came: the Negri Sembilan experience', *Southeast Asian Studies*, 29, 2 (1991), 109–57; Brown, *Capital and entrepreneurship*, p. 37.

way, the recourse of Chinese labourers to the land in times of hardship reinforced the resistance of the rural economy to European manipulation. However, the emerging ethnic patchwork was becoming more rigidly bounded by administrative categories which, over time, took on a political meaning. Whereas the various censi in the States in 1891 referred to the 'nationalities' of different communities, by the first Federated Malay States census of 1911, the primary category of belonging had become 'race', as race became more central to late Victorian understandings of the world. Those responsible for the census had by 1931 acknowledged the arbitrary and shifting nature of this identification.[44] By this time, however, the language of ethnicity, of racial pride, had goaded educated Malays into examinations of the condition of their own 'race'. The other communities of trade, credit and services that arise out of a shared environment and much longer-term patterns of migration and accommodation did, to a large extent, survive. However, a major theme of this book will be the way in which the looser pluralism of the mid-colonial period hardened into new political communities by the later years of British rule. We shall also see how deeply contested these ethnic identities were.

The passing of the Somerset Maugham era

The Great War of 1914–18 exposed many of the stress fractures in the colonial regime. A regional rice crisis led to a drive to make Malaya self-sufficient in foodstuffs. This put new pressure on the Malay peasant economy and provoked fears of land shortage. The depression of the immediate post-war years highlighted the vulnerability of those caught within the vicissitudes of the world economy. The war necessitated the cultivation of new Asian allies. In the towns, the Straits Chinese emerged as the most stalwart compradores of British expansion in Malaya, and the Edwardian empire saw a flowering of their political influence in Malaya. The war itself provoked an outpouring of demonstrations of empire-loyalty through which they affirmed their privileged status. The war also generated a general crisis in Asia. It was in no small part a crisis of Islam: returning students and *hajis* from a Middle East in turmoil were marked as dangerous political threats. Its eddies flowed across colonial borders and spurred politicisation within all communities. The Singapore Mutiny and an uprising in the east-coast state of Kelantan in 1915 were linked in the minds of those who fought them as an attempt to exploit a perceived waning of British power. The Sarekat Islam, Muhammadiyah, and Gandhian *satyagraha* provided templates for new forms of political mobilisation within the diasporas of Malaya. Revolutionary nationalism in China and the rise of Japan reverberated in Malaya. The First World War shook the foundations of European power; a slump and a second war brought it to the ground.

The inter-war years saw a rapid expansion of Leviathan into local life. The British

---

[44] Charles Hirschman, 'The meaning and measurement of ethnicity in Malaysia: an analysis of census classifications', *JAS*, 46, 3 (1987), 555–82.

attempted to decentralise power in the Malay States as a prelude to the creation of a more closely integrated political unit. At its lower reaches, the state was forced to respond to new social pressures. The inter-war slump was perhaps as significant in its political as in its economic impact. Its bite was perhaps not as strongly felt in Malaya as elsewhere in Asia, nor as deeply as many writers have argued. Rice production was rarely disturbed, opportunities for migrants were available and inflows of population from India rose in this period. If there was pressure on the most vulnerable groups, it came from a tightening of credit from moneylenders; the fiscal demands of the state were kinder than they were in the Japanese occupation.[45] Chinese business proved resilient, and new institutions such as the United Chinese Bank and the Overseas Chinese Banking Corporation began to structure themselves on modern lines to cater for the smaller man and help him to share risk.[46] The state placed new curbs on immigration from China and repatriated thousands of unemployed workers. However, the wholesale export of the unemployment problem failed because of the ease with which Chinese labourers fell back on vegetable cultivation on fringes of the industrial areas on the west coast. Resort to these alternatives became a valuable tactic in wage bargaining. The slump is less significant as an external intrusion into local economic life than in how it highlights internal processes of social change and adaptation to a changing economic and ecological environment.[47]

The slump compelled the government to seek to recast the Malay rural economy in order to fulfil its custodial obligations to the Malay, and to produce more of Malaya's food requirements locally. This was nothing new. However, whereas previous attempts to increase food production had been marked by a relative absence of restrictions on non-Malays entering this sector of the economy, between the wars colonial conceptions of Malay economic welfare dictated new controls on land tenure and land use. The notion that rice cultivation was a special economic preserve of the Malays was written into law with the establishment of Malay Reservations. After 1933, the land set aside for these areas and the restrictions on its commercial use were greatly expanded, to encompass by 1941 three and a half million acres. The British strove to create a self-sufficient Malay economy, parallel to the non-Malay one, with its own shops, credit facilities and co-operatives. However, Malay cultivators found new ways to by-pass controls of land and credit and engage in commercial speculation in land. Reservation land ended up in the hands of non-Malays, the heavily promoted co-operatives made slow progress, and colonial officials began to doubt whether their assumptions about Malay land tenure and crop preferences ever had as much validity

---

[45] Ian Brown, 'Rural distress in Southeast Asia during the world depression of the 1930s: a preliminary re-examination', *JAS*, 45, 5 (1986), 995–1025.

[46] United Overseas Bank, *Growing up with Singapore* (Singapore, 1985), pp. 11–14.

[47] Christopher Baker, 'Economic reorganisation and the slump in South and Southeast Asia', *CSSH*, 18, 3 (1981), 325–49; Loh Kok Wah, 'From tin mine coolies to agricultural squatters: socio-economic change in the Kinta District during the inter-war years', in P. J. Rimmer and L. Allen (eds.), *The underside of Malaysian history: pullers, prostitutes and plantation workers* (Singapore, 1990), pp. 72–96.

as they had been invested with. Under the regime of international rubber restriction, Malay rubber smallholders were heavily penalised to the profit of the large European concerns. However, they showed great flexibility in the weighting they gave to rice and rubber in their economy and Malays weathered the height of the depression in 1930–1 better than most by this diversification. Yet there were limits to this adaptability. In 1930 the amount owing by Malay cultivators to Chettiars and Chinese shopkeepers on loans taken out on the security of Reservation land was around $5 million. Indebtedness was not solely a Malay problem; in the second half of the same year $100 million was lent by Chettiars to Chinese rubber smallholders.[48] Those most hurt by the slump were those without opportunity for economic diversification: Indian labourers tied to the strict regime on the European estates, but also the expanding numbers of salaried people in the towns. The most educationally advantaged in Malaya graduated into a world of narrowing horizons.[49]

Despite the hardship of the slump, the cultural and educational gap between Asians and Europeans was narrowing considerably. A problem of poor and outcast whites emerged, which put colonial society on the defensive at the same time as overtly segregationist measures were being challenged and abandoned. Racial indignities became less supportable and it was primarily in the sphere of the colonial bureaucracy that the colour bar was enforced. Elsewhere, Asians adopted or adapted many activities that were previously a European preserve.[50] These distinctly 'modern' activities became arenas of ethnic self-improvement and a training ground for political leadership. The promotion of sports, for example, symbolised dress reform, health and mobility for Malay women. The Malay social critic Za'ba, writing in 1936 identified the birth of the modern, the usage of the new word *moden* in Malay from the 1920s, as a sarcastic reaction to 'Malay girl guides and brownies going about with exposed legs'.[51] Colonial welfare work amongst women forged sisterhoods independent of the affairs of men and bred an inter-communal and international consciousness: post-war campaigners such as Ibu Zain – Zainun binti Hj. Sulaiman, the 'Kartini of Malaya' – were later to acknowledge the training guiding gave in leadership.[52] It was Ibu Zain who led agitation for a Malayan Women's Teacher's Union of Johore in 1929 and for a Malay Women Teacher's College (1934) and Sultan Ibrahim Girls' School in Johore Bahru (1939). By 1939 in Perak there were 62 girls'

---

[48] Kato, 'When rubber came', 143–4; Paul H. Kratoska, ' "Ends we cannot foresee": Malay reservations in British Malaya', *JSEAS*, 9, 1 (1983), 149–68; Lim Teck Ghee, *Peasants and their agricultural economy in colonial Malaya, 1874–1941* (Kuala Lumpur, 1977), pp. 106–16, 209–16; Brown, *Capital and entrepreneurship*, pp. 177–82.

[49] Virginia Thompson, *Postmortem on Malaya* (New York, 1943), pp. 162–3.

[50] Butcher, *The British in Malaya*, pp. 97–125, 167–92.

[51] Za'ba, 'The Malays and religion', in Khoo Kay Kim (ed.), *Tamadun Islam di Malaysia* (Kuala Lumpur, 1980), pp. 103–12.

[52] Janice N. Brownfoot, 'Sisters under the skin: imperialism and the emancipation of women in Malaya, c.1891–1941', in J. A. Mangan (ed.), *Making imperial mentalities: socialization and British imperialism* (Manchester, 1990), pp. 46–73.

schools with 4,000 pupils and 174 women teachers.[53] The colonial state was nurturing the forces – the men and women – who would eventually supplant it.

Although the British placed much store on creating willing native agents of modernity – a secular, Anglophone elite – much of the innovation of this time was disregarded or invisible to British officials. By the 1930s the Malay press was taken in new directions with the appearance of the *Warta Malaya* of Singapore in 1930, owned by the wealthy Singapore Arab family, the Alsagoffs, and edited by Onn bin Jaafar who later founded the *Lembaga Malaya* of Johore Bahru in 1934. An openly national perspective was adopted by the *Majlis* of Kuala Lumpur on its establishment in 1931. In 1939 *Utusan Melayu* was founded as a specifically Malay, rather than an Arab or Indian Muslim concern.[54] These early periodicals not only addressed new problems of identity and belief but their lonely-hearts columns created circles of pen-friends, their publishers new lines of distribution. A new language began to emerge. In Johore modernisers at court formed a literary association to reform the Malay language and expand vernacular publishing. In 1936 they published 10,000 copies of a Malay dictionary, *Buku Katau*, that promoted the Johor-Riau dialect as standard Malay, and was used in the Sultan Idris Training College, the key centre of higher education for Malays in this period.[55] Literary style moved away from poetry to prose and the early Malay novels undertook more direct enquiries than newspapers and primers into the question of how modernist ideas could be translated in the practice of everyday life. They celebrated love of the homeland and confronted the problem of poverty. For the luminaries of pre-war Malay literature – especially journalists and teachers – urbanisation heightened their consciousness of the threat of the alien-dominated city to Malay culture.[56] Malay nationalism awoke in an atmosphere of heightened racial unease.

Debates between the old and the new schools of religion – the *Kaum Tua* and the *Kaum Muda* – dominated these media. From the late nineteenth century, pilgrimage and study in the Middle East led to the rise of exponents of a more '*shari'a*-minded' Islam led by religious reformers such as Shaykh Mohd. Tahir bin Jalaluddin Al-Azhari which challenged much of the prevailing religious practice on the peninsula. The *Kaum Muda* and *Kaum Tua* were not dichotomous, a spectrum of Islamic associations and positions appeared and reformist scholars, many of them Minang-kabau, were drawn into a growing number of religious schools. Malacca was an

---

[53] Asiah binti Abu Samah, 'Emancipation of Malay women, 1947–57' (BA Hons Exercise, University of Malaya, 1960), 5–7.

[54] Nik Ahmad bin Haji Nik Hassan, 'The Malay press', *JMBRAS*, 36, 1 (1963), 37–69.

[55] *Pakatan Bahasa Melayu Persuratan Buku Diraja Bagi Johor* (Johor Baru, n.d.); Nik Safiah Karim, 'Sumbangan Pakatan Bahasa Melayu Persuratan Buku Diraja Johor perkembangan bahasa Melayu', in Jabatan Pengajian Melayu, Universiti Malaya, *Rampaian Pengajian Melayu* (Kuala Lumpur, 1984), pp. 181–5.

[56] Virginia Matheson Hooker, 'Transmission through practical example: women and Islam in 1920s Malay fiction', *JMBRAS*, 47, 2 (1994), 93–118; Ungku Maimunah Mohd. Tahir, 'The rural–urban dichotomy in modern Malay literature: origins and formation in the pre-war period', *Akademika*, 27, (1985), 41–55.

important centre in this regard: many graduates of the Malay College Malacca went on to exercise great influence on a generation of nationalist leaders at the Sultan Idris Training College, Tanjong Malim. Malacca was also a centre of *Kaum Tua* resistance to these new influences, religious practices were disputed at village level here and elsewhere in Malaya, often through discussion forums known as *majlis muzakarrah*. These disputations were widely reported in the vernacular press and were conducted at the heart of the classes of English-educated Malays who were seen as the most reliable allies of the British. These individuals took the lead in a general scramble for new knowledge of the world. In education, the village-level schooling of the *pondok* was overtaken by *madrasah* – and not only those associated with the *Kaum Muda* – which developed new curricula that embraced subjects from logic to book-keeping. New rural institutions such as co-operatives provoked debates on the taking of interest, or *riba*, that explored the practical and ethical application of new economic ideas.[57]

Transmission was not only the province of the elite. Old circuits of communication linked the towns of the peninsula, forged by troubadours, traders, peddlers of knowledge and healing, who thrived in the informal economy of the towns. Itinerant Indonesians – often political exiles – played a part in disseminating radical doctrines. Little has been written about these people. However, they played a central role in change, whether it was through music, comedy, martial arts, or in simply making new attitudes fashionable. The *Commedia dell'arte* of Southeast Asia, the Malay *bangsawan*, introduced vaudeville, new music and challenging Indonesian attitudes to a small-town audience. Its scripted successor, the *sandiwara*, self-consciously set out to celebrate the Malay cultural heritage. The Chinese radical 'New Drama' movement took a revolutionary message out to isolated plantations and mines.[58] In the towns in the 1930s a multiplicity of new things arrived. The great 'Worlds' of Penang, Kuala Lumpur and Singapore, such as Bukit Bintang in Kuala Lumpur, were clandestine meeting places for young Malay intellectuals.[59] The colonial memoir of the Somerset Maugham era is oppressed by anxieties at the effects of idleness and leisure on the population of the towns. The cinema, in particular, rapidly rooted itself in the popular culture of Malaya. After 1910, permanent cinema halls had been established – by the 1930s there were 30 to 40 of them, mostly Chinese-owned – and travelling shows transplanted the medium into the countryside. The prospect of Asians witnessing the spectacle of white men and women cavorting licentiously on the screen was seen by

---

[57] Khoo Kay Kim, Abdul Aziz bin Mat Ton and Baharam Azit, 'Melaka's Malay society in modern times', in Sandhu and Wheatley (eds.), *Melaka*, II, pp. 78–83; Khoo Kay Kim, 'Perceptions of progress and development among English-educated Muslims in pre-World War Two Malaya', *Sejarah*, 2 (1993),147–78.

[58] Fang Xia, *Notes on the history of Malayan Chinese new literature* (Tokyo, 1977), pp. 284–7, 334–52.

[59] Wan Abdul Kadir, *Budaya popular dalam masyarakat Melayu* (Kuala Lumpur, 1988), pp. 131–40; William R. Roff, *The Origins of Malay nationalism* (Yale, 1967), p. 229.

British officials as highly seditious.[60] Through these advances in communications, indigenous popular culture was beginning to find a more public voice.

These channels of communication burst into life during the Japanese occupation. But already by the mid–1930s networks of embryonic nationalist leadership in search of a mass constituency were contending to direct these new forces. The *Sahabat Pena*, or pen-friends league, established by the Penang journal *Saudara*, which published from 1928, developed into the largest countrywide Malay organisation prior to the war. It had 12,000 members at its peak, and held its first national conference in November 1934 which drew together large numbers of articulate young men and women as self-acknowledged agents for social and cultural advancement. However, attempts to create a larger kind of organisation betrayed deep ideological unease, especially at the prominence of Arabs and South Indian Muslims in the movement, divisions which *Kaum Muda* and *Kaum Tua* affiliations intensified and which caused the Penang *Sahabat Pena* to break with other branches. Derogatory terms emerged for those of Arab or Indian blood - *Darah Keturunan Arab* and *Darah Keturunan Kling* – and against such distinctions intellectuals looked to define the nation and measure its progress and reputation in relation to the other communities of Malaya. A Malay association emerged in Singapore in 1924 on the initiative of Mohd. Eunos Abdullah and other *Persatuan Melayu* were founded in Selangor, Negri Sembilan and Province Wellesley. A *Kesatuan Melayu Muda* (KMM) was founded by Sultan Idris Training College graduates in Kuala Lumpur in 1938, led by the government-servant-turned-journalist Ibrahim Haji Yaacob, and its influence spread throughout the peninsula. Ibrahim's writings articulated a clear conception of the Malay nation that challenged old attachments and enunciated a forthright and ideological anti-colonialism: they were a call to awareness and political action. The classic accounts of Malay nationalism make a clear distinction between the radicals and those attached to the court. Yet this was a period of great fluidity: no irrevocable political allegiances were formed, and none, it seems, were sought. Much of the membership of early associations over-lapped, as for example in Selangor in the outwardly *kerajaan*-based *Persatuan Melayu Selangor* and the 'radical' *Kesatuan Melayu Muda*.[61] Congresses of Malay organisa-tions in August 1939 and December 1940 were dominated by the question of fixing the composition of the Malay nation, or *bangsa*. A clear notion of the original sovereignty of the Malays in Malaya was emerging, less tied to the notion of the Malay monarchy, but rooted in a contiguous historical experience from Melaka onwards. The ideologues of this nation were divided on whether it drew its identity from descent, or from history, or as a territorial homeland, or as an *ummah* of Muslim believers. These debates laid the foundations of modern Malay political thought: in them the idea of the Malay *bangsa* confronted that of the modern nation-state.[62] The

---

[60] John A. Lent, *The Asian film industry* (London, 1990), p. 186; Rex Stevenson, 'Cinemas and censorship in colonial Malaya', *JSEAS*, 5, 2 (1974), 44–68.

[61] Roff, *Origins of Malay nationalism*, pp. 212–39; Milner, *Invention of politics*, pp. 257–81.

[62] Tan Liok Ee, *The rhetoric of* bangsa *and* minzu: *community and nation in tension, the Malay*

language of politics that was beginning to emerge underpinned the political dilemmas faced by Malay nationalists in the 1940s and 1950s.

Elsewhere Malayan politics was finding platforms on external issues. By the 1930s leadership within the Chinese community was no longer based solely on social and economic status, on personal sway within dialect associations and Chambers of Commerce, but was founded on politics. The political turmoil in China and her confrontations with Japan were reflected in domestic politics by the formation of the first Chinese revolutionary organisations in Malaya – the *Chung Ho T'ang* and the *T'ung Meng Hui* at the turn of the century. They operated through 'night schools', boycotts and reading clubs. The formation of a Malayan branch of the Kuomintang (KMT) greatly expanded these activities, and although only one Chinese in 200 was a KMT member, it was the largest political organisation in pre-war Malaya. Chinese education was politicised through the 'new life' movement and the formation of youth subsidiaries such as the *San Min Chu Yi* (SMCY) Youth Corps in 1938.[63] By the late 1930s, the Malayan General Labour Union and its offspring, the Malayan Communist Party (MCP), began to win significant support amongst Chinese labour. New research suggests that it was Chinese anarcho-communists – fired by Kropotkin's ideas of 'mutual aid' and encouraged by the May 4th movement – who took the lead in establishing two leftist newspapers: *Truth* in Singapore and the *Yik Khuan Poh* in Kuala Lumpur in 1919. They were rapidly suppressed, but new recruits came from the Overseas Bureau in China, to set up night schools, and to spread propaganda amongst workers and radical KMT cadres, in the spirit of the first United Front in China. It was an urban movement, with branches in the towns of southern Malaya, dominated by networks of Hainanese. Fabled for their clannishness, the community had a disproportionate number of bachelors and poor who were highly susceptible to the self-improvement ethos of the night school movement. Their personalities had been formed by the radical politics of Hainan island, and many took refuge in Malaya from the white terror of the KMT on the island after its break with the Communists. A Nanyang Public Bodies Union was established in 1926, later known as the Nanyang General Labour Union, and a Nanyang Communist Party was formed in 1928 by young Chinese Communist Party activists. Although racially based, a small number of Malay Communists liaised with the Chinese comrades through a Malay section of a 'League against imperialism'. Singapore was a place of transit for Indonesian Communists, and something of a sanctuary for them after the 1926–7 uprisings. The Nanyang Communist Party was reorganised into a Malayan Communist Party in mid-April 1930, at a meeting at Buloh Kesap in Johore, attended by a representative of the Comintern, Nguyen Ai Quoc, alias Ho Chi Minh. The reorganisation of the movement and the Comintern's assumption of its direction was an early step towards

---

peninsula, 1900–1955 (Working paper No. 52, Centre of Southeast Asian Studies, Monash University, 1988), pp. 10–13.

[63] C. F. Yong and R. B. McKenna, *The Kuomintang movement in British Malaya, 1912–1949* (Singapore, 1990).

the domestication of leftist politics in Malaya. It seems to have been prompted by Ho's belief that the strength of the international movement lay in the formation of national movements in the various colonial territories, and by an unease, perhaps communicated by the visiting Indonesians, at the narrow ethnic base of the Nanyang Communist Party. Ironically, the formation of the new party occurred when the Malay leadership was incarcerated; the new party then embarked on its struggle without them. This was to bedevil the MCP in later years. Moreover, the MCP lost many of its key cadres in a police swoop on a meeting in Singapore on 29 April 1930, and it spent the 1930s in the wilderness, harried by the Special Branch, who in 1934 planted an Annamite agent, Lai Teck, in the highest echelon of the party leadership. It was only with the new alliance with the KMT in the National Salvation Movement after 1936 that the MCP began to extend its organisation.[64]

Indian communities concentrated on the rubber estates were caught in the currents that were sweeping the subcontinent. A highly systematised paternalism governed the estates: the key intermediary between management and workers was the foreman, *kangani.* Yet his position was legitimated solely by the company and during the slump it was under threat from changes to his role in recruitment and the withdrawal of his subsidies for religious duties, at a time when outside forces such as the Central Indian Association of Malaya (CIAM) were making their presence felt. Yet this body, founded in 1937, was led by the middle classes of the towns, and lacked a mediating local leadership to assist them to penetrate the authority structures of the estate. New forms of leadership, such as Dravidianism, temple-entry movements and campaigns against toddy gained momentum on estates.[65] Recruitment for the Indian National Army (INA) under the Japanese was to forge links between these different levels of political activity. The Japanese invasion came at a time of growing consciousness of social deprivation. It was reflected in a spate of syndicalism and trade union militancy amongst both rural and urban labour forces. Before the war these lay in several pockets, but involved almost every section of the workforce from Singapore, to the Selangor estates and the collieries of Batu Arang, where the MCP, buoyed by the National Salvation Movement, established soviets. Strikes and riots amongst Indians in Klang in 1941 entrenched an official commitment to strangle any industrial action that they categorised as 'political' rather than economic in nature.[66] Yet as the Secretary for Chinese Affairs prophetically observed, 'the distinction between the social worker who is honoured and the agitator who is executed is not always easy to draw'.[67]

[64] C. F. Yong, *Chinese leadership and power in colonial Singapore* (Singapore, 1992), pp. 203–54.

[65] Ravindra K. Jain, 'Leadership and authority in a plantation: a case study of Indians in Malaya (c.1900–42)', in G. Wijeyewardene (ed.), *Leadership and authority: a symposium* (Singapore, 1968), pp. 163–73.

[66] Yeo Kim Wah, 'The Communist challenge in the Malayan labour scene, September 1936–March 1937', *JMBRAS*, 49, 2 (1976), 36–79.

[67] Khoo Kay Kim, 'A brief history of Chinese labour unrest before 1941'. *Malaysia in history*, 25 (1982), 61.

Malaya in 1941 was on the brink of change. British rule was subject to social pressures on all sides, as it struggled to regulate external migrations and stabilise the population. Malaya's racial arithmetic was delicately balanced: 2,418,615 Chinese; 2,248,579 Malaysians; 767,693 Indians; 30,251 Europeans and 80,035 'others'. The outbreak of the Second World War necessitated new levels of state intervention in political and economic life. The government clamped down tighter on the fourth estate in 1939. A Trade Union Ordinance of 1940 was to lie at the centre of post-war struggles between organised labour and the state. Strikes were outlawed in vital industries in August 1941. Food control measures hit hardest the urban poor and the salaried classes who had already suffered during the slump; the cost of living rose as the rice trade became hijacked by profiteers. The war measures of the colonial state exposed its weaknesses. To many observers a fundamental restructuring of the regime had become inevitable.[68] The British government attempted to raise morale through a noisy propaganda campaign, but on the eve of the Japanese invasion of Malaya few had confidence in it. As the Japanese advanced on Singapore, the British relaxed restrictions and invited the MCP to join the last-ditch resistance to the Japanese. It was too late to save Malaya, but it gave birth to a commitment to reclaim her through a new experiment in colonial partnership.

War and disorder

To Winston Churchill, the fall of Singapore on 15 February 1942 was the greatest military defeat in British history. However, the decisive reverses had occurred in the weeks before this, when British and Commonwealth troops scuttled down the length of the peninsula, pursued by Japanese soldiers on bicycles. However, the terrible fifteenth left a dark imprint on the imperial psyche. To the people of Malaya, the sight of Europeans being marched abjectly through the streets into internment and forced labour shattered the myths of white supremacy. For the Chinese, the fall of Singapore heralded a 'dreadful night' during which they would collectively bear the brunt of Japanese militarism. To the Malays, the British capitulation had broken the mandate of protection; old loyalties were to be reassessed. For all communities, the war was a time of self-sufficiency and considerable individual heroism. It was a time when those in authority made unprecedented demands on the people under them. Japanese rule brought in its wake three and a half years of intensive state-building which shattered the pattern of seventy years of colonial rule. The Japanese introduced new functions and a new degree of centralisation to government. They created a new role for the state in the economy and a new role for ideology within the state. In this they anticipated many strategies the British were to adopt after the war. Japanese rule also accelerated the communalisation of politics and precipitated a massive social crisis: whole communities were uprooted; disease preyed upon the people; and the agrarian economy was in shambles. The forest frontier was breached

---

[68] Thompson, *Postmortem*, pp. 269–300.

by land colonisation schemes and by the flight of townsmen from the reach of the military administration. This experience polarised the politics that had begun to emerge in the 1930s, as new leaders vied to gain a purchase on traumatised populations, and threw the dominant elites of indirect rule on to the defensive.

The Japanese dismantled British Malaya. The northern states of Kedah, Perlis, Kelantan and Trengganu were ceded to Siam in 1943. The other states were drawn together with Sumatra into a new federation, the Southern Region. Its capital was Singapore, which was administered directly by the army and renamed Syonan, or 'brilliant south'. Malaya's economic importance, and its perceived political backwardness, dictated that it was destined to remain a permanent colony within the Southern Region.[69] Initially the Japanese adopted a cautious policy towards the Malay Rulers, leaving their religious authority uncompromised, but refusing to indulge their status as heads of independent domains. A series of royal successions in Kedah, Perlis, Kelantan and Trengganu, and a reversal of the 1936 succession crisis in Selangor, allowed the Japanese to marginalise the Rulers as a focus of opposition. Pro-Japanese and pro-British factions came into conflict in many states, but overall the balance of power within the *kerajaan* shifted away from the Ruler and towards the administrative elite. In Johore, this foreshadowed a bitter conflict between Sultan Ibrahim and his most powerful subjects after the war. Many members of State elites were deeply torn between their empire-loyalty and the need to provide a lead for their people after British protection had vanished; some reached secret understandings with anti-Japanese guerrillas to minimise violence in their backyards. As the war drew on, the Japanese held out a variety of inducements to the Rulers, such as increased remunerations. They also projected a more sympathetic stance towards Islam to harness it to Japanese anti-westernism. This, together with social dislocation, merely aggravated a sense of anxiety within the Malay *ummah.*[70] Japanese indirect rule was an awkward bedfellow with the programme of Nipponisation. Moreover, the military and civil branches of Japanese rule were at odds. The intention was for military government to wither away and usher in a new participatory civil order. As the Japanese grip on Southeast Asia tightened, the Japanese attempted to fashion a more direct relationship between the people and the state, and to cement it by creating a new role for political ideology. Colonialist thinking was to be eliminated by the stimulation of oriental racial consciousness: a new order founded under 'the great spirit of cosmocracy', *Hakko Ichiu.* The new *Malai* was to take its place within the competitive economic system of a Greater East Asia Co-prosperity Sphere with Japan

---

[69] Office of Strategic Services (OSS), Research and Analysis Branch, R. & A. No. 2072, 'Japanese administration in Malaya', 8.6.1944.

[70] Yoji Akashi, 'Japanese Military Administration in Malaya – its formation and evolution in reference to Sultans, the Islamic religion, and the Moslem-Malays, 1941–1945', *Asian Studies,* 7, 1 (1969), 81–110; Abu Talib Ahmad, 'The impact of the Japanese occupation on the Malay-Muslim population', in Paul H. Kratoska (ed.), *Malaya and Singapore during the Japanese occupation* (Singapore, 1995), pp. 24–36.

as its nucleus.[71] Yet imperial vision was always tempered by the needs of war; obstructed by the need to mollify local opinion to secure support for unpalatable measures, and compromised by the lack of consensus as to its ultimate end.[72]

The initial consolidation of Japanese rule was achieved by naked repression: the white terror of the *sook ching*, the vetting and summary execution of perhaps 40,000 Chinese, who paid a bitter price for their prominence in the fight against fascism. Entire communities were detained *en masse* and paraded before hooded informers who marked out members of anti-Japanese organisations, and sowed the seeds for future vendettas.[73] The police and the judiciary came under effective military direction. The physical presence of the state was impressed on Malayan society through the registration of its subjects and controls on residence and movement. In some unsettled areas stockades fifteen feet high were built 'to prevent communications between the village community and the guerrillas', prototypes for the New Villages of the Malayan Emergency.[74] Sections of the population were mobilised into auxiliary police, the *Tekkikan*, and a self-defence corps, the *Jekeidan*. A total of 20,300 men underwent military service in Selangor alone. At the forefront of the militarisation of Malayan life were the *Heiho* auxiliary servicemen, and the *Giyu Gun*, and *Giyu Tai* volunteer army and service corps whose predominantly Malay personnel underwent intensive Japanese training and ideological orientation.[75] These institutions seemed to mobilise one section of the population against another and this fomented communal tensions.

If the new authoritarian machinery was a sudden innovation in the administration of Malaya, even more so were the devices used to draw active gestures of support and expressions of loyalty out of passive and hostile sections of the population. A $50 million military contribution was demanded as 'life-redeeming money' from the Overseas Chinese as atonement for their support for the war efforts of the British and Chiang Kai-shek. The taxation of Chinese property led to a general tightening of credit; lands and goods were disposed of at low prices.[76] New Chinese associations were formed and old ones reactivated to co-ordinate the campaign. The guiding principle of Japanese policy was that 'the Chinese themselves should be held

[71] Lee Ting Hui, 'Singapore under the Japanese, 1942–1945', *Journal of the South Seas Society*, 17, 1 (1961), 33.

[72] Willard H. Elsbree, *Japan's role in Southeast Asian nationalist movements, 1940–1945* (Cambridge, Mass., 1953), pp. 43–54.

[73] Cheah Boon Kheng, *Red star over Malaya: resistance and social conflict during and after the Japanese occupation of Malaya, 1941–1946* (Singapore, 1983), pp. 20–4; N. I. Low and H. M. Cheng, *This Singapore (Our city of dreadful night)* (Singapore, 1946), pp. 15–22; Yoji Akashi, 'Japanese policy towards the Malayan Chinese, 1941–1945', *JSEAS*, 1, 2 (1970), 66–9.

[74] A. B. Walton, 'Malayan forests during and after the Japanese occupation', DF/58/45.

[75] Cheah, *Red star*, pp. 33–6; Karen Lee Li Yeng, 'Japanese occupation in Selangor, 1942–45' (B.A. Graduate Exercise, University of Malaya, 1973), pp. 24–6; OSS, 'Japanese administration in Malaya'.

[76] Y. S. Tan, 'History of the formation of the Overseas Chinese Association and the extortion by the J.M.A. of $50,000,000 military contribution from the Chinese in Malaya', *Journal of the South Seas Society*, 3, 1 (1946), 1–12.

responsible for maintaining security'.[77] As the prospects for rapid Axis victory receded, policy became more accommodating in tone and the Japanese sponsored new community organisations, modelled in part on the night school movement, to stimulate 'voluntary enthusiasm' amongst the Chinese for the war effort, and new civil institutions were mooted to disseminate public information.[78] The phrase *minshin haaku* – winning the people's hearts – found prominence in official utterances. These experiments appeared too late in the occupation to have much success. However, the rhetoric of Japanese state-building was only a step behind the idioms employed by General Templer and his contemporaries during the Malayan Emergency.

This pattern of popular mobilisation was also seen in the economy. Malaya was provider of rubber, tin, bauxite and manganese for the Co-prosperity Sphere. Production was harnessed to the war effort through the establishment of *kaisha* monopolies. In Selangor, for example, 60 per cent of 'enemy' rubber was given directly to the military government and 40 per cent to Japanese firms. Over-production was inevitable: after Japan's needs had been met production was said to be at 20 per cent of pre-war levels. A vicious circle of control and evasion caused prices to escalate. *Kaisha* control over channels of supply and communications raised the pitch of illicit trading. After an initial spree of looting, profiteers took over the market.[79] Malaya's economic isolation catalysed economic diversification. Small-scale import substitution industries met chronic shortages by utilising the products of over-production: rope from pineapple husk; simple shoes from latex; gas from burnt rubber to form petroleum. New commodities appeared: *biak* leaves as a substitute for opium; night soil for manure. In some cases manufacturing output reached high levels: in Selangor, sixty factories produced 23,000 cases of soap a month. 'The day is not far off,' one witness ironically observed, 'when Malaya will knock at the door and seek admission into the family of industrialised countries.'[80]

To exploit Malaya's strategic resources the Japanese sought to organise its people into a series of distinct productive units, wherein each race was to develop its own 'political and economic talents'. Administrative *rapprochement* with the Chinese community was largely motivated by economic priorities. Policy towards the Malay peasant economy was dictated by the need to make Malaya self-sustaining in foodstuffs. This was rendered imperative by the Allied reoccupation of Burma and the recalcitrance of the Thais in providing rice. The Malays were ordered to return to the *sawah*. Malay journals printed lyrical accounts of kampong life.[81] A series of

---

[77] 'Principles for the implementation of security measures', 1.4.1943, cited in Akashi, 'Japanese policy', 79.

[78] Lee, 'Singapore under the Japanese', 39.

[79] OSS, R. & A. No. 1433, 'Political and economic changes effected by the Japanese in Malaya', 1.12.1943; Lee, 'Japanese occupation in Selangor', pp. 36–7.

[80] Chin Kee Onn, *Malaya upside down* (Singapore, 1946), pp. 168–79; Lee, 'Japanese occupation in Selangor', p. 39.

[81] Halinah Bamadhaj, 'The impact of the Japanese occupation of Malaya on Malay society and politics, 1941–45' (M.A. Thesis, University of Auckland, 1975), pp. 2–3.

experiments began in corporatist economic development through colonisation companies, and provision of loans to the 'small man' to liberate him from the clutches of the moneylender.[82] Although many Malays did return to padi planting and vegetable or tapioca cultivation, the aggregate effect of Japanese food-growing efforts was disastrous: the 1945 harvest yielded one third of the 1940 crop. Infrastructural projects were not followed through. Experiments at Sungei Manik in double-cropping with Taiwan padi gave mixed results.[83] High levels of coercion were introduced into the padi trade: troops would search mills for withheld rice. Such controls nurtured black-marketing, as millers evaded regulations, traders smuggled rice from Siam and women spirited away padi into the jungle. Communal harvesting broke down when women were unable to go out into the field because they had no clothes to wear.[84] Buffaloes and locally proven varieties of padi seeds were in short supply. Credit was generally scarce. The enforced sale of surplus padi at low price, a feature of both Japanese and British food control, added to the strain on involved credit relationships such as *padi kuncha*, whereby a shopkeeper supplied goods and finance over a season in return for a portion of the harvest. In Pahang, for example, the 1941 harvest was two-thirds less than normal. The 1942–3 harvests were lost to government as official prices were too low and the government turned to the hated *mata-mata padi*, or rice police, to collect the surplus. In Selangor and Kedah peasants resorted to planting only for their own needs.[85] Yields in 1945–6 remained far below average, due to the neglect of drainage and irrigation. Desperate cultivators agitated for rice rations in the very areas that produced it.

Smallholders or sharecroppers in rubber were badly hit. The collapse of rubber exports cut off the main supply of cash for the rural economy with which essential goods were bought. By the end of 1942 tapping had virtually ceased as dealers were no longer accepting low-grade rubber. From early 1944, smallholders came under pressure to cut down old rubber trees and land was planted on a *gotong-royong* – mutual co-operation – basis.[86] Where they remained standing, rubber smallholdings became overgrown in *lalang* and *belukar*, and the trees diseased with mouldy rot. When Malaya's trade resumed with the outside world, producers were handicapped by the lack of funds, labour and materials, and their indebtedness reached serious

[82] Lee, 'Japanese occupation in Selangor', p. 32.
[83] Van Thean Kee, 'Cultivation of Taiwanese padi in Perak during the Japanese occupation', *Malayan Agricultural Journal*, 21, 1 (1948), 119–22.
[84] J. M. Gullick, 'The British Military Administration of Malaya: some reminiscences from Negri Sembilan' (unpublished paper, 1989), p. 7; Monthly report of the Principal Agricultural Officer, Kedah, for the month of September, 1945, BMA/DEPT/21/1.
[85] Jaafar bin Hamzah, 'The Malays in Telok Gelugur during the Japanese occupation', *Malaysia in History*, 21, 2 (1978), 56–64; Bamadhaj, 'Impact of the Japanese occupation', pp. 8–11; Paul H. Kratoska, 'The post-war food shortage in British Malaya', *JSEAS*, 19, 1 (1988), 27–9; Azahar Raswan Dean b. Wan Din, 'Pengeluaran dan perdaganan padi dan beras di Negri Kedah dari pendudukan Jepun hingga pentadbiran tentera Thai, 1942–45', *Kajian Malaysia*, 5, 1 (1987), 40–62.
[86] Jaafar, 'Malays in Telok Gelugur'.

proportions.[87] Many of them were recent migrants from Indonesia. They were left destitute, and felled rubber trees and jungle to draw a subsistence from the land. In areas such as Ulu Langat, Selangor, and Temerloh, Pahang, they became an obvious target for Japanese militarisation schemes and one of the most politically disaffected groups in the peninsula. These groups had always been responsive to the effects of changing market conditions on their livelihood and the post-war years saw a significant diaspora from these areas to the towns. This became an important component of the new political networks that were being forged in these years.

Adaptation was the key to survival. Chinese squatter communities could take advantage of shortages by growing cash crops on the fringes of the populated areas, and other groups could widen their mix of activities. A survey conducted in Malacca immediately after the war emphasised the variety of sources of income exploited by Malay smallholders: from craft work and the making of medicines, to hawking and trishaw riding in nearby towns.[88] There was a revival of the barter trade; hawkers preferred to be paid in kind. Many individuals, from domestic servants to businessmen and ex-administrators, were driven to undertake low-status tasks they would not have contemplated performing in better days. Much of this kind of work fell upon women. The war years undoubtedly saw an enlargement of their economic role. In the rural areas where women's labour had always been important, their work was intensified. This was especially the case when the men were hostage to Japanese labour schemes.[89] Many displaced labourers and white-collar workers volunteered to work for the Japanese *Giyutai*, a standing labour army. It became a crude device for solving a growing problem of unemployment and underemployment in town and country. In early 1944, compulsory labour service was introduced. Visited primarily on those who had lost their main source of income, the Japanese envisaged it as an arm of social policy: a method of inculcating shared purpose and an Asiatic identity through the spirit of labour. Pressure on subordinate officials to fill quotas for military schemes such as the Bangkok to Rangoon railway fuelled local resentments. Police rounded up tappers from the estates and beggars off the streets.[90] Large resettlement schemes were launched to expel non-essential consumers from the towns: at Endau, Bahau and on Bintan Island. State-enforced colonisation was merely one dimension to a general movement on to marginal land.

Demographic change was the overriding legacy of the war years. The years of slump and war broke a previously paramount pattern of migration within the region. External migration into Malaya in the immediate post-war period was negligible.

---

[87] 'Minutes of the Conference of District Officers of Selangor held on 14.11.1948', SEL.SEC/ 592/49.

[88] R. C. Burgess and Laidin bin Musa, *A report on the state of health, the diet and the economic conditions of groups of people in the lower income levels in Malaya* (Kuala Lumpur, 1950).

[89] Yoji Akashi, 'The Japanese occupation of Malaya: interruption or transformation', in Alfred W. McCoy (ed.), *Southeast Asia under Japanese occupation* (New Haven, 1980), pp. 71–2.

[90] OSS, 'Japanese administration in Malaya'; Akashi, 'The Japanese occupation of Melaka', p. 347.

Chinese and Indians did not, and could not, given the political uncertainty, flock home in large numbers. New census data showed that the immigrant population had stabilised. By 1947, 60.8 per cent of the 'immigrant' population had been born in Malaya. The ratio of women to men amongst the Chinese community was 837:1000, as opposed to only 513:1000 in 1931.[91] A survey in Singapore in 1947 estimated that about 60 per cent of immigrants sent no remittances home.[92] These flows of people had changed direction and the new pattern of movement was an internal one. The long-term repercussions of this change were to be immense; its most immediate manifestation was the people displaced by aborted Japanese public works and resettlement schemes. When the British returned to Malaya, they had to house and feed around 40,000 people. The presence of large numbers of displaced Javanese labourers aroused intense political anxieties. At the end of 1945 there were still over 39,000 Japanese prisoners of war in Malaya. As British officials gradually stationed themselves in the peninsula, estimates of the numbers of people dispersed multiplied. No accurate figures were available. Over 20,000 Chinese had been evacuated from Singapore to 'unknown destinations'; the number of Malayans deported to Siam for railway construction exceeded 80,000; 30,000 were said to have died there. Over 20,000 Malays were said to have taken refuge in southern Siam, and some took years to make their way back home. In October 1945 there were still 27,600 labourers in Thailand.[93] Of the rural areas in the peninsula, perhaps northern Kedah was the most badly affected, especially by the dispersal of Tamil estate labour throughout the padi areas; only 40 per cent of the pre-war labour force remained in Selangor and South Johore; in Malacca the estate population had declined from 25,705 in 1940 to 9,771 in 1945.[94] Communal violence added thousands more to the refugee problem. Over 3,000 Chinese refugees arrived in the west coast area following fighting in Bagan Si-Api-Api in East Sumatra.[95] A similar number descended on Telok Anson after the August disturbances in Perak; 9,000 fled from Muar in Johore after their homes had been wrecked and looted; and there were reports that violence at Batu Pahat had uprooted twice as many.[96] The population of the towns swelled as people gravitated towards food supplies and employment opportunities; vacant land was invaded by

---

[91] M. V. del Tufo, *Malaya: a report on the 1947 census of population* (London, 1949), pp. 57–8, 89.

[92] Singapore Social Welfare Department, *A social survey of Singapore: a preliminary study of some aspects of social conditions in the municipal area of Singapore* (Singapore, 1947), p. 112.

[93] Figures from BMA Fortnightly and Monthly Reports, CO273/675/50822/56/3 and WO220/564; 'Report on situation of labourers etc. imported to Siam by Japanese from Malaya, Java and Burma'; 'Memorandum on repatriation of displaced labour from Siam to Malaya', 14.11.1945, BMA/CA/52/45; Returns on Labour/10/45.

[94] 'Monthly Report for Labour', November and December, 1945, BMA/DEPT/2/1; 'Medical Officer's comments, November, 1945', LAB(Malacca)/45/45.

[95] HQ, ALFSEA to War Office, 15.10.1945, CO537/1669; Malayan Security Service, Political Intelligence Journal [MSS/PIJ], No. 12 of 1946, 15.10.1946.

[96] 'Fortnightly Report No. 4, for week ending 31.10.1945', CO273/675/50822/3; Cheah, *Red star*, pp. 195–240.

squatters.[97] The population of Singapore in September 1945 was estimated at 817,883; by November of the following year it had risen to 928,689.[98] Returning Europeans were outraged by the numbers of destitutes and beggars they found littering the streets. To some extent, such surplus urban labour as was not emaciated by hunger was absorbed into the hawking economy and into the small-scale import substitution industries which had flourished during the war. However, these strategies were increasingly circumscribed by a colonial government bent on restoring order. It was a potentially explosive situation.

The vulnerability of these people was heightened by the breakdown in the apparatus for the distribution of foodstuffs and vital supplies. From the middle of August 1945 prices sky-rocketed in anticipation that Japanese currency would be worthless under the new British regime.[99] The British Military Administration (BMA) attempted to provide a minimum subsistence on a regional scale through its 'Young Plan'. It was a failure. Basic relief was allocated only on paper; in December 1945, the paper allocation was cut, and only a quarter of the original requirements arrived. In Singapore rice rations had been set in October 1945 at a higher level than under the Japanese level, but this was half the minimum level estimated to prevent unrest.[100] By December the average ration per head was a bare 4.5 ounces a day, and imports only picked up by February and March 1946.[101] The supply of rice to rural areas fluctuated; food rotted in dumps due to a shortage of transport. In the first weeks of reoccupation there were serious disturbances in Kuala Lipis, Raub and Segamat, where troops fired on crowds, and there were large, sometimes violent, demonstrations in other towns.[102] In particular the policy of no rice rations for rice-producing areas penalised cultivators who had turned their land to vegetable crops. Restrictions on movement of rice pushed prices even higher. Stocks in Singapore and Kedah were bought up by profiteers and sold for an inflated price in Kuala Lumpur, especially as rationed rice was of poor quality. In Perak the price of rice in Ipoh was 50 per cent more than the price on the coast.[103] An early report of 1945 emphasised that general trade was 'flourishing'; the food shortage underwrote it. Although import controls retarded the revival of Singapore entrepôt trade, smuggling developed from

---

[97] *Kin Kwok Daily News*, 1.1.1946. Citations from the Chinese, Indian and *jawi* vernacular press come from the daily and weekly vernacular press translations and summaries released by the public relations and information departments of the Malayan and Singapore governments. In some cases the original newspapers are no longer extant. Various series of these have been consulted in the Singapore National Archives, the Arkib Negara Malaysia, the Singapore National Library and the library of SOAS, London.

[98] Secretariat for Economic Affairs, 'A report on the damage resulting from the war and the Japanese occupation, and on the past and future difficulties which confront the early rehabilitation of Singapore Colony', 10.12.1946, pp. 2–3, 12–13, CSO/6929.

[99] Chin, *Malaya upside down*, pp. 199–205.

[100] 'BMA fortnightly report for the week ending 31.10.1945', CO273/675/50822/3.

[101] Food Controller, BMA (M) to Hone, 31.12.1945, BMA/DEPT//16.

[102] Cheah, *Red star*, pp. 195–240.

[103] *Min Sheng Pau*, 14.12.1945; *Kin Kwok Daily News*, 11.12.1945.

small-scale business between sampan men and foreign ships, to larger boats trading in the anchorages around the island, into a regular, organised traffic in military stores direct from the warehouses.[104] Controls were evaded at every level: looting was widespread and military personnel were perhaps the most systematic offenders.[105] By December 1945, Chinese merchants had equipped around sixty vessels for Java to buy cereals and sugar; thirty to forty for Siam to buy rice and to trade pepper, coconut and gambier for rice stocks in Rangoon. To evade the legal compulsion to sell rice at the controlled price, merchants made illicit landings at isolated points on the coast.[106] It was a hazardous business: piracy was rife on the sea route that brought Burmese rice to northern Malaya; junks hid in islands north of Langkawi, and over thirty vessels were looted in the first three months of peace.[107] In a sense, the period of the 'Black Market Association' displays the resilience of local economic life to attempts by the state to control it. Much of the apparent corruption and crime was in essence a return to unregulated commercial practice as rice became the only reliable currency in the face of chronic financial instability. Urban populations were caught in a two-way trap: scarcity inflated black-market prices and put further pressure on incomes which were themselves calculated on the basis of an assumed availability of low-cost staples.

Doctors warned that food shortage had wrought 'permanent damage' on the population. Although famine conditions were reached in some areas, a more general 'semi-starvation' and malnutrition was more common. It did not always assume a visible form. A malnourished child of ten looked like a perfect child of six. Yet, on reoccupation, 35 per cent of schoolchildren in Malacca were found to have anaemia and 30 per cent vitamin deficiencies of various kinds.[108] Whilst a tapioca diet had 'passable' calorie value, it did not provide essential vitamins. Moreover, it was unpopular and identified with beri-beri. Newspapers carried spoof recipes for tapioca: skinned and chopped 'Syonan style' – 'a taste not inferior to Irish soda biscuits and good for Christmas presents' – and sweet potato cakes – 'after eating drink cold water copiously to have easy bowel movements'.[109] The ravages of malnutrition were spread unevenly across different social groups. Helplessness was perhaps greatest on the rubber estates. Many Indian families were left without wage earners and, according to one eyewitness report from Negri Sembilan, their children were 'in desperate plight, comparable to photographs I have seen of Biafra or Belsen'.[110] Estate conditions perhaps would have been worse but for the fact that labourers took more legumes and

[104] A. H. Girdler, 'Report on general conditions in No. 1 District, Klang', 10.9.1945, C. H. F. Blake Papers; 'Joint Sino-foreign smuggling', *Nanyang Siang Pau*, 23.11.1945; H. T. Pagden to S.O.1, Chinese Affairs, 10.11.1945.

[105] Hone to F. S. V. Donnison, 1.5.1952, Hone papers.

[106] *New Democracy*, 8.1.1946.   [107] *Straits Times*, 2.1.1946.

[108] T. Matthews to V. Purcell, 22.9.1945, BMA/CH/7/45; 'BMA monthly report for November, 1945', WO220/564.

[109] 'Recipes by Chou Pai', *New Democracy*, 20.12.1945.

[110] J. M. Gullick, 'My time in Malaya', Heussler Papers.

milk and practices of food preparation were less wasteful of nutrients.[111] Deficiency diseases in themselves were not the real killers. Epidemics preyed upon a dehabilitated population. A primary cause was the breakdown of sanitation in the towns. Typhoid was caused by the use of night soil as manure by vegetable gardeners; refuse was dumped in rivers; water supplies were undrinkable; markets were overcrowded and traders unlicensed. In the autumn of 1945 there was a minor outbreak of smallpox in Singapore, and outbreaks of cholera were reported in Kedah and Perak. The biggest cause of death after malaria was tuberculosis, which officials felt 'may in fact prove to be the worst aftermath of war'.[112] A second cause lay in the widened contacts with neighbouring Siam and the Dutch East Indies through the breakdown of quarantine controls and the prevalence of illicit trade. A smallpox epidemic which appeared in the northern States in 1946 spread along the western and eastern trade routes from Siam, particularly affecting coastal villages and staging posts along the railway lines and roads.[113] The cumulative effect of the erosion of mechanisms of disease control during the war was clearly seen in the general resurgence of 'hyper-endemic malaria'. In 1945, it was observed of Selangor 'as regards malaria the conditions in the state were back to what they were in 1890–1900 when our dangerous vectors were not known'. *Anopheline malculatus* bred in the concrete drains on the streets of Kuala Lumpur, and over 52 per cent of a sample of children were found to be affected.[114] The rehabilitation of anti-malarial works was hampered by the shortage of materials. A story later came to light that $175,000 was spent on restoring Royal Selangor Golf Club as 'anti-malarial work'.[115] Although there were indications by late 1945 that vector breeding was stabilising in some places, the connection made between land clearance and disease made in the Japanese period was hard to break, as survivors of labour camps and resettlement schemes 'returned to an uneasy equilibrium with their own environment . . . as they became immune to the malaria and grew their own food under the lash of hunger'.[116]

The generation of 1945

Disease and disorder shaped the world-view of a generation. The Japanese exposed it to new ideological forces. They claimed to have rescued the generation of 1945 from the materialism and liberalism of European thought: to have moulded a generation

[111] Burgess and Laidin, *Report on the state of health*, pp. 27–9; Malayan Union, *Annual report of the Medical Department for the year 1946*, pp. 19–23.
[112] 'BMA monthly report for January, 1946', WO220/564.
[113] E. D. B. Wolfe, 'Smallpox in Trengganu, 1946–47', RHO.
[114] *Report of the Medical Department for the year 1946*; Minutes of a meeting of the Malaria Advisory Board, FMS, 6.3.1946, BMA/DEPT/1/5.
[115] A War Office enquiry was apparently deflected by a threat to remove cut-rate subscriptions for the military. George Houghton, *Golf addict goes East* (London, 1967), p. 118.
[116] A. A. Sandosham, *Malaria in Malai: a handbook for anti-malaria students* (Syonan-to, 2604), p. 10; BMA Fortnightly report No. 4, 30.10.1945, CO273/675/50822/56/2; *Report of the Medical Department for the year 1946*.

'cleansed of all its old shibboleths and superstitions and won over to new beliefs and loyalties'. The Japanese language was a central agent of change: 'the natural recognition of a nation which . . . is now in the process of saving Asians from continuing to be the victims of the English'. Japanese education imparted work-discipline, regimentation, Emperor-loyalty and physical fitness: technical expertise was lauded above academic prowess; manual and artisan skills were celebrated above those of the clerk. Schools were established. Many Malayans avoided them, and rolls fell steadily, especially in the Chinese schools. In Penang 90 per cent of children attended school in 1942, but only 50 per cent in 1945. Teachers defected into other employment, and there was a growing problem of delinquency in the towns.[117] However, the legacy of Japanese indoctrination was a powerful one. New methods of communications were introduced, which helped create the political and cultural milieu for a counter-propaganda against colonial rule.

Japanese propaganda techniques far outstripped those of the Allies, who throughout the war found themselves responding to rather than anticipating Japanese innovations. Japan seized upon the potential of cinema. After August 1942 all English and US films were banned and Japanese films were screened that celebrated the Asiatic spirit. Propaganda traced the historical and cultural links between Japan and *Malai*: similarities of language, parallels in proverbs. They created a legend of Raja Hariman, or *Tani-Yutaka*, 'a Malaian Robin Hood', brought to Malaya when he was one year old, who robbed British and Chinese, gave the proceeds to poor Malays, and then, with 1,000 followers, led the Japanese armies to Singapore, where he was martyred by malaria.[118] Youth training schools, the *Koa Kunrenjo*, reproduced the *Nippon seishin* – the *élan* of imperial Japan. These institutions became forcing houses of racial consciousness. Their alumni included men and women who were to occupy high office in independent Malaya, and they learnt most in the science of communications. Promising students were taken to Japan for study. Yet the Japanese complained of the durable taints of western ideas. The 'racial egotism' of the 'old, cliquish, egoistic nationalism' conflicted with the 'Oriental moralism' of the Japanese *seishin*. Authentic liberation, it was stressed, 'differs from independence based on the idea of liberalism and national self-determination'.[119] The relationship between 'Nipponisation' and

---

[117] Harold E. Wilson, *Educational policy and performance in Singapore 1942–1945* (ISEAS, Occasional paper No. 16, Singapore, 1973), pp. 9, 4, 11–15; Shü Yun-ts'iao and Chua Ser-koon (eds.), *Malayan Chinese resistance to Japan, 1937–45: selected source materials, based on Col. Chuang Hui-tsuan's collection* (Singapore, 1984), p. 52.

[118] Iwao Hino and S. Durai Rajasingam, *Stray notes on Nippon-Malaysian historical connections* (Kuala Lumpur, 2604), pp. 79–81.

[119] Yoji Akashi, 'The *Koa Kunrenjo* and *Nampo Tokubetsu Ryugakusei*: a study of cultural propagation and conflict in Japanese occupied Malaya (1942–45)', *Shakai Kagaku Tokyu*, 23, 3 (1978), pp. 39–66; 'Draft of basic plan for establishment of the Greater East Asia Co-prosperity Sphere', 27.1.1942, cited in Elsbree, *Japan's role in Southeast Asian nationalist movements*, pp. 26–7; OSS, R & A No. 39865, 'The Kempei in Japanese-occupied territory', 13.7.1945.

local nationalisms was deeply problematic. Similar contradictions would later bedevil Britain's attempts to foster a nationalism congruent to its own ideals.

The political legacy of Japanese ideological education was to stem more from its form than from its content. It found resonance in patterns of Malay thought which set *semangat*, spirit, and *pemuda*, youth, above the bureaucratic finesse and elitism which had characterised the relationship of traditional Malay leadership with their colonial counterparts. This rhetoric, and the propaganda techniques learnt from the Japanese, was to shape the Malay radicalism of the post-war years. It borrowed heavily from the *pemuda* spirit that had emerged under similar conditions in Indonesia. The future of the nation lay in its youth, and youth had a special duty to set the pace of national revolution. Important political networks of journalists, actors, film-makers and propagandists were formed in the war. Their worlds cut across each other, and continued to do so in peacetime. Malay memoirs of the Syonan period celebrate the connections that were forged. The Malay newspaper *Berita Malai* brought together in Singapore men who were to dominate post-war Malay radicalism and letters, men such as Ishak Haji Muhammad and Abdul Samad Ismail.[120] This and other periodicals such as *Semangat Asia, Fajar Asia, Sinaran Matahari, Suara Timur* and *Matahari Menacar* fostered the beginnings of a new literature. Much of it voiced fervent support for the New Asia, but it also carried subterranean themes that addressed inner racial awareness and called the *bangsa* to political action. War literature also facilitated a literary crossing-over between Malaya and Sumatra. Nipponisation had taught that language held the key to power, that 'through language the race is known'.[121] Malay drama became rooted in local conditions, and created a mood that embraced the *pemuda* ethos. In particular, the scripted drama of the *sandiwara* rose in popularity, and transmitted new influences from Indonesia. Theatres, such as the 'Bolero' from Sumatra, brought with them radically different kinds of plays – featuring cruel and insane kings, the predicaments of ordinary mortals and the political ideas of the Indonesian revolution. Members of the dramatic society at Sultan Idris Training College, where much of the post-war radical Malay nationalist leadership was schooled, graduated into Japanese propaganda theatre, and helped popularise the *sandiwara*, which embarked on a mission of public information and education, especially as its plays became published.[122] Many *bangsawan* stars were absorbed into the *sandiwara*, and then into the cinema. This multi-form intelligentsia grew in influence at the expense of the old state elites.

---

[120] Melan Abdullah, 'Samad in love and war', in Cheah Boon Kheng (ed.), *A. Samad Ismail: journalism and politics* (Kuala Lumpur, 1987), p. 76. Ahmad Boestamam, *Lambiran dari puncak: memoir, 1941–45* (Kuala Lumpur, 1983).

[121] Abu Talib Ahmad, 'Impact of the Japanese occupation', pp. 12–21; Ahmad Kamal Abdullah et al., *History of modern Malay literature*, II, pp. 3–21, quoting Muhammad Hassan Abdul Wahab's 'Bahasa dan bangsa'.

[122] Cantius Leo Cameons, 'History and development of Malay theatre' (M.A. Thesis, Universiti Malaya, 1980), pp. 181–200; Nur Nina Zura, *An analysis of modern Malay drama* (Shah Alam, 1992), pp. 35–93.

The men and women being nurtured in Japanese schools and militia were not the compliant tools of Japanese imperial interest. One of the most important figures in post-war Malay radical politics, Dr Burhanuddin Al-Helmy, was to emphasise that 'the present spirit of Malay nationalism is not the legacy of Japanese propaganda or Japanese machinations'.[123] The Japanese forged alliances with new Malay political movements, but they were uneasy ones. The *Kesatuan Melayu Muda* (KMM) led by Ibrahim Yaacob, emerged out of the pre-war radical movement, and was utilised by the Japanese as a core group of political agents. However, their position within the New *Malai* remained ambiguous. Many KMM members did not support the Japanese; others co-operated with them only to further the greater end of Malaya's independence within a greater Indonesia, an *Indonesia Raya*. In fact the KMM was banned five months after its creation. The Malay radicals were suffered, rather than encouraged by the Japanese. On the eve of their defeat in August 1945, the Japanese allowed the formation of a new nationalist movement, the *Kesatuan Rakyat Istimewa* – KRIS. Ibrahim Yaacob was at its fore, but other figures such as Dr Burhanuddin, Ishak bin Haji Muhammad and Dato Onn bin Jaafar were involved. Its commitment to *Indonesia Raya* was symbolised by a meeting arranged by the Japanese authorities between its organisers and Sukarno and Hatta. The *Giyu Gun* became a force known as *Pembela Tanah Ayer* (PETA) – defenders of the fatherland – under the command of Ibrahim Yaacob.[124] With Japanese connivance nationalisms were militarised. Malaya became a recruiting-ground for the Indian Independence League and the Indian National Army (INA). When Subhas Chandra Bose visited Malaya in mid-1943, vast crowds, not solely comprised of Indians, flocked to attend what were perhaps the largest political gatherings hitherto held in the country. Young Indian recruits were sent to Tokyo, or to schools such as the Swaraj Institute in Penang, for grounding in propaganda and espionage. Many saw service outside Malaya, and never returned. However, amongst those who remained, the solidarities formed in the Indian Independence League were carried forward into new Indian organisations, which for the first time began to cut across ethnic boundaries.[125] For these men and women Japanese rule engendered a shared sense of the possible.

The Malay radicals and the INA were not called upon to defend Malaya from the Allies. The sudden surrender of the Japanese left them disorganised and disenchanted. The INA was thrown into mourning by the death, on 18 August 1945, of Subhas Chandra Bose, only to revive with the Congress progress to power. The Malay left drew some sustenance from the declaration of the Indonesian Republic.

---

[123] *Malaya Tribune*, 2.6.1947.

[124] Yoichi Itagaki, 'Outlines of Japanese policy in Indonesia and Malaya during the war with special reference to nationalism of respective countries', *Hitotsubashi Academy Annals*, 2, 2 (1952), 190–1; Cheah Boon Kheng, 'The Japanese occupation of Malaya, 1941–45: Ibrahim Yaacob and the struggle for Indonesia Raya', *Indonesia*, 28 (1979), 85–120.

[125] Joyce Lebra, 'Japanese policy and the Indian National Army', *Asian Studies*, 7, 2 (1969), 31–49; and see the old boys' memoir, Netaji Centre, Kuala Lumpur, *Netaji Subhas Chandra Bose: a Malaysian perspective* (Kuala Lumpur, 1992).

Malay radicals rallied openly to the flag of the new state: men such as Abdullah Hussein, A. Samad Ahmad, A. Samad Ismail and Yusof bin Ishak. After the reoccupation many, including Ibrahim Yaacob, and briefly Ishak Haji Muhammad, fled to Indonesia. Indonesians in Malaya were amongst the first groups to organise. Amongst the vast numbers of workers who were stranded in Singapore a *Persatuan Kaum Buroh Indonesia* (PERKABIM) was formed, in which nationalists and communists struggled for influence. In Singapore too, a youth front, *Gerakan Angkatan Muda* (GERAM) was founded by radicals such as A. Samad Ismail and Abdul Aziz Ishak, and a *Pembantoe Indonesia Merdeka* (PIM) was formed in Kuala Lumpur in November 1945 by Sumatran Malays. A new generation had graduated on to the political scene. In many ways the Second World War was a revolution for the young. A generational conflict was unleashed; a perturbation of spirits was in the air. Many young had been deprived of their schooling, and when they resumed it years later they were no longer so young, and did not behave like juveniles. After the war they refused to submit to the sober discipline of study or labour in the manner officialdom expected them to. Mass delinquency was the spectre haunting post-war colonialism.

Its most threatening manifestation emerged from the forests, from the resistance armies that led the guerrilla struggle against the Japanese, and extended their power base amongst the displaced Chinese and aboriginal communities. The British had helped create them. On the eve of the fall of Singapore the Special Branch took up MCP offers of collaboration. The Special Operations Executive established a Special Training School to prepare stay-behind groups that were to remain under the direction of officers of its Force 136. Known as 'Dalforce' after its inspiration – a policeman, John Dalley, who was to command security operations against his own protégés after the war – it produced four classes of graduates: over 200 men. These guerrillas infiltrated back from Singapore into Selangor, Negri Sembilan and two areas of Johore, to become the core of the first four independent regiments of the Malayan People's Anti-Japanese Army (MPAJA). Another four were later raised locally, notably the fifth Perak regiment and the sixth in Pahang, which included veterans of the Chinese Communist Party's (CCP) 8th Route Army. Most fighters were very young: virtually all of them in Perak were under thirty. One platoon was comprised entirely of teenage girls. Of the 1,225 MPAJA members killed in the struggle against the Japanese, 661 had homes in China, or an unknown place of origin. The MPAJA was the military wing of the Anti-Japanese Union, controlled by the MCP through its Central Military Committee – consisting of Party supremos Lai Teck, Lau Yew and Chin Peng – and by political officers attached to each regiment. Where they were strongest, in Perak, they conducted a relentless harassment of the Japanese and their Malay and Chinese 'collaborators', and spread a terror that would cast a long shadow over the post-war years.[126] Although the MPAJA were the most celebrated of the guerrillas, the mountain ranges that form the backbone of the

---

[126] Cheah, *Red star*, pp. 54–64; Hara Fujio, 'The Japanese occupation of Malaya and the Chinese community', in Paul H. Kratoska (ed.), *Malaya and Singapore during the Japanese*

country became a twilight world in which a variety of private armies operated. Some British observers contend that it was the Kuomintang (KMT) guerrillas of the Overseas Chinese Anti-Japanese Army (OCAJA) in the north of the central range who were the greater irritant to the Japanese, and that the MPAJA often seemed to be holding back and concentrating on building up its organisation, as was the case during the last stages of CCP–KMT co-operation against the Japanese in mainland China. The OCAJA had both a political and a criminal complexion, and its gangs dominated the area between Grik, Betong and Sungei Siput, as well as areas across the watershed into Ulu Kelantan. Other bands along the Thai border were engaged in large-scale smuggling with the connivance of customs officials. The '99 Gang', commanded by KMT leader Lee Chee Leong at Sungei Padi, was some 240-strong and was comprised of disparate KMT and MPAJA elements as well as Siamese and Japanese.[127] A graphic memoir by a British officer, J. K. Creer, chronicles the struggles between KMT 'One Star' and MCP 'Three Star' elements around Pulai in Ulu Kelantan and testifies to the complexities of allegiance in these armed bands. The core of the KMT guerrillas he worked with were Hakka. The dominant influence was Lee Fung Sam, a timber contractor for Bukit Betong sawmill. He came from Pahang, but was driven north to Kelantan by Communist attempts to take over his forces, which had escalated into violent conflict.[128] These were most intense around Pulai in Ulu Kelantan: a KMT raid on the town early in the war had led to Japanese reprisals. The KMT had abandoned the area and the MPAJA had gained merit from protecting the villagers in an area of tensions between Hakka hill-farmers facing population pressure from displaced Cantonese *jelutong* tappers. The Lenggong area of Perak was another area fraught with conflict. The KMT was believed to have settled 2,000 supporters in the jungle in February 1945 and saw them as a force to fight the MCP. Produce and poll taxes were collected and a 'Farmers' Native Produce Trading Company' organised.[129] Although the resistance armies were dominated by Chinese, there also existed smaller-scale, but for the British politically reassuring, Malay resistance movements in Pahang (*Wataniah*) and in Upper Perak (*Askar Melayu Setia*). There were private wars, such as the individual resistance of the ex-policeman, Gurchan Singh. However, over much of the peninsula political loyalties were in suspended animation.

The networks of communication laid in these years – the jungle paths that straddled the central range, the courier routes, the secret mailboxes and caches, the systems of intelligence and supply, the smuggling and extortion rackets – survived the Japanese occupation. Many of the guerrilla strongholds of the war – the 'neutral' jungle of the

occupation (Singapore, 1995), p. 45, and Yoji Akashi, 'The anti-Japanese movement in Perak during the Japanese occupation 1941–45', in *ibid*, pp. 83–120.

[127] HQ Malaya Cmmd, WIR, No. 27, 10.5.1946, CO537/2139.

[128] J. K. Creer, 'Report of experiences during Japanese occupation of Malaya', 3.11.1945, Heussler Papers; 'The KMT guerrillas, North Perak', MSS/PIJ, Supplement No. 4 of 1948 to PIJ, No. 10/1948.

[129] 'The KMT Guerrillas, North Perak', Supplement 4 of 1948 to MSS/PIJ/10/1948.

Perak–Pahang watershed, for instance – were to be the principal battlegrounds of the Emergency. The forests bred their heroes and their myths. A genre of rebel literature emerged which enhanced the popular appeal of the MCP. For the British, co-operation between the MPAJA and the British was portrayed as the beginning of a new era of partnership between the British and colonial peoples. However, the motives behind the MCP's position to make alliance were strategic and conditional. They were not to be 'content with begging narrow and factional democratic rights from the British government'.[130] During negotiations between the British and the MPAJA political questions were studiously avoided. The agreement signed between Lai Teck and Force 136 officers on pages torn from an exercise book, armed the MPAJA and placed them under the military direction of South East Asia Command. However, a secret April 1945 directive of the MCP, known perhaps only to a few key cadres, under the slogan 'Establish the Malayan Democratic Republic', dictated a flexible policy to enable the MCP to respond to developments in an interregnum. Arms and supplies were squirrelled away for future use. The main body of the eighty-eight British officers in Malaya at the Japanese surrender, and the bulk of the arms, only arrived between May and August 1945.[131] Given the weakness of British supervision and the fact that there was no responsibility on the MPAJA to restore civil order, a key question has been why the party did not launch a *coup d'état* immediately upon the Japanese surrender. There are several reasons for this. First, there were the difficulties of communicating a co-ordinated strategy swiftly through a secretive command chain and a communications system dependent on overland couriers. Secondly, there was ideological confusion within the MCP itself as to how far to follow the path of 'bourgeois democratic revolution'. Thirdly, these factors were compounded by the treachery of the MCP General Secretary Lai Teck. His story is one of the most remarkable in the history of espionage. He had served the British Special Branch before the war, the Kampetai during the war, and, never it seems having any doubt as to the eventual Allied victory, looked to serve himself by making himself indispensable to the British after the reoccupation. Lai Teck masterminded the Japanese massacre of most of the MCP Central Committee at Batu Caves outside Kuala Lumpur in September 1942. This consolidated his control over policy and allowed him to repeatedly suspend the launching of the Malayan Democratic Republic. A fourth constraint was the MCP's belated recognition of the level of Malay enmity towards it. Ibrahim Yaacob later claimed that his PETA had contracted a pact with the MPAJA to resist the returning British, and that the Lai Teck policy had betrayed this understanding. It is unclear whether the collaborationist associations of KMM–PETA were an obstacle to alliance, or if the MCP was placing its faith in its own recruitment amongst the Malays. However, the communal violence of the

[130] *Nan Dao Zhi Chun* [A brief history of the MCP], Cheah Boon Kheng, *From PKI to the Comintern, 1929–41: the apprenticeship of the Malayan Communist Party* (Ithaca, 1992), pp. 35–9; 103–24.
[131] Anthony Short, *The Communist insurrection in Malaya, 1948–60* (London, 1976), pp. 21–2; Charles Cruickshank, *SOE in the Far East* (Oxford, 1983), pp. 195–209.

interregnum left it beyond any doubt that any attempt to seize power would be met with active Malay resistance.[132] Much of the post-war fiction and histories of the anti-Japanese war – in both Malay and Chinese – emphasises the tense relations between Chinese guerrillas and kampong Malays.[133] It was only after September 1946 that the party embarked on a programme of 'Malayanisation'. The interregnum belonged to the forces of chaos.

Much of the peninsula was liberated by the columns of the 'Three Star' armies, their Force 136 liaison officers struggling to restrain them. As they entered the urban centres of the peninsula, they were fêted and feared. In many areas – Selangor, Negri Sembilan, Malacca, Muar, Johore Bahru and elsewhere – the MCP set up a skeleton local government. However, it rode the crest of a vast wave of disorder and precipitated a communal crisis of unprecedented dimensions. MPAJA kangaroo courts dispensed brutal revolutionary justice, as it took revenge on those – often Malay policemen and minor officials – who had been seen to 'collaborate' with the Japanese. The Malays armed themselves to defend their homes from a Chinese attempt to seize the country. The killings and counter-killings claimed thousands of lives. They were both a local tragedy and part of a wider experience of mass trauma and communal vendetta which followed the collapse of the Japanese empire in Southeast Asia. The full story of the dark days of communal terror has already been told elsewhere.[134] It was not confined to the major flashpoints in Johore and Perak. In the Bukit Besi locality of Trengganu, Malays were driven out of kampongs by fear of Chinese Communists still at large in the area.[135] In Kelantan, a secret Malay Security Force for Self-Protection – the *Pasukan Keselamatan Jaga Diri Kelantan* – was formed to resist the Chinese. There were instances of friction over competing business interests; local relationships of reciprocity had broken down. Yet, confrontation was by no means inevitable, or even general. It was confined more to cases where a closer economic proximity fuelled latent tension for which political uncertainty and an atmosphere of unfamiliarity and rumour within local communities was primarily responsible.[136] A reading of intelligence reports and memoirs emphasises how often rumours of the approach of men from outside a given neighbourhood cultivated an atmosphere of fear and distrust that could spark incidents. The violence would cast a long shadow over the reoccupation period. Rumours of retribution attacks persisted into 1947. The violence was not merely a clash between communities, but a struggle

---

[132] Cheah, *Red star*, pp. 170–240.
[133] See for example, Claudine Salmon's review of Cheah, *Red star*, in *Archipel*, 38 (1989), 156–7.
[134] Cheah Boon Kheng, 'Sino-Malay conflicts in Malaya, 1945–1946: Communist vendetta and Islamic resistance', *JSEAS*, 12, 1 (1981), 108–17; A. J. Stockwell, *British policy and Malay politics during the Malayan Union experiment, 1945–1948* (Kuala Lumpur, 1979), pp. 146–62.
[135] Diary of J. S. Addison, 18.2.1946, DF/63/45.
[136] Kenelm O. L. Burridge, 'Racial relations in Johore', *The Australian Journal of Politics and History*, 2, 2 (1957), 151–68; Gullick, 'The British Military Administration'.

for leadership within them. For the Malays the hold of the old elites on the rural community would be tested by the crisis; their rivals exploited the crisis to forge a new sense of Malay identity. Amongst the Chinese it became a focus for renewed struggle between the MCP and KMT for control of the Malayan Chinese. The MCP was forced to project itself as protector of the Chinese at the very moment it was attempting to widen its support within other communities. If it was the duty of the colonial protecting power to keep the peace, it rationalised, when it failed to do so the people had to defend themselves. Through the MPAJA, it was argued, 'self-defence and self-government go hand in hand'. The KMT was staking a similar claim, the rightist Chinese newspapers urging that the resistance forces be converted into a local defence force 'to keep the unruly Malays at bay'.[137] Further tests of leadership came as community leaders attempted to rein in the violence. In Batu Pahat, the District Officer, Onn bin Jaafar, consolidated his reputation through his courage in confronting the cult leadership of Kyai Salleh. In Perak, Malay Nationalist Party (MNP) and MCP leaders embarked on tours to reduce tensions. The Sultan did the same. In some parts of the State Malays boycotted Chinese coffeeshops and shops. Elsewhere, we find Eng Min Chin of the MCP urging an end to a Chinese boycott of Malay businesses. 'Not all the Malays,' she cautioned, 'are murderers.'[138] Sino-Malay meetings throughout the western States tried to calm communal tensions. In Selangor meetings aired and dispelled rumours and addressed contentious issues such as rampaging pigs. The violence generated much soul-searching amongst MCP cadres. Some argued that as the Malays and Chinese belonged to the same class – the economically exploited – the causes of the violence must be political and not economic.[139] Others identified the fundamental cause in the resumption of colonial rule. Malaya had retreated back into 'the realm of forgotten things'.

> [It] will on the one hand preserve the system of feudalism and on the other bring about a revival of capitalism. The British rulers clearly understand that the Malay Rulers represent the influence of the feudalists, and that the Chinese industrialists represent the economic interests of the capitalists. The unequal economic development brought about by these classes will result in a clash of interests among the people, particularly between the Chinese and the natives, especially the Malays. This will foster the influence of feudalism and encourage interracial friction.[140]

Violence shocked the MCP into addressing Malayan problems. In Chapter 3 we shall chart its attempts to escape from the terrible legacy of September and October 1945.

The Sino-Malay clashes saw a resurgence of millenarianism. In the Malay kampongs most traumatised by the violence, a struggle for leadership was underway

---

[137] 'How to eliminate the hostile attitude of the Malays to the Chinese', *Hwa Chia Jit Pau*, 19.10.1945.

[138] *Min Sheng Pao*, 16.1.1946.

[139] Pa-jen, 'From anti-Chinese incidents to self-government and self-defence in the villages', *Min Sheng Pao*, 19.1.1946.

[140] 'Old policy, new pattern', *New Democracy*, 14.10.1945; 'Beware of new splits', *New Democracy*, 12.10.1945.

in which the main contenders courted the support of preachers and healers of invulnerability cults and *Sabilillah* – 'Path of Allah' – movements. Some of these had their origins in the Red and White Flag societies that had emerged in the later nineteenth century from Penang and become bound up with Triad activity and resurgent Islam in the early twentieth century. The Perak river had been a site of these activities before the war and the area was wracked by violence after it. The *Taslim* heterodoxy was preached throughout the western States. Itinerant Indonesian healers were at the core of invulnerability cults. In Perak, one such man, Sheikh Idris, paraded his followers in remnants of Japanese uniform, with the connivance, it seems, of the *mufti* of the state. There were reports of the formation of *parang panjang* – long knives – gangs throughout Malaya.[141] Local holy men, at the head of *sufi* organisations, expounded doctrines of *Sabilillah*. Chief amongst these was Kyai Salleh of Simpang Kiri, in Batu Pahat district of Johore. Trained in both the *Qadiriyyah* and *Naqshbandiyyah* sufi orders he brought as many as 1,600 Malays together under his leadership in resistance to the MPAJA from June and July 1945 and in the fighting of the interregnum.[142] Millenarian and secret society leadership came to fore elsewhere in the peninsula, and would remain a vital undercurrent of Malay politics throughout the next three years. Millenarianism not only took a grip on parts of the Malay community: it was also in evidence amongst Chinese. Intoxicated by a doctrine propagated by the Nan Sien Temple near Bukit Mertajam, eighteen Chinese men, women and children threw themselves into a nearby river one night in late November 1945 'to learn how to become saints'. Eleven of them drowned. 'Our Chinese,' an Ipoh newspaper warned, 'are being deceived and cheated by various false doctrines and teachings.'[143] In a more sense the period saw a resurgence of secret societies as 'protectors' of Chinese communities groups in the default of other leadership. These shadowy figures were to dominate the politics of the rural Chinese in the coming years.

The communal clashes can only be understood as part of a larger canvas of violence and retribution. Violence was launched against strangers of all kinds. Allegations of looting and rape were general and often levelled at a common outsider: the Indian soldiers of the Allied armies. In these dark months the basis was laid of much political activity that was to dominate the unsettled rural areas in the years that followed. In the interregnum, all the changes of the war years became visible, many of them perhaps intangible to the formal historical record. Unholy alliances were forged; witch-hunts launched; vendettas prosecuted against suspected collaborators. This catalysed long chain reactions of resentment and suspicion; Kampetai and other war criminals were arrested, and so also were many of their mistresses. There were accusations and counter-accusations regarding those who had engaged in the 'shameless trade' of profiteering, an ugly prelude to the confessional politics of the

---

[141] G. H. S. Fripp, 'Sabilallah and invulnerability', 7.10.1946, CO537/1583; Stockwell, *British policy*, pp. 148–56.

[142] Cheah, *Red Star*, pp. 195–230.   [143] *Kin Kwok Daily News*, 28.12.1945.

Emergency. The intense scramble for commodities continued. Economic anxiety did not merely centre on the immediate food crisis, but on the future validity of currency holdings, the prospect of reparations and the securing of labour. Credit was tight; people had nothing left to pawn. Those who had in the confusion of the occupation found relief from debt or litigation, faced a lifting of the moratorium and reconvening of the courts. Within the archives of the British Military Administration some of the most harrowing reading is in the files relating to displaced persons, the voluminous enquiries from families attempting to locate their loved ones, or to find out whether they were living or dead. Fifty years later, bodies of victims of the *sook ching* were still being exhumed. Out of this vast human tragedy, a veneer of normality had to be constructed: homes rebuilt, regular employment resumed, and children sent back to school. Eventually, in Singapore, a cenotaph was raised as a memorial to the civilian casualties of the Pacific war. A more immediate, but equally enduring memorial of the war years, lay in the minds of all who had lived through them: a portent, a terrible nightmare that could never be repeated. It haunted the politicians who attempted to create a new order out of disorder. What this generation of 1945 had in common was their challenge to more established community leadership which was often discredited during the occupation. It was not always so: older leaders could prove resilient to the challenge. Many servants of the Malay *ancien régime* were forced back on to their local power base and revitalised their authority amongst their rural constituency. But what is important to our argument here are the ways in which techniques of militancy, and a consciousness of their wider international application against alien dominance, played a central role in the relationship between these leaderships and the colonial regime. We shall now examine the political concerns which underwrote this struggle.

CHAPTER TWO

The Malayan spring

In the aftermath of war a struggle began for the soul of Malaya. The troubled years between the British reoccupation in September 1945 and the declaration of the Emergency in July 1948 set in motion politics that would dominate the transition to independence. This period has concentrated the minds of a great number of Malaya's historians. Much of their work has focused on the restructuring of the British presence in Malaya under a military administration and the introduction of, and opposition to, the Malayan Union scheme in 1946 and the Federal constitution which succeeded it in February 1948. This period saw the emergence of the movement that became the main vehicle of Malay nationalism the United Malays National Organisation (UMNO). It also witnessed the floundering of a range of radical challenges to its primacy. In the historical writings on the period many of the foundation myths of modern Malaysia have been carved out and contested. A nation is defined by its tragedies as much as its triumphs, and for many the communal and insurrectionary violence of these years set the constraints that would govern subsequent political life and defined the limits of what the structure of Malaya's plural society could tolerate. To others, the constitutional struggles appear as a lost opportunity to effect its transformation.[1] It is hard to exaggerate the importance of these events in shaping the landscape of Malayan politics. However, a preoccupation with the high politics of constitution-making has led the period to be viewed within a paradigm governed by the colonial political framework and chronicled in isolation from the processes of social change at work in post-war Malaya. Historians have shown how local politics reacted to colonial policy, but have said less about the ways in which both were shaped by the trauma of social disorder. In recent years, historians have begun to ask new questions of the profound soul-searching that occurred within Malayan society in this

---

[1] Notably, A. J. Stockwell, *British policy and Malay politics during the Malay Union experiment, 1945–1948* (Kuala Lumpur, 1979); J. de Vere Allen, *The Malayan Union* (New Haven, 1967); Albert Lau, *The Malayan Union controversy, 1942–48* (Singapore, 1991); M. R. Stenson, 'The Malayan Union and the historians', *JSEAH*, 10, 2 (1969), 344–54; Wong Lin Ken, 'The Malayan Union: a historical retrospect', *JSEAS*, 13, 1 (1982), 184–91.

period.[2] This chapter attempts to further this process through a re-examination of post-war colonial rule. It focuses on the reorientation of the colonial state to meet post-war crisis under the British Military Administration (BMA), and the contradictions that lay at the heart of its responses to change. It examines how relief work and social policy were employed to draw reconstructive social movements, born in the cauldron of war, into a new pattern of collaboration. Britain's design was to bolster community life and to place her rule on a more secure footing. Pre-war restrictions on expression, assembly and association were lifted, which seemed to promise a 'Malayan Spring'.[3] The success of the political initiative was contingent on the support of local leaders, through whom Britain aimed to regain her foothold in the region. However, as the public sphere expanded, alternative understandings of the ideological and material priorities of reconstruction were being voiced. The conflicts that erupted, and the competing visions of politics they exposed, illustrate how directly and deeply social crisis shaped the subsequent relationship between the colonial state and Malayan society. The debates of the period were not merely about the shape of a constitution but about the nature of political freedom. In its politics, not only the self-interest of ethnic communities was at stake: their very essence was under dispute.

'A new conception of empire'?

Military defeat transfigured the official mind of the British empire. The 'South Sea Bubble' of reconstruction projects for post-war Malaya which surfaced during the war years was distinguished by the 'muscular faith in reason and progress' in currency in Britain at the time.[4] Territorial rearrangements in the world at large and the formulation of new state strategies on the home front had a history beyond that of the wartime circumstances which launched them. By the 1930s, mechanisms of indirect rule were coming under strain throughout the British empire. The demands of wartime mobilisation substantiated the mounting critique of old institutions. The 'second colonial occupation' of the 1940s created similar kinds of colonial state in various parts of Africa and Asia, as a new generation of technical specialists and anthropologists were harnessed to the imperial enterprise. Out of wartime social change they attempted to create new institutions for new categories of African and

---

[2] Cheah Boon Kheng, 'The erosion of ideological hegemony and royal power and the rise of post-war Malay nationalism', *JSEAS*, 19, 1 (1988), 1–26; Tan Liok Ee, *The Rhetoric* of bangsa *and* minzu (Monash University, 1988); Muhammad Ikmal Said, 'Ethnic perspectives on the left in Malaysia', in Kahn and Loh Kok Wah, *Fragmented vision* (Sydney, 1992)'; Ariffin Omar, *Bangsa Melayu: Malay concepts of democracy and community, 1945–50* (Kuala Lumpur, 1993).

[3] Han Suyin's coinage, 'An outline of Malayan Chinese literature', *Eastern Horizon*, 3, 6 (June, 1964), 6–16.

[4] Paul Addison, *The road to 1945: British politics and the Second World War* (London, 1983), pp. 182–3.

Asian.[5] However, although coloured by broader revisions of colonial policy, planning for post-war Malaya emerged from the debates of a narrow constituency of regional specialists. It was the product of a Malayan official mind, although it was not representative of all its shades of opinion. It focused on the symbols of legitimacy of Great Britain's presence in Malaya: her treaty obligations to protect the Malay Rulers and the social order they embodied. However, they were no longer sacrosanct. Planners were determined to seize the opportunity war presented to rewrite the treaties in new terms. They revised their understanding of the nature of the allegiance the Malays owed their Rulers, and now saw it as less absolute than it had been in the past. They were fortified by a general belief that the fall of Malaya, and reports of local 'collaboration' with the Japanese, represented their own failure to secure the allegiance of the subject populations.[6] This criticism was broadened into an attack on the methods of controlling migrant labour indirectly through the Chinese Protectorate and estate managers. 'The vast bulk of the population,' it was concluded, 'had no organised connection with government.'[7] The new thinking was adopted less to punish the Rulers for their 'collaboration' with the enemy, than to reward the Chinese for their economic achievements and support against Japan. The war had demonstrated, if demonstration were needed, that Malaya's plural society could not be unmade, and that there was a concomitant need to provide a more concrete stake in Malaya for the Chinese through a common citizenship, that would allow them to adopt a fidelity to Malaya that would be strong enough to deflect the irredentist claims of a Chinese nationalist government.[8]

At the heart of the new policy for Malaya was an attempt to replace the confused loyalties of the pre-war period with a direct allegiance to the colonial state. The 'separatist tendencies', the 'corruption and inefficiency' of the unreconstructed system of indirect rule were to be overcome by the arranged marriage of sovereignty and actual power. The story of the evolution of this policy has been well narrated elsewhere.[9] Throughout, the driving impetus was towards the reformation and rationalisation of the colonial presence in Malaya into a strong central government. A new Malayan Union with a uniform administrative apparatus and the direct appeal of common citizenship was to be created to reach over the miscellany of native forms and to be the harbinger of political advancement. The impasse of indirect rule was to be broken by the negotiation of new treaties with the Rulers to acquire full jurisdiction in the Malay States for the British Crown. An attempt was made to align social and

---

[5] See Joanna E. Lewis, 'The colonial politics of African welfare in Kenya 1939–1953: a crisis of paternalism' (Ph.D., Cambridge University, 1993).

[6] A. J. Stockwell, 'Colonial planning during World War Two: the case of Malaya', *JICH*, 2, 3 (1974), 333–51; D. A. Somerville, 'Notes on the future policy and administration in Malaya', 5.2.1944, BMA/RP/1/A.

[7] H. A. L. Luckham, 'Some causes of the loss of Malaya', 30.3.1942, C)865/14.

[8] Albert Lau, 'Malayan Union citizenship: constitutional change and controversy in Malaya, 1942–48', *JSEAS*, 20, 2 (1989), 216–43.

[9] Stockwell, *British policy*, ch. 2.

economic policy with political intentions through a comprehensive series of policy
directives for South East Asia Command (SEAC), drawn up by a Malayan Planning
Unit in London – a kind of court in exile – in close consultation with the Colonial
Office, on matters ranging 'from law to agriculture to electricity'.[10] The new deal
went beyond the writing of constitutions. The British reoccupation of Malaya was
conceived as a vast experiment in democracy. 'A new experiment consequent on the
change of policy towards political societies' was rendered necessary by the recognition
of the MCP during the invasion, and by the latitude given to South East Asia
Command to determine the party's post-war status.[11] If SEAC had given the MCP no
outright assurances of their position after the war, the position was, to say the least,
very ambiguous. It was recognised from the outset that 'Chinese public opinion would
have been alienated by any premature restriction of the rights of freedom of speech
and of association'.[12] Pre-war legislation on registration of societies, trade unions and
control of the press was allowed to lapse. This policy was advocated within the
Malayan Planning Unit by the former Protector of Chinese, Victor Purcell, who as
Adviser on Chinese Affairs embodied the Malayan Spring by his encouragement of all
manner of political societies in the early days of the military regime.[13] The motif of
Malayan politics in this period was the enlargement of the public sphere, in which the
colonial government cast itself as the impresario of new kinds of public opinion.

The new colonialism wore a Janus face. The commitment of the British government
to rehabilitate and advance Malayan social and economic life, although in many ways
driven by 'a new conception of empire', was also shaped by powerful strategic
arguments for a more integrated territory. Policy was further constrained by the
contribution of Malaya's exports to the Sterling Area's balance of payments.[14] The
British had not come to Southeast Asia to collect butterflies. However, economic
calculations were inhibited by a deeper ideological anxiety. The rhetoric of Colonial
Development and Welfare forbade the wholesale plunder of Malaya for metropolitan
recovery. An important by-product of this 'dilemma of trusteeship' was social policy.
This was a blanket term for a complex of concerns – including health services,
nutrition, social welfare and mass education – which reflected emerging domestic
priorities. These lines of activity were not a novelty in themselves. Pre-war welfare
provisions in Malaya had been directed towards research in tropical medicine and
nutrition and attempts by the colonial state to extend medical services and introduce

[10] C. M. Turnbull, 'British planning for post-war Malaya', *JSEAS*, 5, 2 (1974), 239–54.
[11] 'BMA Fortnightly Report No. 1, 20.9.1945', CO273/675/50882/56/3.
[12] 'Minutes of SCAOs' conference session No.1 held on 1.3.1946 at H. Q. BMA', BMA/SEL/
CA/67/46.
[13] Victor Purcell, *Memoirs of a Malayan Official* (London, 1965), pp. 345–59.
[14] The phrase belongs to Capt. L. D. Gammans, 'A new conception of empire', *British Malaya*
(May 1942), 8; for the importance of Malaya to the British economy, see A. J. Stockwell,
'British imperial strategy and decolonization in Southeast Asia, 1947–57', in D. K. Basset
and V. T. King (eds.), *Britain and Southeast Asia* (Hull: University of Hull Centre of
Southeast Asian Studies, Occasional Papers, No. 13 (1986), pp. 79–90.

remedial health measures. An increasing acknowledgement of welfare needs was written into a wider discourse which centred around the need to preserve the norms of community life in Malaya, for example in improving rural conditions in the Malay Reservations, and in maintaining the efficiency of the labouring population.[15] In this limited application, medical and social policy were at once an ornament of modern administration and a by-product of Protection. Elements of pre-war paternalism survived. But under the technocratic regime of reconstruction, welfare assumed the guise of a co-ordinated ideological and practical initiative. As an 'ethical' movement it evolved from official Fabianism and the writings of pundits such as Lord Hailey, Margery Perham and W. K. Hancock.[16] As a developmental strategy, it embraced two patterns of purpose: a kind of welfare state imperialism directed at the structural repair of a strained and discredited system; and a social doctrine prescriptive of a wider attempt to recast colonial relations and remodel local societies along improved lines. In the Malayan context, the contrast between remedial and more visionary interpretations of social policy was particularly marked. The radical argument was forcefully articulated by J. S. Furnivall, an ex-colonial servant in Burma. Furnivall accounted for the 'plural' societies of colonial Southeast Asia in 'the disintegration of social life through the inadequacy of law to control the working of antisocial economic forces'.[17] Social disintegration, Furnivall believed, could only be tended by the careful application of social welfare. The new discipline of social anthropology gave intellectual substance to fears of the breakdown of indigenous social systems. The spectre haunting official thinking was proletarianisation, of huge populations cut loose from the traditional authority and cohesion of village life. A primary aim of social policy was to manage the transition from a subsistence to a mixed agricultural and industrial economy. Although it encompassed preventive measures in rural areas to bolster local institutions and 'to make village life more attractive', the main thrust of policy was to combat delinquency and poverty in the towns where the capacity of these institutions to provide for their constituents in times of distress had broken down.[18] Here new legal obligations were needed to create new 'social opportunities', and to lay the foundations for some kind of social security.[19] In its doctrinaire form social policy was directed towards the restoration of a moral order, and took as its social norm colonial understanding of what that order ought to aspire to.

In Malaya, perhaps more than elsewhere, war was seen to have accelerated the

---

[15] Lenore Manderson, 'Health services and the legitimation of the colonial state: British Malaya, 1784–1941, *International Journal of Health Services*, 17, 1 (1987), 91–112.

[16] J. M. Lee and M. Petter, *The Colonial Office: war and development policy* (London, 1982), pp. 147–63.

[17] Furnivall, *Colonial policy and practice* (Cambridge, 1948), p. ix.

[18] *Papers on Colonial Affairs, No. 5, Social security in the Colonial Territories* (London: Colonial Office, June 1944); *Juvenile welfare in the Colonies: Draft Report of the Juvenile Delinquency Sub-committee of the Colonial Penal Administration Committee* (London: Colonial Office, 8.10.1942), esp. pp. 5–15.

[19] Malayan Union, *Annual report of the Department of Social Welfare for the year 1947*, pp. 2, 7.

process of social change. Local communities were no longer seen as self-sufficient enough to give relief to their members where necessary; war had undermined their 'capacity to support without official help, those who are unable to support themselves'.[20] However, progressive sentiment was outweighed by a reluctance to commit the colonial state to wholesale intervention in social life. The extent of the state's obligations was vigorously contested in the years that followed. An important summation of official thinking, and an attempt to set the perimeters of colonial responsibility, was the Singapore Social Welfare Conference of August 1947, which brought together representatives of Southeast Asian colonial governments and welfare organisations.[21] There, the Singapore delegation sought to establish 'the grounds on which the government justifies its concern of social welfare, and that must come from the central function of the state which is the administration of justice'. However, there was an accompanying danger that the state 'might undermine the foundations of society by destroying people's sense of personal responsibility'. If social welfare was accepted as a duty of government as 'guardian and trustee', there was a corresponding obligation to strengthen and supplement voluntary efforts.[22] The role of the state was, in the final analysis, to be residual. The Malayan Union, for example, was working less for 'a system of state aid and assistance, but for a system of direction and co-ordination and a supplement to private effort'.[23] Policy directives for Malaya emphasised the importance of local initiative. The orthodoxy of social welfare was to help local populations to help themselves.[24] 'The primary responsibility for alleviating distress rests with the family and the local community, and . . . only in the last resort can public assistance properly be expected.'[25] What was proposed was a long-term pledge of partnership heralded by careful groundwork of empirical research, census and survey. Ultimately the success of any governmental provisions was contingent on their capacity to 'create a public demand' for welfare.[26] During the post-war years of dislocation and scarcity, the importance of these policies of relief and social reintegration lie not only as a method by which post-war colonial power could be rendered legitimate, but in the opportunities they afforded for new forms of collective action. The stimulation of a demand for and an organised response to welfare concerns aimed 'to divert energies into socially desirable channels' and create a vehicle for legitimate national and social aspirations.[27] In an important sense, healthy political democracy

---

[20] *Report to investigate the working of the Social Welfare Department*, Federation of Malaya, Legislative Council, No. 41 of 1949, p. B330.
[21] T. Eames-Hughes, *Minutes of Social Welfare Conference*, Singapore, 19–23 August 1947, pp. 2, 7.
[22] 'Singapore Social Welfare Council, Minutes of 13th Meeting', 8.8.1947, SCA/5/1947.
[23] J. A. Harvey, 'Establishment of a Social Welfare Council', Paper No. 15A, *Social Welfare Conference*, p. 296.
[24] 'Long-term policy directive – social welfare', 2.3.1944, CO865/18.
[25] *Report to investigate the working of the Social Welfare Department*, p. B341.
[26] C. P. Rawson, *Social Welfare Conference*, p. 41.
[27] Singapore Department of Social Welfare, 'Social Welfare as a function of government', *ibid*, Paper 2B.

was a corollary of welfare. It was an invitation for Asians to associate, but also a statement of the norms to which these associations were expected to conform, and of which the restored colonial government was to be the arbiter. The old dilemmas of trusteeship were supplanted by a new predicament of partnership.

This predicament was to dominate the period of reconstruction in Malaya. The new welfare-state imperialism's concern for the resilience of local communities was directed not only towards their physical, but to their moral condition. It was not enough to teach imperial virtue by example: Britain had to actively educate its subjects into empire.[28] The fall of Penang and Singapore was the direct stimulus to the formulation of a colonial public relations policy. Unable to make war in Malaya themselves, SEAC's experts in the new field of psychological warfare used radio to encourage others to do so on their behalf. Wartime propaganda was to evolve into a wider scheme of 'social information', anti-materialistic and ideologically neutral in content. Racial and social equality were the driving principles: 'the British Empire', one official remarked, 'will solve the communal problem or be broken by it'. Propaganda had a particular moral responsibility to combat social disintegration, to reconcile the alienated, 'detribalised', labouring classes of the towns with colonial government.[29] Biblical authority was invoked to legitimate the 'Stewardship which God has entrusted to our Nation'. The goal of Christian improvement was the inclusion of the colonies as 'a real part of the Brotherhood of Man within the Commonwealth, which must be achieved if that Commonwealth is to endure'.[30] Yet Christian consciences were troubled as to how the duties of the wise steward to invest profitably the wealth with which he was entrusted could be reconciled with the moral and practical difficulties facing a rich man hoping to enter the Kingdom of Heaven. Edward Gent, Governor-designate of the Malayan Union, believed that Christian doctrine granted rights of equality and self-determination which were ultimately subversive of the colonial connection: 'if we are not prepared to face the results of a genuine Christian policy – bound to be disruptive and in conflict with economic conceptions – we have no right to suborn the Bishops'.[31] Old Malaya hands regarded these appeals as 'meretricious, loud and ungentlemanly', and worried about their propriety.[32] Certainly, the public relations officer held an ambiguous position within the new colonial polity. In the words of Noel Sabine, the metropolitan supremo, the aim was to provide a substitute for politics: 'to bridge the gap which we may expect before the rise of political consciousness and the time, which may be far distant, when some of the political aspirations aroused can be satisfied'.[33] Other officers envisaged a kind of Tribune of the People: 'an extra-administrative instrument of government and

---

[28] E. R. Edmett, 'Colonial propaganda: II – aims and policy', 6.8.1941, CO875/11/1; Rosaleen Smyth, 'Britain's African colonies and British propaganda during the Second World War', *JICH*, 14, 1 (1985), 65–82.

[29] Edmett, minute, 30.12.1941, CO875/11/1.

[30] Sir Donald Cameron, 'Give an account of thy stewardship', 15.5.1942, CO875/19/13.

[31] Undated minute on CO875/19/13.   [32] Purcell, *Memoirs*, p. 317.

[33] Minute, 24.6.1943, CO875/5/15.

also an organ of the people in countries where there are no Members of Parliament and a plethora of nominated members of Council'.[34] The problem was that as a vessel of public opinion the public relations officer could not avoid becoming a political agent; as a disseminator of pure information he needed to employ 'the necessary and inevitable business of selection'; and as the mouthpiece of administration he was the creature of official doctrine.[35] Social policy was an exercise in the reorientation and preservation of colonial power. But whether its sanction was located in Christian or socialistic sentiment, it had great difficulty in sustaining the divorce of social improvement from political engagement upon which its success as an imperial strategy rested.

The rehabilitation of social life

The British Military Administration under the Supreme Allied Commander South East Asia, Lord Louis Mountbatten, had the dual function of maintaining basic subsistence during the period of reoccupation, and also of imposing the state structure upon which post-war imperial power would rest.[36] Essentially a caretaker from September 1945 until the establishment of the Malayan Union at the end of March 1946, the scale of the crisis facing it compelled the BMA to employ new expedients and agencies to perform vital services and execute the provisions of wartime planning. The first test of authority for the British government was its capacity to re-enforce order in trade and employment. From the point of view of a state whose central economic function had been the control of the migrant labour supply for primary production, the most serious kind of anarchy had developed. Not only had controls on the flow of labour from outside Malaya fallen into abeyance, but so also had those governing wage rates and division of labour within the main industries. Wage restraint, directed at controlling inflation and ensuring long-term competitiveness of labour costs, was undermined by a shortage of unskilled workers. The rubber industry was said to be short of 148,604 people, even disregarding the needs of the smaller estates under twenty-five acres. Corresponding unemployment among skilled labour and the clerical classes, most of which were in the public sector, highlighted immense income disparities. Private employers were in no hurry to standardise pay. The British moved to leaven wage rates and pay cost-of-living allowances to their own employees, yet discrepancies widened between and within ethnic groups. Men and women avoided the labour marked out for them, and were working in an 'irregular fashion'.[37] The BMA's initial reckoning with the moraine of war came in the towns. The official mind, particularly in Singapore, was obsessed with the fear of mass delinquency, of

---

[34] Edmett, minute, 30.12.1941, CO875/11/1.
[35] 'Note by Mr. [Sydney] Caine', 31.10.1944, CO875/20/8.
[36] The official history is F. S. V. Donnison, *British Military Administration in the Far East* (London, 1956).
[37] 'Labour Department report for May, 1946'; Deputy Director Malayan Security Service, to Chief Secretary, 3.8.1946, BMA/DEPT/2/14.

the threat from 'a drifting and apathetic population, including many semi-trained artisans of extreme youth'.[38] The resumption of regulation merely aggravated tensions. In particular a drive to control petty trading and tidy up colonial towns fell hard on street hawkers and trishaw riders, the numbers of whom had swelled during the war. There was a noticeable increase in Chinese women working in coffeeshops and stalls, from which they had previously been barred by sanitary by-laws. The police justified their raids on illegal traders on the grounds of throttling the black market and because refuse was blocking the monsoon drains and enabling mosquitoes to breed. Many of these itinerant traders were part-time, supplementing other paid employment, and pleaded that they were a consequence rather than a cause of the black market.[39] In November 1945 the Singapore People's Hawkers' Union claimed that there were 30,000 hawkers in the city and only 1,000 licences available, and that if regulation was reintroduced 100,000 people would face starvation.[40] In Penang, 3,000 hawkers were affected, over 1,000 in Ipoh. They organised to protect their subsistence. In Kuala Lumpur their union established a 'hawkers' bazaar'.[41] In Singapore, trishaws had been acquired during the war by combines, who sold them to peddlers who became 'shareholders' and liable to pay large sums for licences and maintenance which were provided through the combine. After the war a Trishaw Workers' Mutual Aid Association attempted to wrestle control of the licences from monopolists but was constrained by the resilience of past practices and the shortage of licences. It was estimated that the struggle for the control of trishaw licences left 5,000 drivers unemployed.[42] The informal economy was a ripe recruiting ground for leftist parties.

The new regulation was honoured more in the breach than the observance. The failure of the state to ensure an equitable distribution of available resources provoked an extension of welfarism. Initiatives were remedial in outlook and most clearly reflected urban problems. The first was the relief of elementary want. By the end of 1945, $897,992 had been paid out in Singapore to 43,238 cases; in the first year of reoccupation this figure rose to $1,615,538.[43] Public restaurants were established to provide nutritious meals at subsidised prices. By December 1946 there were twenty of them in the main towns serving 30,000 meals daily. In Kuala Lumpur, two meals a day were provided for 10,000 destitutes. School dinners gave some pupils at least one nutritional meal a day.[44] Hawkers saw this as a direct threat to their livelihood and began to advertise the vitamin content in their own food. Often, the ways in which

---

[38] Labour Department, Singapore, 'Monthly report for April, 1946', CSO/44/46.

[39] Leong Yee Fong, 'Labour and trade unionism in colonial Malaya: a study of the socio-economic basis of the Malayan labour movement, 1930–1957' (Ph.D. Thesis, Universiti Malaya, 1990), p. 203.

[40] Enclosures in BMA/CH/48/45.

[41] *Chong Hwa Kung Pao*, 13.4.1946; *Northern Star*, 19.4.1946; *China Press*, 3.6.1946.

[42] Enclosures on BMA/CH/12/46.

[43] BMA, HQ, 'Emergency relief measures in Singapore, 1.10.1945'; 'Summary of statistics for December, 1945', BMA/CH/9/45; 'Minutes of 4th Meeting of Singapore Social Welfare Council, 25.10.1945', BMA/CH/127/45.

[44] 'Minutes of the 3rd Meeting of the Singapore Social Welfare Council', 2.9.1946. 'Minutes of

welfare was targeted had the effect of hindering its recipients from helping themselves. In Kuala Lumpur, an irony of the enforcement of legislation protecting children was that the clearing of the streets of child hawkers hurt hardest the poorest families who had no adult wage earners.[45] These initiatives rapidly transgressed the boundaries of colonial welfare. High unemployment among wage and salaried labour, and the increase in permanent categories of relief applicants, meant that emergency relief was rapidly becoming a dole. Relief centres were ordered to screen the employability of applicants. By the end of 1946 the British claimed that anyone who was unemployed was probably unemployable.[46] Beyond this, as we shall see, the British looked to moderate trade unionism to abate the needs and expectations of labour.

The second urban challenge was the condition of women and the young. Child welfare was a priority and a focus of nutritional work. The fear of 'delinquency' overhung much of the welfare work of the BMA. It was targeted first at young women. The old Po Leung Kuk welfare home in Singapore was turned into a training school to reform girls who had fallen or been coerced into prostitution – as 'comfort women' – during the war.[47] Prostitution was a major preoccupation not least because of the threat it presented to the Eastern Army, 35,000 of whom had been casualties to venereal disease during 1943, sixteen times the number injured in battle. In Singapore, 95 per cent of prostitutes were said to be infected; in Penang, an estimated 2,000 women. By February 1946, the incidence of infection amongst the military as a whole rose above 7 per cent. Medical authorities favoured suppression of brothels, but as their legal powers were inadequate, they relied on 'tactful persuasion' to encourage girls to attend clinics.[48] Remedial work was limited in scope and constrained by the primacy of other demands on colonial resources. However, some innovations did have far-reaching consequences. Training programmes, which incorporated many ex-Red Cross and Mission workers, began to provide for many local personnel an overseas education, and for many Asian women in particular, their first experience of administration.[49] For local women, prostitution and low standards of child welfare were a spur to social criticism and to mobilisation.

The meaning of these schemes went far deeper than their capacity to effect practical amelioration of social conditions. In adopting the rhetoric of welfare the returning

meeting of the Central Welfare Council, Kuala Lumpur', 4.12.1945. BMA/CH/7/45; *Malaya Tribune*, 4.11.1946.
[45] 'Meeting of Central Relief Committee, 15.1.1947', SCA/5/47.
[46] 'BMA relief measures, 14.9.1945'; 'Fifth meeting of Emergency Relief Committee, 25.10.1945'; H. A. Lord, 'Memorandum on emergency relief', BMA/CH/48/45.
[47] 'Scheme to be submitted to the Welfare Council by the sub-committee appointed to consider the rehabilitation of women and girls', BMA/CH/27/45.
[48] 'Special meeting held at HQ, SACSEAC to consider methods to combat VD in SEAC', 7.12.1945; C. E. C. Davies, 'Report on the VD situation in Singapore', 4.3.1946, BMA/DEPT/1/2.
[49] 'The autobiography of Josephine Foss', Mss. in possession of J. M. Gulllick, p. 114. I am grateful to Mr. Gullick for this reference.

colonial power was above all anxious to register itself as a social presence in Malaya. In many places the British were received with genuine goodwill, and the military sought to capitalise on this. The Japanese had suggested ways in which this might be accomplished. The *Nippon sheisin* was to be ousted by a new spirit of empire. Civil administration became a morale-boosting exercise. An entertainments boom was encouraged in the towns, that provided relief from wartime austerity for some and fuelled fears of urban evils in others. A new public relations department worked to correct 'the distortions of world affairs' by the Japanese, and towards the 'inculcation of a sense of Malayan Unity and the sponsoring of civic consciousness'. Declarations of good intentions were made and intimations of allegiance were encouraged. Reading rooms were established at relief centres; theatrical performances extolled the virtues of health education, agricultural efficiency and even 'the Malay feminist movement'. A propaganda war was waged against inflationary spending and to restore faith in the currency. The cinema and the mushrooming vernacular press became targets for government intervention. Film-making equipment was bought from the Crown Film Unit, and a studio set up in an old Japanese paper factory. The escalating expenditure was defended on the grounds that 'public opinion, misdirected as it may be by exceedingly well-trained manipulators and propagandists of other groups, may be so influenced adversely to the British case that the result may well be the loss of the territory before the country is in a fit state to govern itself on democratic lines'.[50] Although this strident tone had its critics, 'social information' had become a new function of government. By February 1946 the BMA had distributed 140,000 posters and notices 'of a political nature' and 45,000 copies of British magazines; public address vans employed Chinese story-tellers. In April the head of the new department sent the Governor a copy of a Kuala Lumpur newspaper in which 90 per cent of the news was supplied by 'PR'.[51]

Imperial vision was undermined by a shortage of European personnel. The scale and cost of the welfare work led to the subcontracting of operations to a range of Asian intermediaries. The government embraced allies wherever it could find them. In mid-October 1945 there were only twenty-one medical officers in the whole of the peninsula. When a smallpox epidemic erupted in Besut, Trengganu, in 1946, it was *bomoh* spiritual healers who were enlisted to supply vaccines that would not be accepted from Europeans. For their part, the *bomohs* were reported to be 'grateful for the simple medicines which were given to them for treating their patients in addition to the usual *jampai-jampai*', or spells.[52] The bulk of initiative and expenditure for relief efforts came from private and charitable sources. This was coincident with longer-term aspirations: a virtue was fashioned out of necessity.

---

[50] Malayan Union, *Department of Public Relations: review of activities. April to October 1946* (Malayan Union Advisory Council, No. 54 of 1946); J. N. McHugh, 'Draft directive of Department of Public Relations, Malayan Union', 31.5.46, BMA/SEL/CA/67/46.

[51] 'BMA monthly report for February, 1946', WO/220/564; Mubin Sheppard, *Taman Budiman: memoirs of an unorthodox civil servant* (Kuala Lumpur, 1979), pp. 144–5.

[52] E. D. B. Wolfe, 'Smallpox in Trengganu, 1946–47', RHO.

Relief work offered scope for the resurrection of voluntary organisations, the emergence of new forms of collective action, and the broadening of the democratic experiment. A formal expression of the relationship between relief and the creation of representative institutions was the BMA Emergency Relief Committee which first met in mid-September 1945 in Singapore, and co-opted the charities, Chinese businessmen, Kuomintang and Anti-Japanese Union (AJU) representatives.[53] This last group, the civil wing of the MPAJA, had already begun to register refugees in 'district centres'. Lee Kiu, the woman who represented it on the Relief Committee, claimed that there were 700,000 refugees on the island, and that by the 26 September the AJU had issued relief to some 80,000 of them at a rate of 300–400 a day. This organisation was integrated into the official operation to the extent that, by 8 October, eight out of the eighteen relief centres were run by Communist or resistance associations, distributing over half the total cash relief. Another two were administered by the San Min Chu Yi Youth Corps, the Kuomintang youth wing.[54] In Selangor the MPAJA-dominated People's Committee, under the guerrilla leader, Soong Kwong, was co-opted for the same purpose.[55] The broad commitment to 'partnership' was promoted through a Welfare Council for Malaya, established in September under the patronage of Lady Mountbatten 'to foster voluntary activity and thereby free itself from the necessity of appealing to government for assistance'.[56] A Malayan Welfare Fund was established to which government gave a dollar for every dollar contributed until the end of 1946. A committee was formed under the chairmanship of the banker Yap Pheng Geck to suggest ways in which the £5 million Colonial Welfare and Development allocation for Malaya should be spent.[57] The burden on private groups such as the Salvation Army, Christian churches and the Red Swastika society was heavy, and their work was hampered by the devaluation of their holdings of Japanese currency. They were the welfare equivalent of the 'sponsored undertakings' which were established in the field of business. In the absence of expatriate leadership, Asian leaders came to the fore. For the church layworkers, welfare work was inseparable from the moral rehabilitation of Malaya. Upon the resumption of civil rule, attempts were made to draw these activists into multi-racial welfare organisations, such as the Malayan Women's Service League under the patronage of Lady Gent, which was formed to 'clean up the mess left by the men of the nations' and whose mainly Malay membership sponsored nutrition schemes and voluntary work.[58] As the colonial regime gradually re-established itself, its relationship with these groups underwent a transformation. Politics – squabbles over representation and corruption – soon intruded into the

[53] 'Minutes of the meeting of the Emergency Relief Committee', 17.9.1945, BMA/CH/9/45.
[54] *Sin Chew Jit Poh*, 26.9.1945; 'Number of cases receiving relief and amount of cash issued up to 11.10.1945', BMA/CA/48/45.
[55] *Min Sheng Pau*, 17.10.1945.
[56] Hone to Permanent Under-Secretary for War, 4.10.1945, CO273/677/50957.
[57] 'Memo – Social Welfare', BMA/CH/27/45.
[58] Virginia H. Dancz, *Women and party politics in peninsular Malaysia* (Singapore, 1987), p. 235.

operations of the welfare committees.[59] Although the post-war regime sought to distinguish itself with a new liberality and to push forward the 'expanding frontier of human progress', there was anxiety as to where the experiment would lead. As the Chief Civil Affairs Officer, Ralph Hone, reflected in the early weeks of reoccupation:

> It will be some time before any definite parties or programmes emerge from the welter of organisations, clubs, societies, pseudo-philanthropic institutions and ex-servicemen's unions which come into existence day by day. Many of their founders are in search of nothing but notoriety for themselves and at this stage it is often difficult to distinguish among them those persons with a real political programme who may become the leaders of the future.[60]

In the prevailing climate of violence and uncertainty there emerged, not unnaturally, a major disparity between the perceptions of the rulers and the ruled as to where the welfare of the latter could be most easily guaranteed, and of the kinds of material and ideological concerns which were to underlie political activity. Notions of social policy and the administrative preoccupations which had developed around them were seen by the government as a paradigm within which political mobilisation might occur. It became increasingly disturbed by the autochthonous and militant politicisation of many of these associations, who were rapidly frustrated by this constrained view of democratisation. 'When each can get six *gantangs* or more a month,' the government was warned, 'then will be the time to talk of moral principles.'[61]

Politics of health and welfare

The kind of politics colonial governors found congenial were rarely the kind they were presented with. Philanthropy, viewed by the British as a surrogate for nationalist ambitions, became a vehicle for their immediate realisation. In the political struggles of the reconstruction period, welfare work was used to boost influence and prestige and to extend an organisation. It was the central way in which social crisis fed political struggle. Charitable work had long been a feature of political mobilisation in Malaya, both in the pre-war period and under the Japanese regime. As civil war deepened in China, Tan Kah Kee and the China Democratic League jostled with Kuomintang and Communist elements for control of the China Relief Fund, sponsoring welfare ventures such as the 'Overseas Chinese China Sanitary Observation Mission' which – although seen as 'screwy' by colonial officials – was an important focus for Overseas Chinese nationalism in this period.[62] Malayan Chinese donations to the KMT, and its patronage of economic recovery in China 'as an insurance against Communism' were

---

[59] For example, the North Johore body, *Northern Star*, 27.2.1946.
[60] 'BMA monthly report for November, 1945', WO220/564.
[61] 'Metropolis of the East' by 'Cosmopolitan', *Comrade*, 24.8.1946.
[62] Yong Ching Fatt, *Tan Kah Kee: an Overseas Chinese legend* (Singapore, 1987); H. T. Pagden, minute, 4.12.1945, BMA/CH/67/45.

largely paid for by the illicit trade. The British government identified collections at charity functions, dialect associations' sponsorship of reconstruction programmes in their respective regions, even the foundation of the Chung Khiaw Bank, as KMT enterprises. The use of charity funds for politics was reinforced by the KMT's accounting, in which money collected for China development capital in Malaya was credited as local party funds, to avoid exchange controls. Machinery and raw materials were shipped to China by industrialists such as Lau Pak Khuan, H. S. Lee and Wee Tiong Kiat in lieu of capital.[63] Much of the relief to rubber estates and destitute Indians was distributed through the Agent of the Government of India, and Congress itself sent a medical mission to Malaya. It ran a hospital in Sentul and doctors toured 274 estates in its first three months of operation.[64] The composition of the Indian Relief Committee, although it purported to be independent, reproduced political divisions. An ex-Lt. Colonel in the INA was despatched to Malaya as an Official Adviser to the Committee at Nehru's suggestion, and used his position to work among ex-INA and Indian Independence League personnel and their organisation, the *Azad Hind Fauj Sabha*, to attempt to form a central Indian political party in Malaya. The Indian community in Penang supported a number of religious and social associations – such as the Ramakrishna Ashram, Hindu *Sabhas* and caste associations – which were drawn into the volatile politics of the town.[65] Good works were also harnessed to other ends as a means by which individuals sought to avoid retribution for some of their more uncharitable wartime activities. Newspapers cautioned the public that many collaborators were taking the lead in welfare bodies.[66]

Politicisation was most overt, and competition most vigorous, in the societies orientated towards youth. There was a stampede to reopen Chinese schools after the war. School numbers had dropped dramatically during the occupation, and the columns of both English and Chinese newspapers were awash with concern at the 'over age boys, the dead-end kids, who are neither in schools nor in steady employment': the Twists and Fagins of the colonial towns. Their socialisation became an imperative.[67] Under the BMA, the main agents for this were the San Min Chu Yi (SMCY) Youth Corps, the Kuomintang subsidiary, which had 2,000 members in Singapore alone, and the Communist-inspired New Democratic Youth League (NDYL) whose inauguration in Singapore in December 1945 was attended by 3,000 people. In the face of delays in opening the schools, both groups assumed educative functions and supported parallel social facilities. The SMCY Youth Corps' sports groups, free letter-writing for illiterate Chinese and night schools had the explicit aim of preserving the youth from Communist influence. 'To build up the revolutionary

---

[63] 'KMT Party funds – their resources and investments', Supplement to MSS/PIJ/8/47.
[64] *Tamil Nesan*, 5.6.1946, 22.6.1946.
[65] MSS/PIJ/5/1947; R. Ampalavanar, *The Indian minority and political change in Malaya, 1945–57* (Kuala Lumpur, 1981), p. 25.
[66] Mau Ping, 'Beware of imitations', *Min Sheng Pau*, 13.12.1945.
[67] Tan Beng Hong in *Malaya Tribune*, 30.4.1947; Eric Mitchell, 'Charter for Singapore's children', *ibid.*, 30.5.1947.

personality' its members had to undertake ten hours of labour service each week. Although the NDYL's sponsors tried to project it as non-partisan, it lay at the apex of the Communist youth bodies, promoting 'free democratic education' and civil liberties through such events as International Youth Week in March 1946. Its Singapore mouthpiece, *New Democracy*, emphasised that in Malaya's 'kaleidoscopic society' different tactics had to be applied by its social workers to different groups, 'based on the subjective aspect of society and in order to elevate the knowledge of the people'. To this end the League ran a wide range of 'free schools', particularly in the towns of Johore, as well as musical and dramatic clubs, basketball teams, secondary schools and training classes.[68] It was a specifically Malayan organisation, although it mirrored similar groupings in China, and attempted to amalgamate Malay parties, such as the *Angkatan Pemuda Insaf* (API) the youth wing of the Malay Nationalist Party (MNP), into a Malay section of the League, the *Barisan Pemuda Bahru*. This society had some success in Taiping in 1946, and spread throughout Perak, where communal tensions were high and membership promised a degree of protection from attack.[69] Where such ventures shadowed colonial provisions, the authorities attempted to absorb them in official welfare projects. When a 'grow more food' campaign was launched to mitigate the effects of cuts in the rice ration, it mobilised organisations such as the Boy Scouts and the YMCA. However, a primary intent was to persuade the NDYL and the SMCY Youth Corps to divert some of their energy into more sedate pursuits such as farming. Agricultural groups along the lines of the English Young Farmers' League were championed as a stimulus to agrarian and civic improvement; as 'a channel for expression', to 'set in proper perspective the political and "gang" differences of the present' and as 'a solvent for interracial differences'. For leadership, the British looked to 'the guerrilla tradition'. 'The anti-social consequences of guerrilla activity are only too apparent,' it was argued, 'but the tradition might be turned to constructive purposes in the present crisis.'[70] Yet when, in 1946, it was proposed to sponsor boys' clubs in Singapore, the Chinese Affairs Officer admitted that 'dubious political parties have already got ahead of us in this matter.'[71] The gambits of social policy were rapidly being forestalled.

To the government, social policy was being obstructed by the lack of 'pure' societies to respond to social needs. British concern at the politicisation of these societies was compounded by their repulsion at their military and extra-territorial complexion. The militarisation of youth that had occurred during the war was not easily reversed. For example, in its strongholds of Penang and Singapore, the SMCY Youth Corps was grouped into regiments which drilled with dummy rifles. The

---

[68] This account is extracted from MSS/PIJ/5/1946 and subsequent issues; *New Democracy*, 23.12.1945; 'List of societies affiliated to the New Democratic Youth League', BMA/CH/19/45.

[69] The SMCY Youth Corps launched a similar experiment in Kelantan in late 1946, MSS/PIJ/15/1946, MSS/PIJ/16/1946.

[70] G. G. Thomson, 'To stimulate food production', 17.9.1946, BMA/CH/31/46.

[71] R. Broome, minute, 2.2.1946, BMA/HQ.S.DIV/34/46.

MPAJA Ex-Comrades Association, whose membership overlapped with that of the NDYL, were reported to be continuing their military training. Among the Tamil estate labour forces, ex-cadres of the Indian National Army developed a powerful blend of syndicalism and social and religious reform in the *thondar pedai* militia.[72] As we shall see, colonial concern over militarism came to a head over the radical Malay youth organisation, API, into whose membership many former members of PETA gravitated. The army regularly reported API drilling and manoeuvres, especially around Malacca, where religious tracts issued in the area exhorted members to create a new system of life based on 'regimented forces'. Nationalist victories elsewhere in the region fired the internationalist and Pan-Asian rhetoric adopted by many of these groups. To the British it was a direct challenge to the territorial nationalism which the Malayan Union scheme was designed to foster. Moreover, the progressive rhetoric of the Labour Government was used as a stick to beat its own back. The newspapers carried detailed accounts of liberation movements beyond Malaya's borders: commentaries that measured Britain's performance within Malaya against its status as a signatory of the United Nations Charter and reflected ironically on her professed sympathy for 'world social consciousness'. It was a sympathy that the colonial government found increasingly difficult to sustain.

Welfare was a spur to social criticism, in which women took the lead. Women were appointed a pivotal role in colonial rehabilitation, through Lady Mountbatten's Red Cross work and Lady Gent's Women's League. However, the impact of these organisations was superficial compared to that of other forms of association for women. From March 1946 large Chinese women's unions were formed in Singapore, Selangor and elsewhere on the peninsula, through which new leaders came to the fore.[73] The Singapore Chinese Women's League, a leftist organisation, claimed over 20,000 members and fostered urban relief work and a militant political consciousness, although it was attacked for becoming a solely Chinese concern and for admitting women with a 'Syonan' past.[74] The Ipoh Women's association, under the MCP leader Eng Min Chin, was particularly strong and women dominated the leadership of the Penang NDYL. These groups campaigned to persuade Chinese housewives not to buy on the black market and tended to the welfare needs of prostitutes.[75] In Penang, it was cabaret girls, confronted with intense public stigma – there were instances of girls walking with servicemen being shied with watermelons – who took the lead in such organisations.[76] In the words of a leader of the Penang taxi-dancers, Tseng Pi Chi:

> We women folk have long been looked down upon. We are being despised because our social system is dark and unwholesome. We who were weak and suffering feel we should be organised in our determined effort to combat the unfavourable circumstances

[72] M. R. Stenson, *Industrial conflict in Malaya: prelude to the Communist revolt of 1948* (London, 1970), pp. 118–20.
[73] 'The emancipation of women cannot be separated from the general struggle', *New Democracy*, 9.3.1946.
[74] Chin Pai, 'Women are going backwards', *Hwa Chiao Jit Pao*, 11.1.1946.
[75] *Malaya Tribune*, 23.10.1946.   [76] *Malayan Post*, 26.1.1946; *Sunday Gazette*, 17.2.1946.

under which we live . . . We don't want to be dancers all our lives; we want only to make a living by dancing. We are waiting until we are the equals of men when we shall quit dancing and seek other opportunities of making a living.[77]

Malay periodicals remarked on a new mood of liberation amongst Malay women. A series of women's magazines was launched, such as *Indaran Zaman* and *Bulan Melayu* in Johore and *Ibu Melayu* in Penang. *Pengasoh*, the voice of the *Majlis Ugama* in Kelantan, celebrated their role as educators 'imbued with the spirit of self realisation and independence'.[78] However, deep divisions over how far this permitted women an active role in politics arose which were to dog the history of the women's movement throughout the post-war period. To Rosmah bte Osman of the Malacca Malay Women's organisation, the duty of Malay women lay solely in the domestic realm, 'in the battle for more children the Malays cannot afford to lose'.[79] Similarly, to Ungku Kamariah of Batu Pahat:

> Realising 'full attainment of democracy' with 'equal rights for women' is commensurate with the teachings of Islam under which men and women are placed on an equal footing, but such advice at the present moment when the Malay women of Malaya are not and have not advanced in education and in other respects . . . is in my opinion inappropriate, misplaced and dangerous.

Politics 'would deprive the husband and children of the soothing hand and caress of an obedient daughter or a dutiful wife'.[80] However, throughout Malaya women were claiming a new voice in public affairs. In Singapore, Zahara bte Noor Mohamed of the Muslim Women's Welfare Association defied the *ulama* by joining public parades – notably on the occasion of the 1947 Royal Wedding. 'We are also Muslims,' she told them, 'and therefore we too know how far we are religiously privileged to act on any occasion.'[81] In Johore, the wife of Dato Onn bin Jaafar took a lead in charity work and encouraged women to go out unescorted. She inverted an old Malay adage in her campaign for improved health care – 'let the custom die, but not the child'. Self-help groups such as the *kampung kumpulan kaum ibu* were rapidly drawn into larger political movements – especially in opposition to the Malayan Union proposals. Under the leadership of women's associations from Province Wellesley, Perak and Selangor – notably Zainab bte Abdul Rahman, Puteh Mariah and Saleha bte Ali – the *kaum ibu* came together at the UMNO General Assembly in 1946 as the organisation's Women's Department.[82] On the radical left of Malay politics the *Angkatan Wanita Sedar* (AWAS) – League of Aware Women – the women's wing of the Malay

---

[77] *The Northern Star*, 6.5.1946.
[78] M.H., 'Awakening of Malay women', *Comrade*, 8.12.1946.
[79] *Malaya Tribune*, 13.11.1947.
[80] N. Mamat, 'Malay women in politics', *Malaya Tribune*, 19.4.1947.
[81] N. Mamat, 'Inche Zahara, Malay woman leader', *Malaya Tribune*, 3.1.1948; *ibid.*, 25.11.1947.
[82] Lenore H. Manderson, *Women, politics and change: the Kaum Ibu UMNO Malaysia, 1945–72* (Kuala Lumpur, 1980), pp. 53–60; Malay League of Perak, *Hidup Melayu: a brief review of the Malay national movement* (Ipoh, n.d.)[1946], pp. 18–20.

Nationalist Party, attracted a number of capable women, many of them schooled in Sumatran *madrasah*, who launched a drive to attack illiteracy, provide schooling for village women and improve hygiene and midwifery, together with other practical initiatives such as the provision of crèches and work amongst prostitutes. The AWAS leader, Shamsiah Fakeh, called on Malay women 'to wake up from their slumber and oppressed state', and the movement encouraged the wives of non-politically minded men to go on strike.[83] In spite of the divergent political affiliations of the Malay women's organisations, they articulated similar concerns. These were often at variance with those voiced by the male leadership who, more preoccupied with controlling women's sexuality, equated the prominent role they had acquired in the occupation years with permissiveness. To such critics, women's education did not mean 'that they should be taught to braid their hair, drink cocktails, or dance the fox-trot'. For all sides of the Malay community, prostitution was a humiliating scandal, and the need to combat it was a paramount charge on political leaders.[84] Yet it was, above all else, the inadequate response of the established elite to the welfare concerns of women which had arisen out of the war that provoked these sweeping attacks on religious conservatism and patriarchy.

Popular culture furthered this social critique. The 'social information' propounded by the colonial government found its parallel in a flourishing of indigenous propaganda forms and an 'unprecedented entertainment boom' in Malayan towns. Cultural renaissance was a common theme: theatre and opera were integrated in a wider didactic enterprise. The Bolero Opera Company, a *sandiwara* troupe led by an ex-Japanese propagandist, toured Malaya 'to put spirit into the Malay people', and Ahmad Boestamam, the leader of API, directed the Sri Noordin Opera Company in 'Berjuang', a bloody tale of Indonesian independence. To its audience, the importation of the *sandiwara* from Indonesia to Malaya symbolised the cultural binding of the two territories.[85] The NDYL also used performance to undermine Kuomintang influence, and plays were a regular feature of fund-raising events and rallies.[86] The propaganda section of the Perak MCP was particularly active, staging shows at sawmills, such as Tronoh, and touring throughout the state. In Selangor a propaganda show, 'The honourable sacrifice', precipitated raids by British troops.[87] The cinema, as we shall see in Chapter 7, took on additional prominence with the importation of large numbers of Malay movies from Indonesia and the expansion of the Malayan film industry. Older forms of political communication also took on a new lease of life: study groups such as the Selangor Cultural Union's 'Social Science Study Group' of government clerks and Chinese schoolteachers, and the All-Perak Writer's Associa-

[83] *Malaya Tribune*, 11.10.1947; MSS/PIJ/6/1946.
[84] Mamat, 'Malay women in politics'; 'Malaya's oldest problem: the wrong remedies', *Malaya Tribune*, 7.4.1947.
[85] Noon-Nim, 'Malay-Muslim Viewpoint', *Comrade*, 17.11.1946; 'From the minaret', *ibid.*, 1.2.1946.
[86] MSS/PIJ/16/1946; *Kin Kwok Daily News*, 26.11.1945.
[87] *Kin Kwok Daily News*, 2.11.1945; *Min Sheng Pao*, 24.11.1945.

tion, which was formed to propagate the 'material of the cultural classes' amongst the masses.[88] Chinese trade unions launched poster newspapers such as the *Vanguard News*, and cartoons in Malay were pasted up in country towns lampooning the Malayan Union.[89] These media created an important bridge between popular images and new political doctrines.

The political exuberance of the Malayan Spring found a ready outlet in a reinvigorated vernacular press. The best and brightest in Chinese journalism – editors of the Penang *Modern Daily News*, *Nanyang Siang Pau* and *Sin Chew Jit Poh* – returned from Sumatra and Java where they had exiled themselves fearing reprisals for their work for the China Relief Fund.[90] The circulation of the Chinese newspapers reached a peak in 1946: the *Nanyang Siang Pau* was the largest at 30,000 daily copies, but the *Sin Chew Jit Poh* sustained two daily editions with a combined circulation of 20,000 copies. By 1947 there was new political investment in the press, competition intensified, and many Chinese newspapers experienced drops in circulation due to a shortage of newsprint. The *Nanyang Siang Pau* dropped to 25,000, the combined editions of *Sin Chew Jit Poh* to 12,500; the smaller papers became dependent on political patronage for survival.[91] The *Nanyang Siang Pau* was edited by Wang Ching Kwang, a dominant figure in the SMCY Youth Corps, and controlled by Hokkien businessmen such as Lee Kong Chian, his brother George E. Lee and Tan Lark Sye. The *Sin Chew Jit Poh* was owned by the Tiger Balm tycoon, Aw Boon Haw, and was also KMT-inclined. In 1947 the KMT gained control of the *Chung Nam Jit Pao*, which had a limited circulation of 4,000–5,000, some of whose owners were KMT bosses such as Wong Shu Fun of Johore and Ong Chin Seong of Perak. The struggling *Hwa Chiao Jit Poh* was reorganised and brought closer to the KMT in early 1947 and its circulation slowly rose. The KMT pressurised newsagents to boost circulation, but the right did not have it all its own way. The *Nan Chiao Jit Pao* was launched in late 1946 as the organ of the China Democratic League and was dominated by Hu Yu-chih, Tan Kah Kee and the writers Hu Wei Fu and Sin Chi Chiu, wife of Hu Yu-chih. Its circulation was around 10,000, much of it on the peninsula.[92] New newspapers were founded – *New Democracy*, *Min Sheng Pau* and *Modern Daily News* – as the central leftist organs in Singapore, Kuala Lumpur and Penang respectively. In addition to this the MPAJA ran a weekly *Combatants' Friend* from Kuala Lumpur, edited by its commander, Lau Yew, which had a circulation of 10,000 copies. Upcountry publications resumed operations – the *Kin Kwok Daily News* of Ipoh, the *Northern Malaya News* of Taiping, the *Kwong Wah Jit Poh* and *Sing Pin Jit Poh* of Penang. Besides newspapers there were around twenty-three kinds of Chinese periodical and pamphlet series: twenty of which emanated from Singapore and fifteen of these from the New Southseas Publishing Company and the New Democratic Culture Service. By far the most outstanding personality involved

[88] MSS/PIJ/7/1947.   [89] Reported in Alor Star, *Warta Negara*, 11.12.1945.
[90] *Chung Wah Kung Poh*, 10.10.1945.   [91] MSS/PIJ/16/1946; MSS/PIJ/13/1947.
[92] Supplement to MSS/PIJ/6/1947; *Malayan Union Government Gazette*, 6.11.1947.

was Hu Yu-chih, a leftist student from Paris who had been editor-in-chief of the *Eastern Miscellany* in Shanghai. Victor Purcell called his *Feng Hsia* 'far above the level of any Chinese journalism which we have had before in Malaya', and it ran to 132 issues until it ceased publication in June 1948. *Feng Hsia*, and other titles such as the *New Era Fortnightly*, *The Student*, *Good Earth*, and *New Democratic Youth*, the *New Women Monthly*, edited by Hu's wife, developed a style of New Democratic polemic, extended the coverage of international affairs, and gave expression to a genre of short story and poetry focusing on the resistance to the Japanese. A prominent theme of Hu Yu-chih's writing was the need to reorientate the Malayan Chinese intelligentsia away from a 'small businessmen's mentality' and 'traditional Chinese feudal ideas', towards national, anti-colonial struggle.[93] These publications led a remarkable literary renaissance: one survey has counted fourteen books of poetry, ninety-six novels and forty-eight books of essays that created a golden age of Malayan Chinese literature during the 'Malayan Spring'.[94] The Malay press also revived. The *Warta Negara* of Penang and the *Utusan Melayu* of Singapore emerged phoenix-like from their wartime incarnations. The Kuala Lumpur daily *Majlis*, under the editorship of Mohamad Yunos Hamidi, took a leading role in awakening Malay opposition to the Malayan Union. New journals appeared: the *Seruan Rakyat* in Kuala Lumpur and *Suara Rakyat* in Ipoh, out of whose editorial office emerged the Malay Nationalist Party.[95] The print-run of the Malay papers remained low in this period – in 1947 *Majlis* had an edition of only 3,000 copies – but this is not an accurate reflection of their effective audience. The growth of the vernacular press was inhibited by paper shortage; both the Chinese and the Malay press saw control of newsprint, and the English papers' privileged access to it, as a thinly veiled form of censorship.[96] Yet, in spite of its advantage in newsprint, the pro-government English language *Straits Times* was forced in 1947 to drop its price from ten to five cents to counter the popularity of the *Malaya Tribune*, in which Asian shareholders such as Tan Cheng Lock held a powerful interest.[97] The British were rapidly disenchanted with the prospects of nurturing a 'responsible' public opinion. They complained bitterly of the 'unbelievably unchecked invective' in the Chinese press. The arrest of the editor and staff members of the *Min Sheng Pau* in Kuala Lumpur at an early stage of the reoccupation under a pre-war law, provoked a huge campaign for freedom of speech. The suppression of these 'voices of sorrow, anger and indignation' marked both growing radical scepticism with the sincerity of the government's commitment to freedom of expression, and the passing of the official

[93] Purcell to Hu Yu-chih, 15.1.1946, CH/1A/45; Tan Eng Teik, 'The development of Malaysia Chinese poetry, 1945–69' (Ph. D. Thesis, Universiti Malaya, 1990), pp. 24–48; A. F. P. Hulswe, 'Survey of Chinese periodicals in Malaya', in *Chinese Press Summary*, No. 60, SOAS; 'The emancipation of Chinese intellectuals in Malaya', *Feng Hsia*, No. 8, 21.1.1946.
[94] Han, 'An outline of Malayan Chinese literature', 14.
[95] Stockwell, *British policy*, pp. 42–3.
[96] G. G. Thomson, 'Newsprint position in relation to the press', 30.9.1945, BMA/PR/2/19.
[97] E. Maurice Glover, 'Our policy and aims for the future', *Malaya Tribune*, 8.4.1947.

belief that such opinion could be created through a position of neutrality on the part of the colonial government.[98] 'The authorities,' commented the editors of one South Indian Muslim paper, 'have their ideas about this freedom and the public have theirs too.'[99]

New Democracy and the '1946 towkay'

The British sought to nurture suitable allies through which to inaugurate a new era of partnership. Their dilemma lay in gauging the measure of political freedom that would permit them to achieve this end with security: political development was a controlled experiment. In the months between September 1945 and April 1946 legal restraints on expression and association were looser than they had been at any time previously in Malaya's colonial history and, for that matter, looser than they have been at any time since. The Malayan Spring saw a widening of the public sphere, whereby new moods, vocabularies and techniques were introduced into political life that would resonate throughout the late colonial period. For the men and women of 1945, the overriding task was to test the limits of the new freedom. To a new generation of journalists and politicians the burning questions of the day did not merely centre on the preservation of communal interests, on the political arithmetic of constitutions, but focused equally on the meaning of freedom and the making of responsible public institutions. Different conceptions of democratisation were explored through debates on civil liberties and the rule of law. An important manifestation of this in the last days of military rule was the struggle between colonial democracy and the 'New Democracy' of the left. This marked the beginning of the passing of the Malayan Spring: the attempt of the colonial government – the '1946 towkay' – to re-establish control by resuming the registration of societies and organised labour.[100] The collapse of the liberal experiment heralded an era when the colonial government moved to narrow the parameters of legitimate public debate at the very time the fate of the flagship of post-war reconstruction – the Malayan Union – was being decided. In an atmosphere of intense political anxiety, many of the wounds of the war years refused to heal. The British looked for new allies, and eventually found them in the resurrection of the pre-war Anglo-Malay alliance. The language of indirect rule, of ethnic interest, was revived, and the language of democracy was stigmatised as the British government collided with a Communist united front for whom it had a very different meaning. Thereafter, the politics of independence was to be explored within much narrower confines.

The public life of the BMA period was dominated by the question of the status of the new agents of public opinion in relation to the colonial state. Different conceptions of popular association were at stake. The British government saw politics in very

[98] 'The Malayan press cases must be re-tried', *New Democracy*, 5.12.1945.
[99] 'Metropolis of the East' by 'Cosmopolitan', *Comrade*, 24.8.1946.
[100] Kor Tat, 'The 1946 *Towkay*', *Min Sheng Pau*, 1.1.1946.

contained terms. The natural leaders of the people would be invited to air the concerns of their communities in colonial welfare councils and legislative chambers. Within these walls constructive political debate might occur, but in the final analysis the participants would bow to the wishes of the British Crown. However, across the expanding political firmament, new organisations had emerged that refused to acknowledge these circumscriptions. The colonial politics of personage were being challenged by the politics of party, by organisations that presented themselves as the embodiment of the popular will, and acknowledged no limits to self-determination. The strongest of these new voices was the 'New Democracy' movement of the Chinese left. It was founded on the political rhetoric of the Chinese Communist Party, and in Malaya it mounted a critique of the new colonial order through which the MCP sought to create space for mobilisation of its united front. The promise of the Malayan Spring played a major part in the MCP's decision to disband its armed forces at the request of the British. An agreement to this effect was signed between the Central Military Committee of the MPAJA and the BMA on 30 December 1945. MCP Central Committee members struggled to account to their supporters for the move. In a statement on 22 November 1945 they argued that although the war had not been waged against Fascism alone, 'it had become the duty of everyone to fight for democracy and peace. The object cannot be achieved by resorting to armed struggle. We must rely on the strength of popular unity and popular consciousness.' Lau Yew explained that at the time of negotiations with Force 136, the MPAJA was concerned to expand its army and to liaise with the Allies. 'Therefore,' he argued, 'we did not raise the political question. But everyone knows that the purpose of our organisation is not so simple. The Malayan people were dissatisfied with the Japanese colonial regime therefore they organised themselves in order to overthrow it and to make a life of democratic freedom attainable.' Above all, what they sought was 'new machinery for public opinion'.[101] Although leftist associations followed pre-war prototypes, under the BMA they glimpsed new possibilities, articulated new ends. They were soon frustrated. The Chinese press was quick to distinguish between the liberalism of some BMA officers and the hostility, the 'improved deceit', of others.[102] Senior Civil Affairs Officers in Selangor, Negri Sembilan and Johore were praised for openly acknowledging the legal status of leftist organisations. Friendships were forged.[103] Yet, behind the progressive façade, it was recognised that the new imperialism remained 'official' and not 'public rule'. As the British had not conceded national self-determination, their encouragement of the people to be 'citizens with all the rights and obligations which that term implies' was meaningless.[104] For this reason the Malayan Union scheme was a betrayal of the wartime accord.

[101] 'Establish democracy in Malaya', *New Democracy*, 13.10.1945.
[102] *New Democracy*, 12.10.1945; *Min Sheng Pau*, 6.10.1945.
[103] 'Government must completely alter its administrative policy', *Min Sheng Pau*, 6.10.1945.
H. T. Pagden's fascinating memoir of his relationship with MCP personalities such as Lee Soong and Wu Tian Wang is 'Unrest in Malaya', 12.10.1948, CO537/3757.
[104] 'Old policy, new pattern', *New Democracy*, 14.10.1945.

If justice, written agreements and the autonomous rights of the weak nations were really respected by the British Government, Malaya would already have acquired a state of democratic freedom and independence. The execution of the [Malayan Union] White Paper proposals today has given five million people a lesson of great meaning.[105]

In practical terms the White Paper citizenship proposals were rejected as being restrictive and fundamentally opposed to the British law of nationality, which was based on *jus soli*.[106] Yet the MCP's attack on the Malayan Union was grounded chiefly on the fact that it meant closer colonial control, and had 'not the slightest odour of democracy'.[107] The Malayan Union would allow the centralisation of executive, judicial and legislative power in British hands, whereas the essence of 'New Democracy' – as embodied in the MCP's Eight Point Programme – was that legislation, justice and administration were based on the popular will.[108]

Right across Malaya, the various representative institutions and self-help societies that had emerged in the interregnum ran into trouble with the new regime. MPAJA shadow local government devolved into People's Associations claiming wide governmental powers; it has been estimated that 70 per cent of small towns and villages were under their control.[109] Although in places like Perak and Singapore the British suffered People's Associations to hold elections to provide a nominee for the Advisory Councils, tension was aroused by the refusal of the government to allow them to assume a wider administrative role.[110] MCP strategy rested on the assumption that the party could acquire a measure of legitimacy in colonial councils. However, the British emphasised that membership of the councils did 'not involve recognition of the right of any person permanently to represent the interests of any community'.[111] MCP representatives on the Advisory Council in Singapore, Wu Tien Wang and Lee Kiu, were told that they were only there as individuals, and were frustrated by the restrained nature of their deliberations.[112] Greater leeway was conceded in the rural areas where the government presence was weak, and where a range of social organisations competed for the allegiance of the rural population. The first confrontations occurred in the towns, as co-operation with various radicalised social organisations broke down and the liberal posture of the BMA became disfigured.

[105] 'Statement of Central Committee of MCP on Malayan Citizenship and Legislative Council', *Combatants' Friend*, 7.5.1946.
[106] 'An analysis of the White Paper', *New Democracy*, 28.1.1946.
[107] 'Mr Wright [Lai Teck] reveals the nakedness of White Paper', *The Democrat*, 1, 1, 9.3.1946.
[108] 'Protect human rights. Fight for democracy', *New Democracy*, 31.1.1946.
[109] Heng Pek Koon, *Chinese politics in Malaysia: a history of the Malaysian Chinese Association* (Singapore, 1988), p. 39.
[110] 'DCCAO's report on the military government of the Malay Peninsula for the period 12.9.1945 to 30.12.1945'; 'Sitrep for week ending 20.10.1945', BMA/GEN/5. For an account of one such committee in Negri Sembilan, see Laurence K. L. Siaw, *Chinese society in rural Malaysia* (Kuala Lumpur, 1983), pp. 72–8.
[111] C. E. Jackson at 'Meeting of the Ulu Selangor District Advisory Council', 25.1.1946, BMA/SEL/CA/66/46.
[112] 'Wu Tien Wang's proposals to the Advisory Council', *Sin Chew Jit Poh*, 20.11.1945.

The peculiar assumption that welfare activities could be channelled into non-political forms was abandoned. BMA officials initially made careful distinctions between the MPAJA–AJU 'recognised organisations', and the 'illegal bands' and 'terrorists' which adopted their names as a cover.[113] They had a naive faith in their goodwill. The Secretary for Chinese Affairs in Singapore, an entomologist by profession, saw these groups as being on probation; he believed that questions of citizenship and the right to speak in internal politics could 'be dealt with and no ill-feeling aroused'.[114] This kind of optimism rapidly evaporated. The political activities of some 'recognised' groups – such as lecture courses by Kuomintang cadres to Taiwanese internees – placed officials in a quandary. Their problem was that 'the SMCY Youth Corps is about our only counter-propaganda to the Communist-inspired NDYL and the policy is therefore to support it up to a point. For its part it is Kuomintang inspired and there will come a time . . . when the Kuomintang will be as big a headache as the Communists'.[115] The situation was in flux throughout late 1945: in October it was felt that the left-wing parties were co-operating more freely with the government, and that it was the Kuomintang which was the most disruptive. A break with the resistance organisation in relief work came with official instructions that forbade the payment of relief to employable workers. The MPAJA opposed what they saw as an attempt to draft labour to break strikes, and argued that men could not be forced to work in this way. Lee Kiu reported that the government was deliberately only making use of resistance relief centres in the rural districts and not in the densely populated urban areas of Singapore: 'an insidious design to increase the prestige of the other relief centres such as charitable bodies and churches appointed by the BMA'.[116] Emergent patterns of association and self-help, the political 'pseudo-charities', began to be seen by the British as part of a wider subversive enterprise and as a threat to social order. 'In view of the daily increase in the number of new Chinese societies,' the Chinese affairs officer now conceded, 'some control over them would appear to be desirable.' Many officers saw the decision not to enforce registration of societies as a 'grave mistake'; the abolition of the Chinese Protectorate was at best misguided, at worst irresponsible.[117] The extent of British obligations to the MCP was being questioned at the highest level. Progressives such as Governor Gent and Purcell evidently felt a commitment had been made – although they could find no record of it in the files in Kuala Lumpur. Enquiries to London in September 1946 produced the reply that although Force 136 had been authorised to give such an assurance, 'we have of course no means of knowing whether any or all of these assurances were given'.[118]

A defining dispute arose over different notions of the rule of law and its violation

[113] H. T. Pagden, 'Sitrep', BMA/CH/3/45.   [114] 'Sitrep No. 2, 21.9.1945', *ibid.*
[115] H. T. Pagden, minute, 7.5.1946, BMA/CH/2/45.
[116] H. A. Lord, 'Memo re. meeting with various representatives of resistance army centres', 30.10.1945, BMA/CH/139/45; *New Democracy*, 2.10.1945.
[117] 'Fortnightly report No. 3, Chinese affairs', 4.10.1945; 'Sitrep, 11.10.1945', BMA/CH/3/45.
[118] Gent to J. J. Paskin, 20.9.1946; Paskin to Gent, 4.10.1946, CO537/1533.

under the 'white terror' of the BMA. Radical frustration focused on press censorship, the exclusion of popular organisations from the Advisory Councils and the arrests of labour leaders and MPAJA personnel on sedition and intimidation charges. The bitter witch-hunt against Japanese collaborators launched by resistance armies threw community leadership into further disarray. Accusation was followed by counter-accusation. In Selangor major public figures were targets, but more often smaller men were marked out, such as the Singapore educator denounced for pushing a Japanese motor car when it broke down, and those who engaged in the 'shameless trade' of profiteering.[119] The leniency of the BMA was interpreted as further evidence of British contempt for the new organs of public opinion and fused with frustration at the lack of recognition given to guerrilla fighters. The Selangor MPAJA Ex-Comrades Association reported in March 1946 that 70 per cent of its members were unemployed. Some had returned to farming, but significantly thirty-three were convicted or being tried for various offences.[120] The *New Democracy* mocked Chinese Affairs Officer Richard Broome's statement that the government had carried out many of the MCP's Eight Points – 'a reference to them shows that there is no clause about arresting AJA personnel'. The case of Soong Kwong, a MPAJA commander in Selangor arrested for running an extortion racket at Bukit Bintang amusement park, escalated into the largest confrontation between the British and the MCP in the BMA period. There were other, similar cases: of the MPAJA leader Chu Kau in Johore for example, and the fact that the offences were committed in the war conditions of the interregnum meant that the very legitimacy of the MPAJA was at stake.[121] It was claimed that the complainant in the Soong Kwong case was not an ordinary citizen but a combatant, a *kampetai* and an assistant of the hated Japanese security chief, Hirota.[122] To Chinese critics, the case discredited and questioned the legitimacy of both colonial and military law. The case was tried under colonial civil law by a military court, and it was argued that if the case had been tried under military law there would have been no case to answer as Soong Kwong was a belligerent. 'Such contradictions and confusion,' it was suggested, 'destroy "the splendid judicial traditions" that have existed for more then one hundred years in Malaya.' The case also raised questions about the powers of a European judge to override local assessors, in a way that anticipated controversies during the Emergency years. What most incensed local commentators was the virtue the British judge made of flouting the popular will, when, in imposing a stiff sentence, he stated he did 'not care whether public opinion think it fitting or otherwise'.[123] The rule of law, as understood by the colonial government, was based on the premise that power is constrained by rules and that the

[119] *Min Sheng Pau*, 16.10.1945; *New Democracy*, 6.10.1945; *Sin Chew Jit Poh*, 13.10.1945.
[120] *Min Sheng Pau*, 8.3.1946.
[121] 'Is the confiscation of the property of traitors and Japanese underlings extortion?', *Min Sheng Pau*, 16.10.1945; *ibid.*, 17.10.1945.
[122] *Sin Chew Jit Poh*, 10.1.1946.
[123] Yeh Wi-Wang, 'My personal feelings about the judgement in the Soong Kwong Case', *New Democracy*, 7.1.1946.

only significant power resides in government impartially administered; as Victor Purcell argued, 'a place cannot be ruled by means of open meetings'. The vernacular press saw the matter differently: 'laws and ordinances are made by man and consequently they are not inviolable. They are subject to amendment and subversion.'[124] When the judge reminded the accused that the British had been fighting for 'freedom', the *Modern Daily News* commented wryly:

> This utterance was no doubt made to convince us of the sacredness of the word 'freedom'. But we also feel that the manipulation and application of the word 'freedom' is only confined to those who can wield power or influence . . . The case of Soong Kwong in particular is yet another patent proof of the subtle use of 'freedom'. After two trials in which the assessors were unanimous that he was not guilty, the presiding judge purposely exercised his 'freedom' by turning down the verdict of the assessors.[125]

Communist policy had been based on the assumption that the government would grant a wide franchise through which the MCP could gain legitimacy as a national political organisation and extend its organisation. In the light of this, the Soong Kwong affair symbolised the redundancy of its attempts 'to enlist the liberal and socialist feelings of the British'.[126]

Frustrations against the BMA erupted in a general strike on 29–30 January 1946. In public the British authorities dismissed the strike as a purely political act, but privately Sir Edward Gent admitted that causes of the December and January unrest were primarily economic, proceeding mainly out of the attempt by the BMA to keep down wages in the face of soaring price inflation. Although there were signs by February 1946 that food prices were coming down, at least in the northern States, wages were still below the recognised minimum 'disease and disorder' standard. As the senior officer in Singapore noted:

> Lowly-paid people cannot possibly subsist on the wages they are getting. The administration cannot have a clear conscience in fighting a general strike on such a basis. Something has therefore got to be done quickly. The next general strike might be effective . . . if force were to be used, it would be disastrous here and for the Empire as a whole.

Employers were led to admit that they would rather face depreciation of the currency 'than fight unrest based on hunger'.[127] Ominously, 700 British troops at Bukit Timah were reported to have stopped work in protest at the suppression of the general strike, and left-wing servicemen made contacts with the General Labour Union.[128] Further protests were planned for 15 February to commemorate the fall of Singapore to the Japanese. The day was marked by violent clashes as police tried to prevent demonstra-

[124] *New Democracy*, 31.1.1946.   [125] 'Where is freedom?', *Modern Daily News*, 10.1.1946.
[126] HQ, Malaya Command, Weekly Intelligence Summary, No. 17, up to 23.3.1946, CO537/1581.
[127] P. A. B. McKerron, 'Minute of the meeting of the Local Civil Labour Employment Committee, Fort Canning, 5.1.1946', BMA/DEPT/2/4.
[128] *Combatants' Friend*, 1.2.1946; MSS/PIJ/1/1946.

tions. To the Chinese left, the incident was a crisis based on a 'misconception of democracy', a 'retraction of promises by the BMA'.

Apparently the democracy demanded by the people in the last few months differs a great deal from the democratic system as specified by the British Army. Hence 'democratic' tragedies have occurred incessantly. Perhaps the BMA may accuse the people of abusing freedom over the past few months, but they must reflect on that which they promised the people. How may the people use the freedom so as to conform with the government specification? There is no definite statement, and so a random use of force is inevitable.

Old laws were reactivated. The editor of the *New Democracy*, Chen Yu-chiu, was detained under the banishment ordinance for the infringement of the 1938 Sedition ordinance. An emergency meeting of associations to discuss human rights was convened on 22 February, chaired by Hu Yu-chih, Liu Woon-sieu, Lee Soong, Lu Cheng and others; a Chinese journalist association was inaugurated to fight for freedom of speech.[129] The launching of a 'democratic united front' was an immediate and ominous backdrop to the publication of the White Paper of Malayan Union constitutional proposals.

For the British, the political will to liberalise colonial politics was already being eroded by the course of the politics of health and welfare. The last days of the BMA were marked by self-division within the colonial state between the dictates of control and political improvement. On 11 February Lord Mountbatten informed the British Chiefs of Staff that the concurrence of Chiang Kai-shek had been sought to expel labour activists to China in anticipation of the 15 February protests. However, he emphasised that:

There is no question of action being taken by the administration to impede the legitimate growth of trade unionism in Malaya, the action proposed is entirely aimed at alien influences wishing to exploit the strike weapon for political ends and thereby to impede the process of rehabilitation which the administration is undertaking in the face of great difficulties.[130]

The 15 February incident raised the level of debate on the extent to which the British were prepared to draw upon reserves of punitive and authoritarian measures to suppress the disturbances. Mountbatten, away at the time in India, was angered at the 'unnecessary brutality' of the police and opposed the arrest of Soong Kwong as 'preventative arrest, which was contrary to my policy'.[131] Conscience-stricken and unwilling to compromise a liberal reputation on the eve of his departure with any overtly repressive measures in Malaya, he confessed that he had got 'carried away'. He refused to approve banishment orders for seven arrested labour leaders and used

---

[129] *New Democracy*, 25.2.1946.
[130] Mountbatten to British Chiefs of Staff, 11.2.1946, CO537/1579.
[131] P. Ziegler (ed.), *Personal Diary of Admiral the Lord Mountbatten: Supreme Allied Commander, South-East Asia, 1943–1946* (London, 1988), p. 296; P. Ziegler, *Mountbatten: the official biography* (London, 1985), pp. 325–6.

his authority of veto to defer the matter to the civil government. 'I felt it would be most embarrassing to His Majesty's Government, particularly a Labour Government, if the Military Administration were to use what would appear to the outside world to be dictatorship powers.'[132] The Chief Civil Affairs Officer, Ralph Hone, however, argued that as policy directives had forbidden the civil government to revive banishment the legality of any detentions would be contentious under the civil regime, and urged swift action before the hand-over of power. The Colonial Office recognised that 'any hint of illegality would be unnecessary and politically undesirable', but prepared to face the consequences under civil law as they were unable to dictate to a military commander who had become convinced that 'it is precisely because the civil government is unable to detain these agitators legally that I am being asked to take action', and that such a move 'would conflict with public conscience today'.[133] On the first day of civil rule Hone informed the Colonial Office with satisfaction that in one of its first acts the new regime had 'despatched ten little nigger boys homeward'.[134]

This episode indicates that by April 1946 a revised pattern of official thought had emerged. The military government had conducted an experiment in democracy through a relaxation of pre-war restrictions on assembly and association. The expectations on the part of the British as to how this might serve to restore social order and revive imperial prestige had been disappointed, and had provoked tensions within the military regime. These tensions were not so much, as is often argued, the direct consequence of a process of repression and reaction. The contradictions and vulnerability of post-war imperialism were exposed through the rise and collapse of a set of assumptions about the nature and direction of improvement of the colonial state. In enlarging the field of social policy the government had invited an extended range of voluntary associations to be called into account by administration. It was making a bid for the support of the social movements which had arisen as a consequence of the dislocations of the war years. Social policy was a means by which the state attempted to equip itself for its new vocation of partnership and was a method by which a rather limited administrative system attempted to transform itself into a polity. As we have seen, this policy had been conceived with regard to the encouragement of tranquil social development and the perpetuation of social norms which were only intelligible against the presumption of a long-term relationship between the colonial power and the society it presided over. This tranquillity was a qualification, a substitute even, for political rights, and proscribed those interpretations of the latter which were disruptive of existing arrangements. For this reason the experiment could not be supported. The political force of the social movements with which the government was confronted had gained too much momentum for them to be gelded in this way. Colonial policy and practice, however, rested on the divorce of

---

[132] Mountbatten to J. Brazier, Trade Union Adviser, 9.3.1946, *ibid*.
[133] H. T. Bourdillon, minute, 10.4.1946, *ibid*.; Mountbatten to Hone, 28.3.1946, Hone Papers.
[134] Hone to G. Gator, 2.4.1946, CO537/1579.

the political from the social, and required that a measure of depoliticisation of social life be sustained if stable political institutions were to be developed. This paradox of post-war colonialism was expressed in a set of regulatory measures which were reintroduced under the civil government.

The end of the Malayan Spring was signalled by one of its principal architects, Victor Purcell, in his review of the BMA. 'We must,' he wrote, 'accept the fact that no compromise can be made with the MCP. Its aims and those of the British Government are in ineluctable opposition.' The question was now how to check the MCP without interfering with 'legitimate' rights of association and 'real public opinion'.[135] In the months that followed, the new civil administration rode the horns of this dilemma. Discrimination between economic and political trade unionism became an index of the uses and abuses of political power, and a test of British authority. As the next chapter will show, the enforcement of wage restraint developed into a prolonged struggle for control of labour not only between the colonial state and the emergent trade unions, but within the labour movement itself. Revived societies legislation became a register of the kind of social formation which would be tolerated in Malaya. Policy towards these associations followed the principle of Hong Kong Societies Law that a society, other than a Triad, should be legal unless declared otherwise, but in Malaya there was pressure from the police and planting industry to reconsider the policy of liberalisation. Their problem was that 'the kind of societies most likely to be affected are those, which really subversive in character, parade their democratic and liberal intentions'.[136] A similar debate arose over the question of banishment. The British remained concerned to distinguish between banishments for Triad activities and for political activities. Gent pleaded that banishment was resorted to primarily against violent crime which the police had little trained personnel to meet. However, the Colonial Office acknowledged in October 1947 that 'the need to draw increasingly in this reserve of arbitrary power has appeared'.[137] As an administrative practice the narrowing of the public sphere allowed for the easy descent of politics into subversion and strategies of self-help into criminality. As the Malayan Democratic Union, the English-educated radicals at the forefront of the United Front, observed, societies had become 'the scapegoats for crime'.[138]

A new dawn fades

It is in the failing light of the Malayan Spring that the fate of its constitutional expression, the Malayan Union, must be understood. The collapse of the Union has had a magnetism for historians of post-war Malaya. A clear narrative has emerged.

---

[135] 'The issues before us: report on Chinese affairs, 18.2.1946', Blythe Papers.
[136] Purcell to H. C. Willan, 17.12.1945; H. T. Bourdillon, minute, 30.12.1946; Gent, minute, 4.2.1946, CO537/1533.
[137] Creech Jones to Gent, 16.10.1946; Gent to Creech Jones, 17.10.1947; O. H. Morris, minute, 11.10.1947, CO537/2139.
[138] *Malaya Tribune*, 23.5.1947.

A mission by Sir Harold MacMichael, shortly after the reoccupation, cajoled and threatened the Rulers into acquiescing in the new constitutional arrangements. The publication of the White Paper proposals in January 1946 ignited a Malay backlash. It was led by a range of state Malay associations which came together under the leadership of the Johore notable Dato Onn bin Jaafar, in a Pan-Malayan Malay Congress on 1 March 1946 and founded the United Malays National Organisation (UMNO). The scale of the agitation against the Malayan Union, and the boycott of its inauguration on 1 April 1946, by Malay politicians and Rulers, who by this stage had been drawn into the agitation, caused the British to abandon the Union and negotiate a Federal constitution with the Malay elites who led the assault on the Union. Within a month of arriving in Malaya the new Governor of the Malayan Union and one of its chief architects, Sir Edward Gent, was convinced of the need to abandon it for a federal arrangement. The result was a *rapprochement* between the British and the Malay elites, through the convening of an Anglo-Malay Constitutional Working Committee on 25 July 1946. Its draft proposals were published on 24 December 1946, and subjected to public scrutiny through a Consultative Committee. Revised proposals were published in July 1947 and the new Federation formally inaugurated on 1 February 1948. The Federation represented a political compromise and a new alliance between the British and Malay elites. The new Anglo-Malay alliance was strong enough to resist a belated opposition campaign orchestrated by a united front of organisations – the All-Malaya Council of Joint Action (AMCJA) – led by the Malayan Democratic Union (MDU), but dominated by the Communist united front, Chinese clan and commercial associations and the Malay left. Historical enquiry has focused on identifying the individuals and motives that led to the formulation of the Union policy; the reasons why the Rulers initially agreed to the scheme, and why it was rejected by the men who created it. However, the fate of the constitutional proposals must also be located within the context of the wider political and social experiments introduced by the British in the reoccupation period. Although historians no longer write of the 'Malay response', the 'Chinese response' to the constitutional proposals as monolithic blocks of opinion, studies locked in the domain of high politics have failed to appreciate the breadth of the issues that were at stake within these communities as they confronted the constitutional dilemmas of the day. Here we examine briefly the political thought of the Malayan Spring; in the next chapter we shall look more deeply into the social roots of its politics.

The foundation of UMNO and its early relations with the Malay Rulers have come under intense scrutiny by historians. For the Malays the Malayan Union years were a period of crisis to which the community had to respond with new political concepts. Malay royal houses were already in disarray after a series of contested successions during the war. The wartime Rulers of Trengganu, Perlis and Selangor were respectively deposed, persuaded to abdicate and exiled to the Cocos-Keeling islands. Kelantan and Kedah were left dependent on recognition by the British. There is little doubt that many Sultans were induced to sign the MacMichael agreement by 'force', or under threat of non-recognition.[139] However, in the backlash that followed, there was a new venom to elite hostility towards the *kerajaan*. Malay elites confronted the charge that this would lead them into treason against their sovereigns by turning the language of divine right on the Rulers: the Rulers had committed treason, *derhaka*, against the nation.[140] Gent himself rapidly realised that Malay opinion was based on popular feeling and not on the personal feelings of the Rulers and that, if anything, the Rulers were a moderating influence on it.[141] The subjects of the Rulers organised themselves in state associations to petition them in protest at the magnitude of what had been conceded. The Malay Graduate Association of Johore, for example, declared the MacMichael treaty null and void: the act of the Ruler went against the constitution of the state. Sultan Ibrahim was informed by telegram in London that Johore Malays no longer considered themselves his subjects.[142] For these Malays, the debate centred on political freedom. When Dato Onn stated that 'the *rakyat* have become the *raja*, the *raja* have become the *rakyat*', he was referring to *rapprochement* of the Rulers and Malay politicians after March 1946, but he was also laying down a principle: popular sovereignty. The people had become the custodians of the Malay nation. The Rulers' power lay not in their personages, but as the guarantors and symbol of the Malay nation. The Malay *bangsa* came before the Ruler. This period marked the height of Dato Onn's prestige as the 'sole spokesman' of his community. The Rulers themselves began to patronise gatherings of Malay associations to secure their position as a core component of Malay identity.[143] Many of the individuals who had led the protests occupied senior positions in the state bureaucracies, and the new ideas were deployed to consolidate this position rather than to dissolve the structures that had created it. Many UMNO organisers, such as Dato Panglima Bukit Gantang in Perak and Dato Onn himself in Johore, took office as Mentri Besar, or chief minister of the Ruler, or in the new nominated Councils. In the years that followed these men continued to benefit from the interpenetration of political and royal power and the Ataturkist rhetoric became more muted. As we shall see in the following chapter, the growth of UMNO was constrained by local loyalties and institutional weaknesses. To take two key states as an example: in Johore, even in a locality such as Muar, a variety of elite associations – the *Kesatuan Melayu Johore*, the *Persatuan Melayu Johor*, the *Pengerakan Melayu Semenanjung Johor* – claimed the mantle of Malay leadership; in Kedah the *Kesatuan Melayu Kedah* vied with the more radical *Saberkas*.[144] However,

---

[139] The Kedah State Government has published private correspondence to emphasise Sultan Badlishah's opposition to the MacMichael agreements: Ismail bin Haji Salleh, *The Sultan was not alone: a collection of letters written by Sultan Badlishah in his effort to repeal the Malayan Union policy imposed by the British Government on Malaya in 1946, and other supporting letters and documents written by others* (Alor Setar, 1989).

[140] Cheah, 'The erosion of ideological hegemony', 1–26.

[141] Gent to Creech Jones, 11.5.1946, CO537/1529.

[142] 'Johore Malays' to Sultan Ibrahim, 22.2.1946, George Maxwell Papers.

[143] Tan, *Rhetoric*, pp.14–15; Ariffin, *Bangsa Melayu*, pp. 49–56.

[144] Ramlah Adam, 'Pergolakan politik di Johor, 1946–48', *Jebat*, 19 (1991), 83–105.

the idea of the Malay community, of its solidarity, took on a new cohesion in this period. The Malays were beginning to see Malaya whole. The pre-war debates on defining the Malay were brushed aside in the face of the wider crisis. However, once this alarum subsided, debates were revived on the place of Indonesians and Orang Asli, Arabs and Indian Muslims within the new nation. The Malay press urged the local-born to become 'Naturalised Malays' rather than 'Malayan citizens'. The immanent census of 1947 brought these divisions to the fore. As *Utusan Melayu* commented:

> The Malays know that there are people trying to disunite them. The people who pretend that Malaya belongs to the Sakais [Orang Asli] are trying to deny that Malaya belongs to the Malays. As the Governor-General has acknowledged that the Malays are the citizens of Malaya and that Malaya is the homeland of the Malays, all Malays should avoid classifying themselves as Javanese, Boyanese, etc., in the census forms to avoid unpleasant consequences.[145]

It was left to the individuals to resolve their identity, and many threw in their lot with the larger political community. However, the new conception of the nation UMNO voiced was not the only one in evidence.

Despite the powerful communitarian appeal of UMNO nationalism, the idea of the nation the elite notables were advancing was not the only political rhetoric available to the Malays. The Malay radicals were left in some confusion after the departure of Ibrahim Yaacob to Indonesia on the fall of Japan. A new grouping emerged. It was not a revival of the KMM, but it recruited much of its old following. It emerged out of the Ipoh newspaper, *Suara Rakyat* – Voice of the People – that had a readership far beyond the town. The moving forces were the Communist Mokhtaruddin Lasso and the journalist Ahmad Boestamam who launched a *Partai Kebangsaan Melayu Malaya* – or Malay Nationalist Party (MNP) – from the paper's offices in October 1945. It had initially supported the Malay Congress, but withdrew on the symbolic issue of its refusal to adopt the Indonesian flag – a protest at the conservative direction in which UMNO was moving.[146] Thereafter it strove to consolidate its independent identity. Yet the MNP brought together men and women of very different temperament and ideological leanings. Mokhtaruddin envisaged a socialist platform for the party, but disappeared to Indonesia in early 1946 leaving the leadership in the hands of Dr Burhanuddin Al-Helmy, as President; Ishak bin Haji Muhammad as Vice President and Ahmad Boestamam as Secretary General and leader of the party's independently-minded youth wing, *Angkatan Pemuda Insaf* – (API). However, this core triumvirate personified very different strains of Malay nationalism. Burhanuddin was a homeo-pathic doctor, educated in a Penang *madrasah*, at Ismaeliah Medical College in New Delhi and at Aligarh, and was steeped in Islamic modernism.[147] Ishak was a secular-

---

[145] 'The population census problem', *Utusan Melayu*, 5.12.1946.
[146] These events are vividly described in Ahmad Boestamam, *Carving the path to the summit* (Athens, Ohio, 1979).
[147] Saliha Hj Hassan, 'Dr. Burhanuddin Al-Helmi, 1911–1969', *Jebat*, 14 (1986), 153–82.

minded social democrat; Boestamam a child of *perjuangan* – struggle, a representative of *pemuda* militancy.[148] However, there was also a significant Communist presence within the MNP – Musa Ahmad, Abdullah C.D. and Shamsuddin Salleh – men who, as we shall see later, would deeply implicate the MNP in the MCP's drive to recruit support amongst the Malay peasantry. Its ideology was based loosely on the Indonesian *Pancasila*. Its aim was to unite the Malays as a prelude to creating a united *Indonesia Raya*. The MNP attacked the UMNO elites, yet also sought to advance a different understanding of Malay nationalism as a more inclusive concept. Dr Burhanuddin championed the *kebangsaan*, a new political concept closer to the western notion of nation than the idea of *bangsa* was. It was a political allegiance that would raise the Malays above the narrow *bangsa* loyalties. In his speeches – published in 1954 as *Asas Falsafah Kebangsaan Melayu* (Basis of Malay Nationalist Philosophy) – he described a political community created by history, and forged by struggle. Membership of it was an act of will, rather than an accident of birth. The citizen of this *kebangsaan* was to be called a *Melayu*, a 'Malay' defined in the broadest sense in the realm of law and politics, but not by race. However, a vision of historical continuity, stretching from Melaka and cruelly broken by colonialism, and the sense of cultural belonging to the *kebangsaan*, were vitally important principles of Dr Burhanuddin's thought. It was a condition of citizenship that a non-Malay had to embrace Malay culture unequivocally, 'to live and die as a Malay.'[149]

The very identity of the Malay was at issue, but so were identities within other communities. For example, there was a debate on the status of Eurasians, especially their ability to hold State office, and the Eurasian Union petitioned the Rulers and UMNO on their claims as 'sons of the soil'.[150] The politics of the Indian community began to root itself in local concerns with the formation in 1946 of a Malayan Indian Congress (MIC). Similarly, the Chinese in Malaya were torn between overseas, *huaqiao* nationalism and the demands of the local political situation. The common citizenship of the Malayan Union – for which over 80 per cent of Malayan Chinese would qualify – opened the possibility for the Chinese to secure a political stake within Malaya. Yet within Chinese thought there remained an important distinction between the ties of the territorial nation-state, *guojia*, and the nation as a cultural community, *minzu*. The Three Principles of Sun Yat Sen had brought these concepts closer together to make China a single nation-state, yet for the Overseas Chinese the distinction remained very problematic as the *huaqiao* sought to reorientate their loyalty towards China as an ancestral *guojia*, and to take advantage of political opportunities in Malaya without sacrificing the essence of *minzu*. Indeed, in these circumstances the rhetoric of *minzu* took on an enhanced importance.[151] For this reason, the community in Malaya, divided between the Straits and China-born, and

---

[148] Abdul Latiff Abu Bakar, *Ishak Haji Muhammad: penulis dan ahli politik sehingga 1948* (Kuala Lumpur, 1977).

[149] Saliha Hj Hasan, 'Dr Burhanuddin Al-Hulaimi: the ideals of a Malay nationalist', *Malaysia in History*, 17, 1 (1974), 1–7; Tan, *Rhetoric*, pp. 18–20.

[150] *Malaya Tribune*, 28.11.1947.   [151] Tan, *Rhetoric*, pp. 21–32.

between the pull of Kuomintang nationalism and Marxist internationalism, spoke with a divided voice. The voice of business, the *Nanyang Siang Pau* urged the Chinese to make a distinction between their race and citizenship, and argued that the term 'Overseas Chinese' itself should be dropped and that 'whether they like it or not' they must devote their political energies to the struggle for freedom in Malaya itself.[152] Yet this new political reality provoked intense soul-searching and intellectual ferment within the Chinese community. A major theme was that the Chinese must reform themselves before they could reform Malaya, that 'the foundation of an inter-racial unity for all the races lies in the unity of the Chinese themselves'.[153] To Hu Yu-chih, the struggle in Malaya was twofold: against servility to colonial 'Fascist' culture, and against racial arrogance within Malaya. 'Cultural workers have to bear the brunt of this struggle. We do not require tanks, guns and hand-grenades now, our weapons are pen and paper only'. Literary polemics took up this theme in a debate on the 'uniqueness of Malayan Chinese literature'.[154] *Freedom News*, a secret publication of the MCP Singapore Town Committee for party members, emphasised the Malayan character of the party, and the duty of members to claim Malayan citizenship.[155] Yet even papers of the left were equivocal on how far the struggle was a local one and the extent to which the non-Chinese were to be equal partners in it. A 'testimony of blood' had been made in the war; 'the Overseas Chinese are undeniably one of the races of Malaya, although we never had power as such'. The Malays themselves, it was argued, were migrants from Indonesia. The Chinese, as the most economically and educationally advanced community, were to dominate a new Asiatic order. They were to be masters of a Malayan People's Republic and other races were to be brought up to the same economic condition. The struggle was for China, for the sake of Malaya, and for all races for the sake of their mother countries.[156] The domestication of Malayan Chinese politics was only just beginning, and in this period it was often expressed in the internationalist terms of anti-colonial struggle. As we shall see in later chapters, there were severe vicissitudes to be faced by the Chinese in reconciling the politics of race and culture and the politics of nation.

These debates on the identity of the Chinese within Malaya were conducted in the face of a crisis of leadership within the Chinese community. The structures of the *shetuan* – the district, clan, or dialect based organisations and professional guilds which were the font of leadership in pre-war Malaya – had been shattered during the

---

[152] Ch'u Che-fu, 'The political crisis of the Chinese race in the Southseas', *Nanyang Siang Pau*, 8.1.1946.

[153] 'Chinese in Malaya unite!', *New Democracy*, 11.10.1945.

[154] Tan Eng Teik, 'Uniqueness of Malayan Chinese literature: literary polemic in the forties', *Asian Culture*, 12 (1988), 102–15; 'Twofold mission of the New Democratic Movement', *Min Sheng Pau*, 12.10.1945.

[155] MSS/PIJ/8/1947.

[156] 'The Malays and the Indonesians', *New Democracy*, 2.12.1945; 'A new understanding indispensable to the Malayan Overseas Chinese', *New Democracy*, 9.12.1945; *ibid.*, 10.12.1945.

war. The trauma and caution over the Sino–Malay clashes reinforced 'a traditional predisposition against overt political activity'. Only by 1948 did the *shetuan* revive to defend the more liberal citizenship provision of the Malayan Union to the Consultative Committee.[157] The alliance was a superficial one. Chinese politics in Malaya was moving in a variety of different directions. Its polarisations are perhaps best epitomised by the China Democratic League (CDL), the only new political organisation among the Chinese to emerge after the war. Dominated by men such as Hu Yu-chih and Tan Kah Kee, it was the most important single initiative to break away from the old system of representing the Chinese interest through *kapitans*, the politics of clique, and to open up new channels of public opinion. Its membership comprised cultural workers and men of business, and it established branches throughout the peninsula. It co–operated closely with the Chinese left whose politics were more rooted in local conditions, and received vocal support from the MCP.[158] The CDL was a response to the skirmishes throughout this period between the KMT and MCP. Both fed their struggle largely on events in China whilst necessarily looking to strengthen their organisations within Malaya, and we shall examine the struggle between them in the next chapter. There is a sense in which the very bitterness with which it was fought led to these parties taking a deeper root within Malayan society, and being shaped in turn by its local dynamics. This was especially true of the MCP, whose newspapers turned their vitriol on the KMT and the Chinese Consuls for importing civil war to Malaya, 'opening factories in Penang, Ipoh and Singapore for the manufacture of false rumours'.[159] As it began to confront local political exigencies, the main instrument of the MCP was the Democratic National United Front for which the China Democratic League was a precedent – a front of independent associations with a common democratic programme.

At the centre of the left's approach to constitutional debates of 1946 and 1947 lay the 'Malayan' nationalism espoused by the Malayan Democratic Union (MDU), a Singapore party of the best and brightest of the English-educated radicals, such as John Eber, Gerald de Cruz, Quek Peng Cheng and Lim Kean Chye. The MDU became a focal point of MCP's united front strategy, and the party operated a cell within the body.[160] Encouraged by the MCP, the MDU took the lead in establishing the AMCJA in December 1946. The new body was an umbrella organisation for a wide range of bodies, including the MDU, the Straits Chinese British Association, the Indian Chamber of Commerce, the General Labour Union, clerical unions, and MCP fronts such as the NDYL and the Women's Federation that sought to campaign

---

[157] Tan Liok Ee, 'Politics of Chinese education in Malaya, 1945–61' (Ph.D., Universiti Malaya, 1985), pp. 48–50.

[158] *Sin Chew Jit Pao*, 10.10.1945; Chui Kwei-chiang, 'The China Democratic League in Singapore and Malaya, 1946–48', *Review of Southeast Asian Studies*, 15 (1985), 1–28.

[159] *Combatants' Friend*, 23.4.1946.

[160] Yeo Kim Wah, 'The anti-federation movement in Malaya, 1946–48', *JSEAS*, 4, 1 (1973), 31–51; Cheah Boon Kheng, *The masked comrades: a study of the Communist United Front in Malaya, 1945–48* (Singapore, 1979).

against the *rapprochement* between colonial officials and UMNO and argue for a united Malaya, including Singapore, with a common citizenship with generous provisions to extend it to non-Malays. The Council secured as its figurehead President Tan Cheng Lock, the veteran Straits Chinese leader, who argued on liberal democratic principles and for a citizenship based on equality, on individual rights. The AMCJA advocated a unitary nationalism on a western model. The MNP had supported AMCJA from the outset, but confronted with taunts from UMNO that it had sold out to non-Malay interests, it pulled out in early 1947 to form the *Pusat Tenaga Rakyat* (PUTERA) – centre of people's power – a united front of the MNP, API and its satellites. AMCJA found some common ground with the Malay radicals. Both were hostile to the exclusiveness of UMNO nationalism. But there was a fundamental difference in their conceptions of the nation. The 'Malayan' nationalism was based on the equal status of individuals; the *Melayu* formula of the MNP on the equal status of the community. A compromise was reached in the People's Constitutional Proposals of the AMCJA–PUTERA that the coalition campaigned on in opposition to the Federation proposals. The *Melayu* citizenship was accepted as was the non-Malays' right to it by *jus soli*.[161] Significantly the ambiguity was glossed over in the English employed by the Malayan Democratic Union leaders who were given the task of drafting the document.

Further ambiguities arose when the coalition sought to co-operate with Chinese bodies such as the Associated Chinese Chambers of Commerce (ACCC). The AMCJA–PUTERA and the ACCC originally adopted different strategies to contest the Anglo-Malay agreement. The ACCC had agreed to participate in the Consultative Committee that was to gauge public opinion on the proposals. However, when few of its suggestions were absorbed into the draft Federation proposals that were published in May 1947, the ACCC agreed to co-operate with the AMCJA. However, the largest demonstration against the Federation, the *hartal* of 20 October 1947, exposed the differences in aim between the AMCJA–PUTERA and the ACCC: they were united only in their opposition to the proposals. The Council viewed the *hartal* as 90 per cent effective, 'a unique method of political education', disseminating over 400,000 copies of its manifesto, 300,000 posters and utilising 300 propaganda groups, backed by support from the *Utusan Melayu*, the 'official organ' of the MNP, *Dunia Bahru*, and the *Combatants' Friend*. The *hartal* displayed the strength of branch organisations rather than of the AMCJA's central authority. It exposed the MNP's strength in Trengganu, and provoked strong UMNO resistance in Kelantan and UMNO counter-demonstrations in Senggaram, Kampong Bahru, in Johore and, in a violent form, in Bagan Datoh in Perak.[162] The Malayan Union government used a survey of participating businesses to acquire evidence of intimidation and to intimidate *hartal* supporters itself. It contemplated radical action to prevent a recurrence, and possible

---

[161] Boestamam, *Carving the path*, p. 109.
[162] 'Minutes of the third delegates, conference of the PUTERA and AMCJA', Kuala Lumpur, 3.11.1947, SP.13/A/7.

outbreak of communal disturbances, on the inauguration of the Federation on 1 February 1948, including the detention of the ACCC leader, Lee Kong Chian. Governor Gent and Governor-General Malcolm MacDonald were reported to be 'at loggerheads' over the matter. In many ways this anticipated their later disagreements over policy towards the MCP. Contrary to later accounts that would label Gent as an appeaser of the left, it was Macdonald who prevaricated over the suppression of the *hartal*. He won the day by arguing that although the form of protest was abhorrent to the western mind, there were many precedents for the *hartal* as a peaceful form of protest in the east and was supported in this by a Secretary of State reluctant to have Britain's liberal intentions maligned.[163] But by this stage there was little support within the Chambers of Commerce for a repeat performance, save in Tan Cheng Lock's stronghold of Malacca. The men of business eventually agreed to accept nominated seats in the Legislative Council. There were fears on all sides that racial tensions could escalate into violence. In the event, beyond a boycott of the Legislation Council and a Sunday strike in Singapore and parts of Johore, little protest materialised.[164] The Malayan government had armed itself for trouble – ready to use a '"shoot to kill" Ordinance' at the last resort.[165] The compass of the political experiment was narrowing.

However, it had set in motion two debates that were to dominate the years to come. Although it was couched in many different terms, a first theme of the political struggles that took centre-stage between 1946 and 1948 was the argument for accountability – Malay opinion argued for the accountability of the Rulers to the *rakyat*; the united front for the accountability of colonial law to the general will. This, in essence, was what the Malayan Spring represented. By its close, many of the players had repudiated the democratic consequences of the positions they had argued for in early 1946. UMNO had emphasised Malay identity and a working relationship with the Rulers and the British government, which tended to bolster old hierarchies. The British had balked at the 'New Democratic' tone to the 'Malayan' public opinion they had sought to generate. A second theme was the identity of the new nation that, through their political experiment, the British had acknowledged must come into being. It was, as we have seen, envisaged in many different ways. Even the identity implicit in the constitutional framework that emerged in 1948 was very ambiguous. Devised in secret by a Working Committee, it retained many features of the Union, and went a long way beyond the looser federation of Malay states envisaged by UMNO leaders. It seems it was acceptable to UMNO as its citizenship did not amount to a nationality and the citizenship rights for non-Malays in no way impinged on the special rights of the Malays. In practice the Federation Agreement fudged the issue by giving limited citizenship rights to non-Malays. 'Malayness' was enshrined in

---

163 MacDonald to Creech Jones, 17.11.1947; Bourdillon, minute, 20.11.1947; Creech Jones to Gent, 21.11.1947, CO537/2149. See also Thio Chan Bee, *The extraordinary adventures of an ordinary man* (London, 1977), pp. 70–4.

164 Gent to Creech Jones, 30.12.1947; to T. Lloyd, 5.1.1948, CO537/3667.

165 O. H. Morris, minute, 8.1.1948, *ibid.*

the constitution, whereas the idea of the 'Malayan' had no status at all. The new political entity was translated as *Persatuan Tanah Melayu*. It contained within it no legal definition of the 'Malayan'. It was a state, but not a template for a nation. For many Malays, after the Union fiasco, 'Malayan' was a dirty word. The united front opposition, although it showed how far the left had travelled since September 1945, were similarly divided on whether the identity they were espousing was the MNP's *Melayu* – now an inclusive category rather than a racial one – or the synthesised 'Malayan' favoured by the Anglophone radicals of the Malayan Democratic Union.[166]

It was perhaps the British who, in the short term, got the most out of the Federation. They felt that 90 per cent of the strategic aims of the Union were achieved within it. There was an underlying consistency: the principle of achieving a level of coherence and unity above parochialisms. The Union was abandoned to secure a unified federal system.[167] The new Anglo–Malay partnership proved durable in the troubled years that followed. However, in the interim, the character of the political experiment had changed. 'The government,' Sir Franklin Gimson, Governor of Singapore, told the Colonial Office, 'would be evading its obligations to citizens if it allowed them to be deprived of conditions favourable to the development of self-governing institutions, as trustees, and I submit that it is our duty to give the necessary background for political education.'[168] The Chairman of AMCJA–PUTERA, Ishak Haji Mohammad, foretold an increasingly tense political climate:

> Our Governor-General and the diehards in Empress Place, the Palmers in the Federation and their mouthpieces in Cecil Street, are all in the game too. You must know that according to these gentlemen we are all Communists and agents of Uncle Stalin . . . This red baiting against the progressive movement is part of the attempt to pave the way for the suppression of the progressive movement in the name of 'public interest and security'.[169]

The unease these social movements engendered in the official mind greatly eased British accommodation with the UMNO moderates. In the aftermath of the politics of Union, in early 1948, the Colonial Office was being reassured that the prospects of a strong independence movement were slight, that Dato Onn would 'put a strong curb' on any such demand, and that the British were destined to 'hold the ring' for many years to come and the main communities remained far apart. The AMCJA was 'fatally weakened' by the loss of rightist Chinese support.[170] The importance of the supersession of the Malayan Union and the conception of nationalism it represented, lies not only in the victory for the Malay elites. It also meant the circumscribing of

[166] Ariffin, *Bangsa Melayu*, ch. 4; Tan, *Rhetoric*, pp. 18–20.
[167] Creech Jones to Gent, 16.5.1946, CO539/1529/Pt. 2.
[168] Gimson to Creech Jones, 2.3.1947, CO537/2171.
[169] Sir Sydney Palmer was the leading representative of planting interests in official councils; Cecil Street was home to the *Straits Times*, 'Minutes of the Annual Conference of Delegates of PUTERA-AMCJA', Singapore, 24–25.4.1948, SP.13/A/7.
[170] W. L. Blythe, 'On the prospect of the emergence of a strong independence movement in Malaya in the near future'; W. Linehan, 'Note', 2.3.1948, CO537/3746.

some of the political opportunities post-war colonialism had initially granted. Official distinctions between 'legitimate' and 'illegitimate' forms of political and social organisations which emerged in this period and the techniques of welfare state imperialism, which in many ways had created them, were written into the strategies of the Emergency period. This reconstruction of the colonial state had a profound impact on post-war Malayan politics. It also confirmed the limitations of the colonial government's capacity to determine the manner in which they were conducted.

CHAPTER THREE

The revolt on the periphery

The political struggles of the Malayan Spring were played out against a backdrop of agrarian crisis and terror. This chapter explores the dynamics of terror, and through this seeks to revise existing accounts of the origins of the Communist rebellion in Malaya. The debates of historians have focused on the extent to which the revolution was planned by the MCP or precipitated by colonial repression. The answer to this question has been sought within high politics, through a mire of intelligence reports and such records of leftist organisations as have survived. Yet key fragments of these secret worlds are missing and likely to remain so. As the former MDU leader, Gerald de Cruz, reminds us, revolutionaries rarely commit their conspiracies to paper.[1] Moreover, as soon as the fighting began a *post facto* rationalisation of events was underway on both sides. We shall see how colonial intelligence reports became an apologia for past failings, and how, through its propaganda, the MCP attempted to regain control of its revolution. Myths were generated to ascribe responsibility for the violence that were to have a profound influence on the way the Emergency was perceived. To expatriate opinion in Malaya at the time – and to many later historians – the Emergency was a product of the confusion and failure of colonial administration and its ignorance of the nature of the challenge facing it. Once the Emergency was subsumed into Britain's global struggle against Communism, it was seen primarily as a problem of policy; as a source of bureaucratic lessons, rather than as a social experience. Yet the uprising no longer looks like a carefully orchestrated design of international Communism. Nor does the revolt seem to be, as the MCP portrayed it, a consequence of the 'improved deceit' of British imperialism, of reaction masquerading as liberalism. As we have seen, during the Malayan Spring, the Labour government did not suppress social movements as a matter of routine. The myths now fail to convince. To uncover the roots of rural revolution in Malaya we must look at more seismic shifts within Malayan society.

[1] Michael Stenson, *The 1948 Communist revolt in Malaya: a note on historical sources and interpretation with a Reply by Gerald de Cruz* (Singapore, 1971), p. 17.

94

The Communist rebellion was not a beer-hall *putsch*, it was a guerrilla war that drew sustenance from a panoply of endemic disorder on the rural periphery. This, as yet, has been imperfectly understood. Historians of the rebellion have described a background of mounting industrial tension and violence without adequately accounting for its internal dynamics. However, new research and new sources are beginning to provide a clearer picture of the upheaval of the war years. This chapter puts the experience of rural terror at the heart of the history of the Emergency. It locates its origins in a long-term pattern of migration and economic expansion against the forest frontier of the central mountain ranges that form the backbone of the peninsula. In particular, subsistence crisis and dispersal of population created conditions of profound social disequilibrium in the immediate hinterlands of the mines and plantations of the west coast which war supercharged and made terrible. Even at the meridian of imperial power in the 1930s, large areas of the peninsula were lawless badlands. During the occupation, old trading relationships and controls on labour were disrupted by a general food shortage which led to the colonisation of marginal land and to an often violent struggle for the control of scarce resources. These volatile social conditions will be examined against the endeavour on the part of the colonial government to reassert its presence in the countryside. This did not only mean a revival of existing administrative controls, but also a drive to conserve the forest, prevent soil erosion, meet a regional food crisis and modernise the plantation economy. At the same time, Asian and European business moved to recapture their control over labour. The strands of authority which had tied the Chinese labourer to European mines and estates or to his *kepala* had been broken by the war. European concerns had collapsed; many big Chinese businessmen had fled abroad; small-town *towkays* had their economic activities curtailed by the Japanese. New centres of authority had emerged. The struggle by which the town sought to regain control over its periphery was interfused by the radicalised political organisations which had gained a foothold in the forests during the Japanese occupation. This chapter emphasises the multi-faceted nature of the contest for the periphery. The Communist revolt was as much the result of power struggles within communities as between the MCP and the British. The Kuomintang and Communist affiliations of the towns were transposed to the countryside. Both sides employed the muscle of Triad societies, which thrived on the smuggling and gang violence of the post-war years. The MCP channelled the anger felt by Chinese squatters evicted from estates and forest reserves. It attempted to tap into agrarian discontent in the Malay kampongs, and intervened at a crucial juncture in the crisis of local leadership within the Malay community. The struggle for authority on the frontier transformed a pattern of endemic unrest in the rural areas into an armed rebellion against the colonial government. From first to last the actions of the British government and the calculations of the MCP were responses to more elemental forces from below: a spiral of rural terror which underwrote the course of political violence throughout the Emergency period. Against this we can read the political circumstances that precipitated the declaration of the Emergency in July 1948.

The political economy of disruption

During the war the British lost control over vast tracts of the countryside. The general disorder on the fringes of forests, concessions and reserves lay at the heart of a range of post-war strategic anxieties. First, the rainforests of the Malay peninsula were a vital imperial resource, accounting in 1945 for 45 per cent of the entire timber reserves of the British Empire, and were guarded jealously. From the 1920s, the British had attempted to create permanent forest estates and to remove valuable timber from unreserved forest at the same rate as land was being alienated to mines, plantations and peasant farmers. Extraction moved at a greater rate than alienation. Therefore, immediately before the war, a scheme of intensive management was mooted over an area of one million acres to promote high yields of timber to meet future requirements and to keep replanting to a minimum. The scheme was under-mined by its high cost and the rising demand for timber.[2] The fear after the war was that timber shortage would retard the rehabilitation of mining enterprise and the urban economy, especially as the most despoiled forests were those which had supplied these industrial areas.[3] The pre-war revenue surplus of the forests was over $1 million, and officials were anxious to resume its collection.[4] They calculated that the area lost to timber production amounted to around 150,000 acres, with the hinterland of rubber and mining areas in Perak, Selangor and Negri Sembilan the most affected areas. In Selangor, areas proximate to Klang and Kuala Lumpur were particularly badly hit; it was estimated that 13,353 acres had been felled by the Japanese for food cultivation.[5] The Batu Arang Concessional Area boundary – including the Colliery farm – was a cleared area of 1,000 acres, all planted with food crops by migrant squatters.[6] In the northern part of Kroh reserve it was reported that 'there is scarcely one tree alive'.[7] Sangkap reserve in Kedah – reported to contain some of the finest forest in Malaya – had become almost entirely tapioca land. Much of the cleared land was never cultivated and much that had been was subsequently abandoned. In Kuala Lipis district clearings followed the lines of communications: 'all along the roads and rivers these *ladangs* have been made – they must run into hundreds of thousands of acres in the whole district'. From Gemas, in Johore, to the Pahang border there were said to be around 150,000 acres of agricultural settlement.[8] Much of this hill-clearing was already underway before the war. In 1939, a survey of

---

[2] E. J. Shrubshall, 'Forest policy in the Federation of Malaya', 12.10.1955, Shrubshall papers.
[3] For example Parit, Kroh, Tanjong Tualing, and Chikus reserves in Perak which supplied the Kinta mines; Sungei Buloh, Kanching, Bangi, Bukit Tunggal which supplied Kuala Lumpur; and Senawang and Sendayan in Negri Sembilan which supplied Seremban, J. P. Mead, memorandum, 'Forest Department', 25.11.1945, BMA/DEPT/11/3.
[4] J. P. Mead, 'Renewed collection of forest revenue', 19.10.1945, DF/90/45.
[5] 'Forest Department Weekly Situation Report for week ending 20.10.1945', BMA/DEPT/11/3; State Secretary Selangor to Commissioner of Lands, 9.4.1948, SEL.CA/282/45.
[6] Assistant Civil Affairs Officer Batu Arang to SCAO, 29.3.1946, SEL.CA/282/45.
[7] Diary of D. F. Grant, 25.6.1946, DF/370/46.
[8] Diary of A. F. Robertson, 8.1.1947, *ibid.*

tapioca planting in Kinta, Perak, showed that planting on steep gradients of land initially fertile and of deep soil, would turn to *lalang* – long, coarse grass – and through erosion the slopes were washed almost bare of soil. In Behrang forest reserve, by 1946, 60 per cent of cleared land was under *belukar* – secondary growth – and not food.[9] The damage was reported to be particularly bad in Sungei Siput district, where steep forest reserve land behind the rubber lands was under crops. As one senior estate manager complained: 'on the plains it is serious enough, but on the hillsides it is a major tragedy and must be stopped at all costs! No penalty could be too severe for such vandalism.'[10] Colonial foresters raised the spectre of environmental catastrophe: deforestation undermined the watersheds and the fragile mechanisms of disease control, silting up the anti-malarial works and the intakes for the water supply. 'The importance of food cultivation,' doctors warned, 'did not justify the opening of land if it was merely to provide a grave for the occupants when they died of malaria.'[11]

A second imperative to recapture control over the frontier was the breakdown of controls on the movement and settlement of labour. The dramatic acceleration of deforestation during the war was not solely the result of the Japanese military's attempts to increase timber and food production, although they were culpable in the extreme. A process of spontaneous population movement into the interior had begun years earlier as a strategy to meet low wage levels and unemployment during the depression. The war and food shortages brought a degree of official acceptance to this, and made it necessary for many Chinese to evade a hostile Japanese administration. The character of these migrations and their repercussions for the wider economy were complex. Although they were to be categorised together as 'squatters', many of the people involved were seasonal cultivators and not permanent settlers. The precise character of their 'migrations' varied from place to place. Many cultivators in the forest travelled some distance from lowland dwellings in the tin areas to tend holdings in the high cleared forest. Others were seasonal migrants at harvest time and worked the rest of the year for labour contractors. Settlers grew mostly cash-crops, vegetables and tobacco, and the seasonal padi growers followed *ladang* cultivation methods. In July 1946, it was reported in Kroh reserve that many of the padi growers swarming into the area and clearing the ground for planting had houses outside the reserve and worked as labourers for nearby commercial concerns.[12] The British were witness to traditional and commonplace practices of diversification. Within the colonial economy, the 'squatters' constituted a kind of self-made reserve army of labour in the hinterland, and for this reason British officials had the initial confidence to dismiss the problem as one which would dissipate when stable conditions of employment returned. After the reoccupation, officials differentiated between the character and composition of squatter communities: they abstained from collecting land rents from

---

[9] Diary of J. C. K. Marshall, 14.3.1946, DF/143/45/Part I.
[10] E. St. Clair-Morford to Mentri Besar, Perak, 22.4.1948, PK.SEC/1006/47.
[11] 'Minutes of a meeting of the Malaria Advisory Board', 6.3.1946, BMA/DEPT/1/5.
[12] Grant diary, 17.7.1946.

the 'humble cultivators who merely grow enough for their own requirements', but charged rent to those 'growing foodstuffs for trading purposes'. One businessman was reportedly cultivating over 1,000 acres of tapioca in Sungei Buloh forest reserve, where he had built a flour mill, the entire output of which was sent to his biscuit factory in Setapak.[13] Lenggong in Upper Perak was home to large concentrations of Kwongsai tobacco farmers. To counter such commercialisation, in early 1946 the planting of rubber, coffee and tobacco was forbidden.[14] British officials minimised the degree of hardship felt by these people. However, Chinese newspapers questioned the profitability of squatter agriculture. Even in the fertile Cameron Highlands, the controlled price for its vegetables was only thirty cents a *katty*, although the black-market price could rise to ten times as much. Yet even at one dollar a *katty* the income per cultivator was only $500 for three months' work and much of the profit was lost to middlemen. Moreover, after a good harvest in early 1946, rice prices generally dropped from $170 to $70 a *picul*.[15] Official reports substantiated the stories of hardship. In Cheras, Selangor, the average income per family, on average six people, was only $28 a month.[16] Moreover, the British conviction that the problem was only a temporary one soon evaporated. The nature of these migrations had changed, and by the end of the war a new demographic pattern had emerged. In Perak, where the greatest concentrations of cultivators were found, previous waves of squatter-cultivators had returned to their previous accommodation upon resumption of their old forms of wage employment as the circumstances that led them to forsake it improved. However, after the war 'the squatter's house with his family remained in the background. To it he returned on holidays, and to it he returns when he is unemployed. Almost all Chinese have their roots in the state in this manner and a great change has therefore taken place.'[17]

A third anxiety was that the problem had become an irritant to Anglo-Malay relations. Malay kampongs on the fringes of reserves were the first to feel the effects of squatter cultivation. In Galah, in Negri Sembilan, Malay villagers complained that soil erosion from Chinese cultivation in the adjacent forest reserve had turned their padi crop into 'an almost total failure'.[18] The cumulative incidence of this is hard to quantify. In the Sungei Kechil area of Kedah, which was badly affected, farmers maintained that silting of padi land began before the occupation when nearby areas had been cleared for rubber.[19] Officials suggested that complaints from the Malay kampongs proceeded more out of jealousy than from any substantial grievance. However, these encroachments worked with the diminishing conditions of personal

---

[13] SFO to RC Selangor, 27.8.1946, SEL SEC/528/46.
[14] 'Forest Department Report for January, 1946', BMA/DEPT/11/3.
[15] *Kin Kwok Daily News*, 15.12.1945; 26.1.1946.
[16] Francis Loh Kok Wah, *Beyond the tin mines: coolies, squatters and the New Villagers in the Kinta Valley, c. 1880–1980* (Singapore, 1988), p. 81.
[17] Perak *Annual Report, 1948*, pp. 14–16, cited in Loh, *Beyond the tin mines*, p. 84.
[18] Diary of A. B. Walton, 28.12.1945, DF/168/45.
[19] Diary of J. Wyatt-Smith, 29.1.1946, DF/36/46.

security in post-war Malaya to raise communal tensions in a number of areas. In Sungkai, Malays were reported to have fled after Chinese began large-scale *ladang* work from the Sungkai to the Erong – a resistance army stronghold.[20] Chinese cultivation in Malay Reservations was undoubtedly at issue in localities where land and the labour to work it were scarce, or credit was tight. In other, often newly opened, areas happier accommodations were made. Chinese established on reservation land often entered into a 'fictitious agreement with Malays by which they paid for the right to cultivate'.[21] The Chinese might work rice smallholdings, whilst the Malays turned to their rubber and kampong land. Such arrangements had undermined land reservation legislation pre-war, and commonly continued to do so after the reoccupation.[22] The Malayan Union scheme had questioned Britain's custodial commitment to the Malays; its defeat subjected colonial agricultural policy to new political pressures. The interests of the Malay cultivator were energetically defended, both in London – by old Malaya hands such as Sir George Maxwell – and by Malay associations within Malaya. To reassure public opinion in the wake of the Union débâcle, the policy of guaranteeing Malay rights through Malay Reservations was trenchantly reasserted. There were land shortage scares in many places, although officials asserted that Malays could not be short of land because colonists were not coming forward for newly opened areas.[23] It was not so much shortage of land but the ability to work it effectively that was retarding the recovery of the Malay peasant economy. However, the British came under intense pressure from Malay associations not to alienate any more reservation land to business interests and to reverse encroachments by non-Malays on reserved land.[24] For example, in late 1946 District Officers in Negri Sembilan warned non-Malays that the planting of permanent crops on Malay Reservation land would not be tolerated. However, no attempt was made as yet to move them.[25]

A fourth voice of alarm came from capitalist enterprise. The rubber industry was anxious to modernise by replanting with high-yielding trees in preparation for its struggle with synthetic rubber for the lion's share of the world market. The London boards of the rubber companies argued, through the United Planting Association of Malaya (UPAM), that 'unless something is done early, the future of the rubber industry in this country will be very seriously affected'. They claimed that 70,000 acres required for replanting by the 1948 season were occupied by squatters.[26] At the

[20] Marshall diary, 19.2.1946.
[21] For one case in Sekinchan, Selangor, see DO Kuala Selangor to RC Selangor, 11.9.1946, MU/1437/46.
[22] Squatters on Malay land in Kalumpang, Ulu Selangor were alienated land by Malays for whom they worked as rubber tappers, DO Ulu Selangor, minute, 26.5.1948, SEL.SEC/479/48.
[23] Commissioner for Lands, memorandum, 18.7.1946, MU/2721/46.
[24] For example, Persatuan Melayu Selangor to State Secretary, Selangor, 1.3.1948; 'Minutes of third meeting of the State Executive Council of Selangor, 6.3.1948', SEL.SEC/1038/46.
[25] 'Minutes of third meeting of the District Officers' Conference, Negri Sembilan, 10.10.1946'; 'Minutes of fourth meeting . . . 11.11.1946', MU/4809/46.
[26] H. K. Dimolene (Secretary UPAM) to Chief Secretary, 26.9.1947; 25.3.1948; A. J. Loch,

outset of the peace, many local managers had adopted a relatively benign attitude towards the squatters, in the face of difficulties in securing labour for rehabilitation work. In Ulu Langat, managers treated squatter cultivation as part of the efforts required of them by the government to contribute to food cultivation, even though most of the food was for urban consumers, rather than estate labour forces.[27] On many estates, the acreage under food-crops was expanding – ragi and sweet potatoes were the main crop, but considerable amounts of tapioca and vegetables, even sugar cane, were also grown.[28] Managers' sufferance of the squatters was short-lived, even in cases where they had entered into written agreements with them. On Bertam Estate in Province Wellesley 1,200 acres were prepared as farm tracts in early 1946 by the government on land borrowed from the estate, which had been used earlier by the Japanese for an agricultural settlement, and it hosted a huge influx of both Malay and Chinese padi planters, mostly from Penang. They had become established agriculturists; they refused to make way for replanting, and returned the next season to resume cultivation. The Chinese Consul demanded that a school and medical facilities be provided for them by the estate. Inducements of up to $150 for a three-acre plot were used to encourage them to move, but Communist cadres and a sympathetic press encouraged them to resist replanting. Their resolve was only weakened by a long drought.[29] When action to evict such squatters was first taken – on Caledonian Estate in Province Wellesley – the MCP-led Farmers' Union of Bukit Mertajam took up the case and demanded land and compensation for some 1,000 Chinese cultivators.[30] Officials assured estates that if squatters were suffered to remain on felled rubber estate land until the end of 1947, it would be a simple matter for the rubber estates to evict them after that date. They held out the prospect of government assistance, even the possibility of offering squatters alternative land, although they did not acknowledge any obligation to them. The estates were sceptical and demanded greater powers of eviction.[31] During 1947 pressure on the land did not ease; there was a heavy demand for land in June for the coming padi season, and it was feared that uncontrolled clearings would result in flooding of the lower reaches of the already overburdened rivers. The planting interest in Selangor protested that deforestation was badly affecting the Sungei Buloh river.[32] The mining industry added its voice to

---

minute, 13.1948; H. Facer (President, UPAM) to Sir Edward Gent, 26.5.1948, MU/4949/47.

[27] 'Report on Labour conditions for November 1946, inland districts of Selangor', EACL.KL/20/45.

[28] 'Minutes of first meeting of the District Officers' Conference, Negri Sembilan', 10.8.1946, MU/4809/46.

[29] Manager Bertam Estate to G. W. Somerville, 20.6.1946; S. N. King, R. C. Penang, to Chief Secretary, 28.8.1946 and 2.10.1946, MU/4592/46.

[30] Farmers' Union, Bukit Mertajam to Governor, 5.8.1947; P. C. Byrne, 'Removal of squatters from Caledonian Estate', MU/3859/46.

[31] C. J. Pyke, Economic Adviser, to John Ramsden, 27.8.1946, *ibid.*; H. K. Dimolene (Secretary UPAM) to Chief Secretary, 26.9.1947, MU/4949/47.

[32] 'Monthly report of the SAO, Selangor, for the month of June, 1947'; 'Weekly food situation

the planters' campaign against illegal occupation. Batu Arang coal mine was overrun by squatters. On tin mines the numbers involved in subsidiary occupations such as *dulang* washing, or panning, had multiplied, doubling from the immediate post-war period, and it was a source of subsistence for many Hakka and Cantonese women who had no husbands in Malaya.[33] They had been tolerated by tin mines in view of acute levels of unemployment in the mining areas, and suppression was confined to cases where damage to mining property occurred. However, officials were increasingly pressurised by the mines to check these practices that were conducted in open defiance of mine employees. In Gopeng, *dulang* washing had extended into extractive work. At one mine at Batu Karang in Kampar a policeman was attacked by *dulang* washers and shot one dead.[34] The rubber and tin industries looked for state support to resume planting and prospecting in isolated areas, and to instil discipline into their labour forces.

In the face of these pressures, the BMA stuck resolutely to its attitude of *laissez-faire*, and deferred the problem on to the civil government.[35] There was little the authorities could do to regularise the situation so long as the main thrust of agricultural policy was towards food production by all available means. The post-war 'Grow More Food' campaign has been described by its historian as 'a dismal chronicle of failure'.[36] Whilst the British deplored Japanese policies to expand food cultivation, they were compelled by the severity of the crisis to resort to the same methods. It was estimated that 170,000 tons of tapioca were to be cropped in the first four months of 1946. Much of it came from forest reserves. Some irretrievably devastated areas were to be converted into new agricultural colonies: 16,000 acres at Bahau, Sungei Buloh, Sungei Patani and elsewhere were allocated for the mechanical cultivation of rice. However, the cleared acreage actually planted was far short of expectations.[37] For example, in Sungei Buloh the soils were light and unsuited to such intense cultivation methods, and deforestation created a grave possibility of erosion. Heavy rains in October 1946 added to the difficulties, particularly in short-term food production areas in Sungei Buloh and Endau in Johore.[38] In Kelantan many recently cleared areas on the coast were abandoned as the soil was unsuited to rice cultivation.[39] To many

report of SAO, Selangor', 15.7.1947; 'Minutes of joint meeting of Kuala Selangor Drainage Boards held on 23.7.1946', SEL.CA/282/45.
[33] Nim Chee Siew, *Labour and tin mining in Malaya* (Data Paper No. 7, Southeast Asia Program, Cornell University, Ithaca, 1953), pp. 13–17.
[34] *Kin Kwok Daily News*, 23.11.1946.
[35] Colin Marshall to Director of Forests, 13.12.1945, DF/119/45.
[36] Paul H. Kratoska, 'The post-1945 food shortage in British Malaya', *JSEAS*, 19, 1 (1988), 27–49.
[37] F. G. Grant-Fletcher, 'Draft: mechanical cultivation of essential foodcrops including dry padi', 19.2.1946, BMA/DEPT/12/9.
[38] 'Minutes of a meeting of the Land Settlement Committee', 21.1.1946; 'Minutes of a meeting of the Agricultural Production Committee', 19.1.1946; 'Minutes of a meeting of the Food Production Board', 6.2.1946, SEL.CA/46/46.
[39] W. Grantham to Chief Secretary, 23.5.1946, SEL.CA/282/45.

observers, the 'Grow More Food' campaign was little short of vandalism. What had begun as a short-term expedient had culminated in the permanent colonisation of marginal and ecologically fragile areas. The British gave squatters two years from early 1946 to cultivate rent-free on forest land, a reprieve that expired on 31 March 1948. In the interim, attempts at agricultural improvement were made. In Kinta, where there were the greatest concentrations of squatters – including those squatting on private land with the consent of the owners – 20,000 Temporary Occupation Licences (TOLs) had been issued, mainly on mining land.[40] However, the short-term title discouraged improvement and when cultivation of short-term crops on newly cleared areas ceased, they quickly went under *lalang*, as regrowth after two crops was poor.[41] Sloping areas were barred to cultivation after the lying crops had been taken. In Kinta officials forbade the growing of tapioca on slopes steeper than 35 degrees; no slopes over 30–35 degrees were to be alienated and those over 25 degrees only on permanent title, as it was 'impossible to enforce anti-erosion measures on any land cultivated on a TOL'.[42] *Taungya* permits were issued: a system that allowed some cultivation combined with a programme of regeneration and reafforestation of damaged landscapes, but this was unsuited to the dry padi planting preferred by many farmers in the higher forest.[43] Another option was eviction. The BMA cleared land required for military purposes with the payment of large amounts of compensation to squatters.[44] Under civil rule, the State governments decided in October 1946 that it would be difficult to eject squatters from such lands, unless there was serious damage to the land and new land was offered to them elsewhere. Governor Gent advised 'that the time was not ripe to declare general war on the squatters. Not only was it beyond our capacity to take energetic action, but also the question of food policy was involved.'[45] An early test case came in Kuala Lumpur, involving a large group of squatters at Cheras Road, where land was needed for a factory. An agricultural location was offered to these people, but it was unappealing to them as most worked as tradespeople, shop assistants and hawkers, and brandished TOLs issued by the Japanese.[46] A sympathetic ruling by a district judge in favour of the squatters was overturned by the Court of Appeal, which affirmed that temporary occupation over a number of years conferred no right of further renewal and could be terminated at any time. Only destitute squatters were to be aided, and there was a resolute body of

---

[40] H. A. L. Luckham, 'Notes on my career in the Malayan Civil Service, 1928–1959', Heussler Papers.
[41] A. J. Fyfe to Secretary to RC Selangor, 28.7.1947; T. W. Cubbitt to Secretary to RC Selangor, 4.9.1947, SEL.CA/282/45.
[42] E. F. Allen to SCAO Perak, 7.3.1946, DF/113/45; D. M. McDiarmid (C.R.E.) to D.C.E., 25.10.1945, SEL.CA/282/45.
[43] G. S. Rawlings to the Secretary to RC Perak, 23.5.1947, PK.SEC/1583/47; R. C. Bernard to Secretary to RC Perak, 6.12.1947, PK.SEC/2283/47.
[44] 'Annual report of the District Office, Kuala Lumpur for 1946', SEL. RC/283/47.
[45] 'Minutes of RCs' Conference held on 8.10.1946', MU/5705/46.
[46] RC Selangor to P. S. to Governor, 14.11.1946; I. B. Mendel to Deputy Chief Secretary, 14.1.1947, MU1437/46.

opinion within the administration against using Welfare Council funds to help resettle them.[47] However, the political mobilisation of the squatters would, within a year, transform the situation.

Conservation and confrontation

Mounting concern about the environmental degradation, the deforestation and soil erosion, created by the expansion of cultivation increased the friction between migrant farmers and the colonial government. However, the trigger for action against them came when control of cultivation became equated with the political control of remote areas. In 1945 the state's legal powers were insufficient to meet the crisis. The occupied forests were often isolated and it was impossible to serve warrants on the 'semi-bandits' – as they were now called – who inhabited them. By mid-1948 the British became convinced that the squatter settlements had become established and entrenched for political reasons, 'because they were Communists and the Communist Party wishes them to be there; or if they are anti-Communist and the anti-Communist political elements also wish them to be there as a counter to Communist activity'.[48] However, it took the British some time to peel away the various layers of disorder and clearly identify an enemy.

From the outset, relations between groups on the periphery and the colonial government were fraught with tension and implied and actual violence. In the confused period of interregnum between the Japanese surrender and the establishment of British garrisons, forest guards were targets for vendetta killings. In early October 1945 two of them disappeared between Kuala Lumpur and Ulu Langat when they tried to prevent fellings, and troops had to be used to prevent the plundering of Ulu Gombak reserve.[49] Widespread intimidation of forest staff was also reported throughout Perak and Johore. As the Director of Forests commented in mid-October 1945: 'these men are constantly being threatened with calamity if they resume working for government. The threats are not empty ones.' Police began raiding areas such as Chikus looking for arms after the Teochews there had threatened forest guards and one had disappeared. In the Gedong valley, as elsewhere in the Tapah Hills, it was noted ominously that the paths were well worn as the area had been used as a guerrilla hideout during the occupation.[50] In November 1945 the help of local *towkays* was enlisted to prevent attacks on forest workers in Tanjong Tualong, Perak. Guards refused to enter the reserve and the State Forest Officer fell into a ten-foot-deep mantrap.[51] The situation remained unsettled at the end of 1946, when looting

---

[47] 'Judgement of Spenser Wilkinson – Criminal Appeal from District Judge No. 64/46'; RC Selangor to Sir Edward Gent, 4.2.1947; 'Minutes of meeting of the Selangor Welfare Committee held on 30.10.1947', SEL. SEC/57/47.
[48] A. J. Loch, minute, 4.6.1948, MU/4949/47.
[49] Forest Department Weekly Situation Reports for week ending 6.10.1945; 20.10.1945 in BMA/DEPT/11/3.
[50] Grant diary, 26.7.1946, 15.8.1946.   [51] Marshall diary, 8.11.1945, 20.11.1945.

and robbery on rubber estates was rampant. The situation stabilised as European managers began to drift back, and guards selected by them were given arms and the authority by the police to patrol properties.[52]

For many months policy was at an impasse. British officials feared their own impotence. 'None of this clearing is authorized,' they complained, 'but it happens within the space of two or three days and the damage is done before we can stop it.'[53] In Selangor, for example, District Officers pressed for punitive powers, such as making illegal occupation of state land a seizable offence. They offered squatters plots with title, on areas of worked-out mining land. However, erosion and neglect had left these areas badly drained and unattractive to cultivators.[54] They recognised the futility of creating a quick method of evicting squatters from the property of one landowner, only to send them off to squat on someone else's property or on State land. To regain administrative control of outlying areas, the squatters either had to be moved, confirmed with legal status or established on new reserves where they would be eligible for permanent title.[55] The difficulty was that the State governments were unable or unwilling to alienate areas of land large enough to satisfy the Chinese.[56] The matter was left to the individual States. In May 1948, the Selangor Kuomintang leader H. S. Lee attempted to get an indication from the State governments as to the free land available. He was told that either no land was available or that States had too many local problems to take in outside settlers.[57] In Perak – where the greatest numbers were involved – there was no land available for the squatters, save forest reserves or Malay reservation.[58] The granting of new land was not always a complete answer in itself. Cohesive new communities had grown up that refused to be dismembered. In Kalumpang, Ulu Selangor, for example, the presence of squatters on Malay reservation land greatly taxed district officials. Various solutions were mooted, but the issue was only resolved when the squatters were offered alienated land by the Malays for whom they worked as rubber tappers. Significantly, this was the only proposal which acknowledged their determination to continue living as one community.[59]

For squatters, agricultural pioneering had become 'a battle against restriction'.[60] After the trauma of the occupation, individuals had the best of reasons to avoid the state and its creatures, even where they were able to prove a right to a legal livelihood. British officials surmised that it was in the natural order of things that the squatter

[52] H. B. Langworthy, Commissioner of Police, to Chief Secretary, 8.4.1946, MU/1251/46.
[53] DO Ulu Selangor to State Drainage and Irrigation Engineer, 21.7.1947, SEL.CA/282/45.
[54] Minute by E. C. G. Barnett, 31.12.1947, SEL.CA/282/45.
[55] Attorney General, memorandum, 18.5.1948; A. J. Loch to State Secretaries, 16.6.1948, MU/4949/47; Commissioner of Lands, minute, 18.9.1946, MU/5705/46.
[56] 'Draft note of a meeting held at King's House on 15.6.1948 to discuss the eviction of squatters on estates', MU/4949/47.
[57] 'Chinese squatters settlement: summary of replies from States/Settlements'; F. Burnett to H. S. Lee, 17.5.1948, FS/2318/48.
[58] Minutes on PK.SEC/1000/48.
[59] DO Ulu Selangor, minute, 26.5.1948, SEL.SEC/479/48.
[60] Marshall diary, 12.1.1946.

'either pays his way through from stump to distant market, or tries every dodge to avoid paying the proper government dues'.[61] The first resort of the cultivator was evasion. In Lenggong, Upper Perak – an area of illicit tobacco-growing where an intelligence officer was kidnapped and the Assistant District Officer (ADO) murdered – arrests were made and the offenders were told to cultivate food under *taungya* permits. Their response was to threaten to move elsewhere.[62] Obstinacy was greatest where alternative land was least in evidence, for example in Perak. Meetings with squatters in forest reserves such as Changkat Jong, Chikus and Sungei Merbau revealed that their resistance to moving out of the reserve was based on the fact that there was no land available in Lower Perak or Batang Padang suitable for the large-scale tapioca planting they pursued. Chinese in forest reserves in the Dindings were demanding either virgin jungle or previously cleared land.[63] Squatters resisted moving from Kroh forest reserve to Changkat Jong as political and criminal societies were known to tax produce and property in the resettlement area.[64] Squatters employed a range of avoidance strategies: many claimed to be merely the employees of some mysterious businessman or simply ran away. Uprooted tapioca plants were strewn on the ground to disguise new and illegal plantings of the crop. 'The local Chinese,' one frustrated Englishman informed his superiors, 'are changing their names as often as it suits them.'[65] In this fashion, piecemeal resistance began from below. In a typical confrontation in Sungkai, squatters stubbornly refused to move: 'one of them brandishing a huge *parang* solemnly affirmed that he would cultivate where he liked'.[66] However, passive resistance and sporadic violence were slow to develop into anything resembling a larger movement of rural revolution.

We know little of the internal dynamics of squatter communities. Some studies have seen them as a 'state within a state': 'the essential anti-government of more or less improvised peasant resistance'.[67] To the contemporary observer the social composition of such groups seemed surprisingly loose. For example in Selangor it was reported that:

> There is no organised group of cultivators, and there is no elected or self-elected 'kepala' in the gang. It appears that anyone can select a plot as he pleases . . . The cultivators generally act on their own knowing as they do that rice is getting scarce and moreover they have planted this land twice before without any hindrance.[68]

However, there is evidence that a shared conception of common predicament was

[61] E. C. Foenander, 'A system for the collection of forest revenue', DF/90/45.
[62] Marshall diary, 12.8.1946, 13.8.1946, 20.8.1946.
[63] Grant diary, 22.11.1947; Diary of P. A. Durgnat, 1.7.1948, DF/371/46.
[64] The Farmers' Union in Kroh was said to have only seven members, but the squatters paid permit fees through the body, Diary of D. Speldewinde, 17.1.1947, DF/375/46.
[65] Diary of G. I. Ironside, 3.3.1947, DF/372/46.
[66] Speldewinde diary, 5.2.1948.
[67] Anthony Short, 'The Malayan Emergency', in Ronald Haycock (ed.), *Regular armies and insurgency* (London, 1978), p. 55.
[68] Report by ADO Rawang enclosed in D. I. Goodwin to Private Secretary to the Governor, 23.8.1946, SEL CA/282/45.

developing together with representative associations through which to advance it. A basic articulation of their viewpoint was that there was a responsibility on the part of the British government to recognise and regularise their position. Squatter representatives reminded officials that their own propaganda was responsible for the situation, and that there was a fundamental confusion over the correct and legal methods of obtaining land.[69]

> Government's 'Grow More Food' campaign has raised our spirits to produce more agricultural products, but government does not keep its word. Government not only cannot relieve the poor, ravaged farmers and save the farming areas from bankruptcy, but on the contrary, re-enforces the regulations of the pre-war days to compel farmers cultivating in forest reserves to evacuate.[70]

These groups appropriated traditional usages of rights to newly opened land as they were understood in the Malay States, whereby the pioneer acquired proprietary rights. This was a notion that the work of colonial scholar-administrators such as W. E. Maxwell had done much to enshrine. The Chinese appropriated it to assert their 'freedom of cultivation' as a form of natural right.[71] This is a common theme of the squatter petitions that survive in colonial records. For example, the farmers of Ayer Kuning, Rangkup, Tanjong Rambutan, Chemor, Manong and Sungei Siput protested to the High Commissioner against the evacuations of the 'farmer-squatters' in these terms.[72] The Central Kedah Peasants' Association demanded suspension of rentals on buildings in reserves and 'that Government should permit the peasants freedom of cultivation and plantation without any periodical limitation'.[73] As squatters in Sawah Sempadan, Kuala Selangor, enquired baldly: 'why do the Chinese have no freedom of cultivation and yet the Malays enjoy such privileges?'[74] The Bukit Selamban Peasant Association in Sungkop, representing 200–300 households in the forest reserve, refused to take out food cultivation permits unless they were given a completely free hand to grow what they wished and a long tenure.[75] A first meeting of the Negri Sembilan Farmers' Association called for the same rations as the urban population; land for clearing and cultivation; burning and planting of felled forest and exemption from quit rent.[76] Farmers stressed that they had become entirely dependent on padi as a sole form of income.[77] As colonial intelligence reports were

---

[69] J. F. Edwards to Deputy Chief Secretary, 6.5.1947, MU/5705/46.

[70] 'Joint representatives of meeting of farmers in various areas of Sungei Siput' to RC Perak, 25.2.1948, PK.SEC/2777/47.

[71] Akimi Fujimoto, *Income sharing among Malay peasants* (Singapore, 1983), pp. 12–15.

[72] *Min Sheng Pau*, 4.4.1948; 'Representative meeting of farmers' to Sir Edward Gent, 31.3.1948, PK.SEC/2777/47.

[73] J. Wyatt-Smith to RC Kedah, 'Land cultivation by Chinese squatters in Kedah forest reserve', 27.10.1946, MU/5705/46.

[74] Petition of Chin Wong Peng and others, 'Cultivation in Kg. Bahru, Kuala Selangor', 29.8.1946, MU/1437/46.

[75] Wyatt-Smith diary, 2.11.1946.   [76] *Min Sheng Pau*, 4.4.1946.

[77] 'The farmers of Pokang (Kampar)' to RC Perak, 1.8.1947, PK.SEC/1006/48.

quick to point out, these demands were presented in a similar form and this indicated that the squatters were being drawn into wider solidarities.

The cultivators had already come into contact with militant organisations through the links with the resistance army that had been forged during the war. Many areas had been an administrative vacuum for some years. In the Bertam Valley, for example, after the reoccupation, the only visible evidence of the existence of colonial government in the area was the periodic visit of a forest officer.[78] It is tempting to look to traditions of social banditry in China itself to explain the hold that the guerrillas and Triad groups had on the squatters. It is a theme that has been highlighted in work on the roots of CCP power in China, and it is undoubtedly the case that in Malaya when the centre fell apart other groups took on the mantle of protector of their communities: the MCP propaganda that we shall discuss in the next chapter elaborated on such themes. Yet folk memories of times of disorder in China do not fully explain the form in which the mobilisation of squatter-cultivators took place in Malaya. The unsettled conditions of peace brought opportunities for new networks of leadership to be established. These were based largely on the rural squatters' links to the industrial labour force, links which were intimate in Malaya before the war and remained so after it. 'Squatters' and 'labourers' were very often one and the same people. With their plots to fall back on workers could ride out periods of unemployment or low wages, take bold strike action, and afford the risk of dismissal. It was through this connection that squatters were drawn into trade union organisations. 'Peasants' unions' were formed in Perak and elsewhere using the offices of mining unions. They gave political and organisational backing to the squatters' demands.[79] The New Democratic Youth League organised a 'Peasant Cultivators' Association at Endau, with a co-operative store and a working capital of $5,000; others were planned in Jemalang and Rompin.[80] Syndicalism existed in some areas: sawmills in particular were outposts of 'lawlessness' and their employees contemptuous of any outside control. The Ipoh Labour Union, for example, was demanding that all fellings of timber be done 'not by contractors but by the democratic workmen'. Trolak sawmill was described as 'another "Republican Sawmill" run by the coolies for the coolies . . . The coolies choose what logs they will saw up . . . and they have to be all in good condition. Their sawmill charges are $10 more than anywhere else.'[81] At Bikam sawmill 'the law of the lawless' ruled; a leftist school and societies flourished, and Malays dared not enter the reserve. At Tronoh mill, loot from a local post office was discovered, and the Chinese there were implicated in the communal violence of the post-war years. The President of the co-operative at the mill was said to have been responsible in the dark days of the interregnum for inciting a mass meeting of 200 Chinese to descend on the Malays at Bota and to burn them alive in their houses.[82]

---

[78] Indeed, the diaries of forest officers provide the primary source material for study of these communities, Speldewinde diary, 28.6.1948.
[79] Loh, *Beyond the tin mines*, pp. 85–7. [80] MSS/PIJ/3/1948.
[81] Speldewinde diary, 13.12.1947.
[82] Marshall diary, 14.3.1946, 15.3.1946, 20.1.1946, 27.1.1946.

This militancy was conflated in the official mind with gangsterism. Infringements of the law became organised and systematic, and the open season in the forests criminalised the squatter problem in the eyes of the government. As a Force 136 officer later explained: 'there were in the Malayan jungle all sorts of camps of Chinese who were under no sort of authority, and would have been classed as gang-robbers at an earlier time'.[83] In the forest reserves, the government competed in its collection of timber royalties with business and political syndicates who made as much as the government on taxation of the timber market. Timber *towkays'* overheads were inflated by various secret charges, such as 'donations' to political clubs and various bad loans. They therefore allowed freelances to cut their compartments under a tribute system – amounting in some cases to four times the government tax – which was used to offset their costs. Gangs stole timber from the roadsides and sold it to foresters who chopped it and acted as fences for it. This 'gangsterism' was widespread in Perak and sustained by the high demand for timber for rehabilitation needs: lorryloads of logs would disappear into secret stockpiles. Thefts of firewood in the coastal areas for the Singapore market were rife, and the cost of collecting timber was so high that many mills on the island threatened to close down. The plundering of dredge and mill machinery was another serious problem. One police raid alone recovered $5,000 worth of machinery.[84] Another source of crime was illicit rubber tapping, which perhaps in mid-1946 accounted for 20 per cent of all rubber tapped, and was seen as a vital perquisite by labourers and squatters, not least because they were short of ready cash to pay government fees and union subscriptions.[85] Gang robbery was endemic to many parts of Malaya. In Perak, police escorts were necessary to travel the Kroh to Klian Intan road. At one stage bandits threatened to cut off Klian Intan unless a ransom of $30,000 was paid, and army jeeps and radio cars were used for kidnappings in Ipoh.[86] In Perak there were twenty-eight murders in the month of January 1946, fifty-three in February, and a general rise in crimes of violence.[87] Much of the violence was an extension of the resistance war. The Siamese border was dominated by ex-guerrillas profiteering from smuggling. As British intelligence concluded: 'It now appears that the armed bandit gangs are merely the 'strong arm' element of a loose but wide-spread commercial organisation designed to exploit the very lucrative possibilities of trans-frontier smuggling.' The KMT 'One-star' guerrillas continued their operations from bases at Grik, Sungei Golok and Betong, together with a sort of administration at Yala. After British troops were sent from the 80th mile on the Grik Road to attack them they withdrew into the jungle. The Grik band was dominated by Tai Man, whose hundred or so ex-KMT guerrillas

[83] R. N. Broome to R. Heussler, 1.5.1982, Heussler Papers.
[84] Marshall diary, 21.2.1946, 22.2.1946, 24.2.1946; 'Monthly progress report for January 1946, Forest Department Perak', DF/119/45; 'Forest Department Report for February 1946', BMA/DEPT/11/3.
[85] LDMR, July 1946, MU/1254/46.
[86] *Chung Hwa Kung* Pao, 11.4.1946; *Malaya Tribune*, 12.9.1947.
[87] *Malaya Tribune*, 24.4.1947.

absconded from Lenggong and Kuala Kangsar prior to the 1 December 1945 disbandment parades. The Sungei Golok gang was formed into two companies of 150 near Tanjong Mat and 50 near Sungei Golok itself. The Betong gang were said to be the connective in the operation: 200–400 men controlling the Betong-Grik area. They were a mixture of KMT and MPAJA people who had moved up the Perak river to avoid troops and dispersed throughout the surrounding kampongs. The MCP were reportedly cultivating an interest in the gang, but it remained in this period a purely commercial organisation. There were other, unconnected, KMT gangs on the upper reaches of the Negiri river in Ulu Kelantan, but these were weakened by attacks from the MPAJA in the later stages of the occupation.[88] The colonial government was increasingly perturbed by what the CID chief called the 'anonymous government' of Malaya: the estimated 20,000 Triad men, an alleged 2,000 of whom were living active criminal lives.[89]

The battle for the forests was not merely a conflict between the squatters and the British government. It was a struggle for political resources. The squatters were not only flouting the authority of the state but also that of private employers, and Chinese businesses felt this most painfully. This, as much as the actions of the colonial government, introduced a momentum of political violence into the struggle for subsistence. The squatter question bore deep into the internal cleavages within the Chinese community. In particular it was an obstacle to the recovery of Chinese capital and the revival of conservative leadership. As we saw in the previous two chapters, this leadership was in disarray. Many pre-war bosses had fled abroad, new men had risen to claim their mantles. For those *towkays* who remained in Malaya, the Japanese occupation had been a time for petty trade rather than production.[90] The hawking economy had expanded with the closure of the mines and estates, and it had forged close links with Chinese middlemen buying from squatters. Some businessmen had, to a point, prospered, trading in conditions of chronic scarcity. They re-emerged into a world of heightened competition. Recovery was fragile and gains had to be resolutely defended. In 1946, as consumer goods from Australia and China flooded the black market, longer-term prospects for recovery were offset by stagnant domestic trade. By the end of the year there was a glut in trade due to the establishment of new import ventures, and many businesses operating on limited capital collapsed.[91] Confronted by these pressures, Chinese business began to reorganise to demand the assistance of the colonial government in restoring pre-war conditions to trade and employment, and to campaign against restrictions in trade. Traders' associations reorganised as a powerful pressure group under the Chinese Chambers of Commerce, to campaign for privileges in distribution of goods.[92] The Kuala Lumpur leftist press, commenting on the formation of a Selangor Chinese Commercial Union, saw fit to point out to

---

[88] HQ Malaya Cmmd, WIR, No. 22, 2.4.1946, CO537/1581.
[89] *Malaya Tribune*, 29.5.1947.
[90] See, for example, Tay Boon Seng, *Recollections of my past* (Melaka, 1970), pp. 12–14.
[91] *Malaya Tribune*, 21.11.1946.   [92] For example, *China Press*, 4.12.1946.

readers that the 'merchant class' had become stronger by the war. The leftist parties attempted to identify and encourage the 'national bourgeoisie': they floated the creation of a pan-Malayan Chinese Chamber of Commerce which would join the united front to campaign for the deregulation of the rice and textile trade and the distribution of goods.[93] However, as we saw in the previous chapter, the alliance between the Chinese Chambers of Commerce and the AMCJA–PUTERA united front involved no meeting of minds beyond a shared resentment of the Federation constitutional proposals. Politics was intermeshed with profit, as it had been before the war in the anti-Japanese campaign. The mounting antagonism between business and the left was fuelled by their competition for resources that both sides drew from the frontier economy. The MCP acquired funds by taxing commercial concerns, and directly ran some centres of production in isolated areas. The KMT was also financed by the illicit trade. These rival political businesses inevitably came into conflict, particularly from mid-1947 as both of them became short of funds. The political stakes were raised further by another problem faced by Chinese capital: labour shortage, to which both the squatter and 'black-market' economy contributed dramatically. Chinese employers reorganised. The largest sector, the Chinese tin mines, were, in some ways, in a better position to resume production than their European counterparts, as they possessed more rudimentary technology that required less rehabilitation work. However, rehabilitation loans were more generous to European than to Chinese concerns. The smaller Chinese mines were under particular pressure and a number of them folded. New levels of mechanisation were needed to compete in the post-war market. Labour costs had to be kept down.[94] In November 1946 a Malayan Mining Employers' Association was founded, dominated by KMT figures such as H.S. Lee and Lau Pak Khuan.[95] Whilst the smaller *towkays* of the hinterland were less successful in combining to represent their interest than their European counterparts, they resorted increasingly to 'extra-legal' means to reclaim control over their labourers.[96] The obvious place to turn was to the Kuomintang and its strong-arm auxiliaries.

One of the most volatile conflicts of the post-war years was the contest between the MCP and KMT and the resurgent Triads. The KMT responded to the MCP challenge in the countryside by opening branches in Communist strongholds like Batu Arang, and by sponsoring parallel social organisations in the town to offset Communist influence – in early 1948 battles for control of schools in Penang reached a crescendo.[97] In 1948 the KMT still boasted a large membership, as Table 1 illustrates. Sixty per cent of the Chinese clubs in Singapore were reported by the security service to be under its control, as well as many Chinese Chambers of Commerce. The KMT

---

[93] *Min Sheng Pau*, 1.2.1946; 21.12.1946.   [94] Loh, *Beyond the tin mines*, pp. 66–74.
[95] 'Minutes of the inaugural meeting of the MMEA held at Ipoh 23.11.1946', MU Labour/ 111/47.
[96] M. R. Stenson, *Industrial conflict in Malaya: prelude to the Communist revolt of 1948* (London, 1970), pp. 194–7.
[97] MSS/PIJ/1/1948.

Table 1 *KMT membership, March 1948*[98]

Region	No. branches	No. members
Singapore	23	5,000
Johore	25	2,190
Negri Sembilan	1	400
Malacca	19	1,315
Selangor	21	2,446
Perak	83	5,547
Kedah	10	1,010
Penang & P.W.	19	3,121
Pahang	12	5,161
Trengganu	4	1,000
Kelantan	2	500
Total	219	27,690

launched an offensive to seize control of isolated rural areas. This was a continuation of the wartime friction between the rival sections of the resistance. Marginal populations were caught in the middle of these feuds, to which the Triads introduced a new level of violence. The history of this is murky, and for evidence we must draw on the reports of colonial specialists who saw the 'secret society complex' as a dark elemental force within Chinese society. They feared that after the war the Triads had become more powerful than at any time in the preceding twenty years. As the ancient rivalry between *Hung* and *Han* societies was perpetuated in Malaya, it seemed that the *Hung* had become linked to the KMT and the *Han* to the MCP. The location of guerrilla strongholds during the war – the KMT in Grik and the MPAJA in Sungei Siput and most of Johore – reflected the territoriality of the rival Triads.[99] The *Ang Bin Hoey* Triad, it seems, had originally been allied to the MPAJA and had helped supply its organisation. However, plans to amalgamate in 1945 had created ruptures, and the society began to work against the MCP, 'not necessarily for political reasons, although its sympathies, if any, are with the KMT'. The *Ang Bin Hoey*, under its president Teoh Teik Chye, applied for registration in Penang as a mutual help society – there were reports of mass initiations at Balik Pulau on the island – and the break with the MCP came to a head after an *Ang Bin Hoey* man gave evidence in a trial of an ex-MPAJA man. The Penang MCP set up a 'Black Face Society' to counter anti-MCP Triads and a cycle of murders began in the town. Conflict over racketeering in Penang led to the inclusion of some KMT men as office-holders in the *Ang Bin Hoey* and the organisation spread its wings through Province Wellesley, Kedah and Perak – bringing together many *Hung* societies that claimed the *Ang Bin Hoey* as a mother lodge. Conflict was especially pronounced in Sitiawan and Pangkor. It was less an

[98] Supplement to MSS/PIJ/8/1947.
[99] J. D. Dalley to H. P. Bryson, 5.2.1965, BAM papers.

ideological conflict, than an attempt to counter MCP domination of these traditionally *Han* areas. However, there was a 'pseudo–mystical' basis to the struggle in that the 'righteousness' spoken of in Triad ritual was directly challenged by the Communist doctrine of the MCP. The British feared that an all-out civil war against the MCP might be initiated, that would spill over into violence against the new constitution and against the Malays. 'This,' the Secretary for Chinese Affairs, W. L. Blythe, concluded, 'would be quite in keeping with the Triad doctrine of righteousness and justice and opposition to alien domination.'[100] Blythe blamed the conflict on the liberalisation of the Malayan Spring. It had, he reported, created an attitude that 'if under the new scheme of government any society is to be permitted to get control of the population, that position rightfully belongs to the Triad and not to Communists'. Although many KMT leaders were heads of *Ang Bin Hoey*, this did not mean that the *Ang Bin Hoey* was a creature of the KMT. Triad was 'something more fundamental and far-reaching' and would always maintain its independent existence. As the President of the *Ang Bin Hoey* told the police:

> If the Triad brotherhood is not allowed to exist all the Chinese shopkeepers will be forced to join the Kuomintang. If the *Ang* Brotherhood is not allowed to exist why are the Communists? The *Ang* Brotherhood is far less dangerous than the Third International. In fact its aims are good, and it will help the government. Not so the Communists.

The KMT realised that the society had powerful political potential, and, as cover, *Ang* men joined the KMT. The British feared that the distinction between Triad and political party was intolerably blurred. The most violent manifestation of these dark struggles was the minor war that flared up in the Dindings between the MCP and the KMT and their Triad allies. The troubles evolved out of labour troubles within the fishing industry on Pangkor Island. The *Ang Bin Hoey* was used by KMT-inclined *towkays* as a strong arm to break up leftist unions, who, *towkays* feared, would buy boats and go into competition with their erstwhile employers.[101] As one Chua Koon Eng, a party to the complex negotiations which resulted from such an incident, asked: 'Are we to discuss the question between employer and labour, or the question between one faction and another? . . . I remember ten years ago this island had no troubles at all, because of increased number in factions and associations, troubles have exploded.'[102]

Violence spread throughout Perak; both parties directed their energies to securing a network of secret society support. The Triads, for their part, resented the 'unchallenged supremacy which the Communists and their satellite organisations had obtained in these areas, a supremacy akin to that of the old Triad societies'.[103] Chinese

---

[100] HQ Malaya Cmmd, WIR, No 27, 10.5.1946; W. L. Blythe, 'Triad, Ang Bin Hoey and Kuomintang in Malaya', 22.1.1947, CO537/2139.

[101] W. L. Blythe, *The impact of Chinese secret societies in Malaya: a historical study* (London, 1969), pp. 380–4; MSS/PIJ/9/1947.

[102] *Min Sheng Pau*, 25.11.1946.   [103] Blythe, 'Triad, Ang Bin Hoey, and Kuomintang'.

employers were increasingly mobilising the KMT and its allies to recover their authority and the violence escalated.

Once the British saw the evasions and obstinacy of the cultivators as part of a wider criminal enterprise, the commitment to enforce land and forest law was pressed home with urgency. Statutes were examined to see if they allowed for the burning of crops and property on State land. Imprisonment was seen as the only deterrent, backed up by banishment even for a second offence. By early 1947 squatters were warned not to plant more tapioca. Its cultivation was prohibited from late August, and forest officers began pulling it up.[104] In the vast squatter domain of Sungei Siput, prosecutions of farmers without a TOL began in earnest in September and October 1947 – in December alone there were 151 prosecutions.[105] It was reported in early October that forty-eight persons were arrested for making fresh clearings in Kroh Reserve alone.[106] A Chinese land bailiff was appointed in Kuala Kangsar and Upper Perak to counter the squatters' hostility to the Malay forest guards. In his first two months of duty he earned over $600 in fines.[107] An estimated 2,600 families, occupying 5,500 acres of land, were given notice in January 1948 to quit by the end of March, and by May suasion had reduced numbers to around 1,100 families, mostly in Piah, Bintang Hijau, Plus and Korbu.[108] One forest officer commented of Hockchu squatters in Raja Hitam reserve that 'this area is becoming more civilised – most of the women now wear *bajus* and even run away if a stranger meets them with only a pair of pants on'.[109] By June 1948 the situation was reported to be improving with little clearing of new land; although in May large areas of tapioca still remained.[110] These administrative successes in mid-1948 did not succeed in reducing tension. In the Rangkup area, there were serious confrontations between cultivators and forest officials who began to pull up their tapioca in early May 1948.[111] The Chinese still 'held land laws in utter contempt'. Officials suspected a conspiracy to ferment disorder. In Jelebu, for example, it was believed that the MCP had taken the trouble to destroy the Land Office records during the interregnum.[112] Cases were reported where frail and impoverished old ladies were able to pay fines of $200. They were, it was observed, 'pawns in a bigger game'. The District Officer in Kuala Kangsar suggested that the events that precipitated the declaration of the Emergency – the murder of three European planters in Sungei Siput – followed from this pattern of resistance. The primary target, a manager called Allison, had been involved in a long strike but had

---

[104] For example, Grant diary, 25.1.1947, 27.1.1947, 28.10.1947.
[105] Enclosures in KKLO/262/47, KKLO/210/47, KKLO/6/47.
[106] R. C. Bernard to State Forest Officer, 8.10.1947, PK.SEC/2283/47.
[107] DO Kuala Kangsar, minute, 8.6.1948, PK.SEC/1006/47; to State Secretary, Perak, 14.5.1948, PK.SEC/2004/47.
[108] 'Annual Report, 1948, Kuala Kangsar Forest District', KKFO/47/48.
[109] Diary of G. I. Ironside, 15.2.1947, DF/372/46.   [110] Grant diary, 6.5.1948.
[111] *Min Sheng Pau*, 12.5.1948; D. Speldewinde, 'Pulling out of tapioca in Compt. 16, Bikam, and Compt. 2, Changkat Jong', PK.SEC/830/48.
[112] C. E. Howe, 'A few memories as DO Jelebu, Negri Sembilan, May 1948 – November 1950', Heussler Papers.

not been warned of any violence; the motive for the killing, he believed, was the eviction of squatters from nearby estates. The man sentenced to death for the crime, Wong Kim Wah, was ex-Secretary of the Rubber Tappers Union of Sungei Siput, and worked on a nearby estate at Karai at the time. 'We only realised a few days later that this incident was much more than banditry of the sort that had been occurring in Johore in previous months, when we discovered that a large proportion of the young Chinese had disappeared from the Chinese mining settlements.'[113]

There were other signals of co-ordination. An article in a Communist periodical on 'The Peasants' Struggle in Perak', lauded the resistance of the Sungei Siput Peasants' Union to the forest workers pulling up their crops, and declared that the squatters had been told to increase their production in preparation for an impending crisis.[114] However, this tension on the periphery could only develop into a more general challenge to the colonial state if there were ways in which this solidarity could express itself more widely. Where there were close links between this informal cultivation and the formal labour of the estates and mines – as in Sungei Siput and parts of Johore where levels of violence on estates were at their highest – unsettled conditions on the forest fringe could spill out into industrial upheaval. The resources of the migrant cultivator lay at the heart of employer's difficulties in controlling labour. Endemic violence was at its height in areas where Chinese employers were calling in KMT and Triad allies to enforce their economic dominance. In later sections we shall examine the ways in which, by late 1947 and early 1948, these connections were bringing conflicts to a head. It is important to note that already, before any formal revolt had begun, rural terror was becoming a burden to be borne internally by these pioneer Chinese, and this, in time, led the Malayan revolution, prematurely, to eat its own.

The sickle and the crescent moon

The anger of squatters was provoked by the colonial state's determination to uphold pre-war controls on land. The land in question was marginal hill forest, and because there was little place else for the squatters to go, there were great obstacles to their establishing common cause with the predominantly Malay cultivators of the settled lowlands. Ethnic and political tensions apart, their agrarian troubles were of a different order. However, there were points at which their problems overlapped. For the Malay cultivator, as for the Chinese, instability manifested itself through a crisis of leadership at a local level. Political uncertainty in the Malay kampongs was a vital dimension to the general crisis. To British officials, at the time, it was perhaps the most disturbing aspect of the whole situation. The nightmare of communal disorder was a symptom of this. The custodial relationship between the rural Malay and the government was under great stress. The post-war problem, as the British understood it, was an administrative one: a need to bolster local government in the countryside, to

---

[113] Luckham, 'Notes on my career'.
[114] *MCP Review*, No. 2, May 1948, reported in MSS/PIJ/10/1948.

uphold the moral authority and natural leadership of the *penghulu*. In practice, however, the *penghulu* had ceased to speak for a coherent local community.[115] In Perak, it was charged that, at the time of grave communal crisis, the *penghulus* had not played their part in informing the government of anti-Chinese activities, particularly of the *parang-panjang* gangs.[116] Alternative institutions were weak: the various loosely constituted councils and consultative boards were 'highly organised "civic" islands in the midst of an ocean of an almost feudal and authoritarian system'.[117] One solution was to grant *mukim*, or parish, councils a more comprehensive sphere of influence. This echoed the urban initiative: elected local committees were to embrace the economic, political and social welfare of their neighbours, and educate a prospective electorate in the proper use of their vote. Although *mukim* councils were originally a Malay preserve, in Perak the Sultan argued that they should include non-Malays to integrate customary and territorial authority and reduce communal tensions.[118] However, attempts to appoint *ketua China* in the squatter stronghold of Sungei Siput broke down due to the lack of willing, and suitable, candidates.[119] In Selangor, Malays were the most vocal members of the councils, although Chinese representatives also attended, and matters relating to illicit occupations of State land and encroachments on Malay reservations figured prominently in the business of the day. In Kelantan, where they were long established, *mukim* councils were held each month and a *penghulus'* conference discussed matters that arose from them.[120] However, there were fierce protests from the Malay Nationalist Party at the appointment of Chinese *ketuas* in Jasin, Negri Sembilan, and resentment at the implication that Malay *penghulus* were not executing their duties effectively.[121] As an attempt to draw the non-Malay population under the authority of the *penghulu*, *mukim* councils worked best in areas where there was 'a homogeneous population mostly engaged in the same type of work'. For this reason they were more effective in Kelantan than in Negri Sembilan, in spite of the latter's larger Chinese community.[122] As a democratic prototype the *mukim* councils proved a disappointment. They were inhibited by the need to acknowledge, in Negri Sembilan and elsewhere, an entrenched tribal hierarchy, 'jealous of any innovation which they consider may detract from the importance of

---

[115] Paul H. Kratoska, 'Penghulus in Perak and Selangor: the rationalization and decline of a traditional Malay office', *JMBRAS*, 57, 2 (1984), 47.

[116] 'Minutes of Penghulus' meeting, Kuala Kangsar District held on 3.1.1946', KKLO/640/46.

[117] DO Dindings, 'Formation of District Councils in the State of Perak', 22.3.1948, PK.SEC/995/48.

[118] 'Racial Harmony Councils' had already been established in Perak to clear the atmosphere of rumour and uncertainty which characterised many communal disturbances, Private Secretary to the Governor to P.A.S.(B), MU/658/46.

[119] J. Jones, minute, 23.6.1947, KKLO/758/46.

[120] RC Selangor to Chief Secretary, 17.1.1947; RC Kelantan, to Deputy Chief Secretary, 9.12.1946, MU/658/46.

[121] *Malaya Tribune*, 19.9.1947.

[122] W. A. Gordon-Hall to Chief Secretary, 7.12.1946; 'Minutes of RCs' conference, King's House, Kuala Lumpur, 1.8.1947', NS.SEC/1550/45.

the customary system'.[123] Plans for direct elections in some areas were aborted by the outbreak of the Emergency. Officials complained that the *rakyat* saw councils less as an inspiration to self-help, than as a vehicle to extract concessions and material aid from the government, and when their demands were not met they generated a dangerous sense of futility. 'I feel,' one District Officer concluded, 'that we should beware of forcing the pace in "democracy" as we did with trade unionism.'[124]

Other vehicles for peasant mobilisation emerged outside of the framework of British administration. Many were local in compass. In Tanjong Karang, an agricultural scheme subject to peculiar administrative attention, there was 'a chain of incipient local self-government', with committees at the different levels of settlement and a Padi Area Advisory Board at its apex. In addition, autonomous expressions of self-help had evolved: planters organised 'padi-saving' co-operatives based around the mosques, erected schools and other works. Their predominantly Javanese members possessed scruples about government pressure to deposit the proceeds of sold padi in the Post Office Savings Bank, an investment which they felt to be unacceptable under Islamic law. Local institutions and government co-operatives kept their distance from one another.[125] Such initiatives reflected a more general mood. There was a peninsular-wide movement to revive the prestige of the Malay community through educational uplift, of which the erection of *sekolah rakyat* – people's schools – by rural communities was a central feature.[126] The post-war years saw the formation of a range of associations amongst Malay schoolteachers and *ulama*. Many of them came to the fore in the struggle against the Malayan Union. In the aftermath of their triumph, it was unclear what political trajectory they would follow. Much has been written on the confusing panoply of associations that emerged within Malay politics in this period.[127] The main 'parties' were themselves loose coalitions and not yet subject to strict collective discipline. They recruited adherents, generously distributed membership cards, but, with the exception of the MCP which recruited some Malay cadres, it is perhaps misleading to think of the associations as 'parties' in the sense of those that were later to emerge. This was Malaya's 'age in motion' in which individual leaders began to mobilise large bodies of opinion, often in experimental ways. Many of the associations were known by dynamic acronyms of Malay words such as 'fire', 'beware', 'the plan', and their leaders sought to introduce

---

[123] J. M. Gullick to Deputy Chief Secretary, 16.5.1947; 'DO Kuala Pilah's Annual Report for 1947', *ibid.*

[124] DO Seremban, memorandum, 7.1.1948; DO Kuala Pilah, 'Mukim Councils', 19.8.1949; DO Jelebu, minute, 10.4.1949, *ibid.*

[125] 'Meeting of Tanjong Karang Padi Area Advisory Board', 4.8.1948, 21.9.1948, 18.11.1948, SEL.SEC/196/48.

[126] Abdul Aziz Mat Tom, 'Persokolahan Melayu, 1945–48: satu manifestasi semangat perjuangan Melayu', Khoo Kay Kim and Mohd. Fadzil Othman (eds.), *Pendidikan di Malaysia: dahulu dan sekarang* (Kuala Lumpur, 1980), pp. 140–64.

[127] An introduction is Khoo Kay Kim, 'The Malay left 1945–1948: a preliminary discourse', *Sarjana*, 1 (1981), 167–91.

new kinds of political language, often by a rich, even theatrical, manipulation of old symbolism.[128]

In 1946, it was an open question whether UMNO would survive beyond the crisis that had given it its birth. After the demise of the Malayan Union, its component elements were slow to show signs of submerging themselves into the larger organisation. Saberkas in Kedah, for example, held on to its separate identity; in Perak and in Johore, a variety of distinct state associations survived. Central direction was weak. Many of the State associations were led by Malay high officials who were not true *anak tempatan*, or sons of the States they represented. The MNP began its trajectory as a party within UMNO's Malay Congress, but it left the Congress in January 1946 when its youth wing API, adopting the cry 'defeat or fame', walked out over the deeply symbolic issue of UMNO's refusal to adopt the flag of the freedom struggle of Indonesia.[129] Connections, conceived before the war, and energised during the occupation, spawned a number of political circles that overlapped in many places. For example, in Chapter 1 we noted that some of the first associations to emerge after the war were among Indonesian settlers in support of the new Republic, in particular the *Pembantu* (later *Persatuan*) *Indonesia Merdeka* (PIM) which appeared throughout Malaya from November 1945 and spawned its own youth subsidiaries; the *Pertubuhan Perpaduan Rakyat Kalimantan Malaya* (PERKAM), formed in areas of Banjarese settlement; and the *Persatuan Kurinchi Peranakan Malaya* (PEKRAP). In addition, in Singapore an Indonesia-minded *Gerakan Angkatan Muda* (GERAM) was created by the journalists Abdul Aziz Ishak and Abdul Samad Ismail. In addition to migrants, a vast body of displaced Javanese and Sumatrans remained in Malaya in which the parties of the Republic, from the *Masjoemi* to the *Partai Komunis Indonesia*, found a reflected image. These associations affiliated to groups such as the MNP and PUTERA, but retained their own identity. The same might be said of the various leftist groupings, and the *alumni* of the religious schools of the peninsula. Into all of these networks the MCP attempted to extend its influence. The Malayan Spring was a period of learning by doing. Periods of co-operation would be initiated and would be broken when political objections and personal differences became insurmountable. Out of this process new, more ideologically distinct, Malay political bodies began to emerge.

The crisis of leadership at the grass-roots of Malay society immediately absorbed the political class of 1945, especially the MNP. It was spurred to this by the sense of drift within UMNO after the end of the Malayan Union agitation. To Dr Burhanuddin, UMNO's repeated calls for unity were 'a guise to dupe the people', which obscured its lack of economic and social programmes.[130] To capitalise on the situation, the MNP launched a spectrum of offshoots that reflected the diverse

---

[128] Cf. Takashi Shiraishi, *An age in motion: popular radicalism in Java, 1912–1926* (Ithaca, 1990).

[129] Ahmad Boestamam, *Carving the path to the summit* (Athens, Ohio, 1979), pp. 67–72.

[130] *Malaya Tribune*, 10.3.1947.

sources of its inspiration. It had distinct regional strengths: in Perak, Pahang, and under its independently minded leadership in Malacca. The party was weakest where Dato Onn's influence was at its strongest: in Johore and Negri Sembilan.[131] In the early days of civil rule, the most dynamic of the subsidiaries was the youth wing – the *Angkatan Pemuda Insaf* (API). API was itself, in theory, divided into several wings. The *Barisan Pemuda Merah* developed the Pan-Asiatic spirit through athletics, scouting, guerrilla techniques, business and agriculture. The *Barisan Pemuda Puteh*, was a similar organisation for sons of fishermen. *Pelupor* was recruited from these bodies as a supervisory section. A final section, *Pertahanian Tanah Ayer* (PETA) was seen as an elite corps, given the task of educating the intelligentsia in eastern thought in preparation for the emergence of a militant movement to challenge the west.[132] API was strongest where the MNP was strong, although it opened its own branches elsewhere, and operated independently in a way that often embarrassed the MNP moderates. From the end of 1946 a struggle was underway to mobilise the rural population, for which API and its allies sponsored a range of self-help initiatives. Many were economic in character. A Selangor Malay Chamber of Commerce was formed and campaigned for a place at the Kuala Lumpur Central Market.[133] The MNP in Malacca also established a Malay Trading Association. Its participation in *pekan* was seen as a stepping-stone to the creation of larger businesses.[134] Its communal farming scheme for underemployed kampong youths in Malacca sought to demonstrate, in the words of one leader, Mohammed Isa bin Haji Taib, 'that the Malay youths are not as *tidak apa* as in the old days. The policeman's uniform does not attract the Malay boy from the kampong any more than does sitting at the wheel of the cars of *tuan besars*.'[135]

The main attempt to orchestrate these activities into a concerted peasant's movement was the *Barisan Tani*. The New Democratic Youth League had already attempted in mid-1946 to draw the MNP, API and PIM into the orbit of its Malay section, the *Barisan Pemuda Bahru*.[136] The *Barisan Tani*, however, was formed under the auspices of the MNP in Selangor in November 1946 to attract the more conservative Malay peasant. A pilot scheme – the North Kedah Peasants' Association – was launched directly under API to develop a system of communal farming 'promising ultimate freedom from quit rents and royalties'. The *Barisan Tani* claimed in mid-1947 to have 1,000 members in Kedah, 1,400 in Trengganu and 50 in Selangor: the *Malaya Tribune* gave the total as 8,700. It was not organised on the same communal lines as the North Kedah society but had a similar flag of the crossed *changkol* and rake within a sickle, with two ears of padi below the sickle. Branches were formed in former API strongholds, often under Indonesian leadership.[137] A conference in Kajang on 6–10 July 1947, addressed by PMFTU and MCP speakers,

[131] WIS No. 17 up to 23.2.1946, CO537/1581.   [132] MSS/PIJ/8/1946.
[133] *Majlis*, 23.1.1946.   [134] *Warta Negara*, 22.4.1946.
[135] *Malaya Tribune*, 12.5.1947.   [136] MSS/PIJ/9/1946.
[137] MSS/PIJ/12/1947; HQ Malaya Cmd., 'Fortnightly intelligence Review, No. 60, w. e. 8.7.1947', CO/717/164/52795/47; *Malaya Tribune*, 10.9.1947.

demanded urgent government intervention to ameliorate the conditions of the peasantry.[138] Although it enjoyed the patronage of the MNP, the *Barisan Tani* was maintained as a separate movement. The cadres and aims of the two bodies, however, corresponded closely. The *Barisan Tani*'s utterances became increasingly anti-imperialist, anti-capitalist and republican in tone. As Ustaz Abdul Rab Tamini argued at its conference at Jeram, Kedah on 25–27 April 1948:

> If there were no *Mentri-mentri Besar* in Malaya we would still eat and live, so it is to the peasant that we should give our respect, not to the *Mentri-mentri Besar*. . . The peasant has overthrown the Malayan Union. Have no fear. Let us be called Communists and so on. We are fighting for our lives and will do so with great determination.[139]

To the journalist S. Rajaratnam, the peasants' front was a bridge between the worlds of the town and country; it reflected the fact that 'many of the urban workers are themselves peasants who have left their fields in the hope of gaining better economic rewards in plantation or in urban enterprises'. Urban workers maintained close links to the kampong and the outlook of the village was changing as a result. 'The Malay peasant,' he declared, 'has been brought into the mainstream of modernism.'[140] Certainly, it was an attempt to find common cause between the urban networks of the Malay intellectuals and the peasantry. However, by early 1948, although progress was reported throughout the country, in Kedah significant obstacles arose: an inexperienced and divided leadership; police harassment, and the opposition of *penghulus* who accused the organisation of being pro-Chinese.[141] At the very period when British concern at endemic unrest in the countryside was growing, the contest for control of the Malay heartlands gained momentum.

It was API, and not the Chinese left, that provoked the British government into passing legislation to narrow the parameters of political activity. The British were obsessed by the existence of secret inner organisations within API, and banned its quasi-military drilling. The trial for sedition of its leader Ahmad Boestamam illustrates the difficulties the British faced in confronting the new languages of Malay politics. The prosecution case was mired in semantic confusion. It rested on whether Boestamam's slogan, '*Merdeka dengan darah*' – 'independence through blood' – invoked revolution, or merely suggested self-sacrifice. The court interpreter admitted that there was 'mistranslation' in the prosecution submission. However, the colonial expert, W. Linehan, overruled him. The API had the distinction of being the first political party to be banned in post-war Malaya.[142] Boestamam himself chose to pay a fine rather than go to prison, a move that tarnished his credentials as a firebrand. However, he continued to be courted by both the MCP and British intelligence.

---

[138] Musa Ahmad, President, All-Malaya Peasants' Union, 'Blue-print for the solution of the food problem', 10.7.1947, CO717/164/52795/47.

[139] Cited in MSS/PIJ/9/1948.

[140] S. Rajaratnam, 'Peasants and workers unite', *Malaya Tribune*, 28.7.1947.

[141] MSS/PIJ/6/1948; MSS/PIJ/9/1948.

[142] *Malaya Tribune*, 20.3.1947; Gent to Creech Jones, 24.2.1947; 1.7.1947, CO537/2151.

Others attempted to revive API under a different name. The most important new body was the *Ikatan Pemuda Tanah Ayer* (PETA), Youth League of the Fatherland, formed on 28 September 1947. British secret policemen saw it as a revival of the elite *Pelupor* and PETA sections of API.[143] However, it was somewhat different in inspiration from its predecessors, and its leadership was in the hands of Malays with a strong MCP connection, such as its President, Wahi Anuar. PETA continued to sponsor subsidiaries at a local level. In November 1947, for example, it was reported that a branch had been formed at Ulu Langat, Selangor, and that the Malay Peasants' Union was planning co-operative stores, *rakyat* schools, and an Islamic co-operative society, a *Syarikat Persatuan Islam*. These ventures were dismissed as 'castles in the air' by the local administration: 'bait' to attract the more 'conservative' Malay peasant into the ranks of the *Barisan Tani*. This organisation flooded government offices with petitions for assistance, such as in the provision of irrigation and seeds, and in the battle against pests.[144] A trading enterprise, *Syarikat Tani*, was launched with a capital of $10,000 and the purchase of a mill. When officials enquired about the legality of the move, the owner of the mill in question, one Haji Ahmad Marjono, professed to be 'most indignant at what appears to be an attempt by the *Sharikat Tani* to make political propaganda out of his mill and to "reap where they have not sown"'.[145] Meanwhile a rival *Barisan Pemuda* toured kampongs advising cultivators on health, religion, and co-operation.[146] The District Officer was pressed to make sense out of all these ventures: 'The so-called leaders of these organisations have called themselves in different ways since the API was banned. They are now variously called the *Kaum Tani* Peasants' Union and the more recent term used was "PETA" . . . Their activities are a nuisance value to all and the *Barisan Pemuda*'s object is to check this tendency as much as possible.'[147] New groups were emerging to resist the radical organisations. MNP collaboration with MCP front groups in Trengganu had built up so strong an influence that UMNO sent a debating team to tour the mosques to counteract it.[148] These local organisations spawned great controversy in the Malay press. The high demand for rubber meant that many spontaneous co-operatives were formed to by-pass the middlemen. There was wide criticism in the Malay press of many of these *kedai syarikat*, especially in Ulu Langat, and the British complained that the adverse public reaction retarded the development of 'legitimate' government co-operatives.[149]

As the struggle for control of the kampongs gained momentum the outlines of a contest between 'left' and 'right' became more pronounced. Certainly, the Malayan press was beginning to speak in these terms.[150] Suspicions of the leftist connections of

---

[143] MSS/PIJ/18/1947.
[144] *Utusan Melayu*, 22.11.1947; DO Ulu Langat, minute, 2.12.1947, RC.SEL/1126/47.
[145] *Majlis*, 2.11.1948; D. Headly to State Secretary, 18.11.1948, SEL.SEC/1819/48.
[146] MSS/PIJ/8/1947 and *passim*.
[147] DO Ulu Langat, minute, 15.12.1947, RC.SEL/1474/47.   [148] MSS/PIJ/6/1947.
[149] 'A matter relating to some Malay co-operative shops', *Majlis*, 3.12.1947; J. G. Crawford, Director of Co-operation to Director of Public Relations, 27.1.1948.
[150] Khoo, 'The Malay left'.

the MNP had been voiced at an early stage. The MNP had more success in the west than in the northeast. To the Kelantan-minded elite of Kota Bahru the MCP connection was the kiss of death to the MNP.[151] Indeed it is important to remember that the MNP was deeply divided on lines of personality and politics, and for this reason, the establishment of branch organisations for larger political bodies can be misleading. The *Perseketuan Persetiaan Melayu Kelantan*, often taken to be a local manifestation of the MNP, contained individuals who diverged dramatically in their later careers.[152] The MCP connection was kept alive through the work of a handful of committed and energetic individuals who were present at the MNP's inception: Abdul Rashid Maidin, who was believed to control the northwestern States; Kamaralzaman bin Teh in the east coast States, and Abdullah Che Dat in the southern States and Singapore. The influence of the core MCP Malay cadres was regionally focused. Although Rashid Maidin, as well as Abdullah C. D., had cultivated an international reputation, he was from Telok Anson, and was especially active amongst the Banjarese settlers of Lower Perak. Contacts with Indonesia were another conduit for Communist influence amongst the Malays, and it was amongst settlers of Indonesian origin that the party had most appeal. Sutan Djenain was active in Malaya until his repatriation in 1948. He attempted to form a Malay Communist Party, separate from the MCP, and when these efforts floundered in 1946 he sponsored a Malay National Socialist Party in Selangor, and joined with Abdullah C. D. in founding the Selangor Malay Labour Union. However, in March 1948 the Malays of the MCP openly broke with him.[153] Ideological disputes played a role in this, and through Javanese intermediaries the influence of Alimin was particularly strong. We can glimpse some of these disputes through the *Balai Pustaka Tanah Ayer Melayu* – based around a caucus of MCP and PETA figures meeting most frequently in Temerloh, Pahang – which published left-wing pamphlets, such as the Malay works of Tan Melaka. However, one of the *Balai Pustaka*'s most important publications was a pamphlet by Alimin, 'Analyst: Alimin versus Tan Melaka', which denounced Tan Melaka as a Trotskyite, and advocated true Marxism following Marx–Engels–Lenin–Stalin, and iron discipline, at a time when Malay MCP leaders broke with the 'Trotskyite', Sutan Djenain. Anti-feudalist propaganda drives were conducted through political classes – *class politik kiri* – which met with opposition by villagers opposed to their lack of conformity with Islamic principles, even in radical strongholds like Ulu Langat.[154] The MCP adapted their approach to local conditions. Communist speakers criticised the fact that much Malay Reservation land in Kedah was fit only for house plots, and that the best land was under forest reserve.[155]

---

[151] WIS No. 17 up to 23.2.1946, CO537/1581.
[152] Khoo Kay Kim, 'Islam and politics in Kelantan', *JSEAS*, 11, 1 (1980), 187–94.
[153] Cheah Boon Kheng, *The masked comrades: a study of the Communist United Front in Malaya, 1945–48* (Singapore, 1979), pp. 62–73.
[154] MSS/PIJ/1/1948, MSS/PIJ/3/1948, MSS/PIJ/6/1948.
[155] Abdul Rasid bin Maideen reported in MSS/PIJ/12/1947.

Elsewhere the theme might be mortgages and debt.[156] Branches were set up in Selangor to capitalise on the reduction in the price of padi. However, the greatest successes were in Pahang under the leadership of Kamaralzaman bin Teh. A Malay section of the MCP was founded in Temerloh, which was also a centre of other left-wing Malay activities, and progress was reported in Kuala Pilah; *class politik kiri* were held in these areas and forty-nine Malays and Indonesians were said to be MCP members, working through a funeral and co-operative society.[157] The MCP attempted to expand its influence amongst the kampongs through the peasants' union and other youth and women's groups. Many of these subordinate associations were an attempt to build downwards a grass-roots organisation for the higher United Front structures of the AMCJA–PUTERA. It had only localised successes. Elsewhere there was robust resistance to the MCP's inroads into the villages.

A further dimension to the struggle for the allegiance of the Malay peasant came from the religious academies. In early 1946, the voice of the MNP, *Pelita Malaya*, made a case for the formation of a central religious body in Malaya: 'As things are these *ulama* are not free agents to give real benefits to the people. They are under the influence of the Rulers above them who claim to be "The shadow of God on Earth" and "Protector of Islam". So these learned men are simply ornaments of the Royal Court.'[158] This intervention reflected the interpenetration between the new genera-tion of politicians and the networks of religious schools. A central institution was Ehya al-Sharif at Gunong Semanggol in Perak. A teacher from the school, Uthman bin Hamzah, had been active in a KMM branch in Perak and had attempted to stir the modernist leadership of the school into active politics. It had contacts with Indonesian radicals such as Sutan Djenain. Dr Burhanuddin himself had been on the staff of Madrasah al-Masyhur in Penang (from whence Musa Ahmad was a graduate) and of Madrasah al-Junaid in Singapore. Many of the approaches to Islamic education that became so celebrated at Ehya al-Sharif were pioneered at Al-Masyhur.[159] Ahmad Azam, founder of the Krian branch of the KMM was a teacher at the more traditionalist Madrasah al-Masriyyah at Bukit Mertajam and Ustaz Abdul Rab Tamini and Haji Ahmad Fuad spent time there.[160] UMNO was initially successful in drawing much of the religious hierarchy into its organisation. However, when the MNP split from UMNO it managed to carry many of the more radical Islamic leaders with it.[161] They constituted one of the several ideological components to the MNP, which was a broad-based anti-colonial front. However, after an initial period of co-operation, the religious element slowly began to carve out their own path. A seminal moment for Islam and politics in Malaya came on 23 March 1947, with the foundation

---

[156] Sheikh Abdul Kadir Ma'ef to 'Brother agriculturalists', in MSS/PIJ/11/1948.
[157] MSS/PIJ/4/48, MSS/PIJ/5/1948, MSS/PIJ/8/1948.   [158] *Pelita Malaya*, 6.4.1946.
[159] Rahim bin Omar, 'Madrasah Masyhur al-Islamiyyah', in Khoo Kay Kim (ed.), *Islam di Malaysia* (Kuala Lumpur, 1979), pp. 75–85.
[160] Othman bin Bakar, 'Haji Salleh Masri: pengasas al-Masriyyah', *ibid.*, p. 72.
[161] Safie bin Ibrahim, 'The Islamic element in Malay politics in pre-independent Malaya, 1937–48', *Islamic Culture*, 52, 3 (1978), 185–95.

of the *Majlis Agama Tertinggi* – Supreme Religious Council – at an all-Malaya conference of *ulama*, chaired by Ustaz Abu Bakar, and attended by representatives of a vast range of political bodies and associations, most pivotally Dr Burhanuddin.[162] It was boycotted by the more conservative *ulama* at UMNO's instigation, although the conference dutifully raised the UMNO flag. However, it soon turned away from the party and embarked on outspoken attacks on the feudal survivals within Malay society.[163] The second MATA conference at Kuar Chempedak in Kedah on 12 July 1947 called on the Rulers to divest religious authority to the Council.[164] MATA also took upon itself responsibility for the economic uplift of the Malays, by establishing a *Pusat Perekonomian Melayu* (PERKIM) at Gunong Semanggol, which incorporated a wide range of business associations, even some UMNO office-holders, and undertook to explore the causes of Malay economic backwardness and to 'demand special protective rights to safeguard the economic stability of the Malay people'.[165] A forerunner of this organisation was the Malay Co-operative Bank of Penang, formed under the auspices of the Penang Malay Association by religious teachers, businessmen and *penghulus* which issued shares at a dollar each, to provide loans to farmers, fishermen and small traders.[166] Tremendous press excitement surrounded PERKIM and its related initiatives, such as the Ipoh-based Ra'ayat Trading Company and the Kuala Lumpur-based Malay National Banking Corporation, which was held by *Utusan Melayu* to be 'the basis of Malay economic revival'. However, it was heavily under-subscribed and employed European managers and accountants to compensate for its founders' inexperience. It was plagued by scandal and mismanagement. In late 1947 its managing director, Kuala Lumpur lawyer Maa'rof bin Haji Zakaria, was found hanging from a tree.[167] Despite the difficulties, these broad-based economic and educational concerns generated a position from which a loose coalition of left-wing organisations might be accommodated to political Islam. A guiding spirit behind this move was Abdullah C. D. 'The backwardness of our race,' he argued, 'has been due primarily to lack of proper education which is directed by the imperialists whose policy has been to afford us only "colonial education".'[168] The possibility of radicalising the *sekolah rakyat* arose when Ustaz Abu Bakar suggested that *zakat* be paid to finance them. MCP established direct links with the 'People's Education

[162] Nabir bin Haji Abdullah, *Maahad Il Ihya Asshariff Gunung Semanggol, 1934–59* (Kuala Lumpur, 1979) is a detailed history of this insitution.
[163] Alias Mohamed, 'PAS platforms: development and change, 1951–86', Ph.D. Thesis, Universiti Malaya, 1989), pp. 13–17.
[164] *Utusan Melayu*, 16.7.1947.
[165] Setia Usaha Agong, *Pusat Perekonomian Melayu* to Creech Jones, 1.4.1947, CO717/164/52795/47; A. J. Stockwell, *British policy and Malay politics during the Malayan Union experiment, 1945–1948* (Kuala Lumpur, 1979), pp. 138–9.
[166] 'At a meeting held on 19.1.1946 at the Al-Mashoor Islamiah, Tek Soon Street, Penang to discuss the formation of an institution along the lines of a People's Bank', Coop/238/46.
[167] *Utusan Melayu*, 29.3.1947; Gent to Creech Jones, 24.11.1947, CO717/164/52795/47; *Malaya Tribune*, 8.12.1947.
[168] Cited in MSS/PIJ/18/1947.

Council' of MATA – the *Lembaga Pendidikan Rakyat*, founded in Kedah in September 1947 – and at the MATA conference of 13–16 March 1948 the Council agreed to collaborate with the left-wing Malay parties. Yet dissatisfaction with the MNP as an instrument of Islamic revival and disenchantment with MATA as a political force led to the coalescing of disaffected elements into the *Hizbul Muslimin*, or Muslim Party, in early 1948. Its President was Ustaz Abu Bakar and, turning to the Indonesian *Masjoemi* for inspiration, it took as its central aim the establishment of an Islamic state. Although the *Hizbul Muslimin* was to meet with an untimely end, many of its leaders, notably Uthman bin Hamzah, Muhammad Asri bin Haji Muda and Abdul Rab Tamini, were to continue their association into the Pan-Malayan Islamic Party in the 1950s.

Many of these political connections were undoubtedly exploratory, experimental and achieved political consequence only in certain localities. However, by 1948 they were provoking a fierce response from both the British and from UMNO. 'We saw the danger coming from the jungle in 1945,' Dato Onn warned an audience at Tangkak, Johore, 'and today we see a similar danger descending from the mountain under the cloak of religion.' 'The mountain' was a clear reference to Gunong Semanggol.[169] Onn's fears were corroborated by British officials who saw these social organisations as part of 'an intensive drive to spread Communism among the Malays'.[170] During the course of 1948, the Malayan Security Service became obsessed with the revival of Malay secret societies and the importation of the ideologies of the *Partai Komunis Indonesia* and the *Masjoemi* into the politics of the peninsula. The British equated the Malay left with Indonesian subversion; its leaders were identified with smuggling and illegal immigration. The Security Service shadowed peripatetic radicals such as Zulkifli Ouni, a Perak man, ex-MPAJA and *Tentera Republik Indonesia*, who returned to Malaya in October 1946 and took a lead in organising API demonstrations.[171] Certainly there was considerable movement between Sumatra and Malaya. Smuggling was a political act. By running the Dutch boycott, Singapore Arab merchants, Malay radicals and Chinese traders attracted by the unregulated trade, came together to support the Indonesian Republic through the dangerous inter-island trade.[172] Leading Malay unionists in Singapore, Abdullah bin Haris and Bizar bin Ahmad, were of Batak and Minang origins respectively. Traditional points of the migratory routes across the Straits of Malacca were hotbeds of radicalism, places such as Malacca and Balik Pulau in Penang. Shamsuddin bin Salleh, for example, a PKI contact working amongst the Malay Harbour Board Workers Union at Muar, passed as an itinerant pedlar; his colleague, Hassan bin Mahiddin, was also a hawker of toothbrushes and combs and a courier amongst Malay communists in Singapore.[173] The geography of settlement in the Malay peninsula became very significant to the

---

[169] MSS/PIJ/6/1948; Stockwell, *British policy*, p. 139.   [170] MSS/PIJ/1/1948.
[171] MSS, 'Note on Zulkifli Ounie (Ownie)', 31.7.1947, CO537/2151.
[172] Suryono Drusman, *Singapore and the Indonesian revolution, 1945–50* (Singapore, 1992), especially pp. 23–7, 45–56.
[173] MSS/PIJ/8/1948.

development of organisations such as PETA: Banjarese areas of Perak, Selangor and Johore were particularly fertile, as were others areas of concentrated Javanese and Sumatran settlement such as Temerloh and Ulu Langat. Many of the leftist propagandists were marginal men and women outside of these areas.[174] British intelligence reports mapped out a clear political geography of kampongs in Pahang largely populated by Javanese and Banjarese into which PETA had made inroads. The PETA branch in Muar, Johore, was also said to be mostly successful with Javanese rather than Malays.[175] It would seem that many PETA members did not have to negotiate the same involved *kerajaan* loyalties as did the peninsular Malays. Moreover, the organisation's successes were in areas in which peninsular associations had not yet taken a firm grip.

This was a source of strength for the Malay left, but also its fatal weakness. The closed session of the MNP Congress in Singapore in early 1948 revealed that the party was in debt to the tune of $2,000; only 40 per cent of members paid subscriptions. It was under increasing harassment from the *ketua-ketua kampong*, the Rajas and the Special Branch. The MNP had worked primarily through its subsidiaries. It was apparent to officials that the MNP's lack of independent success in its efforts to expand were forcing it closer into the arms of the Communists and honing its anti-colonialism. Certainly, it experienced a change in leadership as radicals in the party unseated Dr Burhanuddin and installed Ishak Haji Muhammad. By tendering for the support of organisations like PETA, the MCP was looking to draw MNP and ex-API members into its orbit through joint meetings and propaganda exercises. Some MNP members were resisting PETA for this very reason: the ex-President of API in Kelantan claimed that the PETA Congress was postponed because of suspicions of the Communist leanings of its leadership. When it was held in February 1948 it was revealed that although there were twenty-eight branches of PETA, in every state except Malacca, the leadership had only managed to draw 350 of an estimated 10,000 ex-API members into their ranks.[176] The role of the MCP was very overt in places. In Taiping and elsewhere, the MNP issued NDYL pamphlets and shared their offices. A Perak State Committee member of the MCP claimed that the party had spent between $50,000 and $60,000 on the formation of the MNP, and that in Ipoh money was given for the establishment of its business interests.[177] In the face of the suspicions generated by these links, the various strands of Malay radicalism that the MCP had been attempting to weave together into a unified peasants' movement began to unravel.

From the outset, MCP mobilisation of the Malays advanced under the shadow of terror. The struggle for power in the kampongs after the Pacific war contained dark undercurrents of violence. The MCP's flirtation with the Malay left led it into a

---

[174] Stockwell, *British policy*, pp. 139–40.   [175] For example, MSS/PIJ/1/1948.
[176] At this time the MNP claimed 43,020 members, a quarter of whom were in Perak, with another concentration in Pahang; 6,870 youth members and 1,490 AWAS members, *ibid.*
[177] MSS/PIJ/8/1948.

shadowy world of underground fringe organisations and secret societies. Colonial intelligence reports supplied chilling anecdotes, but shed little real insight into these chimerical militant ventures. There were stories of militarised groups undergoing training in military drill throughout Malaya; displaced Indonesians at Ayer Raja Road camp in Singapore acting as pickets in strikes and cultivating an interest in invulnerability. The MNP was compromised by links of its leaders to invulnerability cults in Singapore and Malacca, where Kiyai Haji Manahar reportedly utilised gold needle rituals to popularise the party. An imminent Third World War was a common image in the political rhetoric of the time. In Kelantan, ex-API leaders preached an impending confrontation with the British; revolution, it was said, would follow an announcement in the *Utusan Melayu* – 'Required: a man who wishes to work for the *rakyat*'. The police and Malay Regiment were expected to join this rebellion, which was said to have leaders in every State, including the followers of the invulnerability guru, Tok Janggut. The API slogan, 'independence through blood', echoed at PETA meetings. Its Kelantan leader, Hassan bin Haji Yaacob, was said to be preparing his own *jihad* against the Federation; the Kuala Besut branch announced it would rather take to the jungle with the Chinese Communists than live under the 'feudal' new constitution.[178] These confused reports were a product of a long-running cold war between the MCP, Malay extremists and the Special Branch, in which informers often indulged British apprehensions and were paid on a piece-rate for it. Couriers were often, like pedlars of invulnerability, itinerant hawkers, and both groups were hounded by the security services. MCP propaganda in rural areas, by striking an apocalyptical note, was echoing the claims of other exponents of invulnerability and this suggested to the British that a common underground front existed between them. In May and early June 1948, Ahmad Boestamam was said to have met with Rashid Maidin to outline a period of planning for insurrection that would not begin until 1950, with a provision to move sooner if the government suppressed the left. However, the return on the MCP's investment in the Malay left was unimpressive: the response in the kampongs to the insurrection was poor, although there were rumours of mobilisation of Malay secret societies and alliances with the Communists. Recruitment in Perak was said to be disappointing save around Taiping and the northern border area. In certain areas of Temerloh there were concentrations of Malay Communists. However, the Emergency declaration had left the MNP divided and without many of its most dynamic political leaders who were either compelled to take to the jungle with the MCP, or, like Ahmad Boestamam and Ishak Haji Muhammad, were rounded up by the British. The party itself was not banned. A 'Special Communiqué' issued by the surviving leadership stressed that it was 'a Party based strictly on nationalism'.[179] It has been argued that Malay radicalism has perhaps

---

[178] MSS/PIJ/3/1948, 4/1948, 5/1948.
[179] Ahmad Boestamam, Kamaralzaman bin Teh, and Zahid bin Karim were detained under the Emergency regulations. Abdul Rashid bin Maidin was arrested but sprung from a camp in Malacca. Wahi Anwar and Abdullah C. D. of the MCP, Yussof bin Salleh of PETA; Musa

never recovered from the embarrassment of the Malay left in this period.[180] Yet, however ill-fitted Malay radicalism was for the revolutionary role appointed for it by the MCP, the unease and disaffection in the Malay kampongs were central components of the rural unrest which underlaid the outbreak of the Emergency.

It has been often argued that the old middle leadership in Malay society, represented by UMNO and its component organisations, deeply sensible to the threat from the mountain, proved resilient enough to survive the challenge of the Malay left by virtue of its foothold in the administration and sway over the village authority of the *penghulu*.[181] However, the ease by which they achieved this must not be exaggerated. One of the catalysts to political conflict in the villages in the first place was the weakness of the administration of many *penghulu* and *ketua kampong* in the face of the challenges facing them. Certainly in places like Perak and Selangor, as recent local studies suggest, the power of local chieftains, their control over their clients, proved very durable. Dato Onn was at the pinnacle of his power and influence. He embodied the Malay nation, and his response to the left was undeniably a critical intervention. However, despite this in many places State elites were deeply divided; their politics highly factional. There were several Malay associations competing in Johore. Kelantanese politics bucked national trends. In the case of Trengganu, the middle and top leadership was from outside the State. The Mentri Besar, Dato Kamaruddin bin Haji Idris, was a Selangor Malay. In the long run, these circles of outsiders were a goad to local men to contest their predominance by joining UMNO. But it was only when ex-MNP men, such as future Mentri Besar Ibrahim Fikri, began to join UMNO that the history of mass local politics began.[182] Perhaps as important as the resilience of traditional leaders was the undercurrent of support from Malay schoolteachers and more conservatively inclined *ulama* for UMNO. There are few studies of such groups, but the indications are that in Kedah, for example, they played a vital role as an organised and reliable bedrock of UMNO support, given the level of influence their members exercised in rural society.[183] Faced with intense competition, UMNO took steps to strengthen itself as a political party. UMNO's main institutional framework was laid down in these years. With the initiative coming from Dato Panglima Bukit Gantang in Perak, a five-year plan to elevate the Malays was mooted, and there were attempts in the States to organise Malay Chambers of Commerce. Hussein bin Onn attempted to make UMNO Youth strong enough to

bin Ahmad of the Kaum Tani; Shamsiah Fakeh and the journalist Mokhtar bin Suleiman all took to the jungle, MSS/PIJ/13/1948.

[180] Firdaus Haji Abdullah, *Radical Malay politics: its origins and early development* (Petaling Jaya, 1985), pp. 110–40.

[181] See especially Stockwell, *British policy*, pp. 156–160.

[182] M. Kamlin, *History, politics and electioneering: the case of Terengganu* (Department of History, Universiti Malaya, Kuala Lumpur, 1977), pp. 18–21.

[183] Mohamed Nor bin Ahmad, 'Suka duka perjuangan guru2 Melayu', in *Persatuan Guru-guru Melayu Kedah, 25 Tahun* (Alor Star, 1971), pp. 131–33; Abdul Manaf bin Saad, 'Persatuan Ulama Kedah, 1365–1376H (1946–1957M)', in Khoo, *Islam di Malaysia*, pp. 148–58.

compete with API and PETA. The *Kaum Ibu UMNO* became a formidable force.[184] However these initiatives took a number of years to bear fruit. It was only in the years after 1950 that Dato Onn had the resources of the Rural and Industrial Development Authority (RIDA) at his disposal and Bukit Gantang an official committee to chart a path for Malay economic advancement. UMNO Youth only became a real fighting force after 1948, in no small part due to it being energised by refugees from the defunct MNP. The *Kaum Ibu UMNO*, the branch of the party which had perhaps demonstrated the greatest grass-roots strength, fought a long struggle for adequate recognition within the party – again incorporating former members of AWAS. UMNO would absorb many of its enemies and become a formidable political machine, but it had not done so by 1948. The processes of social reconstruction which had precipitated the political struggles of the immediate post-war period continued into the Emergency years. UMNO's triumph over its rivals in 1948 was due primarily to its capacity to exploit the British government's fears of the Malay left, amongst whom it was a bitterly held belief that the intercession of Dato Onn was responsible for the arrest of the leadership of the *Hizbul Muslimin* on the outbreak of the Emergency. A further sweep in December 1949 in Krian in Perak, led to the arrest of 107 more activists.[185] UMNO and the conservative religious hierarchy lost no time in taking advantage of the disarray of the Malay left.

The syndicalist challenge

The loosely structured 'Red Peasants' Movement' which emerged in the Malayan countryside was, in itself, an unlikely vehicle of rebellion. But it was symptomatic of the uncertainty which permeated rural life in this period. We have argued that the precipitation of violence in 1948 was related to a much wider series of power struggles than historians have hitherto accounted for. We now look to make more direct connections between this endemic violence and the origins of the Malayan Emergency. They lie in the ways in which the opening of the forest frontier had encouraged the collapse of labour discipline which fuelled the industrial disturbances in the more settled areas. In general, throughout 1946, social disruption and scarcity of labour strengthened the hand of organised workers. However, by 1947, as we noted earlier, a revival of capital was underway. It colluded with a colonial government anxious to restore stability to its internal frontier. Confrontation in the forests supercharged industrial unrest on the estates when it became apparent that the administration was working to restrict the labourer's access to alternative sources of income. These disputes were central to the politics of the Malayan Spring. Building on the displacements, food shortages and political cataclysms of the war years, highly centralised federations of trade unions, controlled by the MCP, mounted a carefully

---

[184] N. J. Funston, *Malay politics in Malaysia* (Kuala Lumpur, 1980), pp. 85–6; Ramlah Adam, *UMNO: organisasi dan kegiatan, 1945–51* (Kota Bahru, 1978).

[185] Alias, 'PAS' platforms', p. 27.

orchestrated campaign to draw together Chinese and Indian labour unions in an attempt to force the pace of the creation of new class solidarities. The British government responded by bringing industrial labour into the mainstream of administration. It sought to promote trade unions, employing a Trade Union Adviser to act as their mentor and to insulate trade unions from the new political forces that were sweeping Malaya. Their concerns were to be confined to the economic welfare of their members, and were not to embrace wider political ambitions. However, the new Asian labour leaders did not accept these narrow conditions of association. A struggle ensued which was the primary catalyst to the outbreak of the Malayan Emergency in 1948. However, as we shall see, the reason why the struggle became so elemental was because disputes on the frontier had gathered their own momentum. They shaped labour relations in the immediate post-war period in crucial ways.

The stormtide of war was slow to recede, especially on the mines and plantations of the industrial heartland of the west coast. Reports from individual rubber estates in Selangor in early 1946 paint a portrait of 'depressed and miserable' Indian labourers lacking suitable plots to grow food, cultivating small amounts of ragi on marginal land, and dependent on buying food from Chinese cultivators. Dehabilitation was universal. In inland Selangor labourers only worked a five-hour day as they were too weak for anything more. On Dominion Estate only two out of the seventy workers who had been sent to Siam had returned.[186] The President of the Selangor Estate Workers Union described 'a life of meek suffering toiling from sunrise to sunset like an automaton, day in and day out leading a life squalid, poverty-stricken, starving, without education, joy or any ray of hope to better ourselves . . . suffering mosquito, leech bites, withered by malaria, and our bones and skinny skeletons shivering in cold from lack of clothing and nourishing food, we lead on this existence'.[187] Even when consumer goods began to be available by the middle of 1946, labourers were poorly placed to deal with market fluctuations, which cuts in rice rations aggravated. Some employers, such as Harrison Barker estates, tried to provide meals or cheap broken rice, but found it hard to procure supplies. Yet even in spite of this hardship it was said that estate labourers were better off than urban workers in Selangor.[188] Similar conditions prevailed in Perak. Inspection reports in early 1947 reported that the effects of wartime dispersal of labour had still not been remedied; in many cases less than half the acreage was being tapped and much of the rest was occupied by Chinese squatters supplying the towns.[189]

The paternalism of the inter-war years had collapsed. In the 1920s and 1930s Malaya has possessed what was perhaps the most regulated labour regime in the British Empire. In 1942 this had been swept away. In September 1947, a columnist in

[186] Enclosures on EACL.KL/20/45.
[187] C. S. V. Krishna Moorthi, 24.3.1947, J. A. Thivy Papers, PUM.
[188] 'Report on Labour conditions for May 1946, inland districts of Selangor', EACL.KL/20/45.
[189] Enclosures on MU Labour/83/47/Pt I.

the Malayan rubber industry journal, *The Planter*, contrasted the insolence of post-war labour with the more compliant workforces of the Somerset Maugham era:

> Labour's relations with managements have suffered a sad sea-change. In the good old feudal times the planter was always metaphorically and occasionally (bad luck, Sir!) literally the father of his flock. Now he is just the embodiment of DAS KAPITAL and considered fair game for all and sundry. As Confucius might have said 'Man who kill chicken, no can eat egg'.[190]

Officials ringed the changes too. The flock were 'fast losing their mental balance and the respect they had for authority'.[191] Tamil trade unionists refused to suffer any longer the usage of the derogatory term, 'Kling'.[192] Estate workers no longer dismounted from their bicycles when a *dorai*, or planter, passed by. Established institutions of recruitment were discontinued as India prepared for Swaraj, and Congress and the Agent of the Government of India provided a new element of accountability, albeit one that diminished rather than increased as Indian politics became domesticated in Malaya. For Chinese workers, too, old systems of bondage had collapsed. The contract labour system had already been weakened before the war. Labourers were more mobile and less dependent on their employers for the necessities of life: many had worked off their debts. More labour tended to be recruited locally, from lodging houses and squatter farms. Smaller estates were already beginning to recruit directly. Contract labour was less willing to tolerate exorbitant charges on food and absconding of contractors. They had an eye on the facilities being provided for Indians on estates, and this fuelled a wave of industrial action in the 1930s.[193] After the war the inequities of the contract system became less sufferable and the power of contractors over their labour forces diminished dramatically. This was at a time when employers were most dependent on contractors and *kepalas*, not least on Chinese mines when there were periods when it was dangerous for managers to set foot on their holdings.[194]

The collapse in labour discipline, so lamented by employers, was due primarily to the fact that the labour market was in disarray and remained so for at least the first eighteen months of the reoccupation. Erratic working patterns emerged. For the labourer this was a strategy to accommodate his livelihood to continuing economic uncertainty. It was apparent, as we have seen, in the towns, where many labourers preferred to work as pay was higher, goods more easily available and there were more opportunities for evening work. Labour in the rural areas exploited opportunities for diversification as best they could. Squatter cultivation was the primary means to this, and not only for Chinese. It was a major theme of the industrial militancy that

---

[190] 'ITBA', *The Planter*, 23, 9 (September, 1947), 235.
[191] R. Gopal Ayer, 'Report on labour conditions for May 1946, inland districts of Selangor', EACL.KL/20/45.
[192] E. A. Ross, minute, 10.2.1946, LAB/92/47.
[193] Leong, 'Labour and trade unionism', pp. 67–75.
[194] Nim, *Labour and tin mining*, p. 20.

accompanied post-war reconstruction. In Johore, for example, when a collapse of the rubber price led the UPAM to decree a 20 per cent cut in tapping rates in July 1947, over half the labour force left some estates. Those who remained supported themselves by illicit tapping. All the Javanese labour vanished and the Chinese went back to planting vegetables.[195] In the Slim river area of Perak many Indians left estates to work in Malay kampongs on a crop-sharing basis. Many failed to return.[196] For employers, squatter agriculture lay at the root of indiscipline.

The unsettled post-war conditions also encouraged the persistence of pre-war differentials in rates of pay for Indian labour against those of Chinese. Contractors, often small operators with no labour of their own, made the most of unsettled conditions and poached workers from the larger concerns and raised their rates. This worked to the advantage of the Chinese, most of whom were employed in this way. This ethnic differential became increasingly insufferable to Indian workers. Officials argued that it was a consequence of the different methods by which Indians were employed, which itself reflected employers' perceptions of their productivity. However, they were compelled to admit that differentials in piecework rates could not be justified.[197] In Ulu Langat, Chinese tappers were paid a maximum daily wage of $2.25, but Indians received only $1.30–1.50 a day. In places, to the annoyance of European managers, Indians were turning to contract work for Chinese to supplement their earnings.[198] With the breakdown of their authority over Chinese labour, employers had no intention of enlarging the problem by dealing also with Indian labour in the same way. The government, in the face of the inability of employers to take action, sought to remedy discrepancies in wage rates by establishing a definite scale that incorporated a basic wage for Indians. However, it resisted giving fuel to its critics by holding a full-scale enquiry into the problem.[199] This issue poisoned labour relations throughout the post-war period.

The aftermath of war, the collapse of old systems for the recruitment and control of labour, and aggravated ethnic discrimination within the working population, fuelled the rapid rise of organised labour after 1945. This began with the revival of what was left of the pre-war General Labour Unions (GLU) in the towns. A Singapore GLU was formed in October 1945, with branches in the States. A Pan-Malayan General Labour Union (PMGLU) was inaugurated on 15 February 1946. The GLUs threw themselves into rehabilitation work, gave support to the embryonic people's representative committees of the MCP, and supplied the massed cohorts for its united front. The collapse of the BMA's minimum 'disease and disorder' standard, provoked the

---

[195] DCL Johore, 'Interim report on Senai and Kulai Besar Estates strikes', 27.7.1947, LAB/139/47.
[196] 'Visiting Report Kati Estate, Kati, 20.5.1947', LAB/83/47.
[197] 'Alleged discrimination in wage rates against Indians in plantations in Malaya', June 1947, CO537/2173.
[198] 'Report on Labour conditions for September 1946, inland districts of Selangor', EACL.KL/20/45.
[199] C. R. Howitt, minute, 6.5.1947, MU Labour/167/47.

GLUs into a series of confrontations with the military regime, which culminated in the general strike of 29–30 January 1946, the abortive protest stoppage of 15 February and the food riots that accompanied it in various towns on the peninsula. The rise of labour has been the subject of a number of monographs.[200] They emphasise how both labour conditions and trade unionism were changing between late 1945 and the declaration of the Emergency in mid-1948. The Malayan left built its bid for power on shifting foundations. From the outset the unions were organised on the basis of large agglomerations of labourers, giving representation and union backing to men and women – and especially the growing numbers of working women – in a variety of trades and where collective organisation and bargaining was either totally non-existent or had completely broken down during the war, such as casual labourers, shop assistants, hawkers and trishaw riders. The GLUs were dominated by, but not synonymous with, the MCP. In fact, after the fateful 15 February incident the central leadership was in some disarray, and the PMGLU chairman, Lu Cheng, was detained. Union organisation developed a spontaneous momentum from below. Indian Labour Unions appeared in the localities. Ex-INA men led these organisations in many States, although there were exceptions to this. The Indian Labour Union in Kedah was led by a driver and coffeeshop owner, A. M. Samy, whose earlier connection with the INA was less pronounced. He exercised dominance over large areas of the State through a *thondar pedai*, a militant Dravidian youth militia, that enforced strike action and picketed toddy shops.[201] *Thondar pedai*-style movements were a feature of Indian Labour Unions elsewhere; for example, in the Johore Bahru division of the Rubber Workers' Union *thondar pedai* orderlies wearing red arm bands organised meetings, and members subscribed a dollar a month to support the organisation.[202] The Indian Labour Unions were absorbed into the larger PMGLU structure. However, this was a protracted and incomplete process. Some unions, most notably the Negri Sembilan Estate Indian Workers' Union, led by P. P. Narayanan, remained independent. The Malayan Indian Congress, established in 1946, had its own labour section, and its leadership, many of whom were old CIAM members and were not Tamil-speaking, tried unsuccessfully to stake a claim to the leadership of estate labour. Although the large federations controlled many public sector employees, pockets of moderate trade unionism existed amongst the clerical groups, as well as amongst the railwaymen and in a Malayan Estate Workers Union, led by men such as M. P. Rajagopal and V. M. N. Menon who represented Malayan labour in the colonial legislative council. However, in 1946 the GLUs had striking successes in absorbing these sectional unions into the larger body. Although the central leaders of the GLUs often had no real trade background of their own, they provided organisational expertise and logistical support

---

[200] Charles Gamba, *The Origins of trade unionism in Malaya* (Singapore, 1960); Stenson, *Industrial conflict* and the excellent unpublished thesis by Leong, 'Labour and trade unionism' are indispensable background for what follows.
[201] Stenson, *Industrial conflict*, pp. 99–100; c.f. Leong, 'Labour and trade unionism', pp. 236–46.
[202] DCL Johore to Commissioner for Labour, 'Kelan Estate', 1.6.1947, MU Labour/139/47.

for local unions, although some union notables, such as Lam Swee and P. Veerasenan of the Singapore GLU could claim a respectable working-class pedigree. Not all the leadership was Communist. The President of the PMGLU, S. A. Gapanathy, was. However, Selangor leader C. V. S. Krishna Moorthi and P. Veerasenan were not.[203] The leadership remained heterogeneous, and was perhaps becoming more so by 1947. Despite this, the unions lay at the core of the MCP's ambitions as a mass movement. As we shall see, the British attempted to channel this unionism into a trajectory of development based partially on the British Trades Union Congress. In response to this, the PMGLUs reorganised into a Pan-Malayan Federation of Trade Unions (PMFTU), established on a craft and industrial basis. This experiment, a component of the larger political experiment of the Malayan Spring, broke down. Unions became subject to more open attacks from employers and administrators of the old school. The full repressive power of the state was invoked at a time when bitter internal struggles were taking place within the trade union movements.

Strike action was intense. In the year after April 1946 there were 713,000 man-days lost in Malaya and 1,173,000 in Singapore, and in the year after April 1947, 512,000 in Malaya and 205,000 in Singapore.[204] In many of these disputes the GLUs used ex-MPAJA and secret society elements as their strong arm, for picketing, intimidating employers and collecting very substantial amounts of funds. Union leaders, in advancing claims to a 'collective livelihood', insisted on the maintenance of discipline in industrial action at all costs, and Workers' Self-Protection Corps became an appendage to their organisation. The Kuala Lumpur unions, it was rumoured, had forged a liaison with the notorious Green Dragon Mountain Gang. By mid-1947 there were indications that the Self-Protection Corps was getting out of control in Singapore and another body, the Steel Star Corps, was set up to police it.[205] It was used to particular effect in the entrepôt. Here discipline and central control were tightest, even when the GLU was working through older established organisations such as the Singapore Traction Company Employees Union. In the bitter conflicts that were unleashed within bodies of workers, the Singapore Harbour Board became a bastion of militant power, as did its equivalent in Penang, where virtually the whole waterfront operation was controlled by the Penang GLU. Yet even here, old divisions were not completely subsumed. Appadurai, the ex-INA head of the Penang harbour workers, based his appeal on an emotional hostility to English-speaking Indians; in 1947 deep conflicts opened up between Hindu and Muslim sections of the workforce, and a rival Muslim union was established.[206]

Much of the strike action in the ports was against attempts to curb the 'privileges' and perquisites that the workers had enjoyed in the time of scarcity. Similarly, on

---

[203] For the structure of the GLU, see Stenson, *Industrial conflict*, pp. 100–8; Leong, 'Labour and trade unionism', pp. 236–46.

[204] Stenson, *Industrial conflict*, p. 200.

[205] GLU document cited in Gamba, *Origins of trade unionism*, pp. 186–7; MSS/PIJ/8/1947, 31.5.1947.

[206] MSS/PIJ/5/1947.

estates and mines, workers struck to retain what scope for adaptability they possessed. Local circumstances varied; strike reports highlight demands for improved pay and conditions, and the provision of maternity leave for women. But if there is a dominant theme of industrial unrest it can be found in workers' assaults on the authoritarian employment regimes of pre-war Malaya, and in their demands to acquire more control over their own labour. This can be clearly seen in workers' targeting of contractors: for example, in the demand that they and not their workers meet the burden of cuts in wages. On the estates resentment towards Indian *mandores* for manifold abuses of their position had accumulated over the years. However, union attacks on the contractor system were not always pressed home by the unions. Often a levy was taken on contractors' costs, which made the unions slow to argue for the abolition of the system. In the Singapore Harbour Board, the organisation of unions was very much bound up with the contractor system, and there were more general fears that eradication of contractors would give managers more control over labour.[207] There was some justification for this concern. For example, after protest strikes at Voules Estate in Tenang, Johore, arrangements arose between labourers and management which eliminated the contractors and paid wages through the elected representatives of the tappers. However, although the manager then became legally their employer, he still regarded the workers as contract tappers and the workers were compelled to strike again for the right to earn a minimum income as tappers and devote more energy to rice cultivation. The average turn-out was only 18–20 days a month.[208] Solidarities across race emerged, especially in areas where mixed labour forces were found, such as Johore. When, in an early estate strike in February 1946 on Wardieson Estate in Selangor, Indian labourers struck for more than 55–70 cents a day, Chinese workers stayed out demanding that Indians be paid the same rate as them and that women be paid an extra 10 cents.[209] However, it was precisely because of the persistence of pay differentials that P. P. Narayanan's Negri Sembilan Estate Indian Workers' Union made the decision to remain communal in organisation.

From an early stage there was friction between the concerns of the heterogeneous grass-roots organisation and the political strategy dictated by the federations. This was not always apparent in 1946, but when it began to emerge in 1947, employers and the administration were quick to exploit it. Throughout 1946 and 1947 severe economic conditions accelerated the momentum from below. On the estates, the main waves of trade union protest ebbed and flowed with fluctuations in the labour market. As Sir Edward Gent pointed out to the Colonial Office during the mid-1947 strike wave, managers contributed substantially to strike situations by crimping labour off each other. Wages varied widely above the recommended $1.30 a day maximum, and estates often kept separate books to disguise the scale of 'bonus' payments.[210] Labour

---

[207] Stenson, *Industrial conflict*, p. 108.
[208] ACL Muar, 'Voules Estate, Tenang', 21.9.1947; 19.10.1947, LAB/139/47.
[209] 'Labour strike on Wardieson Estate', 18.2.1946, EACL,KL/51/46.
[210] Gent to Creech Jones, 24.6.1947, CO537/2173.

was in a strong position to exploit the situation throughout 1946. In 1947 the situation became more contested as the labour supply increased when squatters and laid-off workers in wartime import-substitution industries re-entered the labour market. On the plantations, disputes due to 'wintering' dragged on into a mid-1947 slump in the rubber price. Increased labour costs and rising labour supply led to a series of bitter clashes. Kedah saw the most intense disputes between January and May 1947. They began amongst Indian labour on Harvard and Dublin Estates from July and August 1946, but by early 1947 had spread throughout South and Central Kedah, and were supported by Chinese unionists. They were accompanied by uncompromising picket action: European managers evacuated their families to Penang. The climax came when police opened fire on a crowd at Dublin Estate in April.[211] This marked a watershed in labour relations, and signalled a new period of collusion between employers and the security forces.

Even before the Kedah incident, pressure was mounting on the British government to intervene to restore labour discipline. As in all areas of its social policy, the governing obsession of the colonial state was its desire to contain the politicisation of new social movements. Labour policy was made by a variety of agents – the Colonial Office, the Labour Department, the Trade Union Adviser and a Registrar of Trade Unions – who were increasingly at odds with each other. A passing Colonial Office labour adviser might suggest a need for modern arbitration; statutory tribunals to find people work; for labour affairs to be managed 'through the fresh mind of a convinced socialist'.[212] Old hands in the Labour Department scoffed at such naiveté: 'the House of Commons will be led to believe that there are only a few trade unions in Singapore and Malaya and that they have been organised by the Trade Union Advisers'. The local wisdom was that the principles of collective bargaining were innate to the Chinese; that their traditional 'genius for compromise' worked through conciliation and not through the law. The ends of labour administration were therefore educative, and its touch light.[213] The state should only intervene to determine wage levels and conditions of employment where it had firm evidence of abuse, or an infringement of the law. Otherwise, the head of the Labour Department, John Jeff, wrote, 'the tendency would be for wages to become a political issue and we should lose the whole value of collective bargaining and voluntary agreement'.[214] Yet, by the same token, labour officers accused Chinese unionists of betraying the principles of conciliation. The President of the Selangor Rubber Union, Pan Soo Ching, it was remarked, 'seems to imagine that the mere framing of a demand and the putting of it into writing invests that demand with a sort of inviolable sanctity'. Any deviation from it led to accusations that employers and the Labour Department were in 'an unholy

---

[211] Leong, 'Labour and trade unionism', pp. 269–78.
[212] Eleanor M. Hinder, 'Some comments upon developing labour administration and policy in Malaya', 7.8.1946, MU Labour/48/46.
[213] R. H. Oakeley to Chief Secretary, Singapore, 17.10.1946; John Jeff to Chief Secretary, Malayan Union, 18.4.1946, LAB/48/46.
[214] C. R. Howitt, minute, 6.5.1947, LAB/167/47.

alliance'. This uncharacteristic intransigence smelt of sedition: 'The similarity of attitude, both mental and physical, shown by these leaders and the recognition of the same phrases at each fresh discussion leads one to suspect that a well-planned campaign, aimed at discrediting this department, is underway.'[215]

In the face of demands from planters to act against agitators, from July 1946 the Labour Department began collating information on strikes. However, throughout 1946 the government was reluctant to police labour disputes with a heavy hand. Although it was felt that the new unions struck first and made demands later, it was difficult to take action against activists who encouraged labour to organise and make demands on economic issues, even if planters felt the demands were impossible to meet.[216] The government was accountable to a socialist administration in London, and Governor Gent took this very seriously. Yet despite their recognition that some kind of trade union organisation was inevitable, the cautious policy of the Labour Department was informed by old-style paternalism, rather than new-style welfarism.

However, English Labourism did make an inroad into these debates from another source: a Trade Union Adviser, John Brazier, brought to Malaya by the BMA. A railwayman who had driven the 'Bournemouth Belle', Brazier sought to introduce 'ordinary trade union methods of conciliation' on a British model, and was prepared to countenance strong independent trade unions. Initially he had some successes. After the 15 February 1946 strike the MCP drew back somewhat from its overt control of the trade unions. There was in these months a resurgence of autonomous labour organisation, as witnessed in the revival of pre-war unions and guilds, and Indian Labour Unions. The new PMGLU attempted to work within the colonial system and conform to the requirements of the Trade Unions Ordinance, which was reintroduced in April 1946, by becoming in late 1946 a Pan-Malayan Federation of Trade Unions – the acting General Secretary of which was not a MCP Central Committee member. It argued that a federation, being a body of delegates, could operate legally without registration. The dispute over this was a defining moment in post-war labour relations. In Singapore, Brazier's deputy S. P. Garrett signed an agreement with the Singapore Federation of Trade Unions, reassuring them that a federation would not be obliged to register. The Labour Department and the Registrar of Trade Unions brought a very different perspective to bear on the problem, and responded that it could register under a different Ordinance as a 'society'. Garrett saw the federations as a vital link historically in the transition from a bureaucratic to a democratic government. He rejected the new clamp-down on societies and unions as 'an abrogation of socialistic principles' and resigned in support of the federations.[217] By contrast, on the mainland, Brazier had begun to see registration as a necessary means of bringing the unions to heel. He repeatedly urged the 'top-heavy' PMFTU to

[215] ACL (Chinese) Selangor, 'Strikes on Hawthornden Estate', 27.4.1947, MU Labour/158/47.
[216] John Jeff to Chief Secretary, 2.8.1946, MU Labour/352/46.
[217] *Malaya Tribune*, 24.5.1947; 23.5.1947.

decentralise, as political control of unions was an anathema to him.[218] He threw his weight behind the Registrar's insistence in October 1946 that the PMFTU must apply for registration or exemption from registration. It was eventually told to disband. Brazier heroically attempted to reconcile his responsibilities to the Malayan workforce for the development of independent trade unions and to the colonial government for the maintenance of stable industrial relations. It has been argued that the depth of Brazier's missionary commitment helped allay the scruples of the Whitehall Fabians and legitimised the official policy of control and the suppression of militancy. The appeal of a watered-down TUC-style trade unionism had little appeal beyond English-speaking administrative and technical employees familiar with the administrative procedures for the redress of grievance that Brazier was advocating. For these unions the basis of post-war conciliation machinery was created in this period, but so too were the roots of persistent divisions between public sector and other trade unions. The niceties of 'democratic' unionism, as it was advocated by Brazier in English, were either lost, irrelevant or remained untranslated to the mass of Chinese and Tamil unskilled and semi-skilled labourers.[219] The trial of strength between the government and the federations dragged on throughout 1947, when a new consensus of official opinion began to emerge. It was based on a conviction of the necessity for paternalistic control of labour, restrictions on picketing and a defence of pre-war restrictive legislation in the face of pressures from Whitehall to liberalise – pressures which were, in any case, diminishing. The frustrations of trade union policy mirrored the frustrations of the politics of health and welfare. In both cases, the British had sought to create free, independent institutions unsullied by wider political concerns. Yet to the unions 'politics and livelihood were indivisible'.[220] For the MCP, a strike was 'an instrument for consolidating and extending an organisation'; it had a vital function in political education, and its aftermath was a time for analysis and self-criticism.[221] In the face of new restrictions in 1948 the political objectives of strikes became more explicit. In a close re-enactment of the events of 15 February 1946, the Singapore government banned the May Day parade of 1948. In the face of this, union action, as Lam Swee argued, became a 'fight for freedom of organisation, the right to strike and the right to have processions'.[222] Bureaucratic harassment of the federations was intensified. This phoney war only ended when the federations were declared illegal after the amendment of the Trade Unions Ordinance in late May 1948 – a landmark event in the count-down to insurgency.

Politicised trade unionism was identified with criminality. A pattern of rhetoric emerged which identified the Emergency as a breakdown of law and order, rather than as a social revolution. In the period before July 1948, it was left to the employers to reimpose order. The Malayan Association and the Singapore Association were formed

[218] *Malaya Tribune*, 19.12.1947. [219] Stenson, *Industrial conflict*, pp. 142–8.
[220] Chun-Fei, 'Labour associations and labour troubles', *Sin Chew Jit Poh*, 1.1.1946.
[221] GLU document, 'An account of experiences derived from strikes', February, 1946, in MSS/ PIJ/3/1946, 31.5.1946.
[222] Gamba, *Origins of trade unionism*, p. 330.

to strengthen European interests and straddle the expatriate–official divide. Business pressure was intensified throughout 1947. The Kedah strikes played a major role in the hardening of attitudes, and the harsh policing of them may have been premeditated. Employers demanded 'death, banishment and particularly flogging'. In October 1947 the Incorporated Society of Planters stated its position in strong language:

> It may well be that a guidance of Labour into the tried channels of trade union organisation was calculated to short-circuit subversive movements but the unfortunate delusion that here was an open invitation to disregard authority and dictate at will to employers or their representatives has been used by vicious malcontents masquerading as leaders of an Utopian political faith. Criminal intimidation has emerged as the lifeblood of many labour unions and the power to circulate it has been seized by irresponsible and subversive elements.[223]

In the strikes during the mid-1947 rubber slump, planters insisted that they would deal only with contractors and not with unions. As unions lost ground, the employers began to reorganise and co-ordinate pressure on them, particularly by expelling known 'agitators'. Brazier lambasted the planters for their short-sightedness; Gent told the Colonial Office that many of them should have retired before the war and were 'lost and pig-headed' in the new conditions.[224] After a 20 per cent cut in contract rates in May, the government pressurised employers to introduce collective bargaining. But this was quietly dropped with the arrival of a new hard-line Commissioner for Labour, R. G. Houghton. At the same time, some of the larger employers, such as Batu Arang coal mine and the Singapore Harbour Board were beginning to get a grip on their labour problems. The Batu Arang Mining Labourers Union struggled to be quorate. The unions were particularly losing ground in the more loosely structured trades, amongst hawkers and shopworkers, as the *towkays* experienced a resurgence in authority and government regulation took a grip on the economy of the towns. Throughout the country, as the rubber price dropped, managers began to exercise their powers of dismissal and sought eviction orders to expel labour activists from their properties. By August 1947, it was 'open season for attacks by managers on trade unions'.[225] Notice under various pretexts was given to the contractors of gangs notorious for labour troubles, using existing laws of defamation and trespass. The MIC at times acquiesced in the dismissal of these people as it began to sponsor its own unions on large estates.[226] Appadurai of the Penang harbour workers was arrested; C. S. V. Krishna Moorthi was said to be in hiding. Union actions were made illegal by failure to give notice of strikes. 'Have the labourers,' asked exasperated Chinese unionists in Selangor, 'the right to give the

---

[223] 'Lawlessness and insecurity', *The Planter*, 23, 10 (October, 1947), 241–3.

[224] Brazier to Commissioner of Labour, 19.9.1947, MU Labour/158/47; Gent to Bourdillon, 24.6.1947, CO537/2173.

[225] ACL Klang to Deputy Commissioner, 27.8.1947; John Brazier to Commissioner of Labour, 19.9.1947, LAB/158/47.

[226] For example, ACL Perak, 'Strike amongst labourers on Div III Ulu Bernam Oil Palms Estate', 17.3.1947, MU Labour/40/47.

manager twenty-four hours notice that he will be beaten up?'[227] The Willan Judgement of October 1947 supported the dismissal of some striking rubber workers and placed the right to strike in question. Some factories instituted their own employment regulations which severely curtailed union activity.[228] In Perak, where Chinese labour was available 'in unlimited numbers' some managers refused to engage them, and mines engaged workers from the KMT Perak Chinese Mining Employees' Association.[229] Many estate managers, enthusiastically supported by the Labour Department, revived the old system of *panchayats*, which were constituted so as to give equal weight of representation to older men and isolate the 'irresponsible and undesirable element'.[230] The official line of decentralisation of trade unions, as workers were well aware, gave managers new opportunities to dominate their labour. Their suspicions were aggravated by Brazier's attempts to give Asian estate staff, themselves part of the chain of management, a leadership role in approved estate unions, and by his encouragement of break-away unions, through which the pre-war Indian leadership of the towns attempted to reassert themselves.

In the face of this onslaught, the fissures which had always been below the surface in the union movement began to widen. In Kedah, as the unregistered Kedah Federation of Rubber Workers' Union attempted to force rivals into liquidation, individual estate unions revived and sought to distance themselves from the Federation. A 25 August 1947 general strike was observed by only 50 per cent of the estate labour force in Kedah and it showed that PMFTU support had retreated into local pockets of strength. In Perak there was a high turn-out in Sungei Siput and a low one in Lower Perak; in Johore the strike was only strong in the south of the state.[231] A feature of the 1947 disturbances in Johore – in the old MPAJA strongholds in Sedenak, Yong Peng and Pagoh – was the open lack of support from moderate union leadership, represented by Unni of the MIC and the young General Secretary of the Negri Sembilan Indian Labour Union, P. P. Narayanan. The latter came in for particular praise by the British officials: 'by far the best union leader whom I have so far come across – speaking excellent English, well-briefed, *conciliatory* but firm'. In the face of these setbacks, militant unions attempted to boost discipline. The Sedenak strike was led by leftist ex-MPAJA commanders. The Paloh strikes saw *thondar pedai* picketing of Indian shops and the patrolling of uniformed men. When the leftist Johore Rubber Workers' Union threatened a 'second Kedah' in Muar, any residual reluctance by officials to take police action against activists evaporated.[232] Selangor

---

[227] Reported on Kampong Bahru Estate, Kuala Selangor, 'Report on Chinese Labour, Selangor, February, 1947', MU Labour/54/47.
[228] For example, the Bata shoe factory in Klang, 'Klang Monthly report July 1947', *ibid.*
[229] Estate Inspection reports, Perak 1947, MU Labour/83/47; MSS/PIJ/2/1948.
[230] ACL Perak, 'Estate Committees', 9.1.1948, MU Labour/611/47.
[231] Enclosures on MU Labour/562/47.
[232] ACL Muar, 'Pagoh Estate', 18.2.1947; DCL, Johore, 'Strike on Sedenak Estate', 6.3.1947; DCL Kluang, 'Paloh Estate', 12.3.1947; Harrisons and Crossfield to Commissioner for Police, 20.3.1947, MU Labour/139/47.

supplies an important example of how the way disputes were being conducted was working against the big federations. Here local negotiations between unions and employers embarrassed the central union organisation. A wage agreement was signed in February 1948 between the Malayan Planting Industry Employers' Association (MPIEA) and the Selangor State Rubber Workers' Union on terms unfavourable to the worker, which increased tasks and represented a decline in real wage levels. It by-passed the PMFTU, and was subsequently enforced throughout in Malaya in April 1948. Similarly, on the mines of Perak, the Malayan Mining Employers Association (MMEA) and the Tin Miners' Union attempted to enforce uniform employment conditions over a widely divergent industry. The voice of the MCP, the *Min Sheng Pau*, bitterly attacked this local agreement and drew up alternative proposals.[233] On the estates of Perak, the Perak Estate Employees Union (PEEU) was also losing considerable ground. The dismissal of union activists precipitated industrial action which led to charges of intimidation, dismissal of organisers and renewed strike action. However, this increasingly reflected union rivalry on the estates. The taint of financial and sexual scandals and defections attached themselves to the organisers.[234] PEEU support seemed to be localised: it was strong in estates like Sungkai, Krian Road and Lighterwood; but on isolated estates such as Gedong and Bagan Serai it had little influence. Harewood Estate in Batu Gajah was a battleground for the PEEU and the Malayan Estate Workers' Union – an alternative to the PMFTU sponsored by the Trade Union Adviser. Indeed, in Perak as elsewhere, there was a resurgence of interest in local unions. In Batu Kurau, the Ijok and Batu Kurau Estate Labourers' Organisation set great store on its independence from the PEEU. In Jelai, Perak, the extension of union organisation became wrapped up in Tamil–Telegu conflict, and the Tamil-dominated local unionists' opposition to the PEEU in particular was due to its demands for subscriptions, which ranged between 50 cents and one dollar a week.[235] In the middle of 1947 the PEEU split, and a moderate section under John Emmanuel emerged with the tacit support of colonial officials. Around the same time the ex-MPAJA Communist union organiser, R. G. Balan, returned to Malaya from the Empire Communist Conference in London to organise a rival Perak Rubber Labourers' Union and a new wave of militant action began that resulted in eighty-five strikes in Perak in the first six months of 1948.

These internal disputes illuminate the origins of the Emergency in a number of ways. In particular, struggles over whether labourers should negotiate directly with management or through their contractors were intensified by political contests of the same order as those in evidence on the rural fringe. For example, on one estate in Klang, the contractors and the union leadership included ex-Anti-Japanese Army

---

[233] 'Meeting between Tin Mine Workers Trade Union and MMEA at Kuala Lumpur on 24.4.1947', MU Labour/158/47.

[234] For example, ACL Perak, 'Unrest on Gapis Estate, Padang Rengas', 1.3.1947; 3.5.1947, MU Labour/40/47.

[235] Enclosures on MU Labour/83/47/Pt I and Pt II.

personnel and both groups sought secret society sponsorship.[236] In its struggle with the MCP-controlled unions, the Perak Chinese Mining Employees' Association enlisted Triad backing.[237] Many squatters on estates were dealing in illegally tapped rubber – for example in the Sungkai area – from which resistance army associations drew great benefit.[238] Intense rivalries amongst labour activists, and between labourers and contractors, coupled with administrative and financial problems, led them to resort to violence and strong-arm tactics to resolve them. In May 1948 there were instances of arson in Johore; a European manager held hostage on his own estate in Yong Peng and two KMT-supporting mandores killed on Machap estate; and a Chinese contractor killed and another wounded on Ladang Geddes, men who had been witnesses against the MPAJA. In Perak, a Chinese manager of a rubber factory in Ipoh was shot dead and a subscription collector for the Langkap branch of the farmers' union was arrested in Telok Anson for leading a gang that held up forest guards with spears.[239] Chinese contractors were particular targets. To Michael Stenson, the GLU was at worst 'but one form of racketeering and extortion in a society where such evils were all too common'.[240] The Commissioner of Labour charitably admitted that allegations of coercion in labour disputes often originated from employers, and that 'the fear of assault is innate in most Asiatic labourers and intimidation is at times suggested when there is no evidence of it'.[241] However, in the months leading up to the declaration of the Emergency, these internecine conflicts provoked some of the more alarming incidents of violence which anticipated the confrontation between the Communist-directed unions and the colonial state.

The impact of this competition was augmented by simultaneous moves against squatter cultivation on the estates. In Perak, as the opportunities for cash-crop cultivation diminished, disputes on the estates over rates during the wintering season and wage cuts due to the low rubber price rose in intensity. In late November 1947, in Sungei Siput, a spontaneous strike of all Chinese labour on this issue occurred with no official union support.[242] Rural communities resisted pressures on their subsistence. A vital context for industrial unrest was that by 1947 the opportunities to do so were narrowing. The labour supply was increasing as squatters and workers laid off from wartime import-substitution industries re-entered the labour market. A meeting of the MPAJA Ex-Serviceman's Association in Penang announced that 30 per cent of its members were still unemployed.[243] This, together with moves by employers and the government to reinforce industrial discipline, aggravated the underlying sources of economic grievance. It has been suggested that at this time labour was getting more cautious, that the squatters were less disposed to militant action.[244] However, this

[236] ACL Klang to Deputy Commissioner for Labour, Selangor, 9.6.1947, LAB/158/47.
[237] MSS/PIJ/15/1947.
[238] 'Visiting Report, Sungei Klah Estate, Sungkai', 10.1.1947, LAB/83/1947/Part I.
[239] MSS/PIJ/10/1948.   [240] Stenson, *Industrial conflict*, p. 116.
[241] John Jeff to Chief Secretary, 2.8.1946, LAB/352/46.
[242] ACL Perak, 'Sungei Siput area strike of 17.11.1947', 27.11.1947, LAB/40/47.
[243] MSS/PIJ/1/1948.   [244] Stenson, *Industrial conflict*, pp. 120–1.

trend was reversed when the terms of their squatter style of living and working moved against them. In early 1948, squatter evictions gathered momentum, in a period of alarming surplus of labourers looking for work. Throughout April and May 1948 there were particularly bitter disputes on the Socfin estates at Lima Belas and Klapa Bali in Perak. Strikes were accompanied by threats on the lives of managers and *kepalas.* Evictions aggravated the problem and the Sungei Siput area in particular was inflamed by militant action. Balan's Perak Rubber Labourers' Union was making considerable inroads in this area. Officials expressed the hope that the growing numbers of unemployed and retrenched Chinese would supply a 'natural reservoir' of labour in the peninsula, there was talk of relocating it to elsewhere in the region, perhaps even to the Dutch East Indies.[245] This 'reservoir' of predominantly Chinese labour was caught between new obstacles to a return to life on smallholdings and a world which offered decreasing prospects for employment. These young men and women were a fertile recruiting ground for a mobilising guerrilla army. Anthony Short has written that although the Emergency started in Sungei Siput, it could have occurred in one of a dozen other places. However, from the preceding pages we can see how, at this time, Sungei Siput exemplified conditions on the frontier in the starkest terms. By the second quarter of 1948, the cumulative pressures on the rural periphery had blended with industrial unrest on the estates and mines and heightened levels of anxiety in the rural areas to create a situation of endemic social upheaval. Political organisations of various shades had penetrated these struggles, and circumscribed the efforts of the colonial state to restore order and social cohesion through various social and economic initiatives. This rural unrest remained at the heart of the insurrection in Malaya. It played no small part in precipitating the MCP into a rural revolt for which it was ill-prepared, in creating in the official mind a construction of violence as criminality which denied it a political meaning, and in provoking the colonial state into a massive expansion into the countryside by which it endeavoured to transform the political and social geography of the peninsula.

A revolution reconsidered

It was against this backdrop of actual and implied terror in the rural areas that the crucial political dilemmas of 1948 were addressed. For the British government the question was how far the violence could be suppressed without destroying altogether its post-war plans for the political and social advancement of its colony. For the Malayan Communist Party it was how far it could belatedly rekindle revolutionary enthusiasm when the conditions necessary to sustain it, and its control over its grass-roots support were slipping away. The panorama of social disruption outlined here suggests that the origins and course of rural terror are only intelligible in relation to a wider social crisis over which both the British government and the MCP had little control. Most accounts of the Emergency look to apportion responsibility. Senior

---

[245] LDMR, March, April, May 1948, MU/4181/47.

British administrators have been seen, by turns, as either blind to the magnitude of the crisis, or through their repressive policies forcing the MCP away from a constitutional path and down the road of violence. The MCP have most often been perceived as either 'reluctant insurrectionists' compelled to take up arms by the colonial government's unwillingness to allow them a legitimate political role in Malaya, or as victims of a misguided 'miscalculation' in choosing the path of violence.[246] However, these explanations neglect the extent to which from first to last both sides were responding to events, rather than initiating carefully formulated strategies.

Both sides were, by 1948, in a state of some confusion. The MCP was divided and compromised by informers. By March 1947, the kingpin, Lai Teck, was exposed. Rumblings that he was not all what he claimed to be had begun during the war and continued in the reoccupation period. Rumour must have been abroad in November 1945, when, at a tea party in Ipoh on 25 November, the Perak NDYL leader, Eng Min Chin, was reported to have 'exposed the conspirators' against the General Secretary.[247] Yet the *Overseas Chinese Weekly* of Kuala Lumpur continued to taunt him and asked ironically for him to 'pass impartial view' on Soviet encroachment on China: 'but we do not know what is the nationality of Mr. Lai Teck. We wait for his answer.'[248] The exposure came in November 1945 by a discredited MCP figure, Ng Yeh Lo, in a Penang newspaper, *Modern Daily News*. Ng seems to have been arrested by Japanese with Lai Teck, but made a scapegoat by the party for many of Lai Teck's betrayals. It seems also that the Singapore KMT leader, and aide to the Force 136 hero Lim Bo Seng, Chuang Hui Tsuan, was also aware of the deception, as was the BMA Chinese Affairs Officer, H. T. Pagden, but was instructed by superiors to drop the matter.[249] Lai Teck absconded with party funds; the MCP entered into a period of internal inquisition and, it seems, penury. The man whose name eventually headed the charge sheet against the General Secretary was his former protégé, Chin Peng. Lai Teck's errors were identified as: disbanding the MPAJA, the main source of party power and finance; of having no alternative constitution ready in 1945; his lack of aggression against the Japanese; and his acquiescence in Britain's unopposed return. There were many indications that by early 1947, the united front policy was yielding diminishing returns. Moroever, the intensification of the attacks by Chinese KMT business interests and their Triad allies on leftist organisations had bankrupted the strategy of co-operation with the 'national bourgeoisie'. The core party membership, of which some impression of numbers is given in Table 2, was retreating from the public eye. The MCP began to be concerned that it was losing ground and from March to November 1947 the party, driven by rank-and-file restless at the lack of

---

[246] Respectively, the arguments of M. R. Stenson, *Repression and revolt: the origins of the 1948 Communist insurrection in Malaya and Singapore* (Athens, Ohio, 1969), p. 5 and A. Short, *The Communist insurrection in Malaya, 1948–60* (London, 1976), p. 65.

[247] *Kin Kwok Daily News*, 27.11.1945.   [248] *Overseas Chinese Weekly*, 5.3.1946.

[249] A report by Pagden corroborating Lai Teck's collusion in the Batu Caves massacre was sent to the Colonial Office, 'Appendix 1 – Lai Teck. Communist leader', in CO537/3757.

Table 2 *MCP membership at 1 February 1947 (excluding an estimated 40 Malay and Indonesian members)*[250]

Region	Chinese	Indians
Singapore	750	175
Johore	2,650	180
Negri Sembilan	700	45
Malacca	350	15
Selangor	1,700	190
Perak	1,800	70
Kedah	500	30
Penang	450	35
West Pahang	1,250	20
East Pahang	450	–
Trengganu	225	–
Kelantan	175	–
Total	11,000	760

notable successes of the united front and the leadership's retreat underground, began to reconsider the prospects for direct action. In December, the MPAJA Ex-Comrades' Association was revitalised. Yet it is important to emphasise that the accession of Chin Peng to the position of Secretary-General did not determine an immediate and sudden shift in MCP strategy – it seems that in July to November 1947 and again in February 1948 he was out of the country, in Bangkok and Hong Kong.[251] Colonial intelligence identified Chin Peng as one of the last moderates remaining on the Central Executive Committee. By all accounts, the Party's decision-making mechanisms moved at a very slow pace. A simple account of the MCP's self-examination, drawn from colonial intelligence reports might read something like this: a 20–26 March 1948 Central Executive Committee conference in Singapore discussed the possibility that the party would be banned. It was suggested that the party felt it was losing support on the ground; that it anticipated a lack of resolve in the Labour government; and that outside support would be forthcoming for an insurrection. Directives imparting these views were said to have reached the State leaderships in early May. In the interim, waterfront unions in Singapore and Penang were asserting themselves, and there were reports of backing-up groups being strengthened. In late April, the MCP began compiling lists of MPAJA members in readiness for a sudden call-up. By mid-June this was said to be complete. The troops were not mobilised, but mobile units of 'Special Service Corps' began terrorist operations. The new campaign was to be in three stages: the organisation of industrial unrest; widespread terrorism;

[250] MSS/PIJ/8/1947.
[251] Reported in the recent account by a senior officer of the Malaysian Special Branch, Aloysius Chin, *The Communist Party of Malaya: the inside story* (Kuala Lumpur, 1995), p. 27.

and then armed revolution, supported by guerrillas from the hills, for which the proscription of the MCP would be the signal. After the event, the Malayan Security Service reported that the MCP had, by 20 June, reached the second stage. According to the Security Service, an MPAJA Ex-Comrades Association meeting on 11 June told branch representatives to destroy all documents in readiness to fly to the hills. In Perak and elsewhere, union offices were closed. Arms dumps were reactivated, transit camps established. The open MPAJA forces were said to number around 5,800, and its underground forces about 4,700. Only 10 per cent of the open and 30 per cent of the secret organisation were able to join up – around 2,000 men. The MCP's major financial asset in the peninsula, the *Min Sheng Pau*, desperately tried to find a buyer and then attempted to move newsprint and printing machinery into the jungle. On 15 June a warning order was given. By 20 June, general mobilisation was underway in Johore and Perak; it was imminent in Selangor but precipitate action by government after the Perak murders on 16 June took the MCP by surprise.[252]

How then is the MCP's purpose to be understood? Much ink has been spilt on the question of how far this change of direction was stimulated from outside Malaya.[253] The MCP was well aware of the international situation and the hard line of Cominform and Zhanov. It was well aware also of the revolutionary fires burning in neighbouring countries. It was well-briefed, both by its own leaders who had travelled to international conferences, and by visiting Communists such as the Australian, Lawrence Sharkey. However, there is little evidence that this meant its strategy was *dictated* by the Communist Party of the Soviet Union or by any advice from outside. Recent research has shown that, despite their later adoption of Cold War rhetoric, the British government did not find the evidence convincing also.[254] In fact, it seemed as though the MCP was preparing for the government to move against it. From early 1947, the MCP was confronting the possibility that the political opportunities of the Malayan Spring were an illusion. Even before the exposure of Lai Teck, his line was under fire from within. Indeed, it has been suggested that his removal was more a consequence of political disagreements, in which stories of his betrayals were employed to vindicate the plot against him.[255] Throughout 1947, the campaign against the constitutional proposals and the legalistic mire over registration of trade unions had led to an eschewal of militancy. Both of these campaigns had ended in defeat, and so the earlier triumphs of the GLUs were not sustained. In the localities, workers were tending to make independent agreements with managers, even create independent unions. It was equally uncertain what returns would emerge from the MCP's dalliance with radical Malay nationalism. The MPAJA was becoming con-

---

[252] MSS/PIJ/10/1948; 'Malayan Communist Party Affairs, 28.4.1948 to 26.6.1948', Appendix 'A' to MSS/PIJ/12/1948.

[253] In particular, Stenson, *The 1948 Communist revolt*.

[254] A. J. Stockwell, '"A widespread and long-concocted plot to overthrow government in Malaya"? The origins of the Malayan Emergency', in R. Holland (ed.), *Emergencies and disorder in the European empires after 1945* (London, 1994), pp. 66–88.

[255] By Gerald de Cruz, in Stenson, *The 1948 Communist revolt*, pp. 29–30.

cerned about the dependability of its rural support and sources of supplies. There were many reports of new approaches being made to cultivators to attempt to keep this infrastructure intact. In an important related move, there were reports of an MCP meeting on 20 March that was devoted to discussing the Triad threat to the party's organisation. Reviewing the decisions of the Central Executive Committee (CEC), the *MCP Review* of 19 June 1948 regretted the path of 'rightist opportunism' and admitted that this had been based on the underestimation of the 'reactionary nature of the Labour government', 'and of the popular consciousness of the Malayan masses.'[256] There was a recognition in this that the party had failed to give an adequate direction to the combustion of violence on the peninsula. The *MCP Review* of May 1948 carried a feature on the 'Peasants' struggle in Perak'. It drew particular attention to the uprooting of squatters' crops, particularly in Sungei Siput and lauded the resistance of the Sungei Siput Peasants' Union, which in itself suggests an acknowledgement that the real momentum and leadership for these protests had come from below. As we have seen, it was underway before R. G. Balan's Rubber Labourers' Union led a resurgence of union organisation in the area. In the light of what we know about this violence, the new directives look very much like an attempt to seize control of and employ the undercurrents of violence to a wider political end, in anticipation of decisive moves against the party by the British government. Mobilisation began in stages, and every indication is that it was estimated in June that this was not expected to be completed until August or September at the very earliest. The sheer number and seniority of the MCP personnel who, even in spite of the British government's tardiness, were caught before they managed to abscond to the jungle seems to substantiate this.[257] In June the violence had already reached a crescendo: in the early part of the month there were nineteen cases of attempted murder and three cases of arson. The endemic violence on the frontier had forced the British hand and become a precipitate blow for the revolution. Chin Peng himself, in a self-criticism written in 1961, argued that the climate of suppression and the need to restore the party's credibility after the failures of the Lai Teck years had led plans to be laid. However, the rank-and-file members would not wait for their implementation.[258] In the words of the Malaysian psychological warfare expert, C. C. Too, 'trigger-happy comrades jumped the gun'.[259]

If the MCP's dilemma had been resolved for them, how were the British wrestling with their own? How had they understood MCP intentions? How far would their liberal scruples permit them to act against it? Here, *post facto* justification and recrimination dominate the record. In Malaya, expatriate businessmen and hostile officials who had never forgiven him for the Union episode, placed the responsibility

---

[256] MSS/PIJ/12/1948.   [257] MSS/PIJ/10/1948; 'Malayan Communist Party Affairs'.
[258] Chin, *Communist Party of Malaya*, p. 118. Chin goes further to suggest that Chin Peng's 'wilfulness', his desire to stamp his authority on the Party, led to a decision to mobilise being taken against the advice of other Central Executive Committee members such as Yeong Kuo, p. 29.
[259] *New Straits Times*, 3.12.1989.

on the shoulders of High Commissioner Sir Edward Gent and 'the Fabian element in Whitehall'. This became an article of faith for many, not least for those responsible for security who argued vociferously that their warnings were not heeded.[260] Certainly, there were powerful disagreements and mistrust between Gent and Commissioner-General MacDonald and mounting criticism of Gent in the local press, culminating in the famous headline in the *Straits Times* that called on him to 'Govern or get out'. It seems that by May there were moves to have him recalled pending transfer. Interestingly enough, MacDonald's deepest concern was with Gent's lack of rapport with UMNO leaders such as Dato Onn. In the event the violence in Malaya led to Gent's return being brought forward.[261] He died tragically in a plane crash en route to London and was not able to defend himself. Yet, in the aftermath of revolt, British civil servants in London attributed the blame to failures of intelligence. To them, the main source, the *Political Intelligence Journal* of the Malayan Security Service, 'presented a confused and colourful picture' in which it was 'difficult to see the wood for the trees', let alone concrete evidence of the MCP threat.[262] The Malayan Security Service forecast a rising tide of lawlessness and disorder, but gave little concrete intelligence that the signal for an armed insurrection had been given. It had, as MacDonald pointed out, insufficient time to place agents. Sir Franklin Gimson in Singapore had encouraged the view that the reports were 'too lurid'. John Dalley, its head, Gimson complained, 'tends to assume that any agitation is communist'.[263] Certainly the Malayan Security Service was paranoid about, and in retrospect side-tracked by, the emergence of a trans-Malacca Straits Malay Communist Party. The raw intelligence that was received said more about the momentum that was building up from below in Perak and Johore than about the coming moves of the MCP high command.[264] In an infamous memo, written on 14 June 1948, Dalley reassured that 'At the time of writing there is no immediate threat to internal security in Malaya although the position is constantly changing and is potentially dangerous.' There was no positive evidence of external direction of the MCP – there were 'no problems for which a solution cannot be found' – though if a lenient attitude was maintained towards the Communists for the next five years, there would be certain trouble. The MCP would have to be suppressed before it became too strong, but at a 'psychologically opportune' moment when it makes a tactical error and loses popular support.[265] Two days after this was written three European planters were murdered at Sungei Siput. However, it was not until a month later, on 23 July, that the British banned the MCP and its immediate allies.

Neither the MCP nor the government could agree amongst themselves that a revolutionary crisis had been reached in mid-1948. More important than failures of

[260] For example, J. D. Dalley to H. P. Bryson, 10.2.1965, BAM papers.
[261] Stockwell, ' "A widespread and long-concocted plot" ', pp. 72–4.
[262] Minutes, G. F. Seel, 1.3.1948; J. B. Williams, 22.6.1948, CO537/3751/Pt 1.
[263] Gimson to Bourdillion, 7.2.1948; O. H. Morris, minute, 16.7.1948, CO537/3752.
[264] Short, *Communist insurrection*, pp. 77–90.
[265] J. D. Dalley, 'Internal security – Malaya', 14.6.1948, CO537/6006.

intelligence or inertia on the British side was the fact that high policy did not permit the kind of anticipatory strike against the MCP that the planters and policemen were looking for. To the last the Labour government was reluctant to completely abandon the vestiges of its post-war plans for multi-racial colonial partnership in Malaya and govern by authoritarian instruments. It remained squeamish about the further erosion of civil liberties, as we shall see, well into the Emergency campaign itself. A recent and careful analysis of the links between the violence, the MCP and the British decision to declare an Emergency, drawing on files available in London and Washington, suggests that the Malayan government had incomplete evidence of direct MCP direction of the violence and that Whitehall was unconvinced by it. Attributing the disorder to a communist plot was a 'leap of faith'. It was made first, contrary to assumptions at the time, by High Commissioner Gent, perhaps by the beginning of June. It was made later – perhaps in early July – by Commissioner-General Malcolm MacDonald, and only accepted by the British Cabinet on 19 July because of the need to restore confidence in a local government under assault for inertia and indecision, and in deference to MacDonald's judgement.[266] As we shall see in the next chapter, it was only later that 'Communist terrorism' became the arch enemy of the Emergency campaign. In July 1948 the MCP and the British colonial regime faced each other, internally divided and unsure as to their immediate response to events, events that were increasingly being dictated by escalating conflicts on the periphery. Later historians would orchestrate these events into elaborate conspiracies. However, revolutions are not made in this way. Men and women act, politicians react.

When the British did react, they were still in a position to inflict grave reverses on the incipient mobilisation of the MCP. The first tentative moves were taken against the Federations of Trade Unions. The Trade Union Ordinance was amended on 31 May to limit the composition of federations to a single trade, and to extend the bars on those who might hold office in them. On 13 June the large federations were outlawed. R. G. Balan was arrested on 30 May; the editor of the *Min Sheng Pau*, Liew Yit Fan, on 9 June. The Sungei Siput murders on 16 June signalled the formal declaration of war. A state of Emergency was proclaimed in several areas of Perak and Johore and extended to the whole of the peninsula two days later. Arrests of MCP personnel began on 21 June, and after much soul-searching in Kuala Lumpur and London, on 23 July the MCP was banned. Many senior MCP cadres, including the military commander Lau Yew, never made it into the jungle. By the end of 1948, in the Federation of Malaya there were 1,779 persons detained; 6,374 had already been banished, together with 3,148 dependants. Not only were the MCP and its creatures banned – the MPAJA Ex-Comrades Association, the New Democratic Youth League and PETA – but detentions also dealt terminal blows to the MNP and *Hizbul Muslimin*. The parameters of civil liberties shrunk dramatically overnight. From July 1948, Malaya's march to *Merdeka* would advance in more constrained circumstances.

---

[266] Stockwell, ' "A widespread and long-concocted plot" '.

CHAPTER FOUR

Rural society and terror

———•———

By June 1948 a cycle of rural violence was in motion for which the leadership of the Malayan Communist Party was largely unprepared. Many of its wartime veterans – older, married and re-established in civilian life – were reluctant to follow their old commanders into the jungle. Captured guerrillas confirmed that the party leadership had assumed that any armed struggle would begin from September 1948, and it was only by September that guerrilla mobilisation was deemed to be complete. Against the judgement of some of his commanders, Chin Peng decreed that the MCP should seize power by the 'Yenan Way'.[1] However, its forces – the Malayan National Liberation Army (MNLA) – were denied early successes in establishing liberated areas, particularly in an attack on Gua Musang in Ulu Kelantan and operations around Batu Arang and Kajang on the west coast. A slow revision of guerrilla strategy began which culminated in the October 1951 Directives in which the MCP sounded a tactical retreat to deep jungle bases, especially in northern border areas, and reactivated the united front through labour, youth, educational movements and approaches to the Malay masses, strategies which had been prosecuted to great effect during the party's heyday of the Malayan Spring. It was only after 1951 that the government began to take the initiative: its troops learned the art of 'fighting guerrillas with guerrilla methods', and the bulk of the rural Chinese were resettled into protected areas.[2] Known as 'New Villages', they enabled sophisticated techniques of food control, intelligence and psychological warfare to be targeted on to a captive audience. Civil offensives, through welfare and local representation, began to woo the hearts and minds of the Chinese. MCP terror and subversion continued. The party retained a foothold in labour movements and found effective new vehicles, particularly in its cells in Chinese schools. However, by the mid-1950s, the Malayan government saw the increasingly selective nature of MCP violence as a measure of the effectiveness of

---

[1] Aloysius Chin, *The Communist Party of Malaya: the inside story* (Kuala Lumpar, 1995), p. 31.
[2] Capt J. M. Woodhouse, 'Some personal observations on the employment of special forces in Malaya', *Army Quarterly*, 66, 1 (1951), 70.

its counter-insurgency strategies. The war dragged on: it was only by August 1953 that, beginning with parts of Malacca, the lifting of restrictions and the gazetting of 'white areas' began. In late 1958 the MCP began to demobilise and in 1960 the Emergency officially came to an end. The struggle did not end there, however. A final peace was only signed on 2 December 1989. Survivors of the 1948 leadership – Chin Peng, Rashid Maidin and Abdullah C. D. – now old men, appeared in Haad Yai, South Thailand, to sign separate agreements with the Malaysian and Thai govern-ments. Chin Peng expressed a wish to return to Malaysia and resume open politics, to return to the *status quo ante bellum*; and retired cold warriors, also now old men, warned a new generation of Malaysians to be attentive to the lessons of history.[3]

The Emergency cast a long shadow over the new nation, over its politics and core institutions. It was fought on a vast scale and with considerable imperial resources. Its mythology has dominated the history of modern Malaya. And because Malaya has been seen as a major success story of the end of empire, the history of decolonisation in Malaya was always more than a footnote to the Cold War: it became a counter-insurgency primer.[4] Writing on the Communist war evolved out of the immediate needs of coercion and enforcement. Even recent accounts, which emphasise the social and political components of the campaign at the expense of the military, are permeated with the vocabulary of counter-insurgency.[5] No attempt is made here to chronicle what writers have called the 'shooting war' – this has already been done with considerable skill.[6] Instead, this chapter shifts the focus away from the terrorist campaign, to examine the dynamics of a society living in a state of terror, and the ways in which this indelibly marked the emergence of the independent polity. In this sense, the primary importance of the military campaign lies in its role as a catalyst of social change: in its meaning for the men and women who fought it; for those who attempted to earn a living in its midst; and in the ways in which it scarred and remade the landscape itself, through massive ecological and demographic change. This chapter and Chapter 5 argue that the Emergency entailed a far-reaching militarisation of Malayan society and made the colonial state an authoritative presence in the lives of many Malayans for the first time. The most durable legacy of the conflict was the attempt by the colonial government to fashion stable communities, uninfected by Communism, along its internal frontier. The securing of the jungle fringes permitted the permanent settlement of specialised Chinese agriculturalists on the land, and

---

[3] C. C. Too, 'The Communist Party of Malaya and its attempts to capture power', *New Straits Times*, 3–6.12.1989; Chin, *Communist Party of Malaya*, pp. 249–50.
[4] Sir Robert Thompson, *Defeating Communist insurgency: experiences from Malaya and Vietnam* (London, 1966); Lucian W. Pye, *Lessons from the Malayan struggle against Communism* (Centre for International Studies, M.I.T., Cambridge, 1957); Richard Clutterbuck, *Riot and Revolution in Singapore and Malaysia, 1943–63* (London, 1973).
[5] For example, Richard Stubbs, *Hearts and minds in guerrilla warfare: the Malayan Emergency, 1948–1960* (Singapore, 1989).
[6] Especially Anthony Short, *The Communist insurrection in Malaya, 1948–60* (London, 1976); John Coates, *Suppressing insurgency: an analysis of the Malayan Emergency, 1948–54* (Boulder, 1992).

presented great opportunities for employers to restore labour discipline. The social disruption created by the Emergency campaign itself created new agrarian problems, witnessed most notably in the question of land rights for the Malayan Chinese. For a colonial regime animated with a new sense of purpose, the Emergency created a great field for social experiment in the new settlements and in the workplace. The British proceeded by trial and error. By identifying new local leadership and bolstering their standing as its rural allies, they sought to entrench the obligations of citizenship and to appoint a new role for the individual in society. It was an exercise in moral reconstruction through the fostering of welfare work and community service, and the implanting of civic, and potentially Christian, virtue. The disorientated populations ensnared in these ambitious new initiatives sought to salvage what they could of their livelihood and reconcile themselves to the new order in the countryside. Their efforts to do so can be traced through internal leadership struggles, cultural resurgence through education and the slow recovery of trade unionism. These responses were not always compatible with those envisaged by the colonial authorities. For the Chinese in the New Villages this meant the rise of the predominantly elite-based Malayan Chinese Association (MCA), through which urban business elites sought to regain the authority in the countryside which they had lost in the aftermath of the Pacific war. As the rural Chinese were mobilised into a new era of national politics, its leadership had to reconcile the need to re-educate the new citizenry with the preservation of their communal self-identity.

The official mind of counter-insurgency

Violence embedded stereotypes of the criminal and turbulent Chinese character in the minds of a new generation of soldiers and administrators. These stereotypes – especially of a 'secret society complex' at the heart of Chinese life – were not new. However, the specific understanding of the violence to which they gave birth dictated the political agenda of counter-terror. It confirmed its civil character, and in the early years of the war legitimised authoritarian and sometimes brutal policing. The official understanding of terror had a profound impact on the manner in which the colonial government sought to restrain it. Yet it took some months for the British to be clear in their minds what they were fighting in Malaya. To Sir Henry Gurney, the man who replaced Gent as High Commissioner, Communism in Malaya was 'not a political doctrine; it is banditry and lawlessness'. In private, however, the British were obliged to refute their own propaganda and acknowledge the political dimension to the crisis.[7] In public, the criminalisation of the insurgency gave birth to a careful vocabulary of suppression, in which terror was neither 'war', 'rebellion' nor 'insurrection', and which disallowed any reference to an 'enemy'. At talk of war and insurrection, insurance companies threatened to withdraw their cover; theft and vandalism was

---

[7] Gurney, minute, 31.5.1949; cf. 'A paper on the security situation in the Federation of Malaya – Appendix A: Present attitude of the Chinese population', CO537/4751.

another matter.[8] The guerrillas were therefore 'thugs', 'bandits' and 'terrorists' –
which embarrassed the British Army who still owed many of them pensions. Initially
officials preferred the term 'Communist bandit' for its 'fine minatory ring'.[9] However,
it was abandoned as it found an echo in the Chinese traditions of social banditry
which the MCP exploited. The British government sought to narrow the Emergency's
political parameters. Its international propaganda went to great lengths to dispel any
suggestion that a genuine popular uprising was underway; any part Communism
played in the rebellion came from outside influences. In private, it was admitted that
no evidence could be found to support the idea that the insurrection was directed
from outside. Police Chief Arthur Young thought there was a courier from Moscow
every six months. The Colonial Office was very sceptical about this, and Templer
found no evidence either way beyond reports of visits from Indonesian Malays across
the Straits of Malacca and a trickle of supplies across the Thai border. The MCP
mobilised on its caches of British or Japanese arms, and produced its own guns in
crude armouries.[10]

If terror was merely lawlessness, a major obstacle to its suppression was the
existence of the rule of law. Gurney's problem was that 'in order to maintain law and
order in present conditions in Malaya it is necessary for government itself to break it
for a time'. However, to seek legitimacy for violence through executive decree would
ultimately be derogatory to the rule of law. Terror was civil war, in which the burning
question was how far 'police and soldiers who are not saints' could be restrained.
Gurney's experiences in Palestine had made him nervous of martial law; it was an
admission of defeat. This insistence on fighting a civilian war was perhaps Britain's
most important contribution to the new science of counter-insurgency. Malaya was to
remain a police action, and it was on the police and civilians that the bulk of the
casualties fell.[11] By the beginning of the year of independence, 1957, 2,890 police and
3,253 civilians had been killed, as against 518 soldiers.[12] These legal niceties did not
obscure the ferocity of counter-terror. One reason for resisting the temptation to
declare martial law was that, paradoxically, the police had a freer hand without it as
they were released from their obligations under the rules of war. Atrocities such as
Batang Kali – Malaya's My Lai, in which twenty-five Chinese were massacred by
Scots Guards in circumstances which have never been fully investigated – actually led

---

[8] Andrew Gilmour, *An Eastern Cadet's anecdotage* (Singapore, 1974), p. 173.
[9] Higham to Gurney, 19.5.1950, CO537/5984. J. D. Higham, undated minute, November
     1948, CO537/4762; FARELF to War Office, 22.7.1948, CO537/4751.
[10] See the brief on 'Malaya', circulated to British Embassies overseas, enclosed in T. C. Jerrom
     to R. S. Scrivener, Foreign Office, 13.2.1952, CO1022/2; Ivor Piak (Imperial Defence
     College) to J. G. Tahourdin, Foreign Office, 3.7.1953; T. C. Jerrom, minute, 31.7.1953,
     CO1022/145. M. C. A. Henniker, *Red shadow over Malaya* (London, 1953), pp. 41–2;
     MRSA, April 1955, CO1030/8.
[11] 'BDCC(FE), 16th meeting, 28.1.1949'; Gurney to Creech Jones, 30.5.1949; 'Paper by
     Malaya on organisational lessons of the Emergency', CO537/4773.
[12] J. W. G. Moran, *Spearhead in Malaya* (London, 1959), p. 13.

to the legal powers of the security forces being strengthened.[13] It was a long, long war which produced grisly tallies of kills and public displays of corpses outside police stations.[14] Its brutality was brought home to the British public when the *Daily Worker* published photographs of Royal Marine Commandos in Perak posing cheerfully with bandit heads. The military in Malaya attributed this to 'excessive zeal'; the Admiralty admitted in private that 'a similar action in wartime would be a war crime' and ungenerously and falsely blamed Dyak trackers for it.[15] One British officer complained in his memoirs that hunting tiger or elephant was dull after hunting bandits.[16] Malaya was far enough away to allow the use of Lincoln aircraft to clandestinely drop 1,000 lb bombs on settlements, in the hope that it might not be noticed. In early 1950 it was admitted that there were five cases of air strikes hitting civilian targets, including children at a school in Johore.[17] Few were convinced of airpower's military effectiveness. Aircraft were to be more useful in dropping propaganda leaflets, not bombs.

This understanding of terror allowed the horror of counter-terror to be mitigated by the conviction that armed Communists – and this often meant the Chinese as a whole – were not only criminal, but vicious and evil. In the mind of the soldier, Communism itself was similar to Christianity, except that its ends justified terrible means. Indeed, there were horrendous atrocities, and lurid publication of public mutilations and disembowelments by Communists.[18] A soldier spoke of one senior terrorist: 'even in death the ugly distorted face bore the stamp of cruelty and evil, and stirred little feeling of compassion'. The noted Kajang terrorist, Liew Kim Bok, was said to be 'always deliberate, and was known to enjoy the suffering and the fear which he provoked'. In contrast, to British commanders their soldiers represented 'the innate goodness of the British race'.[19] It was a personalised and intimate war: the life histories of the terrorists were carefully pieced together, their families drawn into the campaign to entice them out of the jungle. In time, the discipline and 'stoicism' that jungle life required, the courage and ambition of the terrorist, the 'semi-Robin Hoods' of the forest, the 'likeable rogues' working with the security forces, elicited

---

[13] This first point was stressed to the planters: 'Extract from record of meeting with the Pahang Planters' Association on 28.5.1950 at Mentakab', CO537/5976; Gurney to Creech Jones, 3.1.1949, CO537/4750. For a discussion of Batang Kali, see Short, *Communist insurrection*, pp. 166–9.

[14] For example, J. B. Oldfield, *The Green Howards in Malaya (1949–52): the story of a post-war tour of duty by a Battalion of the Line* (Aldershot, 1953), p. 149.

[15] *Daily Worker*, 28.4.1952; FARELF to War Office, 30.4.1952; T. C. Jerrom, minute, 30.4.1952; J. D. Higham, minute, CO1022/45. Most military accounts deny that Dyaks took heads, e.g. Oldfield, *Green Howards*, p. xxii.

[16] Henniker, *Red shadow*, p. 196.

[17] HQ, FARELF to Air Ministry, 20.1.1950; Air Ministry to FARELF, 30.1.1950; Gurney to Griffith, 8.3.1950, CO537/5978; *Malay Mail*, 3.3.1950.

[18] Henniker, *Red Shadow*, pp. 38–9.

[19] Richard Miers, *Shoot to kill* (London, 1959), p. 54; Arthur Campbell, *Jungle green* (London, 1959), pp. 53–7; Henniker, *Red shadow*, pp. 10–11.

reluctant admiration.[20] Vast numbers of servicemen, in coming to terms with the sudden violence and exoticism of jungle warfare, utilised a wide range of intermediaries 'to translate for our western outlook the workings of the eastern mind'. Soldiers felt a need 'psychologically to fit in with Chinese customs', and to adjust to the subtleties of the master–servant relationship.[21] The Emergency was a revolt of the houseboys. Arthur Campbell's enjoyment of a meal prepared by his Chinese cook, Ah Soong, gave way to dark reflections:

> Thinking of dinner reminded me that I must have a word with the Police about Ah Soong. I did not trust the man. To begin with he was a Chinese. They were all two-faced beggars, sitting on the fence, waiting to see who was going to get the upper hand. Meanwhile they were as likely as not to be helping one side as the other. He never looked me straight in the face when I was talking to him and his beady eyes were always on the move.

This memoir, and its endorsement by the High Commissioner, General Templer, provoked an outcry from the Malayan Chinese.[22] The primers and dialogues through which the British taught their officers to communicate with the Chinese are revealing documents of applied orientalism in their detailed discussions of Chinese familial and community structures; their keen sense of what a former police chief called 'the usual cruel forms of Chinese terrorism', and in the racial contempt of their fictitious conversations between officials and Chinese with names such as 'Ah Fuk'.[23] The undercurrents of racialism ran deep. However, not all British soldiers were insensible to the predicament of the Chinese. Some acknowledged that the eastern concept of time and space was different, and found a real challenge in coming to terms with the 'incomprehensible mystique' of the Chinese – 'Mr Ping Pong' – their courage, and their willingness to betray colleagues out of mixed motives of self-preservation, hope of reward and bitter disillusionment.[24]

If ethnic difference was quickly mobilised to make terror more comprehensible, the perpetual dilemma of the campaign was how far violence should meet violence. Expatriate business interests always remained sceptical about the government's seriousness in meeting the dangers posed by the Emergency. An attack on Batu Arang mine at the outset of the campaign in July 1948 – and fears that the MCP might establish a liberated area in the industrial heartland of the country – brought the danger close to home. In the early days expatriate managers bore the brunt of the terror, a fear that 'sleep with planters parties' did little to ease. In 1948 their morale

---

[20] Oldfield, *Green Howards*, p. xxi.

[21] Anthony Crockett, *Green beret, red star* (London, 1954), pp. 58, 61, 92.

[22] Campbell, *Jungle green*, p. 53. See Victor Purcell, *Malaya: Communist or free?* (Stanford, 1955), pp. 17, 141–2.

[23] Government Officers' Chinese Language School, Kuala Lumpur, *Malayan Dialogues for translation into Chinese* (Kuala Lumpur, 1957); R. Onraet, 'The prospects for trade unions in Malaya, *British Malaya* (January, 1949), 140.

[24] Miers, *Shoot to kill*, pp. 209–212; Henniker, *Red shadow*, p. 37.

was close to collapse. If more were killed or fled Malaya, Arthur Creech Jones was warned, 'there will be large bands of labour roaming the country panic-stricken, unpaid, starving'.[25] If not for the fortuitous boom caused by the Korean war more would have left; and but for the Pacific war and high UK taxation, many more would have retired. Planters were venomous towards the Malayan Civil Service (MCS) establishment. They were confident that it was their protests that had seen off Gent, and were being increasingly antagonised by Gurney's own 'Fabianism'. His administration was culpable on two accounts: its indirect chain of command, and for running the affair 'as though it were a discussion group when we see it as WAR'.[26] Settler anger reached a head in 1951. Between July and November of that year the Emergency claimed the lives of forty-nine European planters. By the end of the year, economic interests felt the country was heading into 'economic chaos', affecting both industrial efficiency and capital assets themselves – especially replanting, prospecting and inflow of capital. The 'soft-hearted doctrinaires' who put social welfare before the suppression of banditry, and the government's lenient treatment of surrendered insurgents, provoked particular scorn.[27] The mouthpiece of business – *Brown's Malayan Economic Review* – inveighed against the 'premium of lawlessness . . . bandits and their helpers being treated as prodigal sons and daughters and being entertained to ten-course dinners'.[28]

In the face of these attacks, officials argued that 'the Chinese mind' made Malaya unique. Terror had created a new political conundrum.[29] Policy-making was hesitant and reflected profound divisions within the administration. The civil nature of the struggle was severely tested by a series of debates on the extent to which violent counter-terror measures could be sanctioned – for example over colonial policing, collective punishment and capital sentencing. At the outset of the Emergency the police force was in disarray. Its role was ill-defined and bitter professional jealousies surfaced over the importation of reinforcements and a new police chief, Colonel W. N. Gray, from Palestine.[30] Dato Onn complained to the new Secretary of State, James Griffiths, that 'the so-called Emergency has been a convenient instrument to make of Malaya a dumping-ground for more and more expatriate officers'.[31] There were bitter divides between the police and intelligence, the police and the military. In particular, under Gray the force became more paramilitary, and this and jealousy over rank and promotions offended many old Malaya hands, in particular Gray's Deputy,

---

[25] UPAM et al. to Creech Jones, 14.7.1948, CO537/3694.
[26] MacDonald to Creech Jones, 20.4.1949, CO537/4751; Viscountess Davidson to Lyttelton, 1.11.1951, CO1022/1.
[27] 'Memorandum submitted by delegation of joint Malayan interests at a meeting at the Colonial Office on 15.11.1951', CO1022/39.
[28] *Brown's Malayan Economic Review*, I, 3 (14.2.1951), 2.
[29] Gurney to Creech Jones, 30.5.1949, CO537/4773.
[30] Short, *Communist insurrection*, pp. 129–32, 275–91.
[31] Onn to Griffiths, 1.11.1950, CO537/6020.

B. M. B. O'Connell.[32] O'Connell and some of his contemporaries in the State administrations were accused of 'deliberate disloyalty' in co-ordinating a campaign against Gray. An enquiry resulted.[33] O'Connell told sympathetic ears at the Colonial Office that he himself had little confidence in Gurney, who seemed to work only through his chosen instruments: 'He was a sheep farmer, and treats his juniors as if they were sheep.'[34] To other observers the Palestine recruits were of a different type to the Malayan police: 'rough types and adventurers'. 'Most of the breed,' noted Anthony Burgess, 'were a brutal lot. They spoke a little debased Arabic and had learnt ten words of Malay.'[35] To professional soldiers the Special Constables levéed from the kampongs seemed to be 'a horde of hastily enrolled, largely untrained and only partially equipped Malays', many of whom had never fired their rifles.[36] This would change as the local militia became better schooled in police work. The character of the policing also changed dramatically. A new Police Chief, Arthur Young was seconded from the 'Met' to replace Gray in 1952. 'We in Malaya,' the new broom announced, 'will endeavour to establish in a few months the relationship which required more than one hundred years of English history.' The motto was 'Ready to Serve', and sought to identify the police with welfare and youth work.[37] Young aimed to bring the London bobby to the villages and towns of Malaya. He was only partially successful in doing so. However, the police force would be one of the strongest state institutions the rulers of independent Malaya would inherit from the British.

Not only the character of the policing, but the harshness of the punishment – the level of irksome restrictions on movement, on economic life, purchase of commodities that would be tolerable – was constantly under question. The enforcement of these restrictions often provoked public outcry. The manhandling of Chinese women during routine searches at Semenyih New Village forced an official enquiry to appease Chinese opinion. There were dangerous racial undertones to the incidents. It was acknowledged that 'the sanctity of the person' had been violated, that Emergency Regulations were an affront to the human dignity of proud individualistic cultivators.[38] Collective punishment of villages was approved by the British government in November 1950. It had already been used in India, Palestine, Cyprus and East Africa,

[32] A. J. Stockwell, 'Policing during the Malayan Emergency, 1948–60: communism, communalism and decolonization', in D. Anderson and D. Killingray, *Policing and decolonization: politics, nationalism and the police, 1917–65* (Manchester, 1992), pp. 110–13.

[33] Gurney to Creech Jones, 6.10.1949, CO717/162/52745/19/49.

[34] J. D. Higham, minute, 7.10.1949; Shenton Thomas, 'Note of conversation with B. O'Connell', *ibid.*

[35] Harry Miller, *Menace in Malaya: the campaign against Communism, 1948–60* (London, 1954), p. 89; Anthony Burgess, *Little Wilson and Big God* (London, 1987), p. 389.

[36] Henniker, *Red shadow*, pp. 31–2.

[37] A. E. Young, 'Commissioner's Instruction No.36 – Operation Service', 11.11.1952, CS/5235/53.

[38] 'Federation of Malaya Political report for January 1956', CO1030/33; Federation of Malaya, *Report on the conduct of food searches at Semenyih in the Kajang District of the State of Selangor* (Kuala Lumpur, 1956).

and was administered by European officers to minimise its racial aspect. Fines were imposed on villages such as Pusing, Perak and Bukit Selambau in Kedah. In Perak, there were complaints that undesirable and rootless members of the population disappeared before they paid their portion. In Kedah, Chinese 'regarded the payment as something to be expected when entering the District Office'. It became clear that the strategy was best suited to homogeneous communities, and counter-productive if communities insufficiently protected by the police were penalised.[39] The Chinese press emphasised that 'the psychology of the Chinese, as a rule, is to live a peaceful life, and at time of disturbance, to preserve their life by any means'.[40] There was similar awareness of the political dangers of continuing a severe policy of capital sentencing. Mercy was shown to rebels who were not directly involved in killings. However, there was difficulty in distinguishing between complicity and the actual taking of life. The waiving of the death penalty for bandit surrenders was never formally acknowledged in case public opinion demanded prosecution: few were prosecuted, and most were placed under restricted residence orders. By the end of February 1953, 986 insurgents had surrendered, but public discussion of this was avoided, lest magnanimity be interpreted as weakness.[41] When, in 1955, Chief Minister Tunku Abdul Rahman pledged his life against that of any bandit who surrendered this caused considerable embarrassment.[42] A *cause célèbre* was the case of Lee Meng, an attractive and ruthless Communist cell organiser. At her trial, there was a divergence of opinion between the British and local Assessors in the case and it was clear that had Lee Meng the right to be tried by members of her own community – as had Europeans – she might not have been convicted.[43] In support of her appeal to the Privy Council against a death sentence the *Nanyang Siang Pau* wrote:

> This speaks of the dignity of British Law which is not affected by the Emergency in Malaya. It also speaks of the advantage of democracy over totalitarianism, in that the former at least assures the people of their legitimate human rights. Malaya is unfortunately involved in the tragic world struggle between the Communist and non-Communist bloc. In accusing each other, both have gone too far to the extreme. We wish the Malayan authorities would replace this struggle of retaliation by a rule of benevolence. This would win the hearts of the people and would achieve more than a 100,000 troops.[44]

Yet the eventual commutation of the sentence did not obscure the ruthlessness with which the colonial government had pursued a conviction, and the fact that it had repeatedly overridden the verdict of courts to do so. The consolidation of the rhetoric

---

[39] 'Memo on collective punishment'; 'Collective punishment: notes of a meeting . . . on 10.11.1950, CO537/6007; 'Monthly review of Chinese affairs', February, March, 1951, CO537/7280.
[40] 'On the incident at Permatang Tinggi', *Nanyang Siang Pau*, 29.8.1952.
[41] 'Surrender policy', Young Papers; Templer to Lyttelton, 12.5.1952, CO1022/49.
[42] Political Intelligence Report (PIR), January, 1955', CO1030/245.
[43] Short, *Communist insurrection*, pp. 384–5.
[44] 'In support of Lee Meng's Appeal', *Nanyang Siang Pau*, 1.12.1952.

and practice of counter-insurgency fostered new debates on the nature of authoritarianism, in which many of the demands of the Malayan Spring for the accountability of law to public opinion were reprised, albeit in far more circumspect language.

The inner politics of terror

Despite these attempts to ration counter-terror, a continuing legacy of the immediate post-invasion period was a rapidly escalating militarisation of large sections of Malayan society. British regulars and national servicemen did not see the worst of the campaign. Malaya was a Commonwealth war in the widest sense, involving Gurkha, East African, Australian, New Zealand and Fijian contingents. The offensive forces included Gurkhas, Dyaks and Orang Asli. On the front line between the planters and their wives and the Communists, were the Chinese squatters. For these rural Chinese, subjected to extortion on one side, draconian security measures on the other, and occasional atrocities on both, rural terror disintegrated the nascent political solidarities and economic communities in whose name it was launched. In this sense, on both sides the moral validation of violence was severely weakened. Terror also provoked a reaction within the Malay community. The campaign came increasingly to take on a communal guise as thousands of young Malay constables enlisted. As violence escalated, and people's exposure to it became more prolonged, the terms of the struggle underwent a transformation. By 1951, all parties to the conflict were beginning to reassess the way in which the war was fought.

In some places the Pacific war had not yet ended: even in 1989, there were two former soldiers of the Japanese Imperial Army with the Communists in south Thailand. Only in April 1949 did the KMT guerrillas in north Perak surrender, some of them only to resume fighting as Special Constables.[45] General security from gang-robbery was low, especially in border areas such as Perlis, where the Padang Besar area was still a centre for looting of trains, gambling, smuggling and prostitution, killings and kidnappings.[46] Elsewhere, the Emergency was the continuation of organised crime by other means. The relationship between the MCP and the Triads oscillated between aggressive rivalry and cautious alliances of convenience, such as in the Kuala Krau opium trade, and in the absorption of the notorious Green Mountain Dragon Society of Salak South.[47] There is a sense in which their mutual criminalisation and fear of repression brought them together. Some criminal elements were directly absorbed into the MCP, and the MCP-*Ang Bin Hoay* conflict of the immediate postwar years subsided somewhat. In Perak, it was reported that members of the *Ang* joined the MCP 'for excitement'. The MCP attempted to appeal to a shared hatred of

---

[45] *Malaya Tribune*, 22.9.1949.
[46] *Annual report of the social and economic progress of the people of the State of Perlis for the year 1947.*
[47] Monthly Review of Subversive Activities (MRSA), November, 1954, CO1030/7; Pan-Malayan Review of Security Intelligence (PMR), No. 12 of 1949, CO5367/4862; *Malay Mail*, 2.2.1949.

landlordism and exploitation of the poor – evoking common themes of righteousness and brotherhood. However, approaches to Triad elements usually occurred on an individual basis, and the response of the secret societies themselves was governed entirely by self-interest. The MCP remained uneasy about the loyalty of 'robber' elements who might abscond with funds and intelligence. Indeed, for this reason, relations deteriorated again after 1952, as in adversity the MCP strengthened its discipline, and many Triad men joined the Kinta Home Guard. However, reports of the Triad being used to reach the urban masses strengthened the official conviction that the 'secret society complex' remained the lifeblood of Chinese politics.[48]

To the colonial government, Chinese tolerance of secret societies underlaid the effectiveness of the mass organisation of the MCP – the *Min Yuen*. The cultural context of Communist support has yet to be fully researched. As we have seen, Triad leadership came to the fore in the war. Certainly the British themselves continued to make connections between *Ang Bin Hoay* support for the MCP and rival Triads' support for the KMT, and later – as in the case of the *Wah Kee* – with the conservative Malayan Chinese Association. The patchwork of Chinese settlement in Malaya also made dialect differences significant. This was not merely a reflection of clannish loyalties, although this played a part. The Hakka already had made a powerful contribution to the history of rebellion in China. In Southeast Asia, their settlement patterns replicated those of China and the long history of *kongsi* 'little republics' in Southeast Asia perhaps strengthened their sense of partnership and tradition of self-government.[49] The ethnic structure of the MCP also reflected the concentrations of dialect groups in certain tasks. The KMT had strong roots in the Cantonese population of the towns, whilst many, though not all, of the Hainanese and Hakka pioneer communities tended towards the MCP. Dialect groups were also regionally concentrated, in ways that reflected the regional foci of the revolt. Hokkien was the main dialect in Johore and Kedah; Hakka in Negri Sembilan and Selangor; Cantonese and Kwongsai in Perak and Pahang – although Hakka was the second most-spoken dialect in these two States and in Johore, reflecting their dominance in heavy manual labour throughout Malaya.[50] A breakdown by dialect group of detainees at Taiping rehabilitation camp in May 1952 gives: 36.5 per cent Hakka, 30 per cent Hokkien, 15.7 per cent Cantonese and roughly 7 per cent each of Kwongsai and Teochew, only 3.5 Hainanese and a small number of Hockchiew and Luichew. By contrast, according to the 1947 census, Hokkien made up 28.6 per cent of the total Chinese population of Malaya, Hakka, 21.1 per cent, Cantonese 25.7. per cent,

---

[48] See Leon Comber, 'Chinese secret societies in Malaya: an introduction', *JMBRAS*, 29, 1 (1956), 155–61; Wilfred Blythe, *The impact of Chinese secret societies in Malaya: a historical study* (London, 1969), pp. 421–38.

[49] Mary S. Erbaugh, 'The secret history of the Hakkas: the Chinese revolution as a Hakka enterprise', *China Quarterly*, 132 (1992), pp. 937–68; Wong Tai Peng, *The origins of Chinese kongsi* (Petaling Jaya, 1994).

[50] Malayan Christian Council, *A survey of the New Villages of Malaya* (Singapore, 1958), pp. 7–8.

Teochew 11 per cent and Kwongsai only 3.8 per cent. Apart from the very high numbers of Hakka, the MCP forces had a reasonably balanced representation of the various dialect groups in Malaya; more so when only the male population is considered.[51] Dialect was not the primary source of loyalty with the MCP, which came from other, chiefly political, forms of association, but it did give rebellion a much deeper cultural credence within Chinese society in Malaya.

The MCP's success in accumulating funds and resources had a wider economic basis that went beyond any one sectional loyalty. As we saw in Chapter 3, the tribute system which had been a feature of the economy of the expanding frontier was extended to cover the mobilisation of an entire guerrilla army, and was being exploited by existing criminal gangs. Chinese miners in Perak 'regarded [it] as merely a natural and almost inevitable encumbrance on the normal conduct of business'.[52] Eighty per cent of the trading and labouring population were said to be paying contributions. In October and November 1949 an estimated $500,000 was paid.[53] To Gurney this was indistinguishable from:

> the whole vast racket of black-marketeering, smuggling and commercial corruption that go to make up Chinese business methods. In the countries around us where Communist or nationalist banditry is rampant the Chinese flourish. They finance it, because in the short-term it pays and the short-term profits appeal to Chinese philosophy. . . I do not think we yet know enough about how Chinese millionaires in Singapore and the Federation really get their money and how they spend it.

Chinese mining associations were pressurised to call on their members to stop paying protection money, as well as the Chinese bus companies, who were especially vulnerable. This issue, implicating as it did some of the most eminent Chinese in Malaya, was a sensitive undercurrent to colonial politics, and hardened British attitudes towards the Chinese. A number of Chettiars, including one millionaire, confessed to the police; some big Singapore *towkays* were also pursued.[54] Rumour and accusation fostered an atmosphere of recrimination and mistrust reminiscent of the witch-hunts against Japanese collaborators at the end of the Pacific war. These investigations formed the background to British attempts to restore collaborative arrangements with Chinese leaders, helped push them into an attempt to recapture their own authority in the community and forge new systems of clientage.

Yet terror was also reinforcing economic differentiation amongst the rural Chinese. The inflated payments by big business were exceptional: the bulk of the costs of insurgency fell on the small Asian capitalist and the labouring population. The rebels raided isolated shops, and on small Asian-owned estates in Johore absentee land-

---

[51] 'Review of Chinese Affairs, May 1952', CO1022/151.
[52] J. G. Black, 'Note of a meeting between representatives of the Perak Chinese Miners' Association and the BA Perak', 6.12.1948, CO537/3758.
[53] David Rees Williams, minute, 22.12.1948, CO537/3745; 'BDCC(FE), 16th meeting, 28.1.1949', CO537/4773.
[54] Gurney to Creech Jones, 28.2.1949, CO537/4750.

owners only received about 10–30 per cent of the output. In Kajang rubber stealing amounted to $10,000 a month, and in Perak the whole of one 180-acre estate was being tapped by the MCP.[55] MCP earnings were even higher in tin mining than in rubber areas, and in one district only 9 per cent of revenue came from subscriptions.[56] There was little room for Asian businessmen to manoeuvre: there were cases of timber *towkays* selling their lorries to their workers to prevent them from being incinerated.[57] The scope for the worker to resist was even narrower. In Gelang Patah in Johore, the subscription rate was five dollars a tapper, and *kepalas* who tried to stop this were executed. Even in 'White Areas', which the government had officially cleansed of guerrillas, underground organisations quietly collected subscriptions. For the middle class in particular, the MCP's method was to 'teach a monkey by killing a fowl in its presence'. Workers' subscriptions might be reduced when wages fell, but subscribe they must.[58] The course of rural violence tended to consistently undermine the very kinds of solidarities the MCP was trying to reinforce. The effective 'self-tap, self-sell' message was undermined by the party's industrial sabotage which was in effect telling labourers to 'break their own rice bowls'.[59] By this the moral validation of terror was severely weakened. This was a central theme of government propaganda. 'The Communist so-called People's Army,' it trumpeted, 'owes its allegiance to foreign masters, and is run by murderers, thugs and extortioners for their own profit.'[60] Defectors from the party such as the former Vice-President of the PMFTU, Lam Swee, who surrendered at Bentong in June 1950, condemned the 'purely wanton massacre' by the 'undemocratic' MCP. The MCP had destroyed the trade union movement by forcing it into the jungle; it was 'a political conspiracy . . . utilising the workers and farmers as scapegoats for seizing power'.[61] This issue ignited a fierce ideological dispute within the party itself, as 'Deviationists', such as one of the party's leading theorists Siew Lau, began to attack the 'Buffalo Communists' on the Central Committee. Siew Lau was executed for writing a series of pamphlets: 'Rectify our past mistakes'; 'The keynote of the Malayan revolution'; and 'A discourse on the principles of equal distribution of rubber estates'. He claimed that the revolution was premature. The failure to win Malay or Indian support had 'doomed the rising to failure from the start'. By placing the burden of the revolution on the rural Chinese, the party was further weakening itself. Siew Lau advocated a progressive advance to a

---

[55] MRSA, March 1954, December, 1954, CO1030/7; MRSA, January, 1955, February 1955, CO1030/8.

[56] PMR, December 1951, CO1022/187.   [57] MRSA, September 1954, CO1030/7.

[58] MCP, South Malaya Bureau document, 'Opinion on solving the present financial difficulties', March 1954; MRSA, June 1954, *ibid.*

[59] J. N. McHugh, 'Psychological or political warfare in Malaya: II The postwar years', *Journal of the Historical Society of the University of Malaya*, 5 (1966/67), 83–6.

[60] 'Emergency leaflet – No. 202', RHO.

[61] 'A message from Lam Swee to the workers of Malaya', CO537/6015. There was evidence of important defections following Lam Swee's message, e.g. SFWIS, No. 53, 10.5.1951, CO537/7291.

Communist state, through a stage of 'democratic capitalism'. The Central Committee, however, had based its strategy on a reading of Mao which called for 'enemy capitalism' to be immediately nationalised to pave the way for collective farms. To them, 'redistribution' was heretical in theory, and divisive in practice.[62] Doctrinal disputations reflected a mood of self-doubt amongst the party rank-and-file. Disgust at taking from the poor was a recurrent theme in the debriefings of surrendered terrorists.[63] And whilst the poor were in many ways willing to give, deteriorating economic conditions further strained the credibility of terror as a political strategy.

As counter-insurgency slowly began to detach the guerrillas from their main sources of intelligence, recruitment and food, the MCP undertook a profound revision of strategy.[64] 'The petty bourgeoisie and national capitalists have been alienated', it was admitted. More equitable taxation was to exempt small businesses and hawkers.[65] Broad-based cultural and political themes were re-emphasised. The MCP's December 1948 'Strategic Plan' – penned by Chin Peng – had aimed at building bases and supply lines for a large assault on the British.[66] The December 1949 Plan, based on a June Central Committee meeting, ordered the *min yuen* to develop liberated areas. However, the September/October 1951 Politburo Directives were issued to overcome the obstacles to this by establishing deep jungle bases, primarily in three core concentrations: North Perak-Kelantan-South Thailand, South Perak-Kuala Lipis-Raub, and Tasek Bera-Endau-Segamat. Politically this marked a return to united front tactics of enlisting the support of labour organisations, Malay radicals and movements of Chinese cultural resurgence. These directives took nearly a year to filter through to the State leaderships, and in late 1952 and throughout 1953 the MCP began to regroup.[67] The cells of the old united front had never been disbanded. Presses for cyclostyled newspapers like *Vanguard News*, *Malayan War Bulletin*, and in Singapore, *Students' Information* and *Freedom News* or *Freedom Express*, sought to keep alive the front organisation, and it was through the printed word that indirect assistance from the CCP came in the form of publications from Hong Kong. Former MDU radicals such as Eu Chooi Yip and Lim Kean Chye cultivated the Singapore underground – the Anti-British League. Formed in September 1949, it was in many

---

[62] Miller, *Menace in Malaya*, pp. 154–62. A piece of British counter-propaganda, printed by the Craftsman Press in Singapore, describes this dissension in the MCP, purporting to be published by the Malayan Communist Party, Johore-Malacca Border Committee, *Death of a heretic* (Singapore, 1951).

[63] 'Emergency Leaflets – No: 260 – "Target: Enemy"' (Chinese), RHO; 'Interrogation of Chai Soo of 36 Platoon, 8th Independent Company, Perak', in WIS. No. 24, 19.10.1950, CO537/6015.

[64] For an early indication of these difficulties see, Secretariat of the North Johore Area Committee, 'The First Enlarged Conference resolutions', 19–24.2.1949, CO537/4751.

[65] MCP Selangor State Secretariat, 'Opinions on a number of material points connected with the present framework of activity', CO1022/187.

[66] 'Confidential annex to Report No. 17, Eastern department, Colonial Office', 1.6.1949, CO537/4751.

[67] MRSA, December 1953, CO1030/7.

ways the clandestine successor to the MDU and aimed to bring together a range of radical activists – students, journalists, teachers – under the influence of MCP cadres. The colonial authorities took firm action: in a round-up in early 1951 a range of leading left-wing personalities were detained – men such as J. J. Puthucheary, P. V. Sharma, Devan Nair, A. Samad Ismail and John Eber. However, the MCP's efforts to revive the united front did not end there. As early as July 1951 Malcolm MacDonald admitted to Herbert Morrison that the MCP had penetrated schools and trade unions 'to a greater extent that we have been hitherto ready to admit to ourselves'.[68] By 1954 Chinese activists such as the young Tan Chin Siong had revitalised the students' movement through the Chinese High Schools, and their Singapore Chinese Middle School Students' Union was intervening in a new wave of militant industrial action that was sweeping the island, culminating in the momentous riots that accompanied the Hock Lee Bus Company strike in May 1955. The MCP's change of strategy would energise the attempts by the colonial government to create a Malayan national identity through a proactive educational and cultural policy. But also, amongst the terrorists themselves, the experience of violence was necessitating the cultivation of new social and cultural solidarities. For both sides in the struggle this was to become the central lesson of the Emergency.

Although the British and the MCP had become more restrained in their resort to arms, both had to confront the problem of how violence, once loosed, could be restrained. Government operations in one area could displace terrorists to destabilise another; British attempts to recruit rural Chinese could increase guerrilla ranks by leading the MCP to raise the stakes of terror: 'if you join the British,' they would warn, 'we kill you, so you might as well join us first'.[69] Colonial propaganda oscillated between threats and exhortations. 'You can hide your farm for a time,' leaflets informed squatters, 'but sooner or later we will find it and destroy it.'[70] Prolonged insurgency was disintegrative of nascent political solidarities, working both against their maintenance in adversity by the MCP, and the construction of new ones by the colonial government and its local allies. The introduction of the social and political strategies that became the main pillar of counter-terror – especially in the New Villages – proceeded in an atmosphere of mutual distrust. These were days of uncertainty, subterfuge, cunning and betrayal; of great bravery and frailty. Everyone was a potential informer. British appeals for information might be couched in Confucian terms – an appeal to the family – 'communists are like bachelors; they have nothing to lose'. Yet they were also highly mercenary. If the soul of the Chinese was in his purse, then in his purse he was to be punished:

> Why should you have to let your sons, your nephews, your brothers, your sisters or your daughters join the bandits? Why shouldn't they live with you? Why shouldn't

---

[68] In a letter of 24.7.1951, CO537/7262.
[69] SFWIS, No. 35, 4.1.1951, CO537/7291.
[70] 'Notice to all jungle cultivators', 22.10.1952, INF/1036/53.

they work and earn money for you? Why should they die for the bandits? Why should they give their labour free to the bandits?[71]

In his purse the Chinese was also to be rewarded: 'Give more and more information on the bandits. Earn more and more rewards in cash.' Although counter-terror rested ultimately on the guaranteeing of personal security, in the short term it created fear and mistrust. Men and women, in protecting themselves and their families, had to negotiate a world turned upside down by large-scale resettlement schemes, where no one was necessarily who they seemed. The British even reported cases of Communists moving around in drag.[72] It was a time of rumour in which misinformation abounded. The British actively fostered it. In Singapore in 1949, funds were given for officials to recruit a secret network of 'active supporters of democracy', who would initiate whispering campaigns to combat the Communists. By the end of the year 100 agents were on a card index – schoolteachers, clerks, businessmen, priests, trade unionists, members of women's organisations, even racehorse owners – 900 more were planned by the end of 1950. The inspiration for this scheme was obvious: 'it imitates a Communist method of proved success'.[73] And indeed, rumour could still profit the Communists. When in 1949 the British recognised Communist China, the MCP sold bonds of $500 to businessmen who feared being extradited to China as KMT 'running dogs'. In Tumpat in Kelantan, Malays hesitated to volunteer for service against the guerrillas as they feared being sent to work in Burma like they had during the Japanese occupation.[74] 'Pseudo-gangs' were formed whereby surrendered insurgents were sent back to the jungle as bandits to test an uncertain loyalty. Conversely, terrorists would surrender and abscond back to the jungle with information. Even where guerrillas were submitted to elaborate programmes of reform, the detention camps – according to Chinese leaders – were 'nurseries for Communism'.[75] The MCP possessed a remarkable capacity to turn counter-terror to their advantage, and appeared before the public under multifarious guises.

Lam Swee, touring Johore in the second half of 1951 as a government propagandist, noted a 'great fear' in the New Villages; a fear that those who surrendered would give information on those who had helped them in the past. A confessional kind of politics was propagated, in which those who bared their souls would escape the fear of prosecution. British propaganda pointed out that they would still be treated as bandits

---

[71] 'Trends of bandit propaganda', 24.4.1950, CO537/6579; 'To the squatters', in Dept of Public Relations, *Background information for speakers: the Emergency and Anti-bandit Month* (Kuala Lumpur, 1950), p. 21.
[72] 'Seminyih, 23.9.1949'; 'Statements of surrendered Communist bandits', B. P. Walker-Taylor Papers.
[73] A. W. Frisby, 'Objectives and methods of the Anti-Communist Bureau set up by the Director of Education at the request of the Colonial Secretary', 13.10.1949; 'Report on Counter Communist Education Bureau to 31.12.1949', CO537/5982.
[74] *Malay Mail*, 24.1.1950, 9.2.1950.
[75] 'Minutes of the second meeting of the Emergency Chinese Advisory Committee held in the Council Chamber, Ipoh on 11.6.1949', SP.13/A/21.

unless they unburdened their consciences.[76] In a similar way, in return for confessions on the paying of protection money, Chinese leaders demanded a clean sheet for those involved.[77] Surrender policy in fact raised levels of violence. Communist leaflets lashed out at the 'corrupted traitors' and others trying to 'slink back unobserved into civilian life'. People compromised by defectors were urged to escape to the jungle organisation. Ambiguity in official pronouncement regarding the degree of complicity in terror that would make prosecution inescapable encouraged the MCP to keep recruits well-blooded.[78] In the jungle the party was strengthened through 'organisational mobilisation, ideological instruction and having passed through the crucible of revolutionary training'.[79] However, as time went by, steadily less attention was paid by party cadres to legitimating the struggle: new recruits tended increasingly to be uneducated, unskilled labourers, whose political education was minimal. Freedom from disease and endurance became more vaunted qualities than class feeling, political consciousness or even intelligence.[80] An unhappy combination of coercion and self-confession was the mainspring of party discipline. There was an atmosphere of fear and distrust in the camps. Terror became less precise in its application. Surrendered terrorists attacked the lack of freedom of movement, thought or speech in rebel camps. Others complained of being 'treated like a coolie'. The MCP launched its own drive to eliminate police agents with public assistance in 'anti-spy treaties'.[81] On both sides, personal redemption, ideological resilience, and identification with the community were the primary means by which the individual could in some degree constrain terror.

This theme of terror was sharply drawn in relation to the Malay community. The Emergency gave new force to ethnic identity, and Islam a communal edge to counter-insurgency. To the kampong Malays, the Communists were *musang berbulu ayam* – foxes in chicken skins. The narrow mobilisation that the MCP initially achieved amongst Malays was never extended, and was largely confined to localities of recent Indonesian settlement like Batu Kurau and Ijok in Perak, Ulu Langat in Selangor, and particularly Mentekab in Pahang, where the British linked Malay support for the MCP to a long tradition of defiance of authority dating back to the insurrection against British rule between 1891 and 1895. The guerrilla leader there – Wan Ali –

---

[76] 'Psychological warfare', CO537/7262.

[77] 'Minutes of the first meeting of the Emergency Chinese Advisory Committee held in the Council Chamber Kuala Lumpur on 5.4.1949', SP.13/A/21.

[78] 'Surrender policy', Young Papers; MRSA, May 1955, CO1030/8; 'Third further statement of Liew Thian Choy, 10.10.1949', 'Statements of surrendered Communist bandits'.

[79] MCP, 'Mass action – a vital link in the chain of present-day revolutionary activity', CO1022/187.

[80] P. B. Humphrey, 'Confidential ORS(PW) Memorandum No. 16/54 – Some statistics relating to Communist terrorist recruitment in Malaya', CS/5235/53; 'Notes for the Commissioner of Police lecture – the maintenance of the Party', Young Papers. Lucian W. Pye, *Guerrilla communism in Malaya: its social and political meaning* (Princeton, 1956), pp. 248–323.

[81] 'Interrogation of Chai Soo'; 'Yap Seng, 14.10.1949', RHO; PMR, January 1952, CO1022/187.

had a reputation for invulnerability. The KMM had been active in the area and so had API after it. In 1949 there were eighty guerrillas in the area led by Chinese and cases of Malay Special Constables going over to them.[82] *Ketuas* and *penghulus* were forced out of their villages in south Kuala Lipis and Temerloh, 'bad lands' where the British Adviser admitted that 'the reign of terror established by Malay bandits is quite extraordinary'.[83] At the outset of the Emergency Malay leaders such as Musa Ahmad, Wahi Anwar and Shamsiah Fakeh launched a manifesto under the banner of the organisations they headed – the *Barisan Tani*, PETA and AWAS. They attacked UMNO for its support of constitutional politics, and the MNP for indirectly supporting the government.[84] Publications in Malay such as 'Torch of Truth', carried a strongly nationalistic message, and promised to distribute land to Malay villagers and nationalise estates.[85] The Communist high command stressed that the Malays were to be conciliated. In Johore, British control of the State religious affairs department was presented as a 'slow but sure drive toward Christianity' and, in Pahang, *jihad* was proclaimed against an infidel government.[86] It was in Pahang that a secret meeting in May 1949 led to the creation of the MNLA's 10th Regiment. It was commanded by Abdullah C. D. and contained in its ranks Musa Ahmad, Wahi Anwar, and his wife, Shamsiah Fakeh. At its peak it had perhaps 400 members, although perhaps only 200 bore arms. In late 1949 it was ordered north to Gua Musang, and thus began its four-year Long March, during the course of which it was divided into separate companies. Musa Ahmad and his followers were cut off from the main body for a year; Wahi Anwar's group was repeatedly harassed by the security forces, and Wahi Anwar's eventual capitulation in 1951 sparked the mass surrender of 150–200 Malays. The remnant forces, including Abdullah C. D. and Musa Ahmad, only crossed into Thailand in early 1954.[87] By early 1950 the government claimed that the Tenth and East Coast regiments had been largely wiped out as a fighting force, their relatives resettled, and that there was peace on the Pahang river.[88] But even as late as 1954 the MCP claimed that it controlled perhaps 800–1,000 Malays in South Pahang.[89] The government itself responded, through the State religious authorities, with an appeal to Islam. Religious sanction was sought by those Malays who fought the MCP: the Malay fighters sent by the security forces to win the confidence of the Pahang Tenth Regiment cadre, Wan Ali, and murder him first received the personal blessing of the Sultan. On at least one occasion in Negri Sembilan, the British used a

---

[82] *Malay Mail*, 9.8.1949; 'Federation of Malaya – Political report for January 1949', CO537/ 4763; Sabda S. dan Wahba, *Musa Ahmad: kembali kepang kuan* (Subang Jaya, 1981).

[83] In a rare case, money was advanced as compensation for those whose property was destroyed for helping the security forces, W. C. S. Corry to W. E. Rigby, 9.5.1949, BA Pahang/99/49.

[84] PMR, No. 2 of 1949, 19.1.1949, CO537/4763.

[85] MRSA, October 1954, CO1030/7.

[86] *Anatomy of Communist propaganda*, p. 53.

[87] Chin, *Communist Party of Malaya*, pp. 33–41.   [88] *Malay Mail*, 19.1.1950.

[89] South Pahang Regimental Committee, 'Report on Malay department's work', 25.8.1954, in MRSA, August 1954, CO1030/7.

pawang to charm a Malay bandit into leaving the jungle, with success. In Perlis, nearly 200 ex-API and MCP members, mostly from the Pauh area, some wearing UMNO badges, performed *tobat* – ritual repentance – before the Raja.[90] Islam became a dominant theme of colonial propaganda. The British Empire's history as defender of Islam was invoked: 'We, the Malays, embrace Islam, and the Communist aim is to destroy Islam. It means, therefore, that if the Communists were to dominate this country, Islam will be suppressed and it follows that the Malays will be exterminated.' Counter-insurgency inevitably wore a communal guise. 'The Communist Party is trying to steal your country – protect yourselves and guard your kampongs.'[91]

Malay nationalism had never recovered from its experience of communal terror in the aftermath of the Japanese occupation. Occasional MCP retaliatory attacks on Malay policemen and Special Constables, the disappearance of Malay hunters and foresters in the jungle, revived bitter memories of this period and undermined its propaganda. In April 1952, the MCP Central Committee admitted that: 'We are fighting the Islamic religion and our anti-religious approach is angering the Malay masses . . . We cannot go on attempting to impress the Malay peasants with the fact that Communism is a creed which is altruistic, charitable and in accord with the spirit of Islam.'[92]

As the field of permissible political activity narrowed, a primary casualty was the Malay left. MNP branches broke up and its leaders were detained. The realignments in Malay politics which resulted from this will be discussed later; however, it can be noted here that the MCP nationalist appeal to the Malays reached a crescendo in late 1953 when open politics were at their most turbulent. Intimations of communal disorder spread beyond the immediate campaign and into open Malay nationalism. In Johore Bahru in 1954, UMNO Youth formed a secret youth front – *Barisan 33 Perikatan Pemuda UMNO Malaya* – to take over Malay leadership if demands for self-government were frustrated. A network of cadres was to be established, ready to take up arms and root out traitors and informers within the Malay body politic.[93] The British feared that these threats of extremist action were 'conditioning the popular mind to the idea of violence'. Even after the Long March of the 10th Regiment, there were attempts to resurrect API and infiltrate the security forces.[94] In north Pahang the MCP encouraged all parties, took up the issue of *fitrah* payments, and approached religious teachers, especially graduates of *Al-Azhar*. The Malay Communist, Osman China, wrote mildly seditious pieces under a *nom de plume* for *Utusan Melayu* and set

---

[90] Henniker, *Red shadow*, pp. 105–110; *Straits Echo*, 8.6.1950.
[91] 'Emergency Leaflets – No. 258 – "Islam or Communism?"'; 'Emergency Leaflets – No. 222', (Malay), RHO.
[92] Cited in Harry Miller, *Jungle war in Malaya: the campaign against Communism, 1948–60* (London, 1972), p. 119.
[93] MRSA, January, 1954; March, 1954, CO1030/7; mentioned also in Tan Sri Datuk Abdul Samad Idris, *25 tahun UMNO: kenangan abadi kepada bangsa, agama dan tanahair* (Kuala Lumpur, 1984), pp. 250–1.
[94] MRSA, February, April, 1954, CO1030/7; MRSA, November 1955, CO1030/8.

up a *Suara Merdeka* press. According to Osman the nationalist appeal was only adopted after the prospects of military victory receded. However, by this time local allies were not forthcoming. By early 1955, the press had ceased publishing for a year; and the Malay rank-and-file in West Pahang had dropped from forty-five to seven people. Osman himself surrendered in 1955, and ended his career as a car salesman.[95] The security forces, the British recognised, provided UMNO with 'a large ready-made, well controlled audience which would not otherwise have been so readily available'.[96] We shall look in more detail at the roots of UMNO strength in a later chapter. Suffice to say that in the face of violence, the potentially fractious elements in Malay politics moved towards new vehicles: by the mid-1950s, it was political Islam that took campaigns on the *fitrah* issue and the plight of the poor peasants. The complex strands of social upheaval of the Emergency years – the mass mobilisation of the Malays in the police and army; rapid Malay urbanisation; the enhanced position of women in Malay society; movements of economic uplift – acted as a subtle determinant of political realignment in the Malay community. By this time also the MCP's purchase on the rural Chinese was facing a challenge of even greater magnitude.

The domestication of the Malayan Chinese

Terror criminalised the Chinese within the official mind. It disintegrated political loyalties and undermined social cohesion. For the British government this dictated three principles upon which Malaya's internal frontier was to be pacified. First, Malayan Chinese politics was to be domesticated by securing Chinese allegiance to the colonial state. To achieve this the British had to resume collaboration with the post-war *kapitan China* and encourage them to reach an accommodation with the Malay nationalist leadership which went some way to guaranteeing their citizenship status in Malaya. The question of Sino-Malay *rapprochement* will dominate this and subsequent chapters. Secondly, colonial administrators sought to socialise and integrate what they saw as a 'delinquent' population, and to exorcise its tragic propensity towards political violence. They only partially achieved their aims. Their primary tool of integration, the resettlement of the Chinese into protected villages, created new forms of spatial segregation and ethnic separatism amongst the rural population. A third premise of counter-insurgency was that lasting internal security necessitated the provision of a stable subsistence for the rural Chinese. Yet resettlement created new sources of agrarian discontent, especially by severely limiting the range of economic activities which were open to the rural Chinese. These difficulties were only partly met by grants of land. The colonial transformation of Chinese society in Malaya was, for the Chinese, a traumatic process.

The assumptions about the psychology of the Chinese that coloured counter-terror

---

[95] MRSA, January 1955, CO1030/8; Miller, *Jungle war*, pp.145–8.
[96] 'A paper on the security situation in the Federation of Malaya Appendix B: Attitude of the Malay public towards the Malayan Communist Party', 5.4.1949, CO537/4751.

were carried forward into colonial politics. To the Colonial Office, the Chinese mind was 'schizophrenic and ever subject to the twin stimuli of racialism and self-interest'.[97] British Sinologists in Singapore regretted the passing of the Protectorate: the 'secret society complex' could only be overcome by the firm day-to-day presence of government within the community.[98] It was pointed out that many Chinese leaders had been eliminated or discredited during the occupation. Few Chinese who had survived it had enjoyed family life, education or peace and order.

> Chinese racial psychology is essentially individualistic. 'Warlords come and warlords go' is a common expression in Chinese where the peasant for centuries has been caught in the crossfire of opposing factions and wishes only to be left alone. The stalemate atmosphere of the Emergency is an old story to him and the events of the past decade have not been conducive to a belief that the British are invulnerable.[99]

The paying of protection money symbolised their insecurity, and it was over this question that the first *rapprochement* between the authorities and Chinese community leaders – chiefly the dominant business interests – was initiated.[100] The *towkays* complained to High Commissioner Gurney that European business had first call on police protection, and that the Chinese had scant faith in the government's capacity to defend them. There could be little surprise, therefore, that British attempts to persuade the Chinese to commit their loyalty to the government achieved little beyond revealing a lack of organisation and leadership in the rural community. New leadership and a new British alliance with it were required. In the belief that 'most of the squatters would hitch themselves onto anything with a badge of authority, whether Boy Scouts or Methodists', Gurney was midwife to a new Chinese party – the Malayan Chinese Association (MCA).[101] The British urged Chinese Legislative Councillors – H. S. Lee, Leong Yew Koh, Yong Shook Lin, Khoo Teik Ee and Tan Siew Sin – to take a lead in forming a new association with which the British could negotiate. However, within the Chinese community, and particularly in the mind of Tan Cheng Lock, the idea of forming a Pan-Malayan body had been germinating for some time. He had launched pilot schemes: the Overseas Chinese Association in exile in India, and the Malayan Chinese League, floated in the wake of his disillusionment with the AMCJA in May 1948. Another incentive was the inauguration of behind-the-screen discussions with Dato Onn and UMNO notables. The Chinese, they were told, must have their UMNO. Notwithstanding British patronage, once the Legislative

---

[97] J. P. Biddulph, memorandum, 6.6.1951, CO1022/148.

[98] 'Memorandum by T. P. F. McNeice, G. C. S. Atkins and G. W. Webb', 24.11.1948, CO537/3758.

[99] K. J. Henderson, Dpty. Commissioner for Labour Malacca, 'Memorandum', 20.1.1952, Tan Cheng Lock Papers, [SP.13]/A/50.

[100] 'Minutes of the first meeting of the Emergency Chinese Advisory Committee held in Kuala Lumpur on 5.4.1949'; 'A scheme for promoting local liaison and co-operation between squatter areas and local authorities prepared by a Sub-Committee of the Emergency Chinese Advisory Committee on 10.5.1949', SP.13/A/21.

[101] Gurney to Paskin, 10.12.1948, CO537/3758.

Councillors, the Chinese Chambers of Commerce and *shetuan* had come together to form a national unity organisation in April 1949, its leaders were allowed to build up their profile independently of the colonial government. Their relationship to British officials was not always harmonious, especially when the Chinese community were faced with the prospect of mass repatriations.[102] Moreover, there was ambiguity from its very inception as to whether the MCA was a welfare organisation, a colonial tool for collaboration against the MCP, a reaction in the defence of sectarian interests, the Malayan Kuomintang in a new guise, or merely a vendor of lottery tickets.[103]

This ambiguity resulted from the fact that the colonial government's efforts to collaborate with conservative elements in Chinese society was only one superficial manifestation of an internal struggle for authority within the Chinese community. It was simultaneously a political realignment, a process of economic reorganisation and an exercise in moral and cultural refurbishment. Politically, it represented the absorption of the long-running Communist–Kuomintang struggle into the local domain.[104] That the MCA was equated with the Kuomintang in many eyes was a delicate matter for the new body. KMT branches in Malaya existed for seven months after the foundation of the MCA. The government would only accept KMT influence 'properly harnessed', as in recruitment for a Kinta Home Guard which absorbed some of the KMT guerrillas from the Lenggong area, a scheme organised by Leong Yew Koh, who held honorary KMT military rank.[105] But in Singapore fears of a KMT rearguard action lay behind Straits Chinese opposition to the establishment of the MCA branch here, led by the Progressive Party politician, C. C. Tan. There were particularly fierce disputes within the Singapore branch: even fears of rioting when Tan Cheng Lock stood against KMT stalwart Chuang Hui Tsan for election as Singapore MCA President: the clans were mobilised, even the hawkers, with whom Tan Cheng Lock professed 'some ancient association'. Stormy relations between the Singapore branch and the peninsular MCA continued thereafter. The KMT was banned in Singapore after 1949, but its influence continued to be felt through the Chung Shing Club, the *Chung Shing Jit Pau* newspaper and an ill-fated youth party sponsored by the MCA.[106] Outside observers felt that the English–educated element would gain ascendancy over the 'hotch-potch rank and file and KMT refugees in the

---

[102] Gurney to Higham, 10.2.1949. For Gurney's role in the formation of the MCA, MacDonald to Creech Jones, 20.4.1949, 11.4.1949, CO537/4751. Thio Chan Bee, *The extraordinary adventures of an ordinary man* (London, 1977), p. 91.

[103] Lim San Kok, 'Some aspects of the Malayan Chinese association, 1949–69', *Journal of the South Seas Society*, 26, 2 (1971), 32–5.

[104] C. F. Yong and R. B. McKenna, *The Kuomintang movement in British Malaya, 1912–1949* (Singapore, 1990), pp. 199–225.

[105] Templer to Lyttelton, 18.6.1952, 10.7.1952, CO1022/176.

[106] Gimson to Creech Jones, 22.11.1948, CO537/3758; 'Singapore Political Report, November 1950', CO537/5983. R. N. Broome, 'Threat of MCA fracas in Singapore on 28.6.1953', 1.7.1953, CO1022/176; Heng Pek Koon, *Chinese politics in Malaysia: a history of the Malaysian Chinese Association* (Singapore, 1988), pp. 90, 141–2; Yeo Kim Wah, *Political development in Singapore, 1945–55* (Singapore, 1973), p. 185.

MCA out of all proportion with their small number'.[107] Indeed, Tan Cheng Lock's achievement – and that of other English-speaking leaders such as Tan Siew Sin, Khoo Teik Ee, Yong Shook Lin and Ong Yoke Lin – was to bring together the various personal followings which constituted the MCA, and to rise above dialect rivalries. Tan Cheng Lock, who was illiterate in Chinese, was most effective as a figure-head representing 'the spirit of the Malayan Chinese'; senior officials were sceptical about his capacity to hold the alliance together.[108] To the MCP, Tan was the 'Number One Big Dog of the British Imperialists' and in August 1949 he was gravely injured by a hand-grenade in an assassination attempt.[109] The English-educated group were assisted in their leadership role in the MCA by their membership of a network of multi-racial societies, especially in Selangor, and their high status within the community as professionals, within the Chambers of Commerce and *shetuan*, and on the boards of schools. However, their leadership was bitterly contested. Real power lay elsewhere. Approximately three-quarters of MCA members lived outside the main urban centres, where the branches were made up of poorer Chinese: schoolteachers, *sinseh* and merchants. Here the MCA was reliant on older associations for recruitment and for some years the MCA functioned as a *shetuan* and not as a modern political party.[110] A classic account of this period distinguishes between three strata of Chinese politics in Malaya: those who continued to identify with the politics of the motherland; the pragmatic Chinese who worked through the lower-level associations and were content to function through local hierarchies and those who actively explored their Malayan identity. It was the middle group which provided the backbone of support for the MCA.[111]

For the purposes of counter-insurgency, the government refined its analysis of Chinese society in Malaya along similar lines. The lower Chinese-educated echelons of the colonial economy – shop assistants and rubber tappers – were identified as potentially the most dangerous; the uneducated rural Chinese as 'wind-blown'. It was the small *towkays*, estate owners and *kepalas*, dotted across the countryside, that were seen as the key to the government control. A committee of public safety was mooted to pressurise them into supporting the government, by threatening them with detention, deportation or confiscation of property. Thus, the natural constituency of the Kuomintang – the Chinese-speaking trading classes – were potentially the government's foremost supporters, and there were efforts to draw on their natural leaders, men like Lau Pak Khuan in Perak.[112] The British analysis of the social fabric

---

[107] O. W. Wolters, minute, 6.4.1949, CO537/4761.
[108] Gurney to Paskin, 4.4.1949, CO537/4761. For a life, Soh Eng Lim, 'Tan Cheng Lock: his leadership of the Malayan Chinese', *JSEAH*, 1, 1 (1960), 29–53; K. G. Tregonning, 'Tan Cheng Lock: a Malayan nationalist', *JSEAS*, 10, 1 (1979), 25–76.
[109] 'Deliver a more complete blow to the MCA', *Freedom News*, 14 (30.3.1950).
[110] Heng, *Chinese politics*, pp. 54–97.
[111] Wang Gungwu, *Community and nation: essays on Southeast Asia and the Chinese* (Singapore, 1981), pp. 173–200.
[112] O. W. Wolters, minute, 6.4.1949, CO537/4761.

of Chinese politics in Malaya was in many ways heavy-handed, and this created friction in its relations with the MCA. Whilst they assumed that commercial and industrial leaders did not have the general influence they had prior to the war, the revival of the business and professional elite, as noted earlier, was remarkable, and they resented the fact that the government did not appear to listen to their advice. After Gurney's death, they reminded the government that British deafness had 'resulted in bitterness and in a determination not to co-operate any further'.[113] In their slow accommodation with the colonial state, the Chinese leaders delicately weighed the requirements of mediation with their desire for prestige.

The British set these men a series of tests of loyalty, through which they were to draw the Chinese, through the MCA, into the orbit of the state. The first, we have seen, was to dry up the flow of protection money to the Communists. It was inconclusive and bred suspicion on all sides. The second was Anti-Bandit Month in 1950. This was aimed at disrupting *Min Yuen* activities in squatter areas, and registering the presence of the government amongst people who had little contact with it in the past.[114] However, local Chinese leaders often did not provide leadership or attend public meetings. In one Chinese town in Pahang, Karak, not one Chinese came forward, and the Federal government was compelled to keep statistics of recruitment by race a secret.[115] A third trial was the MCA's ability to recruit a Chinese militia. It was not a success: in one instance in mid-1952 a campaign in Selangor only drew thirty-six candidates out of a requisite 300–400. 'We Hokkiens,' complained one local boss, 'were never policemen in China.'[116] When conscripted manpower service was introduced in 1951, applications for certificates of readmission to Malaya after visits to China rose from twenty-five to 160 a day, and it was likely that 5,000 men were seeking to evade their obligations in this way. The MCP was quick to take advantage of this: 'if forced to join up, do not report for duty; go to prison cheerfully, for it is up to the youths of Malaya to unite and resolutely struggle against the British imperialists'.[117] When their time came for conscription youths of sixteen and seventeen years were urged to take to the jungle. Various other schemes were launched to recruit more Chinese, but in the atmosphere of fear there was little incentive for individual Chinese to commit themselves to the bureaucratic

---

[113] R. P. Bingham (SCA Malaya), memorandum, 16.6.1951; 'Record of the conference with the Mentri Besar, Resident Commissioners and British Advisers on the intensification of the Emergency effort', 26.10.1951; 'Note of a meeting held at King's House on 28.10.1951', CO1022/148.

[114] D. C. Watherston to State Secretaries, 19.1.1950, Pahang (MPABM)/22/50.

[115] 'Morale was and is low owing chiefly to intimidation by a certain (it may surprise as how large this is when facts are available) proportion of the populace', Resettlement Officer Bentong, 'Report on Anti-Bandit Month – period 26.2.1950–16.3.1950', Pahang (MPABM)/5/50. Secretary for Defence to State Organiser Pahang, 22.2.1950; State Organiser to Secretary for Defence, 27.3.1950, Pahang (MPABM)/19/50.

[116] 'Review of Chinese Affairs – August 1952', CO1022/149.

[117] MCP, 'Extend propaganda and start the struggle to oppose the Manpower Service Regulations', c. May 1951, CO537/7288.

interest.[118] Although this was deplored by many Chinese leaders, their inability to deliver hard evidence of their strength, as greater demands were made on them, weakened the position of the MCA.

The Association was most successful as a symbolic expression of Chinese unity at the centre. Through the Communities' Liaison Committee, an informal forum for inter-communal understanding organised by Malcolm MacDonald, it established an accord on Chinese citizenship with Malay political leadership whereby the Chinese leadership acknowledged as a token of good faith their allegiance to the Malay Rulers.[119] This period of the Emergency anticipated a pattern of inter-communal bargaining that was to dominate the transfer of power. The origins and workings of the Sino-Malay alliance will be discussed later. However, these political achievements did not dilute the criticism levelled at MCA leaders that they had little natural following in the smaller towns and villages, and that those with influence in the locality were rarely known outside of it. Many Malay leaders felt that they were, therefore, unreliable agents of political control. To the Mentri Besar of Kelantan, the Emergency was 'a war of ideas. A Chinese was by nature a bargainer.' The government had made a fundamental error in making concessions to them. The Malay Rulers lobbied for wholesale repatriations.[120] Gurney himself wrote bitterly two days before his death that 'the British government will not be prepared to go on protecting people who are completely unwilling to do anything to help. These people live comfortably and devote themselves wholly to making money.'[121] If the uneasy *rapprochement* with Malay leadership was to be consolidated, a more fundamental reconstruction of the Chinese position in Malaya had to be undertaken.

A new geography of the peninsula

Although the MCP had been denied quick success in establishing liberated areas, which existed 'merely in embryo', security chiefs admitted in September 1948 that 'there are some areas of the country, for instance south Pahang and northern Johore, where we have little idea of what is happening, and the Communists may already have set up an administration there'. At the very least these areas were 'granaries for the insurgents'.[122] Squatter numbers declined between 1945 and 1950, from around 400,000 to 300,000 in 1948 and to 150,000 in 1950 as families drifted back to the

---

[118] Gurney to Griffiths, 18.2.1951, CO537/7262; Stockwell, 'Policing', p. 117.
[119] Tan Cheng Lock to Yong Shook Lin, 19.1.1950, Tan Cheng Lock Papers, SP.13/A/19.
[120] OAG to Lyttelton, 30.10.1951, CO1022/148.
[121] 'A note in the handwriting of the late Sir Henry Gurney recently found amongst his private papers and known to have been written two days before his death', 19.11.1951, *ibid*.
[122] Local Defence Committee, Federation of Malaya, 'A paper on the dimension and nature of the security problem confronting the government of the Federation of Malaya', 16.9.1948; 'Minutes of the Commissioner-General's Conference held at Bukit Serene on 12.9.1948', CO717/177/52849/41/48; 'Notes of a meeting held at King's House on 17.5.1949 to discuss the Emergency and in particular the squatter problem', CO717/177/52849/41/1/49.

towns, mines and estates. Between 1949 and 1952, detentions had already uprooted as many as 10,000 squatters; deportations had taken 26,000 more.[123] Yet the problem did not evaporate in the way that the government hoped it would. A Squatter Committee investigated and recommended in February 1949 that land policy in Malaya be recast in order to permit the settlement of these rural Chinese for the most part where they stood. The provision of legal titles, a real stake in the land, was seen by the Committee as the only long-term solution to the problem. It was also, for the British, the simplest solution. However, it remained politically unacceptable to the Malay State governments. In Negri Sembilan and Kedah, feelings were said to be particularly high where there were 70,000 squatters on estates that wished to replant with high-yielding rubber. Perak established its own State Squatter Committee. It also recommended that the squatters be given 'normal' title; yet these official surveys perpetuated a fundamental misconception of the problem. Although Perak had the largest numbers of squatters – over 130,000, 94,900 of them concentrated in Kinta – most of them were still viewed by the bureaucracy as primarily industrial labourers, to whom cultivation was only an ancillary occupation. It was not recognised that most of them were now first and foremost agriculturalists, subject to a hunger for land. As normal conditions of trade resumed they had become vegetable and cash–crop farmers rather than cultivators of food staples.[124] From the outset, the needs of security dominated the government's approach to the squatter problem and as it moved to confront the squatters many of the more fundamental questions about the nature of Chinese cultivation and of their future stake in the land remained unanswered.

The Emergency powers enabled the government to take more drastic measures than was previously possible, and allowed greater pressure to be brought to bear on the State governments. A chain of legal instruments – Emergency Regulations 17D, 17E and 17F – were promulgated to allow the rounding up of squatter populations. Chinese Affairs departments, in effect the old Protectorates, were resurrected as far as the chronic shortage of Chinese-speaking personnel allowed. There still remained the question of what to do with these people. MacDonald favoured wholesale banishments as a rapid means of relieving political tensions. However, as the Colonial Office insisted that banishments be reviewed by a cumbersome legal process, repatriation was to be sought rather than banishment. Langkawi, Christmas Island and North Borneo were all considered and rejected as a new abode for the Malayan Chinese as the gateway to China began to close.[125] Given that resolute action against the big men paying protection money would 'cause more of a howl' than the British could

---

[123] Kernial Singh Sandhu, 'The saga of the "squatter" in Malaya: a preliminary survey of the causes, characteristics and consequences of the resettlement of rural dwellers during the Emergency between 1948 and 1960', *JSEAH*, 5 (1964), 145–6.

[124] Loh Kok Wah, *Beyond the tin mines: coolies, squatters and New Villagers in the Kinta Valley, c. 1880–1980* (Singapore, 1988), pp. 108–21.

[125] 'Minutes of the Commissioner-General's Conference held at Bukit Serene on 12.9.1948'; Gurney to Creech Jones, 25.10.1948, CO717/177/52849/41/48; Gurney to Lloyd, 21.2.1951, CO537/7262.

stomach, there was little option but to contemplate the permanent settlement of the Chinese on the peninsula.[126] The experience elsewhere in the British Empire suggested that resettlement was by far the most expensive option.[127] A number of British officials were later to claim credit for devising resettlement. Local initiatives had been taken by enterprising District Officers. The most important of these was in Perak. It was an aphorism that 'the Emergency began in Sungei Siput and will end there'. Perak consistently had the largest concentration of terrorists, and eventually over 220,000 people were resettled in the State.[128] The process began from mid-October 1948 with evictions in Sungei Siput. But of over 5,350 squatters moved, only 2,000 ended up in a resettlement camp. Many moved to the towns or to other squatter areas. Sungei Batu camp in Dindings housed 1,073 in tents, gave them two meals a day and basic amenities. When jungle land in Pantai Remis was reserved for them, there were only eighty takers.[129] Several months later many of the squatters and their crops were washed out by floods.[130] However, the episode, for Gurney, unlocked the secrets of the Chinese mind, and showed that the government's advantage over the MCP lay in the fact that 'a person arrested by the Government gets adequate food and is not beaten up'.[131] This was not fully appreciated by squatters. They were unwilling to move as they feared taxation by political societies in the new area: the early experiments in Perak, and also at Sungei Perangin in Selangor and Mawai in Johore, merely increased their economic and personal insecurity.[132]

A comprehensive strategy slowly evolved, and was to carry the name of the British military commander Lt-General Harold Briggs. The 'Briggs Plan' was to roll up the insurgency from the south to the north of the peninsula with a massive scheme of resettlement, co-ordinated along military lines. It was an attempt by the state to reverse the demographic effects of war. While the deleterious consequences of the occupation to the economic and political position of the Chinese had driven them away from the main lines of communication, resettlement tied them back down to the roads and railways. They were transformed from dispersed pioneers into townsmen. In Johore in 1947, only nineteen towns or villages were classified as urban. By 1952 another thirty-five had come into being, together with another thirty smaller villages mostly on the main Johore Bahru–Segamat road, or clustered around the State capital itself. The psephological consequences of this were to be immense.[133] Statistics vary.

[126] Gurney to Lloyd, 20.12.1948, CO537/3758.
[127] K. E. Robinson, minute, 18.3.1949; V. L. O. Sheppard, 'Squatters', 13.4.1949, CO717/177/ 52849/41/2/49.
[128] 'The Emergency in Perak', C. H. F. Blake Papers.
[129] Harry Fang, 'The eviction at Sungei Siput', *Malaya Tribune*, 7.2.1949.
[130] W. A. Bradley, 'Report on the situation at Pantai Remis squatting camp, Dindings', 28.10.1949, DSW:ER/4159/1/53.
[131] Gurney to Creech Jones, 14.2.1949, CO537/4750.
[132] Chinese Embassy, London to Ernest Bevin, 23.10.1948, CO537/4240; J. W. Humphrey, 'Population resettlement in Malaya' (Unpublished Ph.D. dissertation, Northwestern University, 1971), pp. 76–80.
[133] E. H. G. Dobby, 'Recent settlement changes in South Malaya', *MJTG*, 1 (1953), 7.

A government survey, the Corry Report of 1954, gave a tally of 532,000 resettled persons. The most authoritative academic survey by K. S. Sandhu fixes the resettled population at nearly 572,917 in 1954 in 480 resettlement areas, or 'New Villages' as they were called from March 1952, although a later survey gives as many as 592 villages established with an initial population of 620,785. The confusion over numbers occurs as many more, over 650,000 were 'regrouped' in closer concentrations around towns and workplaces, a phenomenon we will discuss in the next chapter. Over one-seventh of the entire population of Malaya were moved in one way or another during the Emergency. If we take Sandhu's figure of 572,917 for resettlement, it is important to point out that only around 300,000 of these were 'squatters'; most of the others were Chinese legitimately occupying land. Eighty-six per cent were Chinese, 9 per cent Malay, 4 per cent Indian, and 1 per cent other communities.[134] During the course of resettlement, the projections of the numbers involved were consistently underestimated. By the end of April 1951, 220,000 squatters had been resettled at a cost of $27 million, and 221,000 had still to be moved.[135] By mid-1952 new squatter populations were still being discovered.[136] The density of population varied, with the largest settlements being found in Selangor and Perak, closer to the principal urban centres, and the smallest in Kelantan. This vast population was contained in fenced compounds, often on a simple grid-pattern, followed slavishly with little regard for the terrain, resulting in erosion or flooding. The Emergency Ordinances were amended to legalise dangerous electric fences. The perimeters of 161 villages were lighted at a cost of $4.3 million.[137] Vast quantities of raw materials were absorbed – timber, attap, wire and poles – and great infrastructural deficiencies were exposed. Gurney wrote enthusiastically of northern Johore that, 'a piece of virgin jungle becomes a settlement of two hundred houses, complete with roads, water and police post and fencing in ten days'.[138] However, to settlers it meant arriving to the sounds of music from public relations vans, only to scramble on a first-come-first-served basis for a plot, and often to begin to dig their own wells.[139] The poorer villagers had to salvage what raw materials they could from their old homes. As there was a reluctance to appear affluent and attract MCP subscription collectors, early constructions were only slowly upgraded, and many plots were not taken up.[140] It was in the initial uprooting that squatters were left most vulnerable, and privately resettlement officers spoke of the social dislocation, the inefficiency and delay, that resettlement brought in its wake. Opportunities for corruption multiplied. Truckers demanded 'tea money', detectives in north Johore speculated in land, and resettlement officers themselves

---

[134] Sandhu, 'The saga of the "squatter" ', 159; Humphrey, 'Population resettlement', p. 187.
[135] Director of Operations, 'Progress of resettlement', 21.6.1951, CO537/7270.
[136] A. H. P. Humphrey, circular, 26.6.1952, CS/6509/52.
[137] Secretary for Defence, 'Perimeter fences', 28.4.1952; 'Perimeter lighting for New Villages', 18.12.1952; Federation of Malaya, 'Administrative Report, January 1953', CO1022/30.
[138] Gurney to Higham, 13.3.1951, CO537/7270,
[139] S. R. Dawson,'Resettlement in Malaya', CO1022/29.
[140] Humphrey, 'Population resettlement', pp. 214–21.

were notoriously venal.[141] The MCP dubbed the villages 'concentration camps'.[142] However, rather than the MCP, it was more often 'voluble old ladies who appeared to lead the opposition'.[143]

In many cases resettlement uprooted long-established communities. The Hakka population of Pulai, settled in Ulu Kelantan for more than three centuries and an MCP stronghold during the war, was broken up and one group was resettled three times.[144] Where New Villages were founded on the periphery of existing towns and villages, the natural heterogeneity of the settlers was very pronounced when viewed against the relative integration of the host community. Cultivators and rural labourers from a variety of dialect groups such as Hakka, Teochew and Foochow were placed with a compact Cantonese and Hokkien trading and artisanal community. The objective of breaking down unacceptable political solidarities among the squatter communities was compromised as resettlement, by its very nature, worked against the easy re-establishment of alternative social groupings, such as common dialect associations, clubs and temples. Often settlers possessed no natural *lingua franca*.[145] Resettlement not only divided communities, but families themselves, scattering them more widely across the peninsula; and although it did facilitate marriage within the village, family units were often quite independent of each other, and surname associations had a reduced role in the life of the New Village.[146]

Resettlement transformed the human ecology of the interior. The squatter-cultivator had used hillstreams as a water supply and for watering of crops. In the New Villages, piped supplies were inadequate for agricultural needs. Sanitation was imperfect; in the forest, isolation had minimised risk of disease to an extent to which the provision of medical services was unable initially to achieve. Doctors warned of dangerous health risks, particularly from malaria, enteric fever and dysentery. Disease could bring violent protests from settlers, and it revived the bitter memory of Japanese agricultural camps.[147] Pigs, an important capital asset, attracted swarms of flies to the settlement; chickens, no longer free-range scavengers, were plagued by Ranikhet disease in confinement.[148] Assuming the settlements to be temporary, contractors used inferior materials.[149] Some areas became rural ghettos, where people lived in what the London *Times* called 'a urine-tainted poverty, made tolerable only by the

[141] J. Litton, circular letter to friends, 12.9.1950, Litton Papers.
[142] 'Deliver a more complete blow to the MCA', *Freedom News*, 30.3.1950, CO537/5983.
[143] G. H. Jollye, 'Interim account of squatter resettlement in Malacca', Sel Sec/2071/50.
[144] Kernial Singh Sandhu, 'Emergency resettlement in Malaya', *JTG*, 18 (1964), 166–7; S. M. Middlebrook, 'Pulai: an early Chinese settlement in Kelantan', *JMBRAS*, 11, 2 (1933), 151–6.
[145] Judith Strauch, 'Chinese New Villages of the Malayan Emergency, a generation later: a case study', *Contemporary Southeast Asia*, 2, 2 (1981), 129–32.
[146] Ray Nyce, *Chinese New Villages: a community study* (Singapore, 1973), pp. 29–35, 44–6.
[147] 'Prevention of disease in resettlement areas (extract from the proceedings of the Conference of Senior Medical Officers – December 1950)', SCA Pahang/15/51.
[148] Dobby, 'Recent settlement changes', 6.
[149] 'Monthly review of Chinese affairs for March 1951', CO537/7270.

sun'.[150] One medical officer wrote of squatter areas outside of Kuala Lumpur, Salak South that 'the earth drains are choked with rubbish and rubbish is scattered everywhere', and the situation deteriorated with continued squatter infiltration, and the settlement's absorption into the city.[151] The distance of plots from villages meant that they were prey to animals and theft. The MCA were furious after their model scheme at Mawai was closed after it had been opened against the Association's advice but on which they had spent $100,000. To Tan Cheng Lock the people were 'being treated like cattle'.[152]

The economic dislocation of resettlement was immense: 28,282 acres under food-crops were lost by the end of 1951 from a retreat into wage labour, the costs of which were borne by urban consumers.[153] In 1951 alone, Johore's acreage under vegetables dropped by more than half – causing the cost of living in Singapore to rise sharply. 'Before resettlement,' villagers complained, 'Ulu Tiram and Ban Foo supplied Johore Bahru with vegetables. Now Johore Bahru supplied Ulu Tiram and Ban Foo.'[154] Villagers were offered either food or clothing by church relief workers and took food: 'ample testimony of the grim struggle for existence in the New Villages'. The Catholic welfare services in Kinta reported sores and general malnutrition, particularly amongst the young and old, where poverty prevented dietary improvement.[155] The recurring complaints of villagers themselves were malaria and lack of access to dispensaries, chemists, licensed food shops, bus services and vegetable land, especially for the old who were unable to tap rubber. The rural Chinese was not only threatened by terrorism, but 'subject to economic pressures at the narrow margin above the bare subsistence at which he lives'.[156] Once resettled, these pioneer cultivators had difficulty adjusting to settled smallholder agriculture, often on land of dubious quality. Many therefore abandoned serious cultivation for work on rubber estates, ending a process of diversification in the rural economy and becoming dependent on the vicissitudes of the rubber market.[157] In their public statements, officials had grossly overestimated the numbers who were wage earners. Some reports from the ground admitted this. 'Chinese do not normally worry much about living conditions,' it was argued. 'With them earnings are all important, so that the joys of community life are unlikely to be much of a draw. What seems required is adequate land to

---

[150] McHugh, 'Psychological or political warfare in Malaya: II', 87.
[151] R. Calderwood to State Medical and Health Officer, Selangor, 1.6.1949; State Medical and Health Officer to State Secretary, 3.6.1949, Sel Sec/1466/49.
[152] Tan Cheng Lock to Mentri Besar Johore, 30.10.1951, CO1022/29.
[153] Federation of Malaya, Legislative Council Paper No. 33 of 1952, *Resettlement and the development of New Villages in the Federation of Malaya, 1952*, pp. B317–19.
[154] Dobby, 'Recent settlement changes', 6; 'Ban Foo Resettlement Area – Minutes of first Village Committee meeting, 15.5.1951', SCA Phg/91/51.
[155] This group enjoyed the patronage of the Roman Catholic Perak MCA leader, Leong Yew Koh, Catholic Welfare Services, Kinta, 'Report for month of April, 1953', BA Pahang/29/52/Part I.
[156] G. H. Jollye, 'Interim account of squatter resettlement in Malacca', Sel Sec/2071/50.
[157] For one example, D. Gray, 'Paya Lang', 12.2.1952, SCA Phg/9/51.

provide an alternative wholetime occupation to rubber tapping.' This was not to be found. In Salak South, a 1953 survey showed that two-thirds of the villagers had changed their livelihood. By May 1953, unemployment was already seen in Kinta and many other areas – in places as high as 50 per cent of the adult population.[158] New opportunities, such as Lee Kong Chian's massive pineapple plantation in Johore which helped to draw off surplus labour from places hard hit by falling rubber prices such as Yong Peng, were not always to hand. The scale of unemployment was often disguised by the sharing of contract tapping jobs on low wages; for example, widespread odd-jobbing was observed in Kedah, bringing in only $60 a month for labourers. In one village alone – Karangan – 123 regular workers had lost their jobs. It was clear in many areas of Selangor that the new land was much poorer in quality and that it was increasingly difficult to draw a living from it. There were fears of widespread unemployment. Even in fertile Sekinchan, in the Selangor rice lands, twenty-seven families volunteered to return to China.[159] In Negri Sembilan, land shortage was creating renewed illegal cultivation, especially of bananas on slopes. The 1957 census revealed that out of 582 New Villages founded 23 closed and 35 were completely absorbed in towns. Of the remainder, 72 declined, 146 remained static and 306 increased over 5 per cent, in relation to a 28 per cent population growth in Malaya as a whole.[160] These figures mask important variations in local experience. Larger villages experienced more rapid growth, especially those close to urban employment in places like Ipoh. Isolated settlements in Pahang decreased in population.[161] Populations fled to where work was available. Flexible responses to seasonal or varying demands were the bedrock of the economy of the rural Chinese, and as workers went farther afield, directing remittances back to these areas, new patterns of rural–urban migration emerged.[162]

To both Chinese leaders and officials, resettlement was a great psychological experiment. Apprehensions could only be overcome if the Chinese acquired what Tan Cheng Lock called 'a seeable, touchable, tangible stake in the country'. The decisive battle of the Emergency was fought over the rights of the Malayan Chinese to land.[163] 'A just land policy and adequate political rights,' the British government acknowledged, 'are viewed as the cornerstone of Chinese status in the Federation.'[164] Land was the 'social amelioration' that would strengthen the forces for stability.[165] The

[158] M. H. Morgan to SCA, 17.8.1951, SCA Pahang/18/51; Loh, *Beyond the tin mines*, pp. 142–3.
[159] 'Report on New Villages'; 'New Villages and regrouping', SCA Pahang/82/53.
[160] Sandhu, 'Emergency resettlement', 157–83.
[161] Malayan Christian Council, *Survey of the New Villages*, pp. 6–7.
[162] Strauch, 'Chinese New Villages', 126–39.
[163] 'Minutes of a meeting of the Emergency Chinese Advisory Committee held in Malacca on 24.5.1952', SP.13/A/21.
[164] 'A paper on the security situation in the Federation of Malaya, Appendix A: Present attitude of the Chinese population', 5.4.1949, CO537/4751.
[165] O. H. Morris, minute, 21.4.1949, *ibid.*

Malay States, however, resisted any encroachment on their prerogatives over land. In Johore a screen of Malay reservations along the eastern coast was mooted as a barrier to illegal immigration to the new squatter areas. Kedah discouraged Chinese settlement which would invite migration over the Thai border, and in particular the financing of tapioca cultivation by Penang financiers. Kelantan and Negri Sembilan were insistent that Chinese be repatriated.[166] Dato Onn felt the whole scheme was 'cock-eyed': 'the view of the Malays was why did government do something for the squatters and nothing for the Malays'.[167] These utterances reflected the mood of many UMNO divisions.[168] Resettlement revived the older debate about the issue of TOLs to non-Malays on State land inside Malay Reservations, and encouraged a new one over whether leases should be given out or grants in perpetuity.[169] Whilst the permanence of resettlement remained in question, the issuing TOLs continued, on the understanding that once the Emergency was over many Chinese would choose to move elsewhere.[170] By March 1952 – whilst it was stressed that the basic principles of land policy that protected the Malays were unchanged – all States had agreed to permanent titles and leasehold titles, mostly for twenty to thirty years, and many States – the old Federated States, Johore and Trengganu – allowed entry in the Mukim Register.[171] However, obstacles still remained. Land Offices were still in arrears from the occupation period, and from revision of rents in some parts of the country.[172] In the case of New Villages there were delays before land was acquired by the government. There were probationary periods, restrictions on transfer without government consent, cultivation conditions, and fears that some States could close the book on applications at will.[173] In Kedah, while land title had been offered, settlers refused to pay the fees, and officials doubted whether the Chinese wanted title, preferring the 'Golden Age' of uncontrolled cultivation. In fact, as many as 5,000 Chinese returned to this in Sungei Siput and Chemor, squatters 'twice over', until in 1955 and 1956 their crops were destroyed and many of them detained, leaving as many as 4,000 families without a livelihood.[174] By the end of June 1952, 470,509

---

[166] 'Note of a meeting held at King's House on 17.5.1949, to discuss the Emergency and in particular the squatter problem', *ibid.*
[167] 'Notes of discussions of the Communities' Liaison Committee, Ipoh, 14–15.3.1949', TCL/23/3, ISEAS.
[168] Zulkifli bin Mohd. Hashim kepada Tuan Setiausaha UMNO Baghian Kuala Lumpur, 15.12.1951, UMNO/SEL/52/51.
[169] For example, Pahang Executive Council, Paper No. 188 of 1951, 'Issue of TOLs to non-Malays of State land in Malay Reservations', 16.12.1948, BA Pahang/76/50; 'District Officers' Conference, Pahang, 6.1.1954', DO Kuantan/550/53.
[170] 'District Officers' Conference, Pahang, 27.7.1954', *ibid.*
[171] Templer to Lyttelton, 12.8.1952; 'Appendix: Schedule showing types of titles offered by States and Settlements', 'Monthly review of Chinese affairs for July, 1952', CO1022/29.
[172] Federal Government Press Statement, 30.11.1951; Templer to Lyttelton, 10.3.1953, *ibid.*
[173] 'Monthly review of Chinese affairs for January 1952', *ibid*; Loh, *Beyond the tin mines*, p. 147.
[174] 'Monthly review of Chinese affairs for April, 1951', CO537/7270; Loh, *ibid.*

Chinese had been resettled in 410 villages, yet there had only been 4,157 applications, and 2,359 grants of titles.[175] By February 1953, only 6,264 applications had been received and 3,176 approved – only 186 in the whole of Perak.[176] Chinese leaders held that a thirty-year lease was too short a time from the perspective of the Chinese family system. Much of the land was reclaimed rubber land of poor quality – 'poor, bare red laterite looking like an anaemic wound'.[177] Elsewhere, there was either no land available, or the land was unsuitable, or the States did not want them to have it, or they hoped for an early return to lands held elsewhere. And although a title was perhaps a document on which Chinese without collateral could borrow money, the new charges it brought – water rates, alienation and conservancy fees – were an additional economic burden.[178] The government was greedy for land revenues. It saw tenure as a means of tying the cultivator to the village, and preventing the redispersal of pioneer agriculturalists. Yet the distinction between wage labour and cultivation had always been an artificial one. Resettlement had neither tilted the delicate equation of stable subsistence in the squatters' favour, nor provided convincing economic arguments for domestication.

Land shortage undermined British ambitions to exploit the 'New Villages of Freedom' as units of specialised production. Economic opportunities fell to the shopkeeper-traders who had traditionally connected the Chinese farmer to the towns. Quick to take advantage of the isolation of settlements, they supplied credit to evacuees on the strength of the crop they were to plant, the shopkeeper providing seeds. Credit was given over two seasons, and inflated profits were demanded for taking the additional risk.[179] Long-standing arrangements had been greatly disrupted and outside *towkays* and Chettiars attempted to claw back losses by applying for large blocks of New Village land on the grounds that they were the former landlords in squatter areas. Rents were raised once title was acquired.[180] Not all businessmen prospered: small tradesmen experienced decreasing turnover in non-agriculturalist settlements. However, this experience shook the complacent faith that administrators held in the economic resourcefulness and self-sufficiency of Chinese. They were, it seemed, 'more heavily indebted to the middlemen than the Malay *raiats*'.[181] The co-operative movement, seen as a means of indulging socialistic inclinations and for promoting anti-Communist leadership, made few inroads. The raw material – 'simple people with a strain of financial dishonesty' – was not promising, and some co-

---

[175] Templer to Lyttelton, 12.12.1952. CO1022/29.
[176] 'Extract from Executive Council Papers: Applications for land from inhabitants of New Villages', 10.2.1935, *ibid.*
[177] 'Minutes of a meeting of the Emergency Chinese Advisory Committee held in Malacca on 24.5.1952', SP.13/A/21; Purcell, *Malaya*, p. 81.
[178] 'Report on (Johore and) New Villages for December 1953', SCA Phg/82/53.
[179] O. W. Wolters to I. B. Mendel, 30.12.1949, SCA Phg/10/51.
[180] 'Report on New Villages', SCA Pahang/82/53.
[181] R. C. Gates to Secretary RIDA, 20.5.1955, Coop/433/55.

operatives were a cover for racketeering by outside interests.[182] In Kedah, co-operatives applied for government loans merely to pay for subsistence to farmers whose allowances had run out but who had no crops ready.[183] Communal differences in the villages exacerbated the problem. For example, in one village in Pahang, Cantonese and Kwangsai majorities attempted to establish a co-operative, only to be opposed by a minority community of Hokkien traders.[184] Elsewhere established traders fought to preserve their wholesale monopoly, which strict food control measures buttressed.[185] The MCA had taken a passing interest in co-operative shops – at Mawai in Johore, for instance, a Johore businessman had provided the initial capital. However, the main government body for agrarian improvement was the Rural and Industrial Development Authority (RIDA), and its chairman, Dato Onn bin Jaafar, was adamant that 'law-abiding' Malay producers should have first call on resources and was bitterly resentful of the Emergency expenditure on the Chinese.[186] Although, as we shall see, Chinese and Malay cultivators began to share more problems in common, their remedy was expressed in communal terms.

'A rule of benevolence'

Notwithstanding the circumstances of their foundation, the government's grip on the resettlement areas was – as reported in Johore in February 1951 – 'only precariously maintained, and might well be lost with disastrous consequences'.[187] To strengthen its hold on the New Villages, and mitigate against their effects on subsistence, the colonial government drew up co-ordinated principles of after-care.[188] Counter-insurgency evolved into a broader 'socio-economic plan' to build a 'well-balanced community' around the new settlements. The British aimed to provide shops, employment, entertainments, libraries, places of worship – 'the full range of economic, cultural and social requirements of a community'. Town and country planning was combined with new-town planning on a massive scale. The Chinese were to share the benefits of urban living with a rural livelihood, and it was anticipated that social services, especially education, would create more sophisticated aspirations

---

[182] The first was at Tasek Glugor, Penang, 'Federation of Malaya, Monthly Newsletter, 16.12.1950–15.1.1951, CO537/7270; SCA to State Co-operative Officer Pahang, 16.8.1951; SCA to Commissioner for Co-operative Development, 3.9.1951, SCA Pahang/16/51.

[183] 'Report on (Johore and) New Villages for November 1953', SCA Pahang/82/53.

[184] SCA (Pahang) to ADO Triang, 27.11.1951, SCA Phg/16/51.

[185] For example, R. C. Gates, 'Raja Hitam reselement area – co-operative stores society – project', 27.8.1951, Coop Tpg/15/51; J. D. W. Geare, minute, 12.6.1951, FS/9156/51; 'Report on (Johore and) New Villages for December 1953', SCA Pahang/82/53.

[186] T. F. Carey to Secretary for Defence, 18.4.1951; Dato Onn bin Jaafar, minute, 15.5.1951, FS/9156/51.

[187] Director of Operations, 'Minutes of a meeting held in Kuala Lumpur on 2.2.1951 to discuss resettlement matters', SCA Phg/2/51.

[188] For example, E. B. David, Secretary for Defence, 'After-care in New Villages', 5.2.1952, BA Pahang/29/52/Part I.

in the future.[189] For example, to the District Officers, static dispensaries were 'one of the best material features of an active government'. However, the insurgency restricted access to outlying, insecure areas. Medical teams were attached to operations in bad areas, to enhance the popularity of the security forces. These operations were explicitly 'political rather than utilitarian'. The miscellany of new services which emerged in the New Villages were a register of the governmental presence in the interior and of the dispersal of the culture of the towns into the countryside. For example, great faith was placed in village halls as outposts of urban living, meeting a variety of needs as a recreational centre, a meeting place, as a school building or a coffeeshop.[190] By April 1952 eighty-one such centres were built, over two-thirds paid for with government funds, and most run by a village council or committee.[191] The influence of the towns was also felt in less tangible ways; officials attempted to provide a more personal interface with administration, and excursions were organised from New Villages to government departments like the Land Office. The Rotary Club provided entertainment; there were exhibition matches of volleyball and visits from travelling cinemas.[192] Templer himself was particularly impressed by 'clean and bright' New Villages, with white-washed walls decorated in pink, pale green and yellow, and with potted plants.[193] In Sungei Nipah, Negri Sembilan, it was proudly proclaimed that 'the white-washed walls, coloured doors and window frames would be a credit to the Butlin organisation'.[194] However, the extent of this work should not be overestimated. By 1952 only 8 per cent of the $67 million spent on resettlement was spent on social services and amenities: less than half of the New Villages had schools.[195] The scale of the demand meant that most of the welfare provision was the work of voluntary services. The aspirations of colonial power had overreached its means.

The greater part of voluntary assistance was Christian. Although the missionary impact had been profound in the Straits Settlements, the British government had hitherto restricted the activities of missions in the Malay States. However, the secular power turned to them in its hour of need. They became a conduit for new colonial projects on a scale that alarmed the Malay elite: British officials rushed to reassure the Mentri Besars that they were merely 'creating the right atmosphere in the New Villages' for effective counter-insurgency.[196] The churches had a greater vested

---

[189] W. H. Jeffrey, State Medical and Health Officer Pahang, to State Secretary, 22.11.1951, BA Pahang/63/52.

[190] Acting Chief Secretary to Mentri-Mentri Besar and Resident Commissioners, 14.5.1952, CO1022/29.

[191] Templer to Lyttelton, 5.4.1952, CO1022/29.

[192] 'Monthly review of Chinese affairs for August, 1951', CO537/7270; 'Report on New Villages', SCA Pahang/82/53.

[193] D. J. Staples, 'Improvements in New Villages and regrouped areas', 7.3.1953, DO Kuantan/276/53.

[194] 'New Village and regrouping report October 1953', SCA Pahang/82/53.

[195] Loh, *Beyond the tin mines*, pp. 136–9.

[196] D. C. Watherston to Mentri-Mentri Besar, 22.3.1952, 'Notes of the first meeting of the

interest than most in the permanence of the New Villages. 'In a land where the Malay, as a Moslem, is so scrupulously "protected" by his States' laws from even being "exposed" to the Christian message,' they observed, 'the Chinese and Indians are the principal mission field.'[197] The Emergency was, to Methodist Bishop Harry Haines, 'the greatest single challenge that the church in Malaya has ever been confronted with'.[198] It was the culmination of the Christian mission in Malaya. The war had forced local churches to confront new social needs – malnutrition, prostitution and delinquency – often without expatriate direction, in ways that went beyond their traditional educative role. To the Protestant churches, social evils proceeded out of irreligion, and welfare was an occasion for spreading the word of God. Visions of a Christian Social Order in Malaya were not merely a resurrection of old notions of a colonial civilising mission. To an increasing number of American missionaries, influenced by social theologies such as that of Reinhold Niebuhr, the construction of Christian communities, the exorcism of social evils – especially Communism – did not stop with individual redemption: it was a political crusade. The developmental thought of the 1950s buttressed this mission, linking democratic sentiments with capitalism, anti-Communism, overseas aid and progress in the Third World.[199] Before the war, approaches to Chinese and Indian minorities in Malay villages to 'leaven' the protected Malay population had been inhibited by fears of ostracism, persecution or inter-racial tension. The New Villages presented a more homogeneous, captive audience. Traumatised and disorientated communities were a fertile field for evangelism.[200]

Proselytisation was hampered by the Central Welfare Council's refusal to grant funds to religious organisations, on the insistence of its Muslim members. The churches pleaded that mission work was of 'great social value and was part of the campaign against Communism', and that 'Muslim and Buddhist missions should be assisted if they wished to participate'. The Council only agreed to help if the welfare came first and the Christian aspect was 'purely subsidiary'. High Commissioner Templer gave a personal undertaking to the Sultans that Red Cross teams would spend equal time amongst the Malays, and missionary attempts to open hospitals were complicated by the need to match facilities for the Malay kampongs. The scope for missionary work varied from place to place. In Selangor, the Roman Catholic church was assured of assistance in building two schools by the State government; the

Chief Secretary's Co-ordinating Committee of representatives of churches, missionary bodies, and voluntary organisations [CSCC] held on 29.2.1952', BA Pahang/29/52.
[197] Malayan Christian Council, *Survey of the New Villages*, p. 4.
[198] Sungei Durian in Ipoh was the first New Village Methodist church, *Minutes of the Joint Session of the Malaya Annual Conference, 57th Session, and Malaysia Chinese Annual Conference, Singapore, 2–7.1.1952*, Microfilm, Universiti Malaya.
[199] Rev Robert Hunt, 'Historical overview of Christian social service in Malaysia', Paper presented to Malaysian CARE, National Symposium 1988, 'Trends and challenges in Christian social services for the 90s'.
[200] Malayan Christian Council, *Challenges and opportunity: the New Villages in Malaya: What are the Churches Doing?* (Singapore, 1952); *Minutes of the Joint Session of the Malaya Annual Conference, 56th Session, and Malaysia Chinese Annual Conference, Singapore, 3–7.1.1951*.

Methodists were refused permission in Perak. When a mobile film unit toured villages with the slogan 'Jesus Christ, son of God, Saviour' painted on the side of its motor-van in four languages, missionaries were forced to excise the reference to God in Malay.[201] Although British government grants were kept strictly secret, its support for this work was enthusiastic. To Gurney, missionaries were 'each worth a Brigade of troops'; Templer requested missionaries with experience in China from the College of Propaganda in Rome.[202] State co-ordinating committees brought together churchmen and women with government medical and welfare professionals. They continued to meet at a Federal level until 1955, and until 1957 in Johore and Perak, when the meetings broke down as progressive Malayanisation of the bureaucracy led to complaints from Christian organisations that requests for land for churches within these States were being refused.[203]

The missionary contribution to New Villages was, therefore, pronounced, although unevenly felt. The Malayan Christian Council had, in February 1954, 125 resident workers in 65 New Villages, and 150–200 voluntary workers in 43 New Villages; the Catholic Church, 56 workers in 176 New Villages. Clinics in particular provided opportunities for 'unobstructed evangelism'. They were decorated with large Chinese wall texts and Christian messages were printed on medicine packets.[204] Missions brought specialist expertise from Singapore, Hong Kong and China. They created innovative institutions, especially in care for the old – a pressing need in the wake of the disruption of families caused by war and by resettlement.[205] Other opportunities were seized: crèches in tapping areas; 'Little Libraries'; groups of 'Christian agriculturalists'; training in trades or adult literacy with Christian pamphlets.[206] The fight against idleness and delinquency – such as work camps held to 'welcome *Merdeka* with toil and sacrifice' – brought the churches into direct competition with the youth wings of political organisations, and often such initiatives were dropped in the face of the secular challenge.[207] Overall, the churches felt they were unable to

---

[201] 'Notes of the 3rd meeting of CSCC, 22.5.1952', 'Notes of the 7th meeting of CSCC, 3.10.1952'; 'Notes of 8th meeting CSCC, 7.11.1952', BA Pahang/29/52. J. R. Fleming, 'Memorandum on relationships between churches and governments as this affects New Village work (Strictly private and confidential)', November, 1952, International Missionary Council Archives, Collection of Seminari Theoloji Malaysia (STM).

[202] Gurney to Higham, 13.3.1951, CO537/7270; 'Notes of the first meeting of CSCC, 29.2.1952', BA Pahang/29/52; John Cloake, *Templer: Tiger of Malaya* (London, 1985), p. 280.

[203] Malayan Christian Council, *Survey of the New Villages*, p. 9.

[204] 'Notes of the 16th meeting of the CSCC, 12.2.1954'; Catholic Welfare Services, 'Progress report for May–June, 1954', BA Pahang/29/52/Part I.

[205] Bahaman bin Samsuddin, 'Old people's homes in New Villages, regroupment areas and kampongs'; Catholic Welfare Services, Kinta, 'Report for the month of April, 1953', *ibid.*

[206] J. Sutton, 'Malayan Christian Council – Literature Commission: Literature is a vital factor in building the Church in the New Villages of Malaya', 26.10.1954, STM.

[207] Malayan Christian Council, *Survey of the New Villages*, p. 14–17. 'Malayan Christian Council – Report for year ended 31st December, 1952'; 'How to work – and like it!: Third Ecumenical Youth Work Camp in Malaya, 1957', STM.

make the most of the new opportunities.[208] Both villagers and the State governments were suspicious of the churches, and the churches were suspicious of each other. To the rural Chinese, missionaries were government agents. Recognising this, Chinese-speaking workers came independently into Malaya, bringing new denominations such as the American Lutherans, the Southern Baptists, and the China Inland Mission (CIM). This was the largest influx of mission personnel that Malaya had ever experienced. These organisations – especially the Southern Baptists – made the expatriate churches very nervous.[209] In Singapore there was much suspicion of 'the peripatetic evangelist of the fundamentalist type', and churches fought over rival spheres of influence. The CIM, for its part, was antipathetic to the 'very watery sort of modernism' advanced in Singapore, especially its inter-religious conferences.[210] In Johore, because of the ready access from Singapore, a variety of independent churches and itinerant preachers operated.[211] Unwilling to inherit religious divisions that had their origins in Europe, ex-China missionaries led the way in resisting association with the government. The cultural complexion of religion was at issue.[212] The support of the English-educated urban leaders for New Village work was lukewarm on the grounds that such work was communally orientated. The use of dialects advanced evangelism in a sub-culture but spread a distrust of larger organisations.[213] In both English and Chinese churches religion had become a vehicle for expressing cultural identity.

Social disorder offered missionaries little firm ground upon which Christianity could gain a purchase. Many Englishmen believed that in the New Villages, 'a community, in a conscious form, was born of the desire to resist revolution'.[214] Yet, it was a paradox of counter-insurgency that whilst it sought to foster positive expressions of anti-Communism from within communities, colonial policing itself had weakened their capacity for autonomous action. Great faith was placed in welfare work 'as an inoculation against the disease of Communism'.[215] This had wider

---

[208] J. R. Fleming, 'Memorandum on relationships between churches and governments'.

[209] 'Malayan Christian Council – Minutes of the Central Committee, 21.10.1954'; J. W. Decker to N. Godsall, 17.1.1951; H. B. Amstutz (MCC) to N. Godsall (IMC), 1.2.1951, STM.

[210] R. Dawson, 'Spheres of influence', *British Weekly*, 20.9.1951; F. Mitchell (CIM) to N. Godsall (IMC), 23.10.1951; Godsall to J. W. Decker, 14.11.1951; London Missionary Society, 'Report by Revd. R. K. Orchard after a special visit to Hong Kong and Malaya, April–May, 1951', STM.

[211] Malayan Christian Council, *Survey of the New Villages*, pp. 8–10; J. R. Fleming, 'The growth of the Chinese church in the new villages of the state of Johore, 1950/60: a study in the communication of the gospel to Christian converts' (Unpublished Th.D. Dissertation, Union Theological Seminary in the City of New York, 1961), pp. 197–204.

[212] J. R. Fleming, 'IMC Survey', May 1952; Bishop Baines, 'Appendix III – I.M.C. Survey', STM.

[213] Rev W. John Roxborogh, *A short introduction to Malaysian church history* (Kuala Lumpur, 1989), pp. 11–15.

[214] O. W. Wolters, 'Emergency resettlement and community development in Malaya', *Community Development Bulletin*, 3 (1951), 1–8.

[215] M. J. Hayward, minute, 11.2.1949, FS/12222/50.

consequences on the course of colonial state-building, and the Christian churches were not the only voluntary associations taking the initiative. The British Council supported youth service work around Taiping. The MCA provided uniforms for the Boy Scouts and Girl Guides, and after this there was great difficulty in communicating 'a full appreciation of the voluntary and non-political nature of the movement'.[216] The young people of the towns were piloted into projects that aimed to awaken a sense of responsibility for the development of community life in the New Villages. Recruited from schools, churches, the Scouts and Guides, teams were formed that adopted a village and introduced arts and crafts, physical education and converted *padangs* into sports fields. It was a 'game' which the villagers could join in: the youths 'taught' villagers to make saleable handicrafts; they wrote letters to relations in the security forces; and formed badminton and basketball teams. Although it was reported that 'members of the teams are obtaining a great kick out of this form of service', officials were unenthusiastic about the response.[217] The middle-class tradition of philanthropy and public service of the towns was not effectively extended to the New Villages. Although there were around eighty Women's Institutes in Malaya, there were only three in New Villages, where few women had the leisure time or the fluency in English possessed by the wives of the urban elite.[218] It was to children that the new amenities had the greatest appeal. Weighed down by loans and bills, adults had little enthusiasm for community self-help. It was in the nature of resettlement that the innocent were punished with the guilty, and continuity and security could not always be guaranteed. Gambling was rife, especially when the rubber price was high. In two cases villagers requested a longer curfew to stop children playing *mah-jong*.[219] The *Wah Kee* secret society operated openly in the Bentong area; in Jemaluang, a member was elected to the local council, and the society wielded greater power behind the scenes.[220] This was not uncommon. In the Ipoh area, secret society membership peaked in the mid-1950s, especially amongst schoolboys, and independent societies were based on New Villages.[221] In fact there was a growing identification of the *Wah Kee* with the grass-roots organisation of the MCA. As the Kinta politician, D. R. Seenivasagam, was later to assert in Parliament: '*Wah Kee* is *Mah Ching*, and *Mah Ching* is *Wah Kee*.'[222]

The main means by which the government tried to restore the initiative to the New Villages was by allowing the local roots of Malayan Chinese politics to grow in

---

[216] 'Notes of the 3rd meeting of CSCC, 22.5.1952'; E. M. E. Payne, 'New approach to New Villages', 15.5.1953, BA Pahang/29/52/Part I.

[217] 'Youth teams working in New Villages', DO Kuantan/257/53.

[218] 'Notes of the 10th meeting of the CSCC, 6.2.1953', BA Pahang/29/52/Part I.

[219] S. R. Dawson, 'Resettlement in Malaya', CO1022/29.

[220] 'Monthly report for May 1954 – Bentong', SCA Pahang/32/54; 'Monthly report for May 1955 – Bentong', SCA Pahang/15/55; 'Report on New Villages', SCA Pahang/82/53.

[221] Mak Lau Fong, *Chinese secret societies in Ipoh town, 1945–69* (National University of Singapore Sociology working paper no. 42, 1975), p. 3.

[222] Heng, *Chinese politics*, p. 79.

strength. It turned to the MCA and incorporated it in New Village programmes. Complex structures of consultation were created, especially with the appointment of squatter representatives as MCA officials side by side with Chinese affairs personnel. The lessons of colonial welfare policy were not lost on the MCA leadership. As Yong Shook Lin wrote candidly to Leong Yew Koh:

> The best form of propaganda is realistic or materialistic propaganda, talks, speeches and pamphlets are useless as an antidote to this twentieth century menace. Realistic or materialistic propaganda is welfare work amongst the masses. The masses are the squatters and the Malays in the kampongs. We must push ahead with resettlement or regrouping. We can talk politics later on.[223]

The MCA's programme was financed by a lottery, which raised $4 million for New Village work. The impact was most crucial in pioneer schemes, such as the ill-fated Mawai scheme in Johore, in education, dispensing *ang pow*, settling marriage disputes, advice bureaux, contributions to the Red Cross and – mostly Catholic – missions, and Buddhist work. In this way, the MCA sought to reconstruct patron–client relations in the countryside.[224] Yet the MCA's attempts to set up model squatter settlements in safe areas were matched by little enthusiasm from the small and medium shopkeepers, from whom the strongest support was expected.[225] A further obstacle was the rising costs of the completion of resettlement – which in Johore rose from an estimated $2 million to $8 million.[226] Another was increasing Malay unease. The Mentri Besars feared that unacceptable political obligations would be incurred to the MCA for its work in financing resettlement.[227] It was pointed out that the bulk of its membership were not citizens of Malaya, and that those who were eligible to become citizens were slow to register. The limits of the official alliance with the MCA in the New Villages were reached in 1953, when, at the behest of Malay leaders, the primary source of MCA finance, the lottery, was terminated by the Federal government.[228]

The dilemmas of cultural and political identity amongst the rural Chinese fused in the question of New Village education. There was a general crisis in Chinese schools. The Emergency was seen, in many ways, as a problem of delinquency. The number of Chinese youths safely in schools was rising, but very slowly.[229] The MCA were not always able to help finance schools; maintenance costs had risen and the Chinese business community was no longer able to provide the assistance it had once given.[230]

---

[223] Yong Shook Lin to Leong Yew Koh, 26.6.1950, SP.13/A/22.
[224] Heng, *Chinese politics*, pp. 104–12, 127–30.
[225] PMR, No. 12, June 1949, CO537/4761.
[226] Director of Operations, 'Minutes of a meeting held in Kuala Lumpur on 2.2.1951 to discuss resettlement matters', SCA Phg/20/51.
[227] 'Note of a meeting held at King's House on 17.5.1949, to discuss the Emergency and in particular the squatter problem', CO537/4751.
[228] See *Malayan Mirror*, I, 2, 28.6.1953.
[229] In 1947, 193,340; in 1952, 227,694. 'Some notes on Chinese vernacular schools', June 1950; 'Report on Chinese schools – May 1952', SCA Phg/20/51.
[230] B. S. Davis, SCA Selangor, 'Memorandum', 18.12.1950, SCA Phg/20/51; Pahang Execu-

In Penang, it was estimated that between 25 and 50 per cent of school fees remained uncollected. There were four boys to every girl in the Chinese schools; finances were mismanaged; and fund-raising incurred uncommonly high entertainment expenses. Teaching was by rote and indiscipline was a serious problem. In Perak, many schools remained unaccountable to colonial administration.[231] The underlying issue of communalism remained unresolved; British educationalists were disturbed by the portraits of Sun Yat Sen that dominated school buildings. With schools, as in all aspects of resettlement, the difficulty was to locate leadership, in this case to run school management committees. Parents' committees were impossible to convene as most parents were uneducated and had little standing with the average schoolmaster. In Pahang, for example, schools were scattered and community leaders were unwilling to travel the insecure roads to visit them, although in the relatively prosperous Cameron Highlands Chinese put up schools by themselves. 'Outside the schools there is virtually nobody with any Chinese education in the state.'[232] In the eyes of Tan Cheng Lock, the MCA in Pahang had the weakest state leadership.[233] Leaders kept a low public profile in the state capital Kuala Lipis, and exercised little authority elsewhere. Raub, it was said, had 'no local Chinese leadership at all'.[234] This local weakness highlights a wider problem. A survey of rural Chinese in a far less isolated area of Province Wellesley in the mid-1950s stressed the weakness of the links between villagers and the big men of the larger towns.[235] However, Chinese politics in Malaya were already developing in a manner that would allow communal solidarities to be forged in a new fashion.

In September 1952, an MCA report observed that the man in the street 'has but little interest in the organisation'. It was 'a mere basin of loose sand', an urban-based organisation useless for contesting elections.[236] To its Chinese critics it was merely a 'lottery association' – dictatorial, undemocratic, with no records or accounts.[237] For it to survive the Emergency, it had to reorganise itself into a political party through the establishment of a central office, the employment of paid political agents, and the dissemination of propaganda.[238] From 1951 the MCA attempted to do so, and became

tive Council, Paper No. 169 of 1951, 'Grants-in-aid to Chinese schools', 26.6.1951, BA Pahang/76/50.

[231] Malay Peninsula Agricultural Association, 'Observations on Chinese Schools in Penang', FS/13316/49; J. S. Ferguson to Henry Gurney, 22.10.1948; M. Albakiri, 'Schools in rural areas (Perak)', FS/11055/48.

[232] H. M. Morgan to B. A. Pahang, 24.10.1951, SCA Phg/20/51.

[233] 'Two-day visit of Dato Tan Cheng Lock to Pahang', SCA Phg/9/51.

[234] H. M. Morgan to SCA, n.d. August 1951, SCA Phg/20/51.

[235] W. H. Newell, *Treacherous river: a study of rural Chinese in north Malaya* (Kuala Lumpur, 1962), pp. 29–32.

[236] D. F. H. Sinclair, 'Memorandum on democratizing the MCA', 31.9.1952, TCL/1/33a, ISEAS; Leong Yew Koh to Tan Cheng Lock, SP.13/A/22.

[237] 'What is expected of the MCA', *Nanyang Siang Pau*, 26.5.1953.

[238] Tan Cheng Lock to Leong Yew Koh, 24.6.1950, SP.13/A/22; Tan Cheng Lock, 'Memorandum on the organisation of the MCA', 28.10.1951, SP.13/A/22.

less of a *shetuan* and more of a political party. High political developments, of which we will say more in Chapter 8, accelerated this process. In particular it seems as if Dato Onn's attempt to form a multi-racial political party and draw Chinese leaders into it, led to fears that the Chinese community would be irrevocably divided, and provoked the MCA into recasting itself into a more disciplined body. However, the development of branches was retarded by local jealousies. The appointment of salaried 'supermen' to direct the Association exposed bitter personal differences at the centre and the independence of State branches, such as Selangor. There were allegations – in Negri Sembilan for instance – that positions were used for personal gain. In Titi, Negri Sembilan the MCA branch was little more than a core group of key businessmen. Local *towkays* would buy members to advance up a new road to status in the community through political office. Branches inflated their numbers as representation at a national level depended on these figures.[239] To its mass constituency the MCA had to demonstrate, particularly in its resistance to security operations, that it represented all sections of the community. An MCA labour sub-committee was created to foster a community of interest between capital and labour, and rally Chinese labour into unions. In Seremban, it was claimed that 40 per cent of the men were members.[240] However, the MCA higher leadership was still mostly drawn from the elite professions and *towkay* class. 'The common man,' it was observed, 'regards it as an association of capitalists', and to join the MCA through a workers' organisation would be to set oneself up as a Communist target.[241] Although the presence of networks of KMT and Triad men in the MCA gave an element of continuity to conservative Chinese leadership, and although its relationship with the British government gave it a new prestige, these affiliations could render the party unpopular at the local level amongst labouring and peasant populations whose original loyalties had lain elsewhere.[242]

A crucial opportunity to locate and fortify local leadership came with the introduction of elected citizens' committees. The early elected committees were not successful. People were unwilling to put themselves forward, and members had to be nominated. A wider programme began of what the British termed 'democratic education'. Johore was the first state to introduce Chinese citizens' committees in 1951, with proportional representation for different dialect groups, which through co-operation with the *penghulu* were absorbed into local administration.[243] In Pahang,

[239] 'Monthly review of Chinese affairs, January, 1952', CO1022/176, Laurence K. L. Siaw, *Chinese society in rural Malaysia* (Kuala Lumpur, 1983), pp. 96–7; M. Roff, 'The Malayan Chinese Association, 1945–65', *JSEAH*, 6, 2 (1965), 42. I am grateful to Professor Lee Kam Hing for his comments.

[240] 'A note on the Labour Sub-committee of the MCA'; B. H. Tan, 'MCA Labour – March report', 4.4.1953, SP.13/A/50.

[241] K. J. Henderson, DCL Malacca, 'Memorandum', 20.1.1952, SP.13/A/50.

[242] Loh, *Beyond the tin mines*, pp. 211–12.

[243] 'Johore SWEC Directive No. 9 – Chinese Citizens' Committees', 5.2.1951, SCA Phg/91/51; 'Monthly review of Chinese affairs for March 1951'; 'Federation of Malaya, Press Release, 1.3.1951', CO537/7270.

committee chairmen were given prestigious letters of appointment and seats on *mukim* councils. However, MCP intimidation and infiltration of their membership was widespread.[244] An *ad hoc* system of local representative institutions was evolving in some States, which was given formal recognition in the Local Councils Ordinance of 1952. The various informal committees were designated as Local Councils on the basis of their 'social responsibility'. By early 1953 many local village committees were being converted into Councils and levying rates.[245] There were wide regional variations: by 1958 in Johore, 70 per cent of committees were Local Councils, compared with only 50 per cent in Perak. In Malacca, where Chinese New Villages were in overwhelmingly Malay districts, no villages were accorded this status. In this State, local democracy was met with 'stubborn ignorance'.[246] Electoral turnouts varied accordingly. When council elections were held in Pasir Pinji in Perak there was much buying of votes. In Kinta voter turnouts of 4 or 5 per cent were not uncommon.[247] One influential officer involved suggested that, until the material aspects of resettlement were achieved, 'it is play-acting to expect the committee to undertake much more responsibility than for peace and security', and suggested the binding up of MCA branches with these committees.[248] Others were more nervous of the politicisation of these elections. In 1952, the Johore State government discouraged the MCA forming branches in the New Villages, as it would undermine village councils. The MCA did not oppose this, confident that its members would control the committees anyway.[249] The State of Pahang forbade any reference to the MCA to be made in connection with local government. For village elites – shopkeepers, smallholders, schoolteachers – the elections were an opportunity to entrench their position in the new settlements, through the recruitment of clients. Elected office conferred patronage through the allocation of licences, the provision of jobs and the commissioning of public works. These individuals were quick to see the advantage of making alliance with forces outside of the New Villages. The MCA gave the village notables' local ambitions the backing of a national political machine. It was an additional source of funds, funds which fulfilled the 'self-help' conditions of government grants which met local money dollar-for-dollar.[250] The lubrication of new networks of clientage through the new resources available to local notables was a general phenomenon of the Malayan politics in the 1950s. Having promoted the organisation of the MCA, optimistic that it could fashion it in accordance to the needs

---

[244] Assistant SCA, 'Letter of appointment for Chinese headmen and members of Chinese citizens' committees', SCA Phg/91/51; 'Extract from Secret Monthly Review of Chinese Affairs, February–March, 1950', CO537/6017B.
[245] MacGillivray to Secretary of State, 4.2.1953, CO1022/29.
[246] Malayan Christian Council, *Survey of the New Villages*, p. 4; 'Federation of Malaya, Administration Report for January 1953', CO1022/29.
[247] 'New Villages and regrouping', SCA Pahang/82/53; Loh, *Beyond the tin mines*, p. 211.
[248] O. W. Wolters, minute, 22.2.1951, SCA Phg/91/51.
[249] 'Monthly review of Chinese affairs, July 1952', CO1022/176.
[250] Loh, *Beyond the tin mines*, pp. 158–9.

of its social policy, the colonial government became increasingly uneasy at the direction of its politicisation. This was a recurrent nightmare of decolonisation. In many ways the New Villages were isolated from the bulk of the urban Chinese population, and in many cases – paradoxically – closer to the machinery of government. But to observers the preoccupation of Chinese political and business interests moved away from the Emergency, to problems of economy, citizenship education at a national level.[251] This was a measure of their self-confidence; but it gave added impetus to the MCA's drive to entrench itself in the New Villages. It also led to an ideological reassertion of Chinese identity in Malaya.

The *Peranakan* leadership of the MCA took the lead in the domestication of Malayan Chinese politics. Speeches by Tan Cheng Lock were occasions for extended philosophical musings on this. Multi-racialism, he declared at a presidential address to the MCA in 1949, was a 'natural state', and 'that which is contrary to Natural Law cannot be successful'.[252] For Tan neither language, religion nor race was a satisfactory basis for modern nationality. It was based on equal citizenship, on individual human rights.[253] Yet the *huaqiao* view, the view of the Chinese-educated, was different: multi-racialism meant the equal status of *communities* as defined by language and culture. The actual term *huaqiao* was being replaced by 'Malayan Chinese', and domestic political allegiance was recognised. Yet the most important symbol of allegiance – citizenship – was held by only a minority of the Chinese. At the end of 1950, 433,000 Chinese who met the qualifications for Federation citizenship had not registered. A deep unease remained. As the *Sin Chew Jit Poh* commented in April 1953:

> Unity and co-operation is different from assimilation and absorption. For the past fifty years all attempts to form a unified Malayan nation have failed. It is against the trend of human progress in the second half of the twentieth century still to insist on assimilation and absorption especially in culture. The only way out is for all races to unite and contribute separately and jointly to the brilliant whole of the Malayan nation.[254]

The positions of Tan Cheng Lock and the Chinese-educated came together on the defence of Chinese rights against some of the more strident claims of Malay nationalism. But they were fighting for different things, the former for liberal democratic rights, the latter for the rights of the Chinese as a cultural community. The MCA and Tan Cheng Lock took a direct interest in the opposition of Chinese educationalists to the Barnes Report which urged Chinese and Indians to 'set aside their vernacular attachments', and in support of the more liberal Fenn-Wu Report

---

[251] J. B. Perry Robinson, *Transformation in Malaya* (London, 1956), pp. 98–106.
[252] Tan Cheng Lock, *One country, one people, one government: Presidential address by Tan Cheng Lock at a meeting of the General Committee of the MCA held in Penang on 30 October, 1949* (Kuala Lumpur, 1949), p. 2.
[253] Tan Liok Ee, *The rhetoric of* bangsa *and* minzu: *community and nation in tension, the Malay peninsula, 1900–1955* (Working paper No. 52, Centre of Southeast Asian Studies, Monash University, 1988), pp. 42–44.
[254] *Sin Chew Jit Poh*, 14.4.1953.

which gave more space to Chinese education in Malaya. The two Chinese pressure groups that spearheaded the campaign – the United Chinese School Teachers' Association and the United Chinese School Committees' Association – respectively represented the most politically articulate groups amongst the Malayan Chinese: the intelligentsia and the businessmen active in Chinese Chambers of Commerce and clan associations. Educational activism was a means to extend and consolidate the MCA's base as a political party. Although the MCA were unsuccessful in their opposition to the 1952 Education Ordinance, its leaders raised their stock within the community. In so doing they entrenched the MCA's communal posture. During the Barnes controversy, the MCA attempted to bring the educational pressure groups within its own orbit. However, the alliance proved difficult to sustain. In the face of further moves by the government against Chinese education, MCA leaders were inhibited in their opposition by the need to keep high-level political negotiations with UMNO running smoothly.[255]

The consequences of this were profound. To the British, the shrinking employment opportunities for middle school graduates with no command of English was 'an even graver threat to the Federation than the campaign which is being waged by the terrorists who operate in the Malayan jungle'.[256] Both Communist and conservative disaffection was expressed through a resurgence of Sino-centrism. New vehicles of indoctrination appeared. Singapore was a centre for this, and, prompted by the MCP's Anti-British League, student cadres created a network of *hseuh hsih* – or study groups – and combined into Singapore Chinese Middle School Students' Union in 1954. With behind-the-scenes support from *shetuan*, they campaigned on the citizenship issue and in defence of Chinese education and language. The visit of 400 Chinese students from Singapore in July 1955, helped spread the modes of organisation common on the island throughout the peninsula.[257] A Federation of Pan-Malayan Students was created as part of a more general MCP policy of regaining influence amongst labour and the larger schools in the towns, which had been broken in 1948. There were student unions in Ipoh, Klang, Kuala Lumpur and Penang, and intimidation and murder of teachers. Many others were sympathetic: 285 teachers had been detained during the Emergency. In spite of control of textbooks, teachers, who were paid an abysmal stipend, could indoctrinate the young through their lectures, and the police believed that a teacher in a remote area would be unable to stay in his job without subscribing to MCP policy. MCP-inclined Chinese schoolteachers were being elevated to elected office in isolated New Villages. The appointment of MCA men on to school committees, the creation of more politically sympathetic committees, enabled closer surveillance of the home life of students and vetting of teachers and

---

[255] Tan Liok Ee, 'Tan Cheng Lock and the Chinese education issue in Malaya', *JSEAS*, 19, 1 (1988), 48–61.
[256] 'Note on the need for a College to train teachers of English for the Chinese schools in Malaya', CO1030/266.
[257] Yeo, *Political development in Singapore*, pp. 88–120; MRSA, July 1955, CO1030/8.

materials.[258] However, many MCA leaders themselves refused to support the authorities. The party was divided and uncertain of its mass base, and both of these difficulties accentuated a trend towards communal politics. The MCA, in attempting to enforce a distinction between political and cultural identity, was confronted with vocal assertions of communal consciousness. To the Chinese teachers national education and 'the ideal of building a united Malayan nation did not imply that the culture or traditions of any community would have to be sacrificed'.[259] Politically, economically and socially, the domestication of the Malayan Chinese remained an unfinished business.

[258] 'Brief for the visit to the U.K. of the Director of Operations and the Secretary for Defence, Federation of Malaya – Memorandum referring to Communism in Chinese schools'; H. E. Darrenger, Tronoh Mines Ltd, to Lyttelton, 23.1.1952, CO1022/150; PMR, November 1950', CO537/6013.

[259] 'A memorandum from the United Chinese Schoolteachers' Association, Federation of Malaya, to the Secretary of State for the Colonies', August 1955, CO1030/266.

CHAPTER FIVE

House of glass

———•———

The impact of the Emergency on the economy and society of Malaya was felt far beyond the jungle and its fringes. Hitherto, historians of the period have had little to say about this. This chapter attempts to bring some form to a kaleidoscopic picture of change. It argues that the most significant social fact of the last ten years of colonial rule was the growth of the colonial state. Government became a more intimate part of people's lives, yet at the same time it became more formal and impersonal. Its structure was bolted together by the needs of counter-insurgency. Yet its girth was not all-encompassing. The late colonial state was a 'house of glass' through which powerful forces of change can be observed coursing through Malayan society. The foundations for Malaya's post-colonial governance were laid. As commerce began to resume business as usual, the relationship between European and Asian concerns was changing. Whilst the Emergency was a time of economic dislocation for many, by others it is remembered as a period of rare, if fragile, prosperity. Even for those communities that did not live at the forefront of the military campaign, life was changing in myriad ways. For Indian estate labour a process of social reform was underway, which was increasingly bound up with reconstituted trade unionism. Rapid urbanisation was another register of change. It bred social evils and cultural insecurities, but also created new communities. The 1950s witnessed the twilight of colonial society in Malaya, and the emergence of a new Asian managerial class that dominated a wide range of new civic institutions. The Emergency was merely a prologue to a much wider and far-reaching transformation of Malayan society. This chapter follows the flux of change. The ones that follow it delineate the political reconstructions that emerged from this.

The making of the modern Malaysian state

During the Emergency the classic functions of the state – military, fiscal, administrative – were greatly extended and new ones adopted. A centralised federal government grew in strength and its ranks of administrative personnel swelled. War

Executive Committees at State, Circle and District levels produced an integrated chain of command which was mirrored in civilian projects. The stock of the Specialist ran high. The state became, for the first time, a physical presence in the lives of many of its subjects. The extension of colonial authority in this period can be measured by the fuller registration of population, the more comprehensive numbering of individual house-lots and land-holdings and the use of the social survey. An immediate manifestation of this was the issuing of identity cards, and the taking of thumb-prints. These measures were bitterly resented by the MCP and became the focus of many violent incidents. The imprint of government was felt most keenly in the New Villages. In many places, the state even dictated the content of a family's meals, by imposing a shared diet of communal cooking. The body itself was invaded through medical inspections and screening of labourers. Food-searches led to sexual assaults, most famously at Semenyih in Selangor. It is a measure of the tenacity of the colonial regime that its authority was imposed with the minimum of sustained resistance. Protests did occur, and were often led by the MCA. For the squatters there were many excellent reasons why they should submit to the cataloguing of their personal history, and many inconveniences attendant on sharing a diet with the rest of a New Village. It even became difficult to honour the household gods with offerings of food.[1] The evasions of everyday life were everywhere to be found. One of the most common, much to the chagrin of the MCA, was the reluctance of the Malayan Chinese to submit to the inquisitions demanded by registration for citizenship. This lukewarm response fed Malay scepticism of their loyalty to the government.

The Emergency exemplified, perhaps more than any other colonial campaign, the imperialism of power-lines, radio and metalled roads. The Emergency opened up access to remote areas, such as the border tracts of northwest Kelantan. The settled areas became more densely populated, the forests retreated. Infrastructural improvement followed the military columns. The electrification of the Federation proceeded apace. However, the transformation of the state was wrought in stages. Until 1951, the colonial administration was in disarray. The centre was weak. In 1950, the Colonial Office voiced its 'shock' at the extent to which the 'actual administration of the country' was in the hands of the States, in a way unenvisaged by the drafters of the Federation Agreement. They were alarmed at the obstruction of Federal policy, and at the 'inertness' of some British Advisers.[2] However, the centre held, and it was greatly strengthened by the marriage of civil and military authority under the regime of Sir Gerald Templer after 1951. Churchill's apocryphal advice on his despatch was: 'General, to few men in this world is it given to have absolute power, relish it.'[3] Templer did so. Yet in the process, the character of administration was transformed. The Malayan Civil Service establishment was in many ways on the defensive. It was

---

[1] Loh Kok Wah, *Beyond the tin mines: coolies, squatters and New Villagers in the Kinta Valley, c. 1880–1980* (Singapore, 1988), p. 153.
[2] Higham to Gurney, 20.1.1950, a draft despatch that was not sent, CO717/154/52243/25/49.
[3] Sir Robert Thompson, *Make for the hills: memories of Far Eastern wars* (London, 1989), p. 98.

criticised by democratic standards as it became more accountable. The bureaucratic style changed. Appearances in public by the imperial proconsuls of the day became more managed and formal. The public were brought to the capital to visit officials on open days. Lady Templer gave tea parties for Orang Asli. When the *Utusan Melayu* congratulated Templer's successor, Sir Donald MacGillivray on spending a night in a kampong, it was an ironical contrast with the informality of the pre-war era.[4] As the state expanded it became less colonial in character. A slow process of Malayanisation was underway and accelerated by the Emergency. After 1950 Asian Members – two Malays, one Chinese and a Ceylonese – were appointed to executive office. In 1940 there were twenty-two Malay MCS officers; in 1956, 113 – 32 per cent of the heavenborn. Less than a fifth were a *tengku* or a *raja*, compared to nearly a half of the total in 1940.[5] The securing of positions for expatriate staff who wished to stay, and very generous compensation for those who had to leave, was a major part of the negotiations of the transfer of power. However, after the 1955 election the elected masters made it a priority to accelerate Malayanisation at all levels of the administration, which expanded to accommodate them. The debate became more of an internal one as Indian and Ceylonese community organisations lobbied as best they could for the continued prospects for their members who were concentrated in various branches of officialdom. Local government was strengthened. At the lowest level the office of *penghulu* was expanded in scope and became more bureaucratised. The *Johore Penghulu's Handbook* detailed his wide-ranging obligations, from Malay *adat*, implementation of land law to basic first aid, and the bearers of the office became subject to training courses, promotions and transfers on an unprecedented scale.[6] In general, the power and prestige of officials rose above that of *adat* chiefs, and that of politicians above all of them.

The growth of the state was inexorably connected with the expansion of its military function, and it benefited most those on the industrial frontline, rather than the cultivators of the quieter rural heartlands, and many of the latter were angered that, in this sense, lawlessness had its reward. The size of the police force peaked in 1952 with 73,000 full-time personnel and over a million kampong guards. A huge influx of expatriate personnel, especially to manage resettlement schemes, began from the tenure of Lieutenant General Sir Harold Briggs as Director of Operations, creating a garrison of 6,250 policemen by the end of 1951.[7] The function of surveillance expanded in scope. The outbreak of the Emergency was attributed to a failure of intelligence, and great emphasis was placed on creating new techniques of gathering information, which flowed through new channels to new systems of collation and co-ordination. Effective intelligence was the key to the shooting war and a showpiece of colonial administration in Southeast Asia was the Malayan Special Branch, trained by

[4] 'Mr MacGillivray and the kampong Malays', *Utusan Melayu*, 7.8.1952.
[5] J. M. Gullick, 'The Malay administrator', *Merdeka Outlook*, 1 (1957), 81–2.
[6] *Johore Penghulus' Handbook* (Johore Bahru, 1951).
[7] Federation of Malaya, *Resettlement and the development of New Villages*, pp. B314–15.

Britain's MI5.[8] The new police VHF network was perhaps the most sophisticated of its kind.[9] Malayanisation of the security apparatus created problems. There came a point when the British realised they were spying on their new elected masters. Security chiefs told the Colonial Office that they relied exclusively on the police for intelligence as British Advisers could not send political reports through their Mentri Besar, but sent the High Commissioner a confidential report fortnightly. Information was collated by the Director of Intelligence and the High Commissioner and the Chief Secretary.[10] The price of the growth in efficient policing was authoritarianism. There were some 6,000 people detained without trial in late 1951 and the Indian Legislative Councillor, R. Ramani, bitterly attacked 'the new despotism of the executive and newer despotism of the police'.[11] The consequences of this for the new polity will be considered in a later chapter.

As the bureaucracy grew, so did the problem of corruption. Embezzlement increased in proportion to the regulation of everyday life. The Emergency Regulations greatly enlarged the opportunities for petty extortion. Chinese leaders complained of the 'grave corruption' in the lower ranks of the police; British observers of the 'spiritual malaise of the forces of law and order'.[12] Gurney was informed in 1949 of 354 corruption cases in the police force.[13] Much of it, such as the graft associated with the opium trade, was endemic – 'a pool of dirty water'. It was naturally blamed on Asian underlings and not on the British. A statistical breakdown was never released. It was seen to have its roots under the BMA period, and its rising tide was a preoccupation of local newspapers. Malayan politicians paid tribute to British standards of public service. Singapore Legislative Councillor Lim Cher Cheng stated in 1957 that he preferred colonialism to corruption. Many agreed with him.[14] The techniques of counter-insurgency were adapted to fight corruption, such as post boxes to which anonymous allegations could be sent. Although an official enquiry minimised its significance, it was recognised that bribery as an insurance against obstruction or delay would continue until effective central control and simplification of the procedures of state was instituted.[15] For this reason, the British went to great lengths

---

[8] Harry Miller, _Jungle war in Malaya: the campaign against Communism 1948–60_ (London, 1972), pp. 90–112.

[9] G. A. Langley, 'Telecommunications in Malaya', _JTG_, 17 (1962), 79–91.

[10] R. W. Newsam, minute, 4.8.1954, CO1030/244.

[11] A. J. Stockwell, 'Policing during the Malayan Emergency 1948–60: communism, communalism and decolonization', in D. Anderson and D. Killingray, _Policing and decolonization_ (Manchester, 1992), 110–13.

[12] 'Minutes of the first meeting of the Emergency Chinese Advisory Committee held in the Council Chamber, Kuala Lumpur on 5.4.1949', SP.13/A/21; J. Litton, 13.8.1948, Litton Papers; discussed in Anthony Short, _The Communist insurrection in Malaya, 1948–60_ (London, 1976), pp. 149–66.

[13] Gurney to Creech Jones, 6.10.1949, CO717/162/52745/19/49.

[14] _Sin Pao_, 17.3.1957.

[15] Federation of Malaya, _Report of a Commission of Enquiry into the Integrity of the Public Services_ (Kuala Lumpur, 1953).

to promote helpful and accessible administration. A politer state was paraded in 'Operation Service'. Devised initially to combat a 'deep-rooted fear of the police', especially amongst children, it developed into a wider scheme to reform the force.[16] It was seen as a triumph of public information. By mid-1953, the campaign was extended to all government departments 'to convince the public of the government's sincere intentions'. It promoted more attractively decorated offices; it issued merit badges; it encouraged a greater sensitivity to people's feelings and more accessible bureaucrats.[17] At Templer's suggestion, citizen's advice bureaux – *Balai Penasihat Rakyat* – were established on a voluntary basis, with pilot schemes in a 'bad' New Village in Selangor, a small town in Perak and a Kuala Trengganu kampong, to demonstrate the 'helpfulness' of government and to check on corruption. Services were free, to avoid direct competition with established petition writers, and kiosks were planned in all villages and towns.[18] This 'agglomeration of a multitude of trifles' was even extended to the private sector: one large plantation company, Socfin, ordered 12,000 badges for its employees.[19] Acts of kindness may or may not have been provoked by Operation Service; however, it was certainly invoked by the public as a claim to preferential treatment. Coronation Week was promoted at the same time as an opportunity for Malayans to demonstrate their 'unaffected enthusiasm' for the empire. Over 90,000 pictures of the young queen were issued, a second Elizabethan era was proclaimed. Yet many groups bitterly criticised the lavish expenditure. In spite of a propaganda drive, and the throwing-open of government offices in the towns and cities, there was little spontaneous press coverage or public participation. 'The weakness of Operation Service,' commented one of its organisers, 'is that it is being "visited upon" the people: it is an attempt to canalise and exploit a desire which is not widely felt and which is, therefore, not seeking outlets.'[20] Not least of the legacies of the Emergency was that those directing the state learnt to exaggerate its effectiveness as an instrument of change.

The colonial economy under duress

Another register of change was economic, and although the overall picture is one of growth, the Emergency was fought against a backdrop of economy insecurity. It has long been argued that increased revenue receipts from the windfalls of the Korean war boom enabled the colonial government to weather the most challenging years of insurrection. The expansion of the state allowed more effective taxation of its people:

[16] Denis Urquhart, 'Operation Service and the children', *Malayan Police Magazine*, 19, 2 (1953).
[17] 'Notes of meeting held on 10.6.1953 to discuss the extension of "Operation Service" to all departments of government', CS/5235/53.
[18] B. W. B. Chapman, 'Citizens' Advice Bureaux', 14.4.1953, D.INF/TR/93/53.
[19] F. W. Bastin, 'Operation Service', 28.7.1953; Department of Information, 'Operation Service: progress report', 28.7.1953, CS/5235/53.
[20] F. W. Bastin, 'Operation service', 11.3.1954, *ibid.*

a campaign against tax avoidance, especially by Chinese businesses, with efficient tax investigators, was a central platform of the Templer regime. However, the long-term costs of counter-insurgency were burdensome and compounded the large imports of capital needed for post-war rehabilitation. Budget deficits were kept low by internal loans of M$64.5 million in 1946; a loan of £8 million floated on the London money market in 1949, and a contribution of M$42.6 from the UK government. A balance of payments equilibrium did not follow the boom as Malaya's dollar earnings for the Sterling Area were partly the product of restrictions on dollar area imports to enhance the net dollar gain. From 1949 to 1951, the Emergency accounted for 24 per cent to 36 per cent to 42 per cent of gross outlays. Although there was considerable overlap between civil and Emergency expenditure, and although total public works expenditure exceeded estimates by 50 per cent, many exclusively civilian projects were cut back.[21] The benefits of the boom were short-lived, and, as our discussion of the Malay rural economy will show, unevenly distributed. By 1953, a World Bank report revealed the burdensome financial constraints on development.[22] In this year the annual costs of the Emergency peaked at around $250–270 million. This excluded those falling on the police and British and Commonwealth forces – perhaps another $100 million a year. The tin industry spent $30 million defending itself.[23] The Federation government could not bear alone the burden of internal security and the projects of social improvement through which military successes could be consolidated.

The Malayan Emergency was fought in large part to make Southeast Asia safe for British business. Although naked economic exploitation was no longer tolerable, as independence approached, a tight network of expatriate Agency Houses and secretarial firms continued to dominate 'the commanding heights and mouth of the valley' of the Malayan economy.[24] Malaya, of course, lacked the vocal settler interest of the East African colonies. However, there were powerful assaults from European interests on official policy. The Colonial Office was acutely aware of the possibility of parliamentary embarrassment over security issues in Malaya. The 'Old Malaya' lobby remained an irritant. The effectiveness of the planting industry as an organised interest group was undiminished, and may even have been enhanced. The Malayan Planting Industry Employers' Association's (MPIEA) members controlled over 1,600,000 acres of rubber in 1956.[25] Business interests in 1950 successfully obstructed the implementation of a new export duty designed to finance the Emergency; and

[21] Paul Meek, 'Malaya: a study of governmental response to the Korean War boom', in T. H. Silcock (ed.), *Readings in Malayan Economics* (Singapore, 1961), pp. 201–29; Richard Stubbs, *Counter-insurgency and the economic factor: the impact of the Korean War prices boom on the Malayan Emergency* (ISEAS Occasional paper No. 19, Singapore, 1974).

[22] International Bank for Reconstruction and Development, *The economic development of Malaya* (Singapore, 1955), pp. 140–1.

[23] Short, *Communist insurrection*, pp. 346–9.

[24] James Puthucheary, *Ownership and control in the Malayan economy* (Singapore, 1960), especially, pp. 23–59.

[25] Paul L. Kleinsorge, 'Employers' associations in Malaya', *Far Eastern Survey* (August, 1957), 124–7.

fought a running battle against income tax and contributions to replanting. They defended themselves against charges of making outsized profits and against the bogey of nationalisation. Another voice of expatriate opinion, the Malayan Association, challenged the democratisation the colonial regime was fostering. It bitterly attacked the 'socialist technique' of men such as the Trade Union Adviser, John Brazier and the journalist Alex Josey. Encouraged by the 'fanatical theories' of the Labour government, it warned, 'the political atmosphere in Malaya has progressively assumed a pinker hue'.[26] There was uproar when Josey discussed the issue of nationalisation of the rubber industry on Radio Malaya – although it must be said that the attacks on Josey were nowhere stronger than in the Chinese press, and amongst Chinese members of the Legislative Council.[27] This is an index of the revival of conservative politics in Malaya. By the mid-1950s the main source of conservative attacks on British policy came from within Malayan society itself, from the court circles of the Malay States. Their main mouthpiece, the Party Negara, seems to have been financed in part by British business.[28] There was little in the utterances of other parties to threaten the economic status quo. The Alliance made repeated calls for financial responsibility, and sought to vanquish expectations that *merdeka* meant 'free everything'. To Tan Cheng Lock, Malaya had entered the age of 'social man' and some kind of revolution was inevitable. Yet society must remain in balance. Remedial measures based on 'the focal idea of socialism' were necessary to attain this balance, but only in 'equal partnership' with capital. Bismarck's dictum, 'fight socialism with socialism', was quoted with approval, as were G. D. H. Cole's warnings against unnecessary nationalisation. The ideal was 'state capitalism', or as the *Nanyang Siang Pau* put it, a Confucian mean 'between communist and free market democracy'.[29] Similarly, economic teaching in the new University of Malaya under T. H. Silcock was wedded to the Hicksian 'social framework'.[30] Although politicians such as Abdul Razak had fallen amongst Fabians during periods of study in London, the macro-economic policy adopted by the Alliance after their electoral victory in 1955, as outlined by the Selangor tycoon and Finance Minister H. S. Lee, was a cautious mixed market approach which involved no radical break with the past, and his first budget took the unpopular course of raising taxes. It was not until the end of the

---

[26] W. G. C. Blunn, 'Socialization in the Federation', in Brown's *Malayan Economic Review*, I, 8 (30.4.1951), 20–2.
[27] J. N. McHugh, 'Psychological or political warfare in Malaya: II The postwar years', *Journal of the Historical Society of the University of Malaya*, 5 (1966/67), 93.
[28] Nicholas J. White, 'Government and business divided: Malaya, 1945–57', *JICH*, 22, 2 (1994), 265.
[29] Tan Cheng Lock, *One country, one people, one government: Presidential address by Tan Chen Lock at a meeting of the General Committee of the MCA held in Penang on 30 October, 1949* (Kuala Lumpur, 1949), p. 2; MCA, *Presidential address at the fifth Annual Meeting of the General Committee, Kuala Lumpur, 31.1.1953*; 'Confucius' doctrine on ethics', *Nanyang Siang Pau*, 27.8.1953.
[30] Jomo K. S., 'Economic ideas in Malaysian universities', *Malaysian Journal of Economic Studies*, 27, 1 & 2 (1990), 140–1.

1960s that radical new policies of state intervention were mooted and these would be directed primarily at eliminating the inequalities of race, not class.

The continuities were strong because both the colonial and the new Alliance regime saw the future of economic development in the hands of Asian enterprise. In the post-war period, most of the Malayan economy remained in Asian hands, and British business operations remained reliant on Asian expertise. Just as the state was slowly becoming more Malayanised, so too was its economy. Little is known about local intermediaries in the colonial economy and the history of indigenous business is largely unwritten. Yet the 1950s saw the flowering of the comprador system within British banks in Malaya, where Chinese chief cashiers would introduce Asian business to the bank, taking a commission on loans and foreign exchange dealings. In Kuala Lumpur most of them were Hokkien. They amounted to 'a bank within a bank'; many became very wealthy, and, following the lead of the Banque de l'Indochine et de Suez, later became Chinese managers. Chinese-owned banks also began to spread their branch networks through the peninsula. The Kwong Yik Bank claimed that Kuala Lumpur was developed by Chinese using its funds. For the rural majority, however, gaps in the credit structure were filled by Chettiars and pawnbrokers.[31] This is not to say that European investment declined in this period. In fact, the consumer revolution of the 1950s saw the establishment of more European concerns – Unilever, ICI – producing soaps, beer, tobacco and biscuits locally. The construction boom created an upsurge in production of cement, bricks and plywood. This expansion occurred at the expense of the informal sector of rattan, ropes and handicrafts. Manufacturing output grew by 15.3 per cent between 1955 and 1957. Yet it would also be wrong to assume that colonial enterprise necessarily retarded the development of local manufacturing. Chinese workers carried skills they acquired in European firms into their own concerns, and the Pacific and Korean wars increased the demand for locally manufactured products, especially rubber-based goods, shoes and pottery. In the absence of state subsidies it was the smaller firms, enjoying low overheads, that benefited most from diffusion of technology, using the labour of own-account and family workers. These firms benefited from the sub-contracting which many European businesses relied upon for the provision of services. Although by 1955 primary production still dominated the Malayan economy, manufacturing was quite diversified, and local products were being exported throughout Southeast Asia.[32] Singapore continued to grow as an entrepôt, although the value of its trade with the peninsula was subject to large fluctuations, reaching a high of $2,127.5 million in 1951, and a low of $1,023 million in 1954. There was a flood of Singapore capital to the Federation, especially to Petaling Jaya and Johore Bahru.[33]

[31] Supriya Singh, *Bank Negara Malaysia: the first twenty-five years* (Kuala Lumpur, 1984), pp. 33–8, 49.
[32] Rajah Rasiah, 'Foreign investment and manufacturing growth in pre-independent Malaysia' (unpublished paper, 1992).
[33] Ow Chwee Huay, *Singapore's trade with West Malaysia, 1950–68* (Ministry of Finance, Singapore, 1969); *Sin Pao*, 19.3.1957.

The buoyancy of business had a profound impact on society. The growth of the leisure industry did much to alleviate the more terrible aspects of the Emergency. Public lotteries loomed large in the popular imagination. There was a wave of consumerism in the big towns. The newspapers of Kuala Lumpur began to carry shoppers' guides to the expanding city. The Chinese spent more and saved less, and layed out heavily on *wayangs*, festivals and gambling. Women spent more on clothes and *coiffure*. Off-duty Special Constables affected a new style in baggy pants and sports shirts.[34] The Korean war brought rapid inflation. By the beginning of February 1951 there were $663 million currency notes in circulation, a jump of $260 in twelve months. There were waiting lists for cars and a heavy demand for bicycles, most of which were supplied by Japanese firms. Building programmes were hit by a shortage of materials such as steel, which retarded electrification.[35] When relative prosperity came to industry, its benefits were distributed in unequal measure. A 'prosperity award' during the Korean war boom in late 1950 was offset by the rising cost of food and clothing. Although the availability of more rice mitigated against this, meat, fish, coconut oil and fresh fruit were not as protected as the basic diet. The cost of living for estate labourers had risen by December 1951 by 40–50 per cent since the beginning of the boom. By April 1953 newspapers and business journals were full of trepidation of an impending slump. When it occurred, fifty Chinese mines were closed in Perak and 10 per cent of tin workers dismissed.[36] The bleak industrial conditions that nourished Communism in the 1930s and 1940s had not entirely evaporated by the 1950s.

The guerrillas remained capable of disrupting the plantation economy, and of exposing the vulnerability of its management. The wealth most at risk was that of Asian absentee landowners. A register of Asian unease was the rise in remittances abroad from US$16 million in 1949 to at least US$130 million in 1951. The private non-banking sector was responsible for a wholesale capital exodus of another US$300 million (M$920 million). Indian businesses were reportedly transferring wealth out of Malaya, and Indian bankers believed that this could lead to the loss of 60 per cent of the $666 million Indian capital in the country over five years. Three-quarters of this wealth was owned by Chettiars; they were attracted outside of Malaya by Indian industrialisation and the relaxation of tax on remittances. They had already lost money in Burma, Ceylon and Indo-China, and did not intend to lose more in Malaya, where many were not eligible for citizenship. Big sums were also being sent home by Indian labourers.[37] Asian businesses were exposed to the full force of the MCP's revolution. It was small Asian estates that provided the bulk of payments to the MCP and where the authority of managers and *kepalas* was in decline and wage rates most disturbed.[38] There was a fall in rubber production in late 1948. October production

---

[34] *Malay Mail*, 4.4.1950; Amynedd, 'A planter's journal', *ibid.*, 11.3.1950.
[35] *Brown's Malayan Economic Review*, I, 4 (28.3.1951).
[36] Short, *Communist insurrection*, pp. 348–9.
[37] Meek, 'Malaya', 224–5; *Straits Times*, 19.6.1951.
[38] Labour situation in Perak North', January 1949; March 1949, Lab Tpg/13/49.

was down over 40 per cent on the previous month. Officials were reluctant to attribute it to the Emergency directly; however, enquiries reported a decline on medium estates of 25–100 acres due to the departure of owners and foremen on account of terrorist threats. There were other factors also, but in the south a medical officer reported that many smallholders had stopped tapping altogether, and those in bad areas had moved to safety. The quality of the rubber was generally poor and tapped merely to give a little cash income. The expansion of the security forces provided an opportunity to move to more profitable wage employment.[39] The area of uncertain control of labour was estimated in 1949 at a quarter of a million acres. The colonial state acted to restore labour discipline. Officials suggested that absentee landlords be expropriated and the land divided into smaller plots, and given 'to those who will cultivate and defend them'.[40] Certainly many small owners, burdened by the cost of building new lines and falling prices, closed their estates.[41] In the event, committees representing the larger industrial interests were established, and community leaders demanded to be allowed to assist in screening of labour forces.[42] At Batu Arang a private registration scheme was introduced by managers that led to the evacuation of 5,000 squatters.[43] The pacification of the countryside which had begun with resettlement was now taken to its logical conclusion.

Labour and the new paternalism

The colonial state and employers exploited Emergency powers to restore standards of labour discipline which had been broken during the Pacific war. They struck at labourers' economic independence by confining them to secure concentrations at their place of employment. The population affected by this process of 'regroupment' was even larger than that of the New Villages: an estimated 650,000 people; 71.5 per cent of them on estates, 21.5 per cent on mines and the remainder on factories, sawmills and timber *kongsis*. Although most people involved were Chinese, 255,000 Indians were regrouped on estates, that is 50 per cent of the estate population. The priority for regroupment was the Asian-owned estates without resident managers, but exposed European estates were also affected. Their labourers were moved to larger, usually European, estates to join the existing labour force.[44] In Johore alone, labourers and squatters from 450 properties were transferred to forty-seven regroupment areas on large estates. New dwellings were funded by employers, or by the government if

[39] W. D. Drysdale to CLR, 7.12.1948, Controller of Labour (Malacca) 12/45.
[40] Memorandum by Chief Secretary, 'Absentee landlordism', 10.5.1951, CO537/7282.
[41] 'Labour situation in Perak North, October, 1952', Lab Tpg/14/52.
[42] 'Deputation of leading members of commercial interests in Malaya interviewed by the High Commissioner at King's House on 11.1.1951', CO537/7262.
[43] 'State Labour Department Selangor, Annual report for 1948', Sel Sec/311/49.
[44] K. S. Sandhu, 'Emergency resettlement in Malaya' *Journal of Tropical Geography*, 18 (1964), 174; Director of Operations, 'Minutes of a meeting held in Kuala Lumpur on 2.2.1951 to discuss resettlement matters', SCA Phg/20/51.

irregularly paid labourers or smallholders were involved, and the cost of enclosure was shared on this basis.[45] Malay communities were also affected. There are no clear figures, but in Kelantan alone there were twenty-five Malay regroupment areas and thirteen in Johore. Here, the Malays left behind their own land and carefully constructed houses. They were left badly out of pocket, and a journalist visiting Malay regroupment areas near Tangkak in Johore commented on the prevalence of skin disease amongst their inhabitants.[46]

Regroupment had a profound impact on patterns of work. Curfews and food restrictions reduced labour productivity by about 10–15 per cent.[47] In Pahang, regroupment upset the life of Malay kampongs by confining Chinese tappers who worked on the Malay smallholdings.[48] Chettiar estates in Perak, caught in a similar situation, recruited increasingly from the kampongs themselves. There were reports of unemployment as a result of regrouping in Perak and Selangor. This was often a result of absenteeism from the smaller estates, due to the disincentives of poor yields for sharecroppers and long distances to travel.[49] There were great variations in conditions, particularly between internal regroupings on estates and those where outsiders were brought on to the larger plantations. Undertaking regroupment in a period of labour shortage, managers in Kedah for example paid more attention to the quality of the scheme in the hope of securing a stable workforce after the Emergency. One large scheme in Kulim, in late 1950, involved over 100 estates.[50] In north Johore at the end of 1952, of the twenty-six large estates regrouped, twenty-three claimed to have schools, and most had radios, cinema shows, playing fields and a crèche. On smaller estates amenities were less in evidence: 'few can appreciate living further from their task in inferior accommodation, with the added inconvenience of a curfew, redressed only by the convenience of a perimeter fence and Special Constable protection'.[51] The government encouraged employers' associations to improve conditions by establishing schools and nurseries in the workplace. This met with limited results. As independence approached the UPAM began to better its public profile by professing a paternalistic interest in the social life of labourers and sponsoring cultural and sporting activities, such as a football challenge cup.[52] Some estates and mines had leisure facilities – in one case a swimming pool – but these were exceptions to the rule. Only by the mid-1950s were employers starting to provide football pitches. A housing crisis was often met by converting old back-to-back cottages into four-

---

[45] Director of Operations, 'Directive No. 10: Labour regrouping schemes and "Controlled Areas" under E.R. 17FA', 15.1.1951, CO537/7262.

[46] Paul Markandan, *The problem of the New Villages in Malaya* (Singapore, 1954), p. 15.

[47] K. S. Sandhu, 'The saga of the "squatter" in Malaya', *JSEAH*, 5 (1964), 169–70.

[48] 'Report on labour regrouping measures now necessary in Lipis District', 14.2.1951, SCA Phg/8/51.

[49] Labour Department Monthly Report (LDMR) November 1950, FS/12314/50. 'Monthly Report for October, 1953 – North Johore', LDM/27/53.

[50] LDMR, August 1951; December 1950, FS/12314/50.

[51] J. D. H. Neil to Commissioner for Labour, 23.12.1952, LDM/112/52.

[52] UPAM, *55th Annual Report*, 1956.

roomed houses. Yet the new dwellings were still found to be 'very poorly suited to family life'.[53] In some areas there was a growth of insanitary shanty towns with inadequate facilities. Health conditions remained poor. On the whole regroupment caused malaria to retreat, and new replanting methods were less likely to produce concentrated breeding of *Anopheles maculatus*. However, controls could swiftly break down; a severe epidemic occurred in Kuala Lipis in 1953 as a result of the disruption to anti-malarial work by guerrilla activity, and natural immunities had weakened since the war. In 1950, although the malaria rate on estates as a whole was 12.1 per thousand, it amounted to 35.3 in Kedah and 74.8 in Trengganu. Although officials insisted that malnutrition occurred only 'by long established prejudice or from want of discrimination', at the end of 1949, deficiency diseases were still prominent amongst estate workers and infant mortality was high – in coastal Selangor at a rate of 63.8 per thousand.[54] In the same area an average of only 68 per cent haemoglobin levels was found amongst estate labourers; women were the greatest sufferers. Colonial doctors blamed extravagant expenditure on liquor, wireless sets and expensive jaunts to town by taxi for the under-nutrition. However, although they argued that the diet of South Indians had improved, their poverty meant it lacked variety, and when shops were opened to widen the range of available foodstuffs dietary standards actually dropped as families sold off their own domestic produce to them.[55]

The re-establishment of labour discipline allowed employers to negotiate from a position of renewed strength. They took advantage of the Emergency to cut wages and harass activists. In particular, they obstructed any attempt by Chinese labourers to organise themselves.[56] Resettlement and regroupment provided a reservoir of labour that enabled estates to dispense with resident labour when prices were low.[57] Resettlement dealt a powerful blow to the economic resourcefulness of the labourer. However, management did not have it all its own way. It was possible for some labourers to retain a degree of adaptability. In Johore in 1951, Chinese in the New Villages waited on their savings for better work than that offered by the estates. Only with higher wages did labour return to the larger estates. When, two years later, wages fell again, an official remarked that recession could not be biting so hard 'if tappers

[53] 'Conference of Deputy Commissioners for Labour, 2–4.12.1954', DCL Sel/65/53'; State Labour Department Selangor, 'Annual report for 1948', Sel Sec/311/19.

[54] Federation of Malaya, *Annual Report of the Malaria Advisory Board for the year 1950* and for 1953; Labour Department Annual Report, 1949, FS/12373/50. 'Health of labour forces in the inland districts Selangor, 1949'; 'Report on health conditions of estates and other places where labourers are employed, coast districts', DCL Sel/430/19.

[55] R. D. Eagland, 'A report on anaemia in estate labourers in Malaya', *Medical Journal of Malaya*, 7, 1 (1952), 36–8; I. A. Simpson (ed.), *Applied nutrition in Malaya: a collection of papers issued for the use of participants at a training course in applied nutrition held at the Institute for Medical Research, Kuala Lumpur from 26.11.1956 to 4.12.1956* (Kuala Lumpur, 1957), pp. 65–7; B. A. Lamprell and Elizabeth Check, 'Anaemia in South Indians employed on Malayan plantations', *Medical Journal of Malaya*, 7, 2 (1952), 107–14.

[56] Charles Gamba, *The origins of trade unionism in Malaya* (Singapore, 1960), pp. 358–68.

[57] For example in Muar, 'Monthly Report for October 1953 – North Johore', LDM/27/53.

are willing to take so many holidays', and suggested that other incomes continued to offset low earnings.[58] Indeed, when slump hit, as it did by the second half of 1953, it revealed a variety of ways in which labourers diversified their sources of income. In Krian, labourers were given leave to help with the harvest, and managers complained that they overstayed in the kampongs. Many contracted malaria there.[59] Survival strategies were acquired at great cost, and much of it was borne by women. Pressures increased on women of all communities as wage earners. Unequally paid in all industries, women mostly did piecework as it gave them an opportunity to earn as much as the men. On rubber estates in 1948, women constituted 40 per cent of the total labour force, children 8 per cent. An International Labour Organisation (ILO) survey reported that many employers regarded women as the best tappers, although they were limited by the amounts of latex they could carry. However, they were only paid, on average, 80 per cent of the male wage.[60] Too frequently forays into wage-earning by women led to sweated labour. The government was alarmed at its incidence. Conditions in sweated industries were diabolical. In the shoe manufac-turing shops of Malacca only $2 was earned for an eight-hour day, with no accommodation, sickness or maternity allowances, or workers' compensation.[61] In north Perak the main sweated industry was tobacco-rolling at piece-rates which earned women $30–50 a month, less for leaf selectors. In one case in 1949, wages were only $5–18 a month: only the very old and young would take this work.[62] In the vicinity of Kuala Lumpur, it was found on one estate that women began to tap rubber at dawn and moved on to factory jobs in a biscuit factory.[63] This was not uncommon. Shop assistants, male and female, campaigned against a widespread practice of working fourteen-hour days. However, dispersed throughout the towns and villages, it was difficult for them to unionise and the fact that their employers were equally disorganised made the ten-hour day doubly difficult to enforce.[64] It was precisely these scattered groups of workers that found organisation and leadership in the proscribed General Labour Unions.

The outbreak of the Emergency had decimated the unions. Much of the FTU leadership took to the jungle in 1948; 185 unionists were arrested. The registration of the unions whose leaders absconded was cancelled, and their funds frozen. Many of the labour officials of the Malayan Spring had been committed socialists; some, such as John Brazier, remained at their posts. However, after 1948 men of the old regime came to the fore, and the needs of counter-insurgency became the driving force

---

[58] LDMR, August, 1951, DCL Sel/9/51; 'Monthly Report for October, 1953 – North Johore', LDM/27/53.
[59] 'Labour situation in Perak North, March 1954', Lab Tpg/3/54.
[60] Children still provided 8 per cent of labour, 'Enquiry on work on plantations', FS/13622/49.
[61] R. H. Oakeley, circular, 18.10.1954, Lab Tpg/3/54.
[62] 'Labour situation in Perak North, March 1949', Lab Tpg/13/49; November 1954, Lab Tpg/3/54.
[63] 'State Labour Department Selangor, Annual report for 1948', Sel Sec/311/49,
[64] 'Labour situation in Perak North, August 1954', Lab Tpg/3/54.

behind labour policy. Officials argued that 'the labourers appeared to have been somewhat appalled at the Frankenstein which had grown out of trade unionism'.[65] Emergency powers gave the British the opportunity to put down the monster. In the absence of effective trade unions, the British government attempted to be the arbiter of labour conditions. It targeted racial discrimination towards Indian labour. However, employers continued to insist that inequities in income were a reflection of different skill tasks, and argued that discrimination was declining without the need for state intervention.[66] Amongst officials, too, old stereotypes died hard. As the Labour Department spelled them out to the ILO in 1949, the Chinese were 'pushing, hard-working, independent people'. The Indian 'has to be closely supervised. He looks for security and a settled life, and has little ambition because of his background' and caste. The Malay was 'not attracted to work'.[67] The incidence of wage differentials was to some extent masked by the fact that after the war a greater number of estates were employing Indians on piece-rates – especially in Selangor and Perak. In Kedah also, the large Harvard and Dublin estates changed to piece-rates and encouraged other estates to do the same. However, the new system did not secure a parity of income between Chinese and Indians.[68] The drawing up of a new employment code to standardise practices was retarded by the mood of distrust between labour and employers, and by the government's inability to finance the system of labour exchanges and the expansion of the Labour Department necessary to operate it.[69] A mainstay of the improvement of labour conditions was the introduction in 1952 of an Employees' Provident Fund (EPF) to which labourers and their employers contributed. However, it was resisted by both parties. Asian-owned estates ran down their labour when faced with the need to pay EPF subscriptions, and shops reduced their staff below the minimum workforce of four that the scheme required. Labourers were suspicious that employers were not paying their share, and employers claimed that they were refusing to apply their fingerprints to the EPF forms.[70] Distrust remained very deep-rooted.

Attempts to mould the Asian labourer into a reasonable facsimile of the Great British Worker had begun before the Emergency, and remained central to its successful prosecution. The approach was strongly paternalistic in tone. 'The government,' propaganda leaflets stated, 'is like a parent to the people.'[71] A return to the old informal pattern of relations was encouraged. A surviving South Indian Harbour Workers' Union in Selangor settled disputes through a variation of the

[65] 'State Labour Department Selangor, Annual report for 1948', Sel Sec/311/49.
[66] R. D. Houghton, Commissioner for Labour, to Secretary, MMEA, 9.7.1949; MMEA to Houghton, 27.8.1949, DCL.Sel/397/49; Federation of Malaya, Labour Department Annual Report, 1949, FS/12373/50.
[67] 'Enquiry into work on plantations', FS/13622/49.
[68] LDMR, January, 1949; April 1949; March 1949, FS/13151/49.
[69] Federation of Malaya, Labour Department Annual Report, 1949, FS/12373/50.
[70] 'Labour situation in Perak North, May 1952'; August 1952; September 1952, Lab Tpg/14/52.
[71] 'The workers and the Government' (Chinese), 9.9.1952, INF/1136/52.

panchayat system, and in Perak managers stated that they preferred it, and claimed that their workers did too.[72] Even by 1955, when strong trade unionism in the rubber industry had re-emerged, officials were recommending welfare committees on estates, independent of the union, as 'wet nursing for the labourers'.[73] A labour officer in Pahang reported this conversation in 1950:

> Deputy Commissioner for Labour: Do you have any trade unions here among the three thousand employees?
> Andy: No, thank God.
> District Officer Commanding: No, they all rely on Andy's strong sense of justice![74]

In 1949 trade union membership was declining dramatically. In the Federation as a whole trade union membership had slumped to 70,037 in December 1948, and by May 1949 to only 40,434.[75] This was not a reflection of workers' apathy, but of the intense scrutiny and surveillance under which the surviving trade unions had to function. The workers had lost the political and financial support the MCP had given for schools and for clerical and executive officers.[76] When the MPIEA attempted to revise wage rates in May 1949, it was impossible to begin collective bargaining as there was no federation of Chinese unions to deal with; in the end they dealt with a 'workers' group' of surviving unions.[77] Management blamed the Trade Union Adviser for industrial unrest.[78] The unions complained of an erosion of grass-roots support and of harassment. Many labourers felt that the British encouraged trade unions merely to dupe Communist sympathisers into coming forward. As the Adviser confessed: 'it is inevitable . . . that they have their fears when one knows the suspicion, hostility and in some cases hatred of other sections of the community towards their aims and purposes and leadership'.[79] Unionists chafed at the patern-alism of the Labour Department. Its officials, they pointed out, were non-specialists drawn from the MCS establishment. Distrust was compounded by the retirement of a succession of senior departmental officers – A. D. Aheare, R. Boyd and R. G. D. Houghton – to positions in the MPIEA. The last-named was an object of particular vitriol: 'Men like him,' one unionist complained to the Colonial Office, 'are bringing disrepute to the British.'[80] The British government had, in fact, pressed for

---

[72] 'State Labour Department Selangor, Annual report for 1948', Sel Sec/311/49; 'Labour situation in Perak North, August 1949', Lab Tpg/13/49.
[73] 'Welfare Committees', 8.3.1955, CO1030/365.
[74] DCL, Bentong, 'Monthly report for October, 1950', BA Pahang/24/50.
[75] LDMR, May 1949, FS/13151/49.
[76] Gamba, *Origins*, pp. 352–395.
[77] LDMR, May 1949, FS/13151/49; Federation of Malaya, Labour Department Annual Report, 1949, FS/12373/50.
[78] 'Memorandum of meeting between a deputation for the Rubber Growers' Association and the Secretary of State for the Colonies at the Colonial Office on 15.11.1951', CO1022/39.
[79] John Brazier to Tan Cheng Lock, 9.3.1950, SP.13/A/24.
[80] 'MTUC statement submitted to Mr E. Parry', 16.3.1953; M. Arokiasamy to E. Parry, 16.5.1953, CO1022/120.

Houghton's appointment. High Commissioner Templer was severely embarrassed by this and launched a personal campaign to get him out of the country.[81] Templer cut through much of the antipathy and red tape that prevented the revival of unionism. Yet he was driven to it primarily by concern at labour's passive attitude to the counter-insurgency campaign. Employers were persuaded to adopt a more concilia- tory attitude towards unions by Templer's personal assurances that they would be kept free from Communism.[82] He impressed on plantation interests the extent to which wage reductions in the post-Korea slump in the rubber price would 'complicate the Emergency position'. The Colonial Office backed his attempts to achieve industrial stability, and pressed him to institute permanent wage-fixing machinery.[83] Thus, in a limited way, the Emergency could improve the bargaining position of estate labourers. In 1953 Whitley Council machinery was introduced in the public sector. However, there was confusion as to whether this was to supersede or bolster the development of trade unionism.[84] The future of trade unionism in Malaya was to be shaped by counter-insurgency, and the Emergency greatly diluted the post-war government's commitment to encourage robust and independent trade unions.

There were limits to the new paternalism. The spirit unleashed by the INA and the post-war Indian labour unions could not be wished away. Englishmen observed the changes on every estate they visited. Indians, they noted, decorated their houses with pictures of political personalities; the men wore shorts and shirts when visiting town. Local-born women were also particular about their dress – they wore blouses and plaits, whilst their mothers had preferred saris and a simpler hair-style. Cigarettes were preferred to cheroots, beer to toddy; women chewed less betel. 'Local born Indian labourers want to keep up with the times, and not be the old-fashioned "Ramasamy" and "Maniammah".' The change was not all for the better. To British observers the Indian labourer spent too much on the cinema, money that could be spent on food.[85] More and more employees on estates were becoming 'holiday conscious', and making enquiries about their leave entitlements.[86] Behind these changes lay social reform. In Perak it was observed that there was less expenditure on marriages and social gatherings. Inter-caste marriages were very common, and contracted on a linguistic basis only.[87] Opposition to toddy consumption remained a powerful stimulant to the organisation of labour. Dravidian reform movements had

[81] A. M. Webster, minute, 21.5.1953; A. M. Mackintosh, minute, 21.5.1953, CO1022/121.
[82] John Cloake, *Templer: Tiger of Malaya* (London, 1985), pp. 265–6, 286–7.
[83] A. M. MacKintosh to Templer, 17.6.1953; Sir Thomas Lloyd to Templer, 23.12.1953, CO1022/121.
[84] Charles Gamba, 'Staff relations in the government services of Malaya', *Malayan Economic Review*, 2, 2 (1957), 12–32.
[85] 'State Labour Department Selangor, Annual report for 1949', DCL Sel/430/19; 'State Labour Department Selangor, Annual report for 1948', Sel Sec/311/49.
[86] 'Labour situation in Perak North, January 1953', Lab Tpg/20/53.
[87] 'Labour Office, Perak North, Taiping, 1949 report', Lab Tpg/83/49; S. Arasaratnam, 'Social reform and reformist pressure groups among the Indians of Malaya and Singapore, 1930–1955', *JMBRAS*, 40, 2 (1967), 62–3.

taken hold on the estates, and when strong estate unions emerged, such as the National Union of Plantation Workers, they provided a new route through which the Pan-Malayan Dravidian Federation could exercise its influence. A wider process of Tamil revival was underway. It mobilised estate labour, initially in Perak and then more widely, into national politics, and eventually secured Tamil leadership for the Malayan Indian Congress.[88] The history of trade unionism in post-war Malaya is not merely the story of a struggle between official paternalism and a rehabilitated labour movement; it was also shaped by internal debates within labouring communities themselves.

The MCP renewed its attempts to capture the support of labour. In Kedah and elsewhere, as labour shortages occurred Communist 'shadow' unions appeared. In Negri Sembilan, Tamil workers were said to be joining the Communists through MCP sponsorship of Dravidian associations.[89] There were reports of secret militant cells in the Harbour Workers' Union, Port Swettenham and at Batu Arang.[90] In November 1951, there were strikes in the vast estates around Bahau, involving 1,000 tappers.[91] Strike action provoked a sharp reaction from the authorities. However, although there was some evidence of leftist intimidation, it was recognised that much of this unrest was spontaneous, and articulated real grievances. There was a school of opinion in the colonial administration – although very much on the defensive – that still felt that encouragement of trade unions was the best means of preventing renewed Communist dominance of labour. On 27 and 28 February 1949, a Conference of Malayan Trade Union Delegates was convened by the labour representatives on the Legislative Council, with 160 delegates representing 84 registered trade unions. The new movement worked under great constraints. There were suspicions of the dominant Indian leadership of men such as P. P Narayanan, V. M. N. Menon, M. P. Rajagopal and X. E. Nathan – some of whom had been 'official' representatives of labour throughout the struggles of 1945–8. Local leaders also tended to resist any challenge to their parochial power. Government unions were not permitted to federate with private sector unions, but this rule had to be relaxed to allow a trade union working committee to be formed as an embryonic federation, although not as a federation with a right to organise strikes.[92] This body, the Malayan Trade Union Council (MTUC) took shape at a second conference in March 1950, after union participation in arbitration on wages in the rubber industry had reassured the government of their 'responsibility' and won for them 'a growing acceptance of the trade unions' right to speak for, and act on behalf of, the workers of

[88] R. Ampalavanar, *The Indian minority and political change in Malaya, 1945–57* (Kuala Lumpur, 1981), pp. 33–7; M. R. Stenson, *Class, race and colonialism in West Malaysia: the Indian case* (Queensland, 1980), pp. 175–7.
[89] LDMR, January 1951, DCL Sel/9/51.
[90] MRSA, February, 1954, CO1030/7.   [91] SFWIS, 22.11.1951, CO1022/43.
[92] Malaysian Trades Union Congress, *History of the MTUC* (Kuala Lumpur, 1974), pp. 15–18; LDMR, February 1949, FS/13151/49; Federation of Malaya, *Labour Department Annual Report*, 1949.

Malaya'.[93] Education lay at the forefront of union activities. To the MTUC, the education system needed a complete reorientation to 'meet the demands of a new and settled society'. In 1949, the Penang Municipal Services Union started adult education classes that evolved into a national movement. The plantation workers' union published its newspaper, *Union Herald*, from 1952, and offered classes on a large scale from 1954.[94] The MTUC annual conference in August 1951 resumed demands for a new Pan-Malayan federation, or for a single Pan-Malayan union. It called for a minimum wage; a maximum working week of forty-two hours; twenty-one annual holidays, and a contributing social insurance scheme.[95] Delegates voiced their resentment at the sacrifice of political influence unionists were expected to make because of the Emergency. As the MTUC argued in 1952:

> If they enter a wage claim or object to some proposals calling for greater sacrifices, they are lacking in statesmanship, reactionary and determined on defending their privileges against the interests of the public. If some section of the membership, enraged by provocative action on the part of an employer, takes action without going through procedure, then the members are abused as anarchists and the trade union leaders as bureaucrats, incompetent to control their organisations.[96]

However, the MTUC remained moderate when it came to strike action. It initially had no executive authority: its role in collective bargaining in the rubber industry was only consultative. However, resistance to the 1952–3 wage cuts directly stimulated the formation of a national estate union.[97] In 1950 the surviving plantation unions had agreed to co-operate in a Pan-Malayan Rubber Workers' Union to negotiate with employers. Encouraged by the Trade Union Adviser, the big three of the estate unions – the Perak Estate Employees' Union, the Johore State Plantation Workers' Union and the Negri Sembilan Indian Labour Union – together with two smaller Malacca unions, amalgamated to form the National Union of Plantation Workers (NUPW) in 1954 which claimed 80,000 members. It met with resistance from state leaderships in both Perak and Johore: in particular there was rivalry between the Negri Sembilan Unionist, P. P. Narayanan, and the Johore leader, Rayal Jose.[98] With the active support of Brazier, Narayanan assumed national leadership and was to dominate trade unionism for several decades. Fiercely anti-Communist, Narayanan carved out an international reputation for himself through his association with the right-wing International Conference of Free Trade Unions. He stood for a disciplined and

---

[93] 'Report of the Working Committee to be submitted to the Malayan Trade Union Delegate Conference on 25 and 26 March, 1950', SP.13/A/24.
[94] International Labour Office, *Report on workers' education in Malaya* (Geneva, 1960), pp. 1–3.
[95] X. E. Nathan, General Secretary, MTUC, to Chief Secretary, 5.11.1951, CS/12507/51.
[96] MTUC, *Malayan Trade Union Council report for the period 1.7.1951 to 31.3.1952.*
[97] Martin Rudner, 'Labour policy and the dilemmas of trade unionism in post-war Malaya', RIMA, 16, 1 (1982), 101–18.
[98] Charles Gamba, *The National Union of Plantation Workers: the history of the plantation workers of Malaya, 1946–1958* (Singapore, 1962), pp. 25–6, 92; S. Arasaratnam, *Indians in Malaysia and Singapore* (London, 1970), pp. 140–6.

gradualistic approach to the improvement of estate conditions, and began collective bargaining with employers through a Joint Consultative Council.[99] This conciliatory style coloured the first major campaign by the union in 1956 for a minimum guaranteed wage. The industrial action launched by the NUPW consisted solely of a go-slow in May, and rapidly it was confronted by spontaneous, more radical action from below in the shape of lightning wildcat strikes which the NUPW leadership refused to endorse. The new wave of unionisation encouraged a preference for non-Indian labour amongst managers. It also met with a challenge from Chinese-dominated rivals, the Malayan Estate Workers' Union in Seremban district, and the Pan-Malayan Rubber Workers' Union, which labelled the NUPW as 'racist': it was denied registration by the government.[100] The communal aspect of the struggle between the rival leaderships was pronounced, and it was a backdrop to the trade unions' re-entry into politics.

The MTUC grew in political status, yet it was divided as to where it should place its loyalty. A Labour Party was formed in Singapore and in Penang in 1951. However, it was opposed by P. P. Narayanan and the Council of the MTUC on the grounds that it divided the nationalist movement and they cast in their lot with Dato Onn's Independence of Malaya Party (IMP). However, other activists went ahead to launch the Labour Party in Selangor. In the early stages it drew support from public sector unions, such as the Municipal and Government Labour Union and the Clerical and Administrative Staff Union, and a national party was formed on 14 August 1952.[101] In 1953 the MTUC was allowed political funds, but no unions took advantage of them. Although the MTUC continued to assert its political independence, its members supported the Labour Party in growing numbers, to the concern of officials. By late 1955 the spectre of a new pan-Malayan federation, dominated by People's Action Party activists in Singapore and financed by their money, had raised its head once more. A Pan-Malayan Trades Union Congress was formed by Chinese unions, headed by Tan Tuan Boon, as a direct challenge to the MTUC. In the same year the National Union of Factory and General Workers (NUFGW) took a lead in advocating industrial action and a more active political role for trade unions. To the British government, the powerful NUPW was the only bulwark against full-scale industrial warfare. Yet they possessed a formidable armoury of legislation to hinder the resurgent left: the Willan judgement was still in force; employees still had to give two weeks notice of a strike, and in 1957 NUFGW was deregistered.[102] At the same time the security forces made increasing demands on the MTUC for active participation in

---

[99] J. Victor Morais, *P. P. Narayanan – the Asian trade union leader* (Petaling Jaya, 1975).

[100] P. Ramasamy, *Plantation labour, unions, capital and the state in peninsular Malaysia* (Kuala Lumpur, 1994), pp. 97–103; K. S. Jomo and P. Todd, *Trade unions and the state in peninsular Malaysia* (Kuala Lumpur, 1994), p. 100.

[101] V. David, *Freedom never came* (Petaling Jaya, 1989), pp. 40–2.

[102] Jomo and Todd, *Trade unions*, pp. 95–101; 'Colonial Labour Advisory Committee – draft minutes of 55th meeting, 18.6.1953', CO1022/120.

anti-subversive measures. As independence approached, trade unionists trod a careful path between the elected representatives of labour and the ruling Alliance, who regarded them with no less suspicion than their colonial predecessors. This delicate position muted their demands for the MTUC's right to political funds, and for 'economic *merdeka*'.[103] Despite official attempts to revive and guide trade unions, the basic economic structure which had been the target of the federations of the immediate post-war period remained unreformed. Unions in the tin industry remained especially weak and divided. A visiting British trade unionist found the Chinese mineowners a particularly canny lot: 'they argued just like employers in Manchester'.[104] The authorities' overriding resolve to impede the trade union movement's participation in national politics was undiminished. It is unsurprising, then, that the most powerful unions such as the NUPW became communal enclaves, that with the avenue towards the politics of class closed to them, estate populations in particular looked elsewhere for their collective betterment, and to the advancement of a communal interest. Religious and social reform was already a deep-rooted component of local leadership on the estates. The goads to communal uplift were still in evidence. For example, unions complained that toddy shops were actually growing in number: from 105 in 1951 to 168 in 1952.[105] Colonial rule did not create the ethnic politics of labour. However, it imposed severe constraints on the possibilities for the formation of alternative kinds of solidarities. 'The plantation worker,' P. P. Narayanan observed in 1951, 'still lives in a surrounding that reminds one of indentured labour days.' Those groups who had been most militant prior to the Emergency, remained the most disadvantaged as it drew to a conclusion.

The twilight of the colonial town

For much of the population, and especially as insurgency rolled back with the establishment of 'white areas', the Emergency was represented less by the appearance of police posts, armoured cars and militia in the countryside, than by the flourishing of the towns, which often flaunted a new affluence. A British visitor to Malaya in 1955 was amazed at how open a city Kuala Lumpur was – 'Cafes are full, cinemas crammed.'[106] By 1957, Malaya was the most urbanised country in Southeast Asia, and the second most urbanised country in Asia. Taking the census definition of an urban centre as a settlement of over 1,000 persons, the urban population rose from 26.5 to

---

[103] MTUC, *History of the MTUC*, pp. 74–5; 78–103; Martin Rudner, 'Malayan labour in transition: labour policy and trade unionism, 1955–63', *MAS*, 7, 1 (1973), 22–8; Charles Gamba, 'Labour and labour parties in Malaya', *Pacific Affairs*, 31, 2 (1958), 117–29.

[104] E. W. Barltrop to MacGillivray, 27.1.1956; 'Minutes of a meeting between representatives of the TUC and Overseas Employers' Federation and the Colonial Office, 14.11.1955', CO1030/365.

[105] Gamba, *The National Union of Plantation Workers*, p. 45.

[106] J. B. Perry Robinson, *Transformation in Malaya* (London, 1956), p. 46.

42.3 per cent of the total population between 1947 and 1957. If some of the larger villages are removed by taking 2,000 people as the minimum for a town, the rise was 24 to 38.8 per cent – an increase of 105.9 per cent – greatly exceeding the natural growth of population.[107] This was by no means solely a consequence of resettlement: larger forces had been set in motion. The distribution of urbanisation was very uneven. Johore Bahru, Alor Star and Batu Pahat, grew much faster than Kuala Trengganu, Taiping and Muar. The most pronounced growth was in towns with a population of between 10,000 and 25,000, places such as Butterworth, Bukit Mertajam, Kluang, Sungei Pattani, Kota Bahru and Telok Anson. Conurbations grew around State centres such as Ipoh. The growth of lesser settlements showed their continuing importance as centres of education, administration, trade and services. Even sleepy Malacca reported a minor property boom amongst its middle-income groups. Furthermore, the Emergency fuelled the growth of military cantonments such as Port Dickson, Sungei Besi and Terendak.[108] These small towns were staging-posts in the migrations of country people to the larger centres, which on the west coast at least tended to follow established routes.[109] Some older centres entered a period of relative decline. The Penang Indian Chamber of Commerce complained in 1950 that with the loss of free-port status, the customs barrier at Mitchell Pier and the neglect of its harbour facilities, Penang had become merely an appendage of the mainland. Its entrepôt trade had shrunk, whilst that of its rival, Port Swettenham, had expanded along with the economy of the Klang Valley.[110] The development of an urban sub-system in Kelantan was arrested by its isolation as a result of the closing of its only effective link with the west, the east coast railway, during the Japanese occupation. The railway did not reopen until 1953. However, Kota Bahru grew as a result of Malay urbanisation. Traditional centres of Malay power were fused into the structure of an urban system subservient to the interests of the colonial economy as a result of political and developmental initiatives. The fishing economy of both Kelantan and Trengganu was from the pre-war period being drawn into external market networks, and this had consolidated the development of small urban centres with the creation of town boards in the 1930s and the increasing provision of an administrative and developmental infrastructure in the post-war period. The fishing industry of Trengganu lent itself more to a sophisticated marketing system than the more self-

[107] The table in Kernial Singh Sandhu, 'The population of Malaya: some changes in the pattern of distribution between 1947 and 1957', *JTG*, 15 (1961), 88, has an arithmetical error, and gives this figure as 34.4 per cent.
[108] Hamzah Sendut, 'Patterns of urbanization in Malaya', *JTG*, 16 (1962), 114–30; W. D. McTaggart, 'The distribution of ethnic groups in Malaya, 1947–57', JTG, 26 (1968), 69–81.
[109] For example, Kedah-Penang-Perak; Perak-Selangor; Selangor-Negri Sembilan, Robin J. Pryor, *Migration and development in Southeast Asia: a demographic perspective* (Kuala Lumpur, 1979), p. 80.
[110] *Malay Mail*, 29.3.1950; P. P. Courtenay, *A geography of trade and development in Malaya* (London, 1972), pp. 210–16.

Table 3 *Urbanisation by race, 1947–1980*[111]

Year	Urban population	Malay (%)	Chinese (%)	Indian (%)	Others (%)
1947	929,928	19	63.1	14.7	3.2
1957	1,666,969	21	62.6	12.8	3.6
1970	2,530,433	27.6	58.5	12.8	1.1
1980	4,073,105	37.6	50.3	11	0.7

contained rice economy of inland Kelantan. In the case of Kelantan, with its narrower coastline, Kota Bahru became the commercial centre, whereas the long coastline of Trengganu allowed for the development of the commercial and service functions of smaller centres along the coast. The pushing through of a road network from Pahang also meant the decline of some traditional centres such as Kuala Besut, at the expense of other towns better served by road, such as Jerteh.[112] However, in many such cases, the extent to which conditions in the villages were radically divorced from those of the smaller country towns can be exaggerated – a point to which we shall return in our discussion of the Malay rural economy.[113]

The effects of urbanisation were most dramatic in the growth of Kuala Lumpur during the Emergency. The Municipal unit of Kuala Lumpur was expanded to take in marginal settlements and this put additional pressure on public services. By 1957, the city had thrust upon it – in the nation-building parlance of the day – a new integrative role as the focus of the political and cultural life of the transmogrifying colonial system, and its burghers moved to decorate the capital with the architectural, horticultural and monumental ornaments of civic life. The racial complexion of the towns in general was changing, as Table 3 illustrates, and changing in Kuala Lumpur in particular. The increase in urban population between the 1947 and 1957 censi was greatest in the case of the Malay population – 116.5 per cent – but this was only 18.2 per cent of the total population increase which was dominated by the Chinese. Around 50 per cent of the total increase was due to in-migration. Many of the newcomers were labourers who, faced with an unfamiliar environment, tended to settle with others of their race and class. The towns were the province of young men: 68 per cent of the inhabitants of the main centres were under thirty years of age. In 1957, over 50 per cent of Kuala Lumpur was under twenty. Immigrant Malays were

---

[111] Goh Ban Lee, *Urban planning in Malaysia: history, assumptions and issues* (Petaling Jaya, 1991), p. 23.

[112] Urbanisation grew at a much smaller rate than in neighbouring Trengganu, 7.85 per cent compared to 23.5 per cent in 1947, but by 1957, 22.7 per cent as compared to 33.5 per cent. Lim Heng Kow, *The evolution of the urban system in Malaya* (Kuala Lumpur, 1978), pp. 113–52.

[113] Hamzah Sendut, 'Patterns of urbanization', 122–3.

mostly males in their twenties, taking jobs in the public sector where they predominated; their increase in commerce and finance was slight. This was reflected in urban incomes: over 34 per cent of Chinese earned more than $300 a month, only 22 per cent of Malays and Indians earned that amount. Amongst the Chinese the fastest growing group were Hokkiens – who extended their commercial and trade specialisations from the declining centres of Malacca and Penang to the boom town of Kuala Lumpur – and Hakkas from the New Villages. Much of the rising affluence of Kuala Lumpur was due to the growth of its European population. Ironically, Kuala Lumpur in the last stages of colonial rule was more of a colonial city than ever before: the inter-census increase in its European population – from 1,794 to 6,645 – was due to the large military presence and the increase in staff in European commercial firms and diplomatic missions. Chinatown, Brickfields and Kampong Bahru were the foci of Chinese, Indian and Malay urban life respectively. The Chinese areas had dense concentrations of people: residential space and niches for business were highly fractionalised. Labour was absorbed into specialised trades in a way that reinforced the footing of different dialect groups in certain trades. The traditional framework of trade and craft guilds, sports and dramatic clubs, temple and cemetery committees and communal associations, which had always been a characteristic of Chinese urban life in Malaya, remained largely intact.[114] A housing crisis was reported in all the major towns. In Penang, housing had been destroyed during the war and new arrivals converted what had survived into tenements.[115] As controls on land tightened, the growth of urban squatting created new ethnic concentrations. In 1951, the number of squatters in Kuala Lumpur was estimated between 75,000 and 140,000, most of them Chinese, although Indian families settled near the workshops of Sentul. By independence squatting was for the first time becoming a Malay problem. The use of the term 'squatter' with regard to Malays – and indeed a Malay word for the phenomenon – came with the movement of rural Malays to the towns in this period as *tempat mancari makan* – a place to look for food. Hostels were founded to house these young men but their late arrival put them at a disadvantage in the legitimate acquisition of land. In Kuala Lumpur, settlements such as Kampong Kerinchi took in large numbers of migrants.[116] These ethnic concentrations were only partially broken down by the construction of low-cost flats in places such as Kampong Dato Keremat. As squatter settlements proliferated, areas of mixed middle- and upper-class housing expanded, in the areas of government bungalows, the Palladian homes of Kenny Hill and Ampang Road, and to a lesser extent in Pahang Road and Tong Shin Terrace. The classic form

---

[114] T. G. McGee, 'The cultural role of cities: a case study of Kuala Lumpur', *JTG*, 17 (1963), 178–96; James C. Jackson, 'The Chinatowns of Southeast Asia: traditional components of the city's central area', *Pacific Viewpoint*, 16 (1975), 48–9.

[115] Goh, *Urban planning*, p. 64.

[116] Michael Johnstone, 'The evolution of squatter settlements in peninsular Malaysian cities', *JSEAS*, 12, 2 (1981), 370; Azizah Kassim, 'The genesis of squatting in West Malaysia with special reference to the Malays in the Federal Territory', *Malaysia in History*, 26 (1983), 60–83.

of the colonial city – with the colonial elite on the hills overlooking the segregated areas of the plain – survived. By 1957, however, more Malayans of the new administrative and commercial elite had made it up the hill, separated from their countrymen by residence, wealth and social preference. Town planning was brought to Malaya by disciples of the Garden City movement in the United Kingdom. They sought to eradicate ribbon development and zone towns around central shopping centres. A master plan for a new city centre for Kuala Lumpur was unveiled by the planner T. H. H. Hancock in 1950.[117] In the event, improvements were piecemeal. As the capital swelled with newcomers, the main response was the establishment of a satellite town, Petaling Jaya. The grand design for an integral new town, although shelved in the short-term when squatter resettlement had priority, took shape with the financing of large-scale housing projects by the Malaya-Borneo Building Society. Units of urban living were constructed, consisting of basic housing built around a school and a *padang*; five units composed a neighbourhood. The construction of a Federal Highway to Port Swettenham heightened the attractiveness of the Klang Valley as a dormitory area for those that could afford to pay to live there, to the detriment of conditions in the centre of the city. When, in 1953, squatters evicted from the Cochrane and Peel Road area of Kuala Lumpur were told to move to $2,000 and $3,000 houses in Petaling Jaya, they found this way beyond their means.[118]

Fears of overcrowding stimulated a mood of urban anxiety. For example, the 'long-standing social evil' of hawking assumed a special significance in the expatriate imagination as a symptom of disorganised urbanisation and impending chaos. The displacement of population as a result of resettlement operations had caused the recent history of the Japanese occupation to repeat itself in the influx of unlicensed hawkers who terrorised the good burghers of the major towns. Expatriates bewailed the flouting of urban codes by the squatters, the parking violations and the spectacle of foodstalls blocking the five-foot ways. They blamed this on the irrepressible economic individualism of the Chinese. In Kuala Lumpur, statistics for 1957 reported at least 7,500 unlicensed hawkers, twice as many as the legitimate traders. In Singapore, only between a quarter and a third of hawkers were licensed. In both cities they were reported to be the focal point of corruption. Police actions in Kuala Lumpur had little impact. The hawker, one health officer complained, 'regenerates with the facility of an amoeba'. Moreover, they were well-organised and a significant force in municipal politics. When the city fathers moved against them, the Kuala Lumpur Hawkers' Association flooded the towns with pictures showing heavy-handed

---

[117] T. A. L. Concannon, 'Town planning in Malaya', *Quarterly Journal of the Institute of Architects of Malaya*, 1, 3 (1951), 49–52; *Malay Mail*, 8.3.1950.
[118] T. A. L. Concannon, 'A new town in Malaya: Petaling Jaya, Kuala Lumpur', *MJTG*, 5 (1955), 39–43; T. G. McGee and W. D. McTaggert, *Petaling Jaya: a socio-economic survey of a new town in Selangor, Malaysia* (Pacific Viewpoint Monograph No.3, Wellington, 1967), p. 35; Ray Nyce, *Into a new age: a study of church and society in Kuala Lumpur, Malaysia* (Singapore, 1973), p. 11; *Malay Mail*, 2.4.1953.

police raids on their members.[119] Deteriorating economic conditions in the New Villages in the 1960s further aggravated this problem.

The exaggerated economic differentiation of the city nourished other urban blights of disease, destitution and vice. A visiting tuberculosis specialist complained that 'housing is the blackest spot in the social structure of Malaya'. The design of the local shophouse was seen as 'fundamentally wrong', especially where they were broken into cubicles with no access to air and light. Spitting on the floor spread contamination, as did the Chinese habit of closing shutters at night, through fear of cold and bad spirits.[120] The anti-TB movement was one of the most vocal Asian pressure groups, and towns and cities launched 'Do not spit' weeks.[121] Yet the campaign was contested ground, not least because of the economic and social penalties that came with being diagnosed. The severest of these were ostracism and destitution – ubiquitous features of urban life. The full extent of destitution remained uncovered. Colonial surveys identified begging as the soliciting of alms from the public at large, and were silent on the occasional recipients of charity – the petty criminals and extortionists, purveyors of hard-luck stories, medicine men, match sellers, street entertainers, odd-jobbers and *jaga kereta* boys, car attendants – who inhabited the streets. The British did distinguish between the 'professionals' – who 'look upon begging as a respectable and worthwhile trade' – the 'amateurs' and the 'casuals'. Yet all groups were disorganised, and few earned more than a dollar a day, or were fit for other work.[122] A survey of beggars in Kuala Lumpur in 1957 revealed that over two-thirds were over sixty years old; over half had spent most of their lives as unskilled labourers – especially on tin mines – and the vast majority earned less than $30 a month. Most were Chinese: stranded migrants from China, without any dependants, bereft of social ties, who 'lack the means, the will, and the incentive to return'. But for a 'semi-systematic dole' from shopkeepers on Friday mornings, and the most elementary forms of co-operation between them, it was felt many would not survive at all. They swelled into the towns at Chinese New Year.[123] The Social Welfare Department would only contemplate institutional relief, yet it was unable to fund homes for the aged. In the towns as much as in the countryside there was a reliance on voluntary aid, at a time when it was doubted that clan associations amongst the Chinese continued to help the old – many

---

[119] James M. Anthony, 'Urban development planning and development control: hawkers in Kuala Lumpur (1940s–1960s)', *Sojourn*, 2 (1987), 112–24; Colony of Singapore, *Report of the Hawkers Enquiry Commission* (Singapore, 1950); Paul Chan, 'The political economy of urban Chinese squatters in metropolitan Kuala Lumpur', in Linda Y. C. Lim and L. A. Peter Gosling (eds), *The Chinese in Southeast Asia* (Singapore, 1983), vol. I, p. 233; *Malay Mail*, 24.3.1954.

[120] Dr. A. Morland, 'Tuberculosis in Malaya', 26.10.1949, FS/13394/49.

[121] *Malay Mail*, 20.1.1950.

[122] Federation of Malaya, *Beggars in the Federation of Malaya: a factual report on the results of a pilot survey instituted by the Department of Social Welfare and carried out between November 1954 and March 1955* (Kuala Lumpur, 1955).

[123] Central Welfare Council, Federation of Malaya, *Social survey on beggars and vagrants* (Kuala Lumpur, 1958).

of whom had never been settled down long enough to join an association.[124] Urban problems were a direct stimulus to new philanthropic projects and civic action.

To townspeople, all this betokened the erosion of direct administrative contact with the public, the collapse of civic standards and moral corruption. The cosmopolitanism of Singapore, the allure of the brightening lights of Kuala Lumpur, were a threat as much as an opportunity. Crime and Triad protection rackets increased and the government's capacity to maintain order was called into question.[125] The opium problem was undiminished; there were 80,000 addicts in Singapore in 1952.[126] Although fears that hawking and begging were branches of organised crime were probably exaggerated, gangsterism was undiminished, and the efficiency and secrecy of the organisations involved were, if anything, enhanced. The effects of the post-war explosion in delinquency and prostitution had not yet subsided. In a four-month period in 1948 there were 582 cases in the juvenile courts in Kuala Lumpur. The vast majority of offenders had lost their parents, and social workers attributed the growth of the problem to the Emergency.[127] Vice of all kinds was almost certainly on the rise, in the Federal capital – Jean Cocteau's *Kouala l'impure*, where in 1953 there were a reported 500 prostitutes – and in other provincial centres. Sleepy Kota Bahru 'was known, pathetically, as the Paris of the East because of the sexual licence that was believed to prevail there'.[128] Traffic in juveniles from the mainland was a major problem in Singapore: in 1952, seventy-six were detained in raids, and prostitutes would shelter from police raids in the *chaitongs*, or nunneries.[129] Eleven per cent of adults in Singapore were said to be suffering from venereal disease.[130] Although trafficking in women from China had come to an end after the war, the trade continued internally. An obstacle to its eradication, officials stressed, were the 'fear and superstition' that preyed on the women involved. There was only one home in the country to which they could be entrusted, and it was difficult in cases of *de facto* 'adoption' to verify allegations of ill-treatment. A mobile population and the disruption of old communities had led to a growth in independent prostitution. These women resisted the professional keepers. In Penang, as the old kind of brothel became uncommon, it was more usual to send women out to clients at lodging houses and hotels. However, under these conditions, it was more difficult to track the organisers down and to encourage women to seek medical attention. In Singapore *pipa bai* –

---

[124] 'Minutes of Bentong District Welfare Committee, 7.8.1953'; P. Bishop to State Welfare Officer, 13.12.1955, SCA Phg/72/53.
[125] A theme of Mak Lau Fong, *The sociology of secret societies: a study of Chinese secret societies in Singapore and peninsular Malaysia* (Kuala Lumpur, 1981), pp. 111–13.
[126] *Nanyang Siang Pau*, 10.11.1952.
[127] C. P. Rawson, 'Probation – Selangor: interim report, 1.3.1948–31.7.1948', FS/10743/48.
[128] *Malay Mail*, 25.4.1953; Anthony Burgess, *Little Wilson and Big God* (London, 1987), pp. 388, 397.
[129] Singapore, *Report of the Social Welfare Department*, 1952, p. 31; *Straits Echo*, 11.3.1953.
[130] 'Again on venereal disease and anti-vice activities in Singapore', *Nanfang Evening Post*, 26.9.1952.

women in domestic servitude – graduated into dancehalls, and there was a mushrooming of dance classes to train them.[131] Singapore was deluged with semi-nude shows drawing large crowds to singing cafés, advertised in a proliferation of illustrated 'mosquito' papers.[132] Another dilemma for social workers was the flourishing of the *joget moden* cafés in the towns, at Lucky World and Bukit Bintang in Kuala Lumpur, home to a dance that by 1948 was fusing *ronggeng* with samba, rumba, congo and tango. There was consternation that young Malay girls would be drawn into the business as hostesses and taxi-dancers, that the long hours would take their toil on constitutions already weakened by malnutrition, and that their morality would be undermined. This was balanced by the fear that if the *joget* was forbidden to them, the girls would gravitate towards prostitution.[133] There were cases of Malay *joget* girls organising to demand better wages in Singapore, but it was their Chinese counterparts in Penang who were the most vocal, striking in February 1953 for higher fees, and for a reduction in the management share. In the cabaret business, as elsewhere, earnings were squeezed by the post-Korean war slump.[134] A window on the individual casualties of urbanisation is the great increase in suicide in the period after 1948 – especially amongst women. Although medical reports showed that suicide was a greater affliction to the Chinese population than to other communities, it was a general truth that members of minority groups without community support, faced with unalleviated poverty, were especially vulnerable. The Chinese press in Singapore launched a campaign to reduce its incidence. 'During the short period of seven years after the liberation,' lamented the *Chung Shing Jit Poh* in 1952, 'how many people have risen or fallen!' The towns were a focus of high aspirations and robust competition, and left many disappointed. One survey noted a very high suicide rate amongst Singapore dance hostesses: thirty-one in the thousand.[135]

Civic life and the origins of a post-colonial bourgeoisie

Rapid social change nurtured moral anxieties. Mobility, and an unequal measure of prosperity, combined to produce a late imperial mood of decadence. Colonial society was under pressure, although – or perhaps because – the number of expatriates was higher than ever before. In Singapore, military housing estates such as Serangoon

[131] Koh Choo Chin, 'Implementing government policy for the protection of women and girls in Singapore, 1948–66: recollections of social worker', in M. Jaschok and S. Miers (eds.), *Women and Chinese patriarchy: submission, servitude and escape* (London, 1994), pp. 122–40; F. Brewer, 'Notes on prostitution', 20.10.1954, SCA Phg/79/54; *Straits Echo*, 11.3.1953.

[132] *Chung Shing Jit Pao*, 31.3.1953.

[133] Che Abdul Khalid, 'Joget modern in Kuala Lumpur', 21.5.1952; Che Abdul Khalid, memorandum, 2.6.1952, DCL Selangor/155/52.

[134] *Utusan Melayu*, 18.4.1953; *Straits Echo*, 6.2.1953.

[135] H. B. M. Murphy, 'The mental health of Singapore: part one – suicide', *Medical Journal of Malaya*, 9, 1 (1954), 1–45; 'The tide of suicide must be suppressed', *Chung Shing*, 18.8.1952.

Gardens and Frankel dominated the local economy. As one Chinese memoir puts it, 'the British presence was visible, audible and palpable, overseeing every stratum of society and every walk of life'.[136] Yet, one could tell the world was changing when educated Asians solemnly renounced neckties, and the British Commissioner-General abandoned 'the tyranny of the dinner jacket'.[137] An American observer remarked on the insecurity of whites in 1953, the public mockery of their clubs and the resentment of soldiers who 'drank too much and were too obtrusive'.[138] The social distance – the master–servant relationship – between the Asiatic multitude and the new classes of conscript soldiers and technical personnel which constituted the bulk of the European presence was breaking down. 'The *tuans*,' it was observed, 'are much less *besar*.'[139] In the military cantonments of Kuala Lumpur and Singapore, there was a series of scandals, as what remained of the Somerset Maugham era gave way to the Anthony Burgess era. The repercussions of liaisons across the colour line between expatriate wives and locals perturbed even the Chiefs of Staff in London. British tabloids made much of reports that service wives in Singapore were involved in a large prostitution racket. Indebtedness to local shopkeepers and boredom were said to be the causes. White women were no longer sacrosanct; white men were no longer desirable. British soldiers complained bitterly of the lack of interest shown in them by the 'snobbish' local girls, who replied that they found the national serviceman vulgar and boorish.[140] The towns were looking less colonial. In Singapore a young generation of local architects emerged in the 1950s versed in Le Corbusier, Gropius and Mies. Their work can be seen, for example, in Ng Kheng Siang's landmark Asia Insurance Building in Singapore (1954). Firms such as Kumpulan Architek and Alfred Wong began to shape the face of a post-colonial city. Europeans also began to develop local styles in housing, 'translating them into the terms of ferro-concrete'.[141]

New wealth, education and access to power were creating new categories of Asian who tested the boundaries of European racial prestige. The racial slights they encountered were a powerful goad to nationalist struggle. For even the most influential the barriers of race were not always easy to traverse. Malay public opinion was inflamed in 1952 when the Sultan of Selangor was barred from attending a St George's Society Dinner in a European club in his own State. The President of the Kuala Lumpur Lake Club informed the organisers that 'it has been the traditional policy of Lake Club for many years that the introduction of Asian guests is unwelcome'. The government took firm action and the committee members resigned

[136] Peter H. L. Wee, *From farm and kampong . . .* (Singapore, 1989), pp. 115–16.
[137] John Drysdale, *Singapore: the struggle for success* (Singapore, 1984), pp. 54–5.
[138] George Edinger, *The twain shall meet* (New York, 1960), pp. 22, 40.
[139] F.D. Ommanney, *Eastern windows* (London, 1960), p. 17.
[140] *Malay Mail*, 25.3.1954.
[141] Robert Powell, *Innovative architecture of Singapore* (Singapore, 1989), p. 18; C. Northcote Parkinson, 'Houses of Malaya', *Quarterly Journal of the Institute of Architects of Malaya*, 4, 4 (1955), 20.

at its instigation.[142] When Malcolm MacDonald brought the Chinese banker Tan Chin Tuan into the Tanglin Club in Singapore, he received a letter of complaint from its committee.[143] In sport, racial segregation was as rigid at it had been in the 1930s. In Singapore, it was symbolised by the rival European and Eurasian cricket clubs at either end of the Padang. After 1948, Singapore officials such as Andrew Gilmour promoted sport as a stimulus to multi-racialism. However, by 1959, of over 1,000 members of the Singapore Cricket Club, less than 10 per cent were Asians.[144] Although traditionally as much the sport of kings in Malaya as in Europe, the first Asian member of the Singapore Polo Club took the field only in the late 1950s.[145] Malcolm MacDonald promoted the Singapore Island Club as a multi-racial enclave, to foster the 'gracious spirit of inter-racial good will' that thrived on the golf-course.[146] Golf rapidly became the defining pastime of a new elite; clubs flourished under royal patronage. Most of Tunku Abdul Rahman's cabinet members were players and the core negotiations of the Merger crisis were conducted on the fairway. To Lee Kuan Yew, 'golf is valuable reprieve from the pressures of smoky committee rooms which appear to be the inevitable lot of those who have to decide the policy of corporations or governments'.[147] Whilst cricket and rugby were the classic colonial sports, team games that the British saw as cementing the cultural bond of empire, it was the introduction of soccer and badminton, mostly by Indians, that had the most enduring effect on leisure patterns. Non-'colonial' sports such as hockey and 'Chinese' basketball and table tennis, which flourished in the constrained space of the New Villages, represented a break from colonial conditioning, and even a challenge to public policy. Soccer flourished rather than rugby. To the British, sport was the main way of neutralising the energies of emotional adolescents before it could be channelled into leftist politics. However, they noted with concern the Asian preference for individual sports rather than the team games of the English public schools. During and after the war badminton flourished in detention camps and villages and Thomas Cup victories in 1949, 1952 and 1955 galvanised national pride across ethnic communities and sparked public celebrations on an unprecedented scale.[148]

Sport, however, was only one aspect of civic life in which Asians were playing a larger part. Even the secret societies that had provided such an important support structure for colonial expansion were open to privileged Asians – 'permanent residents' was the Freemasons' euphemism. This process had begun earlier: a history

---

[142] OAG to Secretary of State, 29.6.1952, CO1022/464.

[143] Drysdale, *Singapore*, pp. 55–6.

[144] Ilsa Sharp, *The Singapore Cricket Club, 1852–1985* (Singapore, 1985), pp. 107–21.

[145] Wendy Hutton, *The Singapore Polo Club: an informal history, 1886–1982* (Singapore, 1983), p. 102.

[146] Alex Josey, *Golf in Singapore* (Singapore, 1969), pp. 56–9.

[147] Noordin Selat, 'Class status and golf in Malaysia', in *Renungun* (Kuala Lumpur, 1976), pp. 73–8; George Houghton, *Golf addict goes East* (London, 1967), p. 114.

[148] Stephen A. Douglas, 'Sport in Malaysia', in Eric A. Wagner (ed.), *Sport in Asia and Africa: a comparative handbook* (New York, 1989), pp. 165–82; Ong Kah Kuan, *We were great: Thomas Cup badminton* (Kuala Lumpur, 1984), pp. 13–46.

of the Lodge Johore Royal, consecrated in 1919, published at the expense of the Ruler, noted with satisfaction that 'the Universality of Freemasonry requiring only a Belief in a Supreme being, has appealed very strongly to those professing the Mohammadan Faith'. A considerable number of state officials were initiates, including the 'State Commissioner', Dato Abdullah bin Jaafar, father of the founder of the United Malays National Organisation, Dato Onn bin Jaafar. It was a meeting place for the Anglo-Malay elite.[149] After the war, this process was greatly accelerated, yet it carried its own caveat, the District Grand Master warned Masons in 1955 to be careful about who they recommended for initiation: 'With the changes that are already taking place in Malaya our whole Masonic structure may be questioned from time to time by those who know little or nothing of it, and we must exercise the greatest care that untoward action of ours can ever be used by anyone to testify against the practices of the Craft.' The lists of colonial servants who were Masons in 1955 read as a 'who's who' of the MCS establishment and show how freemasonry continued to incorporate the higher echelons of the Malay-Muslim elite. A *mufti* was consulted on how to adapt Masonic initiations for Islamic sensibilities. There was a preponderance of Asian members at Lodge Baldwyn Lowick which was consecrated in 1951 in Kuala Lumpur. Indeed, in 1957 it was boasted that Masonry's 'roots are becoming more firmly embedded in the soil of Malaya'; new lodges were being created to allow for more office-holders, and a Malay was Assistant District Grand Master.[150]

The last years of colonial rule saw a dramatic increase in fora for sociability: from the Rotary Club, the Malayan Association for the Prevention of Tuberculosis, to book clubs, parent associations, ratepayers' associations and even Psychology Clubs in Malacca and Kuala Lumpur.[151] Many were multi-racial, and the prestige of leaders of political parties such as the Independence of Malaya Party and the MCA was often rooted in their membership of these bodies. Other clubs – Tamilian physical culture associations, temple restoration societies, Chinese reading circles and benevolent associations – reflected ethnic identity, and often the divisions in these communities. For example, within the Indian community there was a mushrooming of education, religious and ethnic associations after 1948: for example, the Dhama Institute (1949), the Malaya Hindu Sangam (1956), the Petaling Jaya Hindu Association (1956), the Ceylonese Federation of Malaya (1946) and the Malayan Ceylonese Congress (1950).[152] In the Klang Valley, Eurasians were bitterly divided between the Eurasian Union and the Selangor Eurasian Recreation Club, with the former attacked for its

---

[149] A. J. S. T. [A. J. Shelley-Thompson], *By-Laws and history of the Lodge Johore Royal No. 3946 E.C.* (Johore Bahru, 1922), pp. 4–9.

[150] *The Masonic Year Book for the Districts of the Eastern Archipelago (E.C.) and the Middle East (S.C.)*, II (1955); IV (1957), SNL.

[151] *Societies in the Federation of Malaya: applications for registration as a registered or exempted society (as at 31 December 1950, which supplement list ending 31 December, 1952)* [n.d.].

[152] Tham Seong Chee, *The role and impact of formal associations in the development of Malaysia* (Bangkok, 1977), pp. 111–17.

snobbishness of its fair-skinned members towards dark and poor Eurasians, and the discriminatory high cost of its social events.[153]

A common theme of urban sociability was the defence of traditional values that were felt to be under threat. Rapid Malay urbanisation, for example, bred new cultural challenges as youths crowded to dance the *joget moden* at amusement parks, to the detriment of their minds and morals, and were tempted to hitherto unheard-of practices such as whistling at Malay girls in public places – 'girls', the Malay newspapers reported in horror, 'who are the same race and religion as they are'.[154] Youngsters were even indulging in 'dangerous kissing' in public places.[155] This catalysed movements of Islamic resurgence as reconstituted religious authorities in a number of States moved to ban *ronggeng* and *joget moden* dances, particularly on Thursday evenings.[156] Malay writers seized on this theme of urban decadence for their fiction – for example, Harun Aminurashid in *Minah Joget Moden*; Ishak Haji Muhammad in *Jalan ke Kota Bahru* – and in film – *joget* café scenes abound in films of P. Ramlee.[157] But not only the Malay community detected the change. So distant did the Emergency seem from the vantage-point of fortress Singapore that the good burghers of the city were constantly urged to be vigilant against an inner malaise. 'There is,' the *Ih Shih Pao* commented, 'only a skeleton of democracy inheriting many traditional political weaknesses.' The people of Singapore, it argued, were materialistic, selfish and ignorant; the pioneer spirit of the Nanyang Chinese was in danger of disappearing under a wave of materialism.[158] 'Money-worshipping' and 'English education, which trains only clerical workers', were blamed for Singapore's cultural backwardness.[159] The press waged a campaign against the showing of obscene shows and films. The Singapore Punctuality and Austerity Association inveighed against the lavishness of private and business entertaining and Buddhist and Christian groups launched morality campaigns.

In a sense, municipal issues provided a focus for political energies outside of the intensely policed Emergency. Campaigns of civic-mindedness were launched: for example, anti-spitting and anti-corruption drives. Philanthropic traditions continued to flourish, especially for large-scale educational projects like the new University of Malaya and Nanyang University, and biographies of Chinese business figures place great emphasis on civic virtue. The life of Yap Ah Loy was celebrated in literature to entrench his status as the founder of Kuala Lumpur. Yet, in the representations of him that were published in the 1950s, the basis of his legend had changed: his achievements were no longer the result of charisma, but of work; in remembrance he

---

[153] *Malay Mail*, 16.3.1950.   [154] *Utusan Melayu*, 5.10.1951.
[155] 'Kissing in public', *Asmara*, February, 1955.
[156] For example, 'Perak General Circular No. 6 of 1954', 29.6.1954, DO Batang Padang/709/54.
[157] Harun Aminurrashid, *Minah Joget Moden* (Singapore, 1968 [1949]); Anwar, *Jalan ke Kota Bharu* (Kuala Lumpur, 1956).
[158] *Ih Shih Pao*, 3.7.1952, 5.9.1952.
[159] 'Talk of the town', *Nanfang Evening Post*, 27.5.1953.

was no longer a warrior, but a city father. The Chinese community was advancing towards a more secular understanding of itself.[160] In a similar way, a contemporary biography of the Penang merchant prince Yeap Chor Ee described his life as 'a romance of character, enterprise and industry'.[161] A network of charitable bodies emerged, in many of which women took the lead in combating delinquency and disease: organisations such as the YWCA, the Singapore Chinese Women's Association and the Women's Institutes. Family planning associations brought together a range of highly motivated individuals. Many women felt that their welfare work was incompatible with membership of the women's wings of the main political parties.[162] To the British, the towns had a key role in cultural integration, especially in fostering a small, but significant Asian middle class, upwardly mobile and secular in outlook. The bureaucracy was to supply its nucleus. A survey of the Malay political elite in 1955 revealed that over 55 per cent came from a background in the government service, and over three-quarters from towns with a population in excess of 20,000 people.[163] The British placed great faith in these people as agents of modernity. It was hoped they could afford an element of empire-loyalism that was projected as being in some sense 'national' and in their interest. It was said of the Malay notable Dato Panglima Kinta Eusoff that he 'shunned' politics devoting himself to working for no less than fifty-six public organisations, especially the Rotary, to promote a 'Malayan consciousness'. He earned the hostility of UMNO for urging a cautious pace in the march to independence, for which he felt Malaya was ill-prepared, and was a sponsor of the National Association of Perak, a prototype for the party of other like-minded notables, the Party Negara. Eusoff's biographer, his daughter, admits that his political views are hard to decipher, but has stressed that the reasoning behind his position on independence was motivated by a deeply felt patriotism.[164] Other critics have been less kind. They see the embryonic middle class as a heterogeneous group, each member 'chained to his own segmental society'; confused, immature, they were unable to give a lead to the new nation.

> The Malay middle class adopts the British model because there is no Malay model of middle class life. They take it wholesale complete with big houses, big cars, servants, trips to hill resorts, appreciating Beethoven and Picasso, doing the cocktail rounds, and wearing coats and ties in the equatorial heat. They even build their houses on hilltops as the Europeans did, preferring cooler places. Certainly this is not a Malay ruling class

---

[160] Sharon A. Carstens, 'From myth to history: Yap Ah Loy and the heroic past of Chinese Malaysians', *JSEAS*, 19, 2 (1988), 201–7.

[161] *Biography of Towkay Yeap Chor Ee* [n.d., 195?].

[162] I am grateful to Lenore Manderson for showing me her unpublished paper, 'Historical notes on the establishment of family planning associations in Singapore and peninsular Malaysia' (1979).

[163] S. Neuman, 'The Malay political elite: an analysis of 134 Malay legislators, their social background and attitudes' (Ph.D. New York University, 1971), pp. 80, 203.

[164] Datin Ragayah Eusoff, *Lord of Kinta: the biography of Dato Panglima Kinta Eusoff* (Petaling Jaya, 1995).

tradition. The old chiefs used hilltops for fortresses but built their houses by the riverside.[165]

It was upon this narrow bourgeoisie that the colonial government sought to promote non-communal politics. We shall examine the political expressions of this in later chapters. However, the point to emphasise here is that urbanisation was not necessarily a spur to multi-racialism; in many other ways urban sociability reinforced ethnic loyalties, and often revealed the divisions within these communities.

Urbanisation has been introduced in some detail as it is illustrative of the larger processes of social change to which the Emergency was a catalyst. In this and the previous chapter we have outlined the ways in which a decade of insurrection disrupted social and economic life. The colonial state, to secure its internal frontier, attempted to reconstruct rural communities – a process I have called the domestication of the Malayan Chinese – and to stabilise labour conditions in primary industries. It was a pattern of state-formation that encompassed the permanent settlement of Chinese pioneer agriculturalists and the introduction amongst them of new official agencies that sought to bind their allegiance to the state. Its consolidation rested upon the response of indigenous leadership to the challenge of disorder and the sudden appearance of the state and its energetic servants in the midst of their communities. At every level, the process was incomplete. The specialist skills of the labourer-cultivators of the New Villages were sorely tested during a period of economic dislocation. The Christian experiment in the New Villages failed and the Chinese leaders of the old regime exercised an unsteady grip on their inhabitants. On the estates and elsewhere non-Communist trade unions re-emerged. However, the long-standing dilemmas as to the degree of their politicisation and of the communal character of their leadership remained unresolved. The phenomenal growth of the state moulded the framework of power which the nationalist leaders would inherit at independence. Yet this new aggregation of political resources did not preclude the persistence of administrative clumsiness, corruption and insolvency. Above all, the social history of Malaya in these years was not solely the history of the Emergency. The social fall-out of terror was merely prologue to a much wider and far-reaching transformation of society and polity in late colonial Malaya. Urbanisation, for example, created its own momentum in the fostering of new economic and cultural identities. For the Malays in particular, this meant a great change in the family: women were encouraged to participate more fully in the domestic economy as breadwinners; young men educated in the countryside moved to find their rightful place in the towns. In many ways, however, they remained accountable to the values of the country. The break with the village was not a sharp one. Of all the changes of the Emergency years, perhaps the greatest was in the frequency in which the life of the towns began to enter that of the countryside. The opportunities this brought did not fall on all in equal measure. In both town and country, more fundamental questions of communal and cultural identity were still to be contested. To these we now turn.

---

[165] Noordin Selat, 'The Malaysian middle class: a few alarming patterns', in *Renangan*, p. 52.

CHAPTER SIX

The advent of the 'bumiputera'

Counter-insurgency gave birth to new networks of clientage. These were demanded of the people of Malaya by the British to bind communities to the colonial state. They were also required by the people themselves as they faced crises of leadership and collective identity. Hitherto, we have focused primarily on the Chinese and Indian populations on the industrial front-line of the Communist war. However, the social repercussions of the Emergency also provoked British officials and Malay leaders into attempts to recast the economic structure of the peninsula through reform of the Malay rural economy. British understanding of the economic predicament of the Malays was couched in the language of Protection. Administrators underlined the historical and cultural obstacles to Malay material progress: idleness, an aversion to business and reluctance to innovate had allowed the Malays to be overrun by the economically aggressive Chinese – 'the locusts of commerce' as Sir Richard Winstedt called them.[1] This understanding of the Malay economy was more lyrical than scientific. The image of statis, for example, disguised an incomplete appreciation of Malay land tenure and the diverseness of the rural economy; what was dismissed as rural conservatism often merely indicated the Malays' reluctance to follow blindly the direction of change ordained by the colonial state.[2] However, these assumptions became deeply imbedded in administrative practice and modern scholars have suggested that many of them have been reflected in Malay understandings of their predicament; for example, in Dr Mahathir Mohamad's diagnosis of the 'Malay dilemma'.[3] Many of the remedies for Malay economic backwardness which have been propounded in modern Malaysia have their origins in the colonial period. Malaya has long been taken as a classic example of a bureaucratic system attempting to stimulate

---

[1] In *The Spectator*, 12.3.1948.
[2] J. Overton, *Colonial Green Revolution? Food, irrigation and the state in colonial Malaya* (Oxford, 1994), pp. 85–98.
[3] Syed Hussein Alatas, *The myth of the lazy native* (London, 1977).

modernisation through a variety of complex para-statal organisations.[4] However, the colonial origins of a corporatist approach to development, and its relationship to the creation and mobilisation of a Malay political community, have never been fully explored; nor too have the ways in which perceptions of Malay poverty shaped Malayan politics on the eve of independence.

The resettlement and regrouping of the rural population, as we have seen, not only witnessed the re-establishment of colonial authority in the countryside, it was a much broader process of social reorganisation of which colonial policy was an imperfect arbiter. In the same way, encouraged by a new faith in technology, the British government attempted to chart the largely unexplored territory of rural development. However, the 'development decade' of the 1950s was also a time when changing patterns of social and economic life provoked Malay intellectuals and politicians into their own undertakings to advance their community, and into an examination of the root causes of Malay poverty. In the debates that emerged, many of the conflicting currents of nationalist thought of the 1930s and 1940s found expression. These debates had a profound impact on Malay nationalism and on an emerging pattern of inter-communal bargaining. The core notion that arose out of these debates, that of the Malay *bumiputera*, or son of the soil, and of his entitlement to special rights and privileges in economic life, became the ideological cornerstone of the modern Malaysian state. The political import of the advent of the *bumiputera* is measured by experience of the Orang Asli, who in the 1950s were confronted by a new logic of state-building, to which ideologically they were an impediment, and which challenged their rights to ancestral land and to a cultural existence independent of the Malay community.

The anatomy of poverty

Many of the assumptions held by the British about the nature of Malay poverty were to be challenged in the 1950s by commercialisation, diversification and the entry of Malays into wage labour. However, the basic characteristics of much of the country-side throughout the late colonial period remained isolation, disease and malnutrition. These were years of ecological disturbance: a spate of serious floods, together with population pressure on the Malay heartlands of the eastern coastal plains, forced cultivators upstream where they soon started to pay the price for trespassing on the forest fringe, and were driven back down into the lowlands. One of the biggest problems facing the Malay rural economy were the rats, pigs and elephants that had multiplied and became emboldened during the occupation. In Ulu Lebir, Kelantan, it was reported that the food shortages in the kampongs were directly due to the loss of the firearms which they had to surrender to government in 1941. As a result elephants and pigs walked where they would, and tigers preyed on buffaloes. In Lanchang,

---

[4] Gayl D. Ness, *Bureaucracy and rural development in Malaysia: a study of complex organizations in stimulating economic development in new states* (Berkeley, 1967).

Malacca, eighteen villagers were taken by crocodiles in one year.[5] The Emergency brought stricter controls on arms and assisted nature to encroach on settlement. In Trengganu in 1947 one was still more likely to be killed by a tiger than in a motor accident; in Pahang in 1950 a single man-eater took fifteen lives.[6] Villagers demanded military protection against the beasts of the forest. In East Pahang, Gurkhas were diverted from tracking terrorists and sent hunting. The Emergency also added to the isolation of many rural areas, on the east coast in particular. Roads were often too hazardous to travel; passenger ships were withdrawn from the Tumpat run; even air links were unreliable in the monsoon.[7] In one *daerah* of Kelantan, there were only three motor-cars, and three trishaws.[8] The bicycle was the pre-eminent technology of the countryside, the main means of movement for people and produce. In time communications expanded, often through the collective efforts of rural communities themselves: in Kelantan volunteers built 105 bridges in 1949.[9] However, Malay cultivators would complain throughout the period of the difficulties and expense in marketing their produce. The struggle for control of transportation would be a crucial skirmish in the battle for Malay economic advancement.

The war years witnessed a resurgence of endemic and epidemic disease. On the fringes of settlement malaria remained rife, and in many areas was on the ascendant. It was only low in incidence where stable conditions of padi cultivation prevailed; in pioneer areas there were sharp confrontations with the mosquito, for example where land was opened for rubber smallholding. By the end of the colonial period it was reported that 'the impact of malaria on the mass of the rural population has not changed from pre-war days', especially in the Malay kampongs. In one area of Ulu Kelantan, after the war, a local matron guessed the malaria rate at 95 per cent.[10] In 1949, 28–40 per cent of children in Negri Sembilan were affected; 40 per cent in coastal Selangor in 1953. DDT spraying of malarial areas was first used on a large scale as an offshoot of resettlement, yet controls could also break down due to terrorism, and epidemics occurred, such as the several hundred cases in Kuala Lipis in 1953. When controls broke down the effects were pronounced as the natural immunities of individuals had disappeared. There was a particularly high incidence of malaria in the security forces.[11] In 1956 the population protected from malaria was very low, and of the protected rural population, 40 per cent were on estates (see Table 4). Research showed that immunity, where it existed, was never complete; fever

[5] Diary of J. S. Addison, 1.5.1946; 3.5.1946, DF/63/45; Diary of A. B. Walton, 13.1.1946, DF/168/45.

[6] For this remarkable beast, DO Kuantan/265/49.

[7] *Malay Mail*, 12.1.1954, 27.4.1949.

[8] 'Daerah Tanjong Pauh, Kelantan', in E. H. G. Dobby, 'Padi landscapes of Malaya', *MJTG*, 10 (1957), 37.

[9] *Malay Mail*, 24.1.1950.

[10] M. R. Jellicoe, 'Report of expedition to valley of Sungei Pergau, Ulu Kelantan, 1–9.10.1946, DSW/207/46.

[11] *Annual Report of the Malaria Advisory Board for the year 1955*, pp. 5–6; 'Minutes of a meeting of the conference of SMOs held at Penang, 6–8.12.1951', CS/12549/51.

Table 4 *Population protected from malaria, in millions, 1956*[12]

	Total	Protected	Unprotected
Urban areas	1.6	1.4	0.2
Rural areas	4.4	1	3.4
Total	6	2.4	3.6

attacked both young and old and preyed on their constitutions.[13] In Trengganu the 'malaria barrier' was seen as responsible for the state's underdevelopment, and this barrier had been pushed forward in the Emergency as Malays moved out of the hinterland and back to overcrowding, unemployment and poverty on the coast. 'If casual visitors say that the population is lazy,' the British Adviser challenged, 'then the answer is to invite them to get there themselves and try to do the same things.'[14]

Under the Emergency regime medical services gradually expanded. The campaign opened up access to remote areas such as the border tracts of north-west Kelantan, and the Malay kampongs also benefited from the expansion of health services to the rural areas and the training of local nurses. People visited the doctor more often and lived longer. In 1949 there were two million attendances at government doctors and travelling dispensaries, with an additional 750,000 attendances at fixed and mobile child welfare centres.[15] The aggregate indices of medical advance were impressive. However, these figures disguise massive regional and ethnic variations in the impact of health care. It was reported of Kelantan that 'there is still a vicious circle of poor health leading to inability to cultivate the fields properly, which in turn leads to poor crops, poor nutrition and slow recovery'.[16] Although officials believed that enlistment in the security forces was beginning to break the cycle of disease, investigations in Pahang revealed chronic malnutrition amongst Malay schoolchildren.[17] Filariasis, highly endemic in many rural areas otherwise attractive for settlement, was said to be even more of an obstacle to development than malaria, and its impact was unmitigated by natural immunity.[18] Children perhaps suffered the most, from hookworm, yaws, and an acute shortage of doctors and trained *bidans*.[19] Trengganu perhaps had the lowest standard of living, especially amongst its fishing population. 'This State,' it was reported, 'has fewer doctors per head of the population than any other part of the

[12] 'A proposal to establish a malaria training centre as the first step towards countryside malaria control in the Federation of Malaya', 1956, CS/12549/51.

[13] Ooi Jin Bee, 'Rural development in tropical areas, with special reference to Malaya', *JTG*, 12 (1959), 51–2, 56.

[14] Derrick Fenney, 'Trengganu is Malaya's forgotten state', *Malay Mail*, 20.4.1954.

[15] *Malay Mail*, 11.2.1950.

[16] R. B. Macgregor, 'Notes on my visit to Kelantan', 10.3.1948, FS/9459/48.

[17] 'Minutes of DOs' Conference, Pahang, 6.1.1954', DO Kuantan/133/53.

[18] Ooi, 'Rural development', 60–5.

[19] Chief Medical Officer Kelantan to DO Pasir Mas, 3.1.1951, DO Pasir Mas/201/50.

Table 5 *Selected health and demographic indicators, 1947–1957*[20]

Indicator	1947	1957
Population at census	4,908,086	6,278,763
Doctor: population ratio	1: 17,361	1: 7,252
Medical assistants: population	1: 48,309	1: 5,397
Birth rate (per 1,000)	43.2	46.2
Infant mortality rate (per 1,000)	102	75.6
Death rate (per 1,000)	19.5	12.4

world . . . one to 75,000.'[21] By 1956, tuberculosis was the biggest killer. And as in 80 per cent of cases the cause of death was unrecorded, it was felt that TB could account for four times more deaths than the statistics showed. By the age of fifteen, two-thirds of the population of Kuala Lumpur was tuberculosis positive, and half of the kampong population. There were an estimated 360,000 sufferers and 120,009 in an advanced infectious state. Fighting TB became a priority of colonial medicine: from only 709 vaccinations in 1950, the number of BCGs reached 144,216 in 1952.[22] Much of the credit for this rested with voluntary workers. The women's detachment of the British Red Cross in Kuala Lumpur, for example, was involved in welfare projects in outlying areas and in nutritional and anti-TB work.[23] Prominent Malays mooted an army of trained 'Home Guardians' – 'the feminine counterpart of the Home Guards' – to protect Malay babies from disease.[24] Malay doctors – including the first women medics – challenged traditional gynaecology. Not Islam but 'primitive superstition' was to blame; new *fatwah* were called for to combat rural attitudes.[25] Local girls were trained and sent back to their home areas, so they would be accepted as *bidans*. Malays became more willing to travel to dispensaries for external ailments, although much serious illness was still treated at home.[26] In spite of these advancements, there were fears that the Malays were, quite literally, dying out as a race. Ungku Abdul Aziz alarmed UMNO in Johore Bahru in 1949 by announcing that there were more deaths

[20] Jomo K. S. and Chee Heng Leng, 'Public health expenditure in Malaysia', *Journal of the Malaysian Society of Health*, 5, 1 (1985), 73–83; *Report of the Registrar General on population, births, deaths, marriages and adoptions* (1947) and (1957).
[21] *Annual Report on the social and economic progress of the people of Trengganu, for the year 1947*, FS/9411/48; 'State of Trengganu Annual Medical Report, 1949', SUK.Tr/118/50.
[22] 'Talk given to Kuala Lumpur Rotary Club by Dr. J. S. Sodhy, T.B. Specialist, Selangor, 12.12.1956'; 'Federation of Malaya BCG Campaign', Leong Yew Koh Papers, SP.3/A/23.
[23] *Malay Mail*, 22.1.1954.
[24] Ghazali Shafie to President, Women's Institute, 30.6.1953, FS/13157/49.
[25] Dr Siti Hasmah binte M. Ali, 'Effect on a basic attitude: health', *Intisari*, 1, 4 [n.d., 1961], 27–36.
[26] 'Mukim Four, Province Wellesley', in E. H. G. Dobby, 'Padi landscapes of Malaya', *MJTG*, 6 (1955), 32.

than births amongst the Malays, in a State which spent twelve times more than Trengganu and six times more than Kelantan on health and education. Many members of the Malay religious and political establishment were very suspicious of the family planning associations for this reason.[27] Labour ministers such as David Rees-Williams demanded measures to arrest 'the slow increase of Malays in relation to the Chinese, with its obvious political implications'. For the Malays, 1947 was a post-war high for mortality rates at 129 per 1,000; the worst hit area was Trengganu where the rate was 176 per 1,000. Although a mean for all states of 111 was obtained for 1948, the mean for Chinese was sixty-seven. Although doctors felt that 'the political aspect is rather questionable', reports highlighted the higher nutritional standards and easier access to western medicine enjoyed by the Chinese.[28]

Dehabilitation was an underlying cause of poverty, but it was not the only one. To senior officials, given reasonable prices for padi, there could only be two reasons for the poverty of the planter: 'an inherent characteristic which makes him content with *cukup makan* [enough to eat] and inclines him to no more exertion than is necessary to obtain a bare livelihood', and an ignorance of business methods – or rather, unresponsiveness to the market economy. Both factors made him a more or less willing slave to the middle-men.[29] These ideas were recurring motifs of colonial thought towards the rural economy. They were taken up by many nationalist leaders. It is unnecessary to restate here all of the cultural explanations which have been advanced for the conservatism of the rural Malay and his attachment to padi.[30] The point is that cumulative pressures of social change were modifying tradition, and had been for a long time. These illustrate the complexity and contrariness of the economic forces working on the rural Malay economy, and serve to dispel the 'myth of the lazy native'. As we have seen, diversity and change had always been features of the rice economy of peninsular Malaya. For example, ritual practices often reflected utilitarian as much as religious values, and as such were subject to adaptation. Although observance of the lunar calendar meant that many festivals were not attuned to the seasons, even in the 1947–9 seasons when the fasting month occurred during ploughing and field preparation, intense periods of work reconciled religious obligations with needs of cultivation.[31] Similarly, traditions of rice-planting varied greatly over time and place, and were evaluated by farmers within their own immediate

---

[27] *Malaya Tribune*, 16.2.1949; Lenore Manderson, 'Historical notes on the establishment of family planning associations in Singapore and peninsular Malaysia' (unpublished paper, 1979), pp. 14–17.

[28] Higham to Gurney, 2.2.1949; 'Infant mortality rates per thousand births, 1935–1940, 1946–8', 7.5.1949; R. B. MacGregor, 12.2.1949, FS/13157/49.

[29] T. F. Carey to State Secretary, Perlis, 28.1.1949, Coop/628/48.

[30] Brien K. Parkinson, 'Non-economic factors in the economic retardation of the rural Malays', *MAS*, 1, 1 (1967), 31–46; William Wilder, 'Islam, other factors and Malay backwardness: comments on an argument', *MAS*, 2, 2 (1968), 155–64; Brien K. Parkinson, 'The economic retardation of the Malays – a rejoinder', *MAS*, 2, 3 (1968), 267–72.

[31] Lim Joo-Jock, 'Tradition and peasant agriculture in Malaya', *MJTG*, 3 (1954), 44–7.

environment.[32] In the mouth of the Pahang river, official planting schedules were not followed, not because of the fasting month as officials complained, but because they failed to recognise local conditions, especially the irregularity of the co-operative labouring practices which were necessary in view of the shortage and cost of hired labour.[33] In Negri Sembilan, although co-operative workgroups maintained customary practices in padi cultivation, the *sarekat*, in this case a temporary work association, had become by the 1950s a rationalisation of traditional methods. It was devised as a means of minimising labour input on food crops to allow for a diversion of energies to cash-crops, whilst retaining cherished elements of group working patterns.[34] Although officials deplored the amount of time farmers spent arguing in coffeeshops, acute observers of their communities suggested that what was dismissed as leisure encompassed a wide range of activities that buttressed community life, and the position of individuals within it, during a period of great dislocation.[35]

Nor is it useful to speak of resistance to modernity in areas where access to modern education was often totally lacking. Although Malay newspapers chided parents for not encouraging their children to seek betterment through English schooling, such opportunities were open only to a few. In 1953 there were only 26,215 Malays in English schools, that is only a quarter of the total pupils. The alternative, rural Malay schools, were rarely in evidence. Where they were, it was often through the efforts of the people themselves. These *sekolah rakyat* – people's schools – were, by their very nature, makeshift and saddled with escalating maintenance costs. Of the 146 Malay schools in Pahang in 1950, over one-third had been erected by the people themselves. However, local communities could provide the buildings but not the human resources. In any case, as there were few facilities for the learning of English in rural schools, they were inadequate feeders for the English schools of the towns.[36] In outlying areas of Pahang there was no schooling at all: in Ulu Tembeling the *penghulu* had built a school but no literate person had remained in the *mukim* to teach in it.[37] In Kuala Kangsar, Perak, the District Officer wrote of his shock at the condition of kampong education; sixty schools under his jurisdiction were in decay and disrepair, and the government only built three or four new schools every year. Disillusionment was especially high when it became clear that government policy favoured the establishment of new schools in areas where no schools were in existence; self-help was seen to be penalised. In Larut District, there were twelve communities with over fifty

---

[32] J. C. Jackson, 'Rice cultivation in West Malaysia: relationships between culture, history, customary practices and recent developments', *JMBRAS*, 45, 2 (1972), 76–96.

[33] Rudolph Wikkramatileke, 'Mukim Pulau Rusa: land use in a Malayan riverine settlement', *JTG*, 11 (1958), 18–25.

[34] Diane K. Lewis, 'Rules or agrarian change: Negri Sembilan Malays and agricultural innovation', *JSEAS*, 7, 1 (1976), 74–91.

[35] Rosemary Firth, *Housekeeping among Malay peasants* (second edition, London, 1966), p. 189.

[36] 'Schooling facilities: note for DOs' conference to be held on 3.2.1950', BA Pahang/96/49.

[37] DO Lipis, 'Sg. Tembeling tour, 11th–17th May, 1949', BA Pahang/33/49.

children that had no school.[38] In Kelantan, where the *madrasah* or *surau* were the main points of public assembly, schools were dilapidated and offered little protection from the weather; there were no textbooks, and students learnt on slates or by rote.[39] Some modernisers targeted *pondok* education as a bulwark of rural conservatism. However, their criticisms of it were provoked less by its failings than by its successes. The survival of rural Islamic schooling nourished elite fears that young men with an incomplete Arabic education, who could find no place in the religious bureaucracy, would put pressure on secular Malay nationalism. Colonial efforts at educational improvement were frequently contradicted by the survival of pre-war paternalism. Many British officials still saw education as merely a means of teaching the rural Malay to be a better cultivator. They continued to complain – in places like Trengganu for example – that it was impossible to get holders of school certificates to take up farming.[40]

Another allegation against the conservatism of rural tradition was that savings were unproductive, that they were kept as hoarded cash, or gold jewellery. If they were kept in a less liquid form it was as an inheritable asset such as padi land, or as cattle later disposed of for the purchase of land, and this land was often heavily encumbered by loans. In all the northern padi-dominated states only 5 per cent or less of households had bank accounts. Yet even the British appreciated that less institutionalised saving met many rural needs through its convenience, security and informality. Nor were Malays unresponsive to modern banking where it was available. In fact, the provision of facilities for postal savings was insufficient to meet growing rural needs. By 1959, 80 per cent of deposits in rural co-operatives were from the padi-producing states of Kedah, Perlis and Province Wellesley.[41] Religious obligations were also seen as a great drain on rural savings – especially the *haj*. After the war, large numbers made the journey to Mecca, disposing of assets to meet costs. During the 1950 pilgrimage season over 4,000 hajis were expected to spend in excess of $600,000. However, in post-war Selangor, in the more prosperous rubber-growing areas, the upper stratum of rural society provided the most pilgrims, in contrast to the 1920s when many participated who could not really afford it. The urban elites increasingly sought *haji* status; financial reforms made it more difficult for other groups to participate, and pilgrimage became less of a drain on the resources of rural communities.[42]

At the root of many colonial criticisms of Malay society was a belief that Islam retarded the productivity and economic advancement of the Malays. A central charge

[38] DO Kuala Kangsar to State Secretary, Perak, 8.6.1955; DO Larut to State Secretary, Perak, 23.4.1955, DO Larut/128/55.
[39] 'Daerah Tanjong Pauh', 38–9.
[40] SAO Kelantan to State Secretary Trengganu, 20.12.1950, SUK Tr/1675/50.
[41] Federation of Malaya, *Report of the Pilgrims Economic Welfare Committee*, Cmd. 22 of 1962, pp. 4–9.
[42] *Straits Echo*, 6.6.1950; Mary Byrne McDonnell, 'The conduct of Hajj from Malaysia and its socio–economic impact on Malay society: a descriptive and analytical study, 1860–1981' (Ph.D. Columbia University, 1986), pp. 416–18, 433–7.

was that the Islamic law of inheritance created fragmentation of land-holdings.[43] Parts of Kelantan provided a classic case: in Daerah Tanjong Pauh the vast majority of holdings were worked by owners, and the average was only one and three-quarter acres a household. Although the extent to which lots were borrowed was uncertain, absentee landlordism was low and an even but meagre distribution of land was effected.[44] This exasperated the managers of land colonisation schemes, whose resort to expedients such as tied titles did not modify inheritance customs.[45] Both British and Malay officials railed against these 'fantastic denominations' of land. They felt that only drastic action, with the sanction of religious leaders, would compel heirs to accept a cash inheritance, or to auction the land. At the centre of fragmentation, they recognised, was 'the desire on the part of the heirs to possess, for sentimental reasons, a share in the ancestral holding regardless of the smallness of the share'.[46] An investigation in Kelantan in 1958 found one beneficiary inheriting three square feet – 'and he insisted on having it' – and in the State legislative restrictions were placed on subdivisions below a quarter of an acre.[47] Yet compliance with Islamic rules of inheritance did not necessarily imply the physical partition of a holding, nor was it the only factor making for fragmentation. The situation varied widely and was consistent only in its complexity. Lands could be jointly inherited but cultivated by one person, or lent to one person, with or without a consideration, as part-owner, part-tenant. Surveys in Perak suggested that fragmentation was of little significance as beneficiaries came to understandings whereby a holding was either given to a person wholly, or cultivated jointly, rarely by more than three parties, each sharing at least half an acre. In Krian, co-ownership was predominant and the size of larger holdings shrunk as a consequence. The effects of fragmentation on efficient farming were mitigated by land sale. The important question was what the part-owners did with their land.[48] Above all, the fact that fragmentation was seen as one of the most obstinate barriers to the betterment of the condition of the Malay cultivator, suggested a growing demand for scarce resources of land in the late colonial period. For many Malays land-holding was more than a sentimental attachment, it conferred status and a modicum of stability and subsistence in an uncertain world; for women especially it was an insurance against divorce.[49] Even where there was land hunger, Malays were unwilling

---

[43] See Ungku A. Aziz, 'Land disintegration and land policy in Malaya', *Malayan Economic Review*, 3, 1 (1958), 22–8.

[44] 'Daerah Tanjong Pauh', 32–6.   [45] Enclosures on SUK Tr/1193/50.

[46] Dato Mahmud bin Mat, 'Fragmentation of holdings: measures to be taken to stop it', 13.6.1952, PU&A Phg/352/52.

[47] Cited in K. S. Jomo, *A question of class: Capital, the state, and uneven development in Malaya* (Singapore, 1986), p. 128.

[48] 'Answers to subjects on which the Rice Production Committee desires information: District of Larut and Matang', DO Larut/1066/52. Discussed in T. B. Wilson, 'Some economic aspects of padi-land ownership in Krian', *Malayan Agricultural Journal*, 37, 3 (1954), 125–35.

[49] Robert Ho, 'Land ownership and economic prospects of Malay peasants', *MAS*, 4, 1 (1970), 91–2.

to move to new areas because of the considerable interests tied up in kampong land and houses. Where there was migration to wage labour in the towns, a stake in the kampong was maintained. And whilst commercialised cultivation of padi was not a viable prospect for many rural Malays, for others – often commercial or salaried interests – subdivisions created opportunities for the accumulation of land. The colonial anatomy of poverty masked far-reaching processes of change within the Malay economy.

Stagnation and diversification

At the root of British perceptions of the Malay dilemma was the assumption they had to choose between the rational pursuit of economic interest in the modern economy or the inertia of tradition. Yet for the Malays themselves, no absolute choice of lifestyle had to be made. It did not make sense to make it. Traditional patterns of subsistence and participation in the cash economy evolved side by side; old moral economies and newer political economies could coexist; both were rational responses to fluctuating economic opportunities and the uneven impact of commercialisation. Where there were opportunities, they would be taken. Where there was not, there was a bolstering of subsistence strategies. The 1950s were the best of times and the worst of times. They saw the rise of new wealth – even short periods of prosperity for rubber smallholders – yet overall in the traditional sector, the 1950s were a period of declining productivity. Between 1950 and 1958, smallholder rubber production fell by 14 per cent, copra by 34 per cent, fishing landings by 9 per cent. Only padi production rose by 14 per cent, yet the average income of planters in 1960 remained the same as it had been in 1947.[50] The beneficiaries of agrarian change prospered at the expense of the less-advantaged Malays, creating more pronounced economic differentiation in the countryside. Moreover, the policies of the colonial state played a significant role in shaping the range of economic possibilities for the Malays.

In many areas padi was eclipsed as the primary source of subsistence: Malay agriculturalists were investing their energies elsewhere. Diversification, as noted earlier, had always been a feature of the Malay rural economy, but the scale of the move into other forms of employment in this period increased considerably. The decline of padi was in part due to the disruptions of the Emergency and the attractions of other cash-crops, but pressures came from within the rice economy itself. Whilst fragmentation represented an agricultural involution of a kind, the primary concomitant of agrarian change was an increase in tenancy. The Rice Production Committee – appointed to investigate means of increasing production – revealed in 1953 that rates of tenancy for Province Wellesley, Kedah and Krian were 75 per cent, 70 per cent and 50 per cent respectively.[51] Between 1950 and 1955, some 40,000 acres had changed

---

[50] E. K. Fisk, 'Rural development policy', in T. H. Silcock and E. K. Fisk (ed.), *The political economy of independent Malaya* (Singapore, 1963), p. 165.

[51] Federation of Malaya, *Report of the Rice Production Committee*, I (1953).

Table 6 *Number of wet padi farms reporting various tenure systems, 1960*[52]

Area	Total	Owner	TOL	Tenant	Others	% tenants
Federation	132,276	72,282	10,930	68,564	15,838	51.83
Johore	1,200	460	480	0	340	0
Kedah	44,910	20,918	1,092	27,710	5,442	61.7
Kelantan	20,554	14,470	666	13,126	2,906	63.86
Malacca	3,128	2,246	160	824	180	26.34
Negri Sembilan	2,980	2,480	80	500	160	16.77
Pahang	3,940	2,420	460	880	800	22.33
Penang & P.W.	11,290	4,470	440	8,000	580	70.85
Perak	20,772	10,202	2,976	8,106	2,444	39.02
Perlis	8,540	5,054	1,306	4,438	2,086	51.97
Selangor	7,996	5,056	2,608	1,720	280	21.51
Trengganu	6,966	4,506	642	3,260	640	46.8

from owner to tenant operation.[53] Table 6 gives the situation in 1960. As a series of local, often informal arrangements tenancy was not new, but declining production – especially during the war years – rising demand for land, and a growing insistence on cash rents and 'tea-money' made the situation precarious for many. The incidence and character of tenancy varied widely, as did the ability of cultivators to resist it. District Officers claimed there was little concrete evidence of increased charges or unscrupulousness by landlords. Yet there were many ways in which pressures could be exerted on tenants. In the north, in Krian for example, the more usurious landlords increasingly demanded cash rents before planting started. Cultivators lost lands when a landlord offered lands to the highest bidder; others retained their lands only after great difficulty, borrowing dangerously from financiers, defaulting if the harvest was bad or government reduced the minimum price for padi, as it did in 1954–5. The better the land, the greater the danger. There were other reports that the flexibility and sympathy which were felt to be characteristic of pre-war landlord and tenant relations had been maintained in the modified form of bargaining in the collection of cash rents. There were reports that cultivators occasionally absconded with the harvest, or more often evaded payment, and thus could force down the rent. This was said to be one reason why the landlords were demanding cash advances.[54] However, where land was in short supply the tenant had little bargaining power.

The deterioration of the traditional padi sector was generally portrayed in

[52] T. B. Wilson, *Type, tenure and fragmentation of farms: Census of Agriculture, Federation of Malaya, 1960, Preliminary report No. 3* (Kuala Lumpur, 1961), table 66.

[53] R. D. Hill, 'Agricultural land tenure in west Malaysia', *Malayan Economic Review*, 22, 1 (1967), p. 107.

[54] ADO Krian, minute, 23.7.1951; Co-operative Supervisor Parit Buntar to DO, 20.8.1951, Coop Krian North/39/51.

communal terms. In Kedah, the Malay press reported, half of the padi fields were mortgaged to Chettiars and Chinese, and padi was sold to them at one-third of the price to repay loans. Government loans were an additional burden on the cultivator.[55] Saberkas in Kedah demanded land reform to free Malay lands 'pawned to non-Malays'.[56] From the earliest years of colonial rule, the vulnerability of rural Malays to economic exploitation and indebtedness had been laid at the feet of the Chettiar moneylender. By the end of the war, the situation had changed, and it seemed that the Chinese shopkeeper had replaced the Chettiar as the local exploiter of the Malay padi farmer. Certainly, the expansion of Chinese cultivation had in many places created more intricate relations between the rural Chinese and the Malay cultivator. In some localities where land and the labour to work it were scarce or credit was tight, it had placed a strain on them. In other places, often newly opened areas, happier accommodations were made. Even in 1949, M. V. del Tufo, then Chief Secretary, admitted that rural indebtedness was not as serious as ' "white-collar" indebtedness in the towns, as the rural trader has to keep on literally close terms with his clients and, being himself a relatively small man, cannot afford to sink substantial sums in long term loans'.[57] For the cultivator there were advantages in forming a credit relationship with a middle-man rather than with the state or a co-operative, not least their ability to pay for a product in advance, albeit at a lower price. In Malacca in late 1948, the government paid $15 a *picul* for padi, and black-market buyers $20; however, few peasants had padi to sell as they had already sold to shopkeepers at $5–12 a *picul*.[58] The senior government co-operative officer reflected years later that often Malay co-operators preferred to sell rice to Chinese millers rather than a government mill.[59] There were few alternative sources of credit. In Perlis, Province Wellesley, Kedah and Krian there were an estimated 180,000 planters, and $20 million a year was needed to finance them. Only 17,666 were members of rural co-operative credit societies or seasonal co-operative credit societies, and the 385 societies gave out only $2.4 million in loans. In Sungei Manik, the 3,660 planters required $988,000, and only sixty-three were in co-operatives. In Tanjong Karang and Sabak Bernam, there were 12,000 planters. In Tanjong Karang many provided their own capital without borrowing, and there were four co-operatives. In Sabak Bernan, *padi kuncha* was rampant. It was estimated that even if banking unions could distribute as much as $5 million, it would

---

[55] *Utusan Melayu*, 24.4.1947.   [56] *Malaya Tribune*, 26.4.1949.

[57] M.V. del Tufo, minute, 19.12.1950, FS/13187/50.

[58] 'Report on the activities of co-operative societies for the quarter ending 31.12.1948', Malacca circle, Coop/670/47. *Padi kuncha* and *padi ratus* were 'behind the *nipah* palm' transactions, based purely on trust. Both were forms of crop-mortgage, *padi ratus* being based on 100 gantangs of the crop sold in advance of the harvest for around $30, as against around $60 for the government price; *jual jangi*, a form of land mortgage, practised by rubber and copra smallholders as well as padi planters, was a common form of indebtedness of Malays to Malays. Although usurious they allowed planters to borrow, in the absence of any other source of capital. Abdul Majid, 'Co-operative movement amongst Malays', *Intisari*, 1, 2 (n.d.), 44–5.

[59] R. C. Gates to Robert Heussler, 31.5.1976, Heussler papers.

take eight years to reach all the planters.[60] Certainly the Malay Reservations Enactment did not stop other races entering them and using a vehicle as a place of business.[61] As in the pre-war period, the Malay Reservations were often circumvented by Malay proprietors concluding an unregistered lease with a non-Malay. The government lost the fees accruing from such a transaction and the ability to carry out proper land administration, whilst the parties involved lost nothing, except the protection of the law. In Lenggong, Ulu Perak, the practice was common as Chinese sought Malay lands for the erection of houses and the cultivation of tobacco.[62] Often shops were built on an island of land within the original reservation. Malays themselves leased land to non-Malays for shophouses, often for a period as long as ten years or more, 'aided and abetted', it was said, 'by corrupt or inept *penghulus*'. In Selangor, this was the state of affairs in every Malay Reservation in the State, save for one where the headman absolutely forbade the leasing of land to Chinese. It 'sapped the moral fibre of the Malays' as there was little incentive for the Malays to attempt their own marketing and dealers bought directly from the Chinese.[63] Yet, 'rigid communal separation deemed too dramatic for inclusion in the law forty years ago', recognised a senior civil servant, 'can hardly be adopted in the age of the "Malayan Nation" '.[64]

However, the underlying trend cut across communal lines. Although the problem was a mote in the eye of Sino-Malay relations, relationships of tenancy and indebtedness were on the increase within the Malay community itself. There were allegations in Krian and Kedah that smallholders were paying high rents to Malay absentee landlords. Surveys in Province Wellesley showed that owners of large holdings were Malay, that the land was divided into multiple lots, and that only on three lots were Malays working the land for Chinese. On 218 lots they were working Malay-owned land.[65] In Mukim Dulang in Kedah, although the incidence of *padi kuncha* seemed to be low and government loans were financing the crop, most of the larger landowners were Malays, with Malays working their lots. These landlords tended to demand cash rent, and over 50 per cent of households were landless.[66] In Perak, in large *bendang* areas such as Batu Kurau and Bukit Gantang in Larut, the average area of padi land was two to three acres per family, but elsewhere the figures were extreme – either the cultivator held three acres or above, or below one acre per family – in the majority of cases having no *bendang*.[67] The logic of subdivision in

[60] R. C. Gates to Private Secretary to High Commissioner, 16.5.1955, Coop/208/55.

[61] E. R. Ellis, minute, 11.11.1950, FS/12737/50.

[62] R. J. C. Wait, DO Upper Perak, to State Secretary, Perak, 7.7.1953; ADO Larut, minute, 3.5.1954, DO Larut/184/54.

[63] E. Ll. Jones, 'Memorandum on the present Sino-Malay population ratio of Malay reservations as a potent obstacle to the progress of cooperative marketing', 28.4.1950, FS/12737/50; *Malaya Tribune*, 26.4.1949.

[64] J. M. Gullick, Secretary RIDA, minute, 25.1.1951, FS/12737/50.

[65] 'Mukim Four Central, Province Wellesley', 29–31.

[66] Dobby, 'Padi landscapes of Malaya', *MJTG*, 6 (1955), 53–4.

[67] 'Answers to subjects on which the Rice Production Committee desires information: District of Larut and Matang', DO Larut/1066/52.

Malay Reservations enabled Malays who had land and spare capital to invest in land at low prices. Official reports were chary about revealing the scale of evictions, although it was warned of Kedah and Perlis that 'in time an army of landless tenants devoid of any security may lead to social unrest'. When Tengku Yaacob of Kedah reported 'ruthless ejections' in the State, he was exposing landlords within the royal family. The British agreed that land was up for auction and that its ownership was 'drifting towards being a speculative investment'.[68] They mooted protective legislation, but as control of land was vested in the States, and 'in view of the grip which the Kedah royal family and its offshoots have on Kedah cultivable land', it had little chance of success.[69] British officials in the State attempted to assure the Federal government that the evictors would be opposed by sentiments inside the kampongs and that tenancies were 'not necessarily agreements between capitalists and peasants but frequently both parties are of peasant status'.[70] In a similar fashion, to contemporary observers the Rice Committee Report, 'delicately side-stepped ill-defined issues of domestic sensitivities', especially evidence of increasing charges by landlords.[71] Its critics believed that growing economic differentiation within the Malay community was at stake, rather than issues of communalism. Moreover, in 1949 the government drew back from rice-milling and instead issued licences to private concerns. The granting of licences became a hotly contested political issue, and an important source of political patronage. Malays were often the beneficiaries.[72] A tendency to concentration of wealth, increasingly through land purchase, worked in many places to consolidate a rural elite that had its roots in commerce or a salaried position. It was often bound up with local administrative office, and its emergence is a theme of many anthropological studies of the period.[73] An early field study of five regrouped villages in Malacca in 1955 found them to be less self-sufficient than before: villagers' incomes had fallen; they had less opportunity to turn their time and energy into capital; and a wide gap in prosperity was opening between the majority and the fortunate few in government service.[74] This was neither a uniform nor unchallenged process. A survey in west Johore showed that wealth and village leadership did not always sit side by side.[75] Strong traditions of peasant equity persisted. However, the unfolding effects of the commercialisation of Malay peasant agriculture were bound up with the new forms of political influence that were brought to bear on these localities which, as we shall see, could ultimately be divisive of communal political loyalties.

For those denied access to land on favourable terms, padi cultivation was an

---

[68] Director of Agriculture to Economic Secretary, 12.8.1948, FS/2255/48.
[69] M. V. del Tufo, minute, 23.7.1949, *ibid.*
[70] E. G. Barrett, minute, 22.7.1949; State Secretary, Kedah to Chief Secretary, 7.12.1949, *ibid.*
[71] Dobby, 'Padi landscapes of Malaya', *MJTG*, 6 (1955), 1.
[72] Mohamed Yusof, 'Tanjong Karang', n.d., Coop/442/49.
[73] Syed Husin Ali, *Malay peasant society and leadership* (Kuala Lumpur, 1975), pp. 71–101, 162–3.
[74] Ungku A. Aziz and Raja Mohar, *A survey of five villages in Malacca* (Kuala Lumpur, 1955).
[75] K. O. L. Burridge, 'Managerial influences in a Johore village', *JMBRAS*, 30, 1 (1957), 108.

increasingly insecure livelihood. Tenancy was not the only issue. Peasants were harshly treated by the post-war rice market. In south Krian, during the period of post-war rice shortage, the predominantly Banjarese planters found that the proceeds of sales – even sales on the black market – were insufficient to meet the costs of purchased commodities. As black market prices rose, they increased their sales, and their domestic consumption declined to the point where they were forced to purchase rice. 'Fathers put on scowling faces,' a Malay official recalled, 'and mothers who could hear the cries of hunger cursed the fathers for their madness in pursuit of Mammon.'[76] The government's minimum price for padi remained unrealistically low, especially when imports of cheap rice resumed from elsewhere in Southeast Asia. In the 1954–55 season the official price, set after fields had been planted, was much lower than that anticipated by cultivators and they suffered severe losses. The minimum price seemed to promise security and prosperity for the Malay peasant, yet the main beneficiary from cheap rice was industrial enterprise, and it has been argued that the guaranteed price only served to deflect Malays away from more remunerative employment: an important example of how state policy could perhaps restrict economic opportunity.[77] Moreover, yields were low due to the perennial problems of pests and lack of water. In 1949, 65,000 tons of padi in Province Wellesley and Kedah, worth around $10 million, were lost to poor irrigation, and only 237,500 of 800,000 padi acres were irrigated.[78] The government attempted to meet this shortage of economically viable holdings by launching land colonisation schemes. Significantly, in the implementation of these schemes, officials were compelled to revise upwardly their estimates of the acreage necessary for successful peasant agriculture. They realised that to set an acreage of, say, five acres, was to project a static standard of living for the cultivator, whereas the object of these schemes was to constantly raise it.[79] Diversification was increasingly seen as a requirement for a successful rural economy.

Not only was land in short supply, but also the labour to work it. This was an effect as much as a cause of the unattractiveness of padi cultivation. The scale with which rural Malays took to wage labour was symptomatic of the changes in the rural economy. After the war, opportunities for rural Malays to earn a daily wage increased dramatically. Overall employment in the padi sector 1947–57 dropped from 470,692 to 398,295, that is by 15.4 per cent.[80] The amount of effort given over to padi had never been static; migrant labour had long been built into the economy of the countryside. Even in the padi heartland of Kelantan, coconuts, rubber, vegetable, tobacco and

---

[76] Ahmed Tajuddin, Malay Cooperative Officer, Krian South, 'Economic survey of the padi planters in Krian South', 22.11.1946, Coop/1045/46.

[77] Donald M. Nonini, *British colonial rule and the resistance of the Malay peasantry, 1900–1957* (New Haven, 1992), pp. 120–1.

[78] *Malay Mail*, 15.3.1949.

[79] Department of Agriculture, 'Economic size of padi smallholdings', SUK Tr/1193/50, D. S. Ferguson, 'The Sungei Manik irrigation scheme', *MJTG*, 2 (1954), 9–16.

[80] Nonini, *British colonial rule*, pp. 15, 122.

other crops occupied over a third of available land and a variety of industries used local materials and labour: tile-making, copra and sugar production. Seasonal out-migration was an established feature of rural life: to Siam and Kedah, where vast amounts of seasonal labour were required.[81] After the war, this existing mobility was compounded by the mobilisation and urbanisation of Malays during the Emergency. Even in rice-bowls such as Kedah, Malays were thrown on to the labour market as a consequence of bad harvests, and there was evident depopulation due to shortage of land, increasing rent, movement to settlement schemes such as Tanjong Karang and Krian, and recruitment in the security forces.[82] It was, however, in the areas of secondary padi land that the balance of subsistence shifted decisively away from rice cultivation, and it was here that government was making its strongest demands on labour for the police, army and Special Constabulary. Headmen urged young men to 'leave everything and come forward to shoulder arms'. Malays responded in great numbers. In one district of Malacca, which had a tradition of such service, 70 per cent of eligible men volunteered. Families followed breadwinners, and there were fears that whole kampongs would be abandoned.[83] Women and the aged formed the backbone of labour in the padi fields. By mid-1950, there was in many areas a serious neglect of harvesting of padi lands as labour costs rose. In West Pahang, in one season alone, the cost of cultivating an acre of padi rose from $40 to $100.[84] In Tanjong Karang, three-acre plots were not fully harvested. In the broken, hilly areas of Negri Sembilan and inland Selangor, poor to average yields were obtained from holdings of second- or third-class land in small valleys or of padi surrounded by kampong lands where rubber and fruit were grown. The first-class land was found only on the coastal plains where the way of life was becoming very different from that of the small valley *sawah*.[85] This kind of geographical contrast is crucially important. From the field reports, one central theme stands out. Planters were either becoming – in core areas of rice production such as Kedah, parts of Perak and Selangor, and in Province Wellesley where a second crop of Taiwan padi was introduced – specialised growers, with a surplus for trading, but not always in a position to prosper at it, or they were moving into other employment.[86] For the dominant groups in the countryside this meant the acquisition of larger holdings; for the disadvantaged cultivator this meant tenancy or agricultural labour, or migration towards wage labour opportunities. The countryside was ceasing to resemble, if it ever had done so, the idyll of kampong life that figured so largely in the imagination of British officials.

In the competitive atmosphere of the rubber market the processes of change bearing on the Malay rural economy were visible in a most pronounced form. A trend

[81] 'Daerah Tanjong Pauh, Kelantan', 22, 28–31.   [82] 'Mukim Dulang, Kedah', 44.
[83] Raja Musa, minute, 10.9.1948, Coop/661/46.
[84] 'Quarterly progress report for third quarter ended 30.9.1950 for West Pahang circle', Coop/659/46.
[85] SAO Selangor to State Secretary 27.10.1950; State Secretary Selangor to Chief Secretary, 28.6.1951, Sel Sec/1911/50.
[86] 'Mukim Four Central, Province Wellesley', 21.

towards economic concentration within rural society was underway before the war. Pressures on land entrenched the position of certain core groups, such as the families of *penghulus*, who were best placed to get access to rubber land, register titles and expand their holdings. Recent migrants and younger sons were obstructed by absentee owners who retained parcels of land and by the escalating costs of opening up new land.[87] Also, as rubber required little supervision, it was an especially attractive investment for the townsman: over 48 per cent of owners lived in towns. Eighty per cent of rubber farms were operated by owners with permanent title, 1 per cent on mixed ownership and tenancy, and 2 per cent were operated by owners on temporary title. Many were without legal title, especially in Kedah and Perlis, and there were large-scale illegal plantings of rubber in these areas. Fragmentation was the norm, often as a subterfuge to enable larger farms to qualify for government assistance to smallholders. A 1960 agricultural census reported that only 47 per cent of farms were a single parcel of land; 40 per cent were two or three parcels.[88] It was suggested that Europeans were selling land to investors who divided and sold it to land-hungry smallholders.[89] The concentration of ownership did not mean that diffusion of wealth ceased altogether to be a feature of rural communities. The persistence of *bagi dua* – or share-tapping – is in part evidence of some degree of income-sharing. The growing importance of rubber as a resource meant that land transfers were becoming rarer, but it did require the sharing of that property with others. Under the *bagi dua* system, the tapper retained between 40 and 60 per cent of the crop; and usually kept control of its processing. Smallholders without capital to open up a holding would sell rights to the crop for one or two years to contractors, or absentee owners would rent land to contractors for an agreed amount of rubber. In some areas, such as Temerloh, it seemed that *bagi dua* was more common when prices were low.[90] During the Emergency, the fact that levels of production were sustained was mainly due to the contribution of smallholdings, and they benefited from rising prices.[91] During the Korean war boom, the high rubber prices were reflected in new houses, more pilgrimages, and large profits in the towns. In West Pahang in October 1950, 'this easy money seemed to have been spent by the people lavishly on extravagant clothing such as linen and sharkskin, etc., and on sports bicycles'.[92] However, the boom in the price of rubber did not benefit the majority of the rural population who possessed no

---

[87] Syed Husin Ali, 'Land concentration and poverty among the rural Malays', *Nusantara*, 1 (1972), 100–13; Margaret L. Koch, 'Rubber in the district of Temerloh: unequal access and growing economic disparity', *Kajian Malaysia*, 3, 1 (1985), 1–31.

[88] J. M. F. Greenwood, 'Rubber smallholdings in the Federation of Malaya', *JTG*, 18 (August 1964), 81–100.

[89] UPAM, *56th Annual Report, 1957*, p. 28.

[90] Rubber Research Institute, 'Minutes of the 5th meeting of the smallholder rubber advisory committee, 4.12.1946', Coop/1454/46/Part I; Koch, 'Rubber in the district of Temerloh', 25.

[91] Barlow, *Natural rubber industry*, p. 80.

[92] 'Quarterly progress report for third quarter ended 30.9.1950 for West Pahang circle', Coop/659/46.

rubber at all. General prices rose and many found it hard to maintain a decent standard of living. Some farmers who had rubber trees were in no position to exploit the windfall. In the Jasin District of Malacca, in the early years of the Emergency, many smallholders had leased their land to Chinese to tap at very low rates, or to financiers, often the local shopkeepers.[93] The very readiness of Malays to venture into the commercial economy, highlighted both their disadvantaged position in certain key areas of it, and the uneven distribution of their gains within their community.

Financial vulnerability was seen in its most extreme form in the poverty of the Malay fishing communities. The greatest weakness lay in marketing. In Perak, five Ipoh wholesalers had succeeded in outbidding their competitors for the coastal catch and had secured a virtual monopoly. The actual auction prices were shrouded in secrecy – 'imparted by whisperings in the ears, quick scribbling on slates and rushing on abaci'. The losses fell on the fishermen as their price was determined by the price of the wholesalers who alone had the town board licences for market space, and who unseated competitors. Neither the local *towkay* nor the fishermen possessed the leverage to raise their price, as the cold storage facilities available to wholesalers helped them to regulate demand. They also controlled much of the transport. A survey on the west coast gave 59 per cent of the purchase price going to the fishermen, 18 per cent to the distribution chain and 23 per cent to the retailer.[94] It was not a simplistic picture of Chinese shopkeepers advancing money and goods at usurious rates to Malay fishermen, which the latter paid for with their catches. They were bound together in a complex nexus of dependence, and both were prey to the larger operators of the towns. On the Pahang coast, the British found no evidence of the indebtedness of fishermen to either the government or the 'middle-men'. Rather the reverse was true. Middle-men were indebted to the fishermen due to outstanding payments for fish received: one individual in Nenasi claimed that $1,000 was owing to him. A *towkay* would, by mutual agreement, buy all the fish brought to him at a price set on a week to week basis, providing a ready buyer and a guaranteed supply which enabled the *towkay* to draw advances from Singapore wholesalers. The *towkay* paid only a small advance and his indebtedness lay in the fact that the balances were often withheld. The *towkays* stressed that they too faced hardship: prices were low, there were export restrictions to Indonesia and Hong Kong, and monies due were slow in coming from Singapore. The fishermen, however, were trapped by the *towkay's* virtual control over the price of fish, which was set by verbal arrangements. They attempted to break out of this by selling first-class fish to boats from Endau in Johore for cash, but residual catches of small fish, often uneconomic to cure, were often refused by the *towkay*, and fishermen had no alternative but to dump them at sea.[95] In

[93] 'Quarterly report on the activities of urban and rural co-operative societies in Malacca for the first quarter of 1950', Coop/670/47.
[94] Fishery Inspector, Kuala Kurau, 'Development of the fishery industry in Perak'; minute, n.d., Coop Tpg/39/50.
[95] Abdul Rashid, 'Report on the investigation of the fishermen on the Pahang coast south of Kuala Rompin', *ibid.*; 'Report of visit to Nenasi', 2.9.1948, Coop/598/48.

Kelantan, a survey showed that fish landed on the beach passed through seven different stages of middle-man and the price rose five and a half times by the time it reached Ulu Kelantan: 'it goes by *picul* pole, bicycle, bullock cart and bus'. Yet here, the problem was not one of Sino–Malay relations. In Kelantan the whole of the trade and industry was in the hands of Malays, 'many of the capitalists being old Malay ladies'. In 1951 a Colonial Development and Welfare scheme set up a fishmarketing syndicate to take over from these middle-women. It was opposed by vested interests.[96]

Accused of being too trusting and reliant on the benevolence of the *towkays*, fishermen had little opportunity but to accept the price they were given by the lack of alternative sources of income. At the mouth of the Kelantan river in 1946, families complained that they ate only once every three or four days. Rice cultivation was insufficient to tide them over the monsoon; craft work brought poor returns; traditional women's occupations of preparing salt fish were declining.[97] A survey of fishing kampongs south of Kuala Pahang in 1950 revealed appalling poverty. Fishermen undertook rice cultivation under threat of starvation as fishing incomes barely exceeded expenditure during the fishing season and savings for the monsoon season could not be made. There was little alternative employment; fish for curing were scarce, and this work was for the most part the preserve of elderly women.[98] Often land was unavailable nearby and men fished in rivers, or went south to look for wage labour. Around two-thirds could not scrape together enough to buy rice, some bought tapioca, and others, who could not even afford this, subsisted on wild fruits. Here, the circle of poverty was complete. The harsh subsistence struggle was intensified all along the east coast by the fact that many fishing areas drew in large amounts of migrant labour. In Pahang, migrant fishermen came from Trengganu, usually in groups with their own boats and equipment, and were housed by the Chinese fish dealers in a shed for the duration of their stay. Further south, in Mersing, Johore, in one month as many as 500 migrants could arrive seeking work. Yet here, landings during the monsoon season decreased by over 70 per cent in 1949–50 and migrants were forced to return to their homes; in Pahang the decrease was 90 per cent.[99] Overfishing and the increasing incidence of *kelong* fishing took a further toll on incomes. These off-shore platforms required considerable capital; they cost around $8,000, and all twenty licensed *kelongs* in Pahang waters were owned and operated by Chinese, selling to boats operating from Endau. Malay fishermen complained that they damaged boats and nets; that the intensity of the fishing made it impossible to fish between four to eight fathoms from the coast; and that the Endau operators by-passed them to exploit the guaranteed supply from the *kelongs*. The government was urged to ban them. Change was further advanced on the west coast. Fishing grounds in Perak

---

[96] *Malay Mail*, 21.1.1950; Gurney to Secretary of State, 30.1.1951, CO537/7261; *Report of the Committee to investigate the fishing industry* (Kuala Lumpur, 1956), Appendix 'D'.

[97] M. R. Jellicoe, 'Monthly report for November–December, 1946', DSW/207/46.

[98] Abdul Rashid, 'Report', Coop Tpg/39/50.

[99] Director of Fisheries, 'Monthly Report for December, 1949'; January, 1950; April, 1950, DO Kuantan/67/50.

were being fished to the limit, the population was increasing and there were struggles over sites. Fishermen were pushed into untouched off-shore waters, but the expertise, gear and organisation needed to do this were in short supply.[100] Restrictions were placed on licences, and a dilemma arose whether to issue licences for off-shore fishing to Chinese or Malays. The west coast Malay fishermen were seen by officials as a poor minority 'unable to identify their problems and difficulties'. Leaders had to be found for co-operative ventures, which would not succeed unless fishermen were making enough profits and broke the rings of fresh fish distribution.[101] Tensions ran high in some places: in Kuala Kedah a Sino-Malay committee was formed to mediate on the issue.[102] In the same area in 1951, Malay fishermen went on strike, demanding a revision of the rates for the catch, the writing-off of all debts, and a $10 advance to resume work. Some were successful, and on seeing this Chinese fishermen struck in return.[103] Despite this resistance, the composite picture was of the fishermen sinking progressively into a state of torpor and financial servitude in an increasingly uneconomic pursuit. These inequities, despite their complexity, were portrayed in communal terms and were to become a testing-ground both for colonial policy and nationalist resolve.

Perceptions of development

Confronted by processes of change within the rural economy which were both creating new forms of wealth, and confirming old kinds of poverty, colonial development policy sought both to strengthen the resilience of Malay communities against economic uncertainty and to nursemaid their entrance into the commercial economy. British strategy was contradictory. Born out of the recent memory of chronic food shortage, it looked backwards to the pre-war goal of self-sufficiency in rice production. In this sense, it was an eleventh-hour attempt to restrain urbanisation and the growing of commercial crops. Yet, in another sense, looking ahead to equip Malays for independence, the British attempted to strike at the roots at what they saw as the unsophisticated attitude of the Malays to modern economics. They remained uncertain as to their ultimate goal, as to whether it was the creation of a sturdy yeoman peasantry, or the nurturing of a Malay capitalist class. In the end they achieved neither. The history of rural development in the 1950s followed a course similar to the other grand social experiments of late colonial rule. Its success rested on the fostering of local initiatives. These did not materialise in the manner the British desired, yet their long-term impact was to be immense. The late colonial state had by the mid-1950s initiated a pattern of corporatist intervention in the rural economy. This was a significant contribution to the Malay debate on Malay poverty, and the

---

[100] Abdul Rashid, 'Report'; Fishery Inspector, Kuala Kurau, 'Development', Coop Tpg/39/50.
[101] 'Notes of a meeting held in the State Council Chamber, Ipoh on 5.9.1950', *ibid.*
[102] *Straits Echo*, 15.7.1950.
[103] LDMR, September 1951, DCL Sel/9/51.

Malay politicians who were absorbed in the British machinery of development looked increasingly to the state to redress communal imbalances in the economy.

Colonial officials were distressed at the failure of Malay business, although the demise of the largest-scale effort at Malay self-help – the Malay National Bank – was at least partly due to the efforts of its Co-operative Department in actively dissuading Malay cultivators from investing in it.[104] A secret report in 1952 revealed it to be on the brink of collapse. It made a loss in every year of operation. The accounts for the year ending 1 July 1951 showed that all of its capital was expended. By 1 July 1952, its issued capital was $138,605.00, its liabilities $175,175.41 and its assets $166,226.53. Loans and overdrafts had been given without security, and it had not merely lost its shareholders' money but also much of its depositors'. Cheques were only cleared as deposits were received. The Registrar of Companies repeatedly advised it to go into liquidation and in September 1951 its directors were faced with court action for failing to hold a general meeting. When an extraordinary general meeting was held in May 1953, the company's articles of association were altered to permit the holding of up to 50 per cent of the shares by Chinese, and it was feared that if this offer was taken up it would be a damaging blow to Malay prestige. In the event a new Banking Ordinance compelled it to cease operations.[105] The overall picture of Malay business (see Table 7) was bleak and reports by visiting Colonial Office mandarins in no way departed from the old stereotypes of the Malays as 'lacking the nous', slaves to 'old family custom', and prey to an 'inferiority complex' as regards the Chinese. Senior Malay figures added to this image: the *Yang di-Pertuan* of Negri Sembilan told Sir George Maxwell in 1951 that to 'teach a Malay to keep a shop – you might as well teach a chicken to swim; you would only drown it'. Dato Onn bin Jaafar told T. C. Jerrom a year later that the Malays could not compete with the Chinese as they did not understand bribery.[106] The bureaucratic vision was profoundly paternalistic. Yet the British and their closest local allies were unsure as to whether they ought to be turning the Malays into *kulaks* or capitalists. Given this confusion of collective intent it is unsurprising that, in many ways, the failure of Malay business was less due to a failure of entrepreneurial energy than a consequence of the muddled political priorities of the state that tended to suppress it. In the countryside, official discrimination as to the kinds of self-help it would tolerate ultimately restricted economic opportunity. These levels of confusion marked the landmark colonial development initiatives: the Rural and Industrial Development Authority, co-operative credit institutions, assistance to smallholders and the stimulation of wage employment. The returns of these policies were disappointing and the question of Malay economic betterment came under much closer scrutiny by the politicians.

British policy – as laid down in a grand Development Plan – gave precedence both

---

[104] 'Report on activities and progress of co-operative societies in Kinta for June 1947', Coop/ 661/46.

[105] 'The Malay National Banking Corporation Ltd.', ExCo Paper, 24.7.1952, CO1022/463.

[106] Maxwell to Lyttelton, 22.12.1951; T. C. Jerrom, minute, 22.1.1953, CO1022/463.

Table 7 *The condition of Malay business, 1956*[107]

Business	Companies in existence	Subscribed capital ($)	Companies in liquidation	Companies ceasing to exist since 1945
Transport operators	18	540,212		
General traders	12	653,821	4	3
Rice millers	5	581,632		1
Real estate dealers	3	66,750		2
Rubber dealers	1	254,700	1	2
Saw millers	2	102,010		1
Cinema operators	1	31,880		
Copra dealers				1
Poultry farmers				1
Total	42	2,231,005	5	11

to revenue-earning schemes in settled areas, and the opening of remote areas such as the east coast, aims which were assumed to be complementary.[108] The draft plan was costed assuming British, private and UN assistance, but pressure for more health, welfare, and technical education was outweighed by 'a real danger of a "white-collar" class growing up without sufficient outlet for its abilities', and the plan's authors were adamant that Malaya 'cannot have a Welfare State unless she pays for it'.[109] However, the indignation of Malay politicians at the high expenditure on Chinese in rural areas during the Communist Emergency made a larger official initiative focused on the kampongs inevitable. The price of Malay loyalty was the establishment of a Rural and Industrial Development Authority (RIDA) in August 1950. From the outset, its rationale was political and military, rather than developmental. The choice of RIDA's first chairman was particularly important. The post went to the architect of Malay resistance to the Malayan Union, Dato Onn bin Jaafar. RIDA's creation was a tactical movement on the part of the colonial government to find him prestigious, but politically harmless, employment. It was a token through which the British sought to convince Malay opinion of its good faith, as it sought to win acceptance from it for the liberalisation of the citizenship law for non-Malays. Dato Onn's growing antagonism to the Malay Rulers helped prompt the move, and the resistance of the Malay States

---

[107] D. E. M. Fiennes, *Report on Rural and Industrial Development Authority, 1950–1955* (Kuala Lumpur, 1957), Appendix 'E'.

[108] Federation of Malaya, *Draft Development Plan of the Federation of Malaya* (Kuala Lumpur, 1950); 'Draft Development Plan, Chapter II National Resources and Utilities: record of a meeting at King's House', 12.10.1949, Sel Sec/2223/Part I/49.

[109] DO Kuala Langat to State Secretary Selangor, 20.1.1950; H.A.L. Luckham, 'D.D.P. Federation of Malaya: Comments', 14.3.1950', *ibid.*; State Financial Officer Selangor to State Secretary, 3.8.1950, Sel Sec/2223/Part III/49.

to the Authority's influence worked against its success. Onn sharpened his anti-colonialism in the field of rural development. RIDA was envisaged as an attack on official paternalism. Decades of British rule had corrupted the self-sufficiency, initiative and co-operative spirit of the kampong Malay. RIDA was to provide new leadership. In affecting the reconstruction of village life, RIDA aimed to create a 'systematic channel' of opinion from the kampongs to government. New institutions were to be introduced into rural areas and old ones revitalised. *Penghulus* and *ketua kampong* in particular had fallen from being the leaders of their people to becoming administrative subordinates. RIDA was an opportunity for them to rekindle their leadership role. *Mukim* conferences and kampong development boards were vehicles for the democratisation of rural life. All initiative was to reside in the kampong. 'First place,' it was stressed, 'should be given to the principle of Self-help in the achievement of results.'[110] RIDA mooted rural markets; agricultural and industrial development; domestic and rural education; and leadership training. To complete the chain, State councillors were to be allotted 'constituencies', members of the RIDA Board allotted regions.[111] Ex-soldiers and policemen, the most disciplined members of the rural population, were to take the lead.[112] As the colonial administrative system began to transform itself into a polity, dominant local interests moved to take responsibility for distributing the largesse of government.

RIDA did not conform to Onn's vision, nor did the conception of self-help it evinced find acceptance in the Malay community. In many ways, despite Dato Onn's anti-colonial mood, it was a parochial vision which envisaged little more than making kampong life more attractive. It aimed to restore the village to its former state of health, to affirm the Malay cultivator in his faith in the padi economy and to moderate his economic expectations.[113] Malay public opinion grew in hostility to Dato Onn, and many felt that all the talk of 'self-help' was in some way a device to cheat them. State governments resisted RIDA, especially through their control of land. There was a slow retreat from the principle of self-help as the emphasis moved to constructing amenities, providing loans to the small producer and to education and training. This only had the consequence of taking Malays out of the kampongs and moving them to the towns.[114] RIDA provided rural marketplaces, but neglected transport and

---

[110] J. M. Gullick, 'My time in Malaya', Heussler Papers. Gullick was Onn's assistant as Secretary to RIDA. Onn bin Jaafar, 'Proposal for the reorganisation of the Rural and Industrial Development Authority', 2.3.1951, Sel Sec/174/50/Part I. For an account of RIDA, see Ness, *Bureaucracy and rural development*, pp. 125–33.

[111] Keeper of Rulers' Seal to Mentri Besar Selangor, 29.6.1951, Sel Sec/174/50/Part I.

[112] Mahmud bin Mat, 'Memorandum: proposal to make a model Malay kampong or settlement', 5.2.1950, DO Kuantan/104/50; DO to Penghulu Assam Kumbang, Kamunting, 29.9.1955, DO Larut/338/55.

[113] See Martin Rudner, 'Agricultural policy and peasant social transformation in late colonial Malaya', in James C. Jackson and Martin Rudner (eds), *Issues in Malaysian development*, (Singapore, 1979), pp. 22–30.

[114] Ness, *Bureaucracy and rural development*, pp. 127–8.

marketing of rural produce.[115] Visionary land schemes were to be opened after the Emergency was over, and there were attempts to improve the economic prospects and social services available to settlers on earlier schemes such as Tanjong Karang.[116] However, a scheme to meet land hunger in Perak, especially in Krian, by the resettlement of Special Constables who could be interspersed with more experienced, otherwise landless, agriculturalists, was abandoned through lack of finance.[117] Schemes to link the sale of consumer goods on credit with the co-operative marketing of padi met with some success in places like Perlis where there was an established co-operative organisation to oversee the work. Yet even here there were problems. RIDA did not approve a further loan in 1953, due to late repayments of the previous year's loan, and planters reverted to *padi kuncha*.[118] Prestige projects, such as latex marketing, ran into considerable difficulties, and rubber replanting projects failed due to multiple ownership of land, absentee ownership and consequent lack of supervision.[119] This last scheme for agrarian betterment, the replanting of rubber holding with high-yielding varieties, was a wider initiative, encompassing both estates and smallholdings. Launched in May 1952, the aim was to replant 500,000 acres over seven years. However, it was mostly the estates and larger smallholdings – those of 25–100 acres – that benefited. The small estates could not ride out the loss of income whilst the new trees came to maturation. Many smallholders were reluctant to take replanting loans, and the grants available were in instalments and slow to be disbursed. First instalments were paid only on 27,000 acres in 1953, as opposed to a target of 40,000. *Utusan Melayu* commented that at that rate replanting would be completed only in 1990.[120]

To those charged with carrying out its dictates, RIDA had 'a purely propaganda value'; it was a political gift to Dato Onn and his allies. Senior colonial officials admitted privately that they were pouring money into a hole in the ground.[121] By the first half of 1955, the situation on repayment provoked a reduction in the scope of RIDA's activities. Loans were only made for increased productivity of some sort, or to businessmen of proven entrepreneurial talents, and by July 1957 much of this work had passed to a new Bank Ra'ayat (RIDA).[122] As its first priority was to develop existing rural communities and stem the swelling tide of urbanisation, RIDA did little

---

[115] Mohamed Hussein bin Ibrahim, 'Marketing of rural produce', 19.4.1955, Coop/433/54/4.

[116] 'RIDA participation in planned development of new areas'; J. M. Gullick to State Secretary, Pahang, 28.5.1951, Pahang/1068/51.

[117] State Development Officer, Perak, E. K. Fisk, 'Colonization of new agricultural settlements', DO Larut/502/53.

[118] *RIDA Monthly Bulletin*, 1 (August, 1951); *Utusan Melayu*, 24.9.1953.

[119] *RIDA Monthly Bulletin*, 18 (June, 1953).

[120] IBRD, *The economic development of Malaya* (Singapore, 1955), p. 184; *Utusan Melayu*, 22.1.1954.

[121] J. P. Blackledge, 'Diary as State Development Officer, Johore, 1956/7', 12.2.1956, RHO; J. M. Gullick, interview, November 1987.

[122] J. H. Beaglehole, 'Malay participation in commerce and industry: the role of RIDA and MARA', *Journal of Commonwealth Political Studies*, 7 (1969), 216–45.

to break down the barriers of ethnicity in the economy. It became the corporate representative of the aspirations of the rural Malays, and it was to set a vital precedent in the manner in which the state would allocate resources. The Federal Land Development Authority, established in 1956, began large-scale settlement schemes which would dominate post-colonial rural development strategy and accentuate the attachment of the Malays to the land.[123] When such schemes were first mooted in Pahang, the chairman of the State Development Board, later the 'father of development' of Malaysia, stressed their political dimension:

> the immense importance from the political point of view of initiating a scheme of this nature as it would serve as a tangible expression of the sincerity of the government to fulfil its promise to improve the social and economic conditions of the Malays and would counteract any feeling of despondency among them.[124]

The failure of many RIDA-financed schemes provoked a move away from self-help; though it aimed at fostering economic independence, it convinced many Malay politicians that they had to look to the state for the salvation of the kampong Malay.

This trend is clearly reflected in colonial government's most sustained attempt at 're-educating and remoulding the individual villager's thoughts and character' – the co-operative movement.[125] Indigenous forms of co-operative activities such as *berderau* were already less in evidence as wage labour became more common. The official co-operative movement began in the 1920s. It was hit by falling prices in the inter-war depression, and all but wiped out by the war. In Negri Sembilan, which had a strong tradition of communal life, there were in mid-1948 only 745 members of co-operatives.[126] Although the obduracy of the middle-men was often cited as the reason for this failure, British officials squarely blamed the 'racial characteristics' of the Malay peasants: their 'total lack of business ability'.[127] Certainly, few co-operatives owned transport; it remained firmly in non-Malay hands. Even when they did, private haulage companies could outbid them for produce, as they were licensed to travel further to the large urban markets where prices were much higher.[128] Chinese businesses were prepared to finance large temporary losses to break co-operatives. Competition was stiffest in rubber smallholding. When a scheme was mooted in Kuala Lumpur district, rubber dealers let it be known that they were prepared to sacrifice $100,000 on the 'struggle'.[129] Yet it is misleading to attribute the failures of

[123] Robert Ho, 'Land settlement projects in Malaya: an assessment of the role of the Federal Land Development Authority', *JTG*, 20 (1965), 1–15.

[124] Abdul Razak bin Hussein in 'Minutes of the first meeting of the Pahang State Development Board, 14.3.1951', DO Temerloh/80/51.

[125] 'Quarterly report for first quarter ending 31.3.1949, Selangor Inland Circle', Coop/432/46.

[126] 'Negri Sembilan - Quarterly Progress Reports for the period 1.4.30.6.1948', Coop/630/46.

[127] T. F. Carey to Deputy Chief Secretary, 9.5.1950, FS/12737/50.

[128] For example, Tasek Glugor Co-operative Society, *RIDA Monthly Bulletin*, 4 (November, 1951).

[129] DO Kuala Lumpur, 'Scheme for the purchase of latex from Malay rubber smallholders in Kuala Lumpur District by Mr. H. B. Talalla, JP', 24.7.1950, Sel Sec/1515/50.

the movement, as the British did, solely to peasant irrationality and thraldom to the middleman. The more perceptive observers admitted that 'it is idealistic to expect the producer, be he a member of a cooperative society bound in agreement to sell his product through his society or not, to be swayed by any motive than the expectation of getting as much money and as quickly as possible for his produce'.[130] Moreover, the western institutional nature of RIDA credit facilities were not consonant with traditional practices. Co-operative shops in Pekan, for example, had higher prices than their Chinese neighbours and insisted on cash payments. Rice milling co-operatives in Kelantan competed with small illegal mills brought in from Thailand, and in Malaya as a whole 95 per cent of mills remained in Chinese hands.[131] However, in retrospect, one co-operative officer noted that local contention between the primary producers' co-operative and the middle-man was inevitable and natural; its racial dimension, he stressed, was magnified by external political forces.[132]

This belief that co-operatives were sabotaged by communal interests disguised other weaknesses. Emergency food control and terrorist threats disrupted co-operative stores and their organisers. Farmers had problems accumulating capital, savings were difficult and few had coconuts or rubber to give in lieu of cash. Some co-operatives resorted to collecting two eggs daily, suggesting that the profits be invested in joint business ventures, or given as a subsidy to the poor.[133] Another problem was the moral unease that *riba*, or interest, was forbidden by the *shari'a*, especially after a 1952 ruling by the Mufti of Johore, and in places like Kedah where the religious men opposed to co-operatives were the natural leaders of the village community. Co-operation was a challenge to local leadership. Few *penghulus* were helpful. Instead, support for the movement was found amongst salaried men – Malay schoolteachers and police pensioners – and on occasion the valuable assistance of religious leaders was secured. Attempts at co-operative farming in the Krian area were attempted by the territorial chief of the Dindings, with group title held by the society, buying large areas of cultivated land that no Malay could cultivate individually.[134] Most of these schemes, although driven by rhetoric about the need for local initiative, were sponsored by the colonial government. It was, for many officials, missionary work. Much was made of successes of co-operation, in cases in which the role of government officers and Malay notables had been crucial to success.[135] Malay private businesses in Trengganu established latex collection centres, making profits on higher-grade rubber produced in bulk, paying smallholders the same price they would get for low-grade

---

[130] Mohamed Hussein bin Ibrahim, 'Marketing of rural produce', 19.4.1955, Coop/433/54/4.
[131] Tjoa Soei Hok, *Institutional background to modern economic and social development in Malaya (with special reference to the East Coast)* (Kuala Lumpur, 1963), p. 142.
[132] R. C. Gates to Robert Heussler, 31.5.1976, Heussler Papers.
[133] 'Quarterly progress report for Lower Perak co-operative circle, for period ending 31.3.1948', Coop/660/46.
[134] DO Krian, minute, 23.9.1950, Coop Krian North/36/50.
[135] Mohamed Hussein bin Ibrahim, 'Sungei Buloh Co-operative Rubber Marketing Society Ltd', 8.11.1952, Coop Tpg/62/47.

rubber they produced themselves. As the chances of failure in assisting commercial schemes were high, State governments distanced themselves from such concerns. Where they were successful, co-operatives provided the best means of lessening risk, and the best method of accumulation for small men with no business experience. Society meetings became a more general forum for the discussion of kampong affairs.[136] There were some successes with Malay women's co-operatives. For many years kampong women had been participating in the informal credit system of the *kuttu*. As a system of accumulating capital it was unsatisfactory, quarrels ensued when dishonesty appeared, and the system lost support to co-operatives.[137] The first women's co-operative to be registered was in Bagan Serai, Perak, where the women wished to be self-supporting with their own co-operative and their own rice fields. They were a mixture of ethnic Malay and Banjarese, and the community possessed relatively high levels of literacy. Homecraft and education were dominant themes.[138] In Malacca, another area of reasonable literacy, women made better co-operators than men: this was especially the case in areas like Naning where women had traditionally more influence in kampong affairs. By 1960 there were fifty-eight co-operatives for women, with an aggregate membership of 2,668. Most were small thrift societies, but there were also three weavers' societies, two land purchase societies, and one rice mill in Sungei Bayor, Perak. Most savings came out of saving from the family budget; development was qualitative rather than quantitative, and there was little borrowing for productive purposes.[139] Other success stories built on the rich traditions of *gotong-royong* that survived in west coast areas such as Ulu Langat in Selangor. Here *surau* were community centres for a patchwork of Indonesia settlers – Minangkabau, Kerinchi, Palembang and Javanese and the dominant Mandailing – whose recent migrant past had perhaps fortified a sense of collective enterprise. In 1951, co-operatives had 1,389 members out of a population of around 7,000. Yet here, the largest co-operative, the Ulu Langat Rubber Marketing Society, was divided by misunderstandings and inter-group rivalries; until 1953 the secretary ran it as a private firm.[140] The whole co-operative experience identified key weaknesses of Malays within the commercial economy. Political organisations began once again to fashion their own response to this. This reflected disenchantment with state agencies

---

[136] 'Quarterly report for quarter ending 3.6.1949, Malacca', Coop/670/47.

[137] For example in Padang Sebrang, Malacca, 'Quarterly report for quarter ending 31.3.1949, Malay Co-operative Officer Malacca'; 'Quarterly report on the activities of urban and rural co-operative societies in Malacca for the quarter ending 30.9.1949', *ibid.*

[138] Ahmad Tajuddin, 'Proposed formation of a Women's Seasonal Cooperative Credit Society, Ltd. at Simpang 4 Selinsing', 21.12.1946; Senior Malay Co-operative Officer, minute, 28.7.1947, Coop/1648/46.

[139] 'Quarterly report for quarter ending 31.3.1949', Coop/670/47; International Labour Office, Expanded Programme of Technical Assistance, *Report to the Government of the Federation of Malaya on the promotion and organization of co-operatives among women* (Geneva, 1963), pp. 7–8, 14–16.

[140] Laidin bin Alang Musa, 'The story of co-operative development in the Ulu Langat valley', *Malayan Cooperator Magazine*, 1, 3 (January 1955), 6–8.

such as RIDA. Musing on why the co-operatives had not caught on in spite of the co-operative principle in Malay customs, the Kuala Lumpur newspaper *Majlis* concluded that they had to be based on prevailing customs and not on European models.[141] New bodies began to emerge by the late 1950s such as farmers' associations which aimed to develop rural leadership and became an important counterpoint to the bureaucracy and formal development structures.[142]

A register of failure of agrarian improvement schemes was the rapid growth of a Malay wage labouring class. To some extent this was a deliberate consequence of colonial policy. As the Emergency broke, the government in Malaya were reminded by the Labour minister, David Rees-Williams, that the primary goals of policy were to extend representation, diversify the economy and 'industrialise' the Malays.[143] This process was accelerated by the post-war labour shortage, which led employers to seek to harness local, or failing that, Javanese labour. At the end of 1938 there were 21,000 Malays and Javanese employed, ten years later, 70,000, that is 20 per cent of estate labour. There were ambitious plans to combine recruitment with a land alienation scheme and actively foster a 'Malay middle class'.[144] The prospect of increased Javanese immigration to Malaya was less offensive to Malay interests than renewed Chinese or Indian immigration. However, the British hesitated to import volatile East Indies politics into the country.[145] The active role Indonesians played in Malay radical movements substantiated these fears. In the event, new sources of labour emerged within Malaya. The Emergency provided multiple opportunities for Malays to earn wages. In 1948 32,000 Malays were recruited into the security forces. Yet there was more to it than this. The increased tenancy and fluctuations in the international rubber market forced Malays on to the labour market.[146] In Malacca, although there was a decrease in the estate labour force at the outset of the Emergency – from 21,300 to 19,800 between the end of 1947 and the end of September 1948 – the number of Malays had increased by 600, and 500 of these were women. Opportunities, and wages, were higher in Johore and Negri Sembilan as planters attempted to recruit Malay labour in competition with the security forces. Here many smallholders had stopped tapping, and those in bad areas moved to safety, and the expansion of the security forces provided a cushion of profitable wage employment. By the early 1950s, there was a shortage of Chinese artisanal labour as workers fled to the jungle to evade the manpower regulations, at the same time as demands from the authorities for manual labour for resettlement and related schemes increased.[147] In industrial areas,

[141] *Majlis*, 10.11.1953.
[142] F. J. Fredericks, G. Kalshoven and T. R. V. Daane, *The role of farmers' associations in two paddy farming areas in West Malaysia* (Wageningen, 1980), pp. 11–17.
[143] Minute by David Rees-Williams, 27.5.1948, CO537/3746.
[144] *Malay Mail*, 29.4.1949.
[145] 'Labour population statistics'; John Jeff, 'Immigration of labourers', 13.7.1946, LAB/230/46.
[146] G. R. Percy to Chief Secretary, 13.10.1946, LAB/484/46.
[147] W. D. Drysdale to CLR, 7.12.1948, Controller of Labour (Malacca) 12/45.

such as Klang, Chinese factory owners developed a preference for Malay labour as a means of reducing union agitation.[148]

For Malays, wage labour involved a tremendous adjustment in patterns of work. As Malay estate workers in Perak, recruited from unemployed trishaw men in Malacca, remarked: 'when we were in Malacca all we had to do was pedal our trishaw. We could stop when we wanted to, eat when we wanted to . . . Here we must work hard for many hours in order to earn as much.'[149] When wages slumped, Malay labour on smallholdings dispersed back to the kampongs and on one Johore estate alone in October 1953, 180 labourers beat a retreat from wage employment.[150] Dublin estate in Kedah had recruited Malays – apparently political refugees from Thailand – but they found that earnings of two dollars a day could not meet their costs. Some turned up destitute at Jitra mosque; others pawned their jewellery to return home; others refused to move on after having worked for two years for nothing.[151] The stereotype of the Malays as unamenable to industrial work-discipline remained embedded in the colonial mind. However, by the early 1950s it had begun to break down. Selangor led the way in Malay employment, due, a survey suggested, to its 'progressive and hardworking' population of Indonesian migrants – Minangkabau and Palembang who launched themselves into the business opportunities of Kuala Lumpur.[152] In Selangor, Malays were proportionately better represented in the European industries, especially in the processing of agricultural products, comprising around 16 per cent of the workforce, as opposed to only 9 per cent in the non-European sector which comprised twice as many factories, almost all of them Chinese-owned. Employers remarked that with 'kind but firm' handling, they were excellent industrial operatives: 'once the beauty of the work is appreciated the Malay labourers will stick to it'. Women were at the forefront of this change. Men had led the rush to the cities, but as urban earnings were insufficient to support large families, wives and daughters were forced into the labour market. They preferred factory work, as this left the evenings free for domestic work. Factory work accounted for 42 per cent of Malay women in all places of work in Selangor. 'Frankly speaking,' remarked one employer, 'the Malay women work harder than the men. Their aptitude for work is greater.' This post-war trend was encouraged by high levels of divorce. The benefits were not large. It was discovered that the Malay factory worker consumed only 1,500 calories instead of the required 2,500–3,000, and the food they ate had insufficient nutrients. 'The Malays cannot be branded as lazy. The fact is the Malays in the majority of cases are underfed; consequently they cannot work vigorously at a stretch. Guide the Malays to take a complete and balanced diet and the Malays of the next generation will surely be able to withstand longer hours of hard work.' By 1951 half of the Malay population of

[148] ACL Klang to Deputy Commissioner, Selangor, 28.11.1947, LAB/154/47.
[149] LDMR, April 1949, FS/13151/49.
[150] 'Monthly report for October 1953 – North Johore', LDM/27/53.
[151] DCL Bentong, 'Monthly report for May 1950'; June 1950, BA Pahang/24/50.
[152] Laidin bin Alang Musa, 'The background to the Ulu Langat valley in Selangor', *Malayan Historical Journal*, 2, 1 (1955), 8–11.

Selangor were wage earners, and more than 68 per cent of urban Malays were employed either directly or indirectly by government departments.[153]

Individual responses to the call of wage labour, by themselves, were insufficient by themselves to break down larger patterns of economic inequity. A theme of village anthropologies of the 1950s and 1960s, even those of areas of high security force recruitment and proximity to Kuala Lumpur, is the reluctance of Malays to unquestioningly embrace the values of the city and their desire to retain a foothold in village life. In Jenderam in Selangor, for example, there was no sharp transition to city life for Malays who had already been exposed to the cash economy for a long period. They already possessed a wide experience of towns of intermediate size, settlements that grew rapidly in this period. Yet they still made a clear distinction between the values of the *orang kampong* and those of the city dweller, the *orang môden*. It was retained amongst those who migrated to the city to *cari makan*. Amongst these people, the fiction of eventual return remained powerful.[154] This scepticism towards the stability of wage employment was entirely rational in a time of great upheaval and political uncertainty. It did not signify a resistance to change, rather a profound concern at its direction and its morality.

Nor, conversely, did initiatives at a local level meet with a unified response from communities that were ceasing to reflect the idealised norms of kampong life that these schemes attempted to preserve. Some British officials recognised this. Their main preoccupation was self-help, and this made them sceptical about RIDA. Not only was it a political creation, but it was also constructed on the wrong principles for inspiring the cultivator to help himself. Dato Onn himself became increasingly negative about his accomplishments. However, from the debates surrounding rural development, several strands of thought emerged. One was a kind of state paternalism, to which British officials and men such as Dato Onn subscribed. It was to have an enduring effect on bureaucratic attitudes. Yet in tandem with this, the experience of RIDA – the public expectations of it, and later disappointments with it – had also intensified indigenous debates on economic advancement. These pre-dated RIDA and were bound up with broader political struggles. The Malay press became increasingly contemptuous of RIDA in general and Onn in particular. RIDA was staffed by inexperienced government servants who knew little of business: 'they want to teach the Malays to do something which they do not know how to do'.[155] This critique had its roots within the Muslim entrepreneurial and literary classes of the towns, in their disdain of colonial protection and the assumptions of the Malay character that went with it. Much of the criticism of colonial development policy was articulated in

[153] Abdul Khalid bin Abdul Osman, 'Survey of Malays as factory workers in Selangor', 10.1.1952, DCL Sel/174/51; 'Preliminary report: the Malay wage-earners economy survey', 28.6.1951, DCL Sel/169/51.
[154] E.g. Peter J. Wilson, *A Malay village and Malaysia: social values and rural development* (New Haven, 1967), pp. 39–48; M. G. Swift, *Malay peasant society in Jelebu* (London, 1965), pp. 157, 161.
[155] *Utusan Melayu*, 11.8.1952.

communal terms, but also there were those who rejected colonial policy on the basis of wider, class solidarities. In the face of agrarian change, and the questions of identity to which they gave rise, nationalist leaders were mooting larger initiatives to reconstruct the Malay economic community. A wide spectrum of ideas were floated for them to draw upon. In the new prescriptions that emerged, the role of the state loomed large. This was because during the Emergency it was seen to be a decisive arbiter of social conditions. In the face of British failures, Malay politicians were arguing for its power to be harnessed in a new direction. However, they were as divided as their erstwhile colonial masters as to the ways in which it might be wielded.

'Wake up and be active'

Malay cultivators had always been responsive to the effects of changing market conditions on their livelihood. What was new about the post-war period was the degree to which Malay elites politicised their predicament. The various movements of economic uplift that emerged after the war are indicative of a mounting appreciation of Malay weakness in the commercial economy. The new conception of the state that arose in the Emergency years invigorated the debate on the economic position of the Malays. Yet it was a potentially divisive debate for the Malay political community. Entrenched local elites, it has been suggested, were in an advantageous position to benefit both from the economic opportunities of commercialisation in the rural economy, and from the patronage of State governments. From the political perspective of the centre, both UMNO and its rivals saw programmes of rural development, which could challenge these interests, as a means of establishing a mass base on the eve of the introduction of electoral politics. Yet the co-operation of the powerful local intermediaries would also be necessary in the coming struggle. Therefore nationalist politicians were careful to voice their demands in broad corporatist terms. Yet this too was problematical. The political realities of constitutional politics meant that there was a need to balance an appeal to communal interest with a constructive approach to inter-communal partnership. This section examines these dilemmas of development and the shaping of a *bumiputera* ideology that was to underpin the political economy of independent Malaya.

At an early stage of the Emergency the position of the Malays in the economy was written into debates on citizenship and the constitution. The question dominated the Malay nationalists' accommodation with Chinese leaders. A meeting in August 1948 between British officials and Malay leaders, called under the shadow of Dato Onn's threat to move into active opposition to the government, discussed ways in which the Malays could take a fuller part in the economic life of the country. The British were told that 'until the middle range was shared by Malays, there would be little real advantage in their providing administrative officers and labourers, for without economic security political power would be of little avail'.[156] The Colonial Office was

---

[156] 'Meeting called by H. E. the OAG at Carcosa on 10.8.1948', CO537/3756.

alarmed at the course the debate had taken. They felt that Malcolm MacDonald, the man primarily responsible for driving forward the policy of political development, 'seems to have gone to the limit of concession to Malay special interests'.[157] These 'special interests' were to become more explicitly defined during the proceedings of the Communities' Liaison Committee (CLC). The Committee was mooted at the height of the *hartal* action against the Federation in 1948. A Straits Chinese schoolteacher, Thio Chan Bee, was later to claim that he took the initiative in working to bring Tan Cheng Lock and Dato Onn together. He sought the mediation of Malcolm MacDonald to do so and the two leaders, together with other leading Chinese and Malays, met informally at Dato Onn's house in Johore Bahru on 29 December 1948. During the meeting, frank exchanges took place during which Malay leaders brought forward the principles on which they felt Sino–Malay accommodation might be reached. 'The Chinese,' they argued, 'have economic power. The Malays now have political power. If the Chinese will help the Malays to rise economically, then surely the Malays must share with the Chinese their political power.'[158] Further, more substantive meetings took place in Penang in January 1949, in which the CLC expanded to include Malay representatives from the north of the peninsula who did not attend the original meeting, and the Ceylonese, E.E.C. Thuraisingham, who acted as chairman. It set a precedent by which the cardinal principles of public policy would be composed by a process of bargaining in private, and then marketed for popular opinion. The Committee's main goal was to reach an accord on the burning political question of citizenship rights for the Chinese. We shall consider this in a later chapter. From the outset, the price of political compromise was calculated in the economic advancement of the Malays.

During the Committee's crucial meetings in Penang in December 1949, Dato Panglima Bukit Gantang of Perak was one of the most vociferous of the Malays in demanding a proper share in the economic life of the country. A Chinese member observed that he 'appeared to think that the implementation of this policy should have priority to the consideration of the citizenship question and other political matters'.[159] Indeed, the early proceedings of the Committee were dominated by attacks by Malay leaders on the 'systematic corruption' of Chinese business. Chinese economic success, it was argued, had been achieved at the expense of the rural Malays, especially through Chinese control of transport and manipulation of licensing. What then was the measure of equity? Tables of formulae were drawn up, such as a 51:49 parity for ownership of transport in Malay areas.[160] The Chinese members pleaded that it was beyond their capacity as individuals to deliver a remedy to the problem. They blamed economic imbalance on the British, and both communities looked to the British to provide an answer for it. The government announced steps to 'improve the social and

---

[157] J. B. Williams, minute, 4.9.1948, *ibid.*
[158] Thio Chan Bee, *The extraordinary adventures of an ordinary man* (London, 1977), pp. 80–8.
[159] Tan Cheng Lock to Yong Shook Lin, 19.1.1950, SP.13/A/19.
[160] 'Notes of discussions of the Communities' Liaison Committee held at Kuala Lumpur, 18–19.2.1949', TCL/23/2, ISEAS.

economic well-being of the Malays, with the object of ensuring their full participation in the economic life of the Federation', and recommended the establishment of a Malay Affairs Development Board.[161] Indeed, one of the Committee's concrete achievements was the establishment of RIDA, the announcement of which was timed, at the suggestion of Dato Onn, at the moment that UMNO was asked to accept the recommendations on citizenship drafted by the Committee. In the later words of the Chinese newspaper, *Kwong Wah Yit Poh*: 'What is holding back political organisation is the unequal political status of the Chinese and the unbalanced economic status of the Malays. This problem will be solved if the Malays assist the non-Malays in their fight for equal citizenship rights, and the non-Malays help the Malays to improve their economic position.'[162]

As political pressures grew on the dominant Chinese and Malay interests to weld themselves into an inter-communal alliance to prepare to receive power, a new principle of state-building was accepted by both parties. It has been argued that the economic vision of the CLC was essentially capitalist; that it was the direct precursor of the New Economic Policy of the 1970s and 1980s and that, in the long term, it undermined the status of the Malayan Chinese.[163] This is perhaps a little misleading. At this point it was unclear as to what the agreement actually entailed in practice, and this was the focus of a growing divergence of opinion both between and within ethnic communities. A case in point was the controversy over a $500,000 gift from the Chinese to the Malays. Malcolm MacDonald planted the idea in the mind of Tan Cheng Lock that such a gesture would be a welcome token of good faith, 'as long as the generous financial offer does not appear to be a political bribe'.[164] Tan reassured him that to unselfishly help others was 'the essence of the teachings of Bishop Butler and Lau Tze'.[165] This was a little disingenuous. The intellectual foundations of Tan Cheng Lock's approach to the economic position of the Malays were steeped in Social Darwinism. 'Inferior races,' he argued in 1949, 'are raised by living in political union with races intellectually superior. Exhausted and decaying races are revived by the contact of a younger vitality.'[166] In view of this, it is unsurprising that the gift was viewed with great hostility by many sections of Malay opinion. Moreover, although the intention was to keep the gift non-political, as the sponsors Lee Rubber insisted, the issue became drawn into the political disputes that were opening up within UMNO itself. In particular, Dato Onn's insistence that the money be administered by RIDA was fodder to the growing body of his critics. After Onn left UMNO in mid-

---

[161] 'Statement of the Communities' Liaison Committee', SP.13/A/64.

[162] *Kwong Wah Yit Poh*, 17.3.1953.

[163] Heng Pek Koon, *Chinese politics in Malaysia: a history of the Malaysian Chinese Association* (Singapore, 1988), pp. 151–4.

[164] MacDonald to Tan Cheng Lock, 1.4.1951, TCL/4/1.

[165] Tan Cheng Lock to MacDonald, 20.4.1951, TCL/4/la.

[166] Tan Cheng Lock, *One country, one people, one government: Presidential address by Tan Cheng Lock at a meeting of the General Committee of the MCA held in Penang on 30 October, 1949* (Kuala Lumpur, 1949), p. 2.

1951, the work of the CLC came to an end. Its debates were reopened as UMNO's new leadership sought common ground with the MCA. They became more deeply politicised, and were voiced in several ways.

The first was the formation, in December 1952, of a government Special Committee on Malay Participation in Commerce and Industry. Its chairman was the Dato Panglima Bukit Gantang, Mentri Besar of Perak, a close associate of Dato Onn, and a central figure in orchestrating opposition to the inter-communal Alliance which emerged to challenge Dato Onn's new Independence of Malaya Party. Dato Onn and many of those who had followed him into his new party, most of them senior officials, dominated the Special Committee. They were dismayed at the rapid compromises that were being made by UMNO as it sought alliance with the MCA. They favoured a slower approach to independence, and tended towards the view that independence should be postponed until a greater level of economic parity had been achieved. The statements of Bukit Gantang are illuminating. For Bukit Gantang the claims of the Malays to a more equitable stake in the commercial economy were rooted in history as their forefathers had been great traders throughout Asia. However, in the modern period Malay leaders had failed the community.[167] It was their duty to brook no compromise until a remedy to this had been achieved. There could be no political equality, no concession of Malay political privileges, no 'Malayan' nation, without economic equality.[168] However, Bukit Gantang also recognised that the solution to the problems of Malays was inseparable from the general economic framework:

> No doubt Malays should be encouraged to turn to business and the lucky and able ones would make a success of it. But unless non-Malay businessmen are discriminated against there can be no hope of the Malays as a racial group making a success in a competitive economy . . . The Malays must certainly get more of the wealth of this country than they do now, but this they can get only as part of a general economic programme to better the lot of all under-privileged.[169]

Bukit Gantang articulated a central dilemma in Malay thought towards the Malay economic predicament. It recognised the need for the community to strengthen itself internally, by its own efforts, but, at the same time, the leaders immersed in these debates were seduced by the promise of the resources of the state that soon would be at their disposal to assist them to achieve this end.

One position, then, articulated in many newspapers and public forums, was based on unswerving communal solidarity. In this rhetoric, Malay progress was obstructed by outside interests: the colonial government, Chinese and Indian middle-men had subverted the historical heritage of the Malays as traders. In the colonial period, the Malays had been treated as 'mere tools for obtaining raw materials, while the work of marketing the raw materials is done by the other races'. In commerce and transportation, Malay industry had been throttled by prohibitive monopolies.[170] The Malays lived in a state of 'economic suppression' by other interests. They were under siege

---

[167] *Warta Negara*, 11.12.1952.   [168] *Malay Mail*, 4.12.1952.
[169] *Singapore Standard*, 5.12.1952.   [170] *Majlis*, 21.3.1953.

and the siege had to be lifted. This had to be done immediately, before the free-for-all of open competition that would follow independence; it would be far more difficult for the Malays to free themselves thereafter. The struggle for freedom from 'economic chains', therefore, took precedence over the struggle for political *merdeka*.[171] Government assistance would be useless without action against middle-men. In this critique the obligation on the Chinese to assist the Malay *bumiputera* was neither philanthropic, nor political, but absolute: 'The trust of the Malays in the Chinese could not be bought with money . . . The best way for the Chinese to gain the confidence of the Malays is to leave these things alone. They should acknowledge that the administration of the country is the absolute right of the Malays.'[172]

Significantly, the deliberations of the Bukit Gantang Committee began as the post-Korean war slump placed Malay inroads into the commercial economy in jeopardy. It was showered with memoranda demanding economic safeguards for the Malays: UMNO branches called for 50 per cent quotas, and Malay business preserves in the towns. The Selangor *Ketua Kampong* Association's memorandum to the Committee demanded that aliens be barred from Malay kampongs.[173] *Sarekat* – such as the 'Sharikat Pekan Rabu' in Alor Star – demanded all the above, together with the abolition of RIDA conditions on loans.[174] The Kelantan Malay Chamber of Commerce saw a 50 per cent stake in the import–export trade as essential, as well as a Malay commercial bank sponsored by the government, and courts of arbitration in all states to safeguard Malay interests.[175] For *Melayu Raya* – a major voice in the debate – it was the import–export trade that would 'test the sincerity of the promises made by the non-Malays to give the Malays economic aid'.[176] As Dato Onn and his Party Negara veered to a more hardline advocacy of Malay rights it took up many of these demands – for example in proposing that Malays receive 51 per cent of transport licences in areas where they were dominant, and 49 per cent where they were not, through state aid.[177] It found allies in a range of splinter parties that broke away from UMNO, disenchanted with its policy of compromise.

Yet there was another school of thought. It was most clearly reflected in the pages of the more radically inclined Malay newspaper, *Utusan Melayu*. From this perspective, 'not even legislation will help the Malays to improve their economic position if they do not change their habits and attitude'.[178] This line of argument can be traced back to the first discussions of the problem in the pre-war vernacular newspapers. Although the paper at times responded to the public mood by calling on businesses which have connections with the Malays to be given to Malays, especially in government contract work, it was prepared to see the problem in much broader terms:

---

[171] 'Let us free ourselves', *Warta Negara*, 23.2.1954.
[172] *Melayu Raya*, 2.2.1953.   [173] Reported in *China Press*, 31.12.1952.
[174] *Utusan Melayu*, 24.1.1953.   [175] *Utusan Melayu*, 15.1.1953.
[176] *Melayu Raya*, 16.1.1953.   [177] *Malay Mail*, 8.4.1954.
[178] 'Change our Attitude', *Utusan Melayu*, 25.2.1953.

To improve the living conditions of the Malays does not rest on legislation to create a group of Malay capitalists, Malay banks and Malay merchants in order to compete with foreign capitalists which already have a strong foundation in this country. By asking for special legislation to control the rise of one group of Malay capitalists, it will mean that we will only cause a clash because such legislation may be meat for community and poison for another.[179]

Utusan Melayu – in a clear attack on Bukit Gantang, Dato Onn and the IMP – was also deeply suspicious of the defence of Malay rights by vested interests. As an editorial put it:

Besides the Rulers, Datos, Territorial Chiefs and high Malay officials totalling not more than one thousand, we cannot completely see what 'Malay rights' are all about . . . The truth is what is regarded as the 'rights' of the Malays is only a dream. The sooner we forget about our 'rights' and work very hard to improve ourselves, the sooner will we Malays be recognized by the World.[180]

The Malay elite had failed the community in this respect. Their obligation was to the welfare of the Malay farmers, who constituted the bulk of the Malay population. Yet they were the products of colonial education; they had adopted a 'discriminate evaluation of anything connected with the interests of the masses', and, in their frustration, had 'shut themselves in their rooms'.[181] Malay businesses came under critical scrutiny – especially those in the crucial transport sector – and their internal weaknesses were exposed. *Utusan Melayu* reported that the six Malay bus companies that had come to their attention were all running at a loss. Shareholders would claim excessive privileges; drivers, often relatives of the directors, would take liberties. 'The fault with Malay business is that sentiment is allowed to interfere with discipline.'[182]

It was a clarion call to the Malays to 'Wake up and be active'. A wide range of grass-roots efforts were launched to stimulate the Malay economy. The All-Malaya Islamic Association announced that it was launching a company at Morib with capital of $50,000 to engage in agriculture, rearing of livestock, handicrafts and tailoring. The Selangor *Ketua Kampong* Association announced a similar scheme at Tanjong Karang, and both looked to employ Malay ex-detainees.[183] The *Ketua Kampong* association held a round-table conference in April 1953 that established a Selangor Malay Economic Committee. It identified transportation as the key interest to be secured by the Malays, but also evinced a direct interest in establishing printing and farming companies. Branches were established in places such as Tanjong Karang; it produced a 'Business Guide' for would-be entrepreneurs and formed a Malay businessmen's association in September, with the radical journalist Abdul Aziz bin Ishak as President. With support from the *Majlis* newspaper and the Malacca Malay Chamber

---

[179] 'Improve the living conditions of the Malay', *Utusan Melayu*, 4.5.1953.
[180] *Utusan Melayu*, 25.9.1952.
[181] 'Appeal to educated Malays', *Utusan Melayu*, 3.6.1953.
[182] *Utusan Melayu*, 26.3.1953.   [183] *Utusan Melayu*, 23.1.1953.

of Commerce, there were attempts to set up a national body.[184] Private companies issued shares exclusively to Malays: for example, a Kelantan concern of Mahmood Mahyiddeen's and Tenaga Ra'ayat Ltd, which wanted to mine in Malay Reservations with the consent of the owners. Its policy was to issue shares only to Malays, except in special circumstances, and it provoked a debate as to whether the company was a 'Malay' under the Malay Reservations Enactment.[185] There were attempts to form or revive Malay Chambers of Commerce. Smallholders' associations – for example in Johore and Negri Sembilan – were formed to bring a new impetus to problems of marketing and replanting. For example, a smallholders' association in Gunong Semanggol, the scene of earlier experiments in developing the Malay economy, established a limited company in March 1953.[186] A Malay graduate from India, Haji Mokhtar bin Haji Ismail – a State Councillor and an Islamic scholar – planned a Malay colony on Gandhian lines at Sungei Chuckok, in Kangar, Perlis. This *Sharikat Pembinaan Kampong dan Pakebunan Melayu* allotted each Malay member ten *rulongs*, seven of them for rubber.[187] Some of these locally devised forms of co-operative enterprise horrified administrators, such as the appearance of *sarekat tani* – land companies – in Selangor, Perak and Malacca. The Malay press spoke of the dishonesty and collapse of some of these *sarekat*, including one run by religious men. Officials stressed that these were capitalist and not co-operative ventures, and a propaganda campaign was directed against them.[188] However, their reappearance is significant in that they were a revival of the experiments by the Malay left prior to the Emergency to establish broad-based peasants' movements. Ulu Langat in Selangor had been a centre of this activity, and there remained political opposition there to official co-operatives.[189] On 23 August 1953, a Malay Farmers' Congress was held at Kepala Batas in Province Wellesley, sponsored by the Malay Association of Province Wellesley. This area was to become a heartland for support for the Islamic Association. Its chairman, Tuan Haji Zabidi bin Haji Ali, demanded protection for Malay tenant farmers, land redistribution, and agreed to co-operate with the Labour Party towards these goals.[190] Parallel economic development committees were formed by political organisations.

The Bukit Gantang Report incompletely reflected these aspirations. However, the interventionist mood of the committee succeeded in alarming the only non-Asian member, the Member for Economic Affairs, O. A. Spenser.[191] It suggested that at least $15 million be spent 'to help the Malays take a full part in the economic life of

---

[184] *Utusan Melayu*, 29.9.1953; *Majlis*, 'Malay economy', 5.5.1953, 29.9.1953.
[185] 'Prospectus of Malay Realty and Development Corporation Ltd.', 27.2.1952, CS/8715/52; Idris Hakim to State Secretary Selangor, 29.11.1949; minute, 17.1.1950, Sel Sec/2752/49.
[186] *Warta Negara*, 31.3.1953.   [187] *Straits Echo*, 12.8.1952.
[188] 'A matter relating to some Malay co-operative shops', *Majlis*, 3.12.1947.
[189] 'Progress report of rural co-operative societies in Selangor, 1.10.1945–30.9.1947', Coop/ 432/46.
[190] *Utusan Melayu*, 25.8.1953, 27.8.1953.
[191] Spenser to Paskin, 24.4.1953, CO1022/463.

the country', such as in commercial training and the establishment of marketing boards for kampong produce.[192] It was apparent that many Malay leaders were looking, not to the kampongs, but to Malay business to revitalise the community. And it was the question of quotas in employment, 'feather-bedding' as it was called, which drew powerful resistance from commercial lobbies.[193] The report of the Special Committee was quietly shelved, and an exploratory White Paper on the transport industry was published. Transport interests pleaded with the government to resist the intrusion of politics into business.[194] Most British administrators were convinced that guaranteed preferential awards of contracts and employment were not the way to bring Malays into business, and favoured a longer-term approach through trade apprenticeships. In Bukit Gantang's Perak, however, pressure from Malay politicians led to the introduction of a prototype scheme for contracting and licensing, whereby Malay contractors were circulated before tenders were made public. This was done in the face of recognition that labour quotas tied the hands of Malay businessmen, that government would not get the cheapest price, and that there were insufficient Malay contractors to make the scheme operable. A committee appointed by the Perak State government to consider greater participation by Malays in the field of business undertook special projects such as the training of Malay mining *kepalas*, and the acquisition of a prime site in Ipoh for shophouses for Malay businesses, allocated through a process of natural selection.[195] British officials were furious. One District Officer lamented the 'repeated signs that the Malays are demanding privileges for themselves which are far in excess of anything under hated "colonialism"!!' and forecast the demise of their culture and heritage.[196] In Perak also, embryonic 'Ali-Baba' concerns arose, in which rubber dealers' licences were sold by Malays to Chinese or passed to Chinese managers. It was an effortless method of making money, although in practice it was difficult to decide who was servant and who was master.[197] In Kuala Lumpur, Malay members of the Municipality campaigned for more market stalls for Malays, but they were rented to Chinese friends. A prominent member of the Selangor Businessman's Association, the editor of the *Panduan Rakyat*, Ramly bin Tahir, warned that 'the Malays should not be permitted to become profiteers', and there was friction within the UMNO and MCA Alliance in the city over allocation of vacant stalls in Central Market.[198]

In the eye of this storm of speculation, the Sino-Malay consensus of the

---

[192] *Malay Mail*, 4.3.1954.

[193] 'The economic position of the Malays: summary of the views of the Associated Chinese and Indian Chambers of Commerce and the F.M.S. Chamber of Commerce', SP.3/A/100.

[194] *Malay Mail*, 10.3.1954.

[195] E. K. Fisk, reported in 'Minutes of the 35th meeting of the State Development Board, Perak, 14.6.1956', DO Larut/134/55.

[196] Marginal note by DO Larut, on 'Preferential awards of tenders for works to Malay contractors', Larut/102/56.

[197] *Malay Mail*, 8.4.1954; DO Larut to Mentri Besar, Perak, 2.3.1956, DO Larut/102/56.

[198] *Malay Mail*, 6.3.1954, 30.3.1954; *Majlis*, 17.10.1953.

Communities' Liaison Committee was shaken. An early warning of trouble was the departure of Dato Onn from UMNO in mid-1951, which in itself was provoked by a groundswell of internal opposition to his conciliatory policy towards non-Malay interests. The new leader, Tunku Abdul Rahman, had not been a member of the Committee and clearly felt that he was not bound by its decisions. Sino-Malay understanding had to be renegotiated. However, as the new leadership forged its own alliance with the MCA through a series of round-table meetings, they had, as had their predecessors, to reconcile the burgeoning demands of Malay indiginism with the *Realpolitik* of inter-racial accommodation. At a meeting on 3 March 1953 that began this process, UMNO and MCA leaders again immediately focused on the question of the Malay economy. Tan Cheng Lock reminded UMNO that the real responsibility for the economic plight of the Malays lay with the British. 'The Chinese were the country's retailers,' he admitted, 'but if the British big businesses wanted to, they could pass the retail trade onto the Malays tomorrow.' He argued that the Malays would be rich if there were twenty Malay millionaires. His son, Tan Siew Sin, went further: the Chinese too were poor and faced 'not only political but economic extinction'.[199] This position of anti-colonial solidarity proved to be a basis on which accommodation with UMNO leadership could be reached during a period of turbulent politics in 1953 and 1954. To this we shall return in a later chapter. At this point it is important to note that in the light of the Bukit Gantang Committee it was recognised that a common position on the economy had to be clearly formulated. The fact that its members were in opposition to UMNO made the UMNO leaders deeply suspicious of its recommendations. Under these circumstances, its approach to Malay betterment read like a subterfuge to put independence on a slower track. This brought the UMNO-MCA alliance together. 'Compelling people to employ others,' Tunku Abdul Rahman conceded, 'might have been alright forty years ago. Today compulsion was most undesirable.'[200]

The famous communal bargain that emerged from these discussions was an equivocal one. Although the answer for UMNO did not lie in individual accumulation of wealth, the party committed itself to wider government intervention in the marketing of rural products, education, training, and in quotas in employment.[201] MCA leaders such as Leong Yew Koh were more sceptical. In a crucial memorandum on the question of economic assistance to the Malays – a response to the UMNO position – he argued that 'hard work and actual participation' were the only ways to fit Malays for business. 'Malays,' he added, 'are very often tempted to take short cuts to wealth.' Yet he also accepted the need for a commercial equivalent of Malay Reservations in land.[202] In the discussions of a common election platform, the MCA succeeded in muting much of UMNO interventionism. The principle of Malay

[199] *Malayan Mirror*, I, 2 (28.6.1953).
[200] 'Sixth informal meeting of UMNO and MCA representatives held at 11 Heeren Street, Malacca on 8.5.1953', SP.3/A/100.
[201] 'UMNO - A memorandum on the economic position of the Malays', UMNO/SEL/28/53.
[202] Leong Yew Koh, 'Memorandum on economic aid to Malays', TCL/9/2, ISEAS.

economic advancement was conceded. However, as politicians worked to achieve this, elements of the old paternalism survived. Economic redistribution in the widest sense was ruled out: more limited internal readjustments became the presiding objective. During the final stages of decolonisation, the ambiguity of the Alliance bargain came under direct attack. Advanced as a means of accommodating the political demands of the Malayan Chinese to the entrenched political privileges of the Malays, the acceptance of their special economic rights could only be guaranteed by the maintenance of that political dominance. In seeking to rid itself of 'national stigma' through the strengthening of the community initiative in commercial life, Malay opinion looked increasingly to the assistance of the state. The promise of the transfer of power brought assured administrative capacity, and with this came patronage. In 1955, a Singapore journalist, S. Rajaratnam, expanded on this argument:

> The underlying assumption seems to be that the economic lot of the Malays should be improved by fostering a Malay capitalism . . . In theory it is possible to create a Malay capitalism. But in practice this can be done, paradoxically enough, only by resorting to 'uncapitalistic' methods. The State must forego its neutrality and intervene in favour of one group of capitalists against another . . . A Malay capitalism molly-coddled by the State will remain feeble and inefficient because the only stimulus to efficiency – the threat of being ousted by a stronger competitor – would have been removed. The Malay capitalist would expect the State to intervene to protect him against a strong rival.[203]

This central paradox of Malaysian political life was later acknowledged in the constitutional entrenchment of the status of the *bumiputera*.[204] It was a product of a period of social change which revealed, to both the British and Malay politicians and opinion-makers, that the long and intermittent engagement by the Malays with the commercial economy had become an irreversible process. It exposed the growing disparity of economic interests within the Malay community itself as much as between ethnic groups. However, the advent of the *bumiputera* was to become the touchstone of post-colonial state-building.

The experience of the Orang Asli

The cumulative impact of rural violence, and the ideological pressures of the ethnic mobilisation of the economy, can be measured in the predicament of the Orang Asli during the Emergency. Before the outbreak of the rebellion the Orang Asli, most vulnerable to upheaval and violence in the forest, were drawn increasingly into larger relations of trade and labour with those exploiting its resources. Most easily unsettled by the uncertainties of these new relationships, they were to bear the brunt of rural terror. The battle for the forests compelled Orang Asli communities not only to face the internal trauma of terror, but often clumsy attempts by the government to recruit

---

[203] 'Malay capitalists', *Raayat*, I, 5 (10.1.1955).
[204] Gordon P. Means, ' "Special rights" as a strategy for development: the case of Malaysia', *Comparative Politics* (1973), 29–61.

non-Communist leadership in a period when the Orang Asli were most exposed to confrontation with insurgents. Recruited by both sides in the guerrilla war, they were as communities the most internally torn by the moral trauma of terror, and as victims of both terror and counter-terror, gained the least security from its containment. State-building intruded into the forests in the form of resettlement, which had tragic effects on many communities removed from the forest, but also in the shape of colonial outposts in the forest which changed the life of those that remained. The culmination of these encounters was a massive enlargement of scale of the social life of the Orang Asli. Treated almost solely as an adjunct to the problem of counter-insurgency, the debate over their rights to traditional lands was to mark their future position, and is illustrative of the new dispensation of economy and society to which the Emergency had given birth.[205]

The full extent of the violence inflicted on the Orang Asli remains unclear as is their participation in it. A new study has sought to uncover the depth of their involvement in the violence. It seeks to challenge anthropological assumptions about their pacific nature, especially the 'myth' of the non-violent Semoi, and highlight the active violence through which they responded to the Emergency.[206] Yet there is a danger that one 'myth' may be replaced by another. Terror divided all communities. It divided the Orang Asli in ways that are still inadequately understood. They came under immense pressure to take up arms against wayward members of their own communities. Here, violence – or the problem of evil – was particularly disruptive of social life, and this has yet to be the subject of an anthropological study. The guerrillas were *orang jahat* – evil ones – of whom many Orang Asli lived in terror. In one incident alone, thirty-four Orang Asli working on the Boh Tea plantation in the Cameron Highland were strangled by a gang of forty terrorists in August 1949.[207] A recently published eyewitness account has described the massacre of virtually an entire village in Ulu Kenyor in 1950.[208] There were revenge attacks on Chinese: for example, after murders of Orang Asli in Kampong Kikai, Perak fourteen Chinese were killed in a nearby village.[209] Although Orang Asli ex-guerrillas formed the backbone of an Orang Asli anti-terrorist force, the *senoi pra'aq*, their employment as trackers and guides was marked by a reluctance to create unsettled conditions in their own neighbourhoods.[210] Dyak trackers from Borneo had an undeserved reputation for

[205] See T. N. Harper. 'The politics of the forest in colonial Malaya', *Modern Asian Studies*, 31, 1 (1997), 1–29.

[206] John D. Leary, *Violence and the dream people: the Orang Asli in the Malayan Emergency, 1948–1960* (Athens, Ohio, 1995).

[207] *Malay Mail*, 22.8.1949. For newspaper citations I am indebted to Colin Nicholas, et al. (eds), *Orang Asli in the news* (Kuala Lumpur, 1989).

[208] 'Massacre at Ulu Kenyor', *Pernloi Gah: Orang Asli news*, 1 (December, 1990).

[209] Gurbey to Creech Jones, 16.7.1949, CO537/5985.

[210] John Leary, *The importance of the Orang Asli in the Malayan Emergency, 1948–1960* (Centre of Southeast Asian Studies, Monash, Working Paper No. 56, 1989), pp. 17–20; Alun Jones, 'The Orang Asli: an outline of their progress in modern Malaya', *Journal of Southeast Asian History*, 19 (1968), 301.

head-hunting that may have attached itself to Orang Asli troops. The Europeans who liaised between the Orang Asli and the security forces were simultaneously their protectors, and actively prosecuting a counter-insurgency war. The two roles were not always compatible. Informal bargains were made where the peace would be kept in return for information. These were often broken. Officials recorded grim testimonies of physical abuse and feared that more would come to light.[211] Confronted with such traumas it is unsurprising that the loyalty of many communities was uncertain, and that perhaps in some cases traditional leadership was in disarray. Solidarities that had emerged in the war were not easily broken. The MCP portrayed themselves to the Orang Asli as the victorious party in the Japanese war. In many places the guerrillas remained the only form of external authority, and their agents were experienced jungle traders. Their influence was institutionalised in *asal* clubs, organised on a *saka*, or hereditary territory, basis – a technique imparted by the anthropologist Pat Noone during the war. Their propaganda invested the Orang Asli with the status of legitimate heirs to the land, and exploited the British association with Malay State administrations to discredit colonial rule.[212] British intelligence reports credited the MCP with completely dominating Temiar communities in north and west Kelantan in 1951–2. There the Orang Asli acted as guides and cultivators; each village had an elected committee under MCP supervision, which discussed changes to custom, in which elementary Communist theory was expounded.[213]

The reintroduction of colonial authority into the forest was a protracted process. The social cost of military attacks was immense. The resettlement policies pursued by the British government had tragic effects. The psychological trauma and weakening of health involved in moving a highland population to insanitary and cramped conditions in the lowlands, on an unfamiliar diet, broke down natural checks on disease and claimed the lives of hundreds of Orang Asli. When Semai from the Ulu Bertam and Sungei Jeklai regions settled in the Bukit Betong area, there were 213 deaths to only 38 births in the fifteen months between November 1949 and January 1951 only twenty-four of whom were over the age of fifty – 'the whole group will be extinct shortly if this continues'. The smallpox which had spread down the east coast after the war, had backtracked inland to prey on the Orang Asli. Not only epidemics were to blame: the Orang Asli complained of the heat and the *hantu*, the spirits; they suffered from dysentery, chest disease, and very high levels of malaria, especially amongst young children. Amongst the 2,000 Temiar at Plus river there were sixty-four deaths and only eight births in a four-month period.[214] At Semenyih, sixty had

---

[211] 'Statement taken by Major P. D. R. Williams-Hunt . . . at Paya Senayan, Lipat Kajang Mukim, Temerloh District, Pahang from Batin MAT headman of a Semaq Semang community . . . and from TAN, another of the same group at the same place', DO Temerloh/92/50.

[212] Richard Noone, *Rape of the dream people* (London, 1972), pp. 150–5.

[213] MRSA, July 1954, CO1030/7.

[214] Ivan Polunin, 'The medical natural history of the Malayan aborigines', *Malayan Medical Journal*, 8, 1 (1953), 160–2; Williams-Hunt to del Tufo, n.d., FS./12072/50.

died in two and a half months and more were dying. A rate of 10 per cent deaths was forecast overall.[215] An unknown number, hundreds – perhaps thousands – died. Much of the disruption remained invisible to the colonial government. The response of many isolated communities to the Emergency was evasion. Even on the eve of independence new communities were being encountered.

The Emergency reopened debates on the future of the Orang Asli. By degrees, it created an administration to govern them: a Protector of Aborigines became guardian of the social and economic interests of the Orang Asli, watching over their relations with other communities. The dominant personality of this period was the anthropologist P. D. R. Williams-Hunt, who campaigned for a more humane and measured response to the Orang Asli. Welfare professionals poured into these areas, but their work was dominated by the priorities of counter-insurgency. By 1952, jungle forts were established to provide a tangible government presence in these isolated areas. By 1955 there were 529 Orang Asli attending schools at forts and outside the jungle; this increased to 1,162 in 1956. Forts also opened small shops which enabled the Orang Asli to spend cash income, and rotated employment opportunities.[216] Fort Shean, however, which claimed 8,000 Orang Asli in its sphere of influence, displayed the unsettling effect the forts were having on their economy, by disrupting cultivation and integrating them further into the cash economy.[217] The Orang Asli's scope to manage their own affairs was severely restricted by the Emergency. For the Orang Asli, displacement, resettlement and the jungle forts represented a massive enlargement of scale which threatened to rapidly transform their lifestyle and material culture. Men like Williams-Hunt fought this 'detribalisation': the natural rhythms of their community life had been broken and their very survival was at stake. Williams-Hunt demanded that evolution take its natural course. The only real guarantee of this was Orang Asli land rights similar to Malay Reservations.[218]

> They themselves only wish to be left alone and to be allowed to develop in their traditional way of life with the minimum of outside interference. They ask for protection for their lands, freedom from religious interference of which there is a considerable and growing amount and a gradual development of standards of living and education. These people are the original inhabitants of the country and have largely contributed to the Malay population. They have a right to special consideration for their protection and preservation above all other peoples of the country.[219]

Williams-Hunt died tragically after a jungle fall in 1953. His immediate successor

---

[215] Raya Ayoub, 'Note', 28.4.1950, FS/12665/50.
[216] Alun Jones, 'The Orang Asli', 297–301; Gordon P. Means, 'The Orang Asli: aboriginal policies in Malaya', *Pacific Affairs*, 38, 4 (1985), 644–5; Dr Ivan Polunin, reported in *Straits Times*, 13.10.1950.
[217] 'War for the aborigines', *Singapore Standard*, 3.4.1954.
[218] Department of the Adviser of Aborigines, Circular Memorandum No.15, 'Some notes on a suggested policy for aboriginal advancement', September 1950, Sel Sec/1411/50.
[219] 'Confidential memo from Advisor on Aborigines, Federation of Malaya: aboriginal policy', FS/12663/50.

favoured long and detailed research into Orang Asli social structure, and was dismissed within two weeks. The eventual appointee, Richard Noone, took a pragmatic line. The policy of government was a holding operation to assist the Orang Asli to protect their culture for as long as possible to ensure that 'as being the original inhabitants of the country' they received equal rights to other communities and that none should be moved from traditional territory 'for any economic or political reason', and in the case of jungle communities that 'no culturally subversive influences' be brought to bear on them. Border communities were to be assisted in commerce and in learning Malay; the outer communities encouraged to follow a Malay way of life.[220] These ideas found expression in the Aboriginal People's Ordinance of 1954. The legislation strengthened the legal definition of Orang Asli and mooted reservations to protect them from outside exploitation. The States were, however, jealous of their powers over land, and proposed a cess on aboriginal areas, or reserved land, leased or alienated for any other purpose be abandoned.[221] The redrafted bill felt that the welfare of the Orang Asli was more an administrative problem than a subject for legislative provision.[222]

The decisive conflict came over land. Prior to the war, some privileges had been granted to the Orang Asli, in Perak and Pahang and elsewhere, but very few were gazetted. Communities had, moreover, been displaced or moved on. The government's intention was to survey these areas and gazette them as reserves.[223] However, much of these lands were forest reserve, and the heated debate as to whether forest reserve could be included in an aboriginal reservation revealed the central ambiguity and insecurity of their position.[224] The Protector of Aborigines was concerned to provide 'a right to *ladang* cultivation' in areas 'entirely their property'.[225] The *saka*, or hereditary areas, it was argued, were bound up both with topography, and the material and ritual life of communities. They covered almost 'every square inch' of the central range from Selangor to the Thai border. Shifting cultivation was 'not a haphazard, indiscriminate affair', but bound up with the religious life of the Orang Asli on a five- to fifteen-year cycle. The Protector stressed that fellings were in high forest unsuited for logging; simple planting techniques did not break up the soil; felling and burning produced natural soil retainers.[226] Against this it was argued that the new concentrations that had appeared in the Emergency – for example on the Perak–Pahang watershed – were wreaking immense damage on forests. Foresters calculated that the estimated 6,000 Orang Asli involved required 6,000 acres of new *ladang* a year, which

---

[220] Dept. of Aborigines, 'Suggested long term policy towards the aborigines', 29.10.1955, DF/787/54.
[221] *Malay Mail*, 27.1.1954.   [222] *Straits Times*, 28.1.1954.
[223] P.A.S.(B) to Williams-Hunt, 6.6.1950, FS/12865/50.
[224] E. J. Shrubshall to State Forest Officer, Pahang, 18.1.1955, DF/787/54.
[225] 'Precis (Executive Council, 12.1.1955): Aboriginal Reserve at Langkap', *ibid*.
[226] R. O. D. Noone, 'A note on the conflict of interest between the Forestry Department and the Department of Aborigines as exemplified by the Forest Enactment Cap. 153 and the Aboriginal Peoples Ordinance Cap. 3/1954', 24.3.1956, *ibid*.

cost $600,000 in lost royalties, and ten times that in timber.[227] A 1938 survey of the
Tapah Hills Reserve had exonerated the Orang Asli. However, the new orthodoxy was
that it was the duty of government not to preserve a lifestyle disruptive to production
and to 'alter the aboriginal way of life – by force, if necessary'.[228] The Malay
smallholder was the ideal. 'The choice,' it was suggested, was 'between settlement and
extinction.'[229]

The conviction that Malay life was the destiny of the Orang Asli was a more
powerful determinant of policy than environmental concerns. As independence
approached, these political concerns became more explicit as the British sought to
integrate the Orang Asli into the administration. The British sought to create leaders
by appointing headmen. However, as independence approached, the Orang Asli were
reliant on others to voice their interest. The Perak notable, Dr Haji Mohammed
Eusoff, represented them at the Reid Constitutional Committee. He recommended
placing the Orang Asli on an equal footing with other communities, with security of
land tenure through trusts on aboriginal reserves, to include surface as well as mineral
rights, legal protection from missionaries, and representation on State and federal
councils. 'I intend,' he announced, 'to bring civilization to them, rather than them to
civilization.'[230] The Orang Asli representative to the Legislative Council, Toh Pangku
Pandak Hamid, a Temiar from Sungei Korbu in Perak, and a government field
assistant, in a maiden speech went further and demanded rights for the Orang Asli as
the 'true sons of the soil'.[231] However, this assertion went to very core of the political
and ideological foundations which were being laid for the new polity. The logic of late
colonial state-building was towards assimilation. To Malay indiginism – based on the
absolute rights of the *bumiputera* – the claims of the Orang Asli were an embarrassment. The pressure from both sides was to make the development of the Orang Asli
congruent to that of the Malays. Malay was defined by habitual use of the Malay
language and by Islam. By independence an estimated 90 per cent of Orang Asli could
understand Malay.[232] Several States and the All-Malaya Muslim Missionary Society
launched conversion drives.[233] Yet by the end of 1957, only 108 Orang Asli in Perak
were Muslims. Nor were Christian churches especially successful. Approaches to the
Orang Asli had been forbidden, 'as a matter of politics' after the war.[234] After
independence a new policy followed 'suitable measures designed for their protection

[227] Colin Marshall, 'Perak State Aborigines Advisory Board – Comments on memorandum by
the Protector of Aborigines', 1.4.1957, *ibid.*
[228] D. S. P. Noakes, Director of Forestry, 'Memorandum', 14.5.1957, *ibid.*
[229] State Forest Officer, Negri Sembilan and Malacca to Director of Forests, 5.8.1955; E. J.
Shrubshall to State Forest Officer, Negri Sembilan and Malacca, 26.11.1954, *ibid.*
[230] *Malay Mail*, 21.7.1953; 21.7.1956; Datin Ragayah Eusoff, *Lord of Kinta: the biography of
Dato Panglima Kinta Eusoff* (Petaling Jaya, 1995), p. 81.
[231] *Singapore Standard*, 13.12.1957.
[232] *Straits Times*, 14.7.1957.
[233] *Straits Times*, 22.8.1956; *Malay Mail*, 11.12.1956.
[234] 'Notes of the nineteenth meeting of the CSCC . . . 6.8.1954'; 'Twentieth meeting of the
CSCC . . . 8.10.1954', BA Pahang/29/52/Part I.

and advancement with a view to their ultimate integration with the Malay section of the community'.[235] New land settlement schemes and new forms of political patronage increased the pressure on the Orang Asli, as they trod a precipitous path between absorption into the Malay population and an increasingly fragile existence outside it.

[235] Jabatan Hal Ehwal Orang Asli, *Statement of Policy regarding the administration of the Orang Asli of Peninsular Malaysia* (Kuala Lumpur, 1961).

CHAPTER SEVEN

The politics of culture

In the face of the new assertions of communal identity that the Emergency seemed to be fostering, the British attempted to construct a new 'Malayan' political community. They had failed to impose this community from above during the Malayan Union débâcle. During the Emergency they therefore looked to foster new cultures of belonging from below. Their aim was to fashion a 'Malayan' nation, infused with patriotic spirit. The capacity of the state to create identity is a central issue in modern Malaysian history. Both the colonial and the post-colonial state attempted to build a nation, but in rather different ways. To explain their successes and failures, historians have looked to the politics of culture. However, they differ profoundly on the extent to which primordial political loyalties or more recent class formation have dictated the politics of culture. A key point of contention is the part colonial rule played in this process. A long-standing argument has been that late colonial nation-building was insufficient to reverse the legacy of divide and rule. Yet the people of Malaya were not passive bystanders in this process. Anthony Milner has argued that the opening of the public sphere in the later colonial period, the emergence of 'politics' as a language of public life and as a strategy for social action, allowed old identities and old divisions to be articulated in new ways. 'Although colonialism promoted the practice of politics,' Milner stresses, 'it did not create this politics.'[1] Other writers date the rise of a dissonant and 'fragmented vision' of politics and culture in Malaysia from more recent state authoritarianism, from the rise of an urban middle class and the reconstructions of identity it provoked within communities.[2] A clear historical context for these different visions is needed. With this in mind, I want to suggest that the kind of politics promoted in the late colonial period had far more influence in shaping the landscape of post-colonial politics than existing accounts have allowed. Its legacy

---

[1] A. C. Milner, 'Inventing politics: the case of Malaysia', *Past & Present*, 132 (1991), 104–29.
[2] Joel Kahn and Francis Loh Kok Wah (eds), *Fragmented vision: culture in contemporary Malaysia* (Sydney, 1992), esp. pp. 1–15.

lay not so much in what the British achieved, as in what the British allowed others to accomplish.

During the last years of colonial rule, the British promoted the 'Malayan' by introducing new techniques of collaboration. Late colonialism was not merely a project of political education. It did not rest with the introduction of electoral politics and the establishment of an Anglophile, Anglophone successor state. In 'the borrowed robes of nationalism' it promoted an explicit ideology of citizenship.[3] This was a general theme of post-war imperial thought, but in the conviction with which it was pursued in Malaya in the shadow of a Communist insurrection, it was perhaps the most ambitious undertaking of any late colonial regime. This chapter investigates colonial cultural policy: the quest for an Anglicised vision of the 'Malayan' in active citizenship and in art and literature. It shows how it was defeated by an upsurge of explorations in ethnic and religious identity that emanated from networks within the vibrant popular cultures in the towns. Despite Emergency censorship, perhaps even because of it, these debates were conducted deep within society. They required intellectuals to define the legitimate sources of their inspiration. In a situation where Malaysian political leaders inherited political power rather than won it by force, it was in these debates on national culture that some of the most intense struggles for independence occurred. They questioned the capacity of the English language to weld polyglot communities into a multi-racial whole, they questioned the nature of 'multi-racialism' itself. Of the alternative reconstructions of national identity – through education, art, performance, literature – the most important was the reformulation of the Malay language as an agent of national mobilisation. It was the establishment of Malay as the singular idiom of public life, and the processes of social and political change which underlaid this, that finally defeated the colonial project. Yet the new ways in which colonial power was wielded left a deep impression in the political imagination of Malaya. The devices of colonial state-building became tools to plague their inventors' heads.

The quest for the 'Malayan'

The success of colonial social policy rested on fostering a national culture, or a culture for multi-racial politics. To senior officials Malaya was 'a cultural desert'. The arts had been 'practised in communal isolation' by a population of pioneering coolies and shopkeepers with no common language. Malaya lacked the adornments of a civilised nation: zoos, museums and libraries. General Templer set to remedy this by launching a national museum and an Arts Council. He envisaged a cultural renaissance under British patronage.[4] Expatriate publishers such as Donald Moore produced guides to

---

[3] The phrase comes from D. J. Enright's poem 'In hot water', written with Mr Lee Kuan Yew in mind, in *Instant chronicles: a life* (Oxford, 1985), p. 19.

[4] J. Cloake, *Templer: Tiger of Malaya* (London, 1985), pp. 187–8; 'Help to discover Malaya's history', INF/1316/52; Tony Beamish, 'Art exhibitions in the Federation of Malaya', *The Singapore Artist*, 1, 2 (1954).

every aspect of Malayan culture. Research on the history and geography of the peninsula was begun in the University of Malaya and local historical societies.[5] The 'Malayan' ideal was projected abroad. In the face of riot and revolution, the Singapore Public Relations Office promoted tourism.[6] Europeans took the lead in condemning the cultural starvation they felt in insular expatriate communities and the materialism of cities such as Singapore. They shared a generous vision of cultural fusion: 'the chance is here for the cultures of the Far East, India and the West to learn from each other and to merge and fuse into a Malayan national form'.[7] Colonial memoirs and novels of the period are animated by these possibilities – Anthony Burgess's missionary schoolmaster, Victor Crabbe, exemplifies the spirit of the age. Expatriates sought out and celebrated the 'Malayan' in art, music, architecture and fashion. Amateur dramatical troupes, for example, articulated 'emotions, experiences that are purely Malayan', through a 'purely Malayan style of English'. But in essence fusion meant Anglicisation – Macbeth in Malay dress; Eliot and Priestly – fortified by a robust anti-Americanism. As one critic noted, 'our plays come from the West End, our books from Bloomsbury, our music from the centres of western Europe. Very little comes from Malaya itself.'[8] To another it seemed as if the British were scrambling 'to fulfil a kind of myth, the myth of Malayanisation'.[9]

In practice 'Malayanisation' meant entrenching the English language as the first language of the post-colonial elite. The unifying potential of English had been seized upon before the war, especially as a means of bringing Chinese schools into the mainstream of colonial education. The Protector of Chinese in Singapore, Victor Purcell, was convinced by I. A. Richards, of Magdalene College, Cambridge, that the true *lingua franca* of Malaya was Basic English – a rudimentary language in common. The Colonial Office half-heartedly promoted it, but it became clear that Basic English could not compete with the established local patois.[10] However, during the Emergency, English schools took on a special role as 'nurseries for the more Malayan-minded'.[11] A vast range of English primers were produced. Publishers provided

[5] For example, *The New Malaya* (ed.) Joanna Moore (Singapore, 1957–); the fruits of the local history work of the Malayan Historical Society can be found in the *Malayan Historical Journal* from May 1954. In the second issue S. Durai Raja Singham celebrates Templer's work for 'heritage', in the Natural History Museum, arts and crafts exhibitions, and in promoting a 'distinctive Malayan style of architecture', 'Sir Gerald Templer's work for a cultural revival in Malaya', *MHJ*, 2, 2 (1955).

[6] Vincent Lim Chooi Hin, 'A history of tourism in Singapore, 1950–77' (B.A., Academic exercise, NUS, 1979), pp. 17–24.

[7] Tony Beamish, *The arts of Malaya* (Singapore, 1954), pp. 12–13.

[8] 'Editorial' and David Allen, 'Occupation', in *Singapore Arts Theatre Review*, 1, 1 (1953).

[9] Barrington Kaye, *A manifesto for education in Malaya* (Singapore, 1955), p. 15.

[10] Victor Purcell, *Basic English for Malaya* (Singapore, 1937). pp. 13, 64; Ronald Hyam et al., *A history of Magdalene College Cambridge, 1428–1988* (Cambridge, 1994), p. 265.

[11] David Bloom, 'The English language and Singapore: a critical survey', in Basant Kapur (ed.), *Singapore Studies: critical surveys of the humanities and social sciences* (Singapore, 1986), pp. 370–3.

'controlled original reading material' for Malayan consumption: Malay legends and jungle adventures against the terrorists.[12] *A Young Malayans* magazine was published under official patronage to promote the English language amongst educated youngsters, and it contained the first publications of a number of prominent intellectuals who were later to emerge from the University of Malaya.[13] Mass education had a similar aim. Illiteracy was identified as the main obstacle to full participation in the new political process. Malay literacy in any language was 30 per cent; only 2 per cent in English. UMNO ran some classes in Johore in Malay, English, religious instruction and craft skills; the *Kaum Ibu* had some classes for women in the kampongs, and there were some government and private night schools in the larger towns. However, the beginnings of a formal adult education movement in Malaya lay in the People's Educational Association of Penang, a body established at the urging of public sector trade unions, and at the expense of rubber dealers.[14] Its mainly Chinese organisers regarded fluency in the English language as their primary objective. It was to elevate the under-privileged to citizenship, be a 'training ground of the future leaders of the country', and to cultivate 'a spirit of nationalism'.[15] By July 1951, a country-wide Adult Education Association was formed. The Pahang organiser, Abdul Razak bin Hussein, invoked Disraeli: 'we must educate our masters'.[16] Adult education was, in theory, apolitical. The President of the Penang association, Heah Joo Seang, had warned of the dangers against 'making the association a forum for political parties or a hotbed for subversive propaganda or activity. The association should be strictly nonsectarian and non-political in character.'[17] However, the backbone of the movement were the political supporters of Dato Onn and his Independence of Malaya Party and its successor the Party Negara, men such as Raya Ayoub, Heah Joo Seang and Zainal Abidin bin Haji Abas, conservatives who enjoyed the sympathy of the colonial government. A further impetus came from the MIC, and moderate trade unionists such as M. P. Rajagopal and P. P. Narayanan. The Barnes Report on education encouraged such activities, and had insisted on 'a conspicuous absence of official

---

[12] For example, M. C. ff. Sheppard, *The adventures of Hang Tuah* (Singapore, 1949), written during internment in Changi Prison. See also introduction to H. J. Kitchener and A. R. B. Etherton, *Malayan jungle adventures* (Kuala Lumpur, 1953). Primers included Thelma Hale, *Speech training for Malayans* (London, 1957); P. M. Clements and L. I. Lewis, *Now we can read* (Macmillan's Standard English Course for Malaya, London, 1953); Michael West and H. R. Cheeseman, *The new method Malayan readers* (London, 1947 and 1957).

[13] Edited by Richard Sydney. It seems that the term 'Engmalchin' was first used in its pages, Anne Brewster, *Towards a semiotic of post-colonial discourse: University writing in Singapore and Malaysia, 1949–1965* (Singapore, 1989), p. 3.

[14] 'Minutes of a meeting of the AEA Committee held at Penang on 6.10.1955', INF/1067/51/Pt. I.

[15] People's Educational Association, Penang, 'Report of the discussion with Mr C. P. Purcell, Senior inspector of schools Penang, on the method and system of adult education', 9.7.1951; Heah Joo Seang, 'Memorandum on the future plans of the Adult Education Association, Federation of Malaya', 10.8.1951, INF/1081/51.

[16] Abdullah bin Sultan, 'Pahang AEA, Annual Report, 1952', INF/1067/51/Pt. I.

[17] Heah, 'Memorandum on the future plans', INF/1081/51.

control'; but by the end of October 1952 the 587 classes were backed by a grant of a quarter of a million dollars from the Federal government.[18] Yet the assumption that the medium of citizenship was English was soon challenged. In the face of mounting rural demand – and encouraged by a visit of the adult education guru Dr Laubach – an important decision was made to teach Malay as a *lingua franca*, directing it at social problems such as peasant economy, and leadership training.[19] By the beginning of 1955, 40,000 new Malay literates had brought 'A new element into the life of the country's kampongs in many villages where no such regular gatherings for secular purposes have ever before been known, the literacy class has became a starting point for new community effort, and is a forum for discussion of local affairs.'[20] Literature was imported from Jakarta, and the new literates added new momentum to Malay publishing in the romanised, *rumi*, script.

The political undercurrents of the campaign were challenged. The Malay verna-cular newspapers and rival parties attacked it as a vehicle for Party Negara influence. By September 1954 adult education was dying a slow death in most States except Kelantan, a stronghold of the Party Negara.[21] From mid-1953 to mid-1954 the number of classes outside Kelantan dropped from 371 to 127, whilst the number in the State rose from 13 to 213. Other critics condemned its failure as an anti-colonial movement, as an instrument to raise the consciousness of the masses. By 1955 it had an impact on only 5 per cent of the population; and was responsible for less than 2 per cent of the total literates; the first primer – *Membasmi buku huruf* – listed only 122 words, insufficient 'literacy' to read a newspaper or a government notice.[22] In Singapore, Chinese educationalists objected that all state aid for adult education went to English language education, and the Singapore MCA moved to fill the breach. Yet when other political parties applied for assistance they were obstructed and were told that all classes must come under the supervision and control of the Adult Education Association. It became an acrimonious political dispute. The Adult Education Association campaigned for the MCA's activities to be confined to the New Villages.[23] The MCA had the lottery which financed its 1,200 classes banned in August 1953, on the grounds that it had become a political party. The move was instigated by the Party Negara leaders who continued to benefit from state funding. This compromised the

---

[18] *Adult Education: news bulletin. Adult Education Association Federation of Malaya*, I, 1 (November 1952).

[19] 'Minutes of the third meeting of the Executive Committee of the AEA, 24–25.5.1952', INF/1067/51/Pt. I; 'Programme for the National Conference on Adult Education in Malay, 17–19.12.1954', CS/5209/53.

[20] AEA, *Annual Report, 1954*.

[21] Especially in Kedah, Trengganu, Johore and Negri Sembilan, 'Sub-Committee on Malay Literacy Campaign – minutes of meeting held on 24.9.1954', INF/1067/51/Pt. II.

[22] AEA, *Annual Report, 1954*; Siao Ping, 'Adult education in the Federation of Malaya', *Workers' Education Association, Singapore Bulletin*, V (February, 1955).

[23] 'Minutes of the third meeting of the Executive Committee of the AEA, 24–25.5.1952'; Minutes of the ninth meeting of the Executive Committee of the AEA, 21.12.1952'; AEA, 'Annual Report for 1953', INF/1067/51/Pt. I, INF/1067/51/Pt. I.

party's non-communal posture, and, at a crucial juncture, closed the possibility of it recruiting key Chinese leaders. A Social Welfare lottery superseded the MCA lottery. Its critics claimed that it would be undersubscribed, and that, given that most who would subscribe were of lower income, it was founded merely 'to finance public welfare with the money of the poor to the indirect advantage of the rich'.[24] The MCA reacted by broadening its cultural efforts, establishing libraries and women's and youth sections. It was instrumental in the foundation of the Malayan Public Library Association in 1954, whose libraries were often housed in community centres and became a focus of cultural activities.[25] In this way, the MCA strengthened an alliance with Chinese educational and cultural associations which was to mount a powerful challenge to national education policy.

A revolution in communications

These initiatives were supported by the colonial state, which by the 1950s had become a formidable propaganda machine. Counter-insurgency was a revolution in communications: the technological prowess of the British lay at the heart of the civilising mission of late colonialism. It opened up new possibilities for governance. Although colonial policies of civic advancement eschewed 'the realm of political doctrine', their success depended on control of the dissemination of information and culture, and the public's affirmation of colonial rule.[26] The British provided ideological resistance to Communism. Yet their ambition rose above this: they sought to breathe democratic sentiment into what they saw as the corrupted lungs of nationalist politics. It was a 'moral offensive': a direct appeal to the public, an explanation of 'how the wheel goes round, who keeps it in motion, and the part played by Ahmad, Ah Seng and Ramasamy in its revolution'.[27] In Malaya, by 1953, the Information Department was publishing ten regular newspapers and periodicals.[28] Black propaganda was released; 'whispering campaigns' set in motion, whereby material not of apparent official inspiration was distributed to Chinese story-tellers for them to read out between stories to arouse sentiments of loyalty to Singapore and Malaya.[29] In 1950 a cartoon strip version of *Animal Farm* in Chinese was distributed.[30] The precedent had been set in the war. A vastly wider range of media were now exploited. The generous budgets for counter-insurgency meant that large areas could be saturated with leaflets by air: when an amnesty was announced in September 1955, 1,318,000 leaflets announcing this rained down on the State of Perak alone. In 1948, 50 million, and in

---

[24] *Nanyang Siang Pau*, 3.12.1952.
[25] MCA, *MCA, 20th Anniversary souvenir, 1949–69* (Kuala Lumpur, 1969), p. 70.
[26] J. N. McHugh to Chief Secretary, 21.2.1950, FS/12290/50.
[27] Director, Information Services, 'Memorandum on education in citizenship', Coop/505/55.
[28] 'Department of Information, Weekly Publicity Co-ordination Meeting, 17.11.1953', PRO/58/53.
[29] C. W. Lyle to G. Thomson, 12.8.1952, PRO/Conf/47/53.
[30] John Rayner to G. G. Thomson, 27.12.1950, INF/1232/51.

1957, 116 million leaflets were distributed.[31] However, the written word was said to be 95 per cent ineffective; a government press release in English reached less than 2 per cent of the population.[32] Low adult literacy, especially in the northern states – where it was only 20 per cent of adult males – was an obstacle to effective communication. In early 1949 cutbacks in government expenditure meant that all but one of the Public Relations reading rooms and half of the information centres were forced to close down. That there was a demand for them was evident when others remained open through private funding; in Perak and Kedah the institutions were said to be flourishing.[33] New technologies were enlisted. Messages from voice aircraft spoke to the aboriginal communities in their own tongue, and a 'Thunderer' – a large speaker with a minimum four-mile range – was used to broadcast messages to the heart of the jungle. In March 1949, the first-ever recording of the voice of a Sultan was broadcast in Pahang to rally the Malays behind the government.[34] Speaking tours of surrendered Communists were reported to be 'more valuable than any other form of propaganda'.[35] Major figures had defected to the government camp: Lam Swee, the charismatic former General-Secretary of the Pan-Malayan Federation of Trade Unions; Osman China, the surrendered Malay ideologue of the Malayan Communist Party, who, ravaged by malaria, toured the Malay villages, preaching that Communism was anti-Islam.[36] Surrendered Communists and other officially sponsored parties also put on theatrical shows. A 'New Malaya Operatic Service' active in Perak and the New Villages of Johore, exploited Hakka folksong, *san ko*. Popular songs such as 'The Tapper' detailed Communist atrocities and praised New Village life. However, populist lines such as 'While the rich people are still having their dreams, the penniless labourers have to go to the mountains', worried officials: they were rather 'too akin to Communist themes'.[37]

As the Emergency progressed these techniques were used increasingly for civil affairs. The potential of radio was quickly recognised. The 30,000 receivers in 1949 probably only reached one section of the population. However, subsequent years saw a massive rise in ownership: in 1950, 48,600 sets and in 1951, 110,800. Rediffusion came to Kuala Lumpur in 1949 and Penang in 1953.[38] Community listening sets were installed by General Electric in the Malay areas and Chinese New Villages; broad-

[31] J. N. McHugh, 'Psychological or political warfare in Malaya: II The postwar years', *Journal of the Historical Society of the University of Malaya*, 5 (1966/67), p. 89.
[32] In early 1950 the circulation of the English papers was 105,000; Chinese, 100,000; Malay, 28,000; Indian, 30,000. J. N. McHugh to Deputy Chief Secretary, 21.2.1950, FS/12290/50.
[33] *Malay Mail*, 4.1.1949.
[34] *Malaya Tribune*, 29.3.1949.
[35] Especially, Department of Information, 'Monthly Report, June 1955, Perak', in DO Larut/82/55.
[36] For example, 'Letter to the Party Members, Min Yuen and armed comrades of the whole State', Malacca, 1.1.1952, INF/76/52.
[37] Syed Zainal Abidin to B. A. Negri Sembilan, 21.1.1955; R. J. Isaac to S. I. O. Johore, 12.8.1953, INF/1305/53.
[38] J. N. McHugh to Deputy Chief Secretary, 21.2.1950, FS/12290/50; Russell H. Betts, *The*

casting began from July 1951.[39] By 1953, well over half of surveyed estates had radio receivers, and a slightly smaller proportion of tin mines. Chinese leaders suspected that the radios would be used to receive Radio Peking, but surveys in the Chinese *kongsis* of the Kinta Valley showed that the popularity of Radio Malaya outweighed that of Radio Peking due to its greater proportion of entertainment programmes.[40] In these the use of classical expressions was kept to a minimum; the announcer was told that 'when he speaks he should feel that he himself is a labourer'.[41] Tamil broadcasts used the simplest Tamil in humorous exposés of current affairs in dialogue – 'Truth Teller'.[42] Friday sermons in Malay were broadcast, although their content was carefully scrutinised. During this period, under Reithian leadership, local radio's characteristic style of 'guided broadcasting' was developed.[43] It became a credo of imperial policy that the cinema was the most powerful propaganda weapon, especially amongst the Chinese who, as Malcolm MacDonald informed the minister, were 'highly susceptible to visual propaganda'.[44] Film-making began in earnest; travelling film shows became an ornament of the new-look rural life, 'familiarising as many people as they can possibly reach with the positive advantages of democratic government, and with the strength and positive achievements of the British Commonwealth of Nations'.[45] Newsreels – 'British Pathe News', 'Gaumont British News', 'Movietonews', and 'News of the Day' from America – reached one of the most enthusiastic cinema audiences in the world.[46] The statistics were impressive. In rural Trengganu in October 1954, a total attendance of 64,880 at cinema shows was reported for the month.[47] Other innovations were more eccentric, such as Templer's employment of the Coldstream Guards Band to attract crowds and raise morale. 'The Chinese,' it was delicately pointed out to him, 'worship noise rather than harmony

mass media of Malaya and Singapore as of 1965: a survey of the literature (Center for International Studies, M.I.T., Cambridge, Mass. 1969), pp. 65, 52.

[39] Secretary for Defence to S. W. E. C. Pahang, 10.3.1951, DO Temerloh/598/50; 'Community Broadcasting', INF/22/50.

[40] Results of 'Emergency and Community Broadcasting "Listener Research"'; 'Report on listening facilities in certain districts of the Kinta Valley'; 'Note', 26.7.1952, in INF/811/53.

[41] Mr Sung, 'Chinese programmes for Chinese workers on mines and estates', 18.3.1949, DCL.Sel/47/49.

[42] Community Listening Division of Radio Malaya, 'Report on a Listener Research Survey into the intelligibility of Tamil programmes for estate workers', INF/811/53.

[43] Asiah Sarji, 'The historical development of broadcasting in Malaysia (1930–57) and its social and political significance', *Media Asia*, 9, 3 (1982), 150–60.

[44] 'Minutes of fifteenth Commissioner-General's Conference held at Bukit Serene on 7.6.1950', CO537/6001; Malcolm MacDonald to Secretary of State, 24.8.1949, CO537/6571.

[45] 'Report on production and distribution of propaganda films in Southeast Asia', *ibid*. Some of the fifteen-minute shorts, such as 'Before the wind' (1953) – about an indebted fisherman who buys a motor boat with a RIDA loan – won international awards. A ten-minute newsreel was produced – 'New Malaya Gazette', Malayan Film Unit, *Catalogue of films* (1955).

[46] Singapore, *Annual Report of the Film Censor's Office for the year 1953*.

[47] 'Return of attendence at P/A cinema shows and P/A announcements for October 1954', D.INF.TR/21/54.

and would, we think, be more emotionally affected by gramophones reproductive of what might be described as Chinese culture.'[48] In August 1955 the first government-sponsored entertainment shows toured New Villages to exploit large captive audiences; British officials penned new words for Malay songs for community singing;[49] lion dances were used by the government to attract an audience for talks by its local allies, Malayan Chinese Association politicians. Both Chinese and Indian associations invested in vernacular theatre. In Kedah, a volunteer Indian Dramatic Troupe was formed to tour the estates, with plays on themes of social reform and 'renewed life'.[50] These operations reached a peak in the second half of 1955, publicising the Federal elections and the Amnesty declaration. In July 1955, in Perak alone it was estimated that an audience in the region of 408,000 was reached. The imperative was to educate. Government encouraged its conservative allies to do the same. The possibilities for integration seemed unbounded.

Popular cultures in transition

However, there was little spontaneous support for the 'Malayan'; the colonial culture failed to lodge itself in the popular imagination. The constituency for the 'Malayan' was a narrow one. It lay in the embryonic Asian middle class of the colonial towns. Yet the towns, as the British continually complained, were places of plebeian tastes. To Donald Moore, Singapore had not yet developed 'that class that lifts itself, intellectually and aesthetically, above the deadening influence of the masses'.[51] It was upon this narrow bourgeoisie that the colonial government sought to promote the English language and non-communal politics. However, social change during the Emergency years created its own momentum in the creating of political and communal identities. Urbanisation, as we saw in chapter 5, was not a spur to multi-racialism; in many other ways sociability reinforced ethnic loyalties and divisions. The Emergency was a time of moral crisis and cultural uncertainty. The colonial state was to set itself in competition with all kinds of nationalist and sectarian imaginings. In many ways it was an unequal contest. Emergency powers of suppression permitted the outlawing of a much wider range of political and cultural activities beside those sponsored by Communists. In other ways, it was not an unequal contest. It was precisely because the opportunities for open anti-colonial politics diminished, that in the arena of cultural life the space was found to mount the most effective challenges to the new imperialism of the 1950s.

Urban popular culture was viewed as unwholesome, even subversive. The new

---

[48] J. D. Mathewson, 'Regimental bands', 25.3.1952; A. M. MacDonald, minute, 7.4.1952, INF/1011/53.

[49] M. C. ff. Sheppard to Director, Malayan Film Unit, 6.12.1952, INF/628/53; State Secretary Negri Sembilan to A. D. C. Peterson, 25.3.1953, INF/1305/53.

[50] Kedah Information Services, 'Indian Dramatic Troupe for estates in South and Central Kedah', 29.11.1955, INF/614/55.

[51] Donald Moore, 'The story of a glorious failure', *New Malaya*, 3 (1954), 18–31.

media which had risen to prominence in the war and Emergency energised this cultural world and helped it to colonise the countryside. During the 'Malayan Spring', after years of wartime austerity, and despite the continuing shortages, the movie theatres, the great 'Worlds' – or amusement parks – did a roaring trade. In 1950 Shaw Brothers opened a new Great World in Penang. In general, Chinese big businesses emerged from the war in remarkably strong shape. Entrepreneurs seized on the opportunities the leisure sector presented, and by 1953, the primary leisure activity – according to an official survey – was the cinema.[52] This provided the incipient film industry with a sizeable business organisation and system of distribution. Although dubbed Egyptian and Filipino films remained popular in Malaya, the war opened the way for local companies to dominate the market.[53] Two firms led the way: the Shaw Brothers, and Loke Wan Tho's Cathay. Their interest in the business had begun before the war. Then, Malay film was a cottage concern; after the war it was transformed into an industry. Shaw Brothers established a Malay Films Production Ltd in Singapore in 1947, buying equipment from Hong Kong and picking up abandoned equipment from Shanghai. It soon employed 400 staff and five full-time directors. Loke Wan Tho's Cathay-Keris Film Production Ltd was founded in 1952. Two competing studios emerged in Singapore, each assembling a rival array of talent and housing them in 'resettlement colonies' – it was perhaps no coincidence that both the Shaws and Loke also owned racing stables. A frenzied period of movie-making ensued. In the ten years after the war Shaw Brothers produced sixty-five feature films and in 1951 owned or controlled the programmes of 70 per cent of cinemas. Hong Kong stars were brought to Malaya to make Chinese films with a local background – such as *Nonya and Baba* and *Rainstorm in Chinatown* – but the majority of films produced were Malay medium.[54] The actors and directors of the golden age of the Malay cinema cut their artistic teeth in the studio system. It brought together many themes of Malay cultural resurgence. Although early scripts and music were often Hindi in origin and translated into Malay, by 1960 Cathay-Keris had four Malay directors. The *bangsawan* tradition was adapted for the big screen: the film companies borrowed its stars, its stagehands and its stories. Many early films had an improvised flavour; their dialogue was richly sprinkled with local dialects. In the 1955 epic *Hang Tuah*, the female lead, Siti Tanjong Perak, lapses into Javanese. The early films were dominated by long, slow shots, actors tended to declaim loudly, and the experience for

---

[52] In one area 20 per cent visited the cinema once or twice a week, 50 per cent at least once or twice a month. 'Diagnostic Survey and Master Plan for Singapore – Report of the survey of leisure activities', 26.4.1954, SCA/95/54.

[53] Singapore, *Annual Report of the Film Censor's Office for the Year 1953* (Singapore, 1954). In 1949, six long films were produced locally, by 1952, fourteen. In 1948, 182 were imported, in 1950, 915. UNESCO, Statistics Division, *Film and cinema statistics: a preliminary report on methodology with tables giving current statistics* (Geneva, 1954).

[54] *Malaya Tribune*, 16.11.1946, 10.3.1947; Thomas Hodge, 'The film industry in Singapore and Malaya', *Report on the Third Annual Film Festival of Southeast Asia, Hong Kong, 12–16.6.1956*, pp. 98–104; Cathay Film Services Ltd, *Films about Singapore* (Singapore, 1958).

the audience was not unlike watching the stage. There were also films in *sandiwara* style, early examples being *Mutiara* and *Terang Bulan di Malaya* (1942–4).[55] Elements of the old stage-craft remained in the insistence on songs (at least five) – and Malay and Filipino musicians were employed to provide them at around \$25–30 a piece. In general, the actors had low wages. Big stars such as Siti Tanjong Perak or Normiadah could earn as much as \$200, but on entering work in 1956, Jins Shamsuddin earned only \$70. The artists' union, PERSAMA, threatened strikes over low pay and dismissals in 1957.[56] But this had the effect of keeping them close to other forms of performance: many continued to support their earnings in the theatre and the cabarets; temporary acting troops were established for charity events – including stars like P. Ramlee and Jins Shamsuddin.[57] Even big film stars did not leave this other world behind and were celebrated by the Malay press for doing more for the welfare of their community than the rich or royalty.[58] Distinctive cinematic styles soon emerged. Maria Menado, born in Sulawesi in 1931, came to Singapore as a teenage model – a *kebaya* queen, and gained a reputation in a succession of *pontianak* – female vampire – movies. She later became a movie producer in her own right.[59] However, the outstanding figure was Teuku Zakaria bin Teuku Nyak Puteh, born in Penang in 1929 of Acehnese descent. He was educated in Penang Free School, and in a Japanese *Kaigun* school during the occupation. He was discovered by B. S. Rajhan, a talent scout for Malay Films, who came across him at Bukit Mertajam, and heard him sing his song 'Azizah' – later featured in the film *Penarik Beca*.[60] Better known as P. Ramlee, he was a gifted comedian and musician as well as a dramatist, and had become something of a national hero by the late 1950s. The advent of social dramas came with films such as *Kaseh Menumpang* and *Merana* (1954) – in which P. Ramlee starred with Siti Tanjung Perak. Malay film began to rework traditional legends; question customary order; criticise new wealth. The outstanding examples of Ramlee's dramatic works were perhaps *Hang Tuah* – which retold the legend in Eastman colour; – and *Semerah padi* – a drama of rural customary order, in which the influences of Satyajit Ray and Akira Kurosawa could clearly be seen.[61] In 1955 his collaboration with Jaffar Abdullah, *Penarik Beca* – 'Trishaw Rider' – told the story of a poor man's love of a rich man's daughter, but set it in a clear contemporary setting, illustrating

[55] Jamil Sulong, 'Bangsawan's influence on early Malay films', in Perbadanan Kemajuan Filem Nasional Malaysia, *Cinta Filem Malaysia* (Kuala Lumpur, 1989), pp. 56–60.
[56] Jamil Sulong, *Kaca Permata: memoir seorang pengarah* (Kuala Lumpur, 1990), pp. 130–4.
[57] Cantius Leo Cameons, 'History and development of Malay theatre' (M.A. Thesis, Universiti Malaya, 1980), pp. 226–9.
[58] *Melayu Raya*, 15.11.1952.
[59] Lim Kay Tong, *Cathay: 55 years of cinema* (Singapore, 1991), p. 120; Rahani Mat Saman, 'Women producers', in Perbadanan Kemajuan Filem Nasional Malaysia, *Cinta Filem Malaysia*, p. 102.
[60] Abi, *P. Ramlee: Seniman Agung* (Kuala Lumpur, 1986) p. 1; Abdullah Hussain, *P. Ramlee: Kisah Hidup Semiman Agung* (Kuala Lumpur, 1973), p. 34.
[61] For a useful discussion of his influences see, Baharudin Latif, 'P. Ramlee: the legend', in Perbadanan Kemajuan Filem Nasional Malaysia, *Cinta Filem Malaysia*, pp. 63–65.

the equalities and injustices of contemporary urban life, and showed something of the world of cabarets, crime and violence. Others followed after him: Hussein Hanif, for example, made a distinct break with the Hindustani tradition. His 1958 film *Dang Anom* was seen as a sharp critique of Malay feudal order. This injection of a new element of social realism ushered in a new role for the Malay cinema, as a mirror to national culture.[62]

A distinctive artistic world emerged in Singapore. The world of the cinema remained closely intermeshed with other cultural and literary activities. The increasing popular obsession with the movies was reflected in the emergence of entertainment magazines such as *Utusan Filem dan Sport*, a *jawi* weekly published by *Utusan Melayu*, and *Filem Raya* published by its rival *Melayu Raya*. They generated a cross-fertilisation of literary and artistic talent. One fanzine, *Bintang*, published by P. Ramlee, and in which the Malay critic Asraf wrote, shared premises with the Malay literary movement, ASAS 50 – the Generation of 1950.[63] P. Ramlee also had connections with other writers such as Masuri S. N., Noor S. I. and Abdul Samad Said – through the magazine *Gelanggang Filem*.[64] Ja'afar Wiryo established *Filem Juita* in 1953. S. Roomai Noor took an active role in the landmark debates on modernising the Malay language, and championed the role of film in popularising the new forms and entrenching Malay as the national language.[65] Nor were these kinds of connections confined to the Malay cinema. As a post-war generation of Tamil writers addressed for the first time social concerns in Malaya, such as the survival of Tamil language and education, they found a ready outlet in local movie magazines – *Indian Movie News*, *Manoharan*, and *Kalai Malar*.[66] The province of the cinema was from the outset invaded by nationalist polemic. This was part of a general revitalisation of the common culture into which many new themes were introduced. Cinema helped foster debates on the nation and played a major role in disseminating their conclusions. Retellings of the *Malay Annals*, for instance, began to question the traditional image of the Malay hero – that of the stormy absolutist Hang Tuah – and rehabilitate the leadership of his rival, Hang Jebat – the rebel. Hang Jebat was first celebrated on the *sandiwara* stage, then in literary polemic, and then in Hussein Haniff's 1961 eponymous movie.[67]

Even in spite of Emergency censorship a wide range of newspapers and shades of

---

[62] Sharifah Zinjuaher, H. M. Ariffin and Hang Tuah Arshad, *Sejarah Filem Melayu* (Kuala Lumpur, 1980), pp. 20–7, and for a catalogue of films produced in this period, pp. 49–82.

[63] Enclosures on PRO/186/54.   [64] Aimi Jarr, *P. Ramlee: dari kacamata* (n.d.), p. 63.

[65] See for example his memorandum for the Third Malay Language and Literature Congress (1956), 'Bahasa Melayu dalam filem dan sandiwara', Abdullah Hussain and Nik Safiah Karim (eds), *Memoranda Angkatan Sasterawan '50* (Petaling Jaya, 1987), pp. 156–64.

[66] N. A. A. Govindasamy, 'The development of Tamil literature in Singapore (an historical perspective)', *Singapore Book World*, 10 (1979), 18–19.

[67] For example Ali Aziz's *sandiwara* play, *Hang Jebat Menderhaka* (1959) portrayed the hero as a modern man. The important literary reassessment was Kassim bin Ahmad, *Characterization in Hikayat Hang Tuah: a general survey of character-portrayal and analysis and interpretation of the characters of Hang Tuah and Hang Jebat* (Kuala Lumpur, 1966). For a discussion of Hang

opinion survived. Some even flourished.[68] In 1954, the dominant English voice was still the British-owned Singapore *Straits Times*, which had a circulation of 55,000. It saw itself as the voice of expatriate opinion, and its sister paper the *Singapore Free Press*, with a smaller circulation 15,000, was more 'popular' in outlook and independent in its sources of opinion. But to Asian critics they remained the mouthpieces of European capital. The Kuala Lumpur *Malay Mail*, with a circulation of only 13,000 was less influential, and probably more conservative. It adopted a *festina lente* attitude to local politics, yet its reporting contained a wealth of social and economic detail from the local scene. Although by 1950 the *Malaya Tribune* was defunct, its last years dominated by boardroom squabbles, there still existed an English-language voice of Asian opinion in the shape of the *Singapore Standard*. Owned by Aw Boon Haw, it had a relatively high circulation of 35,000 in 1954, and although its approach was necessarily cautious, radical writers such as S. Rajaratnam and A. Samad Ismail found column space in its pages. A similar role was played by the Penang *Straits Echo* in the north of the peninsula, which played a part in the secessionist campaign on the island, but by the 1950s it was in a very precarious financial situation. Similar difficulties faced the Malay press, although an important theme in this period is that the most authoritative voices of the community were owned by Malays, rather than by Arabs or Indian Muslims.[69] At the summit of Malay journalism was the *Utusan Melayu* whose contribution to Malay nationalism by this time had become legendary. Its circulation was small – 22,000 in 1954 – but far-reaching as three-quarters of this was in the Federation, and it had risen to 35,000 in 1958. As with all newspapers this is not a measure of the number of people who read it or had it read to them. It benefited from improvements in printing technology in the 1950s. Its editorial line was independent: it saw itself as setting the pace of Malay opinion and was often critical of the political mainstream. However, it waged war on UMNO's enemies. In Kuala Lumpur, a more unreserved supporter of UMNO was the *Majlis*, edited by A. Samad Ahmad, a paper that had played an historical role in 1946 in founding the party. It had a smaller circulation of 8,500 and struggled financially in the 1950s until its collapse in 1955. In Penang, the 5,000 circulation *Warta Negara* had been another strong UMNO supporter, but by 1954 tended towards the IMP/Party Negara axis – Dato Onn's ally, Datin Puteh Mariah, was a director. Another independent voice was the Singapore daily, *Melayu Raya*. Established in August 1950, its guiding personalities were the novelist, literary impresario and educationalist Harun Aminurrashid and Haji Mohd. Dahlan (Hamdan) and, as its name suggests, it drew together journalists of an MNP pedigree such as Taha Kalu. A fierce defender of Malay rights, it took a lead in the campaign for an Islamic College, airing the issue of the participation of women in

Tuah and Hang Jebat see Muhammad Haji Salleh, 'The traditional and contemporary Malay literary hero', in his *The mind of the Malay author* (Kuala Lumpur, 1991), pp. 145–66.

[68] For the data that follows, see PMR, 2/1954, CO1030/244; 'Confidential reports on newspapers', 1951[?], PRO/Conf/286/54.

[69] Arshad Haji Nawari, '*Utusan Melayu* yang dipunya orang Melayu', in Khoo Kay Kim and Jazamuddin Baharuddin (eds), *Lembaran Akhbar Melayu* (Kuala Lumpur, 1980), pp. 105–32.

politics, and most significantly orchestrated the campaign against colonial intrusion in Islamic law that culminated in the Nadra riots. In this period its circulation rose as high as 28,000. For this it paid a heavy price: it was silenced for ten months in January 1951. A condition of its reopening was the dismissal of Haji Mohd. Dahlan and it collapsed in late 1952.[70] It was the Chinese press that felt the full force of the declaration of the Emergency: the *Min Sheng Pau*, *New Democracy* and *Combatants' Friend* were all shut down. Tan Kah Kee's CDL mouthpiece, the *Nan Chiao Jit Pao*, survived until 1950, as did the *Modern Daily News* of Penang, when both were banned on grounds of sedition. In Singapore, the largest circulation paper was the *Nanyang Siang Pau*, with a print run of 50,000 copies. Although big tycoons such as Tan Lark Sye had an interest, it was by the 1950s less *siang*, or merchant-inclined, and the British felt it had moved to the left. The *Sin Chew Jit Pao*, another Aw Boon Haw paper, with a lesser circulation of 30,000, was fiercely anti-Communist but liberal in its approach to local politics. Both papers were to play a significant role in mobilising Chinese opinion on citizenship and language issues. On the peninsula, the dominant force was the Kuala Lumpur *China Press*, a voice of ex-KMT businessmen which, given the presence of H. S. Lee on its board of directors, gave strong support to the MCA. In addition to this there was the Penang incarnation of the *Sin Chew Jit Pao* – Aw Boon Haw's *Sing Pin Jit Pao* (circulation 10,000) – and the *Kwong Wah Jit Poh* (circulation 7,500), the voice of KMT businessmen in the north. The main voices of Indian opinion were the Chettiar-owned *Tamil Nesan* of Kuala Lumpur and the Tamil-owned, and strongly reformist, *Tamil Murasu* of Singapore.

Although publications for China and Indonesia were closely scrutinised by the authorities, periodicals from abroad – the *Reader's Digest* for example – were available at every small news stand for an expanding reading public: they fed public awareness of world affairs and were often discussed in local newspapers. The local press carried an increasing number of syndicated stories. However, what was even more significant was the network of women's, students' and vocational magazines that emanated from both Singapore and small publishers in provincial towns such as Kuala Pilah and Johore Bahru. These have been little studied.[71] Many were published by political parties: the voice of UMNO, *Suara UMNO*, a fortnightly operating out of Johore Bahru was revamped in this period and claimed a readership of 8,000, as did the MCA's *Malayan Mirror* in its combined Chinese and English editions. Others carried general articles, short stories, translations and poetry, and the most important of these were *Mastika*, published by *Utusan Melayu* and *Hiburan Cerita*, edited by Harun Aminurrashid at Royal Press in Singapore from 1946. Other publishers followed suit: Qalam, with *Warta* from 1953, and S. O. A. Alsagoff's *Asrama* from 1955, and

---

[70] Mek Siti bt. Hussin, '*Melayu Raya*' in Khoo Kay Kim and Jazamuddin Bahuruddin (eds), *Lembaran Akhbar Melayu* (Kuala Lumpur, 1980), pp. 167–85; Nik Ahmad, 'The Malay press', *JMBRAS*, 36, 1 (1963), 70–8.

[71] For publication details see A. M. Iskander Hj Ahmad, *Persuratkhabaran Melayu, 1876–1968* (Kuala Lumpur, 1973); Khoo Kay Kim, *Malay papers and periodicals as historical sources* (Kuala Lumpur, 1984).

articles in these more general interest magazines soon occasioned controversy. There was a flowering of current affairs journals, many of them short-lived, on the eve of independence. Smaller publications emerged on the peninsula, such as *Taman Bahasa*, published in 1955 by the *Ikatan Persuratan Melayu*, Malay Writers' League, of Malacca. Other were more religious in outlook: *Qalam* in Singapore, published from 1950, and a range of publications by State Religous Affairs Departments and individual *madrasah*.

Women's magazines were also established in this period, such as the long-running *Ibu*, published in *rumi* script in Johore Bahru in 1952, and *Juita*, published at Abdul Ghani Abdullah's Malay Press in Kuala Pilah in 1949. Schoolteachers' journals, published by their associations, such as *Panduan Murid* in Sebrang Prai, *Peredar* in Johore, and *Majallah Guru* in Seremban, helped fashion a common stand amongst Malay educators and turned them into an effective pressure group on issues of Malay language and culture. Many carried poetry on nationalist themes. A new generation of readers was captured by students' magazines such as *Pelajar* in Kuala Lumpur. Although they were not political in any direct sense, children's magazines - *Utusan Kanak-kanak*, Qalam Press's *Kanak-kanak* - popularised the language, symbols and legends of nationhood. So too did comics, which were an important medium in a society slowly gaining in literacy. Up to 5,000 kinds of fantasy, adventure and educational books were available, chiefly US imports and British publications reproduced in Hong Kong.[72] There was a rising demand for Malay comics, and about six publishers were producing Malay comic books in the 1950s from small presses in Kuala Pilah, Johore Bahru and Singapore. Their output was impressive. The nationalist iconography of the *Sejarah Melayu* – the *Malay Annals* – were reproduced in strip form. 'We publish this comic book,' an introduction stated, 'solely to remember past stories. These past stories will benefit and guide our future hopes. These past stories are related to our aspirations for independence today.'[73] Some even celebrated Chinese heroes of the era of Melaka's golden age in Malay and Chinese.[74] These books were to become increasingly important vehicles of popular consciousness after independence.[75] Lists of 'comics' of a degrading nature were drawn up by the police. After the paper shortages of the war there was a flood of books from Malay printers in Singapore such as Qalam, Harmy, Melayu Raya, Al-Ahmadiah and Geliga. School textbooks, dictionaries and books on commerce figured prominently in their portfolios. But novels by established writers such as Ahmad Lufti warranted a large print run of 4,000 copies; those by the new post-war generation slightly less; Hamzah's breakthrough *Ruma itu dunia aku* – 'This house is my world' – in 1951 had

[72] *Malay Mail*, 17.4.1954.
[73] Zainab Awang Ngah, 'Malay comic books published in the 1950s', *Singapore Book World*, 16, 2 (1986), 19–28.
[74] For example, Abdul Ghani, *Puteri Alang Lipo* (Kuala Pilah, 1957).
[75] Ronald Provenchor, 'Covering Malay humor magazines: satire and parody of Malaysian political dilemmas', *Crossroads: an interdisciplinary journal of Southeast Asian Studies*, 5, 2 (1990), 1–25.

a first edition of 3,000 copies. As with periodicals small town publishers in Kuala Pilah, Johore Bahru and even in the fishing town of Marang, Trengganu, were also extremely productive. As *merdeka* approached, history writing in Malay, the work of Buyong Adil for example, accounted for a large proportion of Malay publications in Singapore. There were at least eight history books published in 1956 alone.[76] Malay historiography moved away from the deeds of State aristocracies and began to address the nation.[77]

The national culture was plainly up for grabs, and the struggle for its soul intensified as many individuals from radical political movements took the lead in cultural life. When a Malay arts and cultural society – *Budaya* – was formed, the organisers stressed that 'the society does not want to be tinged with politics'. But these media were already politicised: cultural revival was an indispensable part of the struggle for independence. The colonial Arts Council was anticipated by a range of local art associations. Some were sponsored by expatriate teachers such as the Wednesday Art Group (1952) and Selangor Art Society (1954) in Kuala Lumpur. Others, such as the *Majlis Kesenian Melayu* (1956), gained a following amongst the Malay-educated artists and, in the words of one critic, 'identified itself with national identity by projecting Malay figurative imagery' and gained patrons such as Tunku Abdul Rahman, Dato Nik Ahmad Kamil and Zainal Abidin bin Hj. Abbas.[78] Traditional arts of self-defence – *silat* – had been transformed from a rural pastime by the Malay politicians, including the founder of UMNO, Dato Onn, into a vehicle for the inculcation of loyalty, discipline and Malay identity.[79] Cabaret and *bangsawan* bands took a lead in fusing local forms with western influences, for example in the *kroncong* which had become the indigenous popular music of the Malay world, and in the music of the Malay movies.[80] The *kroncong* singer Ahmad A. B.'s series of 1948 concerts in the Worlds introduced the modern *joget*, the violinist D. Hamzah spiced up rhythm and the saxophone was introduced to the ensemble. Rubiah's recording of the same year, 'Bunga Tanjong' had an elaborate concert arrangement.[81] In the 1950s popular music began to embrace nationalist themes, for example in Zahara Agus's 'Malaya merdeka'; and even, more controversially, to comment on issues such as

[76] Evidence from *Memorandum of books registered in the 'Catalogue of books printed at Singapore'*, under the Publications and Printers' Ordinance, consulted from 1951–6.

[77] Khoo Kay Kim, 'Local historians and the writing of Malaysian history in the twentieth century', in Anthony Reid and David Marr (eds), *Perceptions of the past in Southeast Asia* (Singapore, 1979), pp. 303–11.

[78] Syed Ahmad Jamal, 'Perkembangunan seni rupa Sezaman', in Persatuan Sejarah Malaysia, *Malaysia: sejarah dab proses pembangunan* (Kuala Lumpur, 1979); Syed Ahmad Jamal, *Seni Lukis Malaysia – 25 tahun* (Kuala Lumpur, 1982); Sudar Majid, 'The Malay artist', *The Singapore Artist*, 1, 2 (December 1954).

[79] Mubin Sheppard, *Taman Saujana: dance, drama, music and magic in Malaya, long and not-so-long ago* (Petaling Jaya, 1983), p. 101.

[80] James D. Chopyak, 'Music in modern Malaysia: a survey of the musics affecting the development of Malaysian popular music', *Asian Music*, 18, 1 (1986), 132–3.

[81] L. Webb Jones, '*Ronggeng* rhythm', *Straits Times Annual, 1953*, pp. 78–9.

polygamy, in the song 'Takut dimadu'- 'Fear of sharing a husband' – and to address religion more directly in 'Cahaya Islam' – 'Light of Islam'. The music of P. Ramlee, a rich fusion of the traditional *asli*, with *joget* and external influences such as the samba, on occasion addressed poverty and 'Kerjam manusia', 'The cruelty of mankind', in ways that sounded distant echoes with Brecht and Weill. 'My art,' he explained, encapsulating the mood of the era, 'is not for money, my art is for society.'[82]

Performance became one of the last refuges of the Malay radicals. The world of the movies, cabaret bands and starlets was a network of gifted individuals who set the tone of anti-colonial cultural politics. Important political networks were formed in the war – of journalists, actors, film-makers and propagandists. After the war, 'Bolero' and other *sandiwara* companies such as the 'Sri Noordin', had become an important propaganda arm of the Malay Nationalist Party. The leader of API, Ahmad Boestamam, had even directed the latter in plays representing the Indonesian independence struggle. During the Emergency these companies raised money for Malay welfare, and their veterans dispersed throughout the music and film scene.[83] UMNO Youth organised variety nights at the New World Penang, featuring *dondang sayang*, *ghazali* and *bangsawan* clowns. The *bangsawan* enjoyed something of a revival as it was employed in UMNO's 1955 election campaign. Tunku Abdul Rahman would address crowds between acts.[84] 'Bolero' actresses were combining movie roles with work in nightclubs, such as an all-female swing orchestra, *Pancharagam Wanita*, led by Abaidah 'Queenie', sister of the Malayan jazz king Jerry Soliano. The Malay film industry presented new opportunities for actor-managers such as Jaafar Wiryo versed in the modern scripted techniques of the *sandiwara*.[85] 'Mr Movie Idol 1956', S. Roomai Noor, born Mohd. Taib bin Salleh, took his alias after a wartime sojourn in Sumbawa. He came from Temerloh, a hotbed of radical Malay politics after the war, and was active in the Malay Nationalist Party. He joined Shaw Brothers studios in 1947, and shot to fame in *Cinta* with Siput Sarawak. He energetically promoted Malay culture in film circles.[86] Luminaries such as Bachtiar Effendi – an active nationalist during and after the Japanese occupation – were taking a role in *Budaya* and a new Actors' Union.[87] Many of these figures were Indonesian, and their influence was a direct way in which the Indonesian example set a precedent for the

---

[82] Craig A. Lockard, 'Reflections of change: socio-political commentary and criticism in Malaysian popular music since 1950', *Crossroads*, 6, 1 (1991), 19–26.

[83] For example, on 6–7 April 1949 a 'Malay Show of Shows' was held at Happy World to raise £50,000 for a Malay Welfare Fund, with arts and crafts; an all-bamboo orchestra conducted by Ja'afar Wiryo of the 'Bolero'; *kroncong* competitions; Javanese, Sumatran, Boyanese and Balinese dance; opera, *wayang kulit* and *ronggeng*, *Malay Mail*, 7.2.1949.

[84] *Straits Echo*, 25.4.1952; Tan Sooi Beng, *Bangsawan: a social and stylistic history of popular Malay opera* (Singapore, 1993), p. 170.

[85] For Jaafar Wiryo's connection with P. Ramlee, see Kalam Hamidy, *P. Ramlee: Pujnaan Nusantara* (Kuala Lumpur, 1973), pp. 55–7.

[86] Lim, *Cathay*, pp. 136–7.

[87] For the union of Cathay-Kris actors, *Persama*, see the memoir of its Secretary, Salleh Ghani, *Filem Melayu: dari Jalan Ampas ke Ulu Klang* (Kuala Lumpur, 1989), pp. 57–64.

radicalisation of popular culture in Malaya. Nor were these innovations confined to the Malay community. Mandarin songs flourished in singing cafés; the *ko-tai* street theatre in the amusement parks of Penang, Ipoh and Kuala Lumpur.[88] The 1950s saw a flood of publications from Chinese *xiao bao*, or small presses, and an official ban on publications in China gave local writers a local monopoly. Throughout the early 1950s groups such as the 'Mayfair Musical and Dramatic Association' were used by the Malayan Communist Party to extend its influence back into the cities. Music and dance were at the forefront of Communist reinfiltration into the Chinese schools. They played a similar role in furthering political consciousness in the Indian community. When the Hindu Youth movement, representing English-educated Indian youths, used ballroom dancing to mount an assault on existing social practices, their opponents scrambled to rediscover traditional dance.[89]

Sarong culture, yellow culture

The response of the colonial government to this surge of activity was conditioned by the fact that colonial society was under pressure. Under these circumstances cinema censorship was a major issue. Hollywood confirmed new stereotypes of the accessible sexuality of the western woman, which from the 1930s had been perceived as a potent threat to imperial authority. Post-war cinematic representations of Jane Russell and Ava Gardner had a remarkable effect, as Anthony Burgess recalls in his 'Confessions':

> The crinolined or embustled mems of the old days had been untouchable, but things were changing in the new age of democracy and equality. All Kuala Kangsar was on fire when a French film called *Ah! Les Belles Bacchantes* was shown. In it French women exhibited pert little bosoms and men of all races united in groans of lust.[90]

Strict directives were given to the Singapore Film Censor to cut scenes of overt sexuality or of the glamour of crime. When *The Heart of the Matter* – in which Trevor Howard depicted the corruption of a colonial policeman – was banned it provoked questions in the House of Commons.[91] Even the colonial government's own propaganda was, on occasion, censored. Moreover, as one British information officer admitted: 'films showing the comparatively high standard of living in European countries and America, whether by design or unintentionally, do little to convince the population that their lot is a particularly happy one'.[92] The vast majority of banned

---

[88] Tan Sooi Beng, *Ko-tai: a new form of Chinese urban street theatre in Malaysia* (Singapore, 1984), p. 4.

[89] R. Rajoo, 'World-view of the Indians with regard to the social identity and belonging in Malaya, c.1900–57', in Mohd. Taib Osman (ed.), *Malaysian world-view* (Singapore, 1985), p. 175.

[90] Anthony Burgess, *Little Wilson and Big God*, (London, 1987) p.387.

[91] *Malay Mail*, 20.1.1954; Sautokh Tripat Kaur, 'The cinema in West Malaysia: a study of basic audience patterns and popular tastes, 1970–73' (M.A. Thesis, Universiti Malaya, 1975), p. 81.

[92] D. W. Stewart, 'Propaganda – a government failure', SCA Pahang/92/51.

movies were in fact American – thirty-seven of them were banned in 1950 alone.[93] Hollywood was both economically and culturally questionable. The Singapore government pressed for a 10 per cent quota of British or English Malayan films.[94] In this way censorship strengthened the Malay medium. Cinemas were graded into English and vernacular. Kuala Lumpur cinema owners resisted showing uncommercial, 'high class' films.[95] 'Can we blame a person for not liking the same things as ourselves?' Europeans asked themselves, 'and do we blame the cinema managers for wanting to eat?'[96] But these anxieties were widely shared. When the censor remarked that absurd fairy-tales defeated the educational purpose of cinema, it was sympathetically received in both the Malay and Chinese press. Cinema was 'detrimental to modern youth'; representations of love affairs on the silver screen were more dangerous than those of violence.[97]

But there was more to it than this. The scandalous and the seditious overlapped. As colonial orientalists debated the finer points of translation of lewd texts, they were aware that the kind of periodicals that carried it – especially Chinese mosquito papers – were deeply politicised. Some were founded by Kuomintang figures, such as the *Hwa Sang Post* established by N. K. Lee, the former Chinese Consul in Penang. It voiced anti-Communist doctrine, and eschewed low taste.[98] Yet at least six or seven formerly rightist papers included more of what translators called 'sex-exploitation': nudes, gossip and innuendo to sustain circulation. The *Yeh Teng Pao, Ta Ching Pau* and the *Sin Pao* were said to be Communist, the latter financed by the Chinese government through the Bank of China in Singapore; but after the April 1955 election all supported the left-wing People's Action Party and seem to have had a wide readership. Ex-China Democratic League journalists who found a home in these papers were accused by the authorities of 'subtle propaganda against the western democracies'.[99] Pornography was utilised to illustrate the corruption of colonial society. 'The tenor of these periodicals, both the literary ones and the others, is to spread the impression that society in the free world is degenerate and bankrupt, and that it is necessary to build a new society from the beginning, as has been done in China. In the final analysis this can only mean revolution.' Even the Chinese Rediffusion service was felt to 'sound like a substation of Radio Peking'.[100] Sheet music circulating in Chinese Middle Schools and Chinese gramophone records were also vetted and many banned. In Singapore in one month only in 1953, 460 of over

---

[93] Singapore, *Committee on Film Censorship* (Singapore, 1950).
[94] Singapore, *Report of a Committee appointed by the Government of Singapore to inquire into the Film Quota Legislation of the Colony* (Singapore, 1954); *Malaya Tribune*, 10.2.1949.
[95] *Malay Mail*, 9.3.1954.   [96] 'E.S.' in *Singapore Arts Theatre Review*, 1, 4 (1953).
[97] *Sin Lit Pau*, 4.10.1952; *Utusan Melayu*, 6.4.1953.
[98] APRO to PRO, 4.6.1953, PRO/Conf/47/53.
[99] 'A note of "mosquito" or non-daily Chinese newspapers in Singapore', 2.6.1955, PRO/Conf/286/54.
[100] F. J. A. Sullivan, 'Star News', 12.2.1953; G. G. Thomson, 'Sin Pao', 6.3.1953; APRO; Sullivan, 'Rediffusion News', 12.2.1953, PRO/Conf/47/53.

1,600 packets intercepted by post were stopped – including dictionaries and primers from China, Kuomintang publications and Chinese publications from Jakarta – even books on accounting, herbs and pathology.[101]

Under these conditions, democratic education and censorship moved forward hand in hand. The liberal regime which had briefly prevailed during the reoccupation of Malaya after the Pacific war had seen a mushrooming of opportunities in journalism and publishing. A series of confrontations between the colonial government and predominantly leftist publications had circumscribed the freedom of speech to which the new colonial government had still voiced commitment. Still, attempts were made by Radio Malaya to develop more sophisticated programming by young broadcasters imbued in the Reithian tradition. It was to unify the collective life of the nation, as the British envisaged it, and mark out a new public sphere for Malayans to identify with. However, it was made clear that whilst large moral questions could be discussed, Malayan matters occupying the attention of the press needed official sanction to be aired. Distanced from operational concerns on the peninsula, greater leeway was afforded to the media in Singapore, where the larger newspapers and foreign journalists were based. Here, future BBC Director-General, Carleton-Greene, urged on administrators a more positive approach to the fourth estate.[102] The press were to retain the maximum independence and freedom, 'but this does not release them from the obligation to help on the lines of material and civic responsibility'.[103] The role of media was to educate, and not to hold its masters to account. Publications were to be tolerated unless there was evidence of subversive intent. Sedition and not opposition was to be the rationale of suppression. Yet as their attempts to build up allies in the vernacular press failed, the British fell back on more authoritarian arguments. In 1950 the government moved against Tan Kah Kee's *Nan Chiao Jit Pao* and the *Penang Modern Daily News*. However, the courts did not uphold the government's position in the case of *Fajar*, a University of Malaya students' journal. The government's assumption that the paper was Communist, and its censorship of it before publication, went beyond the Emergency Regulations.[104] The Chinese, officials concluded, did not understand freedom of the press. They could not understand that the government itself might in some ways be committed to the principle. Liberalism was misguided. It was taken for granted that a government would seek to suppress hostile opinion; not to do so would be interpreted as a sign of weakness.[105] The view that the Chinese did not understand these freedoms was by no means general. 'If we are trying to train them towards democracy and freedom of the press,' it was argued, 'we do not want to be guided by their ideas. Rather we should train them towards our own principles.'[106]

[101] 'Singapore review of imported publications', January–July, 1953, PRO/Conf/153/53.
[102] Sir Franklin Gimson to Higham, 2.8.1951, CO537/7255.
[103] J. N. McHugh to Deputy Chief Secretary, 21.2.1950, FS/12290/50.
[104] SCA to Chief Secretary, 3.12.1954; PRO to Chief Secretary, 4.1.1955, PRO/Conf/286/54.
[105] R. N. Broome, 'Control of newspapers', 22.2.1955, PRO/Conf/286/54.
[106] E. C. S. Adkins, minute, 24.4.1950, CO537/6579.

Although some Englishmen still held to the idea that liberalism was a fighting creed, the logic of counter-insurgency triumphed.

In the policing of the printed word and culture, the 'Malayan' was used as a yardstick to distinguish between legitimate and illegitimate forms of public opinion. Yet the need to promote an Asian public opinion undermined its credibility. The official emphasis on the need for strict control was undermined by the growing ineffectiveness of action. Top secret reports on the ownership and political allegiance of the Malayan press show how powerful the press had become, and also the futility of attempts to suppress critical sections of it entirely. General Templer came very close to banning *Utusan Melayu*, the main Malay daily. Attempts were made to take it over, but as all its shareholders had to be Malay, proxies could not be found. The fact that a Federal Councillor, Abdul Aziz bin Ishak, was behind many offensive editorials made silencing the paper difficult. A strong counter-voice could not be found. Other candidates, for example the periodical *Warta*, had rendered themselves unsuitable in one way or another; few Malays had the capital for such a venture, and shareholders had obstructed attempts by the government to acquire the main rival, *Majlis*.[107] Another candidate, *Asmara*, disgraced itself by exposing a brochure available in Singapore advertising white women available as prostitutes.[108] In the absence of equally strong moderate opinion, repression was futile. The colonial official responsible finally conceded that 'the problem must be seen primarily in terms of the growing politics of the Federation, and not in terms of administrative convenience or anti-Communist activity'.[109] A dissident voice from Singapore, although writing somewhat later on the banning of juke boxes in 1960, famously warned government that it would be as futile to institute:

> a sarong-culture, complete with *pantun* competitions and so forth, as to bring back the Maypole and the Morris dancers in England just because the present monarch happens to be called Elizabeth. The important thing for Singapore and Malaya is to remain culturally open. Who can decide which seeds will fall on barren ground and which will grow?[110]

Colonial policy had rested on the stimulation of a viable national culture and sought to determine individual obligation to it through its civics policy. Its authoritarianism outlived it because the colonial policing of public taste had its echo in a parallel movement to eradicate 'yellow culture' – Americanism and materialism – in Malaya. The rape of a young girl in Singapore in 1953 sparked a campaign against imported, degenerate forms of culture that weakened the individual, led to lavish spending, and corrupted public morals. The 'anti-yellow culture' movement attacked the colonial

---

[107] Abu Bakar bin Pawanchee to PRO, *'Utusan Melayu'*, 8.7.1954; 'Notes of meeting on 9.7.1954', PRO/Conf/286/54.

[108] 'White prostitute', *Asmara*, October, 1955.

[109] PRO to Abu Bakar bin Pawanchee, 10.8.1954, PRO/Conf/286/54.

[110] D. J. Enright, *Robert Graves and the decline of modernism: inaugural lecture delivered on 17 November 1960 in the University of Malaya in Singapore* (Singapore, 1960), p. 4.

government for banning Asian magazines containing what its leaders saw as 'healthy culture'. 'The simplest and shortest way that is used by the colonial power to ridicule the colonised people of Malaya is to allow the unimpeded spread of yellow culture.' Therefore, it was argued, 'the anti-yellow culture movement cannot be separated from the *merdeka* movement'.[111] The movement paralleled the revitalisation of the Communist united front a drive to raise political consciousness. Yet it was supported by a wide range of student bodies, trade unions, radical politicians such as Lee Kuan Yew and Malay and Indian cultural associations, including the Malay literary organisation, ASAS 50.[112] A large public meeting in Singapore on 19 August 1956 requested the government to clamp down on 'pornography' and extend existing censorship of film and performance.[113] For many Malays, scenes of western women cavorting on stage and screen became arguments for restricting the public role of Malay women.[114] This reflected wider unease at the effects of fast urban living on the young, and reconstituted religious authorities moved against public entertainments in many States. Even Malay movies, such as *Chembaru*, and songs by P. Ramlee came under censure. Political rivalries were intruding in these debates. When the periodicals *Warta* and *Qalam* were banned, the hand of UMNO leader Tunku Abdul Rahman was alleged to be behind it.[115] These debates had a powerful legacy. After the première of a Twentieth Century Fox promotional film, *The Big Show*, Cathay boss Loke Wan Tho was confronted by an angry Singapore Chief Minister, Lim Yew Hock and accused of showing US propaganda in his cinemas. Loke later berated the American distributors for their indelicacy in exposing him to such charges: 'at this critical moment in our history there are those of us who are doing our utmost to preserve the link between the western democracies and ourselves'.[116] The arrival of rock 'n' roll in 1957 placed further strain on this connection. The legitimacy of journalism and literature was measured by its educational purpose, and defined by its utility in the development of a robust national culture. Faced with a period of intense disorientation and adaptation, communities drew on their own resources to use culture to reconstruct the responsibilities of the individual to the community. The late flowering of the press in the 1950s sowed the seeds of public debate more widely, and made it more intelligible to a mass audience. Yet a general challenge was needed to sustain the anti-colonial momentum of these varied movements, and draw them together into a more coherent challenge to colonial culture.

---

[111] 'Building an extensive anti-yellow culture movement', an article written in Chinese, translated from the *Malayan Student* into Malay and published in *Utusan Zaman*, 19.8.1956.

[112] See *Tai Pao*, 3.8.1956, 'The Communist front "anti-yellow" campaign in proper perspective', PRO/330/56; discussed in Tan Eng Teik, 'The development of Malaysia Chinese poetry, 1945–69', (Ph.D. Thesis, Universiti Malaya, 1990), pp. 172–6.

[113] 'Meeting in protest of yellow culture at Badminton Hall on 19.8.1956', PRO/330/56.

[114] For example, Omar Abdul Rahman, 'What is the status of women', *Asmara* (February, 1955).

[115] *Utusan Melayu*, 30.10.1953.

[116] Loke Wan Tho to Edward Ugast, 29.7.1957, Loke Wan Tho Papers.

'Language is the soul of the nation'

Alternative agendas for national cultural life came out of the shared problem of language, and of reconciling individual commitment to the nation through literature. Yet there was no natural logic to one alternative form, as the colonial policy seemed to suggest. There were separate debates on the Malayanisation of Chinese and Tamil literature. A rich local tradition of Chinese literature which had emerged in the Malayan Spring immediately after the war was crushed because of its leftist connections. Writers went underground; few works are extant and many writers would later deny ever having written anything. Playwrights such as Tu Pien and Yeh Yeh had exploited the local environment for material, but returned to China by the early 1950s.[117] Conservative Chinese newspaper barons resisted a rising school of writers addressing local themes: Chinese writing in Malaya was to remain a 'tributary of the main stream'. Yet new writing emerging in the 1950s, especially from the schools, completed the political domestication of Malayan Chinese literature. Although the rich Straits Chinese tradition of writing in Malay was not revived, by the 1950s new translations of Malay works were appearing. In 1950 the Saturday Review re-introduced the Malay *pantun* to a Chinese audience, and in 1946 the *Sejarah Melayu* was translated by Hsu Yun Tsiao in *Nanyang Monthly*.[118] However, in the heightened political atmosphere of the period, Chinese writing was forced to confront the forceful demands of Malay nationalism for cultural assimilation and to voice the rights of the Chinese community to retain its own cultural identity within Malaya.[119] Moreover, heavily screened by the authorities, it was inhibited as a vehicle for social criticism. Newspapers were also the main medium for Tamil writing, again dominated by an assertive classical tradition. After a flourishing of Tamil writing on social reform in the late 1930s, and Indian National Army polemics during the occupation, a post-war generation of writers such as P. Krishnan and N. Palanivelu began to address the social concerns of the locality – marriage customs and the survival of Tamil language and education. New journalistic blood infused the Dravidian newspaper, *Tamil Murasu* in the early 1950s, and the paper's 'Bell Club' helped vitalise this movement, as in another way did the appearance of movie magazines – Indian *Movie News*, *Manoharan*, and *Kalai Malar*.[120] Radio Malaya gave voice to the homespun humour of the drama, and took on much local colour by the

---

[117] Wang Gungwu, 'A short introduction to Chinese writing in Malaysia', in T. Wignesan, *Bunga Emas: an anthology of contemporary Malaysian literature* (Kuala Lumpur, 1964); Ang Tian Se, 'The dilemma of Chinese writers in Malaya in the late 1940s', *Proceedings of the First International Symposium on Asian Studies*, 3 (1979), 549–52.

[118] Tan Chin Kwang, 'Chinese translations of Malay literary works in Malaya', *Tenggara*, 1 (1967), 116–20.

[119] Tan Liok Ee, *The rhetoric of* bangsa *and* minzu: *community and nations in tension, the Malay peninsula, 1900–1955* (Working paper No. 52, Centre of Southeast Asian Studies, Monash University, 1988), pp. 22–41.

[120] Govindasamy, 'Development of Tamil literature', 18–19.

late 1940s, with Malay borrow-words and coinages. However, its comic duets for labourers were attacked by urban Indians as sensual and disgusting.[121] On one day alone there were ten letters of complaint in the *Tamil Murasu* alone. Bodies such as the Tamil Reform Association and the Tamils Representative Council jumped on the bandwagon of protests. Tamil purists attacked the imposition of a 'hybrid' Malayan Tamil, and the 'open murder' of the language. *Tamil Murasu* satirised the broadcasts for ending words with 'lae', instead of the usual 'l' sound, which they assumed to a vulgar approximation of the Malay 'lah'. There was resentment at the suggestion that Malayanisation of Tamil culture was a corollary of political Malayanisation.[122]

There were also attempts to mobilise English for anti-colonial ends. The most important centre of writing in English was the new University of Malaya, sited in Singapore. It drew together expatriates and young students from throughout the peninsula committed to creating a new national culture. The University was host to the main literary movement in English – a group which included many individuals who were to rise to high positions in public life in Singapore and Malaysia. The hallmark of this group, as stated by Beda Lim, was their belief that: 'The way to nationhood is through the way to culture. The prospect of a common culture is probably not a predominance of any of the main culture streams present, but rather a courageous attempt at a synthesis between all the conflicting currents.'[123] As independence approached these young intellectuals took a conscious lead in defining a prototype 'Malayan' culture. They articulated a complex identity in which English literature with a local context emerged out of a local heritage in which the western was an important, but not a sole cultural component – for example with verse experiments in a local Esperanto of their own devising - *Engmalchin*. This group – many of them Straits Chinese – found an outlet in students' magazines, the most important of which was *The New Cauldron* – which carried on its sleeve a representation of the weird sisters in *Macbeth* – 'boiling, mixing and melting . . . multicultural elements stirring'. It published literary criticism and poetry, mainly experimental renditions of tropical themes in forms derived from the syllabi of the English schools. The verse of Palgrave's *Golden Treasury* in particular provided templates into which the flora and fauna of Malaya was introduced. More sophisticated verse displayed pronounced borrowings from T. S. Eliot.[124] *Engmalchin*, as the name suggests, was a fusion of English, Malay and Chinese, a literary representation

---

[121] T. Wignesan, 'Origins and scope of Tamil literature in Malaysia', in *Bunga Emas*; *Tamil Murasu*, 22.2.1953. Programmes were 'Truth Teller' and 'Kampong Gossip'; for examples of their contents see 'Radio Malaya: rural broadcasting programmes for week 27.9.–3.10.1953', PRO/58/53.

[122] *Tamil Murasu*, 9.11.1952, 21.11.1952, 7.1.1953 and *passim*.

[123] *The Malayan Undergrad: organ of the University of Malaya Students' Union*, I, 3 (18.1.1950).

[124] See *The New Cauldron: the official organ of the Raffles Society, University of Malaya* (Hillary Term, 1949/50); an anthology is *Litmus One: selected University verse, 1949–57* (Singapore, 1958).

of the patois of everyday life.[125] One of its most effective exponents, Ee Tiang Hong, was later to defend it as a challenge to colonialism: 'Where in the past the Queen's English was held in awe as the language par excellence, as an institution to be revered, and even in its everyday uses unimpeachable, *Engmalchin* implied that nationalising the language and literature was an inevitable aspect of the loosening of political allegiance.'[126]

The search for the Malayan was explicitly political. These debates arose at a time when politicisation of students was under attack from the authorities, amid reports of Communist cells in the new University of Malaya. There were plans to form a Malayan Students' Party.[127] In January 1951, ten students were arrested and permission was not granted until 1952 for political clubs to be formed. A Socialist Club appeared in the same year, publishing a journal, *Fajar*, which became the subject of a fierce legal battle, during which a young Singapore lawyer for the defence, Lee Kuan Yew, rose to prominence.[128] He asserted, at the time, that 'the product of the University of Malaya is likely to approximate to the cultural norm of the true Malayan'.[129] Yet, these products fell into fierce controversy as to how far an intelligentsia, soon to be absorbed into the ruling class of the new nation, could impose a culture from on high.[130] As student politicians and anti-colonialists they had learnt to be suspicious of the state, and this led a generation of writers to abdicate from an active political role. English was 'one tributary of the Malayan literary stream', but as it was a cultural imposition of colonialism it stood between the writer and his national audience, and placed the writer in an equivocal position between personal and national identity. Frustration crept in, with the 'culture-wallahs who have never written a line themselves but who nevertheless greet every piece of work by aspiring writers with "But it isn't *Malayan*, is it?".'[131] Reflecting on *Engmalchin* ten years on, Wang Gungwu, a leading exponent, argued that English had been

[125] For an extended discussion of this term and its seeds of 'dystopian totalitarianism', see Brewster, *Towards a semiotic of post-colonial discourse*, pp. 3–9.

[126] Ee Tiang Hong, 'Literature and liberation: the price of freedom', in E. Thumboo (ed.), *Literature and liberation: five essays from Southeast Asia* (Manila, 1988), pp. 11–41.

[127] Yeo Kim Wah, 'Student politics in University of Malaya, 1949–51', *Journal of Southeast Asian Studies*, 23, 2 (1992), 346–80.

[128] K. Kanagaratnam, 'Extra-curricular activities in the period of transition from College to University, 1940–1955', in A. A. Sandosham (ed.), *A symposium on extra-curricular activities of university students in Malaya* (Singapore, 1955).

[129] Koh Tai Ann, 'Singapore writing in English: the literary tradition and cultural identity', in Tham Seong Chee (ed.), *Essays on literature and society in Southeast Asia: political and sociological perspectives* (Singapore, 1981), p. 163.

[130] For example, J. J. Puthucheary, 'Building the Malayan nation', *The Undergrad*, 1, 2 (1949); answered by Francis Thomas: 'They will fail, partly because they do not know what is the common person's "good", and partly because good is a growth not a gift. We cannot construct good by a managerial process', *ibid.*, 1, 4 (1949).

[131] 'Films', in *Write: an independent student publication of the University of Malaya*, I (1957), edited by Lloyd Fernando. A lively memoir of the period is Patrick Anderson, *Snake wine: a Singapore episode* (Singapore, 1984 [1955]).

adapted to nationalism, not because it was best suited to the task but because it was a convenient tool for young people in a hurry. In retrospect the obsession with a didactic promotion of the 'Malayan' identity had been a distraction and the credibility of new literature had been undermined. 'We had,' he wrote, 'galloped off in all directions on an old steed that had never been tropicalized.' 'Malayan' literature had failed as there were very few 'Malayans'.[132] It had read like an edict from on high. Thereafter a reaction set in against using English literature to address political themes. English writers felt that because of this, and rather than creating an 'artificial compromise' between cultures, they could only indirectly contribute to a national culture, using conscience as their moral code.[133] The poet D. J. Enright at the University of Malaya seems to have encouraged an abdication from an active political role that marked a generation of writers.[134] *Engmalchin* shared the same fate as colonial cultural policy. It illustrated the narrowness of the constituency for its 'Malayan' nationalism and even slenderer support for those who were taking up the challenge for anti-colonial ends. A small privileged group unsure of their politics were unable to match the achievements of the reformulation of the Malay language as an agent of national mobilisation.

A more unequivocal movement to effect national reconstruction through literature was in response to a challenge to the Malay language. The Malay critic, Kassim Ahmad, then a university student, roundly condemned 'we bastard Malayans':

> It is the coming of this monstrous child – the Malayan nation that I'm intrigued by, aren't you? If I may say so, he was conceived in sin, by an act of imperialist licence. The trouble is we can't get rid of him now; no Nazified device of any kind will do. We'll give him a goodly anti-father education and baptise him as the son of our generation sworn to life before the god of *Merdeka*.[135]

Here language reinforced larger communal identities, and acted as the stimulus to new ideologies to challenge colonial civic management. In the 1950s there were calls for the use of Malay in all official matters affecting the Malays, although Malay politicians were criticised for continuing to speak English themselves.[136] The English language was a symbol of the humiliation of the Malay nation. The colonial government was accused of giving precedence to English, although Malay was on equal terms under the Federation Agreement. Criticism of colonial language policy was intensified by British attempts to create a Basic Malay as an elementary *lingua franca* – fit only for the bazaar and rooted in rural life. Colonial educationalists were

---

[132] Wang Gungwu, 'Trial and error in Malayan poetry', *Malayan Undergrad*, 9, 5 (1958).

[133] Goh Kiat Seng, 'Towards a Malayan culture', *Write*, 5 (1958); *Report of the Malayan Writers' Conference* (Singapore, 1962).

[134] One critic has recently argued that by insisting on their artistic independence in this manner they equated society with the state, and in disengaging themselves with both became writers without an audience. Shirley Lim, 'The English-language writer in Singapore', in Kernial Singh Sandhu and Paul Wheatley (eds), *Singapore: the management of success* (Singapore, 1990), pp. 523–51.

[135] Kassim Ahmad, 'We bastard Malayans', *Write*, 5 (1958).

[136] MacGillivray to Lennox-Boyd, 25.3.1955, CO1030/68.

contemptuous of attempts by Malay writers to move the language away from its agrarian origins. Their primers of the period inveighed against the 'unnecessary' innovations of Malay language reformers. Eight hundred words were vocabulary enough.[137] The dialogues in these primers are fascinating sources for European perceptions of the Malays and the conventions of race relations in the period – or rather of what the British thought they ought to be. They showed Malays cheerfully embracing agricultural improvement and joining the police to avenge their race against the Communists.[138] One textbook, *Malay for Mems*, consisted almost entirely of commands.[139] Yet to Malay linguistic nationalists, the Malay medium would triumph after independence and it had to be made fit to become the national language. Primers were produced to the new languages of politics that were sweeping Malaya.[140] To colonial scholars, they were 'more or less artificial and cannot be said to be part of colloquial Malay'. Certainly, the British found it hard to penetrate the language of newspaper editorials. It was here, they complained, that one was 'constantly bumping into the latest innovation'. Malayan Civil Service examinations in Malay ignored them.[141] It would be a tragedy, they argued, if Malay surrendered 'to mass-production in verbal expression'.[142] However, the government was compelled to produce its own political vocabulary in Malay. In it the word 'politics' was given as *siasat*, giving the sense of a policy, an investigation, rather than the more dynamic borrow-word that was gaining currency amongst Malays themselves, *politik*. To the British, politics was a matter of administration, not struggle.[143] The censorship of the Emergency Regulations was actively fostering a new literature, by forcing writers to express their ideas in 'parcels so wrapped up that it became difficult to grasp their message'.[144] This new literature was to be a vehicle for the transformation of the Malay language.

The opportunity to achieve this arose, paradoxically, with the suppression of Malay

[137] O. T. Dussek, *Practical modern Malay, an introduction to the colloquial language* (London, 1953), pp. vii–x.

[138] See for example 'Visit to Tanjong Karang' and 'Time of Emergency', in M. Ali bin Mohamed and A. E. Coope, *Malay dialogues with colloquial grammar* (London, 1952), pp. 22–25, 42–45.

[139] Maye Wood, *Malay for mems* (5th edn Singapore, 1949).

[140] These are fascinating documents, for example, Muhammad bin Hanif, *Kamus politik* [Political dictionary] (2 vols, Penang, 1949) and his *English-Malay dictionary of commodities* (Alor Star, 1951).

[141] A. E. Coope, *A guide to Malay conversation* (3rd edn, Singapore, 1953), p. 113; O. T. Dussek, Ahmad Murad bin Nasruddin and A. E. Coope, *A graduated Malay reader* (2nd edn Singapore, 1953), pp. x–xi.

[142] Gerald Hawkins, 'The Malay language in history and transition', *New Malaya*, 3 (1957), 33–9.

[143] J. N. McHugh, *Words and phrases related to political organizations and procedure at meetings* (Kuala Lumpur, 1948). For the rise of *politik* over *siasah*, A. C. Milner, *The invention of politics in colonial Malaya: contesting nationalism and the expansion of the bourgeois public sphere* (Cambridge, 1995), p. 265.

[144] S. N. Masuri, 'The development of Malay fiction in Singapore', in E. Thumboo (ed.), *The fiction of Singapore* (Singapore, 1993), pp. 13–14.

radicalism during the Emergency. A gifted generation of writers and propagandists came to Singapore from the peninsula – especially from Pahang, Malacca and Johore. Some were avoiding the Emergency Regulations, others had served in the police. They were concentrated in the more liberal environment of Singapore which became a centre of literary revival. As we have seen, it was home to important Malay printing companies, magazines like *Mastika, Hiburan,* and the newspapers *Utusan Melayu* and *Melayu Raya.* The penny novels of writers such as Ahmad Lufti embraced social themes – often moralising out of lurid descriptions of urban vice – the stories of Hamdan and Harun Aminurrashid fed the reading public's appetite for historical romance set in a Malay golden age. Singapore was the centre of a remarkable network of politicians and journalists. *Utusan Melayu,* for example, maintained a system of intelligence that stretched from Singapore – through its stringers and correspondents – throughout the Malay peninsula. Many of these were minor officials and school-teachers in the villages from where they had a vital role in leading villages' responses to outside forces and influences and embarked on careers in politics within UMNO. What was debated in Singapore would be debated elsewhere on the peninsula, and what was said on the peninsula would be transmitted back down to Singapore.[145] The island was also a clearing house for information from the new Indonesian republic. Many of its journalists had travelled in the republic or had family connections there. A minority position nurtured a keen sense of Malay identity. Censorship diverted writers from polemic into a new level of engagement with social themes. With the proscription of the Malay left during the Emergency, many leaders fled to Singapore's less stringent laws and employment opportunities. They were drawn together by a *Sahabat Pena* – association of pen-friends – which appeared in the columns of *Saudara,* a religious paper advocating social and religious reform. Graduates of this circle maintained their association working for Japanese-sponsored periodicals during the occupation, and then in to the Malay leftist parties after the war. Around 1947, one of these men, best known by his pen-name Jymy Asmara, came to Singapore from the mainland as a policeman. He collected addresses of old comrades-in-arms and formed an unofficial revived pen-pal club, which found support amongst journalists, schoolteachers, clerks and students, and a ready outlet for their work in the Malay press. The early writings of these young men were, as one contemporary recalls, not marked by any great seriousness of purpose, they embraced themes of young love, and were often written in response to short-story competitions by magazines such as *Mutiara* and *Belia,* published by the Harmy press, or as fillers by rookie reporters in the newspapers, when, as often happened during the Emergency, news stories did not make it into print.[146] However, influenced by the Indonesian *Angkatan 1945* – Generation of 1945 – and enraptured by the nationalist potential of the Malay

---

[145] Ahmad Sebi, 'Samad's influence', in Cheah Boon Kheng (ed.), *A. Samad Ismail: journalism and politics* (Kuala Lumpur, 1987), pp. 90–1.

[146] A. Samad Said, '1948: Dawn of a new literary era', in his *Between art and reality: selected essays* (Kuala Lumpur, 1994), pp. 57–71.

language, an *Angkatan Sasterawan 50* or ASAS 50 was formed. The aim was, in the words of Keris Mas:

> a style which had new life, a style of language that was more fresh than that of the generation of older writers, using themes from society, politics and culture which had the purpose of arousing a spirit of independence, a spirit of 'standing on your own feet' like a people which were respected and had their own identity, to defend justice and oppose oppression.[147]

ASAS 50 represented a critique of British rule, not only for its cultural impositions, but for its encouragement of a division of Malay society between a Malay bureaucratic elite and the masses. There were both ideological and personal links with the MNP, many of whose members were revitalising the dominant Malay nationalist movement UMNO.[148] ASAS 50 represented a critique of British rule, not only for its cultural impositions, but for its encouragement of a division within Malay society between a Malay bureaucratic elite and the masses. The Malay experience was represented as an interplay between the forces of feudalism and colonialism and the masses. The survival of the suffering and steadfast poor in an inhospitable social environment was contrasted with the lives of hypocritical and callous rulers, obsessed with sensual gratification. This interplay began in the village, where authority figures used their position for selfish ends. The city, no longer an evil in itself but colonised by Malays on the move, was a chalice of corruption, dominated by upper classes in a state of moral collapse. 'Malayness' was associated with values embedded in the rural masses; it rejected elitism. The critic Asraf, for example, saw an obligation to reflect the true position of the masses: through close links with journalism, to ensure that this literature reached them, and through literary conventions, to facilitate identification with the moral. Poems in modern form – *sajak* – and short stories – *cerita pendek* – gave a new directness to its message. In drama full scripted works broke with the improvised and spontaneous traditions of folk drama; themes shifted from historical dramas of courtly life, heroic valour, the love of a man for a woman and for his country, to engage with social issues of nationalism, morality and education.[149]

ASAS 50 was the 'literature of the underdogs', the 'literature of the committed'. A role for the writer and for literature was voiced in the slogan: *Sastera untuk Masyarakat* – 'Art for Society'.[150] ASAS 50 mediated the challenges of the impact of the west – 'the divided self in the ancient mirror'– by taking up old debates on self-improvement, Islam and the position of women. It advanced the new debates which dominated the politics of culture: the extent to which the achievement of the one was

---

[147] Virginia Matheson, 'Usman Awang, Keris Mas and Hamzah: individual expressions of social commitment in Malay literature', *RIMA*, 21, 1 (1987), 108.

[148] Firdaus Haji Abdullah, *Radical Malay politics: its origins and early development* (Petaling Jaya, 1985), pp. 120–4.

[149] Rahmah Haji Bujang, 'Drama in Malaysia: the writer in a changing society', *Sarjana*, 1, 1 (1981), p. 39.

[150] For a useful survey, Ungku Maimunah Mohd. Tahir, *Modern Malay literary culture: a historical perspective* (Singapore, 1987), pp. 39–40.

to be solely directed at the enrichment of the many. However, the movement divided on the degree of autonomy allowed to the individual conscience. The debate reflected divisions in the movement between the more left-leaning writers close to *Utusan Melayu* and those associated with the Harmy press.[151] Within the body of ASAS 50 another style of writing emerged characterised by plot style known as *rasa*, a construction of emotional ideas. Here realism was a kind of expressionism in which 'literature is the picture of the thoughts of a generation', reproductive of the self-development of the individual, rather than society. A split occurred between the progressive wing of Asraf, Keris Mas and Tongkat Warrant, and a breakaway *Persatuan Angkatan Persuratan Melayu Baru*, of Hamzah, Rosmera, Abdul Ghani Hamid and others.[152] However, ASAS 50, as literature born from within society, was insistent that literature should not relinquish its educative function for the masses. But its conception of the powerlessness and helplessness of the *rakyat* amounted almost to fatalism. Culture was the vehicle of collective enablement. Yet a notion of individual powerlessness permeates the writing of the school. One famous story by Keris Mas – 'The would-be leader from Kuala Semantan' – clearly demonstrates this theme. He writes of a young cadre fleeing from the proscription of the Malay left on the declaration of the Emergency:

> 'What significant creatures we humans are!' Hasan added. His words were swallowed up by the silence of the night.
> 'But when we begin to question our convictions, and a change takes place within, then we can no longer think straight.'
> My friend Hasan seemed to be confessing his innermost feelings to the dark silence. He was suffering as only a man does who has his freedom snatched away from him by a force he dislikes, yet is unable to cope with. Hasan hated violence, but violence was rampant everywhere, in the jungle and in the world at large. He loved freedom but was being hunted down by circumstances both forced upon him and upon the society in which he lived. Reasoning should be centred about the truth; yet people who have lost their freedom are no longer capable of comprehending truth.[153]

In many ways this celebration of the spirit of nationalism anticipates the disillusionments of independence.[154]

The contribution of ASAS 50 to the securing and expansion of the Malay language

---

[151] David J. Banks, *From class to culture: social consciousness in Malay novels since independence* (Yale University SEA Series Monograph No. 29, New Haven, 1987), pp. 20–1.

[152] These debates are reproduced in A. M. Thani (ed.), *Esei sastera ASAS 50* (Kuala Lumpur, 1981), especially, Hamzah, 'Kenyataan di dalam sastera baharu', pp. 101–8 and Asraf's reply, 'Nilai sastera', pp. 27–39. Li Chuan Siu, *An introduction to the promotion and development of modern Malay literature, 1942–62* (Yogyakarta, 1975), pp. 24–5.

[153] Keris Mas, 'The would-be leader from Kuala Semantan', translated in the Dewan Bahasa dan Pustaka anthology, *Modern Malaysian stories* (Kuala Lumpur, 1977), pp. 79–80.

[154] I have here drawn on the work of Matheson, 'Usman Awang, Keris Mas and Hamzah'. I am grateful to Dr Matheson Hooker for showing me her unpublished paper, 'Literature as social criticism: the writings of the Generation of the 1950s (ASAS 50)', paper presented to the Malaysia Society Colloquium: Malaysian social and economic history, 8–10 June, 1985.

was achieved in two ways. First, through a process of institutionalisation, ASAS 50 harnessed literature to state-formation. The central role that ASAS 50 played in controlling publications and patronage through a peninsula-wide organisation became the basis of the interventionist cultural agencies of the new nation-state. A key figure was the *Utusan Melayu* journalist, A. Samad Ismail. Seen by many as the mastermind behind ASAS 50, he was remembered by its founders as 'the most ruthless and sharpest critic of the movement'. However, for all his scepticism he lent to ASAS 50 the political heritage of the MNP, and his considerable power-base in grass-roots Malay politics of Singapore, within Singapore UMNO and in the circles of activists that would later form the People's Action Party. He brought Malay writers into contact with the *Fajar* writers of the University of Malaya, where they held meetings communicating in 'bazaar' Malay and fractured English. He introduced new writing in Malay to a larger English-audience through the columns of the *Singapore Standard*, and translated Tolstoy, Checkov and Alberto Moravia into Malay in *Mastika*.[155] The editorial powers of ASAS 50 and its allies, exercised through the *Utusan Melayu*, and its offshoots, *Utusan Zaman* and *Mastika*, largely determined literary development for two decades. Branches appeared in Negri Sembilan, the east coast and Penang. Many of the leaders of ASAS 50 moved to Kuala Lumpur as independence approached to dominate journalism, publishing and the cultural institutions of independent Malaya. Some of the younger poets from within ASAS 50 such as Masuri S. N. began to explore more experimental forms. Later the secularity of its approach would come under attack.[156] However, through its editorial power and influence, ASAS 50 played a critical role in the re-invention of the modern Malay language.

This was the second achievement of ASAS 50. Its writers sought to uproot Malay from its agrarian origins and to incorporate a new technical vocabulary. Other educational and cultural societies played an important role in this process. In April 1953, the grand old man of Malay letters, Za'ba, became Chairman of a new Department of Malay Studies at the University of Malaya. His students, under the encouragement of Ungku Abdul Aziz, founded a Malay language society which published a journal *Bahasa* and embarked on its own collation of 'modern' word lists.[157] A *Lembaga Bahasa Melayu* – Malay Language League, formed by older and more conservative schoolteachers, staff of the Singapore Broadcasting Station and novelists such as Harun Aminurrashid and Abdullah Sidek – worked to meet a shortage of Malay textbooks and to maintain the purity of the Malay language.[158] Other bodies were active on the peninsula such as the *Ikatan Persuratan Melaka* and *ASAS Utara* in Penang. Yet ASAS 50 differed from its fellow-travellers by making

---

[155] Usman Awang, 'Leader of Malay literary movement'; Keris Mas, 'A master of his craft'; M. Rajakumar, 'Malaysia's Jean-Paul Sartre', in Cheah (ed.), *A. Samad Ismail*, pp. 25–42; Nasradin Bahari, 'Cherpen² terjemahan didalan majalah Mastika, 1946–59', *Bahasa*, 7 (1965), 56–93.

[156] For example, Shahnon Ahmad, *Kesusasteraan dan etika Islam* (Kuala Lumpur, 1981).

[157] *Mesurat Agung Ketiga, Persekutan Bahasa Melayu, Universiti Malaya* (20.10.1957).

[158] Li, *Introduction*, pp. 24–30.

Malay more congruent to Indonesian. The post-war years were a period of great innovation in language during which many new terms were circulating in common speech and journalism, especially amongst the young. ASAS 50 dominated the movement by defending and popularising the new Malay words and meanings. Debates began on the fixing of Malay meanings. In the introduction of foreign words in new fields of politics, economy and medicine there was little uniformity: some were pronounced in the Malay fashion, others were introduced through Malay words of similar meaning. New language was used to mount an internal critique on Malay society – as it had in Indonesia.[159] It was a social leveller: the language of rank was to be abolished. ASAS 50 argued for the dropping of honorific forms when addressing Rulers, such as *patek* instead of *saya*; they were an obstacle to the progress of the Malays.[160] ASAS 50 drew Malay closer to Indonesian by adopting the *Ejaan Fajar Asia*, a spelling system which had emerged in the Malay periodicals of Japanese occupation. A series of learning aids were produced for the new Federation citizens.[161] A series of conferences on language and literature advanced this process. The first *Kongres Bahasa dan Persuratan Melayu se-Malaya*, on 12–13 April 1952, was promoted by ASAS 50 and supported by the *Lembaga Bahasa Melayu*, the *Persatuan Guru-guru Melayu Singapura* and in all twenty organisations from Singapore and the Federation. A key debate was initiated on the identity of the Malay language. A committee was formed under Harun Aminurrashid, with Keris Mas as his Secretary, which undertook the groundwork for the momentous decision at a second congress in January 1954 at Seremban to adopt *rumi*, or romanised script, at the expense of Arabic script. Some opposed this new direction, fearing that the Malay identity would be lost. Religious leaders felt that the Malays would learn less religion and that the loss of Arabic script would turn the Malays away from the Islamic world; Pattani Malays feared linguistic isolation. The triumph of *rumi* was a victory of new nationalism over old religion. A *Kongres Bahasa* held at Medan between 28 October and 2 November 1954 fortified the Malay alliance with Indonesian linguistic nationalists. The Congresses' campaign to strengthen the resolve of the government to make Malay the national language, culminated in the Third Congress of September 1956 in Singapore and Johore Bahru – the *Ejaan Kongres* which made spelling more phonetic.[162] To Arnold Toynbee who attended it, it was a display of unity by 100 million Malay

---

[159] Khaidir Anwar, *Indonesian: the development and use of a national language* (Yogyakarta, 1980), pp. 108–35.

[160] *Utusan Melayu*, 12.8.1952, 7.11.1952.

[161] For example Mansor Sanusi's *Bahasa Melayu: the new method course* (Penang, 1953) and *Letter writer in Malay* (Penang, 1956), published under the aegis of the Federation of Malaya Malay Teachers' Association.

[162] *Malay Mail*, 16.1.1954; Asmah binte Haji Omar, 'Towards the unification of Bahasa Melayu and Bahasa Indonesia', *Tengara*, 1 (1967), 112–15; Persekutuan Bahasa Melayu University Malaya, *Laporan tentang bahasa Melayu dan bahasa Indonesia oleh Kongres III Bahasa dan Persuratan Melayu Malaya* (Singapore, 1956); HUSBA, 'The Third Malay Language and Literary Congress', *Magazine of the University of Malaya Students' Union, Sessions 1954/55 and 1955/56*, 53–4.

speakers against 'the insinuating Chinese huckster'.[163] However, a publication annotated in Chinese appeared to publicise its keynote speeches.[164] The Congress adopted the slogan *Bahasa Jiwa Bangsa* – 'language is the soul of the nation'.

By 1955 *Bahasa Jiwa Bangsa* had been accepted by the politicians as well. This was the second contribution of ASAS 50. Malay politicians adopted their slogans as Malay language reform was drawn into a wider pattern of assertive corporatist politics. Through the interlocking political and communications networks that fostered ASAS 50, its goals became incorporated in the dominant strain of Malay nationalism. This is not the place to go fully into this process – the Malay politics of the 1950s will dominate the following chapter. However, access to the systems of intelligence and communications dominated by the networks described here played a crucial role in UMNO's defeat of conservative and Islamic opposition. UMNO articulated a secular view of Malay nationalism and advanced a corporatist approach to Malay education, culture and economic improvement. The linguistic nationalists were vital allies in UMNO's claims to leadership of the nation. When, in the months before independence, UMNO came under new pressure from Malay opposition and from Chinese and Indian opposition to the alliance of ethnic parties it led, linguistic nationalism played a vitally important role in UMNO's ability to dominate the endgame of decolonisation. It was through debates on the national language, that ASAS 50's cultural activism, and its gradual institutionalisation, gained ground.[165] Competing nationalist parties were increasingly responsive to it, and ASAS 50's memorandum to the Razak Committee on National Education, advocating compulsory teaching of Malay in all schools so that within ten years Malay should function fully as the national language in all aspects of life, was substantially adopted. The government converted the recently formed *Balai Pustaka* into a *Dewan Bahasa dan Pustaka* – 125,000 new linguistic terms were created in the ten years after 1957.[166] It was through the agency of the Generation of 1950, and their wholesale absorption into the new national cultural agencies, that *Bahasa Jiwa Bangsa* became a core assumption of the post-colonial polity.

This is a general theme of late colonialism. British attempts to build new communities were subverted at many different levels, because social engineering merely gave new resources to Malayans for their own projects of cultural refurbishment. The quest for the 'Malayan' floundered in a resurgence of alternative identities. These were not primordial or traditional, but forged or remade in a period of intense social change and political speculation. However, although the colonial experiment was frustrated, the rearguard defence of it through propaganda and censorship fostered a precedent of state intervention in political and cultural life. Its partial

---

[163] Arnold J. Toynbee, *East to west: a journey around the world* (London, 1958), p. 59.

[164] '*Pidato² dari orang² yang Terkemuka*' (Singapore, n. d. [1957?]).

[165] Tham Seong Chee, 'The politics of literary development in Malaysia', in Tham, *Essays on literature and society in Southeast Asia: political and sociological perspectives* (Singapore, 1981), pp. 216–52.

[166] Hassan Ahmad, *Bahasa, sastera buku: cetusan fikiran* (Kuala Lumpur, 1988), p. 34.

successes in this regard had a profound impact on the character of the independent polity, as people looked more and more to the state to accomplish the cultural and political ambitions of independence. They seized upon colonial methods of censure and control to develop a robust national culture, and enforce new allegiances. Ironically, the very agencies that had emerged to challenge colonial cultural policy were employed to this end. But they would not have it all their own way. Searching debates on the nature of the national culture they now defended – especially on the position of minority tongues and the place of Islam within it – were left unresolved by independence. The Anglophone bourgeoisie did not disappear from view. Resurgent Islam, by identifying the *ummah* – the community of believers – as the true end of politics, challenged the assumptions of national struggle itself. The enduring paradoxes of the late colonial period were that new patterns of corporatism could exclude as much as they united; new techniques of state-building could foster new methods of undermining authority. A process of democratisation was underway that was carefully policed by the authoritarian machinery that had emerged out of counter-insurgency. The politics of culture helped shape the paternalism of the end of empire, but it also created useful precedents for challenging it.

CHAPTER EIGHT

Making citizens

The fulfilment of Britain's mission in Malaya lay in the establishment of multi-racial politics. This was both a measure of political advancement and a condition of independence. However, schemes to restore the initiative to the locality and to break down ethnic blocs through projects of social engineering and democratisation merely revealed the possibilities of these strategies for communal advancement. The aim of drawing Chinese society in the New Villages into the mainstream of national life was subverted when the government's local allies, the MCA, were implicated in a movement of Chinese cultural resurgence. Resurrected trade unionism became a communal enclave. Increasing economic differentiation within the Malay heartlands presaged a shift from locally based movements of self-improvement to corporatism directed from the centre. Malay political leadership did not merely defend this as a strategy for development, but as a political entitlement, an indissoluble component of Malay identity. In a parallel process, the colonial government's propagation of a 'Malayan' national culture was anticipated by a flood of alternative expressions of community and movements of cultural reconstruction. Powerful cultural and political alternatives emerged which refused to conform to the colonial paradigm, and much of the fabric of Malayan social life stood outside of it. These were not to fuse, as the ideologues of the new imperialism had suggested, but to accommodate after a fashion in a social compact, guaranteed in the last resort by the power of the state.

In this chapter, we examine the core techniques of collaboration: community development and democratic tutelage. The politics of decolonisation in Malaya had two dimensions. On the one hand they belong to the wider realm of imperial relations, and had an international compass. The aim in Malaya was not merely to remain friends with the Malays and the Chinese, but to win new friends throughout Asia. Malaya was, as Dien Bien Phu reminded the British, a forward base against Communism in Southeast Asia, and this strengthened Britain's resolve to secure its defence and ensure its economic strength as a buttress of the Sterling Area. Many of the key questions posed by historians have thus focused on the metropolis – on the motives and course of colonial policy-making, on whether the Emergency accelerated or retarded the devolution of power from the centre. Important new documentary research now provides clearer answers to these questions.[1] There was a second, internal dimension to the politics of decolonisation. The questions here were who was to inherit power and the nature of that inheritance. It is this perspective that dominates our account. For the people of Malaya, decolonisation was a series of profound struggles through which they fought for the welfare of their communities, to secure position and place, and to contest the identity of the nation. Colonial nation-building intruded into a profound crisis within Malayan politics. This chapter examines in particular the crisis within Malay politics which raged at its most intense between 1951 and 1953. It looks in detail at one lasting consequence of this: the resurgence of Islamic politics. It shows how, after 1953, Malayan politics stabilised with the rise to predominance of the inter-racial Alliance. However, although after the Federal elections of 1955 the question of who would receive independence was largely settled, the shape of that independence was not. A fully documented political history of the period has yet to be written, and will not be attempted here.[2] This chapter aims to highlight some neglected themes of the political transition against which the wider shifts in relations between state and society described in previous chapters might be set.

Experiments in democracy

The grooming of Malaya for self-government began in the Malayan Spring. At that time it was a very far distant goal and the liberalisation of politics it involved was cast aside in the face of Malay resistance to the Malayan Union and the flourishing of anti-colonial mass movements. In early 1948, as we noted at the end of chapter 2, British policy advisers felt that the prospect of the rise of a strong Malayan independence movement was remote. However, even in the darkest days of the Emergency, British politicians insisted that political reform could not be repudiated entirely. The colonial archives reveal great continuities in British thinking. After July 1948, Malcolm MacDonald, Commissioner-General in Southeast Asia, in cordial partnership with Gent's successor, Sir Henry Gurney, developed a friendship with the leader of UMNO, Dato Onn bin Jaafar and worked to keep progressive policies alive. This regime had its opponents in both Malaya and London. In 1951 it was shaken by mounting criticism, by the resignation of Onn as leader of UMNO and the assassination of Gurney in October of that year. A new Conservative government took office in London. A major review of British administration in Malaya had been underway for a year or more. In the course of it, MacDonald's stock sank somewhat in Whitehall. The new Colonial Secretary, Oliver Lyttelton, embarked on a tour of

---

[1] Notably A. J. Stockwell's magisterial three-volume survey for the 'British Documents on the End of Empire project', *Malaya* (London, 1995).

[2] Narratives are Gordon P. Means, *Malaysian politics* (London, 1970); Khong Kim Hong, *Merdeka: British rule and the struggle for independence in Malaya* (Kuala Lumpur, 1984).

Malaya in December 1951 and on his return gave his support to a growing consensus in London that central authority should be strengthened. He recommended that the posts of High Commissioner and Director of Operations be held by one man. The man with the plan was General Sir Gerald Templer. However, the change in government, and in the approach to the Communist war, should not mask the fact that the underlying political objectives remained unchanged. Many of the reforms had been mooted before the Conservatives took office, and although the new ministers gave precedence to the language of law and order, they ratified projects of political advancement initiated by the Labour government. Asian Members were introduced into the executive in March 1951; municipal elections were held and plans laid for Federal elections. The goal of British policy was stated in Templer's directive on his appointment as High Commissioner in February 1952, his 'bible' that promised self-government to a 'united Malayan nation'.[3] In early 1952, the principle of self-government had been conceded at a stroke. Templer was given unique authority to make decisions on the spot. He originally envisaged self-government as occurring in 1960 at the very earliest. In the event the British were to transfer power in an unseemly haste in August 1957, and in a manner in which many of the lodestones of post-war policy were jettisoned. After 1952 much of the key momentum lay within Malaya itself.

It was one thing to make grandiloquent statements about multi-racialism in Whitehall, quite another to apply them to the shifting sands of local politics. The overarching theme of British counter-insurgency was the creation of community. Political terror was to be overcome by drawing rising social forces into new civic institutions. Political education and community development were to recruit multi-racial anti-Communist leadership. It was a blend of pre-war paternalism and post-war Fabianism that can be found elsewhere in the colonial empire, and the great experiment for British Africa foreshadowed that for Malaya. Social anthropology, technological advances, wartime planning regimes and a revolution in communications all came to the aid of colonial administration. However, the Malayan experience was unique in its scale. For a colonial regime animated by anti-Communism, the Emergency created a great field for social experiment in the new settlements and in the workplace. By the early 1950s, social policy moved from containment to proselytisation; soldiers turned into visionaries. Indeed, General Templer is the hero of most accounts. Attributed with elevating the phrase 'hearts and minds' into the central axiom of government, Templer was armed with civil power unique to any British soldier since Cromwell. Yet most of the initiatives which are associated with his name were already well underway under previous administrations. He brought, like the Prime Minister who appointed him, a blustering barrackroom style and ripened language to the war effort, which whilst it entertained and refreshed many within and outside government, it patronised and bewildered others. He famously

---

[3] A. J. Stockwell, 'British imperial policy and decolonisation in Malaya, 1942–52', *JICH*, 13, 1 (1984), 68–87.

admonished a Chinese New Village thus: 'You are all bastards', which was rendered by the interpreter as 'His Excellency says none of your parents were married.' 'And I can be a bastard too' – 'His Excellency says his parents were also unmarried.'[4] His own thinking on social problems was unsophisticated and chiefly consisted of planting the ornaments of English rural life in Malaya's fertile soil. It was a species of parish-pump politics: shrubberies, park benches, painting villages in cheerful colours.[5] Templer was an enthusiastic Boy Scout. His contribution was to personalise a Federal administration which had seemed distant and austere under Gurney, to give social policy a rural basis it had hitherto lacked, and to give free reign and resources to enthusiasts and clear the field for social experiment. However, another side to Templerism was a tendency to seek administrative and authoritarian solutions to political problems. To his arch-critic, Victor Purcell, 'whereas at one time it looked as if the General's ambition was that his name should live in Malaya as Oliver Cromwell's name still lives in Ireland, it now seems as if he will be remembered only by his more egregarious blunders'.[6] The little bit of politics he permitted during the Emergency was a dangerous thing. In particular the principle of 'service' was a pernicious concept.

> When a people like this are dragooned and spoonfed, the wheels of society will not turn easily without some substitute for public spirit. General Templer had sought to fill the gap with the idea of 'service', esprit de corps, 'leadership' and youth movements. He himself had set the example of direct action, dispensing with the established process of administration or the law . . . [policies] all of them praiseworthy in their intention but cutting at the very roots of civil administration.[7]

The British post-war experiment in Malaya had begun and ended on the same principle: it invited politics, but the state was to be the arbiter of their legitimacy.

The tool for this was community development. Its antecedents lay in Africa, and a sizeable corpus of metropolitan wisdom was on hand to inform policy by the 1950s. It was a more refined elaboration of the welfarism of the 'second colonial occupation'. It celebrated the Schumpterian notion of promoting decentralisation of leadership and aimed to diffuse modernity from the towns to inert villages and pave the way for development programmes.[8] It was seen as a weapon against Communism and the uncertainties of social change. The Malayan manifesto was:

> (1.) To develop a programme of development in which there are mutual contributions from the community and the Governmment . . . The aims are more food and better living conditions in every sense; (2.) To create active understanding of the rights and

---

[4] Robert Heussler, *British rule in Malaya, 1942–57* (Singapore, 1985), p. 186.
[5] For example, D. J. Staples, 'Improvements in New Villages and regrouped areas', 7. 3. 1953, DO Kuantan/276/53.
[6] Victor Purcell, 'Will Templer stage a comeback?', *Raayat*, 1 (13.12.1954).
[7] Victor Purcell, *Malaya: Communist or free?* (Stanford, 1955), p. 265.
[8] United Nations, *Report on Mission on Community Organisation and Development in South and South-East Asia* (1953), pp. 17–18.

obligations of the individual as a citizen to the community and the State; (3.) To develop an interest amongst citizens in the procedure of participation in public affairs; (4.) To develop effective public opinion in support of improvements in democratic government and politics; (5.) To bring Malayan women and youth into the movement as active participants.[9]

Community development, pundits enthused, was 'a movement which builds up from below', manipulated through subtle social engineering so that 'the natural talents of the community should be evoked to develop those features in their make-up which are desirable'. The people were 'to be suitably instructed towards their emancipation'. What was proper in modernity was to be blended with that which was agreeable in tradition: especially as communities were changing and becoming more heterogeneous.[10] These 'communities' were defined as the demographic and geographical units of British administrative practice. Their representative voice was the elected council; the voice of authority, the District Officer. Malaya was divided into kampong, New Village, estate and urban groups, and different strategies directed at each. In Malay kampongs, for instance, it was recognised that there was 'a traditional pattern of social order and that it works'. New Villages by contrast were 'constructed' communities and had to be taught the value of citizenship. Urban dwellers were to be constantly reminded of theirs. Estate workers were to be taught a mean between resignation to paternalism and 'rushing to the opposite extremes'.[11] After careful research, the reconstruction was begun of 'local indigenous units which would carry on work which had been stimulated mainly from outside'. The objective was a Malayan nation: 'to create, from indigenous and exotic racial groups, a people with a common outlook and a common loyalty sufficient in degree to enable them to assume responsibility for the government of the country. The binding force must be national spirit and patriotism.'[12]

There were officials who shuddered at the thought of government 'putting on new services as a vaudeville company puts on new songs and acts'; at stimulating social needs that were deemed inappropriate for rural communities.[13] However, most could see community development's utility in securing a stable labour force and maintaining gainful employment.[14] In response to a period of immense social change, the aim was to absorb individual citizens, and thereby whole communities, into a common identity with the state, through identifying a constructive civic role for the individual within his community. In return for civil rights the citizen must fulfil his 'civic duties', not only legal, but moral duties 'binding in conscience' on the individual – such as voting, co-operation and personal cleanliness. The ideal was 'a sense of "oneness" with the

---

[9] Margaret Read, 'Visit to Malaya – December 1st, 1953 to January 13th, 1954', INF/1867/53.
[10] D. W. Le Mare, 'Community Development', 28. 9. 1953, *ibid.*
[11] Director, Information Services, 'Memorandum on education in citizenship', Coop/505/55.
[12] 'His Excellency's address to civics meeting – 21st May, 1955', *ibid.*
[13] 'Operation Service newsletter, I', 15. 8. 1953, CS/5235/53.
[14] 'Department of Information and community development', INF/1867/53.

government'. However, the great danger was, in the words of one expert, that 'equally it was potentially a field of awakened interest which could be caught by Communism'.[15] In its desire to forge social resilience out of uncertainty, community development, in the final resort, rested on the inculcation of a faith. Its success rested on identifying local intermediaries, especially in the kampongs. In Perak, the *Tunku Mentri* brought an element of traditional authority into the work of the District team; the District Officer in Larut and Matang mobilised religious leaders, through the *kathi* of Taiping, to tour the kampongs to dispense good advice, and to stay overnight in unsettled areas to raise morale.[16] More sceptical District Officers tended to use community development money for purposes other than community development projects. In 1957 the allowance for the entire State of Perak was only $25,000.[17] This did not seem to matter: small was beautiful. The first experimental voluntary scheme in Kelantan was launched at the start of 1954 by the deputy state information officer, Abdul Aziz Ja'afar, acting in a private capacity, in Kampong Banggol, two miles north of Kota Bharu. A reading room was opened, and twelve acres of land were cultivated to pay for its amenities. This 'semi-official' activity generated unease: officers might exploit it for their personal or political advancement – significantly, the Kelantan case involved a member of the Party Negara.[18] Like other social experiments in the period of post-war reconstruction, there was considerable ambiguity in the degree of politicisation that would be tolerated. However, there were great rewards for those who took up the government's challenge. Wide publicity of successes would be given, especially where election pledges were honoured; outstanding leaders might be trained in public speaking.[19] Courses were devised to inculcate the tenets of colonial democracy in groups of 'key persons': schoolteachers, village headmen, youth leaders, estate conductors, selected estate workers – even prisoners from local jails. As elections approached, the political content became more and more explicit. Graduates from these courses were 'to act as the kernel of pro-Government (rather than merely anti-Communist) groups in their respective areas'.[20] Community development was an invitation to citizenship, but also a statement of the rules to which civic life had to conform.

Community development placed a special obligation on women and youths. Civic duty began in the family. Through their maternal and welfare role women embodied its values. Progress was projected in more feminine terms. Apart from attempts to

[15] Read, 'Visit to Malaya', *ibid.*
[16] Taiping Malay Mosque, 'Minutes of the meeting of the Trustees held on 9. 9. 1952', DO Larut/260/50.
[17] 'Minutes of Conference of District Officers, Perak, 20. 9. 1956', DO Larut/101/56.
[18] Abdul Aziz Ja'afar, 'Report on experimental voluntary community development scheme in Kelantan at Kg. Banggol', 22. 6. 1954; C. J. Stanbury to Ya'acob bin Abdul Latiff, Director of Information Services, 6. 7. 1954, INF/1867/53.
[19] Le Mare, 'Community Development', *ibid.*
[20] 'Report on civics courses held during 1955 under the auspices of Information Services, Perak, and an outline of plans for 1956', DO Larut/82/55; 'Penghulu training course at Kuala Lumpur, 25–30. 4. 1949', SEL.SEC/2170/49.

extend Women's Institutes throughout Malaya, other associations were introduced: such as the Corona Society, a women's international society, and an Association of Progressive Malay Women formed in Kuala Lumpur with an enthusiasm for sports, cookery and handicrafts.[21] Lady Templer was very active on behalf of Women's Institutes, and where she led, other wives of the Anglo–Malayan establishment followed, teased by the Malay press for 'only pretending to work hard for Lady Templer'.[22] This was perhaps a little unfair: a first generation of Malay women administrators played a role in the movement, women such as Raja Teh binte Raja Hj Kamaralzaman Zaitun, who was trained in social welfare in London, and Tengku Zainab binte Zakaria, a Social Welfare Officer in Kelantan. Many of the individuals involved were the wives of civil servants, and welfare work provided for them an opportunity to socialise on more equal terms with expatriates. Many were English-educated, and although some combined welfare work with membership of political groups such as the *Kaum Ibu UMNO*, their work for voluntary organisations took precedence. As we shall see, women had become pivotal to mass political movements, especially as the electoral process developed, and political parties were the main focus of the activities of the greater numbers of Malay-educated women. Their role, however, was obstructed by their lack of representation. The idealisation of their domestic role was exploited by hostile male political hierarchies to limit their participation in the new political opportunities.[23]

The political ambitions of youth were obstructed in a similar way. Fears of mass delinquency continued to motivate colonial social policy. Emotional adolescents had to be kept busy; Communism fed on idleness. Officials such as Mervyn Sheppard in Klang pioneered young farmers' clubs. This caught on elsewhere: we hear of a *Persatuan Pelandang Muda Waqaf Bahru* in Kelantan, its stated aims to improve living standards and health, and 'to realise the importance of time (not to waste it uselessly)'.[24] However, the Malayan Youth Council, the highest expression of hale and hearty adolescence, was divided.[25] The imported associations, such as the Scouts and Christian groups, attempted to set up their own council to expunge the influence of the World Assembly of Youth, and there were dark hints by the colonial youth services adviser of Communist infiltration. Representatives of the Youth Council at international meetings included future political leaders such as Abdul Razak bin Hussain and Mohamed Sopiee.[26] Moreover, as Malay politics began to fracture in the mid-1950s, youth movements were pulled once again into the mainstream of national politics. An All-Malaya Youth Congress in 1955, presided over by Dr Burhanuddin, brought

---

[21] *Malay Mail*, 20. 1. 1954; 22. 6. 1949.   [22] *Utusan Melayu*, 2. 4. 1953.

[23] Wazir Jahan Karim, *Women and culture: between Malay adat and Islam* (Boulder, 1992), pp. 100–1; Virginia H. Dancz, *Women and party politics in peninsular Malaysia* (Singapore, 1987), pp. 87–115.

[24] 'Persatuan Pelandang Muda Waqaf Bahru', RSM/353/55.

[25] For the composition of this body at a local level see Settlement Youth Council, Malacca, 'Third annual report for the Year ending 31.12.1953', RofS(FofM)/101/53.

[26] S. A. Abishganardan to Chief Secretary, 6.10.1950, FS/13288/50; *Malay Mail*, 9. 3. 1954.

together many opposition elements in Malay politics in an attempt to reactivate the Malay left.[27] The leadership that did emerge was rarely that envisaged by the colonial authorities. Areas of concern, from women's associations, youth movements, the adult education movement, family planning, local government, even missionary Christianity, continued to replicate wider political struggles, and acted as the forcing-houses of new ideologies that would challenge colonial civic management. This can be seen in the resistance of Chinese parties to the imposition of a national education policy and in the subtle infiltration of social and cultural organisations favoured by the Malayan Communist Party as it was forced to step down its military campaign. Grass-roots welfare work was a shroud for political mobilisation.

To the colonial sponsors of community development, democracy was to be organic, to begin in the natural politics of the village, and not to be imposed from outside by urban activists. The tensions this dictum generated undermined the development of local government. Its beginnings were informal. In Perak, for example, an early democratic experiment was the formal election of the village headman – the *ketua kampong* – usually after Friday prayers superintended by the *imam*. The results were forwarded to the District Officer for approval, and the victor was issued with a formal letter of authority after a six-month probation. The British lobbied to prevent undesirables coming forward, and when a formal franchise was introduced the District Officer doctored it by discussing the suitability of nominations beforehand with the territorial chief.[28] This system did not prevent the intrusion of politics. Nor did it encourage suitable candidates.[29] Despite the growing rewards attached to the post, a great number of *ketua kampong* resigned before their retirement, due to political pressure for fresh elections from what were naturally seen as 'irresponsible political elements within a community', whose aim seemed to be merely to exploit councils as a channel for demands on the government. This created a crisis of local authority at a period when a great number of *ketuas* were ending their five-year term of service and experienced and politically trustworthy men were needed to oversee the Federal elections. Men of no official standing, exploiting the 'democratic racket', were elected solely on the basis of their affiliation to a political party: a development the British abhorred.[30]

These problems dogged the introduction of more formal structures. A town clerk from Hornsey was employed in 1952 to form town and local councils out of existing institutions. However, their hotch-potch character made this difficult.[31] For example, where local councils were elected, as they were in Trengganu by 1953, responsive

---

[27] N. J. Funston, *Malay politics in Malaysia* (Kuala Lumpur, 1980), pp. 42–43.
[28] ADO Larut and Matang, 'System of election of a *ketua kampong*'; ADO Selama to DO, 14. 6. 51; H. E. Josselyn to Secretary to British Adviser, Perak, 22. 6. 1951; I. W. Blelloch to Sultan of Perak, 4. 9. 1951, DO Larut/626/50.
[29] 'Minutes of Conference of District Officers, Perak, 24. 7. 1953', DO Larut/518/53.
[30] I. D. Irvine, 'Memorandum for Conference of District Officers – Election of *Ketua Kampongs*', 17. 8. 1956, DO Larut/626/50.
[31] MacGilllivray to Higham, 18.10.1951, Stockwell, *Malaya*, II, pp. 402–6.

local democracy was difficult to sustain in areas of dispersed population; it was an economy of scale.[32] Although an exploratory select committee in Johore established a precedent in 1952 that there would be no communal representation, in Perak the Mentri Besar complained that town councils, by their very nature, implied racial minority, and created real problems in securing representation of Malays and Indian minorities. Conversely, he noted, there was a general reluctance by Malays to set up local councils and concede influence in areas where they were strong.[33] By 1956 a distinct falling-off of enthusiasm was noted in many areas, 'mainly due,' as one officer observed, 'to the fact that politics become mixed up with village affairs and party interests are allowed to dominate and disrupt village economy'. Obstacles were erected to the participation of parties, such as the banning of fund-raising fun-fairs.[34] Yet where political parties were excluded, there were instances of councils resigning *en bloc*, and when nominations were called for new elections the meeting was boycotted. A councillor's political ambitions would not permit him to take responsibility for seizing the property of poll-tax defaulters, and this encouraged a 'can't pay, won't pay' stance amongst defaulters.[35] By mid-1956, the minister responsible recognised that more had been achieved in the way of transferring political power rather than financial autonomy, which many authorities were not even seeking. All Town Boards with a population over 10,000 had been converted into Town Councils with elected majorities, but they could not become fully elected unless financial autonomy was granted. In any case, the spirit of the experiment was urban or semi-urban, and large parts of the rural population were unaffected by it.[36] The main rationale of local government was political influence. In the Malay kampongs, local democracy was essentially an administrative exercise. Concentrations of government personnel supportive of UMNO at a local level greatly furthered the party's grip on the electoral process. Older forums such as the mosque were also used to the full, though these – especially in this period in Kelantan – could be exploited for mobilisations that would mount a powerful challenge to the post-colonial order.[37] In Trengganu, observers noted the sophisticated political machinery that was being rolled into place by urban activists, and, significantly in light of the later rise of the Parti Islam to power in the State, there were doubts that councils replaced the

[32] 'Trengganu Government Press Statement', 29.12.1952, D.INF.TR/112/54; P. S. Bolshaw, 'Progress Report on local government in Kuantan district for the period between 1.10. – 31.12.1956', Kuantan/84/55; P. S. Bolshaw to State Secretary, Pahang, 6.10.1956, Kuantan/1456/56.
[33] 'Minutes of the meeting of the State Executive Council, Perak, 9. 5. 1955', DO Larut/440/55.
[34] 'Minutes of Conference of District Officers, Perak, 24. 3. 1955', DO Larut/180/55.
[35] I. D. Irvine, 'Are Local Councils losing their glamour?', March 1956, DO Larut/101/56.
[36] J. Love, 'Proposed review of local government development', 27. 6. 1956, Kuantan/145/56.
[37] Marvin L. Rodgers, 'The politicization of Malay villagers: national integration or disintegration?', *Comparative Politics*, 7, 2 (1975), 205–25; Clive S. Kessler, 'Muslim identity and political behaviour in Kelantan', in Roff (ed.), *Kelantan: religion, society and politics in a Malay State* (Kuala Lumpur, 1974), pp. 284–93.

mosques as the nuclei of village assemblies.[38] Town Board elections in 1954 and 1955 were used as an opportunity to flex party muscle. For the British, federal elections could only follow from schooling at the local and the State level. Only then could a party system be constructed. However, there was resistance in the States to the extension of local democracy: those already in power were reluctant to give place, and there was little public demand from them to do so. The real prizes lay elsewhere. The schedule for State elections was pushed aside, together with the vision of creating model structures of local government by independence, as the British left the parties to thrash it out at the centre.[39] When elections did occur, in Johore and Trengganu in October 1954, and in Penang in February 1955, they merely demonstrated the power of party-political machinery. Wider political struggles dictated the fate of colonial experiments in democracy.

The crisis of Malayan politics

After the drama of the collapse of the Malayan Union and the outbreak of the Emergency, the public debate on the political future of Malaya was reopened in late 1949 with the formation of the Communities' Liaison Committee. As we have seen, the CLC was born out of the need to rally conservative Chinese opinion behind the anti-Communist campaign. It set important precedents for inter-communal bargaining and compromise, especially on the position of the Malays within the economy. However, its most significant political achievement was the reopening of Sino-Malay dialogue on questions of citizenship and Malayan nationality.[40] The object of these discussions was to widen the provisions within the Federation Agreement to incorporate a larger number of non-Malays. There were Malay leaders – in particular Dato Onn – who were prepared to concede *jus soli* to the Malayan Chinese. However, this was acknowledged to be way ahead of Malay opinion and the views of the Rulers.[41] The breakthrough formula adopted by the CLC – Malay concessions on Chinese citizenship, in return for Chinese acknowledgement of allegiance to the Malay Rulers – was thus something of a sleight of hand, which promised more than it gave, as further qualifications for citizenship were added to the formula.[42] Yet, the discussions immediately raised the tempo of Malayan politics. As a grand gesture to placate Chinese opinion, they failed. Moreover, they called into question the authority of the Malay leaders involved. Dato Onn's position as the defender of Malay interests was particularly compromised, and his role in the CLC was the target of fierce attacks,

---

[38] J. M. Heywood, 'Trengganu, 1952–54', and of the general election in Trengganu by Gullick, 'My time in Malaya'.
[39] Jerrom, minute, 7.11.1952; MacGillivray to Lloyd, 14. 3. 1953, Stockwell, *Malaya*, II, pp. 421, 448; Jerrom, minute, 15. 1. 1954, *ibid.*, III, p. 20.
[40] Tan Cheng Lock to Yong Shook Lin, 19. 1. 1950, SP.13/A/19.
[41] Gurney to Paskin, 2.12.1949, Stockwell, *Malaya*, II, p. 188.
[42] Gurney to MacDonald, 24. 4. 1950; 'Papers for consideration by the CLC on 6. 5. 1950', SP.13/A/19.

not least from the Rulers. The impact of the decision on citizenship was undermined by Onn's opposition to the idea that the proposals should be put to the Sultans before the people, and by the implication that different State nationalities had been created. This aggravated the unease within the Malay body politic.[43] The ability of Malay leaders to sell the policy to their constituency became a crucial test of their authority. Onn absented himself from crucial meetings of the CLC in Penang at the end of December 1949 to test the resolve of other Malay members: it was an ultimatum for them to either challenge earlier decisions or shoulder their share of the responsibility of confirming and defending them. The decisions were endorsed by the other Malay members, although they expressed the belief that it would take five to ten years before Malay opinion was ready to accept the idea of a 'Malayan' nationality. When the proposals were finally published in April 1950, it was unclear how successful they would be.[44] The politics of Malaya, and of the Malays in particular, were moving into uncharted territory. A crisis of party arose, during which many wavered in their loyalties to established leaders.

At the centre of the uncertainty was Dato Onn himself. The dilemma for those around him was how to reconcile his powerful personality, his autocratic style, with their dependence on him to broker a political accommodation. Onn himself, it seems, had difficulty in accommodating his sense of his own mystique as the sole spokesman of Malay nationalism to the new tasks that lay ahead. Official correspondence is littered with vivid references to his dangerous 'Jekyll and Hyde' personality.[45] The British were exposed to Onn's continuing bitterness at the Malayan Union fiasco. The Rulers were antagonised by his ambition and arrogance, as witnessed by his notorious speech at the UMNO General Assembly at Arau, Perlis in May 1949, in which, without consulting the Rulers, he called for a new 'Malayan' nationality, and reminded them that their thrones had been saved by UMNO. This helped precipitate Onn's resignation as Mentri Besar of Johore, where Sultan Ibrahim had been angered by Onn's dependence on the facilities of the State government for his career within the party.[46] 'I am aware that Mr MacDonald and Sir Henry Gurney consider him statesmanlike,' the old Sultan told James Griffiths, 'and so he is – at intervals and within definite limits. His experience of administration is very small.'[47] Onn blamed the Rulers for resisting his appointment as Deputy High Commissioner. The Rulers resented Onn's impudence in aspiring to a status above their own. It seems that he clashed with the personalities of some Rulers and not with the institution itself.[48] Certainly resistance to Onn was driven by a deeper-rooted unease about the direction in which he was leading UMNO, and much of it came from within the party itself. It

---

[43] Gurney to Griffiths, 13. 3. 1950, *ibid.*
[44] MacDonald to Creech Jones, 7. 1. 1950; J. Higham, minute, 1. 9. 1950, CO537/6018.
[45] Stockwell, *Malaya*, II, pp. 120–2.
[46] Simon C. Smith, 'The rise, decline and survival of the Malay Rulers during the colonial period, 1874–1957', *JICH*, 22, 1 (1994), 100–1.
[47] Sultan of Johore to Griffiths, 15. 8. 1950, CO537/6018.
[48] Ramlah Adam, *Dato Onn Ja'afar: pengasas kemerdekaan* (Kuala Lumpur, 1992), pp. 138–48.

surfaced when UMNO considered the CLC citizenship proposals at a Special Assembly in April 1950. Before a vote was taken Onn declined to stand for re-election as President of UMNO. He received demonstrations of support from branches reluctant to lose the man who had stood up against the British and the Malayan Union. At the UMNO Annual General Meeting in August, Onn was re-elected President by sixty votes to three. Yet the matter did not rest there. Old enemies, such as former API and MNP personalities, began to join UMNO Youth in large numbers and led the groundswell of opposition to Onn. Onn created new enemies by ruling, in early 1951, that UMNO should not get involved in the Nadra issue, and by refusing to countenance the cry of *Merdeka!*: a slogan that had been enthusiastically adopted by the youth wing. Onn defended his position by insisting on the need for strict party discipline: UMNO members who joined new parties that were forming, such as the Peninsular Malays Union, were expelled.[49] Theatrical, emotional, overbearing, and with an unswerving belief in his capacity to direct events, Onn was, as Abdul Razak later described him, the 'prima donna of Malay politics'. British officials complained of his 'lack of balance', that he would make new proposals out of the blue, 'to stir up Malay suspicions to his own personal advantage'.[50] Yet in spite of it all, they felt they could not live without him. The Colonial Secretary, James Griffiths, reiterated in July 1951 that Onn 'represents the only real hope of the Malayan peoples breaking away from Race and turning to Party', although, he added, not at the cost of a split in the Malays.[51] However, by 1951, this split was occurring. Mistrust of Onn mounted with the introduction of the Member system, which ignited a fierce internal debate within UMNO on portfolios. 'To me in particular it is tragic,' Onn confessed. 'I feel worried and worn out, frustrated and disillusioned.'[52] However, Onn continued to believe that the Malays, too, could not live without him. Confident, it seems, in his mandate, Onn launched a bombshell in June 1951: the opening of UMNO membership to non-Malays. When UMNO rejected this, Onn resigned as its President. The reasons behind it – Onn's attempt to free himself of intra-party feuding and elevate himself into a higher plane of national leadership – underscored his misjudgement of his capacity to carry Malay opinion away with him as a personal following.

Malayan politics was at an impasse. The main attempt to break it came with the formation of a non-communal political party. This chimed with the primary objective of British policy: the creation of multi-racial politics. Senior British officials believed UMNO was disintegrating. Dato Onn saw it dissolving into its component State associations, dominated by conservatives. Nehru's visit to Malaya in 1950 impressed on Onn the political importance of the peasantry. To strengthen his power base, he decided to by-pass the UMNO hierarchy and make a direct appeal to the people. Around June 1951, an initiative took shape in Onn's mind for a new, non-communal

---

[49] PMR, No. 1; No. 2 of 1951, CO537/7297.   [50] Gurney to Griffiths, 17. 1. 1951, *ibid.*
[51] Higham to Gurney, 6. 7. 1951, CO537/7303.
[52] Onn to Corry, 6. 1. 1951, CO537/7297.

political party: an Independence of Malaya Party (IMP). This venture received encouragement from Gurney and MacDonald. Yet they were uneasy at the thought of UMNO being left rudderless, and Gurney pleaded, unsuccessfully, with Onn to continue to lead both organisations.[53] Onn resigned from UMNO at the 25–26 August UMNO General Assembly and the new party was launched on 16 September 1951. However, despite the break, the indications are that the IMP was originally intended to function in parallel to UMNO. The IMP was to be, in the words of its mission statement, 'an efficient non-communal National Organisation and to form a centre of united action', and it was to co-operate with other organisations.[54] It initially claimed support from within the UMNO leadership: in Penang, Selangor, Pahang and Johore in particular.[55] The IMP also secured the backing of MCA grandees such as Tan Cheng Lock, who was offered its leadership. 'We must make the MCA strong to help support IMP', he wrote to Leong Yew Koh in September 1951, and he, Dato Onn and Raja Ayoub drank ten bottles of wine at the Majestic Hotel in Kuala Lumpur to toast its formation.[56] Other Straits Chinese leaders saw it as a means of advancing their demands on citizenship. Onn believed that the MCA leaders were, like himself, in danger of losing their grip on their constituency. Tan Cheng Lock had tried to open the MCA to non-Chinese associate members and, like Onn, was frustrated when his party failed to support him. In particular, the Chinese-educated middle leadership refused to countenance the move.[57] The British saw the IMP as an attempt to revive the CLC on a more formal footing. The party was dominated by an impressive coterie of notables, and received the initial support of many community associations. Yet to *Melayu Raya*, the IMP was 'just like a factory with a manager and some clerks but without machinery or labourers to carry out its work'.[58] It had little grass-roots organisation: at the end of August 1953, UMNO claimed 930,682 members; the MCA, 204,906; the IMP, only 2,200.[59] The IMP had nothing to gain from early elections. Many of its members already held seats on State Councils or the Federal Legislative Council. It won only three of the 134 seats it contested in local elections in 1952 and 1953. A conclusive signal came in February 1952 when the IMP was humiliated in the crucial Kuala Lumpur Municipal elections by UMNO in an *ad hoc* local alliance with the MCA.[60]

However, at the time there was some basis for Dato Onn's lack of confidence in UMNO, and the Malay political community faced a deep crisis after his departure. As the poet Usman Awang eulogised: 'the yellow flag [of UMNO] has lost its

[53] Gurney to Higham, 13. 6. 1951, CO537/7303.
[54] 'Interim rules of the Independence of Malaya Party, approved by the Organizing Committee, 7th October, 1951', Tan Cheng Lock Papers, SP.13/A/32.
[55] PMR, No. 7 of 1951, A. S. Meville, minute, 13. 9. 1951, CO537/7297.
[56] Tan Cheng Lock to Leong Yew Koh, 30. 9. 1951, SP.13/A/22.
[57] Heng Pek Koon, *Chinese politics in Malaysia: a history of the Malaysian Chinese Association* (Singapore, 1958), p. 158.
[58] *Melayu Raya* 11. 1. 1953.   [59] *Malay Mail*, 17. 2. 1954.
[60] Heng, *Chinese politics*, p. 168.

champion'. For a year or more it was very unclear how key figures and sectional interests would declare themselves. The boundaries between different political bodies were yet to be sharply drawn, and many Malays were active in a number of them simultaneously. At the same time the radicals who had been removed from the political scene in 1948 and 1949 were starting to re-emerge from the detention camps or the quiet backwaters in which they had been hiding. Among them were some of the most gifted leaders of their generation. In this time of uncertainty, parties strove to define their distinct identity and create disciplined organisations with exclusive membership, in preparation for federal elections. Although all political parties were loath to release membership numbers, UMNO's were almost certainly waning. Although in 1953 UMNO was said to have over 900,000 members, few paid subscriptions.[61] In Kedah only 8,000 of the 20,000 members had paid, and *Warta Negara* suggested the party was almost defunct in the State.[62] There were repeated accusations in the media that the party elite were complacent and indolent, and that branches were inert.[63] Kota Bahru UMNO was thrown into crisis after the branch failed to replaced its chairman who had refused to continue serving.[64] The IMP attempted to take advantage of declining UMNO power in the kampongs. Meanwhile, the problem of political succession had to be faced. Dato Onn's own choice of successor was said to be either Mahmood Mahyidden of Kelantan or C. M. Yusof of Perak.[65] In the event he nominated Tuan Haji Ahmad Fuad, head of the party's *ulama* section, a move that could be interpreted as indicating that he anticipated that UMNO would decline as a party and become more of a sectional interest group. The leader who did emerge, the Kedah prince Tunku Abdul Rahman, was something of an unknown quantity. He had been a patron of *Saberkas* in the State, but had spent long years away from Malaya studying law in England. He was supported by Bahaman bin Shamsuddin, and younger men such as Abdul Razak bin Hussein, a Pahang notable also recently returned from the London Bar, who stood as Deputy President. Recent research has suggested that Gurney played a role in encouraging the nomination of Tunku Abdul Rahman, who was, at the time, a government servant and carried the *imprimatur* of English politicians such as David Rees-Williams.[66] However, Gurney had little faith in the new leader. He predicted that Tunku Abdul Rahman would not hold UMNO together, that he would not be *persona grata* with the Rulers, and that, as there was little love lost between the Tunku and the Dato, many Malays would place a foot in both political camps.[67] The hope was that UMNO and the MCA would decline into welfare

---

[61] Reported in *KLIMP: Official organ of the IMP Kuala Lumpur Branch*, 1, 1, 21. 8. 1953, in CS/5448/53.

[62] *Straits Echo*, 11. 8. 1952; 31.10.1952.

[63] Tanjong Malim had only sixty members; Muar UMNO Youth had had no committee meeting since 1952; UMNO in Sungei Manik, Muar, Rembau and Jasin were not following the party line, *Utusan Melayu*, 30. 4. 1953.

[64] *Straits Echo*, 1. 9. 1952.   [65] PMR, No. 4 of 1951, CO537/7297.

[66] Ramlah, *Dato Onn*, pp. 210–11.   [67] Gurney to Higham, 29. 8. 1951, CO537/7297.

organisations, leaving the high ground to the IMP.[68] The British were wrong on all counts, not least in their consistent underestimation of Tunku Abdul Rahman and his allies.

The new leader moved quickly to resurrect the party on two fronts. First, he strengthened its organisation. In his first speech as successor to Onn as UMNO President, he trenchantly reasserted the party's identity as the vanguard of communal interests, and dismissed the quest for the 'Malayan', which, he argued, had ended along with the Malayan Union.

> With regard to the proposal of some of our men that independence should be handed over to the 'Malayans', who are these 'Malayans'? This country was received from the Malays and to the Malays it ought to be returned. What is called 'Malayans', it is not yet certain who they are; therefore let the Malays alone settle who they are.[69]

This kind of rhetoric alarmed men of the old-guard leadership, and Tunku Abdul Rahman privately apologised to Gurney for employing it. However, it was well-received by those within the grass-roots who been alienated by Dato Onn's recent pronouncements. The prince was also well placed to heal the breach with the Rulers, as the Ruler who had led the campaign against Onn's attempt to be appointed Deputy High Commissioner was his nephew, the Ruler of Kedah. He also gave up his post in the government service, in a move which sharply distinguished him from the men of position who were attached to Onn. Yet the new leader was faced with a party whose old guard were turning away from it, and he was forced to work through an executive council packed with supporters of Dato Onn, such as Datin Puteh Mariah, Zainal Abidin and Dato Panglima Kinta. Tunku Abdul Rahman was led to depend on a new corps of leaders, many of whom were drawn from the Graduates' Association of Johore. He stayed away from the UMNO Headquarters in Johore Bahru until a purge of its staff had been completed, and moved new men into the key positions: Khir Johari as Secretary General and Syed Jaafar Albar as editor of the party's mouthpiece, *Suara UMNO*, which took on a new vitality. The alliances that supported the leadership of Tunku Abdul Rahman were fraught with tension. Relations with his lieutenant, Abdul Razak, were at times stormy. Although Tun Razak was an 'intelligent man', the Tunku was later to reflect, 'his passion for power remained in his heart'. A kitchen cabinet appeared, in and out of which moved men of a more radical temperament – Saardon Jubir, Abdul Aziz Ishak and Dr Ismail Abdul Rahman – who bolstered Tunku Abdul Rahman against the waverers in UMNO.[70] At the Seventh General Assembly in Butterworth in September 1952, Saardon Jubir put the

---

[68] Note by MacGillivray, 6. 4. 1953, Stockwell, *Malaya*, II, p. 451.

[69] I have taken the translation in *KLIMP*, 21. 9. 1953. A full text of this speech appears in *UMNO: 20 tahun*, pp. 58–65, 89.

[70] This account is drawn from a series of memoirs of Tunku Abdul Rahman and others, in Abdul Samad Idris, *25 tahun UMNO: Kenangan abadi kepada bangsa, agama dan tanahir* (Kuala Lumpur, 1984), pp. 207–15; Abdul Aziz Ishak, *The architect of Merdeka: Tengku Abdul Rahman* (Singapore, 1957), p. 79.

youth at the forefront of an attempt to build up a strong organisation and Khir Johari ordered tighter discipline and the cleansing of the party.[71]

A second front on which Tunku Abdul Rahman and his allies moved to rebuild UMNO was through *rapprochement* with the MCA. Initially it looked as if they were drifting apart. In early discussions with the British, the new leader of UMNO displayed unease at the compromises made by earlier leaders, compromises to which he had not been a party. Fearing proposed provisions for Commonwealth citizenship, he argued that there should be a sole loyalty to Malaya. He also wanted to extend Malay rights by creating Malay Reservations in the Straits Settlements.[72] Matters were not helped by the support Tan Cheng Lock had given to the IMP. Yet, in this he had gained neither political leverage on the citizenship issue nor support from his own community, and it was perhaps more through courtesy than anything else that he continued to give symbolic support to the IMP. It was the MCA leadership in Selangor – H. S. Lee, Ong Yoke Lin and S. M. Yong – who took the initiative in approaching the State UMNO leadership under Dato Yahaya bin Dato Abdul Razak (an old schoolmate of Ong Yoke Lin) with a view to forming an alliance of convenience in the Municipal elections in Kuala Lumpur in February 1952. The electoral arithmetic of the capital and the promise of financial assistance made it an appealing prospect for UMNO. The particular strength of the Selangor MCA and its leadership's commanding position within the guilds and associations of the State enabled them to override the objections of Tan Cheng Lock, and in essence to present him with a *fait accompli*.[73] The *ad hoc* alliance was a resounding success, winning nine out of the twelve Municipal seats. Throughout 1952, the MCA reorganised itself internally as a political party and made further overtures to UMNO to extend the Kuala Lumpur arrangement nationally. Initially, Tan Cheng Lock envisaged that it might be expanded to include the IMP, but this was opposed by Tunku Abdul Rahman.[74] Indeed, an exploratory meeting between IMP leaders and Tunku Abdul Rahman broke down when Dato Onn refused to compromise on his precondition that the Alliance be dissolved and its members join the IMP. The UMNO–MCA alliance was cemented after a visit to Malaya by Victor Purcell, now a Cambridge don and adviser to the MCA. The visit so antagonised UMNO that when Tunku Abdul Rahman was told that Purcell wanted to approach him with a proposal from the MCA, he felt he could not agree to the meeting, and instead agreed to a direct meeting.[75] Beginning with a gathering in the Selangor Chinese Miners' Association Building in February 1953, a series of round-table meetings revived a pattern of communal accommodation. As we saw in Chapter 6, it began with the need to find common ground on the issue of the economic position of the Malays, and then extended into wider political co-operation. Tan Cheng Lock recognised that the elite

---

[71] *Straits Echo*, 16. 9. 1952.
[72] Summary record of first plenary meeting, 13. 5. 1952, second meeting, 14. 5. 1952, CO1030/496.
[73] Heng, *Chinese politics*, 158–63.   [74] Templer to Lyttelton, 10. 7. 1952, CO1022/176.
[75] T. H. Tan, *The Prince and I* (Singapore, 1979), pp. 27–8.

CLC was not enough: what was needed was 'a pyramidal system of Sino–Malay liaison committees starting from the top, right down to the masses'. To UMNO the benefits of co-operation were clear. Colonial secretary Oliver Lyttelton impressed on its leaders on his visit to Malaya in 1951 that there would be no transfer of power until the races of Malaya forged unity. This stung Tunku Abdul Rahman into action.[76] He set aside communal rhetoric. 'We must,' he stressed in 1953, 'live and co-operate with other nationalities and work with them for independence provided they show undivided loyalty toward Malaya.'[77] A mood of pragmatism prevailed. Formal Alliance political machinery was created through its round-table, and MCA funds were diverted to revitalising UMNO branch activities. In Perak, and elsewhere, the Alliance caucus held private meetings before the State Council meetings to stop individual councillors speaking contrary to official policy. Within months a formidable degree of party discipline was generated.[78]

What then were the roots of UMNO's renewed strength? A key development was that many API and MNP men, who were essentially radical Malay nationalists, now saw UMNO as the most effective vehicle for anti-colonial struggle. Men such as Ghafar Baba and Rahman Talib bolstered UMNO Youth, which became a militant uniformed force. There were repeated alarms in colonial intelligence reports at the entry of former MNP men into UMNO branches in old radical heartlands such as Alor Gajah, Malacca and Gunong Semanggol. They strengthened the grass-roots of the party. In the October 1954 State elections, the Alliance secured 80 per cent of the vote. In Trengganu, for example, the top leadership was dominated by men from outside the State, such as the Mentri Besar Dato Kamaruddin bin Haji Idris, a Selangor man. This was a goad to *anak-anak tempatan*, local men such as ex-MNP Ibrahim Fikri, to wrest control of UMNO from them. However, within five years a successful opposition emerged in the form of the PMIP, also led by an ex-MNP cadre, Daud Samad, and which also exploited powerful local allegiances.[79] UMNO was not the sole beneficiary of the re-emergence of the generation of 1945 on to the political scene. However, UMNO did draw into its ranks many members, often of Sumatran or Javanese extraction, who applied the political techniques of the Indonesian revolution to the countryside of Malaya. Within the *Kaum Ibu UMNO* several key cadres had been exposed to Indonesian education: Aishah Ghani had studied at the Diniah Puteri Arabic School in Padang Panjang, West Sumatra, together with Shamsiah Fakeh, who took to the jungle with the MCP, and Sakinah Junid, who later was to form the women's section of the PMIP. Although women had been active in the nationalist movement from its inception, these radical leaders transformed the *Kaum Ibu* from a support group of wives of the political elite into a powerful grass-roots organisation

[76] Tan, *The Prince and I*, p. 30.
[77] Reported in *KLIMP*, I, 1, 21. 8. 1953, in CS/5448/53.
[78] MacGillivray to Lennox-Boyd, 10.12.1954, CO1030/244.
[79] M. Kamlin, *History, politics and electioneering: the case of Terengganu* (Department of History, Universiti Malaya, Kuala Lumpur, 1977), pp. 18–23.

for Malay-educated women.[80] They taught them to overcome their shyness of speaking in public and trained leaders by staying in the kampongs. For those involved, the experiences of sisterhood this generated were very intense. The slogan '*Merdeka!*' was taught to the children in song. As Khatijah Sidek, a gifted leader of Minangkabau origin, recalled:

> I addressed every mother to teach the children that in the morning when they went to school they must first go up to see their mother, and say: 'Mother, I go to school, *Merdeka!*' as a salutation, and to say *Merdeka!* again when they come back from school. For this is how it is done in Indonesia. 'Love the word, and fight for that word'. When the people begin to love a word, they fight for it. This lesson the women and the children learnt very well.

This radicalism was opposed. Khatijah was gently warned by Tunku Abdul Rahman not to be too free with the word *merdeka*. She reflected afterwards that Malay political leaders were very different from their Indonesian counterparts, the word 'freedom' itself was pronounced differently by the Malays, 'longer and slower and it is not *merdeka*, short and sharp'. 'Their independence they want only slower and softer, and perhaps not so independent after all.'[81] Khatijah's leadership of the *Kaum Ibu* was challenged by the party hierarchy in 1954, and she was expelled from UMNO after the failure of her campaign to have five seats at the general elections contested by women. However, the Alliance's triumph in the elections testified to the importance of the *Kaum Ibu* in mobilising the votes of Malay women.

Powerful new political networks were emerging. We have glimpsed some of these in earlier chapters. In Chapter 3 we witnessed the beginnings of the UMNO leadership's creation of a party apparatus. In 1955 this process was further advanced by the strengthening of the State organisations which effectively placed the party on a federal footing, although it also increased competition for place in the locality.[82] Malay nationalists achieved power as much through the colonial state as by organising against it. For a short period in the early 1950s it seemed as if the possession of administrative office would benefit UMNO's opponents within the IMP. Yet this was an exceptional time. UMNO's foothold in the bureaucracy helped it defeat the radical challengers between 1945 and 1948, and helped it regain its paramountcy after 1953. Although in the run-up to the federal elections candidates were unable to hold positions in public service, these strictures did not apply to the lower rungs of the administration where UMNO leaders were particularly firmly entrenched. A survey of the Malay political elite in 1955 revealed that over 55 per cent came from a background in the government service.[83] Anthropological field studies from the 1950s

---

[80] Wazir Jahan Karim, *Women and culture*, pp. 97–102.

[81] Ardjasni [Khatijah Sidek], '*Riwayat hidup saya*: My life – IX', *Eastern Horizon*, 2, 1 (1964), 55–61.

[82] B. H. Shafruddin, *The Federal factor in the government and politics of peninsular Malaysia* (Singapore, 1987), p. 282.

[83] Neuman, 'Malay political elite', p. 80.

and 1960s emphasise that young administrators, and other salaried men with modern education, were taking the lead in politics, supplanting many older leaders. In Muar, for example, it was often young schoolteachers who took the lead; men of 'political efficacy', better able to communicate with the bureaucratic world outside of the village.[84] Schoolteachers were a powerful interest group, which could give local support to UMNO branches, as were the conservative *ulama* whom the UMNO leadership had begun to court after 1950.[85] In Chapter 7 we discussed the flourishing of the Malay press, and it too helped bolster UMNO's recovery. *Utusan Melayu*, although it was to pursue a fiercely independent line, was unrelenting in its opposition to Dato Onn and the Mentri Besars. After the release of its most dynamic journalist A. Samad Ismail from detention in 1953, its support for UMNO in the name of anti-colonial struggle became more pronounced. The press had powerful links with the key groups from which political leaders were drawn in the rural areas. *Utusan Melayu*'s local stringers were often village schoolteachers, active in UMNO branches. The party's political intelligence and political propaganda were in this way closely interwoven. In Chapter 6, we noted that the richer peasants often combined local economic dominance with administrative office, and the penetration of state development agencies into the countryside gave resources to lubricate patronage networks. A recent study has emphasised how, in the 1950s, these rising interests – Malay commercial groups, land-holders and the new government salariat, who themselves often invested in the land – would take a lead in forms of mutual help as a way of mitigating against the emergence of class conflicts. Their works of charity and piety were a way in which the subsistence ethic could be upheld. Politics was another. The very existence of increasing economic differentiation in the countryside served to make UMNO, and the services and support it provided through its local leaders, more essential to the poorer cultivator. It seems as if a nexus of interests of wealth and power was settling into place to underpin UMNO's political primacy. Yet it was not all-embracing; in fact, in many ways, rather fragile. Powerful traditions of egalitarianism survived in rural life. When a rich man and a poor man met in co-operative endeavours, they were sharing a powerful tradition of mutual dependence and reciprocity. Whatever their relative economic status, they met as social equals.[86] In a similar sense, although political efficacy was prized, there seems to have been concern that this should not be exercised at the expense of this common culture. Observers commented that the *orang moden* were viewed as brash and insensitive: they were part of the community, to be sure, yet markedly distinct

---

[84] Marvin L. Rodgers, 'Politicization and political development in a rural Malay community', *Asian Survey*, 9, 12 (1969), 919–33.

[85] For example, Mohamed Nor bin Ahmad, 'Suka duka perjuangan guru² Melayu', in *Persatuan Guru-guru Melayu Kedah, 25 Tahun* (Alor Star, 1971), pp. 131–3; Abdul Manaf bin Saad, 'Persatuan Ulama Kedah, 1365–1376H (1946–1957M)', in Khoo (ed.), *Islam di Malaysia*, pp. 148–58.

[86] D. M. Nonini, *British colonial rule and the resistance of the Malay peasantry, 1900–1957* (New Haven, 1992), pp. 128–34.

in many of their attitudes.[87] Translated in larger political terms, the brashness of high politics, and its perceived insensitivity to deeply cherished perceptions of communal and religious identity bred detachment and undercurrents of resistance to the resurgent UMNO. As we shall see, when vital questions of language and nation were at stake, even the support of key groups such as the Malay schoolteachers could not be depended upon.

UMNO's grass-roots strength allowed it to overcome the challenge from Dato Onn and the IMP. A defining moment in the struggle over who would inherit power from the British came in 1953 with the launching of Dato Onn and the IMP's boldest attempt to regain the political initiative: the 'National Conference' of 27 April 1953. It was mooted by senior Malay administrators, seven out of the nine Mentri Besars, and the nominated representatives of functional interests on the Legislative Council. It was suggested by High Commissioner Templer and Malcolm MacDonald, who had not abandoned hope of reconciling Malayan political leaders in a national unity movement. An informal meeting had been held in early 1952 to attempt to reconcile IMP and UMNO leaders, and there was talk of reviving the CLC by its chairman, E. E. C. Thuraisingham in September 1952. Little came of this.[88] The National Conference was a more urgent attempt to rally 'moderates' in the face of UMNO's demands for federal elections and for an elected majority in the Legislative Council. The Conference appointed its own working committee to examine the question of self-government. Its report gave only two cheers for democracy. It argued that in view of the Emergency and the 'unpreparedness' of the population, premature elections would 'make a mockery of democracy'. The Mentri Besars and their allies stood for the competence, efficiency and order of the existing nominated system, and argued for its retention for several more years. Behind this lay deeper anxieties. In the words of its spokesman, E. E. C. Thuraisingham:

> Therefore, let us pin-point our objective, that is the transfer of power. But I say this: it does not very much matter to whom the power is transferred, but it will be gross treachery if, by that transfer, the integrity and the identity of the Malay peninsula is effaced or that the hospitable Malay people of this land are forced to the position of economic frustration and political subordination.[89]

Individual leaders embraced the National Conference for very different reasons. Many of the Malay notables – Bukit Gantang, Othman bin Mohamed, Nik Ahmad Kemal, Mustapha bin Hassan Albakri – were senior MCS figures, men of unimpeachable patriotism. They were paternalists who embraced the bureaucratic wisdom that

---

[87] For example, P. J. Wilson, *Malay village and Malaysia: social values and rural development* (New Haven, 1967), pp. 39–48; M. G. Swift, *Malay peasant society in Jelebu* (London, 1965), pp. 157, 161.

[88] Deputy Commissioner-General to Lyttelton, 4. 2. 1952, CO1022/184; *Straits Times*, 4. 9. 1952; 5. 9. 1952.

[89] *Report of the Working Committee of the Malayan National Conference* (Kuala Lumpur, 1953), p. 21.

mass politics was moving on a dangerous course and chose to follow Dato Onn, right or wrong. Many were uneasy at the compromises that UMNO had made with the MCA, and feared that to advance the pace of independence, would jeopardise the political and economic survival of the Malays. This was a central premise of the IMP-dominated Bukit Gantang committee on Malay participation in the economy, which was deliberating at this time. As a spokesman for another participant, the Pan-Malayan Islamic Association, remarked, premature independence 'invited self-destruction for the Malays'.[90] Other groups outside of the MCA–UMNO nexus saw the Conference strategy as the best means of securing a voice for minority interests: George Shelley and the Eurasian Association; Thuraisingham and the Ceylon Federation of Malaya; S. Shanmugam and the Federation of Indian Organisations; G. V. Thaver and the Malayan Indian Association; and K. L. Devaser and the MIC – and also the Pakistani, Sinhalese and Sikh Associations. Many of the Conference's supporters had prospered under colonial rule, and achieved a pre-eminence as spokesmen for their communities that they could not hope to attain under open democratic conditions. Leaders of the Straits Chinese British Association, such as Heah Joo Seang, suspicious of the KMT pedigree of the MCA, brought in some Chinese support and sought to raise the political profile of Penang and Malacca and guarantee Onn's commitment to membership of the British Commonwealth: a vital precondition for the maintenance of Straits Chinese privileges.[91]

The National Conference was mocked by hostile sections of the media. Its leaders perhaps protested overmuch that they were not colonial stooges. Of a meeting on 27 September 1953 at which the National Association of Perak was formed – essentially a satellite of the Conference – *Utusan Melayu* observed that 'there were no fiery speeches against colonialism, no praise for democracy, and no mention of the needs and interests of the masses . . . other than speeches directed at justifying their own stand'.[92] Opposition to the National Conference greatly accelerated the co-operation between UMNO and the MCA, and led the two parties to voice a common response – the announcing of a parallel National Convention. The Alliance leaders looked to defeat the Mentri Besars' group at the polls and supplant them on the Federal Legislative Council. The National Conference faltered as many of the larger component parties became bitterly divided on the question of participation in it. Both the Pan-Malayan Islamic Association and the Malayan Indian Congress withdrew at an early stage under pressure from their membership. After the departure of the MIC – which in mid-1953 had around 20,648 members – the combined strength of the Conference's participant bodies was no more than 10,000.[93] The leaders that clung to the wreckage did so merely to retain what individual influence they could salvage. Onn read this trend, and as abruptly as he had broken with UMNO, once again

[90] *Straits Echo*, 1. 9. 1952.
[91] Lee Yong Hock, 'A history of the Straits Chinese British Association (1900–59)' (B.A. Hons, University of Malaya, 1960), 69–78.
[92] *Utusan Melayu*, 30. 9. 1953.   [93] *Malay Mail*, 17. 2. 1954.

changed course. He shaped the remnants of the IMP into a new body, the Party Negara, which was launched in February 1954. It was formed to support the Rulers as they went into conference to discuss the Special Committee report on federal elections.[94] The British welcomed it, but they had lowered their expectations.

> The Federation needs a strong Party Negara; there are few if any who view with any equanimity the presence of a single political party or coalition of parties with no organised opposition. Fortunately the Party Negara has a number of influential leaders, Malays in particular, who may be expected to attract a fair number of votes on a family retainer basis.[95]

It was largely on this basis that the struggle between the National Conference and the Alliance was fought out in the locality. In Perak, the Mentri Besar, Dato Panglima Bukit Gantang, although he retained his post as president of Perak UMNO, held secret meetings in mid-February 1953 to form his own non-communal party. He was elected head of UMNO Perak at an extraordinary general meeting at which only sixteen of the forty-two branches in the State were represented. Bukit Gantang made this move as UMNO and the MCA began to discuss a national Alliance. Like Dato Onn, he felt that UMNO was a spent force: by 1953 its membership in the State had shrunk from 35,000 to less than 5,000. He hoped to attract the cream of the UMNO and MCA membership into his new organisation. UMNO's national leaders bitterly opposed the move and saw behind it the guiding spirit of Dato Onn. Tunku Abdul Rahman warned the Perak Malays that the new UMNO was very different from the old: it was no longer a monopoly of the privileged and feudal class, an instrument by which they might further their own ends, but a party to fight for the interests of the workers and peasants. He embarked on a pre-emptive political tour of Perak, and then on to Kedah and Penang, to visit the kampongs. In the north we find him reassuring the villagers of Balik Pulau that Dato Onn's departure from the party had not affected its strength, rather 'with the exit of the "big names" from UMNO it has become a stronger organisation based firmly on the common man'. No longer were the Malays dependent on the Rulers to protect their own interests but on the strength of a people united. This rhetoric should not blind us to the fact that the high leadership of UMNO was itself elitist – dominated by a few key families. However, plans were laid to decentralise the party to break up large conservative factions such as Perak UMNO and to boost the grass-roots leadership.[96] By mid-1953 fourteen UMNO branches in Perak had direct dealings with UMNO headquarters, whilst eighteen branches remained loyal to Bukit Gantang – that is 11,000 members, one-third of the total. The threat from Bukit Gantang was checked, and a new UMNO office was opened in Perak. When Bukit Gantang's new organisation, the National Association of Perak (NAP), emerged, it was a 'party of personage', drawing its support from *penghulus* and others dependent on the fiat of the Mentri Besar. For example, it pressurised Chinese mining interests nervous about the renewal of their licences. It was, in intent, a pilot

[94] PIR, January 1954, CO1030/244.   [95] Templer to Lyttelton, 16. 3. 1954, CO1030/244.
[96] *Straits Echo*, 19. 2. 1953; 20. 2. 1953.

organisation for the Party Negara, but in State elections in 1954 it was trounced by the Alliance, who won all thirty seats. The NAP was beaten by a superior organisation and its platform was discredited by Bukit Gantang's open canvassing and offering of official favours in return for support, although the Party Negara alleged equally dubious tactics on the part of the MCA. There were other factors: Dato Onn was immobilised by a heart attack and the rural support for the NAP he may have been able to conjure up did not materialise in the face of speaking tours by Tunku Abdul Rahman and Tan Cheng Lock. The NAP survived this débâcle, but drew back to focus itself on the authority of the Sultan. Most of its followers drifted back into UMNO.[97]

This pattern was replicated elsewhere: State elites were embarrassed at the polls and, over time, were reabsorbed in the Alliance organisation. In local elections in Johore and Trengganu the best showing of the Party Negara was its 11.3 per cent of the popular vote in Johore, where the personal authority of Dato Onn still seemed to count for something. Yet it could not match the war chest of the Alliance, which spent $250,000 on the campaign to the Party Negara's $3,000.[98] In Kelantan, the IMP/ Party Negara drew strength from the influence of the former Mentri Besar, Dato Nik Kamil bin Haji Nik Mahmud, whose family had long enjoyed an ascendency in the State. In Kota Bahru the IMP boasted nearly 2,000 members, and the town was virtually its national headquarters. However, those opposed to the old ascendency formed a new youth movement, the *Gabongan Pemuda Melayu Kelantan*, and when the grip of the old order was tested in elections in 1955, the Party Negara did not contest them at State level, as it already had an appointed majority and it feared embarrassment. When it did contest for the federal seats there was a clear trend: its leaders could continue to command some support from an older generation of clients; however, the new salaried men in the rural areas and towns were less susceptible to the same pressures as their forebears. They looked more to the support of political organisations emanating from the federal centre, this translated itself into over-whelming support for UMNO. Afterwards the aristocratic elites began to move back towards UMNO and this unlocked a particularly complex period of elite rivalry within Kelantan UMNO as it faced a new challenge from political Islam.[99] In Johore, the State Councillor, Ungku Abdullah bin Omar, heartened by public utterances by Sultan Ibrahim of Johore, who contemptuously dismissed aspirations for independence and called for a return to the days of the Unfederated Malay States, formed a loyalist *Persatuan Kebangsaan Melayu Johor* in October 1955 and demanded secession from the Federation. It was a reaction against the new networks of power that UMNO had weaved within the State. Ungku Abdullah had a quixotic career which encompassed the MDU, UMNO and a campaign to restore a Sultan to Singapore. He

---

[97] *Utusan Melayu*, 10. 7. 1953. Raj Vasil, *Politics in a plural society* (Kuala Lumpur, 1971), pp. 268–73; PIR, August 1954, CO1030/244.

[98] PIR, October 1954, *ibid.*

[99] *Melayu Raya*, 30. 6. 1953; Clive S. Kessler, *Islam and politics in a Malay state: Kelantan, 1838–1969* (Ithaca, 1978), pp. 109–17.

wrote to other Rulers to urge them to take a similar stand. There was little response beyond an insignificant 'Negri Naning' movement, and the brief emergence of a Kelantan Malay United Front, led by Nik Mahmood bin Haji Abdul Majid, another maverick whose career had encompassed the post-war *Persatuan Persetiaan Melayu Kelantan* and the Peninsular Malay Union. Like the Johore initiative it was a reaction to loss of position and, like Johore, was stillborn. The Johore party was even disowned by its own Sultan, who suggested that its headquarters might appropriately be the local lunatic asylum.[100] In Malacca too, the local UMNO attacked the notion that the Dato Naning could speak for the Malays of the State.[101] In Negri Sembilan the *adat* leaders followed Dato Onn, but attitudes to traditional leadership had changed. Revered in *adat*, the *lembagas* were disobeyed in politics, in which *orang bergelar bernama*, men 'of no name', came to the fore.[102] In fact the pressure from the elites through *penghulus* and *ketuas* for the people to vote for the Party Negara was ignored and perhaps even counter-productive. In areas where UMNO was strong, it was through the party that local communities sought to voice their interest. The greater rewards, the real legitimacy, came from the centre.

By 1954, the British government's attempts to promote the Party Negara were half-hearted and restrained by a fear that colonial patronage was too overt. MacGillivray told Whitehall in the middle of the year that the Party Negara was 'pretty inactive in presenting itself as a political force in Malaya'.[103] In October 1954, Dato Onn and his ally, Zainal Abidin, canvassed the support of Dr Burhanuddin. However, he declined their overtures: he saw the Party Negara as a colonial creation, and looked to left-wing cells within UMNO to carry the torch of Malay radicalism.[104] Onn's political gyrations had also begun to alienate non-Malays. As Member for Home Affairs, he made a speech in March 1953 that questioned the loyalty of the Malayan Chinese to the country and accused them of seeking to make Malaya a new province of China. A motion of censure was tabled against him in the Federal Legislative Council; MCA anger was compounded by the banning of their lottery, and after this any hopes Onn had of attracting a significant body of Chinese support evaporated.[105] The utterances of the Party Negara, its demands for a 'Malay Malaya', became increasingly communal in tone. By the middle of 1954 Onn's party was no longer seen by the British as the natural party of government. Onn attempted to revive his fortunes by returning to his earlier career, journalism, founding a new newspaper in Kuala Lumpur in July 1956 called *Kritik*. The venture survived little over a year. Even

---

[100] Mohamed Noordin Sopiee, *From Malayan Union to Singapore separation: political unification in the Malaysia region, 1945–65* (Kuala Lumpur, 1974), pp. 80–6; PIR, December 1955, CO1030/245.

[101] *Straits Echo*, 20. 4. 1953.

[102] Abdul Samad Idris, *25 tahun UMNO*, p. 96. The author was at the time Utusan Melayu correspondent in Negri Sembilan.

[103] MacGillivray to Martin, 10. 7. 1954, CO1030/315.

[104] MacGillivray to Lennox-Boyd, 10.11.1954, CO1030/244

[105] T. H. Tan in MCA, *MCA, 20th Anniversary souvenir, 1949–69* (Kuala Lumpur, 1969), p. 56.

before his humiliation at the polls, Onn had become irrelevant, in the words of one British observer: 'a leader no longer sure of himself or of who will follow him'.[106]

The residual challenge to UMNO came from the populist and Islamic wings of Malay radicalism. One voice of opposition was the Peninsular Malay Union (PMU). Little has been written about this party. It was formed as a protest against Dato Onn's path of communal compromise in 1950. The British reported that the inaugural meeting was inspired by UMNO separatists and that every Ruler, save the Tengku Makhota of Johore, had donated money to it. Dato Onn accused the Rulers of sponsoring the new party. It was led by a court translator from Malacca, Hashim Ghani: a forceful advocate of Malay primacy. At its Conference in Kuala Lumpur in February 1951 the PMU attacked the single nationality proposals of the CLC.[107] It seemed to be making a bid to attract UMNO dissenters by invoking *kerajaan* loyalties. One Chinese newspaper distinguished the IMP as 'Reformist' and the PMU as 'Restorationist'.[108] It had a distinct populist style: 'fighting for the rights and privileges of each and every Malay and not of any particular group'. Hashim Ghani was ousted as President in May 1952 by Nik Mahmood bin Haji Abdul Majid of Kelantan for carrying out his duties in an unconstitutional manner and for failing to disclose accounts. He was bedevilled by a fraud charge from which he was acquitted in November, but thereafter his influence rose again. A Fourth Annual Congress at Butterworth, on 6–8 March 1953, brought new office-holders with a MNP or KMM pedigree to the fore. The PMU initially participated in, and later withdrew from the National Conference and announced its own All-Malaya National Conference. Held in Johore Bahru on 24 April 1953, it incorporated many dissenting elements. One was the *Parti Kebangsaan Malaya*, formed in Johore Bahru in April 1952, based partly on former UMNO figures and old MNP members who had resigned from the PMU, and other groups such as the *Semangat Pemuda Melayu Penang* and the Union of Johore Malays. The PMU attempted without success to recruit influential personalities in Johore such as Khatijah Sidek and her husband Dr Hamzah bin Haji Taib.[109] Hashim took the PMU into the Alliance's National Convention in August 1953, but the party again withdrew after he launched into a fierce attack on the MCA. Invoking the treaties of protection, the PMU argued that independence was a matter to be resolved between the Malays and British, and its political thinking reflected MNP concepts of a single *Melayu* citizenship, Malay as the official language, and Islam as the official religion.[110] It was a fractious grouping of displaced Malay radicals, and acquired little

---

[106] Templer to Lyttelton, 14. 4. 1954, 16. 3. 1954, CO1030/244.

[107] PMR, No. 9 of 1950, CO527/6020; PMR, No. 3 of 1951, CO537/7297. In the same year it campaigned for a Kesatuan *Melayu Raya*, under a President – at one time suggesting the Sultan of Pahang as a candidate. *Utusan Melayu*, 26. 9. 1951.

[108] *Sin Chew Jit Poh*, 26. 9. 1951.

[109] PMR, No. 5 of 1952, CO1022/190; PMR, Nos. 2, 3, 6, 11 of 1952, No. 3 of 1953; 'Secret Abstract of Intelligence of the period 17.10–16.11.1952'; 'Resolutions of the Round Table Conference of Malaya', Johore Bahru, 24. 4. 1953', CO1022/189.

[110] *Malay Mail*, 5. 3. 1954, reporting the Third Malay National Congress in Penang sponsored

popular support. Yet Hashim Ghani's utterances found echoes elsewhere. A Malay columnist for the *Sunday Times* commended him for being 'under no illusion as to the chances of his countrymen in competition with the superior organisation, financial position and education of the non-Malays'. The writer behind the *nom-de-plume* 'C. H. E. Det' was Mahathir bin Mohamad.[111]

By the early 1950s many former API, MNP and Hizbul Muslimin activists were looking for a new political home. The release of Malay detainees added many more to their number. Indeed, their plight – that of A. Samad Ismail for example – became a *cause célèbre* for Malay politics. Many drifted to Singapore, looking for employment as journalists or educators and they turned to political leaders for help in rebuilding their lives.[112] As Ishak Haji Muhammad wrote in a letter to an ex-detainee: 'my house has become an unofficial club for ex-detainees. It is full daily with people with their respective problems. I have no money, but I do provide them with rice, sugar, salt fish and mattresses.'[113] The Malay left survived, unproscribed but weakened. Many ex-detainees gravitated to the new *Parti Rakyat*. Predominantly Malay in character, it articulated a socialist ideology, based around Sukarno's Marhaenism. Such 'Indonesian' political language immediately awoke British suspicions. It also attracted Ahmad Boestamam when he emerged from his 'seven years of lengthening night', and Dr Burhanuddin, who had retired to his homoeopathy practice after a year in jail following the Nadra riots. Boestamam was very active in the cause of detainees, many of whom were his old supporters. The *Parti Rakyat* also looked to ex-servicemen's associations for support. However, a split developed in late 1955 between Dr Burhanuddin and Ahmad Boestamam, who championed a non-communal approach.[114] To the UMNO elite, the reappearance of these radicals threatened to pull the party to the left, and UMNO Youth were ordered to boycott the Malay Youth Congress of April 1955, another brain-child of Dr Burhanuddin's, by which he hoped to spark a realignment on the nationalist left.[115] However, the various strands of radicalism that existed before 1948 were not to recombine and Dr Burhanuddin's political struggle was to take him on a very different course.

Hitherto, we have been focusing on the internal upheavals within the Malay body politic. Although the structure of politics that emerged was shaped along communal lines, all communities approached independence deeply divided. Within the Chinese population, the politics of the *Peranakan* and that of the *huaqiao* drifted apart. The Straits Chinese mercantile interests of Penang gave their support to a secession movement in order to preserve the Straits Settlements, and the privileges of their

by the Peninsular Malays Union, the Peninsula Malays League, the *Semangat Pemuda Melayu Penang*, the *Party Progressive Melayu*, and the *Perpaduan Raayat Kalimantan*.

[111] Khoo Boo Teik, 'The legacy of C. H. E. Det: portrait of a nationalist as a young man', *Kajian Malaysia*, 11, 2 (1993), 32.

[112] For a vivid memoir, Jaafar Hussein, *Kebenaran* (Kuala Lumpur, 1987).

[113] 'To understand the position of ex-MNP detainees', *Utusan Zaman*, 18. 7. 1954.

[114] PIR, December 1955; March 1956, CO1030/245.

[115] PIR, April 1955, CO1030/245.

subjects, as the Malta of Southeast Asia. The MCA leader, Tan Cheng Lock, although Straits Chinese himself, had set his eyes on wider political ambitions and on Chinese integration, even at the cost of relinquishing special Straits Chinese privileges. This issue was a running sore between the old mouthpiece of the *Peranakan*, the Straits Chinese British Association and the MCA.[116] The Indian community was also divided. The Federation of Indian Organisations, formed in 1950, was an attempt by Indian Legislative Councillors to raise support. It did not succeed in attracting grass-roots support and thereafter Indian politics centred on struggles for control of the MIC, which itself was more an arena of intra-communal rivalries than a symbol of a united community. Under its President, the Punjabi K. L. Devaser, the MIC was taken into the IMP. For a while in 1951, the Indian community, due to its large number of registered voters in the towns, possessed an electoral importance dispro-portionate to its numbers. However, Devaser's confrontations with Tamil chauvinists led to his being supplanted as President of the MIC by V. T. Sambanthan in 1954. Thereafter the party leaned more towards the rural areas and networks of Tamil organisations for support. In 1954 it joined the Alliance as a junior partner.[117] Non-communal parties survived – the Labour Party, the *Parti Rakyat* – yet these often relied heavily on a single community for their support. The Malayan Party, formed in Malacca around 1952, campaigned for 'multi-racial, socialist, property-owning democracy' similar to Switzerland, and joined forces with the Chinese *shetuan* on the citizenship issue.[118] A Negri Sembilan Progressive Party was formed in February 1953 by Dr J. Samuel to represent workers, with a multi-racial leadership.[119] Perhaps the most influential of these organisations was the People's Progressive Party, based on Ipoh and Menglembu in Perak. It was Fabian socialist in outlook and led by two Indian brothers, the Seenivasagams. It achieved success in the 1954 Ipoh town elections and drew impressive levels of Chinese support by its articulation of the grievances of the New Villages of Kinta. However, its elitist leadership and 'Malayan' orientation sat awkwardly with the increasingly communal complexion to its support, and it failed to evolve into a national political alternative.[120]

Voices of resurgent Islam

A more powerful challenge that emerged in these years, both to colonial political development and to the new mainstream of Malayan politics, came from resurgent

---

[116] Mohamed Sopiee, *From Malayan Union to Singapore separation: political unification in the Malaysia region, 1945–65* (Kuala Lumpur, 1974), pp. 56–80; Lee Yong Hock, 'A history of the Straits Chinese British Association', pp. 69–78.

[117] Ampalavanar, *The Indian minority and political change in Malaya, 1945–57* (Kuala Lumpur, 1981), ch. 6.

[118] Oong Hak Ching, 'Perjuangan Partai Malayan, 1956–7', *Malaysia in History*, 18, 1 (1975), 1–9.

[119] *Straits Echo*, 5. 2. 1953.

[120] Vasil, *Politics in a plural society*, pp. 93–120, 167–72, 222–44.

Islam. It was to question the core assumptions of national struggle. A process of religious reorganisation had long been underway. However, the new conditions of social life widened the political and cultural possibilities for Islam, and by 1950 the Maria Hertogh case, and riots in Singapore, had supercharged this process. The beginnings of this can be seen in the welfare associations that tried to meet social pressures in the towns. Their central concern was women. Increased prostitution focused religious attention on high levels of divorce – over 50 per cent in Kuala Lumpur.[121] State authorities moved slowly to reform marriage procedures. 'Until and unless we stop these unfortunate happenings,' the *ulama* argued, 'it is no use trying to prevent non-Muslims belittling the religion of Islam which gave the world science, mathematics, physics, chemistry, astrology and astronomy.'[122] As organisations such as the Malay Women's Welfare Association of Singapore pointed out, the number of Malay girls leaving school was growing each year. The traditional teaching, clerical and caring professions could not absorb all these women.[123] There was a more general issue of their status to be addressed. However, when the Association lobbied for legislation to stop Muslim men marrying non-Muslim adopted daughters, on the grounds that it was intolerable to Muslim women, religious authorities accused its leadership of spreading pernicious western influences, of irreligion, and of ineffectiveness in preventing prostitution and cohabitation.[124] Malay women were chastised for spending too much on jewellery and entertainments, and the Singapore council of *ulama* voted to oppose their participation in politics.[125] This was one of many religious disputations that figured prominently in the media in the early 1950s. From them a more fundamental re-examination of the place of Islam within the politics of the nation was to emerge.

Party politics soon intruded into these controversies. In a famous debate over the position of women within the customary law, the *adat perateh*, of Rembau, Negri Sembilan, UMNO representatives attacked *adat* as 'obsolete', 'fit for heathens', corrupted by the local chieftains for their own ends. They demanded the application of Islamic norms. They were opposed by the head of the PMU in Rembau, the secretary of the tribal headmen's association, who countered that *adat* protected the rights of women.[126] The episode reflected local political competition between the parties, but also betrayed deeper popular dissatisfaction with the *ulama* and State religious bureaucracies for their disproportionate enthusiasm for religious rulings in relation to their idleness in spreading the faith and neglect of religious education.[127] The campaign to establish a central Islamic religious college to train *muftis* and

---

[121] Shirle Gordon, 'Marriage/divorce in the eleven States of Malaya and Singapore', *Intisari*, 2, 2 (n.d.), 23–32.

[122] *Malay Mail*, 26. 2. 1954.   [123] *Utusan Zaman*, 3.10.1951.

[124] *Malayan Nanban*, 8. 2. 1953; *Melayu Raya*, 10. 9. 1952, 24.11.1952.

[125] *Melayu Raya*, 22. 1. 1953; 20. 9. 1952.

[126] PMR, March 1951, April 1951, CO537/7302; M. B. Hooker, *Adat laws in modern Malaya: land tenure, traditional government and religion* (Kuala Lumpur, 1972), pp. 212–13.

[127] For example, *Melayu Raya*, 13. 8. 1952.

teachers, and a missionary drive to the New Villages and the Orang Asli, were channels for religious resurgence. Another was the attempt by States to reform themselves. Selangor established a *Majlis Ugama dan Adat*, religious affairs council, in early 1949, to control its Religious Affairs Department. It prepared legislation to tackle the high divorce rate, which by 1949 equalled the 1937 high of 60 per cent; it registered religious schools; scrutinised teaching to avoid the spread of erroneous doctrine; and supervised the mosques and the collection of *zakat* and *fitrah* religious tax. A standing committee of heads of Religious Departments and *muftis* was formed in 1951, under the Keeper of the Rulers' Seal, to recommend to the Rulers uniform dates for festivals, and the States were pressured to adopt a more regularised administration of Islam. In Perak, before 1949, there were no less than six bodies to advise the Ruler on religious matters. Over a period of several years they were brought together into a Department of Religious Affairs, superintended by a *Majlis Agama dan Adat*, to which UMNO initially supplied a layman nominee. It collected *zakat* and *fitrah* after 1952. There were protests at the collections, and large amounts of interest-free loans were given, particularly in areas where opposition was most vocal. In 1953, $280,000 was lent to padi cultivators, $168,585 of it in Krian. Few loans were repaid and the practice was discontinued in 1956. There was opposition to the new religious regime. *Zakat* collections actually declined, and the legality of the *fitrah* collection was contested in court.[128] Prosecutions began. In late 1952, seven men were convicted for not paying *fitrah* in Perlis. They appealed on the grounds that the Rulers had no authority to collect it, and that of $40,000 collected, only $17,000 was spent on the poor, the rest in shophouses and padi. They argued their case from the texts of religious authorities.[129] It was suggested in the House of Commons that *zakat* collection in Perlis was causing poverty and unrest. Equally contentious were moves against moral laxity in the towns. So too was the pursuit of heterodoxy. In Jerantut, Pahang, Malays were charged with propagating Mahdism without the Sultan's permission and when, in March 1954, the first imprisonment was made in Selangor by a *shari'a* judge for the preaching of Islam without authority, it brought an angry reaction from a self-styled 'Christian Freeman' who asked in a letter to the *Malay Mail*, 'is there no freedom of religion in this country?' 'There could be no churches, synagogues, temples and other places of worship for non-Muslims in this country,' replied an *ulama*, 'if Muslims do not practice religious freedom.'[130] The last years of colonial rule were an anxious time for the Christian churches in Malaya, and local church leaders hesitated to antagonise Malay political interests and thereby compromise the position of the churches after independence.[131] The British cherished

---

[128] Mohamed Khalil bin Hussein, *The department of religious affairs, Perak: present structure, organisation and recent development* (Singapore, 1958?); Esmail bin Haji Mohd. Salleh, 'Pentadbiran Hal Ehwal Agama Islam di Negri Perak sebelum dan selepas 1949', in Khoo (ed.), *Islam di Malaysia*, pp. 118–28.

[129] *Straits Echo*, 31.12.1952.

[130] *Malay Mail*, 21. 1. 1949, 13. 3. 1954, 17. 1. 1954, 18. 3. 1954.

[131] Rev Robert Hunt, 'Historical overview of Christian social services in Malaysia', Paper

hopes for accommodation. In 1950, Malcolm MacDonald established an inter-religious talking-shop in Singapore and Johore to develop ecumenical friendship and tolerance. By the end of the year, however, Islamic resurgence had assumed a much deeper political aspect.

The catalyst was the case of Maria Hertogh, a Dutch girl adopted by Malays and named Nadra. In late 1950 she was reclaimed by her Dutch parents, who refused to acknowledge her recent marriage, conducted legally under Islamic law, to a Muslim. The case was fought over the jurisdiction of religious authority. When the case was decided in favour of the European parents, riots erupted in Singapore. The episode was a profound shock to the British government. In particular, it was disturbed by the depth of animosity shown towards Europeans by groups whom it had taken to be its strongest collaborators. Although moderate leaders, including Dato Onn, were restrained in their response to the affair, there were alarming undercurrents of anger. It illustrated the ways in which Islam could be mobilised to articulate general anti-colonial sentiments.[132] Responsibility for the rioting was quickly placed on ex-MNP figures like Taha Kalu and Dr Burhanuddin, who had induced one of the guiding spirits of the campaign, Karim Ghani, to take up the case. All three were arrested. *Melayu Raya*, the main mouthpiece of the Nadra agitation, was punished by the withdrawal of its licence. The protestors voiced a generally held feeling that the colonial court had overruled Islamic law. Other newspapers responded to public indignation; the circulation of the Penang women's magazine, *Melawati*, jumped to 3,000 at the height of the affair. It was published by Ahmad Azan, another ex-MNP man, and Dr Burhanuddin was a contributor. Searching for a conspiracy, British intelligence reported that police and Malay Regiment rank-and-file were sympathetic to the protestors. Subscriptions for an appeal to the Privy Council on the case were being collected; anti-British feeling was reported strongest in Johore and Kelantan. In Kota Bahru, a group of young warriors were said to be preparing attacks on Europeans; 'well-placed families in the State hierarchy' were rumoured to be involved.[133] The disorder stimulated the colonial government into establishing a Supreme Muslim Council to strengthen central control over religious affairs and to counter-balance the influence of *ulama* in Egypt and Pakistan.[134] However, British attempts to create a more responsible Islamic authority bore unexpected fruit, and they unwittingly acted as handmaiden to a new kind of politics.

Dato Onn was also taking a new interest in the *ulama*. As his authority within UMNO waned, he turned to them for support and encouraged them to take a more proactive role in religious and political affairs. In August 1951 an UMNO-sponsored

presented to Malaysian CARE, National Symposium 1988, 'Trends and challenges in Christian social services for the 90s', p. 16.

[132] A. J. Stockwell, 'Imperial security and Moslem militancy, with special reference to the Hertogh riots in Singapore (December 1950)', *JSEAS*, 17, 2 (1986), 322–35; J. R. Williams, 'Repercussions of the Bertha Hertogh case', 31. 1. 1951, CO537/7301.

[133] PIR, December 1950; SFWIS, 2.12.1950'; PMR, 1/51, CO537/7302.

[134] Gurney to Griffiths, 17. 1. 1951, *ibid.*

conference of *ulama* in Kuala Lumpur formed a central organisation. It was chaired by a committed supporter of Dato Onn, Haji Ahmad Fuad bin Hassan, Chairman of the UMNO religious department and a former student of *Ehya al-Sharif Assahriff*, Gunong Semanggol. Its calls for a supreme religious body, independent of the Rulers, echoed MATA. However, from the outset the *ulama* were deeply divided on how far they were prepared to challenge the State religious hierarchies and on the propriety of taking the path of politics. As UMNO politics splintered in 1951, they confronted the further dilemma of whether to continue to work within UMNO or to strike out in an independent direction. Fuad was committed to following Onn, yet came under increasing attack for this.[135] At a meeting in Butterworth on 24 November 1951, an Islamic Association of Malaya was formed, headed by Fuad. It was an independent body, although many of its members still remained members of UMNO. It presented itself as a community of Muslims committed to unity in Islamic administration, and to reconciling the demands of Islam and democracy by co-operating with political parties whose objects 'were not contrary to the teachings of Islam in achieving democracy, social justice and human dignity'.[136] 'Do not spend too much time in the mosques,' Fuad instructed the *ulama*.[137] However, as the *ulama* left the mosques, they were sucked into the intense rivalries within Malay politics. Disenchantment with Dato Onn, and a lack of faith in the capacity of his IMP to defend Malay religion, drove a rival in Johore, Ungku Ismail bin Abdul Rahman, the President of the State Religious Affairs Council, to contemplate another new pan-Malayan political party to unite the Malays around Islam. The model was the Indonesian *Masjoemi*. Friday sermons in mosques in Johore disseminated this proposal, and it aroused the interest of men from a different background, such as the ex-*Melayu Raya* and MNP figures Mohd. bin Haji Abdul Rahman and Abdul Hamid bin Haji Abdul.[138] Indeed, the Islamic Association had attracted many MNP and *Hizbul Muslimin* activists who had been out of circulation since 1948: Osman Hamzah, Baharuddin Latif and Muhammad Asri. Yet although British intelligence reports dwelt on these continuities in leadership, it is wrong to view the Islamic Association as the direct successor of the *Hizbul Muslimin*. Much had happened in the interim. The *Hizbul Muslimin* emerged out of a wider leftist challenge to UMNO's claims to speak for the Malays; the Islamic Association emerged out of UMNO itself. Nor did the Association claim all the *Hizbul Muslimin* leaders, who were men of diverse ideological persuasions, and divided by personal rivalries. The Islamic Association was beset by conflicting loyalties which Fuad's participation in Onn's National Conference served to bring into the open. He was forced to withdraw and resigned after the Association joined the UMNO–MCA Convention. It was only by late 1953 that the Association began to effectively articulate a distinctive message. Its

---

[135] Alias Mohamed, *PAS' platform: development and change, 1951–86* (Petaling Jaya, 1994) pp. 25–9.
[136] PMR, 12/51, CO1022/185.   [137] *Utusan Melayu*, 18. 4. 1953.
[138] PMR, 8/51, CO537/7302,

leaders – disillusioned with the ability of parties corrupted by secular, collaborative nationalism to unite the Malay *ummah* – resolved on forming a new political party. A Pan-Malayan Islamic Party (PMIP) was born from the General Assembly of the All-Malaya Muslim Association in early 1953. By degrees, a singular loyalty was demanded from its members. In January 1954 it withdrew from the Convention, for much the same reasons as it had broken with the IMP: in protest at the liberalisation of the provisions for citizenship. In December 1953 the PMIP was reorganised, and launched a membership drive. Its new President, Dr Haji Abbas bin Haji Alias, a doctor in colonial service, and a popular figure due to his connection with many sporting organisations, brought a rather passive leadership style to the PMIP. Yet grass-roots support, agitated by cadres of a very different stamp, began to grow. The PMIP's core constituency lay on the west coast, particularly in Province Wellesley, Kedah, Perlis and around Gunong Semanggol in Perak, areas where the increased tenancy described in Chapter 6 was putting strains on peasant society. A membership drive was launched in the eastern States. This was a crucial move for the party. The PMIP was brought to Kelantan in 1953 by a Kedah man, Amaluddin Darus, who opened a branch in Pasir Mas in July of that year, but soon veteran *anak tempatan* such as Muhammad Asri, who had a KMM, PPMK and API pedigree, and who had been absent from the state for many years, seized the initiative. His wife, Sakinah Junid, who had been active in AWAS, was to lead the women's wing of the party. The Kelantan case is an interesting example of how the diaspora of Malay radicals after 1948 could help disseminate political ideas, but also of how, by the 1950s, the presence of locally known grass-roots leadership was necessary for their realisation. The intellectual traditions of the *pondok* supplied powerful networks of *mufti*, *kadi* and religious inspectors who were to be an important bedrock of PMIP support in rural Kelantan and Trengganu. Darus's memoir also speaks of recruiting members in less traditional settings, in coffeeshops, bookshops and at news-stands.[139]

The formation of an Islamic party reflected both a radical departure in the basis for political identification within the Malay community and a rejection of nationalist doctrine as it had been previously understood. Entrenched State elites moved to counter it. Before the 1955 election the Religious Affairs Department in Perak placed a ban on the use of mosques and *madrasah* for political purposes.[140] However, the PMIP became the only non-Alliance party to win a seat in the 1955 Federal elections, and that was in Perak. Influential ex-*Hizbul Muslimin* members continued to be drawn into the leadership and by the end of 1955 Dr Burhanuddin had assumed the PMIP presidency.[141] Many commentators viewed the PMIP as an unlikely home for Dr Burhanuddin; some questioned his sincerity. Yet analyses of his career and writings

---

[139] Mohamad Abu Bakar, 'Ulama pondok dan politik kepartian di Malaysia, 1945–85', *Malaysia masa kini* (Kuala Lumpur, 1985), pp. 103–12; Amaluddin Darus, *Kenapa saya tinggalkan PAS* (Kuala Lumpur, 1977), discussed in Alias, *PAS' platform*, pp. 50–1.

[140] Mohamed Khalil, *Department of religious affairs, Perak*, p. 81.

[141] *Malay Mail*, 5. 4. 1954; N. J. Funston, 'The origins of Partai Islam Se Malaysia', *JSEAS*, 7, 1 (1976)', 70–2.

show that he always had pan-Islamic sympathies, and that the coalition of the MNP and API had always been a marriage of convenience for its leaders. War and social change, the bitterness of the Emergency campaign and the pivotal Malay role in it, the searching debates within all spheres of Malay life and culture, all created room by the mid-1950s for new kinds of political organisation and the cultivation of new political constituencies. The PMIP was divided, as all Malay parties were, over how far accommodations should be reached with regard to citizenship, the Malay language and the position of Islam, and whether the national struggle was prior to the Islamic struggle. Dr Burhanuddin's election was contested by a Perak *ulama*, Zulkifli Muhammad, who, although himself a well-travelled sophisticate with both an Arabic and English education, placed precedence on the fight for the *ummah*.[142] Dr Burhanuddin, by contrast, would advocate a front for Malay parties to challenge the hegemony of UMNO. He brought to the PMIP a practised doctrine of nationalism. For Dr Burhanuddin the PMIP was a vehicle for realising the ideals of Malay nationalism, the notion of *Melayu* nationhood first formulated in his writings of the late 1940s, and incorporated into the AMCJA–PUTERA People's Constitution. In 1956 the *Melayu* seemed a more stringently defined category than it was in 1946. To Dr Burhanuddin, nationalism was merely 'preliminary for realising an ideology . . . Regarding the method of how we organize and run our independent, democratic and sovereign country, the method as to how to form a just society, Islam has its own views.'[143] The 'Malayan', as comprehended by 'pseudo-national' colonial thought, was merely an amalgamation of races, and would condemn the Malays to ethnicity.[144] By identifying Islam as the ideology of Malay nationalism, Malaya would be elevated to an *ummah*, a true community, inclusive of non-Malays. The extent to which it was inclusive of non-Muslims was an ambiguity which was left largely unresolved. However, the PMIP advanced an alternative conception of the individual's obligation to the community that was to haunt the project of secular nationalism. Many years later, Dr Mahathir Mohamad was to call the PMIP a 'time-bomb' left by the British in Malaya.

The path to the summit

By the second half of 1953 the Alliance dominated Malayan politics. Within four years they had carved a path to full independence for Malaya. As partners in nation-building they were not the allies the British would have chosen. The British government was compelled to abandon its aim of transferring power to a non-communal political party. The unity that the Alliance envisaged was not a fusion into a non-communal 'Malayan' entity. Multi-racialism as a condition of independence was not met in the way it had originally been conceived: multi-racialism was to be more in

---

[142] Alias Mohamed, *Malaysia's Islamic opposition: past, present and future* (Kuala Lumpur, 1991), pp. 55–6.

[143] Safie bin Ibrahim, *The Islamic Party of Malaysia: its formative stages and ideology* (Kota Bahru, 1981), pp. 85–6.

[144] *Malay Mail*, 8. 3. 1954.

the nature of a business deal. It took some time for the British to accept this. This process perhaps began in September 1953 when H. S. Lee and Dr Ismail were offered, and accepted, posts as Members, a move which, although it provoked opposition from within some sections of the Alliance, signalled the beginning of its absorption into government. No attempt here will be made to detail the intricate negotiations that surrounded the transfer of power. However, some themes may be highlighted. Most accounts see the end of empire in Malaya as a triumph of planned decolonisation, in which the heirs of the old Malay aristocratic elites inherited the system of government in which they had been schooled. However, this might be questioned on two grounds. First, neither the ascendency of the Alliance nor the exact timing of independence was planned by the British. As A. J. Stockwell's monumental documentary study has shown there were several moments when Alliance pressure won concessions that accelerated the devolution of power and overrode British conditions for devolving it: in debates over elections to the Federal Council; over policy towards the Communists; over defence and control of internal security; over the manner by which the constitution was to be formulated.[145] Secondly, at each stage, powerful divisions within Malayan politics were shaping the responses of the main protagonists of the imperial endgame and the timing of independence. The struggle for the soul of the nation would not end in 1957. *Merdeka* left much unfinished business.

With the easing of some of the internal power struggles within Malaya and the stabilising of the Emergency situation, Templer sought to retain the political initiative by expanding the Member system and the membership of Federal Councils.[146] As he predicted, the Alliance rapidly raised the political stakes by demanding, after their first joint meeting in early 1953, that Federal elections be held in 1954. An Alliance committee began to draft rules for them and submitted representations to the High Commissioner and the Rulers that elections be held to create an elected majority in the Legislative Council. They also decided at their second round-table meeting to boycott the National Conference, thus scotching any hope the British held that they would fall in line with the moderates of the Mentri Besars' National Conference. Templer, who favoured a slower approach to elections, whereby Federal elections would only follow the State and Settlement elections scheduled for 1955, responded by appointing a Special Committee for Federal elections on which the Mentri Besar group secured the greater representation. The conclusions of this Special Committee, published in February 1954, in many ways echoed the gradualistic approach of the National Conference and recommended that only an elected minority be created by elections. The Alliance dug in its heels and demanded a three-fifths elected majority. A compromise whereby a bare majority would be created by elections in 1955 was dismissed as unacceptable by the Alliance. An Alliance delegation, headed by Tunku Abdul Rahman, proceeded to London in April and May of 1954 to petition the

---

[145] Stockwell, *Malaya*, I, p. lxxx.
[146] MacGillivray to Lloyd, 14. 3. 1953, Stockwell, *Malaya*, II, pp. 447–9.

Colonial Secretary. Finding Lyttelton unbudging in his support of the government position, the delegation returned to Malaya, demanding a royal commission to settle the issue. This being denied to it, on 13 June 1954 the Alliance announced a boycott of colonial councils.

Three aspects of this portentous crisis stand out. First, the British capitulated to the threat of civil disobedience. Under pressure from within and without the party to adopt a hard line, Tunku Abdul Rahman announced in February 1954 that 'it will be better for me to go to prison than to accept the recommendations of the Federal elections committee'. Secret instructions were issued to Alliance members to underline this resolve.[147] A Gold Coast judge had suggested to Tunku Abdul Rahman in London that he should 'seek independence through the doors of the prison rather than through the doors of the Colonial Office'. During the boycott, there was a distinct danger that the constitutional struggle would spill out into widespread civil disobedience. As we saw in Chapter 4, it was in this period that militant cells were being established within UMNO to root out informers and condition the organisation for more direct action. Tunku Abdul Rahman warned that the Alliance must persist in its opposition as 'there are those who are opposed to real democratic progress'.[148] Behind the scenes, Templer suggested face-saving political strategies to UMNO. For example, they might withdraw from the Legislative Council debate on elections and then return later for the Executive Council business. However, Alliance opposition was only calmed by an assurance given to Tunku Abdul Rahman, by Sir Donald MacGillivray, Templer's successor, in a meeting aboard H. M. S. *Alert*, that he would have a working majority. An 'emergency exit' was provided for the Alliance by which a nominated reserve would be used to ensure this in the event of an inconclusive poll. 'The longer the present situation goes on,' MacGillivray had concluded, 'the greater the chances of disorder.'[149]

Secondly, the crisis was a formative episode in the Alliance's relations with the Rulers. UMNO and the Rulers were divided in their response to the Federal Elections Committee. The crisis came to a head in mid-1954 with a series of processions organised by UMNO in the States as a show of strength to the Rulers. MacGillivray went to great lengths to emphasise that the political dispute was primarily one between the Alliance and conservative opposition and not between the Malayan people and the British government. He pointed out that the UMNO processions were strikingly reminiscent of the Malayan Union agitation, in that they were directed against the Rulers and their Party Negara allies. Yet this did not lessen British concern. MacGillivray urged British Advisers to ensure that the Rulers, for their own good, received the delegations. Indeed, where they did so the processions often ended with spontaneous declarations of loyalty to the Sultans.[150] In Selangor demonstrators

---

[147] PIR, February, 1954, CO1030/244; T. H. Tan in MCA, *MCA, 20th Anniversary souvenir, 1949–69*, p. 87.
[148] Tunku Abdul Rahman to Lyttelton, 25. 5. 1954, CO1030/311.
[149] Templer to Lyttelton 17. 5. 1954; Lyttelton to Tunku Abdul Rahman, 18.5.1954, CO1030/310.
[150] MacGillivray to British Advisers, 26. 6. 1954, CO1030/311.

were told that the Sultan wanted to see them; they were paid five dollars as expenses, and provided with transport. Yet in Perak there was a public outcry when the Sultan refused to see the delegation and it was received by Bukit Gantang, as Mentri Besar, in his stead.[151] As we saw earlier, the post-war Malayan Union crisis out of which UMNO emerged contained elements of popular rebellion against royal hegemony and its failure to adequately protect the political interest of the Malay nation. The notion of popular sovereignty had assumed even greater momentum by the 1950s. Although in his memoirs Tunku Abdul Rahman was anxious to stress how far he attempted to keep the Rulers in line with UMNO, the fact that he himself was a prince of Kedah seems if anything to have strengthened rather than inhibited him in his demands that the will of the *rakyat* must take precedence.[152] He was careful to blame the breach on the State hierarchies: 'unfortunately the Rulers have been hoodwinked by people who are not sincere with the advice they give to their Rulers'.[153] Rather than a claim for the integrity of the *kerajaan*, the resistance of the Rulers to independence was more accurately an appeal to the British government to protect their status under the terms of the Federation treaties. A private meeting of Rulers and Mentri Besar – save those of Perak and Kedah – was held after the processions. It was presided over by the Sultan of Johore, who attacked the Ruler of Perak for refusing to receive the delegation and advocated that the Rulers campaign to increase their personal following in the States. Mindful of the Indonesian experience, the Rulers of Pahang and Trengganu declared that they would throw in their lot with UMNO in a bid to retain their position.[154] In the crucial constitutional negotiations in late 1955 and early 1956 it is clear that the Sultans' reluctance to be cited by UMNO as a reason for their failure led the Rulers, at the Conference of Rulers on 21 December 1955, to agree reluctantly to a timetable for independence: all, that is, except Johore. The Rulers' representatives at the London talks were to persuade UMNO from breaking them off, and voyaged to the talks with the Alliance leaders to hammer out a common position.[155]

Thirdly, the crisis galvanised the Alliance and illustrated how formidable its machinery had become. MacGillivray observed that the Alliance threat to resign was designed to force a trial of strength with the government. It displayed contempt for the colonial experiment in democracy by 'undermining much of the confidence which was built up in these institutions of democratic government by using them as pawns in a game of politics rather than as training grounds in public service'.[156] Certainly the boycott – which by mid-June involved some 600 UMNO and 400 MCA representatives – illustrates the pressures within Alliance politics and some of the strong-arm methods by which party discipline was sustained. Many branches bowed only reluctantly to party discipline; many council members merely failed to show up

---

[151] PIR, July, 1954, CO1030/244.
[152] C.f. Smith, 'The rise, decline and survival of the Malay Rulers', 101–2.
[153] *Malay Mail*, 5. 3. 1954.   [154] MacGillivray to Lyttelton, 6. 9. 1954, CO1030/244.
[155] MacGillivray to Lyttelton, 9. 1. 1956, CO1030/245.
[156] MacGillivray to British Advisers, 26. 6. 1954, CO1030/311.

for meetings to avoid having their seats declared vacant. Many Chinese feared that they would lose the representation they had gained and it appeared in Johore that Chinese were prepared to elect their own candidates outside of the MCA ticket. H. S. Lee told the Chinese that failure to comply with the boycott would provide an opportunity for Malay opinion to vent its anger on the Chinese. In a speech to Chinese organisations in Selangor on 21 June 1954, H. S. Lee employed very loaded political language, and referred to the need to attack the 'running dogs'. The action committee of the MCA put determined pressure on the Chinese Chambers of Commerce and guilds to join the boycott. 'The methods which the Alliance have been using of late,' MacGillivray concluded, 'savour somewhat of dictatorship . . . a sad augury for the future if the Alliance should sweep into power.'[157]

The next step was the elections themselves. This further strengthened the Alliance's united front. Their continued unity was a condition for a rapid transfer of power, and a rapid transfer of power was a necessity to ensure that it would be the Alliance that acquired that power. The most authoritative analysis of the framing of the Alliance manifesto has emphasised that there were in fact two manifestos. It was all things to all communities.[158] Much has been written on the Alliance's over-whelming victory in the polls, yet it is important to recognise that in many ways the 1955 elections were an unrealistic gauge of future electoral trends in Malaya (see Table 8). After the Alliance landslide there were still 46 nominated seats in the Legislative Council. Moreover, the psephology of independent Malaya was not fully formed. In the 1955 elections, there were approximately 1,600,000 people eligible to vote, only 1,280,000 had voluntarily registered, and of these 85 per cent voted. Over 600,000 Chinese were able to vote, but only 140,000 had registered. Rumours had spread that registration was linked to the registration of manpower and the imposition of new taxes. The combined electorate of the two Kuala Lumpur constituencies was only 22,000. The British argued that as three-quarters of Chinese and Indian citizens were under the age of 21 anyway, even if they had all registered, 75 per cent of the electorate would have been Malay. Only one in eight Chinese and one in seven Indians voted.[159] Moreover, the constituencies were drawn up on an estimate for 1953 on the basis of the 1947 census, and without taking into account the changes wrought in settlement patterns by the Emergency, nor of who were and were not citizens of the Federation. As with the entire British approach to Malayan politics, the committee that had created this electoral geography had adopted an unwavering non-communal line, and it was criticised for ignoring the realities of the local situation.[160] It was left

---

[157] MacGillivray to Lyttelton, 28. 6. 1954, CO1030/310; MacGillivray to Sir John Martin, 25. 6. 1954, CO1030/311.

[158] Heng, *Chinese politics*, pp. 202–12.

[159] Francis G. Carnell, 'The Malayan elections', *Pacific Affairs*, 28, 4 (1955), 315–30; T. E. Smith, *Report on the first elections of members to the Legislative Council of the Federation of Malaya* (Kuala Lumpur, 1955), pp. 9–11.

[160] V. David, *Freedom never came* (Petaling Jaya, 1989), p. 59; K. J. Ratnam, *Communalism and the political process in Malaya* (Kuala Lumpur, 1965), p. 194.

Table 8 *Results of the 1955 federal elections*

Party	No. candidates fielded	No. candidates successful	Votes	Percentage of vote
Alliance	52	51	818,013	79.6
Party Negara	33	–	78,909	7.6
PMIP	11	1	40,667	3.9
NAP	9	–	20,996	2
Perak Malay League	3	–	5,433	0.5
Perak Progressive Party	2	–	1,081	0.1
Labour Party	4	–	4,786	0.4
Independents	18	–	31,642	3

to the Alliance to address this through the political exercise of fielding seventeen non-Malay candidates, in striking contrast to the Party Negara which fielded only one. The Alliance political machinery – masterminded by H. S. Lee – was formidable, although Lee himself did not trust to it and, in an embarrassing incident, withdrew from the polls to seek a place in the Legislative Council by nomination. The Alliance victory was interpreted as an unquestionable mandate. Dato Onn was defeated in his home town of Johore Bahru; Bukit Gantang's NAP wiped out in Perak; Nik Kamil's local notables defeated in Kelantan. The solitary member of the elected opposition was a PMIP man from Krian, Zabidi bin Haji Ali, who as we have seen played a role in the Kepala Batas Farmers' Congress of 1953. However, it must be remembered that many opponents of the Alliance still held nominated seats at both a Federal and a State level. And although on the surface voting patterns seemed to promise a non-communal future, as we saw earlier there were serious undercurrents of opposition within the politics of the majority body of Malay voters. By 1959 they were to take centre-stage. In 1955 voters were casting their votes for independence.

After the elections in 1955, the British government's capitulation to the Alliance was almost complete. The formation of an Alliance ministry, with Tunku Abdul Rahman as Chief Minister, accelerated the transfer of power. Ten Alliance ministers assumed office and plans were laid for further constitutional talks. MacGillivray conceded that if these were not forthcoming the Alliance would try and prove the existing arrangements unworkable. At this point a series of new issues imposed themselves on the discussions.[161] Paramount amongst these was the Alliance's reiteration of its demand for an independent constitutional commission and for full independence, including control of internal security, within one year, that is by August 1957. A further development was the offer from the MCP for peace talks, which were both a test of the reliability of the Alliance leadership and questioned the

---

[161] MacGillivray to Lennox-Boyd, 30. 7. 1955, Stockwell, *Malaya*, III, p. 142.

degree of authority they were to be conceded in internal security. An amnesty was declared in September 1955. It bore little fruit: a month later only twenty Communists had surrendered. After clandestine approaches from the MCP high command, plans were mooted for a rendezvous between Communist and elected political leaders at Baling in Kedah. The British saw it as a continuation of the MCP's attempts to return to methods of subversion and infiltration of nationalist movements. The MCP expected concessions, and Tunku Abdul Rahman was expected to make them. Everything, Commissioner-General Sir Robert Scott told the Prime Minister, turned on the strength of the Communists and the degree to which Tunku Abdul Rahman could be trusted. Although he agreed not to make personal commitments it was feared that he would go further than the British would be willing to permit on the questions of present and future detentions, deportations and political activities. This would be 'the beginning of another crisis graver than any hitherto'.[162] The makers of high policy were thinking the unthinkable. The meeting could be called off by the British government insisting on unacceptable preconditions and observers. The political consequences of such a move might also force Tunku Abdul Rahman's resignation. Control might be regained but at too high a cost. A document drawn up by the High Commissioner's security officials listed the 'possible consequences of a break' with the Alliance, which revealed that they were looking at the end of responsible elected government, mass demonstrations, the end of Malay support for the prosecution of the Emergency, and maybe MCP recruitment among Malays.[163] UMNO's contingency plans included the resignation of its members and the activation of a new underground movement.[164] The Minister viewed this 'with the greatest apprehension'.[165] The danger was that the more the British betrayed their anxiety to the nationalist politicians the stronger the constitutional demands they would be presented with.[166] Behind the scenes a working committee of principal staff tutored Tunku Abdul Rahman for the meeting. The base position was the retention of existing powers of arrest, detention and control; no recognition of the MCP without detentions, and deportation of the hard core.[167] Yet all the British could do was persuade and cajole. Roles, it seemed, had been reversed. At Baling on 28 and 29 December 1955 Chin Peng, Chen Tien and Rashid Maidin emerged from the jungle and were escorted by their former Force 136 comrade, John Davis, to a meeting with Tunku Abdul Rahman, the Chief Minister of Singapore David Marshall, and an ailing Tan Cheng Lock. A dramatic series of meetings began at which it became clear the MCP wished to return to the *status quo ante bellum*. A key issue at the talks was the extent of independence the British were prepared to grant to the Alliance.[168] As the talks progressed Tunku Abdul Rahman kept to his brief and refused to

[162] Sir Robert Scott to Eden, 23.10.1955, CO1030/27.
[163] Martin to Scott, 7.12.1955, *ibid.*   [164] PIR, December, 1955, CO1030/245.
[165] Lennox-Boyd to Sir Robert Black, 27.10.1955, CO1030/27.
[166] Black to Secretary to Lennox-Boyd, 27.10.1955, *ibid.*
[167] A. M. MacKintosh to Secretary Chiefs of Staff Committee, n.d. , *ibid.*
[168] See the records on CO1030/129, 130 and 131.

compromise on the question of detentions for MCP guerrillas. The talks broke down and Chin Peng and Rashid Maidin would not meet Malayan government representatives again until 1989.

The repercussions of this were twofold. First, the Baling incident greatly strengthened the Alliance's hand in constitutional negotiations. It provoked a statement from the British government, in advance of the talks, that the ending of the Emergency would no longer be a precondition for independence – a major policy concession. It also greatly eased Tunku Abdul Rahman into the role of statesman.[169] Baling also intensified the issue of defence. Prior to Baling, the Colonial Office could argue that independence and 'Protection' were not necessarily incompatible.[170] However, at Baling, Tunku Abdul Rahman was deeply struck by Chin Peng's suggestion that the MCP would abandon its armed struggle once internal security was in Malayan hands, and thereafter was deeply exercised by the forms surrounding agreements on defence, the final instrument of sovereignty, as it was discussed over the following months. The Chief Minister exuded the impression that full control would be handed over and that there had been agreement of this in principle before Baling, but Abdul Razak and Dr Ismail saw control as pertaining to the police only, and appreciated the command problems of local forces.[171] The local media celebrated the martial prowess of the Malays and the spirit of *Hang Tuah*. Yet, as Tunku Abdul Rahman admitted in 1957: 'We have at our command an army of less than one division in strength; we have no airforce, not even a single plane or a single man; we have no navy, not even a single sailor and we have not even a sea-going craft.'[172] British Air Marshall Fressayer said Malaya would need eleven squadrons before it could become independent. Yet it had only one Pioneer whose function – the British Secretary of Defence joked – was to carry the Tunku to the races.[173]

Alliance ministers, under pressure to deliver the economic rewards of independence, were anxious to avoid the military expenses independence necessitated. Discussions on defence began in parallel with the constitutional talks, but their conclusions were published only after *Merdeka*, in September 1957. In the interim there were still 25,000 Commonwealth combat troops in Malaya. The Anglo-Malayan Defence Agreement was ratified in October 1957. An Emergency Operations Council was created under the local minister in which the British commanding officer exercised substantial powers. Political change disguised great operational continuities. However, there were serious command problems and an inherent difficulty in separating the spheres of internal and external security. This led to involved negotiations over extra-territorial privileges in areas such as the vast new British base

---

[169] Discussed in Stockwell, *Malaya*, I, p. lccvi.
[170] A draft cabinet memorandum of July 1955, *ibid.*, III, p. 133.
[171] MacGillivray to Lennox-Boyd, 9. 1. 1956, CO1030/245.
[172] J. Saravanamuttu, *The dilemma of independence: two decades of Malaysia's foreign policy, 1957–77* (Penang, 1983), p. 24.
[173] Sir Robert Thompson, *Make for the hills: memories of far Eastern wars* (London, 1989), p. 105.

at Terendak, and the use of forces based there outside of Malaya, which resulted in a mixture of concurrent and exclusive jurisdiction and dual-key arrangements. These were deeply unpopular with Malay opinion, and the Defence Agreement was only ratified after Tunku Abdul Rahman turned the issue into one of confidence in his government.[174] There remained deep unease that the spirit of sovereignty had been compromised by the continued dependence of Malaya on foreign 'Protection'.

These debates underlined how much was at stake for the Alliance ministers. Facing rising expectations from within Malaya for results, and mounting opposition as many of the hasty communal accommodations began to unravel, there was little doubt that they would resort to drastic measures if their progress was blocked by the British government in London.[175] As the negotiations approached, the British became increasingly committed, for these reasons, to ensuring their success, even at the cost of concessions on self-government, in order to 'secure satisfactory agreements on defence and the other issues of particular concern to us'.[176] At the London talks of 18 January to 6 February 1956, the British government acceded to the Alliance demand for a constitutional commission, and settled many of the preconditions for independence, such as the withdrawal of the British Advisers. Athough the British continued to argue that it was an unrealistic timetable, the talks also set a date for *Merdeka*'s realisation: 31 August 1957, 'if possible'. However, once that date was announced, an unstoppable momentum built up towards it.[177] There would be subsequent talks in London, in December 1956 and January 1957, to discuss financial matters and finalise defence issues, and on 13 to 21 May to finalise the constitution. However, it was the return of Tunku Abdul Rahman to a hero's welcome in Malacca and his announcement of the date for the transfer of power that symbolised the beginning of the end of the British Empire in Malaya.

The soul of independence

Most accounts of the period emphasise that it was the Alliance's ability to demonstrate effective leadership and its hold on the bottom rungs of administration that had made this possible. It had recognised the working realities of a political structure of communal aggregations. It is not that politicians aggravated the communal problem to win support. This is symptomatic of a communal system in disarray. It is rather the reverse: the authority of the Alliance rested on its ability to secure communal

---

[174] David Hawkins, *The defence of Malaysia and Singapore: from AMDA to ANZUK* (London, 1972), pp. 13–15; Chin Kin Wah, *The defence of Malaya and Singapore: the transformation of a security system, 1957–71* (Singapore, 1983), pp. 23–36.

[175] D. C. Watherston, 'The London talks: Alliance demands and the extent to which they might be met', Nov. 1955, Stockwell, *Malaya*, III, pp. 197–9.

[176] R. Lennox-Boyd, 'Conference on constitutional advance in the Federation of Malaya, 7. 1. 1956, *ibid.*, III, pp. 135–6.

[177] See the Cabinet paper 'Notes on the main conclusions and recommendations of the conference', 21. 2. 1956, *ibid.*, III, pp. 261–5.

compromise and deliver rapid benefits. This is more symptomatic of a communal system coming into being. It was only when these rewards were not readily forthcoming that communal dissension arose to threaten the Alliance. For the time being it was cultivating political support on credit. This is the paternalism, the 'new feudalism', of the end of empire. Both the character of the politics of decolonisation, and the Malayanisation of the bureaucracy, consolidated an integrated urban leadership, which appropriated the structures of the late colonial state and looked to wield them to deliver *Merdeka*'s promise. The ways in which the colonial and the nationalist elites engaged would shape the methods in which policies were to be formulated and executed in the future. New blood was transfused into old arteries of power as the Alliance took on the task of national integration through the forging of a common identity through culture, education and language. Yet, the same processes of change which had suggested these solutions were opening new divisions, generating movements to assert other identities, alternative visions of the nation. Cultural struggle re-entered the political domain and underwrote the endgames of empire.

Malaya was a state before it was a nation, and there remained fundamental contradictions between the formation of a new nation-state and the cultural basis on which it was to evolve. As we have seen, the contradiction had been clearly articulated by Dr Burhanuddin. 'The conflict between *Melayu* and Malaya will not end', he had written. ' "Malayan" follows the colonial mould, it belittles and destroys the Malay nation or Malay nationalism that demands the return of its rights, that is wider than the "Malayan" demand.' In other words, the idea of popular sovereignty of the independent nation-state was not reconcilable with the 'original sovereignty' of the Malays. In the colonial mould of thought, the Malays were merely one ethnic group, subject to the equal laws of the modern nation-state. The *Melayu* as a cultural nation had been diminished in status. In this sense the Malay nation had yet to be properly realised. Yet, viewed from another perspective, the Malay ideologues of this cultural nation had yet to reconcile its imaginative history to the new historical realities of pluralism that colonial rule had created.[178] This was an item of the outstanding business of the Malayan Spring. These dilemmas were not so starkly enunciated between 1954 and 1957 in the scramble for unity in the interest of a rapid transfer of power. Studies of the political thought of Tunku Abdul Rahman and other Alliance leaders have emphasised their pragmatism. UMNO's leaders, it has been argued, were 'political realists', committed to the 'gradual transformation . . . of the Malay world outlook'.[179] Yet there is evidence to suggest that Tunku Abdul Rahman remained very sensible to the idea of the Malay *bangsa* as a political and cultural entity, and wary of the full implications of the colonial pursuit of the 'Malayan'

[178] Muhammad Ikmal Said, 'Ethnic perspectives on the left in Malaysia', in J. Kahn and F. Loh Kok Wah (eds.), *Fragmented vision: culture and politics in contemporary Malaysia* (Sydney, 1992), pp. 254–81.
[179] Salleh Daud, *UMNO: image and reality* (Kuala Lumpur, 1966), pp. 4–5.

nation. In his famous speech in Malacca on 20 February 1956, when he announced the date of *Merdeka*, he set its realisation within a long historical context:

> Although the course of history changed our fate from an independent and superior race to that of a disgraced and colonial one but we were able to maintain God's gifts in the form of patience of the soul, a feeling of honour, justice and an unbroken spirit while we were colonised for more than four hundred years.[180]

By *Merdeka* the Malay community had been elevated into a nation, and it seems that to Tunku Abdul Rahman the nation was a political and cultural entity based on the concept of original sovereignty. Non-Malays could be admitted to the nation, but Tunku Abdul Rahman did not concede that nationality should be the basis of citizenship. Citizenship had a different foundation: it was merely a legal guarantee of specified privileges. This distinction was played down in the interests of unity, and in so far as the term 'nationality' was used it was used in its restricted legal sense, almost synonymously with citizenship – but the Tunku would not allow the term *bangsa* to be used for it. In 1951 Tunku Abdul Rahman had asked rhetorically who the 'Malayans' were: his answer was that there could be a Malayan nation, but the Malay *bangsa* would exist as a distinct core within it.[181]

The drawing of an Alliance manifesto was merely a prologue to a much deeper debate on the principles of nationhood. Following the announcement of the independent constitutional commission, debates reached a crescendo on language, citizenship and Malay special rights; on the reservation of civil service positions, scholarships and business licences. From April to September 1956, the Alliance leaders went into conclave to renegotiate their compact, and to prepare a memorandum for the Reid Commission.[182] It was a delicate process and at one stage it looked like UMNO and the MCA would perhaps have to submit separate memoranda. Direct attacks were made on the MCA by its most powerful supporters. These had been brewing for some time. The politics of Chinese culture in Perak and Selangor increasingly by-passed the MCA party headquarters. Already in 1955, internal disputes within the MCA had broken into the open. They stemmed from the rivalry in Selangor between Ong Loke Lin and H. S. Lee. Lee was seen as dictatorial, and his criticisms of the KMT had lost him the support of its networks. His rival was young, ambitious and frustrated by being denied high party office, due to Lee's patronage of his colleague S. M. Yong. Added to this were the rise of new men such as Lim Chong Eu and Yong Pung How, son of Yong Shook Lin, who had been brought into the MCA to strengthen the grass-roots which was calling for a more robust defence of Chinese interests. In 1956, opposition to the Alliance compromise was led by a 'Big Four' of Chinese association leaders: the *shetuan* leaders Leong Chee Cheong of the Federation of Selangor Chinese Guilds and Associations, Lau Pak Khuan of Perak and Cho Yew Fai of the Selangor Chinese Assembly Hall, and Lim Gian Geok of the United Chinese

---

[180] Cited in Samad Idris, *25 tahun UMNO*, p. 238.
[181] Funston, *Malay politics*, pp. 137–9.
[182] The fullest discussion of these debates is Heng, *Chinese politics*, pp. 225–30.

Schoolteachers' Association. The combined associations broadened their demands to encompass *jus soli*, equal rights, a five-year residence period and no language test as qualifications for citizenship, and Chinese as an official language. They suggested that the position of the MCA in the Alliance had weakened its advocacy of Chinese rights and discredited its cry of 'One race, one voice and one leadership'. The combined associations, led by Lau Pak Khuan, discussed the formation of a rival to the MCA.[183] Direct appeals were made to London, which received a sympathetic hearing from the Colonial Secretary, but no British intervention on behalf of Chinese interests. The MCA leadership responded by accusing the combined associations of being a KMT threat to the integrity of Malaya, and the vehemence with which Malay politicians questioned the loyalty of the Chinese to Malaya led the Associated Chinese Chambers of Commerce to pull back from the education and citizenship campaign.[184] However, the campaign orchestrated by the 'Big Four' represented far more than the convulsions of KMT die-hards. The Chinese schoolteachers saw citizenship and education as intertwined on the language issue. Their nationalism was not a *huaqiao* nationalism. By the 1950s a deep-rooted change had occurred in their perceptions of the Chinese position in Malaya. Their political rhetoric accepted Malaya as their permanent home and related specifically to the Malayan context. Yet it did not accept that this diluted the rights of the Chinese as a discrete cultural community with the nation. The Malayan Chinese had a right to contribute to and enrich the nation.[185]

The 'Alliance memorandum' that took shape argued strongly for special rights for the Malays – the extension of land reservations and quotas in employment and ownership and the reservation of key public positions. The core position of the Malays was recognised as the 'original sons of the soil'. With the lifting of the colonial mandate of protection, sovereignty would revert to the Malays, and the Alliance acknowledged a special role for the Malay Rulers. Significantly no time limit was placed on the entrenchment of these special rights. Where UMNO and MCA leaders agreed to differ was on the question of the status of minority tongues after independence. The principle of *jus soli* after *Merdeka* day was accepted, but it was not to be retroactive. UMNO branches were instructed to let the matter rest and trust the national leadership. There was no Malay outcry over this issue. But in order not to lose ground to radical opinion, UMNO insisted that the language provisions be tightened. To deflect attention from the citizenship issue, much play was made on Malay special rights – itself a source of tension within the Alliance.[186] In the event, the Reid recommendations differed materially from the Alliance proposal in these key areas. A limit of fifteen years was placed on Malay special rights; Chinese, Tamil and English were to be allowed to function as official languages for ten years; there was no

---

[183] MacGillivray to Lennox-Boyd, 10.10.1955; PIR, October 1955; April 1956, CO1030/245; Lee Kam Hing, 'MCA dalam peralihan, 1956–59', in Persatuan Sejarah Malaysia, *Malaysia: sejarah dan proses pembangunan* (Kuala Lumpur, 1979), pp. 268–83.

[184] Wong Yoke Nyen, 'Chinese organisations and citizenship in post-war Malaya, 1945–1958', *Review of Southeast Asian Studies*, 12 (1982), 13–39.

[185] Tan, *Rhetoric*, pp. 33–41.   [186] PIR, June 1956; August 1956, CO1030/245.

special provision for Islam; the Rulers were reduced to a ceremonial role; and the creation of new Malay Reservations was restricted. After the publication of the Reid Committee proposals in February 1957, the Alliance leaders once again retired to smoke-filled committee rooms, when a Constitutional Working Party began to formulate what was essentially a political response to the views of the jurists. Unsurprisingly it followed the views of the Alliance. From the outset Tunku Abdul Rahman 'argued strongly' for Islam as the official religion, and the question of special rights dominated the discussions of the Working Party.[187] Most significantly it prescribed no time limit to the provision for Malay special rights, although it seems that an informal undertaking was made by Tunku Abdul Rahman to review them after a period. Safeguards were instituted for non-Malays and *jus soli* was accepted, as was dual nationality for Commonwealth citizens, a vital demand of the *Peranakan* Chinese of the Straits Settlements, the status of whom remained a final condition of the transfer of power on which the British government, who had direct responsibility for them, was reluctant to compromise.[188] However, the permanence of Malay special rights was a sizeable change from the principles of the Reid Report, and gave added fuel to the opposition outside the negotiations. For the MCA, however, the issue was a trial of its strength upon which its position in the Alliance would depend. Afraid of losing support to the associations it steeped up its campaign to promote citizenship, and affirmed its support for *jus soli* and the relaxation of the citizenship qualifications. It gained concessions from UMNO, but at the expense of Chinese as an official language.[189] The politics of opposition were organising around the defence of core, inalienable principles. However, the demands of government could not allow these principles to jeopardise the delicate unity that had been achieved.

In 1956, the key constitutional debates – on language, citizenship and Malay special rights – threatened to pull the Alliance apart. All the main parties to that Alliance were under pressure from below. The Malaysian Indian Congress was subject to Tamil claims that Hinduism and Tamilian culture had been 'the torchbearer of civilization', and that they had a special claim on the national culture.[190] When it began to support the Alliance it lost grass-roots support to the Labour Party and the People's Progressive Party in Perak.[191] Secular UMNO nationalism was confronted by the Parti Islam's demands for a single *Melayu* nationality, of which Islam would be the central component. UMNO's policy of compromise was undermined by grass-roots fears – such as that expressed by Malay teachers that education and culture were 'the only political foundation left for the Malay race. If this is gone the Malay race

---

[187] MacGillivray to Lennox-Boyd, 25. 2. 1957; 25. 3. 1957, CO1030/524.

[188] Lennox-Boyd to MacGillivray, 8. 3. 1947, *ibid.*

[189] J. Norman Parmer, 'Constitutional change in Malaya's plural society', *Far Eastern Survey*, 26, 10 (1957), 145–52.

[190] 'Memorandum submitted to the Reid Constitutional Committee by All Malaya Tamils Conference', CO889/6.

[191] Ampalavanar, *Indian minority*, pp. 172–3.

will become extinct.'[192] The Party Negara's demands for the primacy of the Malay language were designed to bring into the open Alliance differences on the subject.[193] However, the key point is that the rise of linguistic nationalism was not so much a consequence of communal politics – of Malay nationalism competing with Chinese or Tamil particularism – rather, it was bolstered by the fissures that were opening up within the Malay body politic itself. The Federation of Malay Teachers' Association was to play an active role in opposition to any attempt to water down the position of the Malay language in the life of the new nation. As with the MCA, when such emotive issues were at stake, UMNO could not take for granted the acquiesence of core groups of its supporters. A Second Malay National Congress was called in April 1957 by Dato Onn, Dr Burhanuddin and others that attempted to rekindle the fire of the First Malay Congress in 1946 and draw together Malay opposition to UMNO.[194] Tunku Abdul Rahman attempted to diffuse the *jus soli* crisis by forbidding UMNO branches to discuss it publicly. It was reported in July 1956 that in addition to the militant underground within UMNO Youth, the MCA too was building up strong-arm support by looking to secret societies as an insurance against political failure. It was suggested that forces existed that could be activated if the negotiations with the colonial government, or between the ethnic parties on *jus soli*, broke down.[195] By late 1956 opposition to Tunku Abdul Rahman was reported 'at all levels' of UMNO. He was charged with being too dictatorial, too ready to make concessions to non-Malay interests and to the British. A symptom of this was the resignation of information chief Syed Jaafar Albar, and there were other critics in UMNO headquarters such as Abdul Rahman bin Haji Taib and Senu Abdul Rahman. The British concluded that Tunku Abdul Rahman was trying to hasten independence by proving the communities were united, even drawing the MIC into the Alliance against his own inclinations, to satisfy them. They had a shared interest and resolve to secure independence whilst he himself was at the helm. Tunku Abdul Rahman was 'bidding against the Malay extremists for his community's support'.[196] In these circumstances, *Merdeka* came first and other considerations second.

The mounting intensity of Malaya's politics had, by 1954, given added urgency to the demand for independence. The Alliance had emerged as its definitive voice. In the ensuing years the British colluded in this mood of urgency. The risks in moving too fast were as nothing to those of moving too slowly. There came a point, at Baling in December 1955, when, in their eyes Tunku Abdul Rahman had achieved a critical mass of credibility, and became seen as the pivotal statesman of the transfer of power. Dato Onn was forgotten. The last months of empire were a period when the worlds of

---

[192] Basir bin Udon, 'Federation of Malaya Teachers' Association, Malay Peninsula', 25. 7. 1956, CO889/6.
[193] PIR, March 1955, CO1030/245.
[194] Ramlah Adam, 'Kongres Kebangsaan Melayu: suata penentangan kepada kehilangaan kuasa politik Melayu di dalam kemerdekaan 1957', *Sarjana* (1994), 159–81.
[195] PIR, July 1956, CO1030/245.
[196] MacGillivray to Lennox-Boyd, 25. 3. 1957, CO1030/524.

the imperial servant and the anti-colonial nationalist inter-penetrated as the latter acquired power within the colonial state. The growth of the state has been a major theme of this book, and as it grew it became more secretive. There is a sense in which the public rituals of the *durbars* of indirect rule were replaced by a confidential world which the colonial rulers and their successors shared. Those outside this world resented the secrecy in which the crucial negotiations on independence were conducted. They formed the impression that public opinion was merely invoked and manipulated to strengthen the bargaining power of those involved in the horse-trading of the transfer of power. The statesmen would reply that this was necessary to allow emotive issues to be aired without unnecessarily inflaming public sensitivities. The secular bureaucratic perspective of colonial government came to be shared by the Alliance high command. Its leaders inherited the notion, a notion reinforced by the spirit of politics which had brought them to power, that they were holding the ring between the various centrifugal forces that, unbridled, could tear Malaya asunder. Their goal had been to lead a movement of controlled anti-colonial protest. Once a taste of power had been acquired, Alliance leaders moved swiftly to contain popular politics. Elite bargaining became an embedded feature of the conduct of politics in Malaya. However, it could also breed mistrust, and public opinion refused to give the new men of public business a free hand.

Although it seemed that the ship of state had, by the final agreement on a constitution, sailed into more tranquil waters, there were matters outstanding that marked indelibly the politics of independent Malaya. Malayanisation created its own problems. On taking office after the 1955 election, an Alliance minister was refused entry to his ministry by the Asian doorkeeper. A new culture of administration emerged, new pressures intruded into the decision-making process.[197] A scramble for high office was underway. The tensions that this would foster in the future were already evident after 1955, and this was a source of great disillusionment to colonial officials. In retrospect, it is extraordinary that this should have surprised them. The specific instances of this that emerge in the colonial records illustrate the underlying tensions within the political structure of independent Malaya. A series of such dilemmas – including controversies over the appointment and method of appointment of offices such as the Paramount Ruler, the *Yang di-Pertuan Agong*, and the Governors of the former Straits Settlements – created pressures for the hand of the federal executive to be strengthened.[198] This became an overriding theme of the transfer of power.

A final unresolved issue was the future of the authoritarian powers that had emerged during the Emergency. 'Political developments,' a British intelligence officer remarked in mid-1956, 'have outstripped the Emergency and the politically-minded are not interested in it.' There was a danger that Communism might be forgotten. 'This danger Tunku Abdul Rahman undoubtedly appreciates, but all his followers do

---

[197] Heussler, *British rule*, pp. 198–205.
[198] See MacGillivray to Johnson, secret and personal, 1. 3. 1957, CO1030/524.

not.'[199] Yet the Emergency had a profound impact on the *Merdeka* constitution. The debates on the proposed constitution, as Malaysian legal scholars have recognised, revealed a restrictive conception of judicial review, and said much about the new government's understandings of constitutionalism. The Working Party in fact overturned many of the provisions in the original Reid constitutional proposals for access to the courts for redress of infringement of civil liberties – provisions on which the Commission itself had not been unanimous – and placed the freedom of movement, speech, association and assembly within the complete discretion of Parliament. This move occasioned a lively debate at the time. Tunku Abdul Rahman denied that there was any 'sinister purpose' behind it, but argued that judicial review would 'unduly fetter' the government in taking actions it might deem necessary. Not merely the Emergency but a much deeper commitment to strong government was at the forefront of the Working Party's amendments. Tunku Abdul Rahman was resolute in his attachment to the unwritten British constitution and confident in his government's good intentions. In preparation for the 'stormy and tempestuous days' ahead the courts were to be kept outside of politics. Yet critics in the Legislative Council argued that 'the fundamental rights of the individual would be better safeguarded by the judiciary than by a political party in power'.[200] Just prior to the Baling talks, Sir Robert Scott wrote a bleak report on the state of the new nation for the Prime Minister.

> Tunku Abdul Rahman has an overwhelming Parliamentary majority, the local forces and police are largely Malay, and for his own ends he will keep legal powers to detain without trial. He is therefore supremely confident of his ability to absorb the Chinese terrorists into the community and to deal with any who give trouble (an assessment which incidentally betrays his lack of experience and which, in my view, is highly questionable) . . . Both Rahman and [Singapore Chief Minister David] Marshall are genuinely anti-Communist, but the former is more afraid of the Chinese swamping the Malays than of the Communists dominating both. He gives the impression of aiming at old-fashioned Muslim dictatorship, with some democratic trappings, ready if need be to deal ruthlessly with Chinese who give trouble.[201]

The British were to discover, as Edward Gibbon had observed, that the end of empire is a melancholy business. The atmosphere of gloom, of course, was not shared by the people of Malaya. *Merdeka* on 31 August 1957 was witnessed by 20,000 people in the new Merdeka stadium in Kuala Lumpur and celebrated by a crowd of 100,000 on the *padang* in front of the old Selangor clubhouse. The new Prime Minister and his Cabinet paraded in their new ministerial uniforms and received from the representative of Queen Elizabeth II, the Duke of Gloucester, the Constitutional Instrument of

---

[199] PIR, July, 1956, August 1956, CO1030/245.

[200] Lim Hong Hai, 'The eve-of-independence constitutional debate on fundamental liberties and judicial review: a window on elite views and constitutional government in Malaysia?', *Kajian Malaysia*, 7, 1 & 2 (1989), 1–37. For Lord Reid's own misgivings see his letter to Lennox-Boyd, 8. 7. 1957, CO1030/486.

[201] Sir Robert Scott to Eden, 23.10.1955, CO1030/245.

the Transfer of Power. More pageantry followed a few days later with the installation of the first *Yang Di-Pertuan Agong* of the Federation of Malaya.[202] It was a medieval sacerdotal ceremony in a month-old throne room; an invention of tradition that projected a pre-colonial sovereignty for the new nation-state.

[202] William Fish, 'The Merdeka pageant', *Straits Times Annual* (1958), 16–21.

CHAPTER NINE

The colonial inheritance

At the height of the political crisis in the middle of 1951 Dato Onn took the High Commissioner, Sir Henry Gurney, into his confidence. 'Independence was not the object,' he told him. 'The object was the good of the people to which independence was only a means.'[1] This was all very true. The struggle for *Merdeka* had left much undone. Those who had led it had quite deliberately left many questions unanswered, and the unfinished business of decolonisation would dominate Malaysian politics in the following decades. It is beyond the ambition of this book to do justice to the post-colonial experience of Malaya. We can do no more than briefly identify some of the forces of change that had their roots in the late colonial period. This final chapter, or afterword, examines *Merdeka* in Malaysian history, rather than the history of Malaysia after *Merdeka*. A first theme is the nature of the colonial inheritance itself and this provokes an outline of the ways in which the British presence in Malaya was felt after independence. A second theme addresses the strategies by which the new state sought to carve out an independent course for itself, in particular the introduction of ambitious programmes to reconfigure Malaya's economy and society. A third theme is the continued attempts to define and inculcate a sense of national identity that development has necessitated: we examine how Malaya has faced the political tensions to which state-building has given rise. This leads us to a final concern which returns to a key theme of the end of empire, the nature of freedom itself. A core political dynamic of contemporary Malaysia, unleashed in the late colonial period, has been how its people have reconciled the pressing demands of state with pressures for its accountability. Yet before we turn to what was left undone at independence, let us recapitulate what has been argued in the preceding chapters.

---

[1] In private conversation with Gurney, reported to Higham, 13.6.1951, CO537/7303.

The end of empire and the making of Malaya

The colonial inheritance emerged out of an experience of disorder that recast the relationship between state and society in Malaya in the 1940s and 1950s. The foundations of the late colonial state were laid during the period of subsistence crisis and political violence that followed the Japanese occupation of Malaya. However, the texture of colonial rule was already changing during the inter-war depression, and many strategies of post-war colonialism were anticipated by the policies of the Japanese. The 'second colonial occupation' of British Malaya that occurred in the aftermath of the war saw the creation of a viable nation-state as the culmination of the imperial mission. The Fabianism of British officials was tempered by the need to secure the vital interests of the United Kingdom in a rapidly changing world. Political advancement was to be slow and rigorously controlled. British strategy focused on creating a multi-racial 'Malayan' national identity: its flagship was the Malayan Union, that aimed to replace the unwieldy structures of indirect rule with a unitary state and a single citizenship. However, the post-war experiment went deeper than this. One of the most important keywords of late colonialism was community development. The British sought to break down the divisions of a plural society, and create an integrated economic and political entity, bound together by a shared allegiance, a common culture and the obligations of active citizenship.

Post-war British policy rested on the collaboration of energetic local leaderships that would take the initiative in social reconstruction. When the British returned to Malaya they seemed to promise a Malayan Spring, through the relaxation of pre-war constraints on freedom of association, assembly and expression. They widened the public sphere in order to encourage individuals to engage in new kinds of public service. Much was expected of these intermediaries. The two facets of the post-war crisis described in chapters 2 and 3 illustrate the demands made on them. First, relief work and social welfare became an arena for political struggle. The political organisations, societies for youth, women's movements, trade unions who came forward to collaborate with the British government found that they had to conform to a series of social norms which would govern their activity. However, many of these associations politicised social life to a degree and in a temper which the British government was not prepared to permit. A distinction emerged between legitimate and illegitimate forms of mass mobilisation that dominated colonial politics, and those groups who refused to conform to colonial paradigms of political development were subject to new regulatory controls. However, in the interim, a debate on the meaning of freedom began. It was led by a leftist united front that had emerged out of wartime resistance to the Japanese, and which asserted the voice of popular will against colonial law. Notions of democracy and accountability were also voiced within the Malay community as it opposed the Malayan Union and asserted the sovereignty of the *rakyat* over that of the Rulers. A second facet of the post-war crisis was the restoration of control in the countryside. This tested the extent to which the elite groups most prepared to accept the colonial challenge could function as agents of social control.

The ties of the Chinese business and service elites of the towns to the labourers and agriculturalists of the hinterland were broken in the war. As they attempted to reassert their influence, the Malayan Communist Party and its allies were extending their authority in these areas by exploiting the natural links between the industrial economy and squatter cultivation. This, as explained in chapter 3, transformed endemic unrest into rebellion against the colonial government. The cadres of UMNO Malay nationalism met with a severe challenge from radicalised leftist, religious and cult leadership. UMNO managed to retain control of the kampongs, not so much by its own strength, as by its ability to take advantage of the colonial government's suppression of radical alternatives. However, the new ideological predicaments that had emerged in these years continued to trouble the Malay body politic.

The response of local communities to social crisis challenged British assumptions as to the proper pace and content of political development for Malaya. The outbreak of the Emergency in 1948 led colonial authority to be buttressed. For many Malayans the most obvious and immediate legacy of the late colonial period was the growth of the state and its agents. Decolonisation created the modern state. The Emergency made it bigger, more centralised and powerful than it would otherwise have been. In 1948 it had employed 48,000 people in 1959, 140,000.[2] Old functions were expanded and new ones appended. The power of the administration was no longer exercised personally through a District Officer but through a host of other agencies. For the rural Chinese this paradoxically brought them closer to the state than their counterparts in the towns. For the Malay cultivator the growth of the state was witnessed in the expansion of scientific and technical departments, and the growing complexity of land administration, lands-in-aid and co-operation through which the state attempted to drive through schemes for rural improvement. It precipitated a revolution in the social life of the Orang Asli, and dragged them into the mainstream of political development on the peninsula. Yet the Emergency meant more than the creation of new structures of authority.

An overarching theme of the British government's response to these pressures was the creation of community. This took three main forms. First, control of the periphery was to be won by the re-establishment of strong Chinese leadership, for which a captive following was created in fortified settlements, which were then prey to a wide range of social experimentation. The objective was to draw the Chinese into the mainstream of Malayan life, to give them a stake in the land, a role in local democracy and even to protect them against the temptations of Communism and ethnic particularism through the spread of Christianity. However, secure tenure did not recompense the squatters for the economic liberty they had lost with the closing of the forests to pioneer cultivation. Village councils enlisted little enthusiasm from their parishioners, and were most successful as a springboard to local influence for urban-based political interests. Even the limited successes of expatriate missionaries were

---

[2] Richard Stubbs, *Hearts and minds in guerrilla warfare: the Malayan Emergency, 1948–1960* (Singapore, 1989), pp. 262–3.

less significant than that of independent churches who saw Christianity as a vehicle for Chinese identity. Indeed, the wider problem for the Chinese of locating their identity within Malaya without compromising its cultural foundations was forcefully articulated by Chinese educationalists, and successfully exploited by the Communists as they attempted to reactivate their united front.

Secondly, in the Malay kampongs the colonial government's objective was the bolstering of the traditional practices of self-help as it understood them. Again, this policy aimed to inspire and invigorate Malay leadership. Malay leaders were chosen to preside over a series of developmental strategies designed at alleviating Malay poverty, mitigating against the unsettling impact of commercialisation in the peasant economy, and above all restoring lost initiative to the kampongs. However, the failure of these schemes, or rather their administrative character, instead encouraged Malay villagers, and Malay leadership competing for their support, to look to the state for assistance. The colonial development decade amalgamated with a long-term movement of economic uplift within the Malay body politic to give voice to a strident economic nationalism. A range of strategies were floated; the diagnosis of the Malay dilemma was deeply contested. However, within these debates the state, instead of being a solvent of communal antagonisms, had become an instrument for the corporate advancement of the Malays. The state most closely reflected the interests of the most economically advantaged Malays, the beneficiaries of growing economic differentiation in the countryside, who consolidated their grip on the politics and bureaucracy of the locality. The corporatist strategy had given birth to a new paternalism.

Thirdly, it is in the creation of community through cultural policy that we see both the strength and the diversity of the challenge to the colonial construction of nationhood. The late colonial state was a formidable propaganda machine. The use of new technologies to cajole the rural population into supporting the government against the Communists soon gave way to a larger scheme of indoctrination. This new cultural imperialism was directed at inculcating an Anglophone 'Malayan' consciousness in the minds of a rising generation of modernisers and nation-builders. Expatriate elites and their local allies led experiments in cultural fusion – through drama, publishing and very public forms of patronage. Yet already in the towns there had arisen a popular culture characterised not only by its diversity and vibrant decadence, but also by an openness to political action and to themes of ideological reconstruction. It was the Malay radicals of ASAS 50 and the wider movement to reinvent the Malay language as the singular idiom of national life which mounted the strongest challenge to colonial constructions of national culture. Language was indeed the soul of the nation. Yet, despite its failures, colonial policy did impart strategies through which Malay cultural activists and politicians would seek to enforce their own vision of the nation.

The idea that, in some direct way, the legacy of colonial rule to Malaya was the creation of a new communal ordering of society is misleading. The local leaderships through which late colonialism worked were themselves attempting to carry their divided constituents into the era of mass politics. In so doing they found community in a variety of movements of ethnic advancement. Yet below the leadership of the towns and dominant rural interests lay other forces that rose to challenge them. As independence approached the elites had to move increasingly to anticipate this challenge. This cemented the high political compromise which, although it recognised a measure of Chinese economic freedom and political status, entrenched Malay paramountcy as the ideological foundation of the post-colonial state. A communal pattern of politics followed from this. This kind of mobilisation was a means by which leadership sought to retain a purchase on its following, and was deepened – not just by the accelerated timetables of *Merdeka* – but by the vitality of the forces unleashed beneath them. At the time of independence the strength of the inter-communal alliance lay in its capacity to evince a measure of social control of these forces. Yet the underlying fluidity within peninsular society was a measure of the internal struggles within ethnic communities, in which other claims could be voiced: more direct appeals to communal sentiment; appeals to Islam as the foundation of social order; appeals to more pluralistic visions of the nation.

Social scientists have argued that the language of ethnicity and communalism is an arbitrary tool with which to anatomise a society; that these notions are artificial constructions that disguise more fundamental conflicts within a society, such as those created by the dynamics of class or prebendalism. Malaysian social reformers have also charged that social deprivation has been manipulated along ethnic lines by the political elite.[3] Such explanations have differed on the extent to which there is a reservoir of primordial sentiment to be so manipulated. Many analysts now insist that these loyalties are continually under construction, being redefined and contested.[4] Yet whilst the historian or social critic can expose how these categories have come to the fore, they must also acknowledge how they take on real import and meaning for communities as they confront powerful currents of social and economic change and the demands of the modern state – forces which promise to transform the manner in which they have lived their lives, the ways in which they have understood the status within society both of themselves and others, and which question old beliefs and challenged existing moralities. The 'imagined communities' of anti-colonial nationalism were not merely the fancies of elite politicians and opinion-makers; there were many moments when they had to confront other imaginings within society. Out of such struggles nations are born, and nations do not necessarily agree on the terms of nationhood. When Tunku Abdul Rahman, in his first speech as UMNO President, asked 'Who are the Malayans?', although his immediate target was the Anglophile notables, he voiced what was to be the central dilemma of political independence. Communalism was not the natural state of Malaysian society, but it is often the language through which its political predicaments are addressed. However, this

---

[3] Chandra Muzaffar, 'Breaking the ethnic trap', *Aliran*, 7, 6 (June/July, 1987), 2–3.
[4] For a discussion of this see Joel Kahn, 'Class, ethnicity and diversity: some remarks on Malay culture in Malaysia', in J. Kahn and F. Loh Kok Wah, *Fragmented vision: culture in contemporary Malaysia* (Sydney, 1992), pp. 158–78.

language was constantly changing as the people of Malaya addressed the dilemmas of social change, the questions of identity to which they gave a new urgency, and the predicaments forced upon them by the very requirements of creating a modern nation-state. It is in the contribution of colonial rule to these internal debates that its inheritance for modern Malaya must be assessed. The late colonial state wrestled with the same forces of social change; it had its own contested view of the nature of Malaya's pluralism; many of those who inherited power were trained within its institutions, and were exposed to, and indeed imbibed their governing assumptions. However, as they looked into the soul of independence they drew very different conclusions from the colonial experience. The rhetoric of communalism divided as much as it united the communities of Malaya.

'They do not understand'

The new political language was abhorrent to many Englishmen, but they were forced to submit to it. In the 1950s, their understanding of multi-racialism drifted from an organic fusion to a negotiated accommodation. Yet, once the logic of withdrawal was irresistible, what did decolonisation mean for the British? As the Union flag was lowered, what did Britain hope to salvage from its Southeast Asian experience? This book has been a study of decolonisation as seen from Malaya and not from London, as an experience that shaped local politics and society, yet it does illustrate some larger themes. Malaya represented the most major metropolitan commitment to empire in the mid-twentieth century, in terms of the people and resources absorbed by the Emergency. This was not just a British but a Commonwealth commitment. In the face of this tremendous investment, Britain, above all, looked to salvage its prestige. Late colonialism, I have argued, was a civilising mission. The dialectic of late colonialism was that the satisfactory conclusion of the business of empire demanded its transfer into trustworthy hands; the need to keep it in those hands made the transfer of power a much swifter process than it was intended to be. Once this dialectic was acknowledged and accepted as unstoppable all the British could do was make the government as pro-western, capitalist and clean as it could. And it is in geopolitics, the fortunes of British investment and the fate of the Westminster democratic tradition that Britain's unfinished business with Malaya lay.

The most important geopolitical legacy of colonial rule was the formation of Malaysia. This was one of the last grand designs of British imperial history. The story of Singapore's merger and separation, and the welding of Sarawak and Sabah to Malaysia lies beyond the scope of this work. Archives are now beginning to open which may have more to say about it. For the British, some level of territorial integration was implicit in the Malayan Union and associated policies of post-war reconstruction elsewhere in the region, most particularly perhaps in the office of the Commissioner-General in Southeast Asia that survived the Union débâcle. When Malaysia was mooted, it was adopted by Britain as a strategy to ease its problems of decolonisation elsewhere in the region and to contain the volatile politics of Singapore.

It provides further indication that the British could not legislate for the ambitions or dictate the momentum of local politics. In the case of Singapore's inclusion in Malaysia, by 1965 the high politics moved too fast for the low, and although the politics of the two states were to be transformed over the next thirty years, separation stands as a memorial of the political arithmetic of the era of decolonisation.[5] Thirty years after merger, the issue was still an emotive undercurrent to Singapore–Malaysian relations. Thirty years after merger, the East Malaysian experience was still somewhat exotic to and independent of what remained the peninsular mainstream. However, the Borneo territories' experience was a formidable accomplishment of political integration that flew in the face of geography and of the claims of other states to these wealthy territories. It too, in a very different way, was a reminder of how durable the legacy of late colonial state-building could prove.

Decolonisation was embarked upon, at least in part, to make the world a safer place for British business. Economic decolonisation was a much slower process than the transfer of political power. In 1958, 25 per cent of Malaya's imports were from the UK, in 1963, 21 per cent. In 1970, 65 per cent of all foreign capital in Malaysia was British. The Agency Houses, the 'commanding heights' of the British economic presence in the region, sustained themselves through diversification and mergers which enabled them to identify themselves with local interests. This process was underway in the 1950s as firms such as Guthrie launched cadet schemes to train local managers; companies were registered locally, and kept separate from the London subsidiaries. This process gained momentum in the climate of economic indiginism in the New Economic Policy years: reorganisation facilitated *bumiputera* ownership; retired politicians and civil servants found seats on the board. However, share ownership was diffused in the process. As with political decolonisation, the substance of power had eventually to be sacrificed in order to safeguard a dwindling stake in the region. Yet this process was not as symbiotic as it seems. By the early 1980s British business in Malaysia was confronted by official resentment at the laggardness of its response to the demands of economic restructuring, especially at their tendency to fall back on cosy accommodations with old compradores, and retired civil servants to meet the requirements for Malay participation rather than train new professionals. Frustration rose with the raising of fees for overseas students in Britain, which dealt a blow to Malaysia's assumption that it could look to the old imperial centre for the training of its people. With the acquisition of the Sime Darby in 1976 and a 1981 dawn raid on the London Stock Exchange to acquire Guthries, government agencies seized control of old British enterprises and Britain's non-recognition of Malaysia's sensitivities was punished by a 'Buy British last' policy. In a similar way, rather reckless newspaper criticism of the Malaysian elite in 1994 was punished by a refusal to grant contracts to British firms. The argument was that if Britain was no longer in a position to aid Malaysia, she could at least respect its needs

---

[5] Mohamed Sopiee, *From Malayan Union to Singapore separation: political unification in the Malaysia region, 1945–65* (Kuala Lumpur, 1974), pp. 125–229; Michael Leifer, 'Singapore in Malaysia: the politics of Federation', *JSEAH*, 6, 2 (1965), 54–70.

and achievements. In 1994, as in 1982, Malaysian leaders 'did not demand "expiation", only equality and understanding'.[6]

This demand came to dominate a third area of unfinished business: Britain's defence of the integrity of its political legacy for Malaya. The aim in this regard was the maintenance of the Commonwealth connection, which in this context meant more for the British than Malaya's adherence to a British-dominated framework of international relations, but symbolised the entire identity of the successor regime: it was a question of political culture, of the principles of democratic institutions and civic values. This was the last bastion of imperial idealism. However, both the outward trappings and the meaning of these institutions were to be challenged by subsequent generations of Malaysian politicians. Before 1957 Malaya's foreign policy was colonial policy. After 1957, projecting Malaya as an independent nation became a central task of government. However, under Tunku Abdul Rahman, Malaya maintained its strong anti-Communist stance, its alliance with the west and its advocacy of the security of the smaller nations. However, it did so through a Third World rhetoric. This policy guided the country through an era of uncertainty in the mid-1960s. The larger Malaysia was born under the shadow of external threat and this helped to cement national identity. However, Sukarno was not Indonesia and the attempts to build up a larger regional identity survived his fall, through Tun Abdul Razak's advocacy of a regional Zone of Peace, Freedom and Neutrality (ZOPFAN). Foreign policy became more internationalist and regional.[7] The Association of Southeast Asian Nations (ASEAN) was seen by the 1980s and 1990s as a springboard for Malaysia's growing international ambitions. By this period, too, ties with the old metropolis and the western powers were weakened as Malaysian leadership slipped for the first time into the hands of men who were not educated at the London Bar, who did not share warm memories of metropolitan life or close friendships with British politicians. Dr Mahathir was the first non-golfing Prime Minister.[8] The drive for sustained development led the Malaysian government into a more activist and high profile foreign policy. In the 1980s and 1990s, the foreign policy of Malaysia turned more to the Islamic world, to its membership of the Organisation of the Islamic Conference and its vocal support for Palestinian nationalism and the plight of the Bosnian Muslims.[9] The Commonwealth was turned to anti-colonial ends, as another voice of the South against the cultural and economic domination of the North, and even used to articulate a different road to and meaning for democratisation than that which the Commonwealth connection had been intended to represent. Above all Malaysia

---

[6] J. H. Drabble and P. J. Drake, 'The British Agency Houses in Malaysia: survival in a changing world', *JSEAS*, 12, 2 (1981), 297–328; Roger Kershaw, 'Anglo-Malaysian relations: old roles versus new rulers', *International Affairs*, 59, 4 (1983), 629–48.

[7] Johan Saravanamuttu, *The dilemma of independence: two decades of Malaysia's foreign policy, 1957–77* (Penang, 1983).

[8] Zainuddin Maidin, *The other side of Mahathir* (Kuala Lumpur, 1994), esp. ch. 1.

[9] Hussin Mutalib, *Islam in Malaysia: from revivalism to Islamic State* (Singapore, 1993), pp. 32–3.

mounted an ideological challenge to the hypocrisy and neo-colonialism of the west in its advocacy of its understanding of human rights, environmentalism, free trade and democratisation.[10] It argued for the legitimacy of its own apprehension of the needs of its society and its own ethics of progress; it demanded the recognition of its own political and institutional experience. The west was demonised, and Malaysians across all ethnic groups drew great satisfaction from this: patriotism, it seemed, had never been stronger. There were those who were uneasy at this stance, those who pointed out its inconsistencies and contradictions, to its underlying pragmatism, but in these years Malaysia shook away the psychological residue of colonial rule.

Forty years after the Alliance government first took office, there was recognition, even in the old seat of imperial power, that Malaysia was lost to the empire and had found a new role as a leader of Third World opinion. Yet Malaya occupied, for all the intensity of British involvement, a curious place in the mythology of decline. In one sense it is seen as a success story – from defeat at Singapore in 1942, to recovery and selfless renunciation. Historians of empire have helped perpetuate this myth.[11] The United States was quick to draw on British expertise for the conduct of its own counter-insurgency war in Vietnam. However, observers of the Malayan campaign rightly pointed out at an early stage the dangers of staking too much on these parallels.[12] And despite the optimistic rhetoric of a stewardship successfully concluded, there was an underlying melancholy to the end of empire. For a whole generation Malaya was, after all, remembered most vividly as a place of defeat and humiliation. The British soldiers who were caught in the maelstrom of the Japanese advance in 1941 and 1942 were the 'forgotten army' of the Second World War, and the half-centennials of the fall of Singapore and of the end of the Pacific War were marked in a sombre mood by those who had survived them. For the man-on-the-spot, that curious creature who occupies such an important part in the history of empire, decolonisation was a disenchanting experience – and the tone of much of the testimonies in this book seems to bear this out. The literature of disengagement reflects a profound preoccupation about the decline of metropolitan institutions and values.[13] Even the best of it, such as the work of Anthony Burgess, evinces a sense of betrayal at the natives' failure to grasp wholeheartedly the agenda of the late imperial mission. It is a theme echoed, in a different way, in the fiction of Keris Mas. A story published in 1959, 'They do not understand', beautifully captures the confusion of a colonial civil servant at the transfer of power.

> These Malays are stupid, so impatient to do everything on their own. They fancy they are already qualified for it. No, not yet. And it is my responsibility, the responsibility of

---

[10] K. S. Nathan, 'Vision 2020 and Malaysian foreign policy: strategic evolution and the Mahathir impact', *Southeast Asian Affairs, 1995* (Singapore, 1995), 220–37.

[11] For example, Robert Heussler, *British rule in Malaya, 1942–57* (Singapore, 1985).

[12] Robert O. Tilman, 'The non-lessons of the Malayan Emergency', *Asian Survey*, 6, 8 (1966), 407–19.

[13] Clive J. Christie, *A preliminary survey of British literature on South-East Asia in the era of colonial decline and decolonisation* (Hull, 1986).

all of us expatriate officers, to see to it that independence does not alienate this country from us – her teacher, her former protector. Let them need us for a long time yet, the longer the better for the security of our relationship with them. Our intentions are good, both for us and for them. But they do not understand.[14]

In the 1980s and 1990s a post-colonial generation of Britons were once again rediscovering Malaya through war memoirs, a new wave of exotica and through tourism. Britons were the largest contingent of western visitors to Malaysia: 120,000 in 1989 alone; in the 1990s the expatriate population of Malaysia swelled once again and many members of a British diaspora sought employment there.[15] When they made their new encounters with Malaysia, it was on very different terms.

Realising independence

For the Alliance politicians the great task of independence was the undoing of the ethnic division of labour that had emerged in the years of colonial rule. A confidence in the capacity of the state to undertake massive projects of economic development and to effect national integration through social policy was perhaps the most substantial legacy of late colonialism. Through these projects, the emerging corporatist ethos we explored in chapter 6 was consolidated through the establishment of a wide range of governmental agencies which undertook to preserve the trust of the Malays. In its early stages, economic development was essentially a continuation of schemes begun in the late colonial period, schemes that were given more urgency by the implementation of the communal bargain between UMNO and the MCA. In the developmental language of the day, ethnic division was synonymous with the rural–urban divide. The emphasis therefore in the late 1950s and 1960s lay in bringing the economic condition of the rural population closer to that of the towns. A central aim was the energisation of the Malay rural economy through large-scale land settlement schemes. The Federal Land Development Authority schemes mooted in the colonial period began to bear fruit in the aftermath of independence and sought to draw the best and most disciplined members of rural society, often ex-soldiers and policemen, into co-operative colonisations of large tracts of land. These settlements exploited economies of scale: initially the base was 400 settlers and their families; by the mid-1980s it was over 1,000 families. The settlers were chosen on the basis of family size, their skill and age, and the schemes demanded of them massive adjustments in routine: the aim was the creation of a new rural elite, 'a viable, cohesive and progressive rural community'.[16] Under the development regime of Abdul Razak, the 'Father of Development', many of the command structures developed in the

[14] 'Mereka tidak mengerti', translated in Muhammad Haji Salleh (ed.), *An anthology of contemporary Malaysian literature* (Kuala Lumpur, 1988), pp. 3–14, 9.
[15] Victor T. King, 'Tourism and culture in Malaysia', in M. Hitchcock, V. T. King and M. J. G. *Tourism in Southeast Asia* (London, 1993), p. 106.
, 'Two variants of the modern plantation: FELDA and Mumias', in Edgar *The modern plantation in the Third World* (London, 1984), pp. 105–27.

Emergency campaign were applied to the civil tasks of creating a co-ordinated and responsive rural development apparatus. In a similar way, the late colonial techniques of political education were adapted to the task of nation-building. A touchstone in this regard was the formulation and implementation of a national educational policy, especially by the provision of vernacular education for the Malay rural masses. However, as the British had earlier discovered, much of the population was unwilling to accept the social paradigms implicit in these schemes.

The returns on the first phase of nation-building were disappointing. The famous bargain, which had seemed to leave the field of politics and administration to the Malays and the world of commerce to the Chinese, whilst guaranteeing political rights to the Chinese and economic assistance to the Malays, no longer reflected, if indeed it ever had, the aspirations of key groups in society. Tensions came to a head in the late 1960s: the 1969 general election brought unprecedented gains for opposition parties, and a nexus of political and economic anxieties came together in the tragic communal riots that erupted in Kuala Lumpur on 13 May 1969. Dissatisfaction with the elite compromises of the Alliance government was registered by all communities, and the problem of poverty was one they all faced. However, resentment was perhaps deepest in sections of the Malay community who felt alienated from the modern, urban-based sectors of the economy. Malay elites were unwilling to accept that the future of the community lay in becoming a yeoman peasantry. The quest for economic alternatives had begun in the inter-war years, and was catalysed by MATA and the political crises of the 1950s. We observed in chapter 6 the growing currency of a corporatist, capitalist vision of Malay economic development. It was contested at the time by those who saw the alleviation of poverty across all communities as the first claim on any national development policy. However, *bumiputera* economic thinking had gained momentum with the 1965 Bumiputera Economic Congress which led to the establishment of a Bank Bumiputera and the dissolving of RIDA into a new agency called the *Majlis Amanah Rakyat* (MARA). In the last years of the decade, dissatisfaction was deepening amongst the Malay business and professional elite at the slow pace of restructuring in the economy, and with what was seen as Tunku Abdul Rahman's excessively accommodating posture towards non-Malay interests.[17] It came to be associated with 'Young Turks' such as Dr Mahathir Mohamad and Musa Hitam and their opposition to the Prime Minister. The conception that emerged from it was that of the Malay *bumiputera* as the 'definitive' people, the first claimants on the nation; the absolute owners of Malaysia, a notion that found its fullest expression in Dr Mahathir's book, *The Malay Dilemma*, a book which was banned at the time but became the definitive text for Malay nationalism during the next twenty years.[18] Similarly the position of English and minority languages relative to Malay linguistic

---

[17] Jomo K. S., 'Whither Malaysia's New Economic Policy', *Pacific Affairs*, 63, 4 (1990–91), 469–99.
[18] Khoo Boo Teik, *Paradoxes of Mahathirism: an intellectual biography of Mahathir Mohamad* (Kuala Lumpur, 1995), pp. 17–48.

nationalism became a hotly contested area, and provoked a new wave of opposition to UMNO. The slow implementation of educational ambitions of independence led the frustrations of Malay intellectuals and teachers to grow in momentum, and they burst into a crisis in 1967 when the National Language Bill failed to meet the aspirations of this powerful constituency.[19]

The day of 13 May 1969, like the interregnum after the Japanese surrender, was thereafter to mark the breaking-point of the Malaysian polity, and forced Malaysia's rulers to make more explicit the principles of state on which the country would be founded. The immediate consequence of the crisis was the suspension of parliamentary democracy, the elbowing from power of Tunku Abdul Rahman and the introduction, under the new Prime Minister Abdul Razak, of new strategies for economic development and national integration. A national ideology, the *Rukanegara* – similar to the *Pancasila*, or principles of state, of Indonesia – was formulated. The Alliance was transformed into a National Front – Barisan Nasional – which in 1974 contained nine political parties. But the real centre-piece of the new regime was the New Economic Policy (NEP), as embodied in the Second Malaysia Plan. There was little that was new about its assumptions. Although it paid appropriate cognizance to the need to eradicate poverty across all ethnic communities, the NEP fashioned a central role for the state to make up the economic deficit of Malay nationalism. In 1969 the Malay stake in the corporate sector amounted to only 2.4 per cent; the NEP aimed to raise it in twenty years to 30 per cent. It created new bodies corporate which managed the economy in trust for the Malays, and in them bureaucrats found a new role. A new Malay business class emerged, fortified by its relationship with the state. The New Education Policy aimed to create the personnel to manage this transition by increasing the presence of the new generation of Malays in higher education, and an elaborate system of quotas sought to guarantee their future prospects. In the 1970s the NEP rode forward on the back of a boom in commodities, notably oil, and by the momentum the state itself had generated. By the 1980s this momentum was slackening, and by the middle of the decade Malaysia was in a recession: state expenditure was cut back, official salaries frozen. The social effects of this were significant, and witnessed in a wave of bankruptcies, in graduate unemployment and in shrinking urban incomes. In the 1980s the emphasis of the NEP changed. In 1983 the Mahathir government launched a new industrial grand plan and a Heavy Industries Corporation of Malaysia to spearhead it. New watchwords were coined: 'Look East' and 'Malaysia Incorporated' as Malaysia looked towards the Japanese experience. Privatisation aimed to restructure the economy without creating a 'subsidy mentality' amongst *bumiputera* business. A new ethos of efficiency swept the public sector and was demanded from private enterprise. It was, in many senses, a move towards a different understanding of the NEP. In the course of the shift, corporations were restructured, only the fittest were to survive. A core group of businessmen emerged out of the larger class that had been created in the first years of the NEP. The rationale had shifted from restructuring to sustaining growth generally; to its critics the mechanics of the NEP had moved from patronage to cronyism.[20] Not least amongst the beneficiaries of this were the political parties themselves. UMNO in particular had become a powerful corporate entity on a similar model to the trusteeships created by the NEP, and this raised dramatically the stakes in political competition.[21]

As the NEP came to the end of its twenty-year course, its social consequences came to the fore. As in previous periods the towns were a window on the changes that were coursing through Malaysian society. The roots of these can be seen in the 1950s: in Kuala Lumpur in 1959, then celebrating its hundredth anniversary, real estate values had risen 40 per cent in two years. New civic conceits were constructed, and the opposition attacked their extravagance.[22] Urbanisation created new Malay constituencies but, as it had done in the 1950s, also generated much social unease. Much of the growth was concentrated in the Klang Valley, and involved migrations over very short distances, but the capital and its environs soon became a powerful draw to Malays from all over the peninsula. Malays were 21 per cent of the urban population in 1957, 28 per cent in 1970.[23] Malay urbanisation accelerated in the early years of the NEP, and the 1970s saw mounting concern at the growth of a Malay squatter problem in the towns. Housing was provided for *bumiputeras*, but there was a slow take-up rate and problems of financing. Women were the focus of a range of civic anxieties: about the effects of work on their dress and morals, on changing marriage patterns and the high levels of divorce. Women's activists such as Marina Yusof of the *Kaum Ibu UMNO*, and the Convention of Muslim Women's Organisations, which first met in March 1974, attempted to boost the rights of women in a way that was commensurate with their new position.[24] The towns were the province of the young, but equally, a rural–urban migration created new levels of stress, and one measure of this was taken to be the escalating drug problem: in 1984, 76 per cent of known addicts were Malay.[25] As it had done in an earlier period, urban problems proved a goad to movements of Islamic resurgence, and the effects of the New Education Policy created a new constituency for their reception. This too had begun in the 1950s, but by the 1970s energetic new missionary groups had established themselves to work amongst what were perceived to be the most vulnerable groups.[26] Although in these

---

[20] Khoo Kay Jin, 'The Grand Vision: Mahathir and modernization', in Kahn and Loh, *Fragmented vision*, pp. 44–76.

[21] Edmund Terence Gomez, *Politics in business: UMNO's corporate investments* (Kuala Lumpur, 1990).

[22] Willard A. Hanna, *Sequel to colonialism: the 1957–60 foundations of Malaysia* (New York, 1965), pp. 261–70.

[23] P. J. Rimmer and George C. H. Cho, 'Urbanization of the Malays since independence: evidence from West Malaysia, 1957–70', *JSEAS*, 12, 2 (1981), 349–63.

[24] 'From sarong to jeans: darker side of success story in rural-urban migration', *Malay Mail*, 14. 6. 1982.

[25] *New Straits Times*, 11. 1. 1984.

[26] Zainah Anwar, *Islamic revivalism in Malaysia: dakwah amongst students* (Petaling Jaya, 1987).

years the towns achieved a new dominance in Malaysia, the countryside was also subject to far-reaching changes. The village anthropology of independent Malaysia has pointed to the continuities between the colonial development decade and the NEP years, above all in the kinds of conflicts they have generated.[27] A 'green revolution' in many areas of peninsular Malaysia gave a greater intensity to the growing incidence of land concentration and tenancy we observed in chapter 6. Again, a rich theme of study of Malay rural society has been how Malay peasants have responded to these changing circumstances. Old strategies of flight, of evasions and protest, were adapted to more differentiated societies and the more intimate penetration of the state and its local agents. The language of protest in the disturbances involving poor farmers in Kedah in 1976 and 1980 was a familiar one, and upon it, especially on the east coast, the Islamic opposition began to build core areas of support.[28]

There was by the 1970s a sizeable middle class in Malaysia. Commentators were obsessed by it as an instrument of change, especially within the Malay community, and with the growing contrast in its lifestyle with the population of the Malay heartland, ageing, and dependent on remittances from the towns. To its critics the middle-class had a dual personality, one part of which was turned towards their colonial predecessors, and these critics mocked their affectations with bush jackets, obsessions with social hierarchy and the social training to which they submitted themselves. A vitally important question was the political direction in which these men and women, living at the forefront of the immense social changes sweeping Malaysia, might move. Within the growth of the Malay middle class there were divisions: between those who had emerged out of the expansion of Malay-medium education in the NEP years, and those, particularly those in the private sector, who had been moulded in the more hybrid and bilingual middle class culture, often exposed to overseas or private education, that had begun to arise in the late colonial period. These divisions gave added urgency to debates on the extent to which the Malay middle class would be strong enough to withstand open competition once the NEP expired after its twenty-year trajectory; the extent to which a critical mass had been created in economic restructuring. The benchmark proportions of 30 per cent *bumiputera* ownership were not reached; in 1988 it had reached 19.4 per cent. In 1990, Malays made up 29 per cent of the professional and 33 per cent of the administrative and managerial positions. It is important to note also that the targets for non-Malay ownership under the NEP were also not reached: the corporate stake of the Indian community, for example, had remained static since independence. By the late 1980s Malaysian politics was consumed by the debate on the future of the NEP. A National Economic Consultative Council was launched – incorporating both supporters and opponents of the Barisan regime – to review the NEP and formulate a new policy.

[27] An exemplary work is Shamsul A. B., *From British to Bumiputera rule: local politics and rural development in peninsular Malaysia* (Singapore, 1988).

[28] James C. Scott, *Weapons of the weak: everyday forms of peasant resistance* (New Haven, 1985); for continuities, Nonini, *British colonial rule*.

The National Development Policy that replaced the NEP, owed less to this body than to the world-view of the executive.[29] Although the original targets for restructuring were kept under review, the new emphasis was on growth, and in 1991 it created a new Perbadanan Usahawan Nasional Berhad – National Entrepreneurs' Development Board – to foster this. New types of rhetoric were adopted to accompany the change. Under the Mahathir administration the debate had become more focused on creating a new kind of Malay society, a new kind of Malay, the *Melayu Baru* – in which the residual feudal bonds of the Rulers and the disruptive claims of pan-Islamic resurgence would have no place. Simply stated Mahathir's consistent political objectives were to mobilise the most progressive and dynamic elements in Malay society, to anticipate and if necessary to oppose western-style democratisation to which he has always been hostile. A new kind of corporatism and social discipline was needed for Malaysia to modernise economically, to entrench a stable Malay supremacy, within which a new Malay community could take the lead in the creation of a new Malaysian nation, which would then take its rightful place in the international community. The new vision was launched by Mahathir at the first meeting of the Malaysian Business Council, in a speech 'Malaysia: the way forward'. It was *Wawasan 2020* – Vision 2020 – the transformation of Malaysia into a fully industrialised country by this date. It created a new goal for national integration: the realisation of a true *Bangsa Malaysia* in which old ethnicities would have no place.[30]

The end of ethnicity?

The identity of the nation remained contested throughout the post-colonial period. As a political project nationalism in Malaya sought to create a modern nation-state, on a model thrust upon it by a European colonial power, where the linguistic and cultural basis of that state had yet to be resolved. Post-colonial Malaya had to cope with the contradictions that arose in this period.[31] The last years of empire saw, in addition to the MCP threat, the rise of movements of opposition to the framework of elite compromises that dictated its agenda. Even within the Alliance there lay very different nations of intent. Nation-building glossed over these different visions. Indeed the maintenance of the Alliance, however one looks at it, was a considerable political feat. However, in the 1950s we can already see the fault lines that were to dominate peninsular politics in the ensuing decades. Moreover, the men and women who dominated politics into the 1980s and early 1990s had the terms of their political struggles shaped in the late 1940s and 1950s. Only by the middle of the 1990s was a

---

[29] Richard F. Dorall, 'DEPAN: an alternative development paradigm for Malaysia in the 1990s', in Azizah Kassim and Lau Teik Soon (eds), *Malaysia and Singapore: problems and prospects* (Singapore, 1992), pp. 123–61.
[30] Khoo, *Paradoxes of Mahathirism*, pp. 327–31.
[31] For an important discussion of this see Muhammad Ikmal Said, 'Malay nationalism and national identity', *Suomen Antropologi*, 2 (1995), 11–31.

generational change complete. The continuing national struggle took place on several fronts.

The first was the struggle for the soul of Malay nationalism. This was both a conflict of interests and an ideological contest. As we have seen, early Malay nationalism had to define itself in relation to the *kerajaan*. At independence the Malay Rulers were seen as central to the creation of Malay political identity and an essential guarantee of its paramountcy. They were a symbol of an unbroken line of sovereignty that reached back to Melaka's golden age. Yet the relationship between the Rulers and *rakyat* was subject to increasing tensions. They rumbled below the surface in the 1960s and 1970s: in 1963 Tunku Abdul Rahman was driven to threaten to reduce the Rulers to 'the King of Hearts, the King of Clubs, the King of Spades and the King of Diamonds'.[32] When Malay nationalism became subject to a new ethos in the early 1980s open clashes erupted. The debates it fostered between nationalist and *kerajaan* interests were both discussions of present political needs and appeals to history. After a series of confrontations between Rulers and their Mentri Besar in Perak, Pahang and Selangor, and an on-going conflict with the ruling family in Johore, a crisis was provoked in 1983 over amendments to the constitution to limit their formal powers of vetoing legislation. The confrontation was reminiscent of the first days of the Malayan Union agitation. The Prime Minister, Dr Mahathir, took on the mantle of the great commoner as he rallied support at huge meetings across the country: in Batu Pahat on 8 December 1983, 200,000 people assembled to hear him speak.[33] However, the confrontation ended in compromise and laws remained in place that forbade any questioning of the constitutional position of the rulers in Malaysia, less to protect them personally than to uphold their role as custodians of Islam and Malay political primacy. Yet in 1993 and 1994 there was a renewed assault on the Rulers, pursued with unprecedented vigour by the national press and by UMNO. The misdeeds of many years were exposed, although different Rulers were challenged for very different reasons. Critics saw the confrontation as orchestrated by Prime Minister Mahathir to increase the centralisation of power, as a reprise of the inconclusive 1983 conflict. However, the 1993–4 crisis of the monarchy had new features, not least of which was the decisive failure of Rulers in their attempt to mobilise popular support outside of party political channels, whose patronage had taken precedence over that of the courts'. The press was firmly under government control, especially under the influence of UMNO ministers who were taking the lead in the challenge to the royal courts. The police forbade Rulers to hold rallies. Where members of ruling houses attempted to canvass rural support, few people turned up to meet them. The rising middle class of the towns were a vital political interest to which UMNO politicians turned in their attacks on the courts, and these new elite interests showed themselves to be largely immune to the claims of the *kerajaan*. However, as we shall see, there was another way

---

[32] Cited in Zainuddin Maidin, *The other side of Mahathir*, p. 77.
[33] Chamil Wariya, *Politik dan Raja* (Kuala Lumpur, 1992), pp. 27–38. Laurent Metzger, *Les Sultanats de Malaisie: un régime monarchique au vingtième siècle* (Paris, 1994).

in which the terms of political contest had changed: it advanced the concept of political accountability. Although the assault on the Rulers sought to confirm Malay allegiance to UMNO, and to the transformation of society demanded by Vision 2020, a more general critique of political power was emerging from all of this.

A second source of conflict lay in the fact that Malay nationalism, as represented by UMNO, remained an alliance of forces, and these forces continued to contest the identity of the party. By 1959, the year of the first fully representative election in Malaya, some of the fissures within Malay nationalism were beginning to open up. In 1958 the slow implementation of the Razak Report on the National Education Policy saw the Federation of Malaya Malay Schoolteachers' Association instruct its members, some 80 per cent of whom were members of UMNO, to resign from the party, and the consequences of this were seen in the 1959 election results which saw losses for UMNO at a State level. In Trengganu, of the 24 seats, 17 seats were lost to the PMIP and 4 to the Party Negara, and 28 out of 30 seats lost to the PMIP in Kelantan. Tensions within UMNO smouldered through the 1960s and erupted in 1969. This bred an intense factionalism within the party that rumbled throughout the Razak years and resurfaced once again after his sudden death in 1975. Bitter conflicts arose between the 'old guard', many of whom remained attached to the old Alliance approach of Tunku Abdul Rahman, and the 'Young Turks' who were ready to challenge many of its assumptions. The new Prime Minister, Hussein bin Onn, brought a rather bureaucratic style to government and appointed Dr Mahathir as his Deputy in an attempt to rise above this factionalism.[34] Yet throughout this period, the dynamism of Malay politics was drawn as much from the internal dynamics of the Malay body politic and within UMNO itself as from the communal dynamics of the nation. As UMNO entered the hour of its gravest crisis in the middle 1980s, as it dissolved and reconstituted itself, we can begin to trace the role underlying divisions played in what was often portrayed as a contest solely of rival personalities and ambitions – a 'Team A' led by the Prime Minister, vying with a 'Team B', led by his rival Tengku Razaleigh, and his disaffected deputy, Musa Hitam. Political writers contrasted Mahathir's 'mandatism' with Musa Hitam's 'bureaucratic tolerationism'; Mahathir's insistence on self-reliance with Tengku Razaleigh's adherence to state interventionism.[35] However, there was more to it than this. The nature of UMNO itself was changing. Its core base of support was changing. In 1981 40 per cent of delegates to the General Assembly were schoolteachers, in 1987 only 19 per cent. The party had become a major business enterprise and struggles for position had intensified. One analyst has suggested that the opposition to Mahathir was perhaps strongest amongst the smaller capitalists, as represented by the Chambers of Commerce, and the middling ranks of civil servants who had arisen in the first years

---

[34] Discussed in Harold Crouch, 'The UMNO crisis, 1975–77', in Harold Crouch, Lee Kam Hing and Michael Ong (eds), *Malaysian politics and the 1978 election* (Kuala Lumpur, 1980), pp. 11–36.
[35] K. Das, *The Musa dilemma: reflections on the decision of Datuk Musa Hitam to quit the government of Datuk Seri Dr Mahathir Mohamed* (Kuala Lumpur, 1986).

of the NEP and were wedded to its bureaucratic approach to development. Their influence in government may have diminished, as the support of the regime shifted to the larger entrepreneurs in the private sector and bureaucratic power towards key technocrats within the Prime Minister's Office.[36] These struggles of interest, a contest perhaps for the future class personality of UMNO, were underpinned by the new ideological dilemmas faced by the Malay community in the wake of the NEP.

The nature of ethnicity and of the national identity remained contested. Cultural life is a window on this third front of conflict. A central goal of Malay nationalism was to make the Malay language the idiom of national life. As we saw in Chapter 7, after *Merdeka*, Singapore declined as centre of Malay culture, and a Malay literary establishment emerged in Kuala Lumpur as the Generation of 1950 was absorbed into the state structure, and rose to a new prominence in the years of the NEP. Yet Malay intellectuals continued to rail against the Anglophile elite, who it was suggested was emerging stronger than ever, in spite of the New Economic Policy. Unlike in an earlier period, ideologues such as Ismail Hussein warned, the middle class was no longer racially based. The result would be class struggle and a 'new feudalism'. 'What the Malays want,' it was suggested, 'is an elite with a non-elitist mind. Aristocrats with a non-aristocratic leaning.'[37] It was a claim for the maintenance of an organic Malay community based on a common culture. To achieve this end the Malay language continued to be reformulated, pushed in virtually all areas of education, in the public sector and encouraged, with more difficulty, in the private sector. It was even pursued in the courts as a preliminary to creating a Malaysian common law.[38] However, despite the many triumphs of the Malay medium, it seemed by the late 1980s that the national language had reached a threshold in its advance. Translators could not meet demand; Chinese educationalists revived their claims; English made a revival. The reassessment of the NEP, attacks on the 'yellow culture' content in television schedules, even the foreign names given to new urban properties to attract middle-class buyers, fuelled cultural anxieties. In Kuala Lumpur, a new generation of English-educated intellectuals, many of them returned from overseas sojourns, injected a new element into the literary, cultural scene, and cast themselves as multi-cultural intellectuals in a manner strikingly reminiscent of the 'Malayan' intellectual of the early 1950s. This was congruent with the expansion of local publishing, and private education in English in the 1990s as the English medium became more acceptable and a passport to betterment for the new middle class. These changes created a mood of unease against which Malay intellectuals mobilised. Fears were expressed that the Malays were becoming a 'race of Creoles': that the rural–urban divide was widening; that the *nouveaux riches* had lost their culture.[39] An Intellectuals' Congress in early

---

[36] N. J. Funston, 'Challenge and response in Malaysia: the UMNO crisis and the Mahathir style', *Pacific Review*, 1, 4 (1988), 363–73; Khoo, 'The Grand Vision', pp. 68–76.

[37] Ismail Hussein, 'Interview with Alina Ranee: anglophiles and the Malay elite' [1985], in *Statements on Malay language and literature* (Kuala Lumpur, 1989), pp. 46–50.

[38] Richard Mead, *Malaysia's national language policy and the legal system* (New Haven, 1988).

[39] Reports by Ismail Kassim, *Straits Times*, 28. 5. 1991, 20.10.1992.

December 1992 brought together these voices: they made it clear that they too stood for progress; they identified with the development of a new Malay ethos emphasising rationality, pragmatism, innovation and sensitivity. Yet they also emphasised that material considerations must be balanced with spiritual needs. Socially they represented the heirs of the politicised educators, students, journalists and writers of the 1950s; smaller-scale entrepreneurs rather than larger corporations – significantly the Congress attracted little response from the Malay corporate giants. Their anxieties focused on the English language: they opposed the decision to allow English in the teaching of science and technology at a higher level and they attacked official references to the national language as *Bahasa Malaysia*. Instead, they argued for *Bahasa Melayu* as a historical *lingua franca*, as a language that would develop in congruence to *Bahasa Indonesia*, the voice of *Nusantara*. It was a living language, not the voice of heritage.[40] There were fears that an entire generation of Malay students who lacked English language teaching at an earlier age might be left behind. Other Malay writers argued that these vested interests no longer reflected the aspirations of their community – the Malay language experiment had been pursued as far as it realistically could be taken – and forecast that bourgeois ambitions would overcome cultural scruples.

Yet many of the old shibboleths of state-building had been challenged. The *bumiputera*, too, was changing his identity. The Portuguese renewed their claim to be *bumiputera* and sought to be eligible for membership of UMNO, as did Christian *bumiputeras* from Sabah, as UMNO became more of a *bumiputera* party. In 1995 the old dream of Dato Onn of fielding candidates whose only party affiliation was to a multi-racial party had been floated within the National Front. This was in part a response to local political difficulties, but all those involved were aware of its symbolic importance. Malay nationalism was being redefined in congruence with new needs and, in the pursuit of the *Bangsa Malaysia*, a nationalism beyond ethnicity, the division between the core and the periphery of the nation had become significantly blurred. It remained to be seen how far the underlying structure of Malaysian politics was changing; how far the momentum of the new *bangsa* came out of the logic of inter-ethnic relations in Malaysia. It was argued that a middle-class consumer culture, shared rituals, even sport, had made the symbols of Malay nationalism the common property of all. A central question of the 1990s was the extent to which the politics of ethnicity had been supplanted by those of class.[41]

In the 1990s the logic of government policy remained, as it had been in the period under study here, the creation of one fused form of national identity. In this, the echoes of the political rhetoric of the 1950s could perhaps be heard; yet still too could its dissonances, and Malaysians were most attentive to them. In 1957 the strongest ideological challenge to the assumptions of nation-building came from Islam. Tunku Abdul Rahman mistrusted political Islam. Onn dallied with it only after other

---

[40] *Straits Times*, 9.12.1992; *New Straits Times*, 29. 6. 1992.
[41] Muhammad Ikmal Said, 'Malay nationalism and national identity', 28–9; Khoo, *Paradoxes of Mahathirism*, pp. 331–8.

strategies of creating a broad-based nationalist movement around his orbit had failed. Nearly forty years later, Islam remained a challenge, although the nature of this challenge had changed considerably in the interim. Scholars have, correctly, drawn attention to the external dynamics of Islamic resurgence. However, the experience of the 1950s might lead us to focus on its internal momentum. As we have seen, the constituency for political Islam grew markedly in the years after independence.[42] Resurgent Islam drew its inspiration from a variety of agencies, some of which – *Jamaat Tabligh*, for instance – avoided open political contest, and the modernism of others – the *Angkatan Belia Islam Malaysia*, or Islamic Youth Movement of Malaysia, for example – led them to drift towards the UMNO mainstream. The Islamic party, PMIP, later the *Parti Islam SeMalaysia* (PAS) also changed its character in the years after independence: it moved away from Malay particularism and towards Islamic universalism. Its leadership by the 1980s had shifted firmly into the hands of *ulama* who challenged the place of secular-minded Malay nationalism within Islam. In government in the State of Kelantan, PAS moved to implement the *hudud* Islamic laws. The contest between UMNO and PAS left the Malay *ummah* visibly divided and deeply troubled. At its height it caused rival sections of villages to pray in different mosques – under 'two *imams*' – and branded UMNO as infidel – the charges of *kafir-mengkafir*. In Besut District in Trengganu the political struggle between PAS and UMNO was reported in 1982 to be the cause of over 200 divorces.[43] On occasion violence erupted. The Memali incident in 1985 was a traumatic event which saw the army clash with a religious community led by the teacher Ibrahim Libya: eighteen people died and were subsequently martyred by PAS. In 1984, UMNO responded with its own 'Islamization of the government machinery.'[44] By the 1990s Islam had moved to a central position within its ideology. The state defined heterodoxy with more precision and it moved resolutely against its challengers. It did so most dramatically with the proscription of the *dakwah* or missionary movement *Al-Arqam* in 1994 and the 're-education' of its members. Scholars have emphasised that Islam and 'Malayness' still lie in tension with one another, and that secularism and class will undermine Islamic universalism.[45] However, the *Al-Arqam* episode also illustrated that radical Islamic resurgence was not solely the doctrine of the under-privileged, but also of highly educated Malays, even Malay technocrats. The PAS challenge remained undefeated and much of the rationalising, internationalist rhetoric of Vision 2020, as well as UMNO's claims to moral leadership, was grounded in Islam. Islam remained a central predicament of statehood.

This brings us to a final theme: the future of the plural society. Again the experience of independence has tended to highlight the divisions within ethnic

---

[42] The fullest account is Hussin Mutalib, *Islam and ethnicity and Malay politics* (Singapore, 1990).

[43] *The Star*, 10. 8. 1982.

[44] D. K. Mauzy and R. S. Milne, 'The Mahathir administration: discipline through Islam', in Bruce Gale (ed.), *Readings in Malaysian politics* (Petaling Jaya, 1986), pp. 75–112.

[45] Hussin Mutalib, *Islam in Malaysia*, esp. pp. 114–19.

communities rather than to provide examples of them acting as monolithic blocks of communal opinion. Amongst the Indian community, whilst the MIC leadership had achieved some success in forging durable political ties with UMNO, core problems of marginalisation and poverty remained, and attempts to resolve them created new fractions within the community. The Orang Asli struggled to maintain their independent identity in the face of the integrationalist pressures on them, and in fact became increasingly plural in religion: not merely in the face of the competing demands of Islam or Christianity, but in some areas to Bahai. Chinese politics remained torn between the demands of nation-building and the deeply rooted belief that a Malayan patriotism did not imply a sacrifice of the Chinese cultural heritage. The MCA was faced with the problem of how to function as the representative of Chinese interests with the Alliance. The tensions created by this reached a head soon after independence in 1958 as the MCA's own 'Young Turks' such as Lim Chong Eu, President of the party from 1958, and Yong Pung How challenged the leadership on this issue and threatened to carve out an independent course for the party. The relative electoral performances of the party in 1959 and 1964 showed the extent to which the party was dependent on its status within the Alliance and on the Malay vote for its survival.[46] In the 1964 election, the PAP campaign for a 'Malaysian Malaysia' questioned the extension of Malay rights and provoked suspicions that it was attempting to supplant the MCA if it did not deliver the urban vote. However, the MCA machinery proved strong enough to meet the PAP challenge on the peninsula, and ironically it was the Socialist Front of the Labour Party and the *Parti Rakyat* that suffered most electorally. The MCA rehabilitated itself, but faced a new wave of recrimination, both from UMNO and from its own constituency in the political crisis of 1969. One response in the ensuing years was the Chinese Unity Movement, which challenged the MCA's ability to safeguard Chinese rights within the Barisan Nasional. Again the MCA responded by creating new community self-help organisations, such as its investment wing Multi-Purpose Holdings Berhad (1977) and by campaigning for a Chinese 'Merdeka University'.[47] Yet it failed to revive its claim to be a grass-roots Chinese organisation, and took on the role of an intercessor organisation with the Malay leadership. The rise of new Chinese business figures, who made alliance with *bumiputera* elites through more informal means, added to this impression. In these years opposition parties such as the peninsular successor to the PAP, the Democratic Action Party, revived the claim for a 'Malaysian Malaysia' and opposed discrimination against non-Malays at the zenith of the NEP. Cultural unease resurfaced in 1987 with a campaign for Chinese education in which a new generation of activists confronted Malay nationalism. There was substantial historical continuity to their struggle, and although the aims of these groups reflected a

[46] M. Roff, 'The Malayan Chinese Association 1945–65', *JSEAH*, 6, 2 (1965), 51–3.
[47] Francis Loh Kok Wah, *The politics of Chinese unity in Malaysia: reform and conflict within the Malaysian Chinese Association* (Singapore, 1982); Heng Pek Koon, *Chinese politics in Malaysia: a history of the Malaysian Chinese Association* (Singapore, 1988), pp. 254–77.

pluralistic vision of the nation, they did not break out of an ethnic framework of politics. Their claim for individual citizen rights had long been embroiled in a campaign for those of a community.[48] By the mid-1990s, however, the situation seemed to be changing. The UMNO leadership felt it was in a position to make some concessions to relieve Chinese educational and cultural anxieties and the MCA profited from this. As noted earlier, the great struggles over language and culture subsided somewhat in a general mood of pragmatism and prosperity. There was a critical measure of acceptance of the changes of the 1970s and 1980s, a sense of relief that some of the main sources of ethnic tension had receded; new prospects were offered by Vision 2020 and the *Bangsa Malaysia*. The milieu of urban middle-class life had regained much of its old plural quality, if indeed it had ever lost it. There was support across all communities for the Barisan leadership, and a substantial personal following amongst non-Malays for Prime Minister Mahathir. Patriotism was a currency available to all. The question of how far the old struggles of Malay nationalism would be reconciled and subsumed within the new struggle of Malaysian nationalism would dominate the politics of pluralism as it entered a new era.

Authoritarianism and accountability

There is a final facet of the colonial inheritance to be addressed. Modern Malayan politics, this book has stressed, was born against a backdrop of war and insurgency creating a system of government, in the words of a Whitehall mandarin, 'combining autocratic rule with the new democratic processes in a typically Malayan way'.[49] The intensity of the social struggles that were encountered in Malaya's formation also made its mandarins very conscious of its fragility. In the shadow of the Communist insurgency the state became a more ruthless and authoritarian instrument of political power. It embedded a powerful rationale of anti-subversion in the official mind and it carved out restraints on political contest. This was a central feature of the mind-set of the post-colonial bureaucracy.[50] The political crisis and communal terror that shook the polity in 1969 seemed to vindicate its anxieties. In this sense the legacy of British rule was immense. It bequeathed a police force possessed of a unique combination of paramilitary force, security intelligence apparatus and prosecuting power. Yet it also meant that the force remained nationally organised: a counter-weight to the power of entrenched State elites. Similarly, the military has remained aloof from civilian politics.[51] Colonial policy, we have seen, lurched between authoritarianism and a missionary adherence to the rule of law. Malaysian politicians were reactive to the

---

[48] Tan Liok Ee, '*Dong jiaozong* and the challenge to cultural hegemony, 1951–87', in Kahn and Loh, *Fragmented vision*, pp. 181–201.

[49] T. C. Jerrom, minute, 27. 3. 1953, Stockwell, *Malaya*, II, p. 437.

[50] James C. Scott, *Political ideology in Malaysia: reality and the beliefs of an elite* (Kuala Lumpur, 1968), *passim*.

[51] Zakaria Haji Ahmad, 'The police and political development in Malaysia', in Zakaria (ed.), *Government and politics of Malaysia* (Singapore, 1987), pp. 116–19.

same stimuli and a strict legalism surrounded the apparatus of suppression. A formidable series of legislative provisions were laid to deal ostensibly with the MCP threat. Many of these were drawn directly from colonial legislation. After the formal end of the Emergency in 1960, its powers of detention were retained in the Internal Security Act of 1960. Between May 1969 and November 1975, 3,454 people were detained 'for internal security reasons'. Further legal instruments were created: most notably a revised Sedition Act (1969), the Essential (Security Case) Regulations (1975); the amended Societies Act (1981) and the amended Official Secrets Act (1986).[52] Added to the momentum of the Barisan government's long period of incumbency, these sanctions have created a constrained role for political opposition. Tunku Abdul Rahman had reluctantly accepted the *Parti Rakyat* as legitimate opposition but by 1959 a government White Paper was attacking its infiltration by the MCP. Periods of political crisis were marked by sudden contractions in the public sphere. The generation of radicals who had looked to Indonesia for inspiration to *Indonesia Raya* as a 'nation of intent' – Ahmad Boestamam, Ishak Haji Muhammad, Dr Burhanuddin – were removed from the political scene during the days of Confrontation; 13 May 1969 provoked a similar backlash, as did internecine conflicts within UMNO in 1976 and the period of heightened ethnic antagonism in 1987.[53] These executive actions have been attacked as an infringement of the fundamental rights of the citizen, but also defended as a necessary surgical tool to be used to protect the stability and harmony of society. A central question was the definition of what constituted national security; by the 1980s, social activists, environmentalists, Christian propagandists and Islamic activists were subject to these executive actions. Citizens' organizations which had come to the fore in the late 1970s and 1980s were attacked as being a conduit for challenges to parliamentary primacy. Similarly, during a major confrontation with the judiciary in 1988 the executive maintained that even the courts could not question the constitution as this would usurp the role of Parliament and politicise the role of judges. The practice of politics in independent Malaya was subject to similar distinctions between legitimate and illegitimate forms of participation in the political process that marked the democratisation of the late colonial period, and similar dissension over their boundaries. It has been asserted that the discourse of politics shared by various competing groups within Malaysian society might be creating new types of unity.[54] It might also be speculated that the extent to which this may occur will also depend on the latitude with which the state – given the logic of its own bureaucratic history – allows this public sphere to emerge. In 1996 the MPAJA bogey was resurrected by the chief of police in response to a *tribunal rakyat* of non-governmental organisations.[55]

---

[52] Chandran Jeshuran, 'Government response to armed insurgency in Malaysia, 1957–82', in Jeshuran (ed.), *Governments and rebellions in Southeast Asia* (Singapore, 1986), pp. 134–61.

[53] Simon Barraclough, 'The dynamics of coercion in the Malaysian political process', *MAS*, 19, 4 (1985), 797–822.

[54] A. C. Milner, 'Inventing politics: the case of Malaysia', *Past & Present*, 132 (1991), 128–9.

[55] *Straits Times*, 18.12.1996.

The 1980s and 1990s were a period of redefining national identity and recasting individual obligations to the nation after the trials of the 1960s and the introspective and bureaucratic 1970s. Public relations survived the Emergency as a central arm of government and retained a proactive role in forming public opinion, educating the peasant in thrift and progressive habits. Indeed, it gained a new lease of life under the Mahathir administration in promoting the grand designs of the 'Look East' policy, 'Malaysia Incorporated', 'Vision 2020', and the new drives for leadership by example and Islamisation.[56] Searching debates on the proper place of communications technology within an emerging Asian polity were left unresolved by independence. But in their attempts to resolve them, politicians drew much on the experience of the late colonial period, and the bureaucratic preoccupations and language of the institutions they had inherited. In Malaysia, the government instituted stronger controls on what was not to be shown, and did its utmost to promote what it felt should be shown. The colonial censorship laws were strengthened in 1974 in terms reminiscent of the crusade against 'yellow culture' in 1957.[57] The legitimate use of such media was measured by its educational purpose, and defined by its utility in the development of a robust national culture. In the 1980s the curbs on politically subversive, retrograde, or, increasingly, anti-Islamic uses of media and performance were strengthened. However, in attempting to create this new political community, the government did not have it all its own way. As in the late colonial period, greater state involvement in these areas also widened the space for individual initiative. Popular culture remained a rich vein through which comments on power could be made. Counterpoints survived, and new media emerged that may even amplify them in the future.[58]

This is a very important theme. Most accounts of Malaysia in this period emphasised the staggering successes that the Malaysian leadership achieved in its social and cultural engineering. However, a subterranean theme was political account-ability. It was implicit throughout the crisis of the Rulers in 1994. Many 'new' criticisms of the monarchy – such as their alleged links with Chinese business interests – were central to the statecraft of kingship since the pre-colonial period. It was a practice which the new Malay political elite themselves adopted. The attack by UMNO politicians on the abuse of royal privileges attempted to deflect political debates away from reflections on their own abuse of power. However, the crisis did concede the notion of accountability: if the Rulers could be censored for their excesses, their lavish lifestyles exposed, so could politicians. If the *rajas* were accountable, so too were elected officials. Moreover, there was unease, a sense of regret that sections of the new middle class seemed to share, that the circumscribed role of the Malay Rulers had increased the political vulnerability of the Malays. New

---

[56] Benedict Morais and Hamdan Adnan (eds), *Public relations: the Malaysian experience* (Kuala Lumpur, 1986).

[57] John A. Lent, *The Asian film industry* (London, 1990), pp. 195–7;

[58] Tan Sooi Beng, 'Counterpoints in the performing arts of Malaysia', in Kahn and Loh, *Fragmented vision*, pp. 282–305; Kean Wong, 'Metallic gleam', *The Wire* (April 1993), 18–20.

political literature mushroomed from small independent publishers in these years, and it began to take up these themes. A new kind of political polemicist emerged: a vast range of analyses and exposés, and biographies and eulogies were produced. Yet whether these texts were partisan, commissioned or a spontaneous response to contemporary predicaments, a general theme of this cottage industry was leadership. They gave the political rivalries of the 1980s and 1990s unique exposure.[59] Leadership struggles themselves took up these ideas. They were not only debates about position and patronage. They were also debates which sought to question the corporatism of the new generation that younger leaders espoused as the way forward for the new Malays; debates that focused on abuse of power, cronyism and corruption; of concerns that machine politics would erode further the more organic political community that UMNO had originally sought to represent. This kind of debate was, as one analyst observed, part of a wider move 'to make leaders more accountable and transparent'. It was perhaps felt that the polity could bear this after a long period of political stability. Although most of the scandals were exposed for strategic political motives, as UMNO sought to recover its moral authority a more general debate on the character and quality of Malaysia's civil society, *masyarakat madani*, especially on the sway of 'money politics', gathered momentum. The task ahead, as the then Deputy Prime Minister Anwar Ibrahim argued, was both to imbibe the lessons the decadent west still had to confer and to entrench a new set of national values.[60] There were indications that the kind of social transformation sought by Malaysia's leaders had made this kind of accountability essential, as they sought to address questions of political legitimacy, not through the inherited language of the colonial inheritance, but through that of their own democratic experience.

It was difficult to escape the sense that Malaysia was at the end of its post-colonial history. A new post-colonial generation was entrenched in the political succession. The restructuring of the NEP lay in the past, and Malaysia was articulating an outward-looking vision, a sense of purpose and cultivating a new patriotism. It was a time of great public works, lit by the torch of technology. The world was coming to Malaysia and applauding its achievements. Political leaders spoke of the birth of a new Malay civilisation: a new Melaka. The 1995 election was a National Front landslide and provoked parallels with 1955. Indeed one could see in it a similar triumphalism, a similar promise of prosperity. Commentators on national affairs were almost unanimous in asserting that a long period of national struggle had somehow reached its culmination. Certainly, nearly forty years after *merdeka* the colonial inheritance was no longer taken for granted. Economic and demographic change was reshaping the

---

[59] An interesting example in English translation of many of these themes, and a robust defence of the genre, is Zakry Abadi, *Why Anwar: political games of UMNO's leadership* (Kuala Lumpur, 1993), esp. preface. Other representative writers and texts are Chamil Wariya, *Pandangan politik era Mahathir* (Petaling Jaya, 1990); S. H. Alattas, *Penimpin, politik dan firasat* (Kuala Lumpur, 1994).

[60] See for example Anwar Ibrahim's speech at the UMNO Youth and Wanita General Assemblies in November, 1994, *New Straits Times*, 18.11.1994.

foundations of Malaysian society. Right across society there was an acceptance of change, even an intoxication by it. But it also generated anxieties, moralities, that had to be addressed. In 1997 and 1998 a new economic and political crisis brought these into the open. To survey the future is to interrogate history, and as Malaysians debated their futures, history offered much that could illuminate their predicaments. The response of the state, too, had its history. As it had done in the past, the government blazoned its vision of nationhood, and exhibited a conviction that it could shape the course of these transitions. Yet a consistent theme of this social history of the nation-state coming into being is that the more sophisticated the technologies of rule become, the more those in power attempt to realise their own imaginings, the more they seem to engender in their subjects a sense of the possible.

Bibliography

UNPUBLISHED SOURCES

Arkib Negara Malaysia, Kuala Lumpur

Federal records
BMA	British Military Administration, 1945–6
BMA/ADM	British Military Administration Secretariat
BMA/DEPT	British Military Administration Departmental
Coop	Director of Co-operation
CS	Chief Secretary
DF	Director of Forestry
DSW	Social Welfare Department
FS	Federal Secretariat
INF	Information Department
LAB	Commissioner for Labour
MU	Malayan Union Secretariat
PR	Public Relations Department
R of S	Registrar of Societies
SCA	Secretary for Chinese Affairs

State records
Selangor:
DOUL	District Office Ulu Langat
DCL Sel	Deputy Commissioner for Labour, Selangor
EAC KL	Extra Assistant Commissioner for Labour, Kuala Lumpur
RC Sel	Resident Commissioner, Selangor
Sel/CA	Selangor Civil Affairs, 1945–6
Sel Sec	Selangor State Secretariat

Perak:
Coop K.N.	Co-operative Department, Krian North
Coop Tpg	Co-operative Office, Taiping
DOBP	District Office, Batang Padang
DO	Kinta District Office, Kinta

DO	Larut District Office, Larut, Matang and Selama
KKFO	Forest Office, Kuala Kangsar
KKLO	Land Office, Kuala Kangsar
KLO	Land Office, Kinta
Lab Tpg	Labour Office, Taiping
Pk Sec	Perak State Secretariat
SFO Perak	State Forest Office, Perak

Pahang:

BA	Pahang British Advisor, Pahang
BA Phg/MPABM	British Advisor, Pahang/Malayan Peoples' Anti-Bandit Month
DO Bentong	District Office, Bentong
DO Kuantan	District Office, Kuantan
DO Temerloh	District Office Temerloh
PU&A	*Majlis Ugama dan Adat*, Pahang
SCA	Pahang Secretary for Chinese Affairs, Pahang

Malacca:
| LAB (Malacca) | Controller of Labour, Malacca |

Negri Sembilan:
| NS Sec | Negri Sembilan State Secretariat |
| DOKP | District Office, Kuala Pilah |

Trengganu:
RC Treng	Resident Commissioner Trengganu
INF Tr	Information Department, Trengganu
SUK Tr	Trengganu State Secretariat
Treng SCAO	Trengganu Senior Civil Affairs Officer

Johore:
| LDM | Labour Department North Johore, Muar |

Kelantan:
| DO Pasir Mas | District Office, Pasir Mas |

Kedah:
| DO Sik | District Office, Sik |

Private records
UMNO	UMNO files
SP.3	Leong Yew Koh papers
SP.13	Tan Cheng Lock papers

Perpustakaan Universiti Malaya, Kuala Lumpur

Methodist Mission Annual Conference (microfilm)
J. A. Thivy papers

Seminari Theologi Malaysia, Kuala Lumpur

Miscellaneous documents from International Missionary Council Archive, and other papers pertaining to the churches in Malaya.

Perpustakaan Universiti Sains Malaysia, Penang

Office of Strategic Services, Research and Analysis Branch, Reports on Japanese occupation of Malaya (microfilm)

Singapore National Archives

BMA/HQ	BMA Headquarters, Singapore, 1945–6
BMA/CA	BMA Chinese Affairs, Singapore, 1945–6
SCA	Secretary for Chinese Affairs, Singapore, 1946–8
CSO	Social Welfare Department/Chief Secretary's Office, Singapore, 1945–7
PR	Public Relations Office
INF	Information Department

Private records:
Loke Wan Tho papers

Singapore National Library

Daily and Weekly Vernacular Press Summaries
The Masonic Year Book for the Districts of the Eastern Archipelago (E.C.) and the Middle East (S.C.), Vols II (1955)–IV (1957)
Memorandum of books registered in the 'Catalogue of books printed at Singapore', under the Publications and Printers' Ordinance, 1950–5

Institute of Southeast Asian Studies, Singapore

TCL	Tan Cheng Lock papers

Public Records Office, London

CO273	Straits Settlements Original Correspondence, 1945
CO537	Colonial Office, Original Correspondence, 1945–51
CO717	Malay States, Original Correspondence, 1945–51
CO825	Eastern Department, Original Correspondence, 1945–8
CO865	Far Eastern reconstruction, 1942–4
CO889	Reid Constitutional Commission
CO1022	South-East Asia Department, Original Correspondence, 1951–3
CO1030	Far Eastern Department, Original Correspondence, 1953–7
WO220	Civil Affairs, 1945–56

Rhodes House, Oxford

Malayan Civil Service papers/Robert Heussler papers
Besut Annual Report, 1947, 1948
J. P. Blackledge papers
C. H. F. Blake papers

John Dalley papers/ Malayan Security Service, Political Intelligence Journals, 1946–8
J. C. R. Denning papers
G. C. Dodwell papers
Sir William Goode papers
L. S. Himely papers
Sir Ralph Hone papers
John Litton papers
H. W. Phear papers
B. P. Walker-Taylor papers
F. Wallace papers
M. L. Webber papers
E. D. B. Wolfe papers
Arthur Young papers

Cambridge University Library

Royal Commonwealth Society Library Collection:
British Association of Malaya papers
George Maxwell papers

Library of School of Oriental and African Studies, London

BMA Chinese Press Summaries

PUBLISHED GOVERNMENT SOURCES

Annual report of the social and economic progress of the people of the State of Perlis for the year 1947
Annual report on the social and economic progress of the people of Trengganu, for the year 1947
Burgess, R. C. and Laidin bin Musa, *A report on the state of health, the diet and the economic conditions of groups of people in the lower income levels in Malaya* (Kuala Lumpur, 1950)
Central Welfare Council, Federation of Malaya, *Social survey on beggars and vagrants* (Kuala Lumpur, 1958)
Colonial Office, *Juvenile welfare in the Colonies: Draft Report of the Juvenile Delinquency Sub-committee of the Colonial Penal Administration Committee* (London, 1942)
Colonial Office, *Papers on Colonial Affairs, No. 5, Social security in the Colonial Territories* (London, 1944)
Department of Information, Federation of Malaya, *Communist banditry in Malaya: the Emergency with a chronology of important events*, June 1948–June 1951 (Kuala Lumpur, 1951)
Department of Public Relations, Federation of Malaya, *Background information for speakers: the Emergency and Anti-Bandit Month* (Kuala Lumpur, 1950)
Federation of Malaya, *Annual Report of the Malaria Advisory Board for the year 1955*
Federation of Malaya, *Beggars in the Federation of Malaya: a factual report on the results of a pilot survey instituted by the Department of Social Welfare and carried out between November 1954 and March 1955* (Kuala Lumpur, 1955)
Federation of Malaya, *Draft Development Plan of the Federation of Malaya* (Kuala Lumpur, 1950)
Federation of Malaya, *Labour Department Annual Report* (1949–57)
Federation of Malaya, *Report of a Commission of Enquiry into the Integrity of the Public Services* (Kuala Lumpur, 1953)
Federation of Malaya, *Report on the conduct of food searches at Semenyih in the Kajang District of the State of Selangor* (Kuala Lumpur, 1956)

Federation of Malaya, *Report to investigate the working of the Social Welfare Department* (Legislative Council, No. 41 of 1949)

Federation of Malaya, *Report of the Pilgrims Economic Welfare Committee* (Cmd. 22 of 1962)

Federation of Malaya, *Report of the Registrar General on population, births, deaths, marriages and adoptions* (1947 and 1957)

Federation of Malaya, *Report of the Rice Production Committee*, I (1953)

Federation of Malaya, *Resettlement and the development of New Villages in the Federation of Malaya, 1952* (Legislative Council Paper No. 33 of 1952)

Federation of Malaya, *Societies in the Federation of Malaya: applications for registration as a registered or exempted society (as at 31 December 1950, which supplement list ending 31 December 1952)*

Fiennes, D. E. M., *Report on Rural and Industrial Development Authority, 1950–1955* (Kuala Lumpur, 1957)

Jabatan Hal Ehwal Orang Asli, *Statement of policy regarding the administration of the Orang Asli of Peninsular Malaysia* (Kuala Lumpur, 1961)

Malayan Film Unit, *Catalogue of films* (Kuala Lumpur, 1955)

Malayan Union, *Annual Report of the Malayan Union for 1946*

Malayan Union, *Annual report of the Medical Department for the year 1946*

Malayan Union, *Department of Public Relations: review of activities. April to October 1946* (Malayan Union Advisory Council, No. 54 of 1946)

Singapore, *Annual Report of the Film Censor's Office for the Year 1953* (Singapore, 1954)

Singapore, *Committee on Film Censorship* (Singapore, 1950)

Singapore, *Report of a Committee appointed by the Government of Singapore to inquire into the Film Quota Legislation of the Colony* (Singapore, 1954)

Singapore, *Report of the Hawkers Enquiry Commission* (Singapore, 1950)

Singapore, *Report of the Social Welfare Department* (Singapore, 1952)

Singapore, *A social survey of Singapore: a preliminary study of some aspects of social conditions in the municipal area of Singapore* (Singapore, 1947)

del Tufo, M. V., *Malaya: a report on the 1947 census of population* (London, 1949)

Books and articles

A. Samad Said, '1948: Dawn of a new literary era', in A. Samad Said, *Between art and reality: selected essays* (Kuala Lumpur, 1994), pp. 57–71

Abdul Aziz Ishak, *The architect of Merdeka: Tengku Abdul Rahman* (Singapore, 1957)

Abdul Aziz Mat Tom, 'Persokolahan Melayu, 1945–48: satu manifestasi semangat perjuangan Melayu', in Khoo Kay Kim and Mohd. Fadzil Othman (eds), *Pendidikan di Malaysia: dahulu dan sekarang* (Kuala Lumpur, 1980), pp. 140–64

Abdul Ghani, *Puteri Alang Lipo* (Kuala Pilah, 1957)

Abdul Latiff Abu Bakar, *Ishak Haji Muhammad: penulis dan ahli politik sehingga 1948* (Kuala Lumpur, 1977)

Abdul Majid, 'Co-operative movement amongst Malays', *Intisari*, 1, 2 (n.d.), 44–5

Abdul Manaf bin Saad, 'Persatuan Ulama Kedah, 1365–1376H (1946–1957M)', in Khoo Kay Kim (ed.), *Islam di Malaysia* (Kuala Lumpur, 1985), pp. 148–58

Abdul Rahman Haji Abdullah, *Gerakan anti penjajahan di Malaysia, 1511–1950: pengaruh agama dan tarikat* (Kuala Lumpur, 1994)

Abdul Samad Idris, *25 tahun UMNO: kenangan abadi kepada bangsa, agama dan tanahair* (Kuala Lumpur, 1984)

Abdullah Hussain, *P. Ramlee: Kisah Hidup Seniman Agung* (Kuala Lumpur, 1973)

Abdullah Hussain and Nik Safiah Karim (eds), *Memoranda Angkatan Sasterawan '50* (Petaling Jaya, 1987)

Abi, *P. Ramlee: Seniman Agung* (Kuala Lumpur, 1986)

Abu Talib Ahmad, 'The impact of the Japanese occupation on the Malay-Muslim population', in Kratoska, Paul H. (ed.), *Malaya and Singapore during the Japanese occupation* (Singapore, 1995), pp. 24–36.

Addison, Paul, *The road to 1945: British politics and the Second World War* (London, 1983)

Adult Education Association of Malaya, *Annual Report, 1954*

Ahmad Boestamam, *Carving the path to the summit* (Athens, Ohio, 1979)
Lambiran dari puncak: memoir, 1941–45 (Kuala Lumpur, 1983)

Ahmad Kamal Abdullah, et al. (eds), *History of modern Malay literature*, 2 Vols (Kuala Lumpur, 1992)

Aimi Jarr, *R. Ramlee: dari kacamata* (n.d.)

Ainsworth, Leopold, *The confessions of a planter in Malaya: a chronicle of life and adventures in the jungle* (London, 1933)

Akashi, Yoji, 'Japanese Military Administration in Malaya – its formation and evolution in reference to Sultans, the Islamic religion, and the Moslem-Malays, 1941–1945', *Asian Studies*, 7, 1 (1969), 81–110
'Japanese policy towards the Malayan Chinese, 1941–1945', *JSEAS*, 1, 2 (1970), 61–89
'The *Koa Kunrenjo* and *Nampo Tokubetsu Ryugakusei*: a study of cultural propagation and conflict in Japanese occupied Malaya (1942–45)', *Shakai Kagaku Tokyu*, 23, 3 (1978), 39–66
'The Japanese occupation of Malaya: interruption or transformation', in Alfred W. McCoy (ed.), *Southeast Asia under Japanese occupation* (New Haven, 1980), pp. 65–90
'The anti-Japanese movement in Perak during the Japanese occupation 1941–45', in Kratoska, Paul H. (ed.), *Malaya and Singapore during the Japanese occupation* (Singapore, 1995), pp. 83–120.

Alattas, S. H. *Penimpin, politik dan firasat* (Kuala Lumpur, 1994)

Alias Mohamed, *Malaysia's Islamic opposition: past, present and future* (Kuala Lumpur, 1991)
PAS platform: development and change, 1951–1986 (Petaling Jaya, 1994)

Allen, J. de Vere, *The Malayan Union* (New Haven, 1967)
'The Malayan civil service, 1874–1941: colonial bureaucracy/Malay elite', *CSSH*, 12, 2 (1970), 149–78

Amaluddin Darus, *Kenapa saya tinggalkan PAS* (Kuala Lumpur, 1977)

Ampalavanar, R., *The Indian minority and political change in Malaya, 1945–57* (Kuala Lumpur, 1981)

Andaya, B. W. and L. Y., *A history of Malaysia* (London, 1982)

Anderson, Benedict, *Imagined communities: reflections on the origins and spread of nationalism* (2nd revised edition, London, 1991)

Anderson, Patrick, *Snake wine: a Singapore episode* (Singapore, 1984 [1955])

Ang Tian Se, 'The dilemma of Chinese writers in Malaya in the late 1940s', *Proceedings of the First International Symposium on Asian Studies*, 3 (1979), 549–52

Anon, *Biography of Towkay Yeap Chor Ee* (n.d., 195?)

Anon, *Pidato² dari orang² yang Terkemuka* (Singapore, n.d., 1957?)

Anthony, James M., 'Urban development planning and development control: hawkers in Kuala Lumpur (1940s–1960s)', *Sojourn*, 2, (1987), 112–24

Anwar [Ishak Haji Muhammad], *Jalan ke Kota Bharu* (Kuala Lumpur, 1956)

Arasaratnam, S., 'Social reform and reformist pressure groups among the Indians of Malaya and Singapore, 1930–1955', *JMBRAS*, 40, 2 (1967), 54–67
Indians in Malaysia and Singapore (London, 1970)

Ardjasni [Khatijah Sidek], '*Riwayat hidup saya*: My life – IX', *Eastern Horizon*, 2, 1 (1964), 55–61

Ariffin Omar, *Bangsa Melayu: Malay concepts of democracy and community, 1945–50* (Kuala Lumpur, 1993)

Arshad Haji Nawari, '*Utusan Melayu* yang dipunya orang Melayu', in Khoo Kay Kim and Jazamuddin Baharuddin (eds), *Lembaran Akhbar Melayu* (Kuala Lumpur, 1980), pp. 105–32

Asiah Sarji, 'The historical development of broadcasting in Malaysia (1930–57) and its social and political significance', *Media Asia*, 9, 3 (1982), 150–60

Asmah Haji Omar, 'Towards the unification of Bahasa Melayu and Bahasa Indonesia', *Tengara*, 1 (1967), 112–15

Azahar Raswan Dean b. Wan Din, 'Pengeluaran dan perdaganan padi dan beras di Negri Kedah dari pendudukan Jepun hingga pentadbiran tentera Thai, 1942–45', *Kajian Malaysia*, 5, 1 (1987), 40–62

Azizah Kassim, 'The genesis of squatting in West Malaysia with special reference to the Malays in the Federal Territory', *Malaysia in History*, 26 (1983), 60–83

Baharudin Latif, 'P. Ramlee: the legend', in Perbadanan Kemajuan Filem Nasional Malaysia, *Cinta Filem Malaysia* (Kuala Lumpur, 1980), pp. 63–5

Baker, Christopher, 'Economic reorganisation and the slump in South and Southeast Asia', *CSSH*, 18, 3 (1981), 325–49

Banks, David J., *From class to culture: social consciousness in Malay novels since independence* (Yale University SEA Series Monograph No. 29, New Haven, 1987)

Barraclough, Simon, 'The dynamics of coercion in the Malaysian political process', *MAS*, 19, 4 (1985), 797–822

Bayart, Jean-François, *The state in Africa: the politics of the belly* (London, 1993)

Beaglehole, J. H., 'Malay participation in commerce and industry: the role of RIDA and MARA', *Journal of Commonwealth Political Studies*, 7 (1969), 216–45

Beamish, Tony, 'Art exhibitions in the Federation of Malaya', *The Singapore Artist*, 1, 2 (1954)
    The arts of Malaya (Singapore, 1954)

Betts, Russell H., *The mass media of Malaya and Singapore as of 1965: a survey of the literature* (Center for International Studies, M. I. T., Cambridge, Mass., 1969)

Bloom, David, 'The English language and Singapore: a critical survey', in Basant Kapur (ed.), *Singapore Studies: critical surveys of the humanities and social sciences* (Singapore, 1986)

Blythe, Wilfred, *The impact of Chinese secret societies in Malaya: a historical study* (London, 1969)

Brewster, Anne, *Towards a semiotic of post-colonial discourse: University writing in Singapore and Malaysia, 1949–1965* (Singapore, 1989)

Brown, Ian, 'Rural distress in Southeast Asia during the world depression of the 1930s: a preliminary re-examination', *JAS*, 45, 5 (1986), 995–1025

Brown, Rajeswary Ampalavarnar, *Capital and entrepreneurship in Southeast Asia* (London, 1994)

Brownfoot, Janice N., 'Sisters under the skin: imperialism and the emancipation of women in Malaya, c.1891–1941', in Mangan, J. A. (ed.), *Making imperial mentalities: socialization and British imperialism* (Manchester, 1990), pp. 46–73

Burgess, Anthony, *Little Wilson and Big God* (London, 1987)

Burridge, Kenelm O. L., 'Managerial influences in a Johore village', *JMBRAS*, 30, 1 (1957), 93–114
    'Racial relations in Johore', *The Australian Journal of Politics and History*, 2, 2 (1957), 151–68

Butcher, John, *The British in Malaya, 1880–1941* (Kuala Lumpur, 1983)

Campbell, Arthur, *Jungle green* (London, 1959)

Cant, R. G., *An historical geography of Pahang* (Kuala Lumpur, 1972)

Carnell, Francis G., 'The Malayan elections', *Pacific Affairs*, 28, 4 (1955), 315–30

Carstens, Sharon A., 'From myth to history: Yap Ah Loy and the heroic past of Chinese Malaysians', *Journal of Southeast Asian Studies*, 19, 2 (1988)

Cathay Film Services Ltd, *Films about Singapore* (Singapore, 1958)

Chamil Wariya, *Pandangan politik era Mahathir* (Petaling Jaya, 1990)
    Politik dan Raja (Kuala Lumpur, 1992)

Chan, Paul, 'The political economy of urban Chinese squatters in metropolitan Kuala Lumpur', in Lim, Linda Y. C. and Gosling, L. A. Peter (eds), *The Chinese in Southeast Asia* (Singapore, 1983), Vol. I, pp. 232–44

Chandra Muzaffar, 'Breaking the ethnic trap', *Aliran*, 7, 6 (June/July, 1987), 2–3

Chandran Jeshuran, 'Government response to armed insurgency in Malaysia, 1957–82', in Chandran Jeshuran (ed.), *Governments and rebellions in Southeast Asia* (Singapore, 1986), 134–61

Cheah Boon Kheng, 'The Japanese occupation of Malaya, 1941–45: Ibrahim Yaacob and the struggle for Indonesia Raya', *Indonesia*, 28 (1979), 85–120

    The masked comrades: a study of the Communist United Front in Malaya, 1945–48 (Singapore, 1979)

    'Sino-Malay conflicts in Malaya, 1945–1946: Communist vendetta and Islamic resistance', *JSEAS*, 12, 1 (1981), 108–17

    Red star over Malaya: resistance and social conflict during and after the Japanese occupation of Malaya, 1941–1946 (Singapore, 1983)

    'The erosion of ideological hegemony and royal power and the rise of post-war Malay nationalism', *JSEAS*, 19, 1 (1988), 1–26

    The peasant robbers of Kedah, 1900–1929: historical and folk perceptions (Singapore, 1988)

    From PKI to the Comintern, 1929–41: the apprenticeship of the Malayan Communist Party (Ithaca, 1992)

Cheah Boon Kheng (ed.), *A. Samad Ismail: journalism and politics* (Kuala Lumpur, 1987)

Cheng Siok Hwa, 'The rice industry of Malaya: a historical survey', *JMBRAS*, 42, 2 (1969), 130–44

Chin, Aloysius, *The Communist Party of Malaya: the inside story* (Kuala Lumpur, 1995)

Chin Kee Onn, *Malaya upside down* (Singapore, 1946)

Chin Kin Wah, *The defence of Malaya and Singapore: the transformation of a security system, 1957–71* (Singapore, 1983)

Chopyak, James D., 'Music in modern Malaysia: a survey of the musics affecting the development of Malaysian popular music', *Asian Music*, 18, 1 (1986)

Christie, Clive J., *A preliminary survey of British literature on South-East Asia in the era of colonial decline and decolonisation* (Hull, 1986)

Chui Kwei-chiang, 'The China Democratic League in Singapore and Malaya, 1946–48', *Review of Southeast Asian Studies*, 15 (1985), 1–28

Clements, P. M. and Lewis, L. I., *Now we can read* (Macmillan's Standard English Course for Malaya, London, 1953)

Clifford, Hugh, 'Life in the Malay peninsula: as it was and is', in Kratoska, Paul H. (ed.), *Honourable intentions: talks on the British Empire in Southeast Asia delivered at the Royal Colonial Institute, 1874–1928* (Singapore, 1983), pp. 224–48

Cloake, John, *Templer: Tiger of Malaya* (London, 1985)

Clutterbuck, Richard, *Riot and Revolution in Singapore and Malaysia, 1943–63* (London, 1973)

Coates, John, *Suppressing insurgency: an analysis of the Malayan Emergency, 1948–54* (Boulder, 1992)

Comber, Leon, 'Chinese secret societies in Malaya: an introduction', *JMBRAS*, 29, 1 (1956), 146–62

Concannon, T. A. L., 'Town planning in Malaya', *Quarterly Journal of the Institute of Architects of Malaya*, 1, 3 (1951)

    'A new town in Malaya: Petaling Jaya, Kuala Lumpur', *MJTG*, 5 (1955), 39–43

Coope, A. E., *A guide to Malay conversation* (3rd edn, Singapore, 1953)

Courtenay, P. P., *A geography of trade and development in Malaya* (London, 1972)

Cribb, Robert (ed.), *The late colonial state in Indonesia: political and economic foundations of the Netherlands Indies, 1880–1942* (Leiden, 1994)

Crockett, Anthony, *Green beret, red star* (London, 1954)

Crouch, Harold, 'The UMNO crisis, 1975–77', in Crouch, Harold, Lee Kam Hing and Ong, Michael (eds), *Malaysian politics and the 1978 election* (Kuala Lumpur, 1980), pp. 11–36

Cruickshank, Charles, *SOE in the Far East* (Oxford, 1983)

Dancz, Virginia H., *Women and party politics in peninsular Malaysia* (Singapore, 1987)

Das, K., *The Musa dilemma: reflections on the decision of Datuk Musa Hitam to quit the government of Datuk Seri Dr Mahathir Mohamad* (Kuala Lumpur, 1986)

David, V., *Freedom never came* (Petaling Jaya, 1989)

Dewan Bahasa dan Pustaka, *Modern Malaysian stories* (Kuala Lumpur, 1977)

Dobby, E. H. G., 'Recent settlement changes in South Malaya', *MJTG*, 1 (1953), 1–8

'Padi landscapes of Malaya', *MJTG*, 6 (1955), 1–94

'Padi landscapes of Malaya', *MJTG*, 10 (1957), 1–43

Donnison, F. S. V., *British Military Administration in the Far East* (London, 1956)

Dorall, Richard F., 'DEPAN: an alternative development paradigm for Malaysia in the 1990s', in Azizah Kassim and Lau Teik Soon (eds), *Malaysia and Singapore: problems and prospects* (Singapore, 1992), pp. 123–61

Douglas, Stephen A., 'Sport in Malaysia', in Wagner, Eric A. (ed.), *Sport in Asia and Africa: a comparative handbook* (New York, 1989)

Drabble, J. H., 'Some thoughts on the economic development of Malaya under British administration', *JSEAS*, V, 2 (1974), 199–208

Drabble, J. H. and Drake, P. J., 'The British Agency Houses in Malaysia: survival in a changing world', *JSEAS*, 12, 2 (1981), 297–328

Drysdale, John, *Singapore: the struggle for success* (Singapore, 1984)

Dussek, O. T., *Practical modern Malay, an introduction to the colloquial language* (London, 1953)

Dussek, O. T., Ahmad Murad bin Nasruddin, and Coope, A. E., *A graduated Malay reader* (2nd edn Singapore, 1953)

Eagland, R. D., 'A report on anaemia in estate labourers in Malaya', *Medical Journal of Malaya*, 7, 1 (1952), 36–8

Edinger, George, *The twain shall meet* (New York, 1960)

Ee Tiang Hong, 'Literature and liberation: the price of freedom', in E. Thumboo (ed.), *Literature and liberation: five essays from Southeast Asia* (Manila, 1988), pp. 11–41

Elsbree, Willard H., *Japan's role in Southeast Asian nationalist movements, 1940–1945* (Cambridge, Mass., 1953)

Enright, D. J., *Robert Graves and the decline of modernism: inaugural lecture delivered on 17 November 1960 in the University of Malaya in Singapore* (Singapore, 1960)

Instant chronicles: a life (Oxford, 1985)

Erbaugh, Mary S., 'The secret history of the Hakkas: the Chinese revolution as a Hakka enterprise', *China Quarterly*, 132 (1992), 937–68

Fang Xia, *Notes on the history of Malayan Chinese new literature* (Tokyo, 1977)

Ferguson, D. S., 'The Sungei Manik irrigation scheme', *MJTG*, 2 (1954), 9–16

Firdaus Haji Abdullah, *Radical Malay politics: its origins and early development* (Petaling Jaya, 1985)

Firth, Rosemary, *Housekeeping among Malay peasants* (2nd edn, London, 1966)

Fish, William, 'The Merdeka pageant', *Straits Times Annual* (1958), 16–21

Fisk, E. K., 'Rural development policy', in Silcock, T. H. and Fisk, E. K. (eds), *The political economy of independent Malaya* (Singapore, 1963)

Floering, Ingrid, 'Two variants of the modern plantation: FELDA and Mumias', in Edgar Graham (ed.), *The modern plantation in the Third World* (London, 1984), pp. 105–27

Fredericks, F. J., Kalshoven, G. and Daane, T. R. V., *The role of farmers' associations in two paddy farming areas in West Malaysia* (Wageningen, 1980)

Freedman, Maurice, 'The growth of a plural society in Malaya', *Pacific Affairs*, 33, 2 (1960), 158–68

Fujimoto, Akimi, *Income sharing among Malay peasants* (Singapore, 1983)

Funston, N. J., 'The origins of Partai Islam Se Malaysia', *JSEAS*, 7, 1 (1976), 58–73

    Malay politics in Malaysia (Kuala Lumpur, 1980)

    'Challenge and response in Malaysia: the UMNO crisis and the Mahathir style', *Pacific Review*, 1, 4 (1988), 363–73

Furnivall, J. S., *Progress and welfare in Southeast Asia: a comparison of colonial policy and practice* (New York, 1941)

    Colonial policy and practice (Cambridge, 1948)

Gamba, Charles, 'Staff relations in the government services of Malaya', *Malayan Economic Review*, 2, 2 (1957), 12–32

    'Labour and labour parties in Malaya', *Pacific Affairs*, 31, 2 (1958), 117–29

    The origins of trade unionism in Malaya (Singapore, 1960)

    The National Union of Plantation Workers: the history of the plantation workers of Malaya, 1946–1958 (Singapore, 1962)

Gammans, Capt. L. D., 'A new conception of empire', *British Malaya* (May 1942)

Gilmour, Andrew, *An Eastern Cadet's anecdotage* (Singapore, 1974)

Goh Ban Lee, *Urban planning in Malaysia: history, assumptions and issues* (Petaling Jaya, 1991)

Gomez, Edmund Terence, *Politics in business: UMNO's corporate investments* (Kuala Lumpur, 1990)

Gopinath, Aruna, *Pahang, 1880–1933: a political history* (Kuala Lumpur, 1991)

Gordon, Shirle, 'Pondok and our peasantry', *Intisari*, 2, 1 (n.d.), 32–3

    'Marriage/divorce in the eleven States of Malaya and Singapore', *Intisari*, 2, 2 (n.d.), 23–32

Gouldsbury, Pamela, *Jungle Nurse* (London, 1960)

Govindasamy, N. A. A., 'The development of Tamil literature in Singapore (an historical perspective)', *Singapore Book World*, 10 (1979)

Greenwood, J. M. F., 'Rubber smallholdings in the Federation of Malaya', *JTG*, 18 (August 1964), 81–100

Gullick, J. M., 'The Malay administrator', *Merdeka outlook*, 1 (1957), 69–83

    'The condition of having a Raja: a review of *Kerajaan*, by A. C. Milner', *RIMA*, 16, 2 (1982), 109–29

    'The entrepreneur in late nineteenth century Malay peasant society', *JMBRAS*, 58 (1985), 59–70

    Malay society in the late nineteenth century: the beginnings of change (Singapore, 1987)

    Rulers and Residents: influence and power in the Malay States, 1870–1920 (Singapore, 1992)

Hadijah bte Rahmat, 'The printing press and the changing concepts of literature, authorship and notions of self in Malay literature', *JMBRAS*, 69, 1 (1996), 64–84

Hale, Thelma, *Speech training for Malayans* (London, 1957)

Hamzah Sendut, 'Patterns of urbanization in Malaya', *JTG*, 16 (1962), 114–30

Han Suyin, 'An outline of Malayan Chinese literature', *Eastern Horizon*, 3, 6 (June, 1964), 6–16

Hanna, Willard A., *Sequel to colonialism: the 1957–60 foundations of Malaysia* (New York, 1965)

Hara Fujio, 'The Japanese occupation of Malaya and the Chinese community', in Kratoska, Paul H. (ed.), *Malaya and Singapore during the Japanese occupation* (Singapore, 1995), pp. 37–82

Harper, T. N., 'The politics of the forest in colonial Malaya', *Modern Asian Studies*, 31, 1 (1997), 1–29

Harun Aminurrashid, *Minah Joget Moden* (Singapore, 1968 [1949])

Hassan Ahmad, *Bahasa, sastera buku: cetusan fikiran* (Kuala Lumpur, 1988)

Hawkins, David, *The defence of Malaysia and Singapore: from AMDA to ANZUK* (London, 1972)

Hawkins, Gerald, 'The Malay language in history and transition', *New Malaya*, 3 (1957), 33–9

Heng Pek Koon, *Chinese politics in Malaysia: a history of the Malaysian Chinese Association* (Singapore, 1988)

Henniker, M. C. A., *Red shadow over Malaya* (London, 1953)

Heussler, Robert, *British rule in Malaya, 1942–57* (Singapore, 1985)

Hill, R. D., 'Agricultural land tenure in west Malaysia', *Malayan Economic Review*, 22, 1 (1967), 99–116

    Rice in Malaya: a study in historical geography (Kuala Lumpur, 1977)

Hino, Iwao and Rajasingam, S. Durai, *Stray notes on Nippon-Malaysian historical connections* (Kuala Lumpur, 2604)

Hirschman, Charles, 'The meaning and measurement of ethnicity in Malaysia: an analysis of census classifications', *JAS*, 46, 3 (1987), 555–82

Ho, Robert, 'Land settlement projects in Malaya: an assessment of the role of the Federal Land Development Authority', *JTG*, 20 (1965), 1–15

    'Land ownership and economic prospects of Malay peasants', *MAS*, 4, 1 (1970), 83–92

Hodge, Thomas, 'The film industry in Singapore and Malaya', *Report on the Third Annual Film Festival of Southeast Asia, Hong Kong, 12–16 June, 1956*

Holman, Denis, *Noone of the Ulu* (London, 1958)

Hooker, M. B., *Adat laws in modern Malaya: land tenure, traditional government and religion* (Kuala Lumpur, 1972)

Houghton, George, *Golf addict goes East* (London, 1967)

HUSBA, 'The Third Malay Language and Literary Congress', *Magazine of the University of Malaya Students' Union, Sessions 1954/55 and 1955/56*, 53–54

Hussin Mutalib, *Islam and ethnicity and Malay politics* (Singapore, 1990)

    Islam in Malaysia: from revivalism to Islamic State (Singapore, 1993)

Hutton, Wendy, *The Singapore Polo Club: an informal history, 1886–1982* (Singapore, 1983)

Hyam, Ronald et al., *A history of Magdalene College Cambridge, 1428–1988* (Cambridge, 1994)

International Bank for Reconstruction and Development, *The economic development of Malaya* (Singapore, 1955)

International Labour Office, Regular Programme of Technical Assistance, *Report on workers' education in Malaya* (Geneva, 1960)

    Expanded Programme of Technical Assistance, *Report to the Government of the Federation of Malaya on the promotion and organization of co-operatives among women* (Geneva, 1963)

Iskander Hj Ahmad, A. M., *Persuratkhabaran Melayu, 1876–1968* (Kuala Lumpur, 1973)

Ismail bin Haji Salleh, *The Sultan was not alone: a collection of letters written by Sultan Badlishah in his effort to repeal the Malayan Union policy imposed by the British Government on Malaya in 1946, and other supporting letters and documents written by others* (Alor Setar, 1989)

Ismail Hussein, 'Interview with Alina Ranee: anglophiles and the Malay elite' [1985], in *Statements on Malay language and literature* (Kuala Lumpur, 1989), pp. 46–50

Itagaki, Yoichi, 'Outlines of Japanese policy in Indonesia and Malaya during the war with special reference to nationalism of respective countries', *Hitotsubashi Academy Annals*, 2, 2 (1952)

Jaafar bin Hamzah, 'The Malays in Telok Gelugur during the Japanese occupation', *Malaysia in History*, 21, 2 (1978), 56–64

Jaafar Hussein, *Kebenaran* (Kuala Lumpur, 1987)

Jackson, James C., *Planters and speculators: Chinese and European agricultural enterprise in Malaya, 1786–1921* (Kuala Lumpur, 1968)

    'Rice cultivation in West Malaysia: relationships between culture, history, customary practices and recent developments', *JMBRAS*, 45, 2 (1972), 76–96

'The Chinatowns of Southeast Asia: traditional components of the city's central area', *Pacific Viewpoint*, 16, (1975), 45–86

Jackson, R. N., *Immigrant labour and the development of Malaya* (Kuala Lumpur, 1960)

Jain, Ravindra K., 'Leadership and authority in a plantation: a case study of Indians in Malaya (c.1900–42)', in Wijeyewardene, G. (ed.), *Leadership and authority: a symposium* (Singapore, 1968), pp. 163–73

Jamil Sulong, 'Bangsawan's influence on early malay films', in Perbadanan Kemajuan Filem Nasional Malaysia, *Cinta Filem Malaysia* (Kuala Lumpur, 1989), pp. 56–60

    Kaca Permata: memoir seorang pengarah (Kuala Lumpur, 1990)

Johnstone, Michael, 'The evolution of squatter settlements in peninsular Malaysian cities, *JSEAS*, 12, 2 (1981), 364–80

Johore Penghulus' Handbook (Johore Bahru, 1951)

Jomo K. S., *A question of class: capital, the state, and uneven development in Malaya* (Singapore, 1986)

    'Economic ideas in Malaysian universities', *Malaysian Journal of Economic Studies*, 27, 1 & 2 (1990)

    'Whither Malaysia's New Economic Policy', *Pacific Affairs*, 63, 4 (1990–91), 469–99

Jomo K. S. and Chee Heng Leng, 'Public health expenditure in Malaysia', *Journal of the Malaysian Society of Health*, 5, 1 (1985), 73–83

Jomo K. S. and Patricia Todd, *Trade unions and the state in peninsular Malaysia* (Kuala Lumpur, 1994)

Jones, Alun, 'The Orang Asli: an outline of their progress in modern Malaya', *Journal of Southeast Asian History*, 9 (1968), 286–305

Jones, L. Webb, '*Ronggeng* rhythm', *Straits Times Annual, 1953*, 78–9

Josey, Alex, *Golf in Singapore* (Singapore, 1969)

Kahn, Joel and Loh Kok Wah, Francis (eds), *Fragmented vision: culture and politics in contemporary Malaysia* (Sydney, 1992)

Kalam Hamidy, *P. Ramlee: Pujnaan Nusantara* (Kuala Lumpur, 1973)

Kamlin, M., *History, politics and electioneering: the case of Terengganu* (Department of History, Universiti Malaya, Kuala Lumpur, 1977)

Kanagaratnam, K., 'Extra-curricular activities in the period of transition from College to University, 1940–1955', in Sandosham, A. A. (ed.), *A symposium on extra-curricular activities of university students in Malaya* (Singapore, 1955)

Kassim bin Ahmad, *Characterization in Hikayat Hang Tuah: a general survey of character-portrayal and analysis and interpretation of the characters of Hang Tuah and Hang Jebat* (Kuala Lumpur, 1966)

Kathirithamby-Wells, J., 'The Johor-Malay world, 1511–1784: changes in political ideology', *Sejarah*, 1 (1988), 35–62

Kato, Tsuyoshi, 'When rubber came: the Negri Sembilan experience', *Southeast Asian Studies* 29, 2 (1991), 109–57

Kaye, Barrington, *A manifesto for education in Malaya* (Singapore, 1955)

Kershaw, Roger, 'Anglo-Malaysian relations: old roles versus new rulers', *International Affairs*, 59, 4 (1983), 629–48

Kessler, Clive S., 'Muslim identity and political behaviour in Kelantan', in Roff, William R. (ed.), *Kelantan: religion, society and politics in a Malay State* (Kuala Lumpur, 1974), pp. 272–314

    Islam and politics in a Malay state: Kelantan, 1838–1969 (Ithaca, 1978)

Khaidir Anwar, *Indonesian: the development and use of a national language* (Yogyakarta, 1980)

Khoo Boo Teik, 'The legacy of C. H. E. Det: portrait of a nationalist as a young man', *Kajian Malaysia*, 11, 2 (1993), 28–43

Paradoxes of Mahathirism: an intellectual biography of Mahathir Mohamad (Kuala Lumpur, 1995)

Khong Kim Hong, *Merdeka: British rule and the struggle for independence in Malaya* (Kuala Lumpur, 1984)

Khoo Kay Jin, 'The Grand Vision: Mahathir and modernization', in Kahn, Joel and Loh Kok Wah, Francis (eds), *Fragmented vision: culture and politics in contemporary Malaysia* (Sydney, 1992), pp. 44–76

The Western Malay States, 1850–73 (Kuala Lumpur, 1972)

Khoo Kay Kim, 'Local historians and the writing of Malaysian history in the twentieth century', in Reid, Anthony and Marr, David (eds), *Perceptions of the past in Southeast Asia* (Singapore, 1979), pp. 299–311

'Islam and politics in Kelantan', *JSEAS*, 11, 1 (1980), 187–94.

'The Malay left 1945–1948: a preliminary discourse', *Sarjana*, 1 (1981), 167–91

'A brief history of Chinese labour unrest before 1941', *Malaysia in history*, 25 (1982), 59–64

Malay papers and periodicals as historical sources (Kuala Lumpur, 1984)

'Malaysian historiography: a further look', *Kajian Malaysia*, 10, 1 (1992), 37–62

'Perceptions of progress and development among English-educated Muslims in pre-World War Two Malaya', *Sejarah*, 2 (1993), 147–78

Khoo Kay Kim, Abdul Azia bin Mat Ton and Baharam Azit, 'Melaka's Malay society in modern times', in K. S. Sandhu and P. Wheatley (eds.), *Melaka: the transformation of a Malay capital c. 1400–1980*, II, pp. 78–83

King, Victor T., 'Tourism and culture in Malaysia', in Hitchcock, M., King, V. T. and Parnwell, M. J. G. (eds.), *Tourism in Southeast Asia* (London, 1993), pp. 99–116

Kitchener, H. J. and Etherton, A. R. B., *Malayan jungle adventures* (Kuala Lumpur, 1953)

Kleinsorge, Paul L., 'Employers' associations in Malaya', *Far Eastern Survey* (August, 1957), 124–7

Koch, Margaret L., 'Rubber in the district of Temerloh: unequal access and growing economic disparity', *Kajian Malaysia*, 3, 1 (1985), 1–31

Koh Choo Chin, 'Implementing government policy for the protection of women and girls in Singapore, 1948–66: recollections of social worker', in Jaschok, M. and Miers, S. (eds), *Women and Chinese patriarchy: submission, servitude and escape* (London, 1994), pp. 122–40

Koh Tai Ann, 'Singapore writing in English: the literary tradition and cultural identity', in Than Seong Chee (ed.), *Essays on literature and society in Southeast Asia: political and sociological perspectives* (Singapore, 1981), pp. 160–86.

Kratoska, Paul H., *The Chettiar and the Yeoman: British cultural categories and rural indebtedness in Malaya* (ISEAS, Occasional paper No. 32, Singapore, 1975)

'Rice cultivation and the ethnic division of labour in British Malaya', *CSSH*, 24, 2 (1982), 280–314

' "Ends we cannot foresee": Malay reservations in British Malaya', *JSEAS*, 9, 1 (1983), 149–68

'Penghulus in Perak and Selangor: the rationalization and decline of a traditional Malay office', *JMBRAS*, 57, 2 (1984), 31–60

'The peripatetic peasant and land tenure in British Malaya', *JSEAS*, 16, 1 (1985), 16–45

'The post-war food shortage in British Malaya', *JSEAS*, 19, 1 (1988), 27–47

Kratoska, Paul H. (ed.), *Malaya and Singapore during the Japanese occupation* (Singapore, 1995)

Laidin bin Alang Musa, 'The background to the Ulu Langat valley in Selangor', *Malayan Historical Journal*, 2, 1 (1955), 8–11

Lamprell, B. A. and Check, Elizabeth, 'Anaemia in South Indians employed on Malayan plantations', *Medical Journal of Malaya*, 7, 2 (1952), 107–14

Langley, G. A., 'Telecommunications in Malaya', *JTG*, 17 (1962), 79–91
Lau, Albert, 'Malayan Union citizenship: constitutional change and controversy in Malaya, 1942–48', *JSEAS*, 20, 2 (1989), 216–43
   The Malayan Union controversy, 1942–48 (Singapore, 1991)
Leary, John, *The importance of the Orang Asli in the Malayan Emergency, 1948–1960* (Centre of Southeast Asian Studies, Monash, Working Paper No. 56, 1989)
   Violence and the dream people: the Orang Asli in the Malayan Emergency, 1948–1960 (Athens, Ohio, 1995)
Lebra, Joyce, 'Japanese policy and the Indian National Army', *Asian Studies*, 7, 2 (1969), 31–49
Lee, J. M. and Petter, M., *The Colonial Office: war and development policy* (London, 1982)
Lee Kam Hing, 'MCA dalam peralihan, 1956–59', in Persatuan Sejarah Malaysia, *Malaysia: sejarah dan proses pembangunan* (Kuala Lumpur, 1979), pp. 268–83
Lee Sheng Yi, *The monetary and banking development of Malaysia and Singapore* (Singapore, 1974)
Lee Ting Hui, 'Singapore under the Japanese, 1942–1945', *Journal of the South Seas Society*, 17, 1 (1961), 31–69
Leifer, Michael, 'Singapore in Malaysia: the politics of Federation', *JSEAH*, 6, 2 (1965), 54–70
Lent, John A., *The Asian film industry* (London, 1990)
Lewis, Diane K., 'Rules of agrarian change: Negri Sembilan Malays and agricultural innovation', *JSEAS*, 7, 1 (1976), 74–91
Li Chuan Siu, *An introduction to the promotion and development of modern Malay literature, 1942–62* (Yogyakarta, 1975)
Lim Heng Kow, *The evolution of the urban system in Malaya* (Kuala Lumpur, 1978)
Lim Hong Hai, 'The eve-of-independence constitutional debate on fundamental liberties and judicial review: a window on elite views and constitutional government in Malaysia?', *Kajian Malaysia*, 7, 1 & 2 (1989), 1–37
Lim Joo-Jock, 'Tradition and peasant agriculture in Malaya', *MJTG*, 3 (1954), 44–7
Lim Kay Tong, *Cathay: 55 years of cinema* (Singapore, 1991)
Lim San Kok, 'Some aspects of the Malayan Chinese association, 1949–69', *Journal of the South Seas Society*, 26, 2 (1971), 31–48
Lim, Shirley, 'The English-language writer in Singapore', in Sandhu, Kernial Singh and Wheatley, Paul (eds), *Singapore: the management of success* (Singapore, 1990), pp. 523–51
Lim Teck Ghee, *Origins of a colonial economy: land and agriculture in Perak, 1874–1897* (Penang, 1976)
   Peasants and their agricultural economy in colonial Malaya, 1874–1941 (Kuala Lumpur, 1977)
   'British colonial administration and the "ethnic division of labour" in Malaya', *Kajian Malaysia*, 1, 2 (1984), 28–66
   'Non-government organizations and human development: the ASEAN experience', in Lim Teck Ghee (ed.), *Reflections on development in Southeast Asia* (Singapore, 1988), pp. 160–91
Lim Teck Ghee (ed.), *Reflections on development in Southeast Asia* (Singapore, 1988)
Lockard, Craig A., 'Reflections of change: socio-political commentary and criticism in Malaysian popular music since 1950', *Crossroads*, 6, 1 (1991), 1–106
Loh Kok Wah, Francis, *The politics of Chinese unity in Malaysia: reform and conflict within the Malaysian Chinese Association* (Singapore, 1982)
   Beyond the tin mines: coolies, squatters and New Villagers in the Kinta Valley, c. 1880–1980 (Singapore, 1988)
   'From tin mine coolies to agricultural squatters: socio-economic change in the Kinta District during the inter-war years', in Rimmer, P. J. and Allen, L. (eds), *The underside of Malaysian history: pullers, prostitutes and plantation workers* (Singapore, 1990), pp. 72–96
Lonsdale, John and Berman, B., *Unhappy valley: conflict in Kenya and Africa* (London, 1992)

Low, N. I. and Cheng, H. M., *This Singapore (Our city of dreadful night)* (Singapore, 1946)

McGee, T. G., 'The cultural role of cities: a case study of Kuala Lumpur', *JTG*, 17 (1963), 178–96

McGee, T. G. and McTaggert, W. D., *Petaling Jaya: a socio-economic survey of a new town in Selangor, Malaysia* (Pacific Viewpoint Monograph No. 3, Wellington, 1967)

McHugh, J. N., *Words and phrases related to political organizations and procedure at meetings* (Kuala Lumpur, 1948)

'Psychological or political warfare in Malaya: II The postwar years', *Journal of the Historical Society of the University of Malaya*, 5 (1966/67), 75–94

McTaggart, W. D., 'The distribution of ethnic groups in Malaya, 1947–57', *JTG*, 26 (1968), 69–81

Mahathir bin Mohamad, *The Malay dilemma* (Singapore, 1970)

Mak Lau Fong, *Chinese secret societies in Ipoh town, 1945–69* (National University of Singapore Sociology working paper No. 42, 1975)

The sociology of secret societies: a study of Chinese secret societies in Singapore and peninsular Malaysia (Kuala Lumpur, 1981)

Malay League of Perak, *Hidup Melayu: a brief review of the Malay national movement* (Ipoh, n.d.)[1946]

Malayan Chinese Association, *Presidential address at the fifth Annual Meeting of the General Committee, Kuala Lumpur, 31.1.1953*

MCA, 20th Anniversary souvenir, 1949–69 (Kuala Lumpur, 1969)

Malayan Christian Council, *Challenges and opportunity: the New Villages in Malaya: What are the Churches Doing?* (Singapore, 1952)

A survey of the New Villages of Malaya (Singapore, 1958)

Malayan Communist Party, Johore-Malacca Border Committee, *Death of a heretic* (Singapore, 1951)

Malayan Film Unit, *Catalogue of films* (1955)

Malayan National Conference, *Report of the Working Committee of the Malayan National Conference* (Kuala Lumpur, 1953)

Malaysian Trades Union Congress, *Malayan Trade Union Council report for the period 1.7.1951 to 31.3.1952*

History of the MTUC (Kuala Lumpur, 1974)

Manderson, Lenore H., *Women, politics and change: the Kaum Ibu UMNO Malaysia, 1945–72* (Kuala Lumpur, 1980)

'Health services and the legitimation of the colonial state: British Malaya, 1784–1941, *International Journal of Health Services*, 17, 1 (1987), 91–112

Sickness and the state: health and illness in colonial Malaya, 1870–1940 (Cambridge, 1996)

Mansor Sanusi, *Bahasa Melayu: the new method course* (Penang, 1953)

Letter writer in Malay (Penang, 1956)

Markandan, Paul, *The problem of the New Villages in Malaya* (Singapore, 1954)

Masuri, S. N., 'The development of Malay fiction in Singapore', in Thumboo, E. (ed.), *The fiction of Singapore* (Singapore, 1993), pp. 1–23

Matheson, Virginia, 'Concepts of Malay ethos in indigenous Malay writings', *JSEAS*, 10, 2 (1979), 351–71

'Usman Awang, Keris Mas and Hamzah: individual expressions of social commitment in Malay literature', *RIMA*, 21, 1 (1987), 108–31

Matheson Hooker, Virginia, 'Transmission through practical example: women and Islam in 1920s Malay fiction', *JMBRAS*, LXVII, 2 (1994), 93–118

Mauzy, D. K. and Milne, R. S., 'The Makathir administration: discipline through Islam', in Bruce Gale (ed.), *Readings in Malaysian politics* (Petaling Jaya, 1986), pp. 75–112

Mead, Richard, *Malaysia's national language policy and the legal system* (New Haven, 1988)

Means, Gordon P., *Malaysian politics* (London, 1970)
' "Special rights" as a strategy for development: the case of Malaysia', *Comparative Politics* (1973), 29–61
'The Orang Asli: aboriginal policies in Malaya', *Pacific Affairs*, 38, 4 (1985), 637–52
Malaysian politics: the second generation (Singapore, 1991)
Meek, Paul, 'Malaya: a study of governmental response to the Korean War boom', in Silcock, T. H. (ed.), *Readings in Malayan Economics* (Singapore, 1961)
Mek Siti bt. Hussin, *'Melayu Raya'*, in Khoo Kay Kim and Jazamuddin Baharuddin (eds), *Lembaran Akhbar Melayu* (Kuala Lumpur, 1980), pp. 167–85
Melan Abdullah, 'Samad in love and war', in Cheah Boon Kheng (ed.), *Samad Ismail: journalism and politics* (Kuala Lumpur, 1987)
Metzger, Laurent, *Les Sultanats de Malaisie: un régime monarchique au vingtième siècle* (Paris, 1994)
Middlebrook, S. M., 'Pulai: an early Chinese settlement in Kelantan', *JMBRAS*, 11, 2 (1933), 151–6
Miers, Richard, *Shoot to kill* (London, 1959)
Miller, Harry, *Menace in Malaya: the campaign against Communism, 1948–60* (London, 1954; 2nd edn. 1970)
Jungle war in Malaya: the campaign against Communism, 1948–60 (London, 1972)
Milner, A. C., *Kerajaan: Malay political culture on the eve of colonial rule* (Tucson, 1982)
'Islam and the Muslim state', in Hooker, M. B. (ed.), *Islam in Southeast Asia* (Leiden, 1983), pp. 23–49
'Colonial records history: British Malaya', *MAS*, 21, 4 (1987), 773–92
'Inventing politics: the case of Malaysia', *Past & Present*, 132 (1991), 104–29
'Post-modern perspectives on Malay biography', *Kajian Malaysia*, 9, 2 (1991), 24–38
The invention of politics in colonial Malaya: contesting nationalism and the expansion of the bourgeois public sphere (Cambridge, 1995)
Mohamad Abu Bakar, 'Ulama pondok dan politik kepartian di Malaysia, 1945–85', *Malaysia masa kini* (Kuala Lumpur, 1985), pp. 92–122
M. Ali bin Mohamed and Coope, A. E., *Malay dialogues with colloquial grammar* (London, 1952)
Mohamed Khalil bin Hussein, *The department of religious affairs, Perak: present structure, organisation and recent development* (Singapore, 1958?)
Mohamed Noordin Sopiee, *From Malayan Union to Singapore separation: political unification in the Malaysia region, 1945–65* (Kuala Lumpur, 1974)
Morais, Benedict and Hamdan Adnan (eds), *Public relations: the Malaysian experience* (Kuala Lumpur, 1986)
Morais, J. Victor, *P. P. Narayanan – the Asian trade union leader* (Petaling Jaya, 1975)
Moran, J. W. G., *Spearhead in Malaya* (London, 1959)
Muhammad bin Hanif, *Kamus politik* (2 vols, Penang, 1949)
English-Malay dictionary of commodities (Alor Star, 1951)
Muhammad Haji Salleh, *The mind of the Malay author* (Kuala Lumpur, 1991)
Muhammad Haji Salleh (ed.), *An anthology of contemporary Malaysian literature* (Kuala Lumpur, 1988)
Muhammad Ikmal Said, 'Ethnic perspectives on the left in Malaysia', in Kahn, Joel and Loh Kok Wah, Francis (eds), *Fragmented vision: culture and politics in contemporary Malaysia* (Sydney, 1992), pp. 254–81
'Malay nationalism and national identity', *Suomen Antropologi*, 2 (1995), 11–31
Muhammad Yusoff Hashim, *The Malay Sultanate of Malacca: a study of various aspects of Malacca in the fifteenth and sixteenth centuries in Malaysian history* (Kuala Lumpur, 1992)
Moore, Donald, 'The story of a glorious failure', *New Malaya*, 3 (1954), 18–31

Murphy, H. B. M., 'The mental health of Singapore: part one – suicide', *Medical Journal of Malaya*, 9, 1 (1954), 1–45

Nabir bin Haji Abdullah, *Maahad Il Ihya Asshariff Gunung Semanggol, 1934–59* (Kuala Lumpur, 1979)

Nasradin Bahari, 'Cherpen[2] terjemahan didalan majalah Mastika, 1946–59', *Bahasa*, 7 (1965), 56–93

Nathan, K. S., 'Vision 2020 and Malaysian foreign policy: strategic evolution and the Mahathir impact', *Southeast Asian Affairs, 1995* (Singapore, 1995), 220–37

Ness, Gayl D., *Bureaucracy and rural development in Malaysia: a study of complex organizations in stimulating economic development in new states* (Berkeley, 1967)

Netaji Centre, *Netaji Subhas Chandra Bose: a Malaysian perspective* (Kuala Lumpur, 1992)

Newell, W. H., *Treacherous river: a study of rural Chinese in north Malaya* (Kuala Lumpur, 1962)

Nicholas, Colin, Williams-Hunt, Anthony and Tiah Sabak (eds), *Orang Asli in the news* (Kuala Lumpur, 1989)

Nik Ahmad bin Haji Nik Hassan, 'The Malay press', *JMBRAS*, 36, 1 (1963), 37–78

Nik Safiah Karim, 'Sumbangan Pakatan Bahasa Melayu Persuratan Buku Diraja Johor perkembangan bahasa Melayu', in Jabatan Pengajian Melayu, Universiti Malaya, *Rampaian Pengajian Melayu* (Kuala Lumpur, 1985), pp. 181–5

Nim Chee Siew, *Labour and tin mining in Malaya* (Data Paper No. 7, Southeast Asia Program, Cornell University, Ithaca, 1953)

Nonini, Donald M., *British colonial rule and the resistance of the Malay peasantry, 1900–1957* (New Haven, 1992)

Noone, Richard, *Rape of the dream people* (London, 1972)

Noordin Selat, *Renangan* (Kuala Lumpur, 1976)

Nur Nina Zura, *An analysis of modern Malay drama* (Shah Alam, 1992)

Nyce, Ray, *Chinese New Villages: a community study* (Singapore, 1973)
  Into a new age: a study of church and society in Kuala Lumpur, Malaysia (Singapore, 1973)

Oldfield, J. B., *The Green Howards in Malaya (1949–52): the story of a post-war tour of duty by a Battalion of the Line* (Aldershot, 1953)

Ommanney, F. D., *Eastern windows* (London, 1960)

Ong Kah Kuan, *We were great: Thomas Cup badminton* (Kuala Lumpur, 1984)

Onraet, Rene, 'The prospects for trade unions in Malaya, *British Malaya* (January, 1949), 140

Ooi Jin Bee, 'Rural development in tropical areas, with special reference to Malaya', *JTG*, 12, (1959)

Oong Hak Ching, 'Perjuangan Partai Malayan, 1956–7', *Malaysia in History*, 18, 1 (1975), 1–9

Overton, J., *Colonial Green Revolution? Food, irrigation and the state in colonial Malaya* (Oxford, 1994)

Ow Chwee Huay, *Singapore's trade with West Malaysia, 1950–68* (Ministry of Finance, Singapore, 1969)

Pak Sako [Ishak Haji Muhammad], *Tiga tahun di Singapura* (Petaling Jaya, 1975)

Pandey, Gyan, *The construction of communalism in colonial North India* (Delhi, 1993)

Parkinson, Brien K., 'Non-economic factors in the economic retardation of the rural Malays', *MAS*, 1, 1 (1967), 31–46
  'The economic retardation of the Malays – a rejoinder', *MAS*, 2, 3 (1968), 267–72

Parkinson, C. Northcote, 'Houses of Malaya', *Quarterly Journal of the Institute of Architects of Malaya*, 4, 4 (1955), 13–20

Parmer, J. Norman, 'Constitutional change in Malaya's plural society', *Far Eastern Survey*, 26, 10 (1957), 145–52

Perbadanan Kemajuan Filem Nasional Malaysia, *Cinta Filem Malaysia* (Kuala Lumpur, 1989)

Persatuan Guru-guru Melayu Kedah, *25 Tahun* (Alor Star, 1971)

Persekutuan Bahasa Melayu University Malaya, *Laporan tentang bahasa Melayu dan bahasa Indonesia oleh Kongeres III Bahasa dan Persuratan Melayu Malaya* (Singapore, 1956)
Mesurat Agung Ketiga, Persekutan Bahasa Melayu, University Malaya (20.10.1957)
Polunin, Ivan, 'The medical natural history of the Malayan aborigines', *Malayan Medical Journal*, 8, 1 (1953), 55–174
Powell, Robert, *Innovative architecture of Singapore* (Singapore, 1989)
Proudfoot, Ian, *Early Malay printed books: a provisional account of materials published in the Singapore-Malaysia area up to 1920, noting holdings in major public collections* (Kuala Lumpur, 1993)
Provenchor, Ronald, 'Covering Malay humor magazines: satire and parody of Malaysian political dilemmas', *Crossroads: an interdisciplinary journal of Southeast Asian Studies*, 5, 2 (1990), 1–25
Pryor, Robin J., *Migration and development in Southeast Asia: a demographic perspective* (Kuala Lumpur, 1979)
Purcell, Victor, *Basic English for Malaya* (Singapore, 1937)
'Will Templer stage a comeback?', *Raayat*, 1, (13.12.1954)
Malaya: Communist or free? (Stanford, 1955)
Memoirs of a Malayan official (London, 1965)
The Chinese in Malaya (Kuala Lumpur, 1967)
Puthucheary, James, *Ownership and control in the Malayan economy* (Singapore, 1960)
Pye, Lucian W., *Guerrilla communism in Malaya: its social and political meaning* (Princeton, 1956)
Lessons from the Malayan struggle against Communism (Centre for International Studies, M. I. T., Cambridge, 1957)
Datin Ragayah Eusoff, *Lord of Kinta: the biography of Dato Panglima Kinta Eusoff* (Petaling Jaya, 1995)
Rahani Mat Saman, 'Women producers', in Perbadanan Kemajuan Filem Nasional Malaysia, *Cintra File Malaysia* (Kuala Lumpur, 1989), pp. 102–5
Rahim bin Omar, 'Madrasah Masyhur al-Islamiyyah', in Khoo Kay Kim (ed.), *Islam di Malaysia* (Kuala Lumpur, 1979), pp. 75–85
Rahmah Haji Bujang, 'Drama in Malaysia: the writer in a changing society', *Sarjana*, 1, 1 (1981), 27–58
Raja Singham, S. Durai, 'Sir Gerald Templer's work for a cultural revival in Malaya', *MHJ*, 2, 2 (1955)
Rajoo, R., 'World-view of the Indians with regard to the social identity and belonging in Malaya, c.1900–57', in Mohd. Taib Osman (ed.), *Malaysian world-view* (Singapore, 1985), pp. 147–83
Ramasamy, P., *Plantation labour, unions, capital and the state in peninsular Malaysia* (Kuala Lumpur, 1994)
Ramlah Adam, *UMNO: organisasi dan kegiatan, 1945–51* (Kota Bahru, 1978)
'Pergolakan politik di Johor, 1946–48', *Jebat*, 19 (1991), 83–105
Dato Onn Ja'afar: pengasas kemerdekaan (Kuala Lumpur, 1992)
'Kongres Kebangsaan Melayu: suata penentangan kepada kehilangaan kuasa politik Melayu di dalam kemerdekaan 1957', *Sarjana* (1994), 159–81
Ratnam, K. J., *Communalism and the political process in Malaya* (Kuala Lumpur, 1965)
Reid, Anthony, *Southeast Asia in the age of commerce, 1450–1680, II – Expansion and crisis* (New Haven, 1993)
Reid, Anthony (ed.), *Southeast Asia in the early modern era: trade, power and belief* (Ithaca, 1993)
Rimmer, P. J. and Allen, L. (eds), *The underside of Malaysian history: pullers, prostitutes and plantation workers* (Singapore, 1990)
Rimmer, P. J. and Cho, George C. H., 'Urbanization of the Malays since independence: evidence from West Malaysia, 1957–70', *JSEAS*, 12, 2 (1981), 349–63

Robertson, A. F., *The people and the state: an anthropology of planned development* (Cambridge, 1984)

Robinson, J. B. Perry, *Transformation in Malaya* (London, 1956)

Rodgers, Marvin L., 'Politicization and political development in a rural Malay community', *Asian Survey*, 9, 12 (1969), 919–33

'The politicization of Malay villagers: national integration or disintegration?', *Comparative Politics*, 7, 2 (1975), 205–25

Roff, M., 'The Malayan Chinese Association, 1945–65', *JSEAH*, 6, 2 (1965), 40–53

'The politics of language in Malaya', *Asian Survey*, 7, 5 (1967), 316–28

Roff, William R., *The origins of Malay nationalism* (Yale, 1967; 2nd edn. Kuala Lumpur, 1994)

'Colonial pursuits', *Journal of the Historical Society, University of Malaya*, 6 (1967/68)

'The origin and early years of the *Majlis Ugama*', in Roff, William R. (ed.), *Kelantan: religion, society and politics in a Malay State* (Kuala Lumpur, 1974), pp. 101–52

'The institutionalization of Islam in the Malay peninsula: some problems for the historian', in Sartomo Kartodirdjo (ed.), *Profiles of Malay culture: historiography, religion and politics* (Jakarta, 1976), pp. 66–72

'Whence cometh the law? Dog saliva in Kelantan, 1937', *CSSH*, 25, 2 (1983), 323–38

Roff, William R. (ed.), *The wandering thoughts of a dying man: the life and times of Haji Abdul Majid bin Zainuddin* (Kuala Lumpur, 1978)

Roxborogh, Rev W. John, *A short introduction to Malaysian church history* (Kuala Lumpur, 1989)

Rudner, Martin, 'Malayan labour in transition: labour policy and trade unionism, 1955–63', *MAS*, 7, 1 (1973), 22–8

'Agricultural policy and peasant social transformation in late colonial Malaya', in Jackson, James C., and Rudner, Martin (eds), *Issues in Malaysian development* (Singapore, 1979), pp. 7–67

'Labour policy and the dilemmas of trade unionism in post-war Malaya', *RIMA*, 16, 1 (1982), 101–18

Sabda S. dan Wahba, *Musa Ahmad: kembali kepang kuan* (Subang Jaya, 1981)

Sadka, Emily, *The Protected Malay States, 1874–95* (Kuala Lumpur, 1968)

Safie bin Ibrahim, 'The Islamic element in Malay politics in pre-independent Malaya, 1937–48', *Islamic Culture*, 52, 3 (1978), 185–95

The Islamic Party of Malaysia: its formative stages and ideology (Kota Bahru, 1981)

Saliha Hj Hasan, 'Dr Burhanuddin Al-Hulaimi: the ideals of a Malay nationalist', *Malaysia in History*, 17, 1 (1974), 1–7

'Dr Burhanuddin Al-Helmi, 1911–1969', *Jebat*, 14 (1986), 153–82

Salleh Daud, *UMNO: image and reality* (Kuala Lumpur, 1966)

Salleh Ghani, *Filem Melayu: dari Jalan Ampas ke Ulu Klang* (Kuala Lumpur, 1989)

Salmon, Claudine, Review of Cheah, *Red star over Malaya*, *Archipel*, 38 (1989), 156–7

Sandhu, Kernial Singh, 'The population of Malaya: some changes in the pattern of distribution between 1947 and 1957', *JTG*, 15 (1961), 82–96

'Emergency resettlement in Malaya', *Journal of Tropical Geography*, 18 (1964), 157–83

'The saga of the "squatter" in Malaya: a preliminary survey of the causes, characteristics and consequences of the resettlement of rural dwellers during the Emergency between 1948 and 1960', *JSEAH*, 5, (1964), 143–77

Sandhu, Kernial Singh, and Wheatley, Paul (eds), *Melaka: the transformation of a Malay capital, c.1400–1980*, 2 vols (Kuala Lumpur, 1983)

Sandosham, A. A., *Malaria in Malai: a handbook for anti-malaria students* (Syonan-to, 2604)

Scott, James C., *Political ideology in Malaysia: reality and the beliefs of an elite* (Kuala Lumpur, 1968)

The moral economy of the peasant: rebellion and subsistence in Southeast Asia (New Haven, 1976)

Weapons of the weak: everyday forms of peasant resistance (New Haven, 1985)

Shafruddin, B. H., *The Federal factor in the government and politics of peninsular Malaysia* (Singapore, 1987)

Shaharil Talib, *After its own image: the Trengganu experience, 1881–1941* (Singapore, 1984)

Shahnon Ahmad, *Kesusasteraan dan etika Islam* (Kuala Lumpur, 1981)

Shamsul A. B., *From British to Bumiputera rule: local politics and rural development in peninsular Malaysia* (Singapore, 1988)

Sharifah Zinjuaher, H. M. Ariffin and Hang Tuah Arshad, *Sejarah Filem Melayu* (Kuala Lumpur, 1980)

Sharp, Ilsa, *The Singapore Cricket Club, 1852–1985* (Singapore, 1985)

Sheppard, Mubin, *The adventures of Hang Tuah* (Singapore, 1949)

    Taman Budiman: memoirs of an unorthodox civil servant (Kuala Lumpur, 1979)

    Taman Saujana: dance, drama, music and magic in Malaya, long and not-so-long ago (Petaling Jaya, 1983)

Shiraishi, Takashi, *An age in motion:popular radicalism in Java, 1912–1926* (Ithaca, 1990)

Short, Anthony, *The Communist insurrection in Malaya, 1948–60* (London, 1976)

    'The Malayan Emergency', in Haycock, Ronald (ed.), *Regular armies and insurgency* (London, 1978), pp. 53–68.

Shih Yun-ts'iao and Chua Ser-koon (eds), *Malayan Chinese resistance to Japan, 1937–45: selected source materials, based on Col. Chuang Hui-tsuan's collection* (Singapore, 1984)

Siaw, Laurence K. L., *Chinese society in rural Malaysia* (Kuala Lumpur, 1983)

Siddique, Sharon and Suryadinata, Leo, *'Bumiputera* and *pribumi:* economic nationalism (indiginism) in Malaysia and Indonesia', *Pacific Affairs* (1982), 662–87

Sidhu, Jagjit Singh, *Administration in the Federated Malay States, 1896–1920* (Kuala Lumpur, 1981)

Simpson, I. A. (ed.), *Applied nutrition in Malaya: a collection of papers issued for the use of participants at a training course in applied nutrition held at the Institute for Medical Research, Kuala Lumpur from 26.11.1956 to 4.12.1956* (Kuala Lumpur, 1957)

Singh, Supriya, *Bank Negara Malaysia: the first twenty-five years* (Kuala Lumpur, 1984)

Siti Hasmah binte M. Ali, 'Effect on a basic attitude: health', *Intisari*, 1, 4 [n.d., 1961], 27–36

Slimming, John, *Temiar Jungle: a Malayan journey* (London, 1958)

Smith, Simon C., 'The rise, decline and survival of the Malay Rulers during the colonial period, 1874–1957', *Journal of Imperial and Commonwealth History*, 22, 1 (1994), 84–108

Smyth, Rosaleen, 'Britain's African colonies and British propaganda during the Second World War', *JICH*, 14, 1 (1985), 65–82

Sng, Bobby Ek, *In his good time: the story of the church in Singapore, 1819–1978* (Singapore, 1980)

Soh Eng Lim, 'Tan Cheng Lock: his leadership of the Malayan Chinese', *JSEAH*, 1, 1 (1960), 29–53

Stenson, Michael R., 'The Malayan Union and the historians', *JSEAH*, 10, 2 (1969), 344–54

    Repression and revolt: the origins of the 1948 Communist insurrection in Malaya and Singapore (Athens, Ohio, 1969)

    Industrial conflict in Malaya: prelude to the Communist revolt of 1948 (London, 1970)

    The 1948 Communist revolt in Malaya: a note on historical sources and interpretation with a Reply by Gerald de Cruz (Singapore, 1971)

    Class, race and colonialism in West Malaysia: the Indian case (Queensland, 1980)

Stevenson, Rex, 'Cinemas and censorship in colonial Malaya', *JSEAS*, 5, 2 (1974), 44–68

    Cultivators and administrators: British educational policy towards the Malays, 1875–1906 (Kuala Lumpur, 1975)

Stockwell, A. J., 'Colonial planning during World War Two: the case of Malaya', *JICH*, 2, 3 (1974), 333–51

British policy and Malay politics during the Malayan Union experiment, 1945–1948 (Kuala Lumpur, 1979)

'British imperial policy and decolonization in Malaya, 1942–52', *Journal of Imperial and Commonwealth History*, 13, 1 (1984), 68–87

'British imperial strategy and decolonization in Southeast Asia, 1947–57', in Basset, D. K. and King, V. T. (eds), *Britain and Southeast Asia* (Hull: University of Hull Centre of Southeast Asian Studies, Occasional Papers, No. 13 (1986), pp. 79–90

'Imperial security and Moslem militancy, with special reference to the Hertogh riots in Singapore (December 1950)', *JSEAS*, 17, 2 (1986), 322–35

'Insurgency and decolonization during the Malayan Emergency', *Journal of Commonwealth and Comparative Politics*, 25, 1 (1987), 71–81

'Policing during the Malayan Emergency, 1948–60: communism, communalism and decolonization', in Anderson, D. and Killingray, D., *Policing and decolonization: politics, nationalism and the police, 1917–65* (Manchester, 1992), pp. 105–28

' "A widespread and long-concocted plot to overthrow government in Malaya"? The origins of the Malayan Emergency', in R. Holland (ed.), *Emergencies and disorder in the European empires after 1945* (London, 1994), pp. 66–88

Strauch, Judith, 'Chinese New Villages of the Malayan Emergency, a generation later: a case study', *Contemporary Southeast Asia*, 2, 2 (1981), 126–39

Stubbs, Richard, *Counter-insurgency and the economic factor: the impact of the Korean War prices boom on the Malayan Emergency* (ISEAS Occasional paper No. 19, Singapore, 1974)

Hearts and minds in guerrilla warfare: the Malayan Emergency, 1948–1960 (Singapore, 1989)

Sudar Majid, 'The Malay artist', *The Singapore Artist*, 1, 2 (December 1954)

Sullivan, Patrick, 'A critical appraisal of historians of Malaya: the theory of society implicit in their work', in Higgott, Richard and Robison, Richard (eds), *Southeast Asia: essays in the political economy of structural change* (London, 1985), pp. 65–92

Suryono Drusman, *Singapore and the Indonesian revolution, 1945–50* (Singapore, 1992)

Sutherland, Heather, 'The taming of the Trengganu elite', in Ruth T. McVey (ed.), *Southeast Asian transitions: approaches through social history* (New Haven, 1978), pp. 32–85

Swettenham, Frank, *British Malaya* (London, 1948)

Swift, M. G., *Malay peasant society in Jelebu* (London, 1965)

Syed Ahmad Jamal, 'Perkembangunan seni rupa Sezaman', in Persatuan Sejarah Malaysia, *Malaysia: sejarah dab proses pembangunan* (Kuala Lumpur, 1979)

Seni Lukis Malaysia – 25 tahun (Kuala Lumpur, 1982)

Syed Husin Ali, 'Land concentration and poverty among the rural Malays, *Nusantara*, 1, (1972), 100–13

Malay peasant society and leadership (Kuala Lumpur, 1975)

Syed Hussein Alatas, *The myth of the lazy native* (London, 1977)

Tai, Hue-Tam Ho, *Radicals and the origins of the Vietnamese revolution* (Cambridge, Mass., 1992)

Tan Cheng Lock, *One country, one people, one government: Presidential address by Tan Cheng Lock at a meeting of the General Committee of the MCA held in Penang on 30 October, 1949* (Kuala Lumpur, 1949)

Tan Chin Kwang, 'Chinese translations of Malay literary works in Malaya', *Tenggara*, 1 (1967), 116–20

Tan Eng Teik, 'Uniqueness of Malayan Chinese literature: literary polemic in the forties', *Asian Culture*, 12 (1988), 102–15

Tan Liok Ee, *The rhetoric of bangsa and minzu: community and nation in tension, the Malay peninsula, 1900–1955* (Working paper No. 52, Centre of Southeast Asian Studies, Monash University, 1988)

'Tan Cheng Lock and the Chinese education issue in Malaya', *JSEAS*, 19, 1 (1988), 48–61

Tan Sooi Beng, *Ko-tai: a new form of Chinese urban street theatre in Malaysia* (Singapore, 1984)
  'Counterpoints in the performing arts of Malaysia', in Kahn, Joel and Loh Kok Wah, Francis
    (eds), *Fragmented vision: culture and politics in contemporary Malaysia* (Sydney, 1992), pp.
    282–305
  Bangsawan: a social and stylistic history of popular Malay opera (Singapore, 1993)
Tan, T. H., *The Prince and I* (Singapore, 1979)
Tan, Y. S., 'History of the formation of the Overseas Chinese Association and the extortion by
    the J. M. A. of $50,000,000 military contribution from the Chinese in Malaya', *Journal of
    the South Seas Society*, 3, 1 (1946), 1–12
Tay Boon Seng, *Recollections of my past* (Melaka, 1970)
Taylor, R. H., *The state in Burma* (London, 1987)
Tham Seong Chee, *The role and impact of formal associations in the development of Malaysia*
    (Bangkok, 1977)
  'The politics of literary development in Malaysia', in *Essays on literature and society in
    Southeast Asia: political and sociological perspectives* (Singapore, 1981), pp. 216–52
Thani, A. M. (ed.), *Esei sastera ASAS 50* (Kuala Lumpur, 1981)
Thio Chan Bee, *The extraordinary adventures of an ordinary man* (London, 1977)
Thio, Eunice, *British policy in the Malay peninsula, 1880–1910* (Singapore, 1969)
Thomaz, Louis Filipe, 'The Malay Sultanate of Melaka', in Reid, Anthony (ed.), *Southeast Asia
    in the early modern era: trade, power and belief* (Ithaca, 1993), pp. 69–90
Thompson, Sir Robert, *Defeating Communist insurgency: experiences from Malaya and Vietnam*
    (London, 1966)
  Make for the hills: memories of Far Eastern wars (London, 1989)
Thompson, Virginia, *Postmortem on Malaya* (New York, 1943)
Tilman, Robert O., 'The non-lessons of the Malayan Emergency', *Asian Survey*, 6, 8 (1966),
    407–19
Tinker, Hugh, *A new system of slavery: the export of Indian labour overseas, 1830–1920* (London,
    1974)
Tjoa Soei Hok, *Institutional background to modern economic and social development in Malaya
    (with special reference to the East Coast)* (Kuala Lumpur, 1963)
Too, C. C., 'The Communist Party of Malaya and its attempts to capture power', *New Straits
    Times*, 3–6.12.1989
Toynbee, Arnold J., *East to west: a journey around the world* (London, 1958)
Tregonning, K. G., 'Tan Cheng Lock: a Malayan nationalist', *JSEAS*, 10, 1 (1979), pp. 25–76
Trocki, Carl A., *Opium and empire: Chinese society in colonial Singapore, 1800–1910* (Ithaca,
    1990)
Tunku Shamsul Bahrin, 'The Indonesian immigrants and the Malays of West Malaysia: a study
    in assimilation and integration', *Geographica*, 6 (1970), 1–12
Turnbull, C. M., 'British planning for post-war Malaya', *JSEAS*, 5, 2 (1974), 239–54
Ungku A. Aziz, 'Land disintegration and land policy in Malaya', *Malayan Economic Review*, 3, 1
    (1958), 22–8
Ungku A. Aziz and Raja Mohar, *A survey of five villages in Malacca* (Kuala Lumpur, 1955)
Ungku Maimunah Mohd. Tahir, 'The rural-urban dichotomy in modern Malay literature:
    origins and formation in the pre-war period', *Akademika*, 27 (1985), 41–55
  Modern Malay literary culture: a historical perspective (Singapore, 1987)
UNESCO, Statistics Division, *Film and cinema statistics: a preliminary report on methodology with
    tables giving current statistics* (Geneva, 1954)
United Overseas Bank, *Growing up with Singapore* (Singapore, 1985)
United Nations, *Report on Mission on Community Organisation and development in South and
    South-East Asia* (1953)
Urquhart, Denis, 'Operation Service and the children', *Malayan Police Magazine*, 19, 2 (1953)

Van Thean Kee, 'Cultivation of Taiwanese padi in Perak during the Japanese occupation', *Malayan Agricultural Journal*, 21, 1 (1948), 119–22

Vasil, Raj, *Politics in a plural society* (Kuala Lumpur, 1971)

Wan Abdul Kadir, *Budaya popular dalam masyarakat Melayu* (Kuala Lumpur, 1988)

Wang Gungwu, 'A short introduction to Chinese writing in Malaysia', in Wignesan, T., *Bunga Emas: an anthology of contemporary Malaysian literature* (Kuala Lumpur, 1964)

    Community and nation: essays on Southeast Asia and the Chinese (Singapore, 1981)

    'Migration patterns in history: Malaysia and the region', *JMBRAS*, 58 (1985), 43–57

Wang Tai Peng, *The origins of Chinese kongsi* (Petaling Jaya, 1994)

Warren, James F., *Rickshaw Coolie: a people's history of Singapore (1880–1940)* (Singapore, 1986)

Wazir Jahan Karim, *Women and culture: between Malay adat and Islam* (Boulder, 1992)

Wee, Peter H. L., *From farm and kampong . . .* (Singapore, 1989)

West, Michael and Cheeseman, H. R., *The new method Malayan readers* (Longmans, 1947 and 1957)

Wheeler, L. Raymond, *The modern Malay* (London, 1928)

White, Nicholas J., 'Government and business divided: Malaya, 1945–57', *JICH*, 22, 2 (1994)

Wikkramatileke, Rudolph, 'Mukim Pulau Rusa: land use in a Malayan riverine settlement', *JTG*, XI (1958), 18–25

Wilder, William, 'Islam, other factors and Malay backwardness: comments on an argument', *MAS*, 11, 2 (1968), 155–64

Wilson, Harold E., *Educational policy and performance in Singapore 1942–1945* (ISEAS, Occasional paper No. 16, Singapore, 1973)

Wilson, Peter J., *A Malay village and Malaysia: social values and rural development* (New Haven, 1967)

Wilson, T. B., 'Some economic aspects of padi-land ownership in Krian', *Malayan Agricultural Journal*, 37, 3 (1954), 125–35

    Type, tenure and fragmentation of farms: Census of Agriculture, Federation of Malaya, 1960, Preliminary report No. 3 (Kuala Lumpur, 1961)

Wolters, O. W., 'Emergency resettlement and community development in Malaya', *Community Development Bulletin*, 3 (1951), 1–8.

    The fall of Srivijaya in Malay history (London, 1970)

Wong, Kean, 'Metallic gleam', *The Wire* (April, 1993), 18–20

Wong Lin Ken, 'The Malayan Union: a historical retrospect', *JSEAS*, 13, 1 (1982), 184–91

Wong Tai Peng, *The origins of Chinese kongsi* (Petaling Jaya, 1994)

Wong Yoke Nyen, 'Chinese organisations and citizenship in post-war Malaya, 1945–1958', *Review of Southeast Asian Studies*, 12 (1982), 13–39

Wood, Maye, *Malay for mems* (5th edn. Singapore, 1949)

Woodhouse, Capt J. M., 'Some personal observations on the employment of special forces in Malaya', *Army Quarterly*, 66, 1 (1951)

Yeo Kim Wah, *Political development in Singapore, 1945–55* (Singapore, 1973)

    'The anti-federation movement in Malaya, 1946–48', *JSEAS*, 4, 1 (1973), 31–51

    'The Communist challenge in the Malayan labour scene, September 1936–March 1937', *JMBRAS*, 49, 2 (1976), 36–79

    'The grooming of an elite: Malay administrators in the Federated Malay States, 1903–1941', *JSEAS*, 11, 2 (1980), 287–319

    'Student politics in University of Malaya, 1949–51', *JSEAS*, 23, 2 (1992), 346–80

Yong Ching Fatt, *Tan Kah Kee: an Overseas Chinese legend* (Singapore, 1987)

    Chinese leadership and power in colonial Singapore (Singapore, 1992)

Yong, C. F. and McKenna, R. B., *The Kuomintang movement in British Malaya, 1912–1949* (Singapore, 1990)

Za'ba, 'The Malays and religion', in Khoo Kay Kim (ed.), *Tamadun Islam di Malaysia* (Kuala Lumpur, 1980), pp. 103–12

Zainab Awang Ngah, 'Malay comic books published in the 1950s', *Singapore Book World*, 16, 2 (1986), 19–28

Zainah Anwar, *Islamic revivalism in Malaysia: dakwah amongst students* (Petaling Jaya, 1987)

Zainuddin Maidin, *The other side of Mahathir* (Kuala Lumpur, 1994)

Zakaria Haji Ahmad and Kernial Singh Sandhu, 'The Malayan Emergency: event writ large', in Kernial Singh Sandhu and Wheatley, Paul, (eds), *Melaka: the transformation of a Malay capital, c.1400–1980* (Kuala Lumpur, 1983), Vol. 1, pp. 388–420

Zakaria Haji Ahmad (ed.), *Government and politics of Malaysia* (Singapore, 1987)

Zakri Abadi, *Why Anwar: political games of UMNO's leadership* (Kuala Lumpur, 1993)

Ziegler, P., *Mountbatten: the official biography* (London, 1985)

Ziegler, P. (ed.), *Personal Diary of Admiral the Lord Mountbatten: Supreme Allied Commander, South-East Asia, 1943–1946* (London, 1988)

UNPUBLISHED PAPERS AND THESES

Alias Mohamed, 'PAS platforms: development and change, 1951–86' (Ph.D. Thesis, Universiti Malaya, 1989)

Asiah binti Abu Samah, 'Emancipation of Malay women, 1947–57' (B.A. Hons Exercise, University of Malaya, 1960)

Cameons, Cantius Leo, 'History and development of Malay theatre' (M.A. Thesis, Universiti Malaya, 1980)

Fleming, J. R., 'The growth of the Chinese church in the new villages of the state of Johore, 1950/60: a study in the communication of the gospel to Christian converts' (Th.D, Union Theological Seminary in the City of New York, 1961)

Foss, Josephine, 'Autobiography of Josephine Foss'

Gullick, J. M., 'The British Military Administration of Malaya: some reminiscences from Negri Sembilan' (unpublished paper, 1989)

Halinah Bamadhaj, 'The impact of the Japanese occupation of Malaya on Malay society and politics, 1941–45' (M. A. Thesis, University of Auckland, 1975)

Humphrey, J. W., 'Population resettlement in Malaya' (Ph.D. Thesis, Northwestern University, 1971)

Hunt, Rev. Robert, 'Historical overview of Christian social services in Malaysia', Paper presented to Malaysian CARE, National Symposium 1988, 'Trends and challenges in Christian social services for the 90s'

Kaur, Sautokh Tripat, 'The cinema in West Malaysia: a study of basic audience patterns and popular tastes, 1970–73' (M.A., Universiti Malaya, 1975)

Lee Li Yeng, Karen, 'Japanese occupation in Selangor, 1942–45' (B.A. Graduate Exercise, University of Malaya, 1973)

Lee Yong Hock, 'A history of the Straits Chinese British Association (1900–59)' (B.A. Hons, University of Malaya, 1960)

Leong Yee Fong, 'Labour and trade unionism in colonial Malaya: a study of the socio-economic basis of the Malayan labour movement, 1930–1957' (Ph.D Thesis, University of Malaya, 1990)

Lewis, Joanna E., 'The colonial politics of African welfare in Kenya 1939–1953: a crisis of paternalism' (Ph.D. Thesis, Cambridge University, 1993)

Lim Chooi Hin, Vincent, 'A history of tourism in Singapore, 1950–77' (B.A., Academic exercise, NUS, 1979)

McDonnell, Mary Byrne, 'The conduct of Hajj from Malaysia and its socio-economic impact on Malay society: a descriptive and analytical study, 1860–1981' (Ph.D. Thesis, Columbia University, 1986)

Mackie, J. A. C., 'Analysing Southeast Asian political systems: changing circumstances and changing approaches', ASAA Conference, Singapore, 1–3 February 1989

Manderson, Lenore, 'Historical notes on the establishment of family planning associations in Singapore and peninsular Malaysia' (unpublished paper, 1979)

Matheson, Virginia, 'Literature as social criticism: the writings of the Generation of the 1950s (ASAS 50)', paper presented to the Malaysia Society Colloquium: Malaysian social and economic history, 8–10 June 1985

Neuman, S., 'The Malay political elite: an analysis of 134 Malay legislators, their social background and attitudes' (Ph.D. New York University, 1971)

Rasiah, Rajah, 'Foreign investment and manufacturing growth in pre-indepedent Malaysia' (unpublished paper, 1992)

Tan Eng Teik, 'The development of Malaysia Chinese poetry, 1945–69' (Ph.D. Thesis, Universiti Malaya, 1990)

Tan Liok Ee, 'Politics of Chinese education in Malaya, 1945–61 (Ph.D. Thesis, Universiti Malaya, 1985)

CONTEMPORARY NEWSPAPERS AND PERIODICALS

Adult education: news bulletin, Adult Education Association Federation of Malaya
Allied Screen Review
British Malaya
Brown's Malayan Economic Review
Comrade
The Democrat
KLIMP
Malay Mail
Malaya Tribune
Malayan Historical Journal
Malayan Mirror
Malayan Police Magazine
The Malayan Undergrad: organ of the University of Malaya Students' Union
Merdeka Outlook
The New Cauldron: the official organ of the Raffles Society, University of Malaya
The New Malaya
New Straits Times
The Planter
Raayat
RIDA Monthly Bulletin
The Singapore Artist
Singapore Arts Theatre Review
The Star
Straits Echo
Straits Times
Workers' Education Association, Singapore Bulletin
Write: an independent student publication of the University of Malaya

Cited from summaries and translations of vernacular press

Chinese:
Chung Shing Jit Pao
Combatants' Friend

Feng Hsia
Ih Shih Jit Poh
Kin Kwok Daily News
Modern Daily News
Nanfang Evening Post
Nanyang Siang Pau
New Democracy
Overseas Chinese Weekly
Sin Chew Jit Poh
Sin Pau

Malay:
Asrama
Majlis
Melayu Raya
Mingguan Melayu
Pelita Malaya
Utusan Melayu
Utusan Zaman
Warta Negara

Tamil:
Tamil Murasu
Malayan Nanban

Index